A SYSTEMATIC
INTRODUCTION TO
THE PSYCHOLOGY
OF THINKING

Under the Editorship of WAYNE HOLTZMAN

SYSTEMATIC
INTRODUCTION TO
THE PSYCHOLOGY
OF THINKING

DONALD M.ᶜᴱᵂᵉⁿ JOHNSON

Michigan State University

HARPER & ROW, *Publishers*
New York, Evanston, San Francisco, London

CONTENTS

PREFACE

he flourishing state of the psychology of thinking is documented by numerous books of readings and reports of symposia on special topics: concept attainment, cognitive development, problem solving, reasoning, creative thinking, judgment, and so on. But the student and the investigator are often handicapped by the independence of research developments, and an integration of these divergent trends is badly needed at this time. Experiments on concept learning and cross-sectional studies of cognitive development do have something in common in spite of the differences in both terminology and procedure. Judging operations are not independent of reasoning operations. The principal aim of this book, therefore, is to pull the significant trends together into a coherent account of the psychology of thinking.

This volume owes something to an earlier one with a similar aim (Johnson, 1955); some of the historical material in Chapter 1 and several figures are taken from there. But whereas the earlier volume was limited by the research data then available, in the present one the author was faced with the problem of selection. The topic of thinking has always held a central position in psychology and for this reason shares common boundaries with several other topics. A survey that claims to be comprehensive could easily stray into such neighboring fields as the psychophysiology of thought, problem solving by animals, and the intellectual activities of social groups. Fortunately, however, the decision not to trespass has been simplified by the good surveys of these fields already available elsewhere.

Each of the topics included here could be probed more deeply, but a compromise between breadth and depth is always necessary. Perhaps the breadth of view chosen by the present account will help to locate promising areas for later, more penetrating investigations.

In the preparation of this book I have been indebted above all to the hundreds of investigators who have struggled to gain tangible evidence on the subtle phenomena of thought, and especially to those who have given permission for the use of figures and tables. In addition, several of the figures attest to the drafting skill of Robert Almli. I am grateful to my colleagues and students at Michigan State University for discussions, often disguised as casual conversation, that have helped to straighten out certain confusions of data and terminology. Finally, the editorial consultants for Harper & Row also were very helpful.

East Lansing, Michigan   D. M. J.
April, 1971

A SYSTEMATIC
INTRODUCTION TO
THE PSYCHOLOGY
OF THINKING

CHAPTER **I**

HISTORICAL
INTRODUCTION

_he intellectual pathways that brought the psychology of thinking to its present status crisscross through several centuries. The pioneers who took the first steps could not know where they were going, but with the benefit of hindsight we can now outline the main routes to the present. This will help to show where the psychology of thinking stands today and to explain both its achievements and its failures.[1]

Ideas in Consciousness

As soon as man became self-conscious, he began to examine his consciousness. One early result of this self-observation was the separation of the mind (or consciousness) from the body. The psychologies of antiquity, at least those of most influence on later psychologies, were dualistic in this sense. By the eighteenth century, many scholars of our civilization had become accustomed to

---

[1] Much of the material in the first part of this chapter is presented more thoroughly in the standard historical treatments, such as Boring (1950), Humphrey (1959), Murphy (1949), and Peters (1953). Mandler and Mandler (1964) have assembled and integrated some of the important historical discussions of thinking.

analyzing their consciousness into ideas: ideas were the elements of thought which could be combined and rearranged to make up the complex thoughts of complex thinkers. Many convincing principles of the association of ideas were worked out by the psychological philosophers (chiefly British) of the eighteenth and nineteenth centuries, through the analysis of their own mental experiences.

INTROSPECTION

The British associationists were philosophers before they were psychologists and their method was logical before it was observational. The careful observation of one's own consciousness was developed in Germany in the nineteenth century and nourished by Wundt and his followers. One of his most influential disciples, E. B. Titchener, brought the Wundtian tradition to America. The Wundtians aimed to make psychology—defined as an analysis of the contents of the mind—a precise science by refining the method of self-observation, or introspection.

Classical introspection, as developed by Wundt, was a special kind of self-examination, which required knowing what to look for and what to ignore. The elements of the mind were sensations, images, and feelings, and training in introspection consisted of practice in identifying these elements. The method was experimental in that the conditions of observation were controlled.

Wundt did not directly concern himself with thinking. He believed that precise introspection of the higher mental processes was impossible because (1) the experiment could not be repeated exactly; (2) introspection could not be directed to the phenomena to be observed; (3) attention could not be properly controlled; and (4) the conditions of introspection could not be systematically varied. Thought could only be studied through its products, such as language.

Many psychologists did not accept these strictures. Indeed, psychologists have always been busy solving problems that other psychologists told them were impossible. So Binet, Külpe, Woodworth, and others went ahead, gave their subjects thought problems, and asked for informal, introspective reports. Some of the tasks used to stimulate thought were quite simple: "Give a word that means the opposite of compact." Some were complex: "What is the more delightful, the smell of a rose or its appearance?" "Can our thought apprehend the nature of thought?" Binet asked his ten-year-old daughter just to close her eyes and think of anything. Woodworth asked his subjects: "Should a man be allowed to marry his widow's sister?"[2] Syllogisms were also used.

THE WÜRZBURG SCHOOL

A concerted attack on thinking was begun about 1900 by one of Wundt's students, Oswald Külpe. Külpe and his followers at Würzburg asked their

---

[2] Titchener commented on this in a footnote: "I may be obtuse; but I confess I can find in this question no food for thought [p. 92]" (Titchener, 1909).

subjects to make judgments (e.g., which of two weights is heavier) and to report what went on in their minds while reaching the conclusions. Or, using the familiar association method, subjects were given a stimulus word with instructions to respond with another word and then to give full introspective reports.

IMAGELESS THOUGHT

One outcome of this work was a controversy centering on the question of imageless thought. This controversy—like so many others in the history of psychology—illustrates the critical influence of the investigator's psychological and philosophical background. The observers who were trained by Wundt and Titchener, when they examined their thoughts, "found" sensations or images of sensations, even though they had to look hard to find them. The Würzburg observers, on the other hand, and observers used by Binet in France and Woodworth in America, did not always find that their thoughts were made up of images, perhaps because they did not look hard enough. Instead of palpable sensations and images, vague unanalyzable experiences were reported, which in Würzburg were called *Bewusstseinslagen* (usually translated as "conscious attitudes"). One result of this controversy was a loss of faith in the introspective method. Today the controversy has lost its pungency, even though there was no officially declared winner. A "final comment" on imageless thought was delivered by Woodworth in 1938 (page 788).

EINSTELLUNG

Previous work on reaction time had emphasized the preparation, or mental set; the reaction itself was considered by several physiologists and psychologists as a *prepared reflex*. Watt, an Englishman working with Külpe, applied this insight to the association experiment. Using *systematic experimental introspection,* he divided the association experiment into four periods: (1) The preparatory period, during which instructions were given (e.g., "When the stimulus word is given, name an opposite"); (2) the presentation of the stimulus word; (3) the search for the response word; and (4) the response itself. Subjects were asked to introspect on only one period at a time. The surprising result was that there was little to report in the third period: the work of thinking, as far as introspection could disclose, seemed to be done in the first or preparatory period. When the thinker is well prepared, the remainder of the sequence runs off automatically, with little conscious content.

Thus the emphasis shifted to preparation. When a subject accepts the task, or *Aufgabe,* he is prepared to respond accordingly. Acceptance of the instructions establishes an *Einstellung,* or, as Ach called it, a *determining tendency.* The term *mental set* was often used as a synonym until the adjective *mental* went out of fashion.

THE SUBTRACTION METHOD

The reaction time experiment suggested a method of analyzing the mental processes that seemed at first quite straightforward. Donders in the 1860s attempted to time the higher mental processes separately by measuring the time of a complex reaction and subtracting the simple reaction time. Others went even further. The time required for cognition was inferred by measuring cognitive response time, as when many stimuli are to be differentiated, and subtracting the simple sensory reaction time. Judgment time was inferred by subtracting association time from total time, which included both association and judgment.

The average times were not consistent, but the chief reason for the abandonment of this method was Külpe's argument against the elementistic assumption. It is true that complex reactions take more time than simple ones. But the change in instructions does not merely add another mental process; it alters the whole task. The mental performance is prepared in advance, and the stimulus word releases an integrated response.

SELZ AND THE SCHEMA

The Würzburgers rejected one assumption of associationism, the assumption that thoughts are always images. Selz, working with Külpe but influenced also by Köhler and the new Gestalt psychology, went further and rejected the associational mechanism. He presented the stimulus word and the *Aufgabe* at the same time on a card—e.g., Poem, Superordinate?—and asked his subjects for an introspective description of their mental activities. The results led him to stress, not the interaction of associations, but the integration of the *Aufgabe* and stimulus word into a *Gesamtaufgabe* (task as a whole). This consciousness of the total task guides the production of a complex of relationships, not just a class of words in a specified relationship to the stimulus word.

When the task is difficult, the complex that is integrated is not complete. The response word is missing, but it is schematized or anticipated in the total *Aufgabe*. Productive thinking consists essentially of completing this incomplete schema. Woodworth (1938) asserted that the anticipatory schema "lays claim to a position of fundamental importance in the psychology of thinking [p. 798]."

THE DECLINE OF *DENKPSYCHOLOGIE*

During the first few years of this century *Denkpsychologie*, the psychology of thought, had some of the characteristics of an exciting new movement that promised to grow and spread to other countries. But this promise was not fulfilled. Külpe's interests changed; World War I impeded scientific communication, and Germany's prestige declined. Most important, the development of behaviorism cast suspicion on all introspective investigations, and this suspicion was generalized to a taboo on thought itself.

Denkpsychologie was not a blind alley; at least, no one proved that it was so. But other routes to other goals appeared more attractive to active psychologists. The problem of understanding thinking has always seemed intriguing, but the revival of interest in this topic came from other directions and the research followed different approaches.

The contents of thought are often disclosed by reports of conscious experience, but the operations of thinking are usually missed and must be inferred by other methods. All the methods that are useful for the study of thinking today will be examined critically in the chapters ahead.

Gestalt Psychology and the Organization of Experience

Gestalt psychology began in Germany with the study of perceptual organization. Wundt and the associationists had pictured complex perceptions as built up by the synthesis of elementary sensations. Wertheimer, a student of Külpe, objected, saying that the perceptual pattern is primary: one perceives a triangle directly, not by adding three sides and three angles. Perception is determined by the given sensory data and by the dynamics of organizing forces in the brain. These brain forces cause some patterns, known as *good figures*, to have priority over others, just as a soap bubble is more likely to take the shape of a sphere than a pyramid. When perception is modified, it is not usually by the accumulation of little changes, but by a reorganization of the perceptual field. When a new force acts on the soap bubble, it does not change a little piece of the sphere; rather, the whole field of forces is reorganized into a new equilibrium.

Gestalt psychologists do not differentiate thinking from other activities; the laws of organization apply to all. Their early experiments dealt chiefly with perceptual phenomena reported by human subjects, but in 1917 Köhler applied the Gestalt approach to the behavior of apes solving problems. His account of these experiments emphasized the perception of relationships and insight into the organization of the solution pattern rather than associative learning of new responses.

Wertheimer in 1920 (and again in 1945) described human thinking, emphasizing and recommending the reorganization of patterns rather than a piecemeal attack on the problem situation. Good thinking, he maintained, consists of seeing the structure of the problem clearly and then restructuring it as necessary. According to Gestalt psychology, those psychologists who treat thought as a subhead under learning, and thus try to study thinking by experiments on learning mazes and memorizing words, are doomed to failure. Such artificial experiments eliminate the possibility of good thinking by depriving the subjects of the opportunity to perceive the significant relationships.

This emphasis on the organization of patterns raised questions in turn about the structure of cognitive and social, as well as perceptual, fields. It was apparently Koffka who, by expanding the concept of *figure and ground*, popularized the idea of "frame of reference," which has been so much used in interpreting political attitudes and other judgments in a social context. Gottschaldt showed how patterns can be embedded in larger patterns, thus becoming harder to disentangle from the whole. And Lewin's topological theory of personality dealt seriously with "regions" of the ego and the "life space," their differentiation and overlapping.

Thought as an Instrument of Adaptation

The associationists began with the contents of the mind as introspectively observed. Darwin published his *Origin of Species* in 1859; gradually, as the implications of evolutionary doctrine became clear, the emphasis shifted from the contents of the mind to the mind as an instrument of adaptation to the environment. The view of man as an active animal, trying to hold his own in the struggle for existence, put the emphasis on psychological functions or processes rather than contents.

FUNCTIONALISM AND FUNCTIONS

As early as 1890, William James complained that the introspective analysis of thought into elementary ideas was too static; it caught the contents but missed the processes. In an oft-quoted passage from *Principles of Psychology,* he says: "The rush of thought is so headlong that it almost always brings us up at the conclusion before we can arrest it. . . . The attempt at introspective analysis in these cases is in fact like seizing a spinning top to catch its motion, or trying to turn up the gas quickly enough to see how the darkness looks."

John Dewey, another philosopher with a psychological point of view, popularized the notion that man's mind and achievements, including rules of logic and systems of philosophy, were human solutions to intellectual and social problems. In an influential book called *How We Think,* he analyzed reflective thought into five stages or processes that were widely accepted as a functional description of a "complete act of thought."

Famous thinkers have often been asked to describe how they made their discoveries or created their masterpieces. Helmholtz, the great physicist-physiologist-psychologist, had done this, as had Poincaré, the great mathematician. Graham Wallas, a British political scientist whose role in British intellectual life was similar to Dewey's in America, was interested in thought as a sideline. He wanted to help the average citizen control and improve his thinking, so he summarized the contributions of the associationists and the Würzburg School, as well as Dewey's analysis and the accounts of the great thinkers. In 1926, in a book called *The Art of Thought,* he systematically described the various steps in creative thinking as *preparation, incubation, illumination,* and *verification.*

These descriptions of functions resulted from logical, subjective analysis. But experiments were soon undertaken to study and differentiate the higher mental processes. Ruger, for example, in 1910 described the activities of his subjects solving puzzles as analysis, conscious variation, and the setting up and testing of a hypothesis. In 1927, Hollingworth separated out judging from perceiving on the one side and guessing on the other. Judging, he concluded, was done with more accuracy and confidence than guessing, but with less than perceiving.

CONTROVERSIES IN COMPARATIVE PSYCHOLOGY

The controversy about evolution stimulated comparisons of the capacities of different species. Thus comparative psychology got its start, with some investigators trying to find similarities between men and the other animals, and others trying to find the differences. Those who claimed to observe higher intellectual activities in lower animals were often quite uncritical about it, so C. Lloyd Morgan laid down the rule that no performance should be attributed to a higher capacity, like reasoning, if it could be explained by a lower one, like experience or instinct. Morgan's canon was supposed to be a special case of the law of parsimony so often invoked in the other sciences.

Instead of relying on anecdotes and casual observation, Thorndike in 1897 put some cats in a problem box and watched them try to escape. He saw no evidence of ideas or reasoning; his interpretation favored rather exploratory activity and accidental success. The cats' performance improved with practice because their successful activities were rewarded. This interpretation, which came to be known as *trial-and-error learning*, was stated in terms of associations; but the associations were between stimuli in the problem situation and overt responses, rather than between ideas.

In England soon afterward Hobhouse, claiming that Thorndike had not given his cats a fair chance, undertook a series of experiments with animals in a variety of problem situations, all of which were visible and rather simple. His observations led him to assert that the higher vertebrates could perceive relationships between objects and respond adaptively to them. Experiments of this kind were continued by Yerkes, Köhler, and others, stressing problem solving by *insight*.

Thus the argument over insight versus trial-and-error was born. It has enjoyed a lively career for half a century, sometimes contributing methods and results to the progress of psychology in general, sometimes going off into special disputes of no interest except to the disputants. There is no need to follow the argument per se, but in one form or another these interpretations are bound to reappear in later chapters.

BEHAVIORISM AND ITS CONSEQUENCES

Working with animals incapable of communication, comparative psychologists and experimental biologists were forced to devise their own techniques, and they found that they were able to perform enlightening experiments on many psychological topics by strictly objective methods. John B. Watson, who began his psychological career working with animals, announced the behaviorist position in 1913 by declaring that psychologists should not use any other methods. For many years experimental psychologists, including those not dedicated to any particular "ism," had demonstrated great ingenuity in inventing objective methods for attacking difficult psychological problems. The methods of Ebbinghaus in Germany and Pavlov in Russia, for example, had been quickly adopted in other countries, especially the United States. Thus the call for an objective study of behavior received a generally favorable reception.

The implications of the behaviorist approach to thought, however, did require some defense. When someone thinks, an outsider may not be able to observe any behavior at all until the results of the thought are announced. Watson got out of this predicament by equating thought with "inner speech." Speech is behavior, to be sure, acquired as an adaptation to social life; but social pressure and ordinary lassitude interfere with overt speech under many conditions. Thus the overt speech of uninhibited children migrates inward, as it were, to become covert or implicit in the socialized adult. Association between one idea and another in consciousness became, to the behaviorist, association between a covert symbol for a stimulus and a covert symbol for a response. Behaviorists began to define thinking as covert behavior, or behavior involving symbols.

To nonbelievers this seemed like obscurantism, pushing the problem inward beyond the possibility of empirical attack. But Watson and his followers believed that inner speech movements are not completely covert. Some efforts were made to record tongue movements during thought. Nothing very specific turned up, either because the recording instruments were not sensitive enough or because they were not attached to where the thought was. The musculature does show more activity in general, however, when the subject is thinking of something than when his mind is blank.

We must conclude that the influence of behaviorism on the psychology of thought was a negative one. Watson showed how some phenomena of thought could be rephrased to fit his system of behavior, but he did not show how to do anything about it. His criticism of subjective methodology scared many psychologists away from the topic of thinking. The distinction between thought as conscious content and thought as a problem-solving function was not always grasped, so that the taboo against introspection spread to a taboo against the investigation of intellectual activities in general.

THOUGHT ACQUIRES MOTIVES

One survival of the dualism of early psychology has frequently been expressed, and more frequently assumed, as a contrast between opposites: between instinct and intellect, or between emotion and reason. Comparisons between species, stimulated by evolutionary doctrine, at first reinforced this survival of faculty psychology: man has the power of reason; the lower animals are controlled by instinct or habit.

But evolutionary doctrine also saw man as endowed with the same instincts as the lower animals. In adapting to his environment he was motivated, like the other animals, toward survival of the species. The unity of the organism was explicitly stated by William McDougall when he wrote that man's power of thought was an adaptive biological function at the service of man's instincts.

Once the artificial distinction between motivation and thought was overcome and the relationship between the two became apparent, it was necessary to work out the details of this relationship. Woodworth powered this movement in 1914, pointing out the connection between interest and ability. Freud, McDougall, and others speculated about the learning of new drives, or at least greatly modified secondary drives, on the basis of primary drives; and the modern behaviorists are attempting to show precisely how this learning occurs in some simple cases. The effects of various drives on attention, perception, imagination, thought, and judgment also are active topics of experimental psychology today.

The Würzburg school discovered the need for dynamic concepts in understanding thinking and tried to fill the blank with the *Einstellung*. Because its only credentials were introspective and because psychologists were interested in other things, this concept did not catch on. Now, years later, when dynamic concepts have become more fashionable and objective methods for their investigation have been devised, the *Einstellung* by one name or another is a favorite topic of investigation.

The disordered mind of the madman has long been an intriguing subject of speculation, and many observers of the insane and the neurotic have attempted to contrast their irrationality with the thought of rational man. The gradual development of Freudian psychoanalysis in the first decades of this century helped to shift the emphasis from thought, in the sense of rationality, to motivation.

Because of Freud's associationist background, he used *thought* in its subjective meaning, as a conscious content. But his shrewd observations forced him to describe, or invent, mechanisms by which conscious thoughts are disguised and symptoms formed under pressure of the censor, or super-ego. The mechanisms are thought processes in a sense: repression, fantasy, symbolism, rationalization. But the emphasis in psychoanalysis has always been on the drives behind thought, their detours and collisions, rather than on the intellectual processes per se.

THOUGHT ACQUIRES CULTURE

When the early anthropologists of our civilization, fascinated by the theory of evolution, began to study less literate peoples, they interpreted primitive thinking as prelogical and irrational. A leader in this movement, E. B. Tyler, stated in 1871 that primitive man was animistic; that he looks at the world anthropomorphically and endows all things with a conscious-ness like his own. But as anthropology gradually became more critical and empirical, the differences between the mind of primitive man and that of civilized man seemed to dwindle away. The final coup, perhaps, was delivered by Paul Radin when he collected many wise and witty sayings from preliterate cultures in a book which he called *Primitive Man as Philosopher*. Anthropologists gradually came to state the differences in terms of cultural background, interests, and information rather than in terms of thought processes, though adequate comparisons between representative samples of different peoples have never actually been made.

The early social psychologists, writers like Tarde and LeBon, were intrigued by man's irrationality in social situations. Illustrations of imitation and mob violence were collected to show that social influences make people suggestible and that membership in a crowd reduces the individual's intellectual powers to the lowest level. When social psychology borrowed the objective methods of experimental and differential psychology, demonstrations of irrationality became very popular.

These bizarre overemphases were brought into better balance when the textbook writers (for example, Gardner Murphy, et al. in 1931 and 1937) undertook their undramatic function of integrating strange facts and diverse points of view. The social psychologists' primitive glee in showing that people are irrational, prejudiced, superstitious, suggestible, and undemocratic was muted by more systematic attempts to discover the origins and operation of values, attitudes, and opinions, whether sensible or foolish. Later chapters will show that research on bad judgment has contributed in a roundabout and incomplete way to the psychology of good judgment.

Just as important as the specific results of these developments in social psychology is the general effect of socializing all psychology. Emerging from his laboratory, the psychologist was occasionally asked by an anthropological colleague how his results would differ if the experiment had been done in New Guinea. Careful investigators then began to consider the implications of their subjects' attitudes toward any experiment or test, the instructions given by the experimenter, the laboratory atmosphere, and the social significance of the responses. In the past, these influences on thinking had been treated as nuisances, to be eliminated by careful control of the experimental conditions; but a nuisance taken seriously often becomes the starting point of more adequate theorizing.

Psychophysics: From Sensation to Judgment

Alongside the dramatic rise and fall of psychological schools, experimental psychology has been steadily expanding its interests and achievements. Introspective procedures have come and gone, but psychophysics since 1860—when Fechner published his *Elemente*—has been predominantly an objective science.

Fechner's interest at the outset was subjective, metaphysical, almost mystical. He wanted to measure the intensity of sensations so that he could tie the inner world of consciousness to the outer world of physical stimuli with the firmness of a mathematical equation. As so often happens, Fechner's aims have been ignored, but his psychophysical methods are in daily use. Experiments were soon undertaken to determine the acuity of each of the senses, acuity being defined eventually as precision of judgment. Sensory capacities under different conditions were charted, and anatomical and physiological correlates explored. Fechner's methods for studying preferences for physical stimuli, for example, rectangles of various proportions, were expanded into a new science of experimental aesthetics.

When psychologists asked how these judgments were made, they naturally turned to introspection for evidence. Careful observers reported images and other conscious contents when comparing a sound or weight with a standard, but as in the *Denkpsychologie* experiments, the results were disappointing. When the observer was well prepared, the judgment seemed to come directly, as soon as the second stimulus was presented. Perhaps the most interesting results were those of Müller and his students in about 1900. They noted that after a series of judgments, the observer was not comparing the lifted weight with an image of the standard weight, but rather with some absolute impression of the whole series for which he had gradually become *set* or *eingestellt.*

Refinement of the psychophysical methods moved toward holding the judging process constant, so that the functional relations between some aspect of the stimulus and some perceptual consequence could be clearly determined. Under ideal conditions, it was assumed that the judging process was standardized, and therefore psychophysical data could be published as "From the left eye of Observer B." But in the effort to improve the psychophysical methods, a number of constant errors and other phenomena of judgment came to light. And when these were taken as the objects of investigation rather than as incidental to the measurement of sensation, the experimental psychology of judgment was born.

An important constant error was often observed when each of a series of stimuli was compared with a standard stimulus. A midpoint or center can be calculated from the series of judgments, which under ideal conditions may be expected to coincide with the standard stimulus. It is called the *point of subjective equality,* or PSE. But it is not always exactly equal to the standard stimulus; the discrepancy is called a *constant* or *systematic error.* Hollingworth discovered (in about 1909) that when several series are used, the larger stimuli are underestimated and the smaller overestimated. The PSEs for each series approach the center of all the stimuli judged. This phenomenon, which he called the *central tendency,* and others called the *series effect,* has been observed in many experiments with different kinds of stimuli.

It is not necessary to compare each stimulus with a standard. The rating method appeared around the end of the last century, applied first to the judgment of affective stimuli and other complex objects of judgment. When the rating method was used in a psychophysical experiment, for instance, on the loudness of sounds, it was called either the *method of single stimuli,* since no standard was available for comparison, or the *method of absolute judgment,* since, as noted above, the judgments seemed to be direct.

Something similar to the series effect was noticed when the method of single stimuli was used, as in rating the affective tone of colors or odors.

Judgment of each stimulus was influenced by the preceding stimulus, in fact by the whole range of stimuli. In the 1920s this phenomenon was termed *affective contrast* and *affective equilibrium*. Then, as Gestalt psychology extended its influence, the phrase "frame of reference" was loosely applied to these facts when they came to light in many fields of psychology. In the 40s, Helson developed a quantitative formulation of frames of reference: this assumes that the organism adapts to a certain level which is a function of all the stimuli and that each single stimulus is judged in relation to this adaptation level. Applications of adaptation-level theory in several areas soon followed (Helson, 1964); in fact, many of the experiments on scales of judgment surveyed in the last chapter of this book were undertaken in support or refutation of Helson's concept of adaptation level.

Other quantitative models and hypotheses about judgment were borrowed from economics, personality research, social psychology, and perception and applied to more complex situations, such as decisions under risk and combinations of stimulus dimensions. Clinical psychologists began to treat diagnosis as a problem in judgment. Thus the psychology of judgment became more complicated, more quantitative, and more integrated with general psychological theory.

Tests and Abilities

People have always speculated about the differences between human beings, but differential psychology had to wait for progress in general psychology. The pioneers in this movement, Galton, Cattell, and Binet, investigated mental processes before they constructed mental tests. Galton and Cattell had been working on simple processes, while Binet had been working on reasoning, studying the thinking of his two daughters as well as that of chess players and arithmetical prodigies. Hence, he characterized intelligence as the ability to understand directions, to maintain a mental set, and to correct one's errors; and the tests he constructed along these lines were most useful in the school situation.

Once the testing movement got started, after World War I, it acquired terminology, methodology, and, to some extent, personnel of its own. Hints for new tests soon followed from the successes and failures of previous tests, as well as from the findings of general experimental psychology. In recent years, the testing of intelligence and the psychology of thought have progressed side by side, with only occasional interdisciplinary contacts.

The generalizations of differential psychology have for the most part been of a statistical nature, based on correlations between test scores; psychological interpretations of the relationships have been secondary and tentative. It was noticed early that all tests that could be called intellectual are positively correlated. In 1904 Spearman announced his two-factor theory, stating that success in any task depends on g, a general ability required for all tasks, and on s, an ability specific to each. Later, he devised methods for computing the amount of g involved in each test and the amount displayed by each subject. When he came to discuss the nature of g, he spoke of a fund of cerebral energy that is manifested in "eduction" of relations and of correlates.

The two-factor theory encountered many objections. In England group factors, intermediate between g and s, had to be recognized. In America Thurstone developed a more general method that analyzed the correlations into a number of factors, none of which need be more general than the others. This method results in many factors or abilities, and a whole new methodology was developed for identifying abilities and purifying them in later tests. The enterprise has been carried forward in recent years by Guilford's (1967) long-term program of test development and analysis. His three-dimensional model of the structure of intellect generated many hypothetical abilities and guided the construction of tests of these abilities. The kinds of intellectual operations performed are: cognition, memory, divergent and convergent production, and evaluation; the kinds of content on which the operations are performed are: figural, symbolic, semantic, and behavioral. And the kinds of products resulting from the operations on these contents are: units, classes, relations, systems, transformations, and implications. These abilities are all involved in thinking, in one way or another, but divergent-production abilities seem to make a special contribution to creative thinking. The tests devised by Guilford and his students and their factor analyses of the test scores brought new excitement to the topic of creative thinking—long neglected by most psychologists and educators—and initiated a new research trend.

Intellectual Development of the Child

The invention and refinement of intelligence tests in England, France, and the United States yielded useful quantitative indices of intellectual status. When norms became available, each child's development could be compared, in a general way, with the development of others. But there were always a few people, including Binet himself, who sought more than a general quantitative index.

Jean Piaget was one who rejected the quantitative measures for a more qualitative approach and, in the 1920s, initiated a long-term program to chart the stages of the child's progress toward adult modes of thought. Although the questions he raised and his research style were unfamiliar, he eventually won a wide audience in both psychological and educational circles. His unorthodox claims about the cognitive schemas that the child constructs and through which he knows the world could not long be ignored and are now, in fact, being integrated with the more familiar notions.

Meanings of Thought, Past and Present

In classical times, thought was a goddess who appeared in many faces, and today the terms *thought* and *thinking* appear in many contexts with several meanings which must be carefully scrutinized. The investigator can dream of one natural unveiled goddess, but he must work with several empirical manifestations. Finer distinctions can always be made, but most references to thought and thinking can be grouped under four headings: (1) Thought as a topic, (2) as mental experience, (3) as solving problems, and (4) as mediation.

THOUGHT AS A TOPIC

Thought has often been used in a very broad way to refer to intellectual activities, intelligent behavior, or abstract operations, just as coordinate terms like *perception* and *personality* are used to refer to other broad divisions of psychology. In this sense, *thought* is a nontechnical designation for the contents of a book or course of study; such usage does not cause much misunderstanding because it is not intended to be precise. The most frequent error consists of treating this topic of thinking as a minor topic, subsidiary to learning, perception, language, or something else.

THOUGHT AS MENTAL EXPERIENCE

Thinking also refers to mental experience or the contents of consciousness, as in the questions: "What are you thinking about?" "What's on your mind?" In this sense, a thought is the object of the verb "to think"; the passive form is also common: "The thought occurred to me that . . ." Thinking in this usage is equivalent to attending, so that the above questions could be rephrased as: "What are you attending to?" When psychology was defined as the study of consciousness by the British associationists and the Wundtians, this was the standard meaning of thought.

Any literate person can report the ideas, images, and feelings that come to mind while he is smelling a rose, dreaming of past failure and future success, or solving a problem. When thinking has this meaning, a distinction is made between *reality thinking*, which occurs during solution of a problem, and *autistic thinking*, which is regulated by personal hopes and fears.

The methods of investigating thinking in this sense are necessarily subjective, and the behaviorists, who insist on objective methods, consequently discard this aspect of thought. Many others are suspicious of the accuracy of subjective methods, simply because the results obtained from different subjects and under different conditions are often inconsistent. But there need be no uncertainty about what thinking, in this meaning, refers to, as long as it is properly circumscribed and differentiated from the other meanings.

THOUGHT AS SOLVING PROBLEMS

Thought, or *thinking,* is also often used today to refer to activities directed toward solution of a problem, in contrast to routine or thoughtless activities. "I don't know what to do; I'll have to stop and think." Many psychologists prefer the more awkward term *problem solving,* rather than *thinking,* to avoid confusion with other meanings of thinking. Synonyms for the verb "to think" in this sense are: to cogitate, deliberate, ponder, reflect, and study. In contrast to thought as mental experience, this meaning stresses adaptive activities rather than the contents of consciousness and does not state whether these activities are or are not open to subjective observation.

Problem solving includes creative thinking, deductive reasoning, and judgment as special cases; under some conditions concept achievement is a kind of problem solving also. The effort to understand a difficult paragraph or a cryptic lecture involves thinking in the sense of problem solving, but here the difficulty lies not in the mechanical aspects of reading or listening, but rather in the abstract concepts or linguistic structures. Thus the problems of problem solving range from the solution of jigsaw puzzles to comprehension of an argument about the meaning of freedom.

THOUGHT AS MEDIATION

Thought is the name of a topic in the first meaning above, a mental experience in the second, and an activity in the next; but in another sense, *thought* refers to the mediation of activity. If one stops to think, to solve a problem, much will happen before the solution is executed, and these internal mediating events also deserve the name of *thought.*

If the subjective method of observation is assumed to be adequate, these mediating events are open to direct observation. Thus thought in this sense overlaps thought as mental experience, except that the emphasis is on those mental experiences that occur during the solution of a problem. William James, the Würzburg psychologists, the early behaviorists, and others exposed the inadequacies of this method for the investigation of problem solving, but there is still some residual confusion between direct subjective observation of mediating events and theorizing about them.

Since the solution of a problem often covers a long period when there is little relevant behavior to observe, mediating events seem to be theoretically necessary; but the practice today is to treat them as hypothetical constructs which, like others, should be tested against observable data to confirm their explanatory utility. Various modern behaviorists, in order to fit mediators into their general theoretical programs, have assumed that these constructs have the properties of implicit stimulus-response associations, observing activities, covert verbal responses, and symbols of observable objects. Berlyne (1965) has put it as follows: "Whenever a symbolic response is implicit and has a preponderantly cue-producing function, we shall call it a *thought*. We shall refer to a string of such cue-producing symbolic responses as a *train of thought* [p. 27]."

Theorizing about hypothetical constructs is good clean fun, but it is not free-for-all speculation. The empirical validation of such constructs requires an explicit statement of the assumptions. Most behaviorists assume, for example, that mediating responses are strengthened and weakened as observable responses are, that they are elicited similarly, and so on. The theoretical links are intended to tie the mediating events to observable antecedents and consequents, and thus to explain the overt behavior. If *thinking* means anything to a behaviorist today, this is usually what it means.

Other theorists can play the same game. Hypotheses about mediating events also refer to cognitive structures, such as concepts, conceptual systems, principles, and logical relations, or, in the context of information processing, self-instructions and programs. Several cognitive processes, as well as a single associative process, are also conceivable. The theoretical status of such cognitive mediators in problem solving is formally similar to that of implicit responses but there are differences that have given this meaning of thought a somewhat different signification.

Concepts, for example, were discussed long before the theoretical apparatus of hypothetical constructs was invented. Education consists in large part of achieving concepts, because they are useful in communication as well as problem solving. The achievement of concepts is therefore tested as a measure of educational progress (without regard to their mediation in the solution of any particular problem) under the assumption that they constitute standard knowledge, which will be instrumental to the solution of many problems in the future. The great distinction of man compared to the other animals is this ability to represent things conceptually, by words and other symbols, and then to use these symbols in communicating and solving problems.

Thought in the sense of conceptual or symbolic processes resembles thought in the sense of cue-producing responses since both have the internal mediating function, but concepts also function in external social communication. Whether concepts, principles, and similar cognitive achievements should be treated under the same heading as response-produced cues and implicit verbal responses may be argued; but they are all mediators in a broad sense, and this is what many people mean by thinking, especially when they contrast it with immediate response to stimuli. And this must also be what people mean by such terms as *conceptual thinking* and *abstract thought.*

AN ATTEMPT AT INTEGRATION

Each of these manifestations of the elusive goddess has its own charm and has attracted, at various times, its own circle of worshippers. But the best scheme, at present, for embracing the complete meaning of thought is a definition that pulls together the coherent aspects of all these diverse manifestations. In this spirit, we can define thinking as problem solving and including mediators and mental experience to the extent that they assist the explanation of problem solving. Since mediators are unobservable and have in the past few decades been notoriously difficult to validate, they are an insecure base for definition of anything. Some mediators are pertinent to problem solving, but not all; some mental experience is pertinent to problem solving, but not all. Concepts are pertinent because the attainment of a concept may be a kind of problem solving and because concepts are instrumental to the solution of many problems. Intellectual history—often called the history of thought—documents the reciprocal relationship between the struggles for conceptual understanding and the solution of concrete problems; so, over a shorter time span, does the educational history of the individual. If we include concepts and the solution of different kinds of problems, we include practically all the activities that are usually discussed under the topic of thinking. But retaining problem solving in the center of the definition emphasizes the adaptive function of thought.

Although an integrative definition like the one just given is plausible and convenient for locating both the center and periphery of our topic, the experiments and discussions to be reviewed here have arisen in fact out of several different conceptions of the meaning of thinking, and clarity often requires that these meanings be identified and differentiated. In questions about thought in the lower animals, for example, the meaning of thought as mental experience is not applicable; but when thought means problem solving, abundant evidence is available. In discussions of language and thought, it makes a difference whether thought means mental experience, problem solving, or mediation. The research trend that treats concept achievement as problem solving overlaps only slightly with the trend that treats concepts as mediators in the solution of larger problems. The subject of this volume is the contribution of diverse experiments and discussions to the topic of thinking. The contribution of each cannot be properly evaluated unless we remember that different investigators may begin with different conceptions of thinking and that the data may be relevant to different aspects of the topic.

Recent Theoretical Trends and Countertrends

Early psychological theorists of the armchair type, such as the British associationists, were preoccupied with the phenomena of thought. They speculated on what happens when someone tries to "think of" a word, how one idea suggests another, and why it is harder to think of some things than others. Then psychology became more experimental. Experimenters found it easier to devise good experiments for studying the behavior of the lower animals and the simpler activities of man than for studying man's complex intellectual activities, and the theories followed the same path of least resistance. Recently, thinking, by one name or another, has attracted more attention from theorists.

We must admit that, in the accuracy of their predictions, psychological theories are not very successful. Predictions based on current theories are only slightly more accurate than those based on the intuitions of an intelligent layman. But psychological theories, including theories of thinking, generate interesting experiments and promise greater understanding in the future. Such theories have some value in explaining the behavior of the subject of an experiment; they have greater value in explaining the behavior of the experimenter who designs the experiment and interprets the results. The three theoretical trends that are most relevant today are the cognitive approach, stimulus-response associationism, and the information-processing approach.

THE COGNITIVE APPROACH

Despite the older meanings, *cognition* is often used today in a nontechnical sense to refer to a division of psychology, and in this sense it is synonymous with thought. When cognitive tests and cognitive abilities are contrasted with noncognitive tests and abilities, this must be the meaning intended.

COGNITION AS KNOWLEDGE
In the more formal meaning that one finds in the dictionaries, *cognition* refers to knowledge or the process of obtaining knowledge. Perception was formerly included under cognition in this sense but it is often treated separately today. Knowing where something is in relation to other things is one form of cognition; knowing what event is likely to follow another event is a second form. Knowledge also consists of knowing names for things, classes of things, and relationships between classes. This abstract knowledge is manifested largely by the use of words and other symbols, in accordance with the standards of the culture or of special branches of knowledge. New knowledge is acquired by the study of words as well as by the perception of subjects. Thus, *cognition* in the *abstract* form implies escape from the domination of immediate perception, and much research on standard concepts fits into this meaning.

Knowledge and observable behavior are reciprocally related. Yet knowledge itself is not observable; it is inferred from behavior, most often verbal behavior, such as the use of words in accordance with cultural standards, answers to questions, and the manipulation of symbols to solve problems. Thus, although cognition is an old, established idea, methods for making inferences about cognition will have to be examined closely in later pages.

COGNITIVE THEORIES
Cognitive theories take many shapes, but in general they emphasize the individual's view of the world: what he knows or believes, what he perceives, what he expects, how he organizes his experience. The European

phenomenological school raised the question of how the individual experiences objects and events and how he represents them to himself. Gestalt psychology emphasized the organization of experience and used cognitive structures, such as the figure-and-ground structure, and reorganizations of these to interpret perception and thought. Lewin extended the Gestalt principles of perceptual organization to social psychology and invoked cognitive structures to explain interpersonal relations, attitude change, and motivation in social situations.

More recent interpretations of attitude formation and change have made much use of quantitative relations between cognitions, as indicated by such terms as *cognitive balance, cognitive congruity,* and *cognitive dissonance.* Thus, although the cognitive message came to America with a foreign accent, these current cognitive theories have the characteristic American love of numbers.

COGNITIVE STRUCTURES

Cognitive theories can be contrasted with stimulus-response associationism in several respects (Ausubel, 1965; Hilgard, 1956; Mandler, 1962; Scheerer, 1954). While the associationists said that the rat in a maze learns a chain of responses from the starting box to the goal box, Tolman—an animal psychologist with a cognitive outlook—said that the rat constructs a cognitive map and learns where the goal box is in relation to the maze as a whole. The theoretical constructs preferred by cognitive theorists are cognitive structures assumed to represent the relevant aspects of the environment: some of the structures that have already been investigated are images, classes, dimensions, systems of classes and dimensions, schemas that represent objects, propositions, and relations between propositions.

According to this view, the environment is known through such cognitive structures, and these structures control our reactions to the environment. The individual does not just respond to the stimulus that he perceives; rather, he constructs a pattern or representation of certain attributes of the environment and then adapts to the environment as he has constructed it. Some cognitive investigations examine how an individual develops his own set of attributes for construing the data of his experience. And some research is focused, not on any particular cognition, but on certain characteristics of cognitive structures, such as the number of attributes an individual uses to describe a person.

COGNITIVE PROCESSES

While associationists talk about only one process, association, cognitive theorists speak of many processes, all of which involve organization or reorganization of the structure. An external structure may be represented by an internal structure, such as an image. A structure may be divided into substructures that are meaningful only as parts of the whole. Several structures may be arranged in a hierarchy that functions as a whole. Cognitive structures are compared with other cognitive structures. Classes may be arranged into a system, and a system of classes rearranged into an alternative system. A plan of action may include constituent acts which would be meaningless, and perhaps could not be executed, in isolation.

Cognitive psychologists often do not explicitly identify and describe the cognitive structures and processes that they assume, and methods for making inferences about these hypothetical constructs are not standardized; but certainly the processes differ from the cumulative learning of associations between stimuli and responses. It is the cognitive psychologists, especially, who object to treating thinking as a kind of learning.

STIMULUS-RESPONSE ASSOCIATIONISM

Modern behaviorism, except for a few followers of Tolman, depends on associations between stimulus and response for the explanation of behavior. The principles of learning, developed in simple situations, often with lower animals, are assumed to apply, with appropriate elaborations, to the behavior of sophisticated human beings in complex situations. But behaviorism has altered its shape considerably in order to escape the limitations of Watsonian theory.

In experiments on lower animals, behavior is controlled by physical reinforcements—such as food, water, and electric shock—but in experiments on human subjects it is initiated and directed by verbal instructions and the reinforcement for success is usually verbal also. Hence, associationist theories of human learning have attempted in one way or another to include verbal stimuli and verbal responses.

Behaviorists, with a few exceptions, now admit hypothetical constructs. Although the early behaviorists tried to limit psychology to the study of observable behavior, most modern behaviorists are willing to state hypotheses about unobservable or implicit responses that determine observable behavior. A hypothetical construct having the properties of a verbal response greatly increases the theoretical potentialities of the S-R approach. A stimulus word may evoke a response word directly, to be sure; but it may also evoke an implicit verbal response, which acts as an implicit stimulus to evoke an observable response word. The early behaviorists treated thought as inner speech and hoped to get records of minimal speech responses during thought; modern behaviorists, on the other hand, deliberately treat verbal mediators as hypothetical constructs, unobservable by definition. Thus it appears that whereas Watson tried to explain behavior peripherally, in terms of muscular and glandular responses, most modern behavior theories explain behavior centrally, in terms of internal unobservable mediators. For this reason, the term *behaviorism* is now misleading, but the term *stimulus-response associationism* is still appropriate.

Once hypothetical mediators are incorporated in the theory, complex activities can be interpreted as due to chains of Ss and Rs. Theoretically, the solution to a problem can occur when some response, perhaps an exploratory one, is fortuitously associated with another response that is in turn associated with the goal response.

In addition to response chains, modern behaviorists often assume response hierarchies: that is, a complex problem situation elicits many implicit responses, varying in strength. The response with the strongest association to the problem stimuli is elicited first, then other responses of less associative strength. If the first response is rewarded, there is no problem. This definition of a problem implies that interfering responses are elicited first and thus that the solution process consists of the cumulative strengthening of the correct association and the weakening of the others. Such a hypothetical hierarchy of responses can be validated most convincingly in the case of verbal problems because word associations can be recorded objectively and a hierarchy of associative strengths of different response words independently determined.

Other modifications of behaviorism have been proposed to apply to complex behavior, the important assumption in all of them being that internal, unobservable stimuli and responses are associated in accordance with the same laws as external stimuli and responses. The pages to follow will document the great flexibility of modern S-R theory in meeting the challenges coming from other theories, especially cognitive ones. With a few simple mechanisms, S-R theorists have been able, at least in theory, to account for many of the complex and abstract phenomena that the cognitive experimenters have forced them to consider.

From this discussion it is easy to see why the older behaviorists preferred to talk about problem solving, or problem-solving behavior, rather than thought, and why modern behaviorists, when they talk about thought, mean mediation, usually verbal mediation.

COGNITIVE AND ASSOCIATIVE THEORIES COMPARED

The outlines of the classic controversy between these two theories are becoming blurred, and current theoretical allegiances are no longer easy to detect (Van de Geer and Jaspers, 1966). Even in the verbal learning laboratory, that ancient citadel of associationism, explanations that invoke cognitive mediators, such as images and linguistic structures, are now being offered. When cognitive psychologists get down to experimental details and when S-R psychologists discuss patterns of response that are evoked as a unit, the differences often seem to be only semantic. If we assume that the solution of a problem involves a hierarchy of alternative cognitive structures, is this a cognitive or an associative approach?

Psychological theories are very general, and interpretations of the results of specific experiments require specific conjectures as well as minor principles of limited generality. Thus experimental tests of hypotheses involving cognitive mediators and S-R mediators seldom lead to results that clearly reject either; mathematical theorists have noted that when these alternative hypotheses are rewritten in mathematical form, they are often indistinguishable. All theories of interest here must account for complex structures of behavior and thought; the method of dealing with such structures is more important than the hypothetical units from which they are allegedly fabricated. How the structures are built up and reorganized, and whether the reorganization process is continuous or discontinuous, is what matters.

The differences between S-R and cognitive views have not vanished, of course. There are still psychologists who dismiss any psychological explanation as devoid of theory if it does not identify the relevant Ss and Rs and suggest how they are associated, and there are others (e.g., Asch, 1969) who assert that the associations themselves require explanation. If one is convinced that mediators must have the properties of responses, he will be reluctant to discuss abstract or "responseless" thought, just as earlier psychologists were reluctant to discuss "imageless" thought. Cognitive psychologists are more willing to accept a contemplative view of thought; that some problems are solved by just sitting and thinking. Behaviorists insist that a response of some sort, somewhere, is necessary.

Vestigial methodological differences can still be observed, if one looks for them. While all students of thinking seem to agree on the importance of mediators, some cognitive psychologists are willing to trust the phenomenological method for obtaining evidence about them. Most behaviorists, however, even those who speculate extravagantly about implicit responses and print many-splendored diagrams of hypothetical associations, consider the inference of mediating events a difficult methodological problem and hope ultimately to tie them to objective dependent variables. Cognitive theorists accept cognition on its own level; behaviorists try to reduce it to something else. The behaviorist approach to concepts, for example, asks how the subject learns to make a common response to superficially dissimilar objects; the cognitive approach asks how the subject categorizes the world of the senses and brings order out of chaos.

THE INFORMATION-PROCESSING APPROACH

Information as a technical term came into psychology in the 1950s, borrowed from telephone engineering. A switch that may be open or closed is wired to a light in another room that may be on or off. The status of the light, which is considered the output of this little communication system, gives information about the status of the switch, the input. The information in the input may, of course, be quite large, as when there are many switches or when the input consists of speech patterns. Then interest turns to the capacity of the communication channel to transmit all the information accurately, without distortion. A special index of amount of information, the bit, was devised to measure information in the input and output and thus to study the amount of information transmitted.

MEASUREMENT OF INFORMATION
Psychologists found such measures useful in standardizing the information in the materials presented in concept experiments, in computing the information transmitted by judgments on a rating scale, and in analyzing language (Miller, 1956). Many experiments gave evidence of an upper limit in the

human capacity for retaining and processing information when measured in this way. It soon became apparent, however, that the usefulness of information measures was restricted by the tendency of human beings to organize information into higher units and then to process these as wholes. If we treat the individual as an information channel, it is what he does to the information between input and output that is important for the psychology of thinking.

PROCESSING OF INFORMATION
Psychologists' interest in information measurement declined while interest in information processing increased, bringing a bright new style to the parade of psychological theories. According to this view, the information in the environment is coded into categories and represented by a system of symbols, such as a set of words or numbers. Thus encoded, the information may be stored in memory and later retrieved and decoded to fit the requirements of the task at hand. But once encoded, the information can be recoded and processed in many ways. The environmental stimuli are not processed, of course, but the symbols that represent the information in the environment. Information coded in a visual system may be transformed or recoded into an auditory system or a system of hand signals. Information from the environment may be matched with information retrieved from memory. If the information matches, a second operation follows; if it does not match, a different operation follows, or the same operation is repeated; some of the processes of information processing are: encoding, decoding, recoding, transforming, matching, scanning, storing, and retrieving. The more complex processes can be understood as strategies for getting around the limitations on the amount of information an individual can attend to at any one moment.

COMPUTER SIMULATION
Information processes were suggested by research on information measurement, by the subjective analysis of intellectual operations, and by the potentialities of electronic circuits, which can recode, store, retrieve, transform, and perform many other operations that go by the name of *artificial intelligence*. Some information-processing theories have been deliberately written in the form of a program for an electronic computer in order to see just how far the computer can go in simulating human thinking. Such programs are as interesting theoretically as other theories even though they may not fit the requirements of any particular computer. It is the black magic of computer simulation, however, that has made possible an exciting and easily misunderstood approach to the understanding of thinking.

Computer-based theories, or models, merit description here because they differ in intent, power, and certainly in style from the more familiar theories that have so long held the center of the psychological forum. Like mathematical theories, computer theories are more precisely stated than verbal theories. Just as one must make precise statements to permit mathematical calculations, one must make precise statements to program a computer. Once the theoretical details are worked out and programmed for the computer, the program constitutes the model, and the computer can be dispensed with—in theory. Usually it is necessary, however, to perform the many involved numerical operations and realize the model. Furthermore, a computer model has so many interacting component operations that after the start button is first pushed, the system's behavior, like that of any other automaton, may not be exactly what its builder expected.

The great power of electronic computers could, of course, be harnessed to any theory that can be stated explicitly. But, as it has happened, most computer programs for the simulation of thinking have been based on an information-processing approach rather than, for example, an association approach, and have aimed at a description of processes rather than the prediction of results of experimental manipulations. These characteristics may not be permanent; Berlyne's (1965) speculations point the way to computer models for a modified S-R associationism.

The most prominent feature of the present computer models for thought is their attempt to simulate in detail the output of a human problem solver. Other theories attempt to predict group means or proportions of successes under different experimental conditions or perhaps the shape of a curve, but computer simulation aims to duplicate the problem-solving efforts of an active subject as recorded in a protocol covering many pages. The subject's final solution, or failure, is only a small part of the record. Thus a program for simulating problem solving is quite extensive, and it is particularly difficult for computer model builders to communicate to others what the theory says. The model is not neatly wrapped up in a few verbal statements or mathematical equations. It consists of many pages of specific details written in a specific language—most often a language elaborated to fit information-processing concepts to the requirements and capabilities of the digital computer. Thus this is no easy way to instant development of a new theory. The writing and checking of a simulation program takes a tremendous investment of time and skill.

Such theories, if they are theories, differ from other theories, and the procedures for verification differ correspondingly. The artificial intelligence of the computer, its capacity for complicated numerical operations—after being programmed by a sophisticated human being—does not demonstrate that its behavior simulates human behavior. A direct comparison is necessary. The observable behavior of the human subject is, of course, his oral or written output, while the computer prints its output in the information-processing language; but the two outputs can often be translated into the same symbol system so that agreements and disagreements can be counted. Furthermore, many attempts at simulation select problems which require the human subject to make responses, such as *Green square, Turn both switches up*, and *LLRL*, that are easy to compare with the computer printout.

Computer simulation experiments generally use only a few subjects and adjust the program to each; the agreement of the computer output and the human output is checked for each subject separately. In another procedure, the two outputs are compared during the first half of a problem-solving enterprise, the necessary adjustments in the program are made to take care of the discrepancies, and then the modified program is checked against the last part of the human output. One small indication of the success of simulation is that, when different problems are solved, the order of difficulty for the computer is about the same as for the human thinker (Hunt, Marin, and Stone, 1965; Simon and Kotovsky, 1963).

Certainly more goes on than is written down by the subject. There is no place as yet in computer programs for casual comments of the subjects, such as "I think you are trying to confuse me," that may or may not indicate something important about the direction of his thinking. But if the elements and the moves of the problem can be symbolized without too much difficulty, the subject's output may represent his moves, and perhaps his hypotheses and strategies for testing them, fairly well. The hypothetical, covert activity is a question for this type of model—as for all others. Any observable output can be generated by more than one set of hypothetical internal operations. The hope of the computer experts is that, if the program simulates the overt aspects of complex problem-solving behavior in detail, then the information-processing operations that produce the computer's output will be similar to the human subject's internal operations that produce his. And these operations can be examined by examining the program.

Like other types of theories, computer models lead to new experiments. If the program solves a problem by a certain operation, a new type of experiment may be undertaken to see if flesh-and-blood people perform such an operation. It is not necessary to assume that neurons work the way transistors work. Designing an experiment for human subjects suggested by the performance of an electronic wizard is no different in principle from designing a experiment suggested by animal research, or a logical proposition, or a theory of social organization. Here, as elsewhere, progress comes from the two-way interaction between theory and experiment.

The reactions to computer models of thought go both ways, like reactions to psychoanalysis, factor analysis, and other new ideas. While some people have hailed the dawn of a new era and rushed to adopt computer terminology as the mark of sophistication, others have viewed the computer as a dehumanizing machine and, more pertinent here, certain psychologists have perceived it as a threat to their theoretical establishment. It is safe to predict, however, that computer theories will not displace other theories any more than clerical applications of the computer have displaced clerks. Computer models do not show that S-R theories, Gestalt theories, or any others are wrong. Instead of attacking, computer simulation is outflanking entrenched theories and opening up attractive new fields for electronic exploitation. Theorizing is becoming more differentiated.

Two consequences of this innovation take the form of the lifting of old taboos. The prohibition of process-tracing experiments, maintained for many years by the S-R establishment, cannot stand against the accomplishments, limited though they are at present, of simulation models of problem solving.

Secondly, words like *thinking* and *thought*, outlawed by some psychologists and treated with suspicion by many, are now being rehabilitated. Since the pioneer Turing raised the catchy question "Can a machine think?" in his celebrated 1950 paper in *Mind*, the computer fraternity has used these terms freely, and psychologists' language habits cannot resist the prestige associated with a machine that makes $400 an hour. Theoretical activity seems to be immune to accusations of teleology and anthropomorphism when so much of the activity is carried on by an electronic computer.

ECLECTICISM AND INTEGRATION

The theoretical approaches mentioned above will be applied to specific topics in the pages to follow, but a large share of the research on thinking proceeds from an eclectic position that can be characterized in negative terms as nondoctrinaire and is not far from functionalism. Many psychologists in planning research and discussing their results slip easily from associationist language into cognitive language and back again, adding a phrase about transformations, with a semantic flexibility that seems irresponsible, or at best superficial, to true believers. The eclectic is likely to be more receptive to new ideas and new language, even to those that do not fit well with the old, than the doctrinaire. The eclectic strategy is organized, not by a grand inclusive theory, but around effects or principles of medium size, such as functional fixedness, and around the diverse influences of important variables, such as word frequency, with the expectation, not usually explicit, of a grand synthesis later.

If we assume that an individual trying to solve a problem will do whatever he can under the circumstances, it is easy to say, with eclectic informality, that he *uses* facts, tools, concepts, knowledge of the situation, knowledge of common errors, strategies of recall, strategies for processing information, and any other tricks he may possess. The controlling influences of attention and set were studied from a nondoctrinaire position before the behaviorists and the cognitive psychologists broadened their systems to incorporate such controls. We could say instead that the situation elicits various response patterns, or that the field forces compel cognitive reorganization, or that the input information is recoded. The functional manner of speaking, which appears to make the individual rather than the situation the master of his behavior, is particularly convenient for discussing the polymorphous activities to be covered in this book. But it is just a manner of speaking. It does not bias the interpretation of the data, and other language could serve as well —though awkward circumlocutions would often be required.

The integration of findings from different approaches is facilitated by translation from one theoretical language into another, but the grand synthesis is advanced more fundamentally by the identification of common principles. To this end, Campbell (1960) has drawn attention, at a very abstract plane of analysis, to the wide variations in behavior and the selective retention of the more adaptative variations at all phyletic levels and all levels of human activity from reflex to creative thought. "A blind-variation-and-selective-retention process is fundamental to all inductive achievements, to all genuine increases in knowledge, to all increases in fit of system to environment [p. 380]." These variations may be genetic variations retained by natural selection; they may be variations in behavior retained by selective feedback. Large cognitive units of knowledge may also be produced in variety, and the selection may be cognitive, based on knowledge gained from previous blind variation and selective retention.

With similar intent at integration but within a more limited range, Mandler (1962) has shown how some cognitive structures can be built out of associations and Berlyne (1965) has used his neo-associationism to explain, in abstract terms, the "structure and direction of thinking." The integration of associationist principles for simple learning with cognitive principles for abstract operations offers a possibility of synthesis that is being explored by many contemporary students of thought.

CHAPTER 2

COGNITION
AND
CONCEPTS

s happens so often in the development of a science, the two terms *cognition* and *concepts* refer to overlapping sets of facts, yet they have not often appeared in the same context. Both have had long and honorable careers in the history of psychology, but they have functioned in different traditions and their paths have seldom crossed. Both will be more clearly understood when they are brought together. This chapter discusses the nature of concepts and summarizes the evidence on conceptual and cognitive achievements, mostly from laboratory research. The next will discuss individual differences and development.

The Nature of Concepts

As a simple illustration of the nature of concepts, let us consider the case of the child who has divided up his environment into things that are animal, vegetable, or mineral. We could say that this is a three-part cognitive structure or that he has learned three concepts. Perhaps he has the animals further divided into large and small, the vegetables into edible and inedible, and the minerals into soft and hard. This organization, represented below, illustrates a more elaborate cognitive structure or conceptual system:

ANIMAL: *large, small*
VEGETABLE: *edible, inedible*
MINERAL: *soft, hard*

His knowledge of the objects of his world has been organized and, within the limits of his ability, he can classify objects according to this system. Furthermore, he knows the words for each class so that he can communicate with other people about them. And he can use this cognitive structure to assimilate new knowledge and to solve problems. For example, if he sees a picture of an unfamiliar object and is told that it is an animal, he will expect it to act as other animals act. Once the child has achieved such a cognitive structure, he can make some sense out of what would otherwise be a meaningless world.

Some of the questions that psychologists have struggled with are: How do children, and adults for that matter, learn classes? How do they acquire more comprehensive cognitive systems? How do they attach words to classes? How do they learn the meanings of words? In a systematic treatment of thinking, it is convenient to consider concepts first because they are the basic elements of thought and because some of the results of concept research will be helpful in later chapters.

THE SPECIAL INTERESTS OF PSYCHOLOGICAL SPECIALTIES

Psychologists were not the first to study the concept; no science or art has exclusive rights to this elusive notion. On the contrary, teachers, philosophers, mathematicians, and other scholars have discussed the concept in general and the special concepts of their disciplines for a long time, and it is only recently that psychologists have devised methods for empirical investigation of the concept and have tried to find a place for it in their theories.

Experimental psychologists have been concerned with the learning of concepts under controlled conditions in the laboratory. They tend to use artificial concepts appropriate to the method, and the experiment ends when the criterion of learning is reached. These concepts are therefore defined to fit this situation.

Developmental psychologists have tried to trace the intellectual growth of the child, charting his conceptual abilities, limitations, and characteristic thought patterns at different ages. To give one example, a prominent trend runs from the concrete thinking of the child to the abstract verbal thinking of the adult.

Educational psychologists, trying to understand and promote learning in the classroom, have always been involved with concepts. Much of education consists of learning the standard concepts of culture, the abstract ones being of course the most difficult. Teachers and textbooks are concerned, not only with a single concept, but also with a system of concepts utilized in discussion of a topic of convenient size, such as the nitrogen cycle. Here the definitions, methods, and criteria of achievement have all been devised to fit the educational situation.

Thus the psychological specialties have looked at concepts from different points of view and have used their own materials and methods of investigation. The concepts studied by educational psychologists and tested by educational achievement tests, for example, have been more realistic and more abstract than those of experimental psychologists. Each specialty has something to contribute, however, and we shall try to integrate their contributions to attain a general understanding of concepts.

THE SEMANTICS OF CONCEPTS

Another specialty that contributes to this understanding is semantics, which studies the relation between words and what they refer to. In the example above, when the child has mastered the concept of *vegetable,* he uses the word *vegetable,* or some other symbol, to refer to this class of objects. The symbols most widely used in intellectual operations are words, of course, and whatever a word refers to is its meaning. The function words, such as *to, of,* and *or,* do not have meaning in this sense; they are used rather as syntactical devices to relate different parts of a communication. It is the object words, mostly nouns, pronouns, verbs, and adjectives, that have meaning in that they refer to other things, such as objects, events, persons, actions, qualities, and classes. Thinking consists in large part of manipulating meaning by manipulating words, and the study of thinking requires a minimal analysis of meaning.

In its most general sense, meaning is knowledge of structure, of the relations between things. When we inquire about the meaning of a historical event, we are inquiring about how it is related to other events, how it fits into larger historical trends. When we ask the meaning of a woman's suicide attempt, we are asking how it fits into her personality structure. Likewise when we ask the meaning of a word, we are asking how it is related to objects and to other words. The meaning of a word is a special case in that the word-referent relation is quite arbitrary, but it is culturally standardized so that speaker and listener know what the word refers to. Communication is facilitated and intellectual capacities are extended because standardized symbols are easy to manipulate in sentences and formulas, while the things they refer to are too heavy, too numerous, or too far away to be easily summoned. Or the referents may be abstract qualities, like truth, beauty, and goodness, that cannot be pointed to or picked up but can be designated by words.

Logicians, who like to use words precisely, speak often of terms rather than words, because a combination of several words may have one referent. Any word or phrase that designates a unitary referent is called a *term.* These may be *singular terms,* referring to one object, such as Socrates or the Statue of Liberty, or *general terms,* referring to a class of objects, such as dogs or small red triangles. Even one object is perceived from several points of view at different times or is described in different books in different contexts, with different associations; hence it is convenient to speak of an *identity class* to which the singular term refers.

When a general term is used to refer to a class, the *extensional significance* or meaning of the term is the set of objects denoted by that term. The extension, or denotation, of the term *dog* includes all members of the class, those actually living and those yet to be born. The *intensional significance* consists of the properties that define the class and characterize the members of it. Dogs, for example, are carnivorous, they suckle their young, they are domesticated, they have four legs, etc. In different contexts, these properties are called *attributes, qualities,* and *dimensions.*

The use of a term to refer to an object or a class of objects is not true or false in any absolute sense. The meanings of terms are a matter of definition or agreement between their users, subject to change over time and place. Nor is the word-referent relation unique, restricted to one word and one referent. All adults use different terms, or synonyms, to refer to a single object, a single term to refer to different objects, pronouns in place of nouns, paraphrases, and other alternative constructions as the situation requires. The usage of words by a speaker (or writer) and the comprehension of them by a listener (or reader), as Olson (1970) has pointed out, depends on the knowledge each has of the alternatives in the context. In domestic situations, *cat* means an animal, or class of animals; on a construction job, *cat* means a caterpillar tractor and if there are no alternatives in view, there is no ambiguity. But when there are alternatives in the listener's context, two cats, for instance, the speaker chooses his words so as to eliminate alternatives: "the black cat." Or if cats have been under discussion, he may refer to the same object as "the black one." Thus the term *cat* refers to different objects, and the object cat is referred to by different terms. This use of alternative constructions by the speaker to communicate with the listener is not a special case but a fundamental characteristic of language, of meaning, and of thought.

Symbols are not entirely arbitrary. Representational signs and symbols have some perceptual properties in common with their referents. When we speak of a bumble-bee buzzing around the clover, the word *buzzing* sounds like more than an arbitrary symbol, presumably because the sound of the word has some attributes in common with the sound of the bee. When the weather man indicates the location of clouds on the weather map, he may draw curvy lines that have some visual resemblance to clouds in the sky. The map also has a basic spatial correspondence to the area it represents. For this reason, some international road signs avoid language difficulties by using pictographs to signal the approach of sharp turns, bumps, and railway crossings.

The meaning of a word includes, not only the explicit characteristics of a class or dimension, but in many cases a suggestive literary meaning or association. *Dove* suggests peace as *hawk* suggests war. *Blue* refers to a color but also symbolizes a mood. Scientific, legal, and logical communication goes better when the linkages between terms and referents are unique and explicit, while the purposes of artistic communication are often better served by the evocation of suggestive verbal effects.

The understanding and use of conventional symbols, such as words, to be discussed in this chapter, is the end of a complex interaction between maturation and learning. The cognitive development of the child, as he gives up his childish ways of representing the objects of his environment and moves into the abstract symbolic world of the adult culture, will be discussed systematically in the next chapter.

AN ATTEMPT AT A COMPREHENSIVE DEFINITION

In past centuries when the concept was considered a generalized mental image, there was no problem of definition. But the overthrow of the image was followed by definitional anarchy. The notion of an internal event of some kind persisted, and various internal stimuli and responses were hypothesized to replace the image, but none was accepted as definitive. Many educated writers use the term *concept,* without explicit definition, to refer to any object of knowledge. Many dictionaries define a concept as a general idea, but this does not please psychologists, who cannot define an idea. While some good research can be done without a good definition, any integration of research from various approaches and any effort at deeper understanding must take the problem of definition seriously. What kind of thing is a concept? Is it a mental experience, a response, a stimulus, a set of objects, a word, or a culture trait? And the problem of measurement follows the problem of definition. How do we know that someone has achieved a concept?

Certainly, a concept is not observable; it cannot be an observable stimulus, or a set of objects, or an observable response. A concept is an abstraction from the world of the senses, and it is this same abstractness that gives a concept its great utility in thought while making definition and measurement so difficult. But psychology has to deal with abstractions.

The best procedure today is to treat the concept as a hypothetical construct, specifically an ability construct. One who "has" a concept can do things that others cannot do. The literate adult can classify objects on the basis of abstract properties; he can use words to communicate with others about abstractions and to solve abstract problems. Standard abstractions are associated with words or other symbols, but the symbol is not the concept. If someone asks, "What is your concept of insight?", everyone understands that the question is not about the word but about the abstraction to which it refers. Each individual learns each concept for himself but, if he communicates with and learns from other people, the cognitive structures through which he views the world will be the standard concepts of the culture.

It is reasonable to think of a concept as a cognitive structure which each individual builds for himself in his continuing effort to impose meaning on the chaotic world of his senses. It is also reasonable to think of a concept as a piece of the culture, handed down, like the rest of the culture, from one generation to the next. But in most cases, the end results are the same. Each individual is confronted with multitudinous experiences that become meaningful during the socialization process as he organizes his cognitive structures to correspond with standard usage. It is true that many individuals make occasional use of idiosyncratic cognitive structures that they do not put into words—the idiosyncratic thoughts of schizophrenics are especially interesting to clinical psychologists—but these are exceptional rather than typical.

A concept, then, is an abstraction, and achievement of the concept is demonstrated by use of the abstraction for classification, communication, and problem solving, according to the standards of the culture. One who has thoroughly mastered the concept of *dog,* for example, has the ability to discriminate dogs from other objects, to describe their characteristics, to understand and use the word *dog* in the conventional way, and to apply this knowledge when planting flowers or approaching a farmhouse. It is not unreasonable to treat concepts as the basic elements of thought when this functional versatility of the full-fledged concepts mastered by a normal literate adult is emphasized.

The Structure of Concepts

A short tour through the arts and sciences will disclose many varieties of concepts, but there are four that must be distinguished here: class concepts, dimensional concepts, explanatory concepts or principles, and singular concepts.

CLASS CONCEPTS

Knowledge is organized: to know the horizon is to know what is above it and what below. A knowledge of the concept of *trees* includes knowledge of their place in a cognitive structure: they are part of the superordinate class of *plants,* and they have subordinate classes such as *oaks* and *willows.*

In this context, class and category are synonyms; we could equally well speak of the categorical concept. Classes are discrete structures that differ qualitatively one from another: circles, triangles, dogs, picnics, prime numbers, angels, limericks. *Unidimensional* classes are characterized by one attribute or feature: red objects, things that break, sharp things. Most classes are *multidimensional,* characterized by two or more attributes: black dogs, one-armed angels, sharp red objects that break. As noted above, classes can be defined extensionally, by identifying the instances included in them, and intensionally, by describing the attributes of the class. In the language of set theory, often used in computer simulation of concept achievement, a class concept can be defined to designate "either a set of elements satisfying some criterion or else the criterion itself [p. 98]" (Reitman, 1965). The set of elements gives the extensional definition and the criterion the intensional definition.

The important properties of classes can be illustrated by Fig. 2.1, which shows a set of cards that were constructed for concept research, with four attributes, three values of each: the shape of the figures (squares, circles,

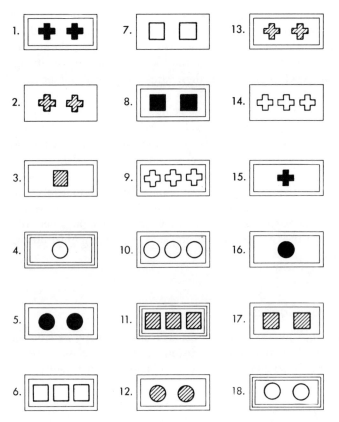

FIGURE 2.1. Cards for research on concept attainment. A selection of 18 from a larger number used by Bruner, Goodnow, and Austin (1956).

crosses), the number of figures (one, two, three), the texture of the figures (open, cross-hatched, solid), and the number of borders (one, two, three).

CONJUNCTIVE CLASSES

In order to be classified as a licensed driver, a person must meet two criteria: he must be above a certain age *and* pass a certain test. Thus the class of licensed drivers is a conjunctive class, made up of the conjunction of two attributes. In Fig. 2.1, Numbers 3, 6, 8, 11, and 17 are instances of a conjunctive class composed of squares with double borders. In this case, we say that shape and borders are the *relevant* dimensions; variations on the other two dimensions are *irrelevant* to this concept. Numbers 2, 12, 13, and 17 are instances of another conjunctive class. What are the relevant attributes?

DISJUNCTIVE CLASSES

Less familiar is the disjunctive class, defined by *either* of two or more attributes. For example, in some states a psychologist is classified as a certified psychologist if he has passed an official examination *or* has practiced for five years. A disjunctive class that consists of circles or solid figures includes

Numbers 1, 4, 5, 8, 10, 12, 15, 16, and 18. Another disjunctive class includes Numbers 4, 6, 7, 10, 11, 18, and no others. What are the relevant features? The reader who works these little problems will agree that disjunctive classes are more difficult to grasp than conjunctive ones.

RELATIONAL CLASSES
A different type of class is characterized by relations between features rather than the presence of features. An example would be married couples in which the husband is taller than the wife. Another example, containing the same features, would be married couples in which the wife is taller than the husband. Such classes appear to be abstract but the relation may be one that is easily noticed. The class of isoceles triangles includes triangles that vary considerably in size and shape, but the equality of two sides is readily perceived. On the other hand, married couples belonging to the same political party would be hard to distinguish from married couples belonging to different parties. In the cards of Fig. 2.1, Numbers 1, 5, 8, 11, 12, 13, and 17 are instances of a relational class in which the number of borders is the same as the number of figures. Another relational class includes Numbers 3, 4, 18, and no others. What are the relevant attributes and what is the relation between them? Relational classes, as well as disjunctive classes, are usually more difficult than conjunctive classes.

DIMENSIONAL CONCEPTS

Cognition of the world consists not only of assigning objects to abstract categories but also of locating them on abstract dimensions. Dimensional concepts have much in common with class concepts, but dimensions are continuous while classes are discrete. Dimensions are continuous properties, qualities, or attributes, abstracted and generalized from specific objects and events; they are associated, like classes, with general terms. Their usefulness is evident when objects are compared in respect to their dimensions and when dimensional terms, such as *helpful, very bad,* and *bright red,* are applied to objects and events. Children use categorical terms like *big* and *small* for two classes at an early age; later, they use dimensional terms like *great big, very small,* and *tiny,* that suggest knowledge of a continuous dimension. The use of general terms, such as *length* and *weight* for the continuous dimension, is a later achievement.

Some of these dimensional concepts are based on salient perceptual qualities, such as size, color, loudness, and fragrance, and are therefore relatively easy to learn. Those based on more abstract properties like acceleration are harder to learn. Many of the technical terms listed in the glossaries of psychology textbooks refer to abstract dimensions: attitude, conformity, intelligence, rigidity, social distance. The multidimensional classes mentioned above are constructed from continuous as well as discontinuous attributes.

EXPLANATORY CONCEPTS

In some contexts the word *concept* means an explanatory concept or principle, such as the frustration-aggression concept. A principle is an abstraction of a higher order of complexity than a concept, since it states a relation between concepts—either dimensional or class concepts. The angle of incidence equals the angle of reflection; cities grow near harbors. A principle takes the form of a proposition and thus, unlike a concept, may be true or false.

Principles are more important than concepts in the long run. Whereas concepts help us to refer to events, principles help us to understand and predict events. Much of the research on the learning of concepts applies also to principles, but it is convenient, because of the nature of the research trends and the problems of measurement, to pass over principles at this point and give them special treatment later under the heading of problem solving and again under reasoning.

SINGULAR CONCEPTS

A singular term refers to a single object or event, and in some contexts the word *concept,* or *conception,* is used for cognition of the object or event designated by a singular term. It is standard usage to speak of one's concept of the moon, or D Day, or the Taj Mahal. The referent of a singular term may be a cluster of memories, perceptions, affects, and associations, based on direct experience and on communication from others. One's concept of the moon, for example, may be acquired by direct perception at different times, in different phases, under different atmospheric conditions. It may be based also on pictures in books, lectures on astronomy, and news reports of lunar exploration. But all these attributes are organized and held together by their association with a singular term.

Singular concepts have not been studied as thoroughly as class concepts, but, as one illustration, Saltz and Sigel (1967) were able to plot age trends in the conceptualization of a single person from photographs taken at different angles.

Procedures for Studying Concept Achievement

Psychological specialties with different interests in concepts have devised different procedures for studying them. It is possible to begin with a variety of objects and ask someone to classify them, to state how to classify them, or to label them with a word that refers to the class. Or one can begin with a word and ask someone to apply it to objects, to give its meaning, or to carry out other verbal operations according to standard usage. Only the more common procedures will be briefly described here as a guide to understanding the results of such studies.

Classes are frequently manufactured for concept experiments from familiar attributes (such as size, shape, and color) that are learned early in life. Experiments of this kind therefore do not include the learning of these attributes; they do include learning which attributes are relevant to a certain class and how these attributes are combined.

METHOD OF PRESENTATION

Tests of knowledge of concepts present the materials once only, while experiments on the learning of concepts present the materials repeatedly. One method of studying concept learning, the *reception method,* presents cards, like those in Figure 2.1, to a subject one at a time. His task is to classify them by stating that each is a positive or a negative instance of the class the experimenter has in mind. The experimenter usually tells the subject after each response whether he is right or wrong. Another method, the *selection method,* lays all the cards on the table simultaneously. The experimenter identifies one card as a positive instance, then the subject is permitted to select other cards and ask the experimenter if each is a positive or a negative instance. By either method, the experiment continues until the subject has reached a specified criterion of learning.

The subject of an experiment by the reception method is in a position rather like that of a student in class listening to the lecturer present the information. The selection method is analogous to the situation of a student who has the same information available but studies it in his own way. As one might expect, the second is usually more efficient, other things being equal (Bruner, Goodnow, and Austin, 1956; Reed, 1946), but occasionally it works the other way, apparently because the selection method makes greater demands on the subject (Murray and Gregg, 1969).

TESTS OF CONCEPT ACHIEVEMENT

How do we know that someone has acquired a concept? There are many tests of concept achievement precisely because concepts have so many functions in intellectual life. The usefulness of each depends on the nature of the concept and of the function to be studied. The scientific yield from an experiment is greater, of course, when concept achievement is measured by more than one dependent variable, and in fact multivariate designs are becoming more common.

CLASSIFICATION

The classification operation consists of making a common response to objects that belong in a class but are superficially dissimilar, and a different response to other objects. It is necessary to stipulate that the objects be dissimilar in some attributes in order to rule out the identity response. For example, when the cards of Fig. 2.1 are classified according to the shape of the figures, the positive instances are similar in their relevant attribute, shape, but dissimilar in respect to the other, irrelevant attributes.

The nature of the response is unimportant. Experimental subjects can associate the key on the right with one class of objects and that on the left with another class; or they can equally well use the terms *dax* and *not dax* or *A* and *B*. The conceptual achievement is not in making the response but in making it to certain objects rather than others.

Conventional concept learning experiments require attempts at classification from the beginning, confirm correct responses, and then plot progress as an increase in the number of correct responses. Hence the response made as a test of achievement is the same as the response made during practice. There are exceptions to this custom, however. Some experiments (these will be described) have used the classification test following practice by other operations.

Many concept learning experiments present the same materials for classification repeatedly until all, or nearly all, are classified correctly. In such cases, it is customary to add a generalization or transfer test with new materials in order to eliminate the possibility of rote learning of specific instances.

Classification is a test of extensional meaning since instances that belong in the class are identified separately. A test of intensional meaning requires a description of the class, by naming the relevant attributes and by the rule of combination. These two aspects of intensional meaning are not the same. It frequently happens, for example, that a subject learns the relevant attributes, such as shape and number, correctly, but learns the wrong rule for combining them; he acquires a conjunctive concept when a disjunctive concept is correct.

The classification operation is often part of a concept learning experiment, but it is used also as an educational achievement test: in zoology classes, for example, specimens of tissue are presented and students are asked to name the class to which each belongs.

Hundreds of experiments on concept learning have been designed around the classification operation, so many in fact that this operation has influenced the definition of a concept, within experimental psychology at least. When the classification test is the only one used, experiments on concept learning resemble those on discrimination learning with human and animal subjects. The learning can be conceived as associating one response to the positive stimuli and another to the negative stimuli. One can go further and define the concept as a *common response* to dissimilar stimuli (Kendler, 1961), but this definition is appropriate only for experiments by this method. Asking the subject to state the basis for the classification would not be a test of concept achievement by this definition, nor would the other tests listed next.

Another approach to the definition of concepts, when classification is the test of achievement, is to treat the concept as the identification of the relevant attributes and the rule of combination. According to Haygood and Bourne (1969), a concept can be understood as a principle by which objects or events can be classified as positive and negative instances. This definition, referring to intensional meaning, is more realistic than the common-response definition, but it is still based on the classification operation and would not include other tests to be listed next. The classification of objects is certainly an important test of concept achievement, but it is not the only operation of interest and it is not sufficient by itself for a general definition of concepts or for a comprehensive evaluation of concept achievement.

ORDERING

The ordering operation, for testing achievement of a dimension, is analogous to the classifying operation but more complex. Some intelligence tests present a child with four blocks, of the same size, to be arranged in order of weight from lightest to heaviest. The effect of knowledge of a dimensional concept on learning a class concept has been investigated by giving children a dimensionality test, which requires them to arrange six blocks in order of size and six other blocks in order of brightness, prior to the learning task (Johnson and White, 1967). Successful performance requires knowledge of the dimension as well as the ability to follow the instructions; failure could be due to lack of either. Unlike artificial classes, artificial dimensions are not easily manufactured for learning experiments under controlled laboratory conditions.

VERBAL OPERATIONS

When one learns to respond to square figures with double borders by the word *dax,* we can say that he is learning a discrimination, a class, a category, or a common response. But, from another point of view, we can say that he is learning the meaning of *dax.* In the context of the experimental situation, the term *dax* refers to square figures with double borders. The versatility of concepts allows the testing procedure to move from objects to words, from words to objects, and from words to words. A child may be given a singular term, such as *moon,* and asked to tell what it means by pointing to the object in the sky or to a picture in a book. If a student is given a general term, such as *evergreen,* he can demonstrate that he knows the extensional meaning (by pointing to examples in view or by giving names of examples), or the intensional meaning (by listing the attributes of the class). The student may give a synonym, a superordinate class, or a subordinate class, or he may use the word in a sentence. Another test of this kind requires the subject to arrange words in levels as a structure of logically related elements (Natadze, 1962). Many abstract concepts of science and law are meaningless unless they are placed within a structure that includes other abstract concepts.

These verbal tests are applicable, with slight modifications, to terms that designate dimensional concepts as well as class concepts. In addition, terms can be ordered in respect to a dimension of their referents; thus, a student is asked to arrange the names of metals in order of hardness, or to arrange the names of eminent psychologists in chronological order.

Tests of word usage, like tests of classification, may be in multiple-choice form for objective scoring, or in open-end form, which requires scoring by expert judges. But the agreement between two independent judges scoring definitions of concepts and the use of concepts in sentences is high under favorable conditions (Johnson and O'Reilly, 1964; Johnson and Stratton, 1966). And many open-end tests can be converted to multiple-choice tests, for example, by asking for a choice from five alternative definitions of a term.

TESTING PROCEDURES IN GENERAL

In general, these methods are used to study concept achievement at any one time, as at the end of a college course, or to record decreases in time and errors during concept learning in the laboratory. The purpose may be either to investigate general principles or to measure differences between individuals, although the latter may require minor modifications. Individual differences in approach or cognitive style are disclosed by the nature of the groups that people form when they are merely asked to categorize a variegated set of objects, by the number of groups they form, by their preferences for classifying by one dimension rather than another, and by their flexibility in shifting from one dimension to another.

The achievement of a concept is a quantitative thing: some people know a concept thoroughly, others partly, others only slightly. This quantitative nature certainly appears in the study of difficult concepts of the arts and sciences, if not in the study of easy concepts. The term *number,* for example, can be variously defined at the level of the fifth-grade pupil, the college freshman, or the graduate student of mathematical logic; similarly, botanical classifications that are acceptable at the fifth-grade level may not be acceptable at the graduate-student level. The proportion of subjects who pass any of the above tests can be raised or lowered by adjusting the test materials and the scoring standards.

If a concept is viewed as an ability construct, the methodology requires that successful performance on any test be mediated by this construct, not by direct association. When the test requires the classification of objects, responses should be mediated by knowledge of the class, not by the memory of specific positive and negative instances. When it requires verbal operations, these also should be mediated by knowledge, not by a memorized definition or a hackneyed illustration. Likewise, the arrangements should be such that failure, when it occurs, can be attributed to lack of achievement of the concept rather than to inability to make the perceptual discrimination, to perform the response, to remember the terms, to pay attention, or to other noncognitive components of the performance.

Each of these methods of measurement has certain advantages; none is infallible. None is more fundamental in any way than the others; none has epistemological priority. A convergence of the results from two or more tests is more convincing than the results of one, and if the present discussion is correct, the results of different tests will converge. That is, the person who scores above average on one test of achievement will score above average on another test of achievement of the same concept. Each measure contains its own specific sources of difficulty, to be sure. The classification test may be the difficult one for some concepts (e.g., schizophrenic), while the definition test may be the difficult one for others (e.g., number); but it is a reasonable hypothesis that, if adequate tests were available, performance on one test would be correlated with performance on the others.

Achievement of Figure Classes

The bulk of the evidence on concept achievement comes from experiments on the learning of classes of stimulus patterns or figures printed on cards or projected on a screen. Hence we will summarize the principal results of research on figure classes first. Later, we will turn to word classes and number classes and will see that the results can be applied, with some exceptions, to these other types of material.

The concept research of the past few decades has been strongly influenced by the pioneer experiments and interpretations of Clark Hull (1920). Other psychologists had presented various figures to their observers and had tried to use the introspective reports to derive generalizations about discovery of the features of a class. Hull put his investigation in the form of an objective learning experiment. The stimulus objects were printed patterns, resembling Chinese characters. The class to be named *li,* for example, contained two sloping lines joined at the top, embedded in different complex patterns of lines. Hull used the familar method of paired associates so that he could plot progress in terms of an increase in the number of correct responses. The subjects were expected to associate a name with each character and, with practice, to learn the correct name for each class. Finally, they were asked to draw the identifying feature of each class.

These experiments produced some objective results that have been verified in later experiments and are still under investigation today. It was quite common, for example, that a subject could learn to classify figures correctly but could not draw the feature that all positive instances had in common. Hull noted also that learning could be speeded up if the common feature of the class was made more salient by coloring it red. But the method and the interpretation were the more important contributions.

Hull's experiments demonstrated that concept learning could be studied as the association of a common response, such as the verbal response, *li,* to figures that are similar in respect to one common feature but dissimilar in other respects. According to association theory, the response to each stimulus will be random at first. But the association between the correct response and the critical feature of the positive instances will be systematically strengthened whenever a correct response happens to occur and is confirmed as such by the experimenter. Simultaneously, the associations between the correct response and other elements of the stimulus patterns will be weakened. Thus, the common feature of the class will be gradually abstracted from the remainder of the stimulus pattern because it is the only feature that is always associated with confirmation of the response.

A few years later, Edna Heidbreder (1924) pointed out that such a theory treats the individual as a rather passive receiver of information from the environment, contributing little to the task but impartial memory of positive and negative instances. The contrasting theory, she noted, views the individual as taking a more active part, formulating hypotheses about the concept and testing them against later instances. Much of our present knowledge of concept achievement has come from attempts to support one or the other of these theories. Under certain restricted conditions, mathematical models can be developed and computer simulation becomes possible also (Hunt, 1962; E. S. Johnson, 1964).

TASK VARIABLES OR CONDITIONS OF ACHIEVEMENT

Aside from theoretical enterprises, considerable solid data on concept achievement has come from atheoretical attempts to improve the methods of studying concepts and to illuminate the conditions that influence concept achievement. We shall consider first the conditions that are known to have strong influences on concept achievement; they might be called general task variables. Then we shall return to some attempts at theoretical explanation.

THE QUESTION OF ABSTRACTNESS

"To abstract" means to pull out or separate something from its entanglements, and this is what Hull's subjects had to do in order to classify Chinese characters according to the presence of a common attribute. In this sense, all concepts are abstract. But Hull's classes were formed from concrete attributes, directly visible, while other classes are formed from more abstract attributes. The relational classes mentioned in connection with Fig. 2.1 are examples of more abstract classes since each is characterized by a relation between attributes. Forming classes of classes is an even more abstract accomplishment. When we compare the Jones system for classifying roses with the Smith system for classifying roses, we are operating at a higher level of abstraction than when we are classifying roses by either system.

The hypothesis that the more abstract concepts are harder to learn is reasonable, and yet experimental demonstrations of this hypothesis have not been as clear-cut as expected. In one of several experiments on this topic, Heidbreder (1947) used line drawings which could be sorted into three classes. Thing classes consisted of common objects, such as a hat; form classes consisted of nonsense figures; and number classes, supposed to be more abstract because they are based on numerical relations, consisted of three, four, or six small designs. In general, thing classes seemed to be the easiest to acquire and number classes the hardest. According to Heidbreder, the perception of concrete objects in man is the dominant mode of cognition because his locomotive and manipulative capacities have priority. The more classification resembles perception of concrete objects, therefore, the easier it becomes. In later studies, however, this *dominance hierarchy* as it was termed was found to be a weak one, often obscured by other tendencies (Heidbreder, 1948; Heidbreder and Overstreet, 1948).

Further evidence on this question comes from the Wisconsin Card Sorting Test, which requires sorting by form, color, and number classes but does not include a class of concrete objects. In one study by this procedure, number classes were easier than form classes (Grant, Jones, and Tallantis, 1949). The inconsistency in research here is probably due to the selection of materials to be classified and to procedural differences. The importance of the procedure comes out in an experiment by Wohlwill (1957) that included two procedures, one intended to depend on abstraction, the other on conceptualization. When the subjects abstracted their own dimensions and classified cards on the basis of these, form classes were used more consistently than color classes. But when the experimenter told the subjects which dimension to use and measured the sorting times in seconds, with discriminability controlled, color gave better results than form.

The question that Heidbreder raised did not receive a satisfactory answer from experiments with figure classes and remains still open. It comes up again in experiments with word classes, in studies of cognitive development, and in tests of cognitive style.

POSITIVE AND NEGATIVE INFORMATION

Is a *No* the opposite of a *Yes?* This question has intrigued psychologists for decades—since Smoke (1933) reported the results of his experiments on positive and negative instances. The subjects were presented with circles of different sizes and colors, together with dots in various positions. Those circles with one dot inside and one dot outside were to be classed as *dax*. Each positive instance was presented with a plus sign and each negative instance with a minus sign, but the information for learning the class seemed to come more from the positive than from the negative instances. Furthermore, classes formed from positive instances were often too general; the contribution of negative instances was mostly to sharpen the concept derived from the positive instances.

This demonstration is not altogether convincing, years later, because it is not obvious what the subject could be expected to get from each instance. More clear-cut experiments can be arranged, however, by telling the subject in advance what dimensions and what values of each are to be presented. Suppose the subject is told, for example, that there will be eight objects varying in size (large and small), shape (circle and triangle), and color (red and yellow). These can be represented by their initial letters as: LRC (large red circle), LRT, SRC, SRT, LYC, LYT, SYC, and SYT.

Let us say that the class to be learned is a conjunctive class of two dimensions and the subject sees LRC with the information that it is a positive instance. He can guess that L and R are the relevant attributes, hence LRT would also be positive, or he might guess that L and C are the relevant attributes, hence LYC would be positive. The other possibility is that R and C are relevant, hence SRC would be positive. Thus this information has logically narrowed the positive instances down to four out of eight.

Suppose, on the other hand, that the first card presented was SYT and the subject was informed that this was a negative instance. He could logically exclude the SY, ST, and YT combinations and thus eliminate SYC, SRT, and LYT. Counting SYT, this information has logically eliminated four out of eight possibilities and four out of eight remain, exactly the same as in the previous example with a positive instance. The number of alternatives was cut in half, hence in technical terms the amount of information in each instance was one bit. Yet the positive information is more useful to the average subject than the negative.

More complex sets of materials require more complex calculations, but the amount of information in positive and negative instances can still be equated. When experiments were carefully designed in this way, it was shown that negative information was utilized to some extent but not as much as positive information (Hovland and Weiss, 1953). Negative instances were more helpful when all instances were presented simultaneously than when they were presented successively.

These findings have been verified by other experimenters. Apparently, most people distrust negative information; it is indirect. Choosing one attribute because of the elimination of two others requires an additional operation, with the risk of making a mistake, and requires also the firm faith that there are only three attributes to be considered. This goes counter to ordinary habits of thought because life teaches us to avoid closed systems and a statement from the experimenter that there are only so many dimensions may not be enough to overcome such old habits. This is probably the reason why simultaneous presentation increases the use of negative information.

Whatever the explanation for the reluctance to utilize the information in negative instances, it can be definitely reduced by practice. Freibergs and Tulving (1961) equated the information in their instances, as Hovland and Weiss did, but they gave their subjects advance instructions about using negative instances, as well as positive, to discover classes. Then one group practiced on positive instances and another on negative; the classes based on positive instances were learned quickly while those based on negative instances took longer. But, as Fig. 2.2 shows, after 20 trials the 2 groups were about equal in number of errors.

Some recent hypotheses about difficulties in concept learning have led to recommendations for pretraining in analyzing information in the situation, as we shall see later; this procedure also reduces the differences between the use of the two kinds of information (Bourne and Guy, 1968; Davidson, 1969). Such results do not erase the differences that others have found, but they demonstrate that the difficulties of negative information can be reduced by thorough instructions and a little pretraining.

When we turn from conjunctive to disjunctive classes, the contribution of negative instances is quite different because it is the negative instances that are more informative. (The reader can verify this statement by going back to the disjunctive problems of Fig. 2.1.) Hence Chlebek and Dominowski (1970) arranged an experiment similar to that of Freibergs and Tulving but with disjunctive classes and found that those who were shown only negative instances discovered the concepts much earlier than those who were shown positive instances. In addition, as in the case of conjunctive classes, the differences between the value of negative and positive information decreased as practice continued.

Although we can describe the factors that influence the difficulty of concept learning, such as the nature of the class, the kind of information, and the stimulus materials, one by one, complex research designs have demonstrated that the effects of these factors are usually not independent. The

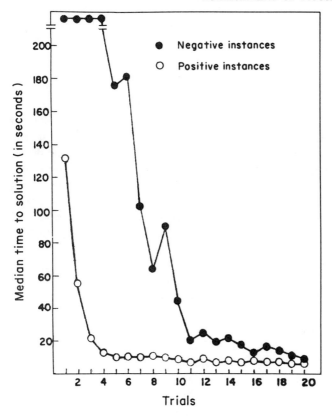

FIGURE 2.2. *Solution time for 20 concept problems for subjects with positive instances and other subjects with negative instances. From Freibergs and Tulving (1961).*

special relation between negative instances and disjunctive classes is only one illustration of this.

RELEVANT AND IRRELEVANT DIMENSIONS

The acquisition of a conjunctive class based on two relevant dimensions, such as size and shape, would obviously be more difficult than that of a class based on only one. And a class based on three relevant dimensions, such as size, shape, and color, would be even more difficult to grasp. But the presence of irrelevant dimensions raises difficulties also. If the objects vary in size, shape, and color, and the class to be learned is the class of black circles, size is an irrelevant variable. Large and small objects are positive instances; large and small objects are negative instances. Increasing the amount of relevant information in the materials presented for classification increases difficulty, of course, and so does increasing the amount of irrelevant information (Haygood and Stevenson, 1967; Walker and Bourne, 1961). These effects are not peculiar to visually perceived objects, because parallel experiments can be done with auditory stimuli by varying the frequency, intensity, steadiness, presence of background noise, and location of the ear-

phone through which the sound is heard; here again the difficulty of classification depends on the amount of irrelevant as well as relevant auditory
information (Bulgarella and Archer, 1962).

SALIENCE AND SIMILARITY

In his early concept experiments, Hull (1920) was able to help his subjects abstract the critical feature out of the complex patterns by making it
more salient, that is, by outlining it in red. This is an old trick often employed in teaching anatomical and other spatial relations. A similar device
to emphasize the figure is to vary the background so that the figure stands
out. The classification of patterns is easier when the critical figure is shown
with varying backgrounds than when the same figure is shown with a constant background (Turnure and Wallach, 1965). Likewise, if the critical
feature is a simple drawing of one or two curved lines, combining three of
these in a complex pattern makes classification according to any one feature
quite difficult—as predicted by the Gestalt principle of good continuation
(Wallach, 1962).

When synthetic classes are systematically constructed of familiar attributes,
such as size, shape, and color, abstraction from background entanglements is
not difficult but it is still possible that the values of one attribute may be
more impressive than the others. The difference between a large and a small
square, for example, may contribute more, or less, to the difficulty of the
task than the differences between a white and a black circle. This question
can easily be examined by varying the difference between the two values
of a binary dimension. Archer (1962) arranged a set of designs in which
the two squares, for example, differed by ¼ inch and another in which the
two squares differed by ⅛ inch. Although the smaller difference was large
enough for easy discrimination, in a set of objects that varied in many
dimensions, some relevant and some irrelevant, the large difference was more
obvious and was more readily grasped as a basis for classification. The results of several experiments of this nature led to the general statement that
the optimum condition would maximize the obviousness of the relevant information and minimize the obviousness of the irrelevant information. This
comprehensive statement seems reasonable enough but there are some exceptions. When the set of stimuli included a few irrelevant features that
were highly salient, they were quickly examined and eliminated from further
consideration; learning was actually faster than when these irrelevant features were less salient (Fishbein, Haygood, and Frieson, 1970).

This factor of salience can be important when children have to classify
shapes on the basis of subtle variations. Rommetveit (1960) required children
of twelve to classify curved line drawings that resembled the outlines of a
cup and saucer and included a recognition test as well as a sorting test. He
found that under some conditions the children had learned to recognize the
shape just exposed when sorting was not yet above the chance level of accuracy. In one experiment (Rommetveit and Kvale, 1965), attempts to
verbalize, that is, to describe the shapes, early in the learning process had a
detrimental effect on later sorting.

This factor of salience does not necessarily negate the findings reported above because it is common practice to rotate dimensions within conditions. But when classification by one dimension is compared with classification by another, or when concrete classes are compared with abstract classes, the factor of salience becomes critical. Classification by color could be made easier than classification by shape merely by increasing the color differences; equally, classification by shape could be made easier by increasing the shape differences.

In general, we may say that the salience of a dimension may be an intrinsic property of the stimulus patterns or it may be a consequence of prior experience. Various kinds of practice directed toward increasing knowledge of the stimulus patterns prior to discrimination learning, technically called *stimulus predifferentiation,* do facilitate concept learning (Tighe and Tighe, 1966).

MEDIATED ASSOCIATION AND CONCEPT SHIFTS

The classical discussions of the concept, based on introspective evidence, treated it as a generalized mental image; this is analogous to a composite photograph, which emphasizes the common feature of a set of faces and blurs the specific features. If such a generalized image is aroused by perception or recall, present instances can be compared with it and judged as members of the class or not.

Modern psychology distrusts introspective evidence but permits the notion of a mediator as a hypothetical construct to be validated by behavioral data. Hypotheses about mediators, to fill the gaps in stimulus-response behaviorism, are as old as behaviorism itself (Goss, 1961). The mental image, which was buried alive a half century ago and is now being revived, can also be considered a mediator between S and R. Hypothetically, this mediator has some of the properties of the stimulus pattern; other mediators have been hypothetically endowed with some of the properties of responses, words, or cognitions.

Modern hypotheses about mediators replace so-called single-unit association with two-unit association. The mediator is pictured as associated with the S on one side and the R on the other, the two associations being acquired separately. The mediator acts as a response to S and a stimulus or cue to the next R, thus: S———$\boxed{r—s}$———R. This picture is probably too simple; the chain of associations may be longer. But two-unit association illustrates the nature of mediation hypotheses. While single-unit associations might account for the simple behavior of lower animals and young children, mediated associations are more plausible for complex behavior.

The need for a mediated association theory is apparent when the subject classifies figures to fit the experimenter's criterion for a correct response and then the experimenter shifts his criterion. Suppose, to take a simple example, that the figures to be sorted vary in size, shape, and color, and that choice of large figures is rewarded, shape and color being irrelevant. After the subject is sorting correctly, the experimenter may, without informing the subject, shift and reward on some other basis in order to analyze the classifying process more thoroughly. There are two types of shift in this situation: a *reversal shift* requires the subject to shift to the opposite value of the same dimension; that is, if large figures were correct, small figures are now correct. This is also called an *intradimensional shift* since size is still the relevant dimension. A *nonreversal* or *extradimensional shift,* on the other hand, requires the subject to shift to some other dimension; perhaps triangular figures of any size or color will be called correct.

The behavior of children and adults following such shifts led Howard and Tracy Kendler and their associates (Kendler and D'Amato, 1955; Kendler and Kendler, 1962) to a series of new experiments and an attempt at theoretical explanation in terms of mediated association. A reversal shift seems to necessitate the relearning of all associations between figures and responses: what was positive is now negative and vice versa. Yet the experiments have shown that reversal shifts are easier for adult human subjects than nonreversal shifts, though nonreversal shifts are easier for animals and young children.

Consider a simple situation in which a few figures are displayed and the subject has to learn names for classes. It is reasonable to suppose that the first response is an orienting one, for example, looking toward the figure at the right. This response brings into view a figure, which in turn acts as an implicit cue or mediator for the next response in the chain that leads to the terminal naming response. If this terminal response is confirmed, the whole chain, including the mediating response of orienting to the right, is strengthened. More often, of course, the critical element is an attribute rather than a location. The critical attribute of a large red triangle may be the color, with size and shape being irrelevant. In this case, the orienting response that mediates the next response and thus is strengthened by success is not one of head and eye movements but a perceptual orienting response which might be described as observing color rather than size or shape. Such a differential mediating response would be strengthened by association with a terminal confirming response just as other responses are.

This mediation hypothesis has received some support from several experiments resembling those on discrimination learning. One by Kendler, Kendler, and Learnard (1962) illustrates the nature of the research. Two pairs of stimuli are used: one consists of a large white square and a small black square, the other of a large black square and a small white square. Two training phases and one test phase are required. In Phase I, the two pairs of stimuli are presented sequentially and different subjects are rewarded for selecting a square from each pair on the basis of one of the four stimulus elements: *black, white, large, small.* For example, if the correct dimension is *color* and the correct value is *white,* the large white square in one pair and the small white square in the other pair will be rewarded. After the subject meets the criterion of learning in this phase, Phase II presents only one pair, and the subject is rewarded for choosing the previously negative stimulus; for example, if *white* was correct in Phase I, *black* is correct in Phase II.

But the choice in Phase II is ambiguous because the small black square could be chosen either for its color or its size. If the choice is for color, the subject has reversed from black to white, hence this would be called a reversal shift. It is also an intradimensional shift, since the subject continued to orient to the color dimension. If the choice is on the basis of size, it would be called a nonreversal or extradimensional shift. Phase III is intended to determine which it was. After the subject is responding consistently in Phase II, the other pair is reintroduced as a final test. If the subject chooses on the basis of color, presumably he was using color throughout Phase II; therefore he reversed.

The mediation hypothesis states that the subject orients to a dimension, such as *color,* and a value of this dimension, such as *white,* is associated with the next response in the chain. If the final instrumental response is mediated by orientation to this dimension, a shift on this dimension (e.g., from *black* to *white*) would be easier than a shift to some other dimension (e.g., from *black* to *small*). The difficulty of the nonreversal shift is that it requires learning to orient to a different dimension. The hypothesis that a reversal shift is easier defies intuition and simple single-unit associationism, because after a reversal shift an association that was right becomes wrong and one that was wrong becomes right. A number of experiments on reversals have shown that, while the simpler associationism may be adequate to explain the discriminative behavior of animals and young children, the mediation hypothesis, or something similar, must be added to it to explain the behavior of older children and adults.

Kendler, Kendler, and Learnard (1962) included different age groups in their experiment and found that children of ten made more reversal shifts than the younger children. They take this result as evidence that the older children have verbal mediators, such as the words *color* and *shape,* that help them maintain their orientation to a dimension. Such research results do not mean that the young children lack the vocabulary to describe the simple concepts used. Rather, they do not use these as implicit cues for the instrumental response, at least not as much as older children do. Tracy Kendler (1964b) has been able to increase the number of reversal shifts at younger ages by requiring kindergarten children to verbalize labels for the positive and negative stimuli: "The square is the winner and the circle is the loser," or "The black wins and the white loses." Kendler believes that "at this developmental stage overt verbalization has the same effect that the model ascribes to covert verbalization among more mature human Ss [p. 434]."

The results of other experiments agree that reversal shifts are often easier than nonreversal shifts, but the explanation in terms of the mediation of implicit cues is not beyond dispute. An experiment with college students by Isaacs and Duncan (1962) disclosed the usual superiority of the reversal group over the nonreversal group, but in comparison with a control group the reversal group showed a significant negative transfer. They interpreted the results in terms of nonspecific transfer of practice on tasks of this kind and a specific transfer, which may be negative, on the dimension reinforced in training. Erickson (1971) was not satisfied with the general belief that reversal shifts are easier than extradimensional shifts even for adults; he reported, after a series of experiments, that the critical condition was the completeness of the instructions. When he gave college students a figure concept problem with the usual brief instructions, the extradimensional shift problem was learned after about three times as many errors as the reversal shift. With more thorough instructions—explaining in a general way how to use the information given by confirmation and nonconfirmation—the difference in difficulty was in the other direction and the reversal shift required about twice as many errors. The activities of the subjects with brief instructions seemed consistent with mediated association theory, while those with thorough instructions were more consistent with a hypothesis-testing model (to be described next).

A reversal shift is an intradimensional shift, but an intradimensional shift is not necessarily a reversal shift. To keep things simple, many experiments have used only two values of each dimension: the colors are red and green, the shapes square and triangle. But a dimension may have more than two values. If red figures are positive and green figures are negative, a shift to *yellow-positive* and *blue-negative* would be an intradimensional shift but not a reversal. Thus when classes are constructed from four colors and four shapes, there are three types of shift to be compared: extradimensional (or nonreversal), intradimensional, and reversal. Systematic comparisons by P. J. Johnson (1967) disclosed that reversal shifts were relatively easy for college students, causing only 8.00 errors on the average before they adjusted to the shift. Intradimensional shifts were also easy, 9.58 errors. But extradimensional shifts were quite difficult, 22.75 errors. Such results suggest that the mediator is rather general, a dimension rather than a specific value of a dimension. Reversal from *red-green* to *green-red* was about the same in difficulty as a shift from *red-green* to *blue-yellow*. To put these results in terms of attention, one could say that the subject learns to observe color (or shape) rather than a specific color (or shape).

Reversal shifts in children of four, six, and eight can be increased, as in college students, as a result of verbalization that calls attention to the correct dimension (Jeffery, 1965). Tighe and Tighe (1968b) also taught young children to make reversal shifts, simply by giving them predifferentiation training to familiarize them with the independence of the different dimensions. Thus these writers find it possible to account for much of the research on discrimination learning in terms of perceptual differentiation: learning to distinguish the different stimulus patterns is more important than learning the responses to them.

The design of the early experiments emphasized specific stimuli, cues, or bipolar values of a dimension; but recently it has appeared that the dimension can be the mediator—or the focus of attention. It is also possible that mediators representing stimulus values are nested in a superordinate set of mediators representing dimensions (Kendler and Kendler, 1970).

It is clear that the mediation hypothesis has generated some instructive research designs, whatever the final interpretation of the results may be. At present it seems that the results can be interpreted alternatively in terms of selective attention, perceptual differentiation, and verbal mediation (Kendler and Kendler, 1966; Tighe and Tighe, 1968a; Wolff, 1967). This research trend may be more relevant to attention, perception, and discrimination learning than to concept learning.

SELECTING CUES AND TESTING HYPOTHESES

The more active approach to concept learning, which Heidbreder (1924) described many years ago as a search for common features, attributes more complicated problem-solving activities to the subject of a concept experiment. Single-unit and mediated association theories assume that the subject is alert and observant, to be sure. But the more dynamic theories assume that the subject takes the initiative by looking for similarities in a series of instances, formulating hypotheses about common features, and testing these on later instances. It has been known for some time (Reed, 1946) that instructing the subject to look for common features facilitates concept learning in comparison with merely instructing him to learn correct responses. Thus, association theories portray concept learning as a continuous improvement in performance, the correct associations being gradually strengthened, while hypothesis-testing theories portray it as a discontinuous process. Formulating and testing an incorrect hypothesis would produce no consistent improvement; formulating the correct hypothesis, however, would be followed by rapid improvement.

SELECTION AND RECEPTION STRATEGIES

The hypotheses that people formulate and the procedures by which they test them were examined by Bruner, Goodnow, and Austin (1956) in a series of experiments from which the cards of Fig. 2.1 were taken. They looked at concept attainment as the coding of experience into categories. The subject's task is to discover which attributes of the perceived objects are useful cues for distinguishing the objects that belong together in a category from those that do not. One way to study the subject's categorizing efforts would be to ask him to describe what he is doing, but this method is open to many criticisms and has not, in the past, yielded convincing evidence. If the subject is doing his best to discover the concept, he cannot also take on the experimenter's task of scientific investigation, at least not without some sacrifice in efficiency of one or both tasks. If the dimensions are familiar ones, like size and shape, however, and the subject chooses to test a hypothesis that the class is a simple combination of these, then statement of the hypothesis is not too much to ask. Sequences of responses can, of course, be objectively recorded and analyzed; and the subject's statements about his hypotheses can be checked against his actual responses.

As one can see from Fig. 2.1, familiar attributes were used in these experiments. The difficulty consisted not in learning the attributes but in the cognitive strain or memory load involved when the information pertinent to a hypothesis was gathered over a period of time from a series of instances.

Any method of collecting pertinent information and organizing it so as to evaluate a hypothesis is called a *strategy*. When the selection method of presentation was used, with all cards exposed, the experimenter helped the subject to get started by giving him one positive instance. After that, the subject selected one card at a time and was told whether it was a positive instance or not. The experimenter could reconstruct his strategy fairly well from records of cards selected, and, in addition, the subject was encouraged to hazard a hypothesis after each selection of a card. Thus, in this type of experiment the subject knew the materials in advance and what he was supposed to do. What he did not know was the concept the experimenter expected him to acquire.

The possibilities for approaching such a problem are numerous; 50 people working on such a complex problem could use 50 different strategies. Fortunately, the variation is not that large. It is possible to describe a few logically ideal strategies, and then to observe whether the subject's behavior conforms to one of these types. One ideal strategy would be to collect and integrate all the information simultaneously and work out a solution logically. But this *simultaneous scanning*, as it is called, is beyond the memory capacity of most people. None of the subjects of this experiment, who were college students, really tried it. A more feasible strategy is to begin with a hypothesis, and then to select cards that yield information pertinent to it. This strategy, which is called *successive scanning* or *part scanning*, because the subject needs to scan and remember only the part of each card that is relevant to his hypothesis, was frequently employed by the students. It has the disadvantage that the subject concentrated only on part of what he saw and was not likely to learn much while he was following a hypothesis that proved to be wrong, although under some conditions some subjects were able to remember a little even about cards irrelevant to that hypothesis.

A very efficient strategy known as *conservative focusing* consists of beginning with the first positive instance and collecting information around it. One has to have a correct instance to begin with, and in this experiment the subject was given a positive instance as a starter. He did not understand at first why this card was a positive instance but he could find out by maintaining his focus on the card and selecting another card that varied from the known positive instance in only one attribute. If this second card was also a positive instance, the attribute varied must be irrelevant, and thus one possibility had been eliminated. (Some subjects were not so easily convinced. If the positive focus card had two red squares with one border and the subject then chose a card with two green squares with one border and was told that this card was also positive, he had logically eliminated color as an attribute of the class. But a few subjects preferred to choose a card with two black squares and one border next, just to be doubly sure.) If the card chosen was a negative instance, the attribute varied must have been relevant. In either case, this focusing is wholistic; the hypothesis is based on the first positive instance as a whole.

These strategies were investigated in the context of attaining figure concepts, but some of the lessons learned here may be applied elsewhere. The difference between simultaneous scanning and conservative focusing should be familiar to any student who has searched the scientific literature in order to write a term paper because he is bothered by the same effect of too much information. One could go through the recent issues of a likely journal and scan each article briefly. Or one could, as soon as he came across a useful article, focus on it and then choose other articles in the light of the information obtained from this first positive instance. Each method has its advantages, but the second is more efficient in general.

Conservative wholistic focusing requires a positive instance to begin with and a little patience. If the subject is in a hurry and is willing to take a chance, he may change two attributes at once. This is a risky kind of focusing, called *focus gambling*. He will reach a solution sooner by this strategy if he makes a lucky guess; but if he makes a bad guess and selects a negative instance, he will not know which of the two changed attributes is responsible for the error. He may even forget the positive focus card. As the names imply, conservative focusing was followed by moderate gains and losses, while focus gambling was followed by big wins and costly errors.

The other situation, in which the subject receives information regularly but cannot choose what information he receives, was also studied by these experimenters in order to describe reception strategies. They used the method of successive presentation, making the experiment more like a conventional learning experiment. The subject could not pick his cards but he could formulate a hypothesis and test it against the cards as they came to him. The same two types of strategies could be identified in their choices. The wholistic strategy, concentrating on the first positive card as a focus card, was found to be more frequent and more efficient than the part scanning strategy.

Similar experiments by Bourne (1963) and others have also found the conservative focusing, or wholistic, strategy to be more efficient, but it is not always the most frequently used. Most subjects can profit from information just received, but many errors come from the failure to remember earlier instances well enough to see their implications for testing a hypothesis (Cahill and Hovland, 1960). This is one reason, no doubt, why concept achievement by successive presentation takes longer than by simultaneous presentation.

The effectiveness of the conservative focusing strategy has stimulated efforts to use it in teaching, but an attempt to teach it to children in the fifth and sixth grades was not successful (Tagatz, 1967). Some of the sixth-grade children tried to follow the strategy as programmed but soon reverted to the simpler procedure of merely trying to generalize from the positive instances. The fifth-grade students, who used the simpler strategy, actually achieved better average performance. When university students, however, were instructed in various procedures for solving concept problems, it was the conservative focusing strategy that was the most successful (Klausmeier and Meinke, 1968).

The generality of these descriptions of information-processing strategies is complicated by the results of experiments by Bruner, Goodnow, and Austin (1956) with thematic materials. The thematic cards bore drawings of people who differed in sex (male or female), in dress (day clothes or night clothes), and other attributes. Concept attainment with a set of these materials went slower than with a parallel set of meaningless abstract figures. The subjects used similar strategies, but they were distracted by reasonable and familiar hypotheses about possible groupings. They clung to certain attributes, classifying by sex, for example, after these attributes had logically been eliminated.

In general, the wholistic focusing strategies were more efficient than the scanning strategies, especially under difficult conditions, as when time pressure was applied and the display of information restricted. But the question of efficiency is an ambiguous one that cannot be clearly answered unless we know the subject's motivation. In these concept attainment tasks and in the tasks of later chapters, the motivation may usually be described as cognitive. The subject tries to maximize his successes and minimize his errors. Yet some situations emphasize the attractiveness of success and others emphasize the cost of error. In the experiments of Bruner, Goodnow, and Austin, the subjects adjusted their approaches to the situation at hand with some flexibility, adopting a risky strategy when they had only one try and a more conservative strategy when they had several tries. When the experimenters arranged conditions so that the subjects' guesses were right, they adopted more risky strategies.

PROBABILISTIC CUES

After a system of categories has been thoroughly mastered, each element of the system—that is, each value of each dimension—seems to belong in its proper place. But during the learning process an element is only a cue that may or may not be a criterion to define a category. Most experiments are planned so that each feature has exceptionless validity as a cue to the category. If a class of triangular objects is to be learned, choices of other objects are never confirmed. Considerable difficulty is introduced when the validity of a cue is neither 100 percent or 0 percent. In such experiments, 75 percent (or some other proportion) of the choices of triangular objects and a few choices of square objects or green objects are confirmed. Bruner, Goodnow, and Austin found that such variations slow down learning considerably and the difficulties due to the factors mentioned above are magnified.

Shifting the confirmation of cues from 100 percent to some less probability is not as irrational as it may seem, nor is it an arbitrary scheme to confuse the subjects. Life is like that. Most of the classification systems that one has to learn could be described as useful but less than perfect. The 100 percent condition is an interesting special case, but probabilistic conditions are more common and must be considered not only here but in other chapters to come.

It is worthwhile at this point looking back to observe how far this type of concept research has progressed from the early experiments by Hull. Instead of associating names with figures exposed at regular intervals in a memory drum, the subjects try to solve a problem, to discover the defining attributes of a class, with a considerably flexible approach. Since they know the dimensions of the problem in advance, they can proceed more or less rationally and adjust their strategies to the information given. Their reports of their hypotheses are consistent with their hypothesis-testing moves (Schwartz, 1966), and those subjects who are explicit about their strategies are the most efficient (Eifermann, 1965). The subjects examine the stimuli and choose their responses, not only by association with a reward, but in part by balancing probability of success against probability and cost of error. The series of experiments by Bruner, Goodnow, and Austin, which was called *A Study of Thinking,* described the subjects' activities in such terms as *inference, choice,* and *strategy,* and thus played an influential role in shifting concept research from the associative-learning framework to the problem-solving, decision-making framework. Subsequent inquiries have been concerned with methodological improvements and variations of both practical and theoretical significance.

A TWO-PROCESS DEMONSTRATION

The instructions and materials of the experiments described above were chosen so that the concept would be acquired in an active, problem-solving manner rather than by the gradual strengthening of associations. But the demonstration of one process does not negate the other. The relation between the two concept attainment processes was clarified by Podell (1958) by means of differential instructions and more complex materials. During the learning phase, both of her groups saw complicated meaningless figures; but one group was instructed to evaluate them aesthetically (unintentional set), while the other group was instructed to look for common features (intentional set). Both groups were later asked to write the defining characteristics of the class of figures, and these definitions were scored for the number of correct common features mentioned.

Presumably, whatever concept learning occurred under the unintentional set would be a summation of positive and negative associations, whereas the intentional set would promote active search and a more efficient concept achievement. The other important variable was the variety of instances. Some subjects received only 2 examples while others received 12. The expectation was that the unintentional set would be sufficient for the small-variety condition when only 2 figures were seen repeatedly, and that the intentional set would be better for the larger variety of instances, because the subjects would be trying to formulate and test hypotheses to account for all instances. The results, as shown in Table 2.1, confirmed both expectations, at least for these intricate figures. The possibility of concept learning by two processes, long suspected, thus received strong support from these data on definitions.

TABLE 2.1. MEAN NUMBER OF COMMON FEATURES MENTIONED IN DEFINITIONS ACCORDING TO INSTRUCTIONAL SET AND VARIETY OF FIGURES

Instructional Set	Variety of Figures	
	Large	Small
Unintentional	7.12	11.87
Intentional	17.37	10.37

From Podell (1958).

SERIAL EXPOSURE

If we treat concept attainment as a problem to be solved rather than as the learning of responses, the main independent variable need not be practice. Another method for studying concept attainment processes requires the subject to select a common dimension in a display of figures and then to test his selection by applying it immediately to a second display of figures (Johnson, 1961). For the serial analysis of problem-solving activities, the apparatus is so arranged that the subject can illuminate either display but not both at once. Thus hypothesis formulation is separated from hypothesis testing. Fig. 2.3 shows a problem that is ambiguous since the common dimension of the figure on the left side may be shape or texture, and subjects who select either will find a satisfactory solution on the right side. Subjects who had seen several displays of figures that were easily classified by shape selected the shape solution to all ambiguous problems. When the display of figures on the right contained only a texture solution, those who had selected the shape dimension could not find an appropriate solution.

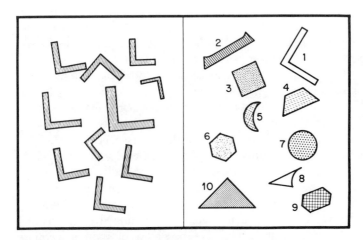

FIGURE 2.3. Figure concept problem. Instructions: "Examine the figures on the left and note what they have in common. Then look at the figures on the right and find another of the same class." From Johnson (1961).

They might have perceived and remembered both dimensions but apparently they did not—all the subjects had to switch back to the left side to observe the other dimensions, then return to the right side and identify the correct figure. Thus this experiment emphasized the discontinuities in solving a concept problem by allowing the subject to interrupt his own activity and seek more information when he saw that he had selected the wrong dimension.

ATTEMPTS TO DEFINE THE CLASS
Many ordinary citizens can classify oak trees and maple trees but cannot describe the identifying features of each. Laboratory reports have also noted, since the beginning of concept research, that many subjects after learning to classify objects cannot define the class. Subtle theoretical implications have been elaborated around this common occurrence, but an interpretation that takes account of the methodology of concept experiments is more convincing.

When the classification test and the definition test are treated as coordinate measures of achievement of the concept, any expectation of consistency between the two assumes that both are adequate measures of the achievement. But typically the defining task is introduced at the end of the experiment, with no practice, while the classifying task is practiced from the beginning. Furthermore, good definitions are hard to write at best, and the complex figures used in some of the early experiments were patterns of almost indescribable shape. The scoring of the definitions presents a methodological problem that has usually been overlooked.

In many recent experiments, when the attributes are familiar shapes and colors, definition is much easier. If the attributes to be considered are explicitly denoted in advance, then the universe of discourse is restricted to them and a statement of the rule of combination suffices as a definition of the class. If the subject states that the class consists of red triangles, *triangles* and *red* need not be further defined. In such experiments, an attempt to formulate a rule of combination of the attributes, either to communicate to the experimenter as a measure of achievement or to retain as a hypothesis for testing in subsequent trials, amounts to an attempt at a definition. Are such attempts worthwhile? In attempting to describe the class, do the subjects learn more than they learn in just classifying the instances?

One experiment on the effectiveness of practice in defining required children of about twelve years old to learn the concept of *gunkle bird* (Johnson and O'Reilly, 1964). Pictures of birds on cards had red, yellow, or blue wings, orange, green, or black tails, and short, long, or hooked beaks; there were 27 cards in all, with black tail as the defining feature. A parallel set of 27 cards had verbal phrases, such as red wing and orange tail, in the same combinations. Each child in 1 group was given the pictorial cards, 1 at a time, asked to guess whether it was a gunkle bird or a bunkle bird, and told when he was right. After attaining the correct classification, each subject was asked the defining question: "How do you think you can tell a gunkle bird from a bunkle bird?" Another group practiced classifying the verbal cards by the same procedure. A third practiced on the pictorial cards and, in addition, was asked after each 5 trials to attempt to state how to tell a gunkle bird from a bunkle bird. The results demonstrated that this small amount of practice in defining, even without knowledge of results, increased the quality of the definitions.

The explicit stating of a hypothesis is good for college students, too. In the typical concept experiment with college students, the subject states a hypothesis whenever he thinks he is beginning to catch on; but when he is required to state a hypothesis systematically after each trial, he is likely to achieve the concept more quickly (Byers and Davidson, 1967). If the hypothesis that is offered is called wrong, however, the subject hesitates before offering another (Byers, 1965; Wallace, 1964). Disconfirmation of a hypothesis has an aversive effect. After some discouragement of this kind, most subjects tend to offer a hypothesis only if it is firmly established.

HYPOTHESIS-SAMPLING MODELS

When concept achievement is treated as the formulation and testing of hypotheses, it is possible, with certain simplifying assumptions, to describe the subject's activities in mathematical terms. Mathematical models based on hypothesis testing, which are quite different from those based on associative learning, have been rather successful in accounting for the data of concept learning experiments and have made a strong impression on the psychological theorizing of the past decade (Bower and Trabasso, 1964; Kintsch, 1970; Levine, 1970; Restle, 1962; Suppes, 1965).

These models employ a variety of mathematical manipulations which need not be considered here. But the assumptions about psychological processes deserve our consideration because the success of a model supports the validity of the assumptions on which it is constructed. In general, a model of this type assumes that the subject samples the attributes or cues that he perceives in the stimulus materials until he finds a cue, or a combination of cues, that is consistently confirmed as correct. Since he is actively trying to solve the problem, the selection of a cue amounts to a hypothesis that the cue is worth trying, so these models are called *cue-sampling* or *hypothesis-sampling models*. When the subject's hypothesis is confirmed, he continues to use it, and his percentage of correct responses remains high. Until this time, on what are called *presolution trials*, he shifts from one cue to another, sampling and resampling at random and, if the materials are complex, he does not remember anything useful about the instances he has seen. Therefore, according to the model, the subject makes no progress until he formulates the correct hypothesis. An analysis of the responses will show correct responses and errors with chance frequency up to the last error. It is not always necessary to identify the subject's specific hypothesis; in well-defined sets of figures, one wrong hypothesis leads to the same proportion of errors as any other wrong hypothesis. However, the experimenter can infer what hypothesis the subject is acting on by skipping the usual informative feedback and observing a few responses that are neither confirmed or disconfirmed.

Whereas associative theories portray progress in concept learning as a continuous strengthening of the reinforced responses, hypothesis-sampling models portray it as a discontinuous, all-or-none phenomenon. Obviously, this model requires analysis of the responses of each subject individually because the last error is made by different subjects on different trials, and group data show a continuous improvement which obscures the individual discontinuities.

Bower and Trabasso (1964) found support for the all-or-none assumption in data from college students learning a class defined by one binary dimension, among several irrelevant dimensions. For any one subject the proportion of correct responses prior to the last error was no greater following a single correct guess than following an error. This proportion, actually, remained constant at the chance level during the presolution trials. Various patterns of multiple-reversal and dimensional shifts in what the experimenter called correct did not influence the error rate prior to solution (Trabasso and Bower, 1964). Several studies of children learning mathematical concepts also support the all-or-none assumption (Suppes, 1966).

The difficulties that have arisen to plague models of this type involve some of the assumptions mentioned above, especially the question of when and how the subject formulates the hypotheses that he tests. It is not certain that a subject remembers nothing from hypotheses he has tried and rejected (Trabasso and Staudenmayer, 1968). Apparently, what is remembered depends partly on the time allowed the subject between trials to think about the information just received (Bourne, Dodd, Guy, and Justesen, 1968). Most hypothesis-sampling models assume sampling without replacement, but under some conditions the subject will resample a hypothesis he has previously tried and rejected (Erickson and Zajkowski, 1967), and he may even change his hypothesis after a response has been confirmed as correct (Dodd and Bourne, 1969). Under some conditions the alert subject will formulate and test two hypotheses concurrrently or he may adopt a working hypothesis for his responses but also monitor other hypotheses of interest (Levine, 1970). Thus the focusing strategy and the scanning strategy are not so sharply differentiated as they seemed to be ten years ago. Furthermore, multidimensional concepts may be acquired in two or more stages, which has the consequence of decreasing the difference between continuous and discontinuous models.

The hypothesis-sampling models have already demonstrated their vitality as explicit statements about the formulation and testing of hypotheses and as mathematically sophisticated alternatives to the associative approach, although, when the situation is complex, the possibility of associative learning at some stage cannot be overlooked (Overstreet and Dunham, 1969). This is an active, intriguing area of research at present; further limitations on hypothesis-sampling assumptions will no doubt be discovered and more complicated models elaborated to meet the criticisms.

COMPLEX CLASSES AND RULES OF COMBINATION

The difficulty of acquiring classes increases, as we have seen, as the number of relevant and irrelevant attributes increases. But the difficulty is determined also by the structure of the class, that is, by the way the relevant attributes are combined. For a systematic comparison of the difficulty of different types of concepts, Hunt and Hovland (1960) arranged an experiment with stimulus materials that varied in color, shape, and number in such a way that each subject could organize the instances in a conjunctive, relational, or disjunctive class with equal validity. Each subject received first a training series that familiarized him with one example of each type of class, and then a test series. The test series could be classified in any of the three ways, but it was found that conjunctive and relational solutions were used much more frequently than disjunctive ones. It is possible, of course, to arrange special training in the use of disjunctive classes; this increases the proportion of subjects who offer a disjunctive concept when a conjunctive concept is also available and it even increases the number of disjunctive rules given for forming the classes (Wells, 1963). The training does not render disjunctive classes as easy as conjunctive, however.

COMPLEXITY AND DIFFICULTY

Actually, there are many ways in which a set of objects can be classified, some of which seem to be more complex than others. To evaluate the effects of complexity systematically, Shepard, Hovland, and Jenkins (1961) used several sets of eight stimuli—including pictures of familiar objects as well as meaningless designs—arranged in six levels of complexity. The least complex were unidimensional classes; next came classes with two dimensions. Classes with three dimensions increased in complexity as disjunctions and exceptions were added. The experimental results showed that the classes which the experimenters considered complex were, in fact, learned more slowly. Neisser and Weene (1962), using strings of four consonants, also found that the difficulty of a concept varies directly with the complexity of the rule of combination. These experimenters pointed out that the order of difficulty does not appear when a computer program is used to attain the concepts by simple elimination. "It seems to reflect a hierarchical organization of conceptual processes in the Ss themselves [p. 645]."

But if a class appears complex to the experimenter, does it also appear complex to the subjects who have to learn it? An enlightening outcome of the Shepard, Hovland, and Jenkins experiment was obtained by having the subjects write rules for constructing the classes. It turned out that there was a close correlation between complexity of rules and difficulty of acquisition. An example of a rule written for the construction of a simple class was: "All circles on the left; triangles on the right." A rule written for a more complex class was: "All black figures on the left and white figures on the right *except* the large black circle should be exchanged with the small white triangle [p. 15]." A correlation of .90 showed that those classes which were difficult to learn, in terms of time and errors, were the ones for which the subjects wrote complex rules of classification.

ATTRIBUTE LEARNING AND RULE LEARNING

If the class is unidimensional, defined by one attribute, that is all there is to be learned; but if the class is multidimensional, the subject must learn the relevant attributes and also the rule for combining them. These two aspects of the conceptual task may alternate or overlap under ordinary conditions, but Haygood and Bourne (1965) have shown that they can be separated quite easily. Attribute learning can be studied by telling the subjects the rule but not the relevant attributes—as was done in most of the experiments reviewed above. Rule learning can be studied by telling the subjects the relevant attributes but not the rule of combination.

When college students learned several types of classes, constructed from the conventional geometric figures, this analytic procedure showed that attribute learning required more time and contributed more errors than rule learning. The acquisition of conjunctive classes consisted mostly of learning the attributes; learning the simple conjunctive rule was so easy that it made a negligible contribution to time and errors. For example, those subjects who had to learn the attributes made an average of 4.0 errors before mastering the first problem, while those who had to learn the rule made 0.2 errors, and those who had to learn both made 3.6 errors. Rule learning was a more important part of the acquisition of disjunctive and other complex classes because, although the attributes were the same, the combinatory rules were more complex. On disjunctive classes, for example, those who had to learn the attributes made 12.1 errors, those who had to learn the rule made 8.0 errors, and those who had the complete problem made 37.0 errors. Adolescents, in grades six and seven, are also capable of learning rules for conjunctive and disjunctive classes and of transferring their skill to new problems (Youniss and Furth, 1967).

When the inquiry moves from attributes to rules for combining attributes, many complex cases taken from symbolic logic can be investigated. The conditional rule is particularly interesting because it involves implication: If A, then B. Suppose the relevant attributes are *square* and *red,* with other attributes being irrelevant, and the rule is: If square, then red. Square red figures are obviously positive, that is, they fit the rule, and square figures that are not red are obviously negative. The rule does not imply that figures that are not square must be red, so red figures of other shapes are positive instances, and so are figures that are neither red nor square. The latter two instances are the ones that make the conditional rule a difficult one to learn. In the Haygood and Bourne study, for example, those who had to learn the attributes of a conditional problem made 26.8 errors on the average, those who had to learn the rule made 16.4, and those who had the complete problem made 38.4 errors.

INSTRUCTIONS AND TRAINING

Concept research has usually followed the tradition in experimental psychology of keeping the subject in a condition of innocence for the duration of the experiment. In educational circles this condition is supposed to promote "learning by discovery." But in fact when the subject is given detailed knowledge of the materials, the task, and the concept to be attained, his performance is generally improved—though the reasons for the improvement may be obscure. Simply giving more explicit instructions and a brief demonstration improves performance even on the difficult conditional rule (Laughlin, 1969). These conditions can be experimentally manipulated, like other experimental conditions, to clarify the reasons for the improvement.

PRETRAINING

Much of the difficulty of the more complex classes, according to Bourne (1967), is due to the inexperience of the subjects in making use of the information provided. Teachers of logic have worked out several schemes for systematic representation of the information to be used in deductive reasoning; one such scheme, the *truth table,* can be used also in inductive reasoning, or concept and rule learning. Bourne gave some college students preliminary training by having them sort geometrical figures into two categories, positive and negative, on the basis of presence or absence of relevant attributes. Students who had pretraining on some simple problems developed strategies that helped them with more complex problems. In one study, for example, the trained group required only about a third as many trials as a comparable untrained group in order to attain the more complex rules of combination.

We have seen that the difficulty in using negative versus positive information decreases with practice, and so does the difficulty of disjunctive versus conjunctive classes. Practice in mapping the available information into a truth table (or into any systematic scheme for representing the data) simplifies the logical use of the data and reduces the vulnerability to interferences of one kind or another. If a subject represents all instances in a two-by-two table, for example, he is more likely to consider it a closed system and be willing to use the negative information along with the positive. For pretraining, Guy (1969) had children of seven and nine sort figures into a box with four panels, two by two, labeled according to the presence or absence of the positive values on two dimensions. Then the children were shown how to collapse the two-by-two table into just two categories, positive and negative. The pretraining did reduce the differences between the difficulties of various rules of combination—for children as well as college students. Some aspects of the problem became mechanical, so that the subjects could apply their conceptual abilities more efficiently to all types of problems. If we regard the following of a complex rule as a high-level task and the coding of figures into classes as a low-level component of this task, then practice in coding is a helpful first step toward the higher performance (Lee, 1968).

The most illuminating effect of pretraining, however, with a revealing sidelight on concept learning theories, is the effect on the processes by which the concept problems are solved. It appears from an experiment by White (1967) that the activities of college students will be consistent with either an associational theory or a hypothesis-testing theory, depending on the pretraining they have received. White gave some students pretraining on an unsystematic set of figures, assuming that these would be learned by a gradual increase in correct associations with the appropriate responses. He gave other students a systematic set of figures, assuming that these would encourage students to look for the system and thus employ a discontinuous, hypothesis-testing approach. On the test problem, which was the same for all subjects, subjects with 25 pretraining trials on either systematic or unsystematic materials performed about the same way. But 75 pretraining trials separated the 2 groups of subjects on the test problem. Those with pretraining on unsystematic materials acquired the second concept gradually, as if by associative learning, while those with systematic materials acquired it in a discontinuous fashion, as if by hypothesis formulation and testing. As the author put it, "Hypothesis testing theories describe the behavior of sophisticated Ss, while associational theories have more applicability to the untrained S [p. 13]."

VERBAL LABELS

The concept learning experiment can be modified for young children, either to pursue the theoretical questions discussed above or to evaluate alternative classroom practices, by the technique called *matching to a sample*. Wittrock and Keislar (1965) projected slides with three figures varying in four dimensions: color, size, shape, and number. The sample figure or model appeared at the top of a slide, the other two figures at the bottom; the child's task was to choose the bottom figure that was most like the top figure. This is, in effect, a reception method of presentation, with all three instances shown simultaneously. The top figure, for example, might be three small green circles while the bottom left figure is two small green diamonds and the bottom right three large red circles. When *color* is the correct dimension, and size, shape, and number are irrelevant, the correct choice for this example would be *left*.

Wittrock and Keislar examined the effects of verbal hints or cues, given orally when the slides were shown, on helping children discover concepts and transfer their skill to new concepts. For children in the second and third grades, general hints about concepts were useless but class cues, such as *color*, and specific cues, such as *red*, facilitated learning on transfer to new concepts as well as to additional instances of the same concept, and even on a follow-up test three weeks later. One might expect that general hints about concepts would be most helpful in the transfer to new concepts, but there was some evidence that the general hints merely confused the children.

Similar slides, with simple line drawings of familiar objects such as trees, birds, and toys, were prepared by Stern (1965) for children in kindergarten and first grade. The top picture might be a bird, for example, and the three bottom pictures a toy, a tree, and a different bird. The children's task was to select one of the bottom pictures to "go with" the model above, and in this experiment the children were given labels for the instances, for example, *robin*. It was not a case of learning the labels as such; it was more a matter of using them conceptually, to apply to a class and thus to solve a problem. The same superiority of class names as verbal cues has been reported in an experiment on teaching French words for pictures to kindergarten children (Wittrock, Keislar, and Stern, 1964).

When complex rules are to be learned, one efficient procedure is to learn the components separately. The complex rule that Lee and Gagné (1969) taught to high-school students was the relation between certain A attributes, such as size and color, and certain C attributes, such as shape and texture. It is reasonable to suppose that the A-C rule is acquired in two stages: categorizing the A attributes and associating them with appropriate labels (the B components), then learning the B-C rule that relates the labels to the C attributes. A subject might learn, for example, "When a red large figure, choose the shape of the figure and read the value of the shape dimension." The experimenters assumed that the B labels acted as verbal mediators in the chain between the A and C attributes. They supported this assumption by demonstrating that consistent training with the mediators facilitated acquisition of the A-C rule more than inconsistent training. The implication is that a concept is more likely to be integrated with others when it is properly labeled.

These experiments leave no doubt about the generally helpful effects of verbal labels when appropriately applied to classes of figures. There are exceptions, of course. Furth and Milgram (1965) reported that asking children to supply verbal labels for pictures facilitated correct classification at age nine but not at age six when verbal skill was less developed. And the controversy over mediated association and reversal shifts sketched in the preceding pages suggests that even when labels have proved helpful, there is room for argument as to whether these effects are due to verbal mediation or to verbal control of attention.

STRATEGY TRAINING

Children's problem-solving processes also can be improved by proper training which is directly suggested by the theoretical investigations of concept learning. One error that children, as well as adults, often make is to repeat a hypothesis they have already tried. In technical terms, they sample cues by a replacement strategy when a nonreplacement strategy would be appropriate. Wittrock (1967) was able to train second-grade children, 12 minutes a day for thirteen days, on a nonreplacement strategy for simple figure concept problems with good success and with transfer to other problems. Children with training on a replacement strategy were more successful than a control group, but not as successful as those with nonreplacement training.

In general, anyone who is looking for a comprehensive theory to explain the acquisition of figure classes and rules is likely to be disappointed. One sees progress in the direction of sophisticated and differentiated theorizing but no conclusive agreement. The more satisfying progress consists of the description of cognitive processes, such as hypothesis formulation and testing, focusing strategies, nonreplacement strategies, systematic representation of the information, and verbal labeling. Any comprehensive account of concept acquisition must include the alternatives and the flexibility: thus, verbal labels are useful but not always necessary; hypotheses are helpful, especially for sophisticated subjects, but others get by without them. A pluralistic description is more satisfying when one recalls that the conditions under which each of these activities occurs have been partially determined and so have their contributions to improvement in overall performance. Clearly, a whole theory of concept learning will be more than the sum of its interchangeable parts.

LEARNING MEANINGS OF CONCRETE WORDS
THROUGH INFORMAL COMMUNICATION

The experiments reviewed above, analyzing complex abstract human accomplishments, are a triumph of psychological methodology. They have been criticized, however, as experiments on artificial classes associated with artificial names. The advantages of such materials are obvious to an experimental psychologist, but the range of application of the results must be limited. Since the concepts that everyone acquires and uses are the standard concepts of the culture, such acquisition may be considered, at a gross level of analysis, as one aspect of the lifesize enterprise of learning the culture. If the aim is to investigate this extensive and tangled learning process, then culture-free concepts peculiarly suitable for research are no more to be hoped for than culture-free intelligence tests.

And if the experiments described above are intended to yield generalizations that apply to concept learning as it takes place outside the laboratory, they are open to another criticism. They have been designed, almost exclusively, as experiments in learning to classify. Hence the subject observes some objects and learns to give the class name as a response to the positive instances, and later a definition or rule of combination. Concept learning proceeds in this direction, to be sure, but it also proceeds the other way. The subject hears the class name or definition and then observes the objects to which it refers. Concept learning goes from words to things as well as from things to words.

Suppose a man brings home a dax and shows it to his wife and five-year-old daughter. Later, he asks his daughter to get the new dax to show a visitor. If the child does so, she demonstrates that she has learned something about the meaning of *dax,* the extensional meaning at least. It is what her father refers to when he says *dax.* We need not assume that she likes or dislikes the dax or makes any response to it as a dax. The reinforcement is contingent not on her response to it but on her father's response to her when she attempts to follow his instructions. If she brings him the object that he calls a *dax,* she will receive social reward; if she brings him something else, she will be disappointed. If she is rewarded in this situation, she may later be heard telling others that her father brought home a new dax. Reinforcement and nonreinforcement of her attempts to use the new word in other situations also reside in the communicative process. In general, it is meanings, information about referents, that are communicated.

The meaning of a singular term is probably learned by simple association between the term, such as *Daddy,* and a perceptible referent. But even this is a polymorphous association: the child hears the word and then sees the referent of the word, he sees the referent and then hears the word, he sees the referent and speaks the word, he speaks the word and observes a rewarding response by the referent.

The referents of a concrete general term, such as *toy,* are probably learned most often by extension or denotation, as when parents point to toys and tell the child to pick up "this toy," and "this one too," and "all the toys." But intensional meanings or properties of the class are communicated also: "This is medicine. You have to take it to get well." Children also hear many adjectives that refer to dimensions, such as *heavy, red,* and *large,* and soon use them with fair accuracy. These are the familiar dimensions from which synthetic classes are later constructed for laboratory research.

Certainly positive instances occur more frequently in communication between the parent and the child, but the occasional negative instances may be especially valuable. It is not uncommon for a parent to tell a child: "This is not a toy. It's a sharp knife that can cut you." Word usage is sharpened through continued two-way communication with more positive and negative instances, through deliberate correction by parents, and perhaps through ridicule by other children. The referents of some terms are broadened while others are narrowed. Some singular concepts become general concepts, as when the child explores the neighborhood and finds that other children have daddies too. In all probability, adjectives that adults use to refer to bipolar dimensions, such as *clean* and *dirty,* are used as class concepts by children at first and only later as dimensional concepts.

A well-known theory of the acquisition of word meanings by the preschool child is the mediation theory of Osgood (1957), which begins with an unlearned or previously learned stimulus-response association. The taste and feel of warm milk in the mouth of a hungry infant, for example, are strongly associated with swallowing, salivating, and digestive activities. Considering the stimulus pattern as the significate, Osgood states that when another stimulus is associated with this significate and the association is reinforced, the new stimulus acquires an increment of association with some fractional portion of the total behavior elicited by the significate. Thus a visual stimulus, a bottle, can become a sign of the taste and feel of the milk because it can elicit a portion of the response to the milk. Likewise an auditory stimulus, the word *ball,* becomes a sign of a ball when it elicits part of the manipulatory response pattern elicited by the ball. This association generalizes to other balls and other objects like balls that elicit similar response patterns. The mediator represents the objects in the sense that it is a fraction of the response to them.

But words and other symbols, unlike signs, are produced as well as heard. After the child has acquired the skill to produce words like those he hears, the spoken word as well as the heard word is associated with the fractional response that represents the object or class of objects.

Since the fractional representational response has not been tied to distinctive experimental operations, discussion of this theory has been on the speculative level. Lennenberg (1962) has pointed out that any theory of verbal comprehension that depends on speech movements is questionable because of the existence of children who learn to comprehend quite well without being able to talk. Fodor (1965), a linguist, is critical of psychologists' theories that conceive of words or verbal cues acting as implicit stimuli and responses, because a word is not really a response in the sense that it is under stimulus control. Different words, synonyms, have approximately the same meaning, and the same word in different contexts has different meanings. Some words, such as *dragon,* have no corresponding stimuli. Thus fractional components of the response to a word as such are too unstable to support a theory of meaning; in the example above of the girl learning the meaning of *dax,* it was successful communication that was reinforced, not any particular response (also see Osgood [1966]). There is general agreement that any theory of the relation between words and meanings must include the flexibility between words and referents in different contexts; the disagreement is whether a mediation theory of the S-R type, or any other, can be flexible enough to account for the facts without being too abstract to be testable. But psycholinguistic research, inquiring about sentences as well as words, is increasing in amount and sophistication, hence it is not too much to hope that we shall gain a deeper understanding of the acquisition of word meanings.

At any rate, by the time he goes to school and enters a more formal education program, the average child has learned to use many common terms to refer to classes and dimensions and to understand these terms as referring to such abstractions when others use them. It is a fair guess that some of the results of laboratory research on the learning of figure classes, as reviewed above, are applicable to this extralaboratory preschool learning, but the range of applicability is not known at present. At this young age gradual associative learning seems more pertinent, intuitively, than hypothesis formation and testing.

Achievement of Word Classes and Meanings from Other Words

The acquisition of word classes is more typical of man's distinctive intellectual accomplishments than the acquisition of figure classes. Word classes seem to be more abstract than figure classes because each word is itself a symbol that refers to an abstract class or dimension. But verbal and pictorial stimuli differ in many ways; we cannot assume that what we know about figure classes can be directly applied to word classes. In the Johnson and O'Reilly (1964) experiment mentioned on page 57, children who had verbal phrases describing birds learned to classify them in fewer trials and gave better definitions than children who had corresponding pictorial dimensions. Compared to the pictures, the verbal materials are easier to analyze and to describe in verbal terms.

The materials for experiments on word classes are not constructed as systematically as those for experiments on figure classes, because the attributes to which a word refers cannot be listed as a closed set of elements, explicitly known to experimenter and subject. And the stimulus materials are complicated, of course, by the associations between words. Nevertheless, some of the experiments on word classes have followed the same designs as experiments on figure classes, and have confirmed the importance of some of the same conditions.

Classes of words are familiar to literate people: words that refer to vegetables, or to animals. But words can also be ordered along dimensions of meaning. A standard procedure for doing this systematically with bipolar scales, known as the Semantic Differential (Osgood, Suci, and Tannenbaum, 1957), is widely employed in investigating the meaning of words and other symbols. Fig. 2.4, illustrating the data obtained by this procedure, shows that along most of these 20 scales *man* and *woman* are quite similar in meaning. The

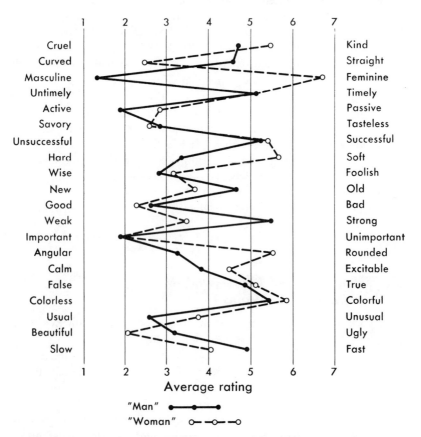

FIGURE 2.4. *Semantic profiles of two words:* man *and* woman. *Average ratings by 15 college men and 15 college women on 20 scales. Data from Jenkins, Russell, and Suci (1958).*

larger differences appear on the Masculine-Feminine scale, of course, and on the Hard-Soft, Weak-Strong, and Angular-Rounded scales.

The most prominent dimensions of meaning, in ratings of many words on these scales, are Evaluation, as represented by the Good-Bad scale, Potency, as represented by the Strong-Weak scale, and Activity, as represented by the Active-Passive and Fast-Slow scales. These 3 basic dimensions account for a large share of the difference in ratings of words on the Semantic Differential, and distinctly different word classes can be constructed from such ratings. A class of 40 words can be selected from words that have been rated high on the Evaluation dimension, for example, and another class of 40 from words that have been rated low on this dimension (Haygood, 1966). When the 80 words, printed on cards, are shuffled, variations of meaning on many irrelevant dimensions are apparent, but college students quickly learn to classify the words on the relevant dimension, as "good" and "bad" words.

Ratings of words on various dimensions of meaning are used in the construction of materials for an experiment (as in the above example) and also as the dependent variable at the end of an experiment to measure what meaning has been learned. The evidence of a subject's achievement of the meaning of a word comes also from observing his use of that word in oral or written communication and from his comprehension of the word when used by others. The multiple-choice vocabulary test is a familiar device for testing word comprehension.

CONDITIONS THAT INFLUENCE THE ACQUISITION OF WORD CLASSES

Reed (1946) made a start on the investigation of the learning of word classes by printing groups of four words on cards. One word, for example, was *monkey*; other four-word groups had other animal words. All groups that included one animal word were to be called a *kun*. Other four-word groups in the list were characterized by the presence of one word of another class. Some word groups and class names are shown in Table 2.2 Note that these

TABLE 2.2. SELECTIONS FROM THE MATERIALS OF A CONCEPT LEARNING EXPERIMENT

Group of Four Stimulus Words (on card shown to subject)				Name (to be learned)
horn	*leaf*	*monkey*	*debt*	*kun*
brook	*leave*	*claim*	*precious*	*vor*
roses	*suit*	*juice*	*plum*	*yem*
fight	*tablet*	*chair*	*poppy*	*yem*
fame	*ought*	*tiger*	*saucer*	*kun*
lover	*borrow*	*flower*	*point*	*vor*
horse	*circle*	*paid*	*scholar*	*kun*
banana	*haste*	*dear*	*minutes*	*vor*
laden	*daisy*	*disgust*	*cranky*	*yem*

From Reed (1946).

are simple classes, characterized by one element, and that this one element characterizes the class because of its meaning, not its physical attributes. The subjects of Reed's experiments, who were college students, knew the meanings of the critical words as well as the noncritical ones. The task was not to learn word meanings but to abstract the one critical word out of each group of four and to generalize across four-word groups.

THE PREPARATORY SET

In learning word classes, as in learning figure classes, the set or preparation for the task, established usually by the instructions, makes an important contribution to efficiency. If a subject does not know that there are classes of words, he may simply associate one word with another. This may, in fact, be the most efficient procedure if the classes are hard to learn and there are only a few instances in each class. When studying French, for example, it is worthwhile learning the classes of regular verbs because there are only a few classes and many verbs in each; but there is also a small number of irregular verbs that must be separately memorized. The materials of the usual concept experiment are chosen so that acquisition of the classes facilitates performance. Under such conditions, a set to learn classes is more efficient than a set to learn correct associations and, unlike associations between nonsense syllables, these conceptual achievements are retained very well (Reed, 1946).

METHOD OF PRESENTATION

Simultaneous presentation has certain obvious advantages over the more common serial presentation—for word classes as for figure classes. In a comparison by Reed (1946), the simultaneous method led to the discovery of more correct concepts, presumably because when the subjects can study several examples of a class at once in their own way, they can easily detect similarities and check hypotheses. This advantage did not hold, however, when so much material was displayed that the subject could not grasp it simultaneously and had to fall back to a serial method. Furthermore, the subjects spent considerable time studying the words presented simultaneously, hence this method increased accuracy rather than speed.

ABSTRACTNESS

The old question of the abstractness of concepts can be examined with word classes as with figure classes, but the materials for the former are perhaps easier to standardize. In an experiment along the lines of that given above, Reed and Dick (1968) compared the learning of classes of abstract words with classes of more concrete words, using high-frequency words equated for judged familiarity. As an example of abstract words, *second, minute, week, decade, year,* and *night* were to be grouped under the label *paf,* and, as an example of concrete words, *bread, milk, salad, cereal, sugar,* and *cream* were to be grouped under the label *mev.* The abstract classes were clearly more difficult for college students to learn, judged by number of failures, promptings required, and generalization errors.

This finding is consistent with the recent research on verbal learning, summarized by Paivio (1969), showing that concrete words are more easily learned than abstract words. Paivio's interpretation, that concrete words arouse more facilitative imagery than abstract words, is also pertinent to the learning of word classes.

RELEVANT AND IRRELEVANT WORDS

Irrelevant words interfere with the formation of word classes just as irrelevant dimensions interfere with the formation of figure classes. This interference has been demonstrated by a serial-exposure technique (Johnson and Hall, 1961) like that described earlier for figure classes. The subject is presented with a list of words, with instructions to observe what they have in common, then turn to a second list and find another word of the same class. Attaching a label to the class is not required. An illustrative problem follows:

bark	1. *birch*
salt	2. *number*
pepper	3. *wood*
cement	4. *pot*
paprika	5. *cloves*
thyme	

The important measurement, for present purposes, is the time spent on the first list. The number of irrelevant words contributes far more to the time required than the number of relevant words; problems with six relevant words, for example, required a median time of 3.3 seconds. With five relevant and one irrelevant words, median time was 3.6 seconds. In problems like the one given here, with four relevant and two irrelevant words, 6.3 seconds was required. In general, the interfering effect of the irrelevant words was less when the number of relevant words was large.

This method yields measures of the difficulty of forming classes more efficiently than conventional learning methods, but the experiment is open to the criticism that the associations between words were not standardized. An experiment of similar design by Mayzner (1962), but with better control of the materials, presented two, three, four, or five words in the first list, in addition to the correct word. These problems were more difficult than the one above. Their solution was aided by an increase in the first list, which offered more associations with the correct response word, and impeded by an increase in the second list, which offered more competing associations.

SIMILARITY OF MEANING

A previous section on salience and similarity in the achievement of figure classes noted that the dimension on which objects differ is more obvious and therefore more useful as a cue to classification when the differences on that dimension are large. It is reasonable to ask if this principle applies also to the achievement of word classes where the dimensions of interest now are dimensions of meaning. Taylor and Haygood (1968) investigated this question by selecting words that were close together in ratings on the evaluation dimension for comparison with words that were well separated. The words differed, of course, in other semantic dimensions irrelevant to evaluation. Their results showed that learning to classify 60 words into 2 classes proceeded more rapidly when the separation in meaning was large. It is relatively easy to classify words for their evaluative dimension of meaning when the differences on this dimension are large. The same results were obtained for words close together and far apart on the potency dimension.

Three semantic dimensions—evaluation, potency, and activity—are prominent in children's classifications of words also (Di Vesta and Ingersoll, 1969). The evaluative dimension is basically salient, of course, hence fifth-grade children learn word classes rapidly if this dimension is the relevant one. But whatever semantic dimension is relevant, the learning goes faster when the differences on the relevant dimension are larger than the differences on the irrelevant dimensions.

COMPLEX CLASSES AND RULES
The first experiments on word classes constructed simple classes characterized by one dimension of meaning, but the fact that words can be rated on several dimensions of meaning makes it possible to construct complex classes as well. Di Vesta and Walls (1969) constructed multidimensional classes from words rated on the evaluation, activity, and potency dimensions, presented these to fifth-grade children to learn, and found, as expected, that disjunctive classes required more trials for learning than comparable conjunctive classes. The expected differences between attribute learning and rule learning, which has been demonstrated for figure classes, also appeared, as shown in Fig. 2.5.

Thus it appears that several of the generalizations which have been worked out with figure classes apply also to word classes. But words, unlike figures, are often strongly associated with other words, and this raises questions that are, as far as we know, peculiar to word classes.

WORD CLASSES AND WORD ASSOCIATIONS
Reed departed from tradition in constructing classes of words but followed tradition in naming the classes by nonsense syllables. When the names of word classes are also words, the responses as well as the stimuli are words, and a multiplicity of previously learned associations may be aroused—to facilitate or to impede concept formation. The relevant and irrelevant dimensions that affect the achievement of figure classes may differ in salience, as noted above; but the differences between words in terms of previous associations to other words are larger and more specific. This special nature of word classes means that a careful standardization of research materials is needed. It also couples concept research with verbal learning research and generates fruitful new hypotheses for both.

DOMINANCE OF ASSOCIATIONS
Underwood and Richardson (1956) investigated the influence of previous relationships by presenting their subjects four names of common objects

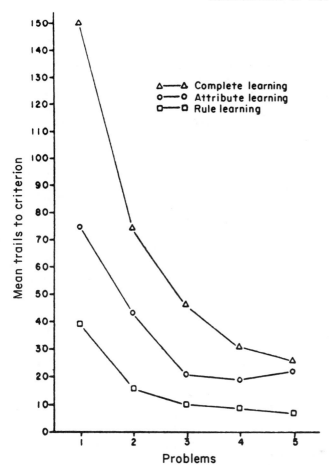

FIGURE 2.5. *Attribute learning and rule learning of word classes by fifth-grade children. From Di Vesta and Walls (1969).*

(e.g., *tomato*), with a request to discover what single dimension, represented by an adjective, described all four of them. In a situation like this, when the subject has nothing else to go by, no specific set, he is likely to respond with a word that has been associated with the stimulus word in the past (e.g. *red*). The experimenters began with the hypothesis that concept learning will occur quickly if a descriptive response word has previously been strongly associated with all four stimulus words. Hence, a pool of response words of different strengths of association to stimulus words had to be collected first. A long list of nouns was presented to college students: they were instructed to give a free association word to each, but with the restriction that the associated words must be adjectives descriptive of sense impressions, such as *round, small,* and *white.* From this list four words were selected, such as *barrel, doughnut, knob,* and *balloon,* to which the word *round* was an associate of high dominance. That is, *round* was the response word given first

TABLE 2.3. EXAMPLES OF ASSOCIATIONS OF HIGH, MEDIUM,
             AND LOW DOMINANCE

High Dominance		Medium Dominance		Low Dominance	
barrel		bread		baseball	
doughnut	round (66%)	flannel	soft (42%)	fang	white (12%)
knob		jellyfish		paste	
balloon		moccasin		sugar	

From Underwood and Richardson (1956).

with an average frequency of 66 percent. Examples of descriptive response words of high, medium, and low dominance are displayed in Table 2.3 in order to show how such experimental materials are prepared.

For the main experiment, other students were given 6 such groups in various combinations and instructed to describe 4 nouns by 1 adjective, 4 other nouns by another adjective, and so on. Correct responses were confirmed. The subjects easily learned to group words like *barrel* and *balloon* together and to label them by a response associate of high dominance level. Learning word groups with a common response word of low dominance was much harder, so much so that many of them were not learned even in 20 trials.

In these experiments, the process is not so much a learning of new associations as a shuffling and reorganization of previously learned associations of varying strengths. Competing associations play an interfering role somewhat as the irrelevant attributes in the learning of names for synthetic classes of geometric figures do. If *baseball* is to be put in the class named *white* but *white* is an infrequent associate to *baseball,* then other, more frequent associates will be given first; the learning will consist of inhibiting the strong association and replacing it with one that was initially weak. Underwood and Richardson illustrated this effect of the associative response hierarchy by recording the errors made by their subjects. The weak strength of the class names of low associative dominance permitted other class names to be given more often at first, and these erroneous responses were most often class names of high dominance.

The effect of competing responses was demonstrated more explicitly by Kendler and Karasik (1958), who assembled word groups in which the irrelevant words varied in dominance and relatedness. The easiest groups to learn were those in which the irrelevant words were of high dominance and formed a class of their own that was easily differentiated from the correct class.

Over and above the associative dominance of class names, according to Freedman and Mednick (1958), is the variance of this dominance. In order to examine these associations more closely, they made up two types of word groups. The first consisted of groups of four words, from the lists of Underwood and Richardson, each word being associated with a common adjective at the same dominance level; the second of groups of words that had the same average dominance level but contained one word of high dominance and thus had more variance in associative dominance. (An example of each type of word group is shown in Table 2.4.) The results of their experiment, following the method of Underwood and Richardson, came out as expected: with average associative dominance equated, word groups of high variance in dominance were learned faster, with fewer errors, than those of low variance. The most frequent response to one word in a high-variance group is soon confirmed as a correct class name, and this gives the subject a cue or focus that helps him find others to which this name can be applied.

A later experiment (Mednick and Halpern, 1962) tested the same principle, stated more precisely in terms of associative rank. The adjective *metallic* is a first-rank associate to *pail* because it occurs with higher frequency (24%) than any other adjective; the adjective *soft* is associated with the same frequency (24%) to *belly*, but it has second rank in this associative hierarchy because *round* has first rank (43%). Word groups containing a word with a first-rank associate were easier to learn than word groups of the same mean dominance without one.

The perceptive reader will detect an analogy between the helpful effect contributed by a high variance of associations in the learning of word classes and the focusing strategy in the learning of figure classes. Whether this is more than an analogy is the question. There is a difference in the labeling of the two interpretations, to be sure, which reflects the difference between the cognitive and the associative traditions. The notion of focusing implies that the subject takes the initiative in formulating a hypothesis and testing it; the notion of associative dominance suggests that it is the stimulus word which elicits the response word. The subjects of word association experiments are not forbidden to formulate hypotheses but neither are the experiments designed to place them on record. Hence the available data do not reveal whether the acquisition of word classes in these experiments is continuous or discontinuous.

MEDIATED VERBAL ASSOCIATION

The function of verbal mediators in the achievement of figure classes was discussed earlier; their function in the achievement of word classes is more

TABLE 2.4. ASSOCIATIONS OF HIGH AND LOW VARIANCE OF DOMINANCE

High Variance			Low Variance		
gnat	76%		*sauerkraut*	24%	
needle	9	*small* (24%)	*hospital*	23	*smelly* (23%)
stone	7		*tobacco*	23	
canary	5		*gym*	21	

From Freedman and Mednick (1958).

obvious and less controversial. In the learning of word classes, the first word associate is considered a mediator if it is not the correct response but is a cue to which the correct response is associated. (If the correct response word is directly associated with the stimulus word, the hypothesis of mediation is unnecessary.) The verbal mediator is usually conceived not as a complete response word but as an implicit response having some of the properties of a word. Fortunately, there is considerable information on the properties of single words and of associations between words. This information has been used in designing the experiments on word classes described above, and also in designing experiments on verbal mediation. In fact, much of the research on verbal learning is concerned with hypothetical associations and chains of associations between observable stimulus words and observable response words. The success of such hypothetical explanations has encouraged application to the concept experiment.

A recent experiment by Duncan (1965) illustrates this well. He had college students learn which was the correct word on each of 24 cards containing 3 words. The correct words were in pairs forming disjunctive classes: in one condition, for example, the correct cards contained either *wait* or *give,* the other words being irrelevant. This task was easy when the two correct words were members of a familiar class, such as *circle* and *square,* and especially easy if the irrelevant words were not members of a familiar class. The mediator in this experiment could be either member of a class, *circle* or *square,* because such words are commonly associated with each other and when one is reinforced, the occurrence of the other is strengthened also.

Pairs of words vary more in associative strength than pairs of geometrical figures, hence the effects of verbal mediation suggest interesting hypotheses about concept shifts involving word classes. Kendler and Watson (1968) designed a concept shift experiment, like those of Kendler and others described in an earlier section but using classes of words as in the experiments just mentioned. The important part of their results is that after the shift, the relearning was facilitated by high associative strength between previously correct words and correct responses to the new problems. In this situation, when the cues are words, it would not be accurate to say that cue selection is random.

Similar effects of verbal mediation were demonstrated in a concept shift experiment by Schvaneveldt and Kroll (1968). If the subject has learned that groups of words containing the word *horse* are positive and those containing other animal words negative, then a shift of reinforcement to groups of words containing *cow* would be an intradimensional shift, while a shift from *milk* to *cow* would be an extradimensional shift. The results of figure concept research with adults suggests that intradimensional shifts would be easier. But words are associated along many lines, more so than figures, so lists of high and low association were also included in this experiment. A shift from groups containing *horse* to groups containing *cow* is facilitated by the high association between these two words, while a shift from *rabbit* to *cow* is not so facilitated.

The results of this experiment indicated little difference between intra-dimensional and extradimensional shifts, but the difference due to the associative strength of the words was considerable. Shifts from one word to another strongly associated with it required about half as many trials as shifts to a weakly associated word. The authors take these results as evidence that concept shifts can be mediated by associations between the words and as a lack of evidence for second-order mediation by the dimension. Thus the fact that *horse* and *cow* as animals are on the same dimension, or in the same class, was evidently not as significant as the fact that *cow* is a close associate to *horse* but not to *rabbit*.

LEARNING THE MEANINGS OF ABSTRACT TERMS

The broad view of concepts proposed in this volume looks at a concept as a part of the general culture and at concept achievement as an aspect of socialization. It follows from the flexibility of the human mind and the versatility of concepts that concept learning will proceed along several routes. We have noted that young children can acquire a concept by beginning with perceived objects and learning the word that refers to them in ordinary domestic conversation or by beginning with the perceived word and learning what objects it refers to. But domestic communication refers to intangible classes and dimensions also. Children pick up such concepts as *good, bad, gone, tomorrow, grow, love,* and *work* from hearing these words in sentences with other words. This is usually called *incidental* rather than *intentional* learning.

A child who hears an unfamiliar word in an interesting context may go to an adult or an older child and ask what the word means. When this happens, he may be given the denotative significance, through a few positive and negative instances, perhaps accompanied by pointing. In the case of abstract concepts the instances must, of course, be described in words, and considerable previous conceptual learning is assumed. The child may even be given a synonym or a definition, depending on the adult's skill and the child's patience.

When children go to school and learn to read, their incidental learning does not stop, but there is a big increase in their intentional learning, or study, a large share of which, at all educational levels, consists of the acquisition of meanings for terms. The direct applicability of conventional concept learning research to concept teaching practice appears, however, to be quite limited (Carroll, 1964; Gagné, 1965) because the role of instructions from one person to another, in speech and in writing, has not received the study it deserves. Concept research has been concerned with discovery learning, but concepts are also presented, or "given," to students by teachers and text-books. As Carroll put it, concepts are acquired deductively as well as inductively.

An examination of the textbooks reveals that most writers employ several techniques, though not systematically, in order to communicate a new concept. One common technique presents a definition first, then some positive examples, and a negative example for differentiation; thereafter, the term is used in context to fixate it. Occasionally, a writer will introduce a new term in the context of a sentence, perhaps to arouse interest, before defining it.

The sequence of events does make a difference, in the second and third grades at least. To demonstrate the superiority of a hypothetically optimal sequence, Eustace (1969) wrote a hierarchical program for teaching the concept of *noun,* beginning with names of things and progressing to word groups, a definition, position of nouns in sentences, and so on, through eight levels. This systematic order proved somewhat more efficient (in terms of scores on a posttest) than the same materials arranged in other orders.

It is informative also to consider the case of the ordinary adult who wishes to classify the trees, rocks, or birds that he sees on a walk through the countryside. He has heard terms, such as *oak, sugar, maple, sandstone,* and *robin,* and he has observed many colorful instances but, if he is serious, he will not try to attain concepts alone. He will get help, by oral communication from an expert if he is fortunate, or by written communication. Field manuals or guides to classification of birds, trees, minerals, and other natural phenomena are well worth psychological scrutiny.

Such guides to classification usually begin by describing the distinguishing features: the songs and wing structures of birds, the leaf outlines and bark of trees, and the color and specific gravity of minerals, and so on. Standard symbols are assigned to these perceptible features in order to facilitate verbal reference. Then the classes—major divisions, subdivisions, and finer distinctions—are described on the basis of such attributes, and scientific names, together with local synonyms, associated with them. Features that are perceptually salient but irrelevant to the classification may be given special attention. It is safe to assume, as the authors of such books do, that learning the critical attributes, a kind of stimulus predifferentiation, facilitates learning the classes, and learning the classes and their names facilitates perception of the critical attributes in the field. After study of the system, the rockhound's perception and conceptualization of any specimen will be mediated by a hierarchical cognitive structure. The meaning of a term will depend on his location of the term in this structure, and he will communicate with other rockhounds in the terms of this structure.

ACQUISITION OF MEANING BY VERBAL CONDITIONING

In order to examine the development of the meaning of a symbol, Staats and Staats (1957) began with nonsense syllables, such as *yof,* to see if they could acquire meaning by association with familiar words of known meaning. As the subject saw *yof,* he heard the word *beauty.* And he saw *xeh,* he heard the word *thief.* In this way *yof* was associated with "good" words, such as *beauty, sweet, honest,* and *smart,* while *xeh* was associated with "bad" words, such as *thief, bitter, ugly,* and *sad.* Other syllables and other scales were included in the experiment as controls. Later, when these subjects rated the syllables on the Pleasant-Unpleasant scale, *yof* was rated more pleasant than *xeh*.

The same procedure was employed to give nonsense syllables more specific meaning (Staats, Staats, and Heard, 1961). *Laj* was associated with words that had previously been judged to be "angular," such as *square, box, roof,* and *triangle. Giw* was associated with words that had been judged to be "round," such as *coil, globe, hub,* and *barrel.* Later, when the subjects rated these syllables on several scales, *laj* was rated at the "angular" end of the Angular-Round scale and *giw* at the "round" end.

Although these two experiments were designed to demonstrate classical conditioning of meaning, other interpretations are possible. When the adult subject's awareness of the experimental contingencies and the demands of the social situation are scrutinized, it appears that this learning is frequently more than simple conditioning (Page, 1969; Staats, 1969). The criticism does not deny that children may learn meanings by simple conditioning in some circumstances; it is very difficult, however, to be sure that a college student learns by conditioning when he can diagnose the experimental expectations and reach the same end in his own way.

ACQUISITION OF MEANING FROM VERBAL CONTEXT

Learning the meaning of a word from the context of the sentences in which it occurs is a common mode of acquisition; children acquire many words in this way. To investigate this process, Werner and Kaplan (1950) printed artificial words and several contexts for each. One task was to discover the meaning of *corplum* from six sentences such as the following:

A corplum may be used for support.
Corplums may be used to close off an open place.
A wet corplum does not burn [p. 3].

The sentences were presented to children one at a time and each child was asked for a meaning of the artificial word that would fit all six sentences. The younger children, as one would expect, were not yet capable of "decontextualizing" the unfamiliar word. The most childish attempts, by children around age eight, fused the meaning of the artificial word with that of the whole sentence. Other children, a little older, could give a meaning that fitted the context of one sentence and later another that fitted the next sentence. Or, at a later age, they might give a meaning appropriate to two sentences but not a general meaning appropriate to all. Even at age ten, when children are using single words quite grammatically in their own speech, parts of the verbal context surrounding the artificial word crept into the meaning assigned to it. But by age eleven most children were able to make use of the context of all the sentences to derive a general meaning for the artificial word that was independent of any specific sentence.

Learning from the context often lacks precision. Many objects that are big, for example, are also heavy and strong. When a child hears one of these adjectives in a sentence, the meaning he attaches to it may be the meaning that adults attach to one of the other adjectives. A differentiation of meaning comes slowly when the dimensions of meaning are correlated in the environment and discrepant instances are seldom encountered. Thus when opportunities were created for children to make such confusions in describing simple objects (Ervin and Foster, 1960), *strong* was used where *big* would be correct with a frequency of 66 percent in the first grade and 21 percent in the sixth grade. In describing faces, *pretty* was used where *clean* was appropriate with a frequency of 91 percent in the first grade and 41 percent in the sixth grade.

College students continually encounter new concepts, but a single encounter is usually not enough for adequate learning. One of the earliest studies of context learning (Gibbons, 1940) presented such sentences as:

In the beginning the teacher traveled from one locality to another to meet the students, thereby bringing into existence the *itinerant* school master [p. 29].

Only two-thirds of a sample of college freshmen were able to give the culturally accepted meaning for *itinerant* after reading this sentence. The other third gave such replies as a research schoolmaster, an immoral schoolmaster, and a rural schoolmaster.

The information for contextual learning comes from the other words and the sentence structure; but more than one sentence is necessary to strengthen the standard meaning and eliminate other meanings peculiar to a single sentence. In this respect, learning verbal concepts from a verbal context resembles learning figure concepts in the conventional laboratory experiment. A context learning experiment was arranged, therefore, with frequency of occurrence of each word in a sentence as the independent variable (Woolum and Johnson, 1969). Coherent paragraphs were constructed of sentences each containing 1 unfamiliar but genuine English word, such as *posset, pharisaical,* and *amerce.* The dependent variable was the score on a 5-item multiple-choice test of word meaning, hence the maximum score for any concept would be 5. Under these conditions, college students acquire some concepts faster than others, of course, but the results indicated a general increase in achievement with an increase in frequency of occurrence in context. With no exposure to a word the mean score was 1.5, with 1 sentence the mean was 2.3, 2 sentences 3.0, 4 sentences 3.1, 8 sentences 3.7, 12 sentences 3.9.

Obviously some sentences are more informative than others. The sentence *A pujoy is alive* tells us something but not as much as *A pujoy eats worms.* Woolum (1970) developed a measure of the information communicated by a sentence by asking her subjects to read sentences in which such artificial nouns were described by familiar adjectives and then to guess the meaning of each noun. The number of subjects who changed their conceptions after reading a sentence was taken as a measure of the information in that sentence. Thus some of the subtleties of learning from the context could be quantitatively investigated. It was possible, for example, by constructing positive and negative sentences of equivalent information, to verify the expectation, from previous work with figure concepts, that the subjects would acquire concepts more readily from the positive sentences.

Other variables that are influential in the achievement of figure concepts, such as the subject's set and the amount of irrelevant information, are no doubt influential in this situation also; but there are some other variables, such as the syntactic structure in which the new word appears, that are peculiar to verbal context. Prentice (1966) was able, in fact, to separate the syntactic aspects of the acquisition of word meaning from the semantic aspects by varying the training given to fourth-grade children. Semantic training was given by showing three pictures in association with a syllable, such as *fud,* referring to all three. The syntactic training consisted of presenting a syllable in a sentence that indicated little more than its grammatical function as a noun, adjective, verb, etc. So, when *sim* was to be an adjective, three sentences were presented, along the lines of: "This is a *sim* dog," and "This is a *sim* house." Later, the achievement of semantic meaning was measured by a test of word equivalents, and achievement of the syntactic function of each syllable by a test of use in a sentence. As one might expect, those with semantic training made an average score of 12.9 on the semantic test and only 6.7 on the syntactic test; while those with syntactic training made 7.4 on the semantic test and 10.1 on the syntactic test. It is especially interesting to note that those children who did not learn what *sim* referred to could still put it in its proper grammatical place in a sentence.

These experiments on learning from the context are pertinent to the activity of a student trying to puzzle out the meaning of an unfamiliar term in a textbook but, like the experiments on learning figure concepts, they are less pertinent to the incidental learning that children do for many years outside school. Students in high school and college are accustomed to formulating a hypothesis about the meaning of a word and testing it on later instances. Young children depend on associative processes, which are less efficient but nevertheless adequate for learning the meaning of words that they hear very frequently in many contexts.

SYNONYMS

If we try to look up the meaning of a word in a dictionary, we often find a synonym rather than a definition. Teaching materials frequently include familiar synonyms when introducing an unfamiliar concept, perhaps with an explanation of the variations in usage. And the conventional multiple-choice vocabulary test is often nothing more than a comparison of words to see which one is most similar in meaning to another.

Concept research has ignored synonyms, but we may speculate that the use of two terms alternatively to refer to a class of objects would complicate learning from oral or printed context. Or let us suppose, in a conventional concept learning experiment, that the labeling of a class of objects by *either* of two terms was confirmed. By analogy with disjunctive classification, we would expect that this disjunctive labeling would retard concept attainment.

There are also conditions under which the availability of synonyms helps concept learning; at least, explanations of meaning often include one or two synonyms. Such explanations seem to be based on the assumption that all synonyms have a general meaning component in common and that each has a special component. By this assumption, as synonyms are added to the context, the general component is strengthened while the special components cancel each other out.

A COMPARATIVE EVALUATION

A recent experiment treated several of these methods of communicating concepts together in one experiment for purposes of evaluation (Johnson and Stratton, 1966). The meanings of four words, moderately difficult for college freshmen, were to be learned: *alacrity, altercation, chide,* and *opulent.* One group was given definitions of the words, then told to rewrite the definitions in their own language. Another group read a simple story in which each word appeared twice, then used each to complete a sentence. A third group was given practice in classifying short descriptions of events as positive and negative instances of these four concepts, with knowledge of results. A fourth had practice in identifying synonyms for these four words, also with knowledge of results. And a fifth group had a mixed program, including a little of each method, requiring the same overall time, about 20 minutes. Nine days later, all five training groups and a control group took a battery of four different tests constructed so as to correspond to the four different training methods.

In their total score on all tests, all the groups improved as compared to the control group with no training; but the group with mixed training improved the most. In fact, all groups exceeded the control group on each of the four different tests. The four training methods were equally effective; only the mixed training surpassed the others. The question of transfer was phrased as follows: How much of what was learned by one method transferred to the tests corresponding to the other methods? And in this experiment, unlike most others, the answer was that transfer was 100 percent. For example, the group that had practice on definitions did as well on the classification test as they did on the definition test. Apparently these college students, who were accustomed to studying concepts, did not stop at learning specifics; they learned concepts.

Achievement of Mathematical Concepts

Number classes differ from figure and word classes in some respects, and the investigation of numerical achievements has consequently taken somewhat different paths. Nevertheless, the number concepts of the preschool child in our culture can be described in the same terms as the others. Number classes, to begin with, are relational classes: what two dogs and two blocks have in common is not a directly perceptible feature but a numerical relation between perceptible features. The child learns these abstract relational properties of perceived objects and the symbols, such as *one* and *three,* that refer to them. By the time he goes to school the average child, when shown sets of two or three objects, can give their number and, when asked for two or three objects, can select that many from a pile (Russell, 1956). The troublesome question of definition does not arise in this context. If a child can pass both of these tests, he has the concept *three*—by any reasonable definition.

Since young children learn so much in diversified domestic interaction, recording what has been learned at different ages is easier than manipulating the conditions of learning. The simple number terms are probably learned at first just as other terms are. The child hears "one apple" as he hears "an apple" and "the apple," often accompanied by pointing or handling. The same terms are applied in the same way to many other objects, associated with singular nouns. Probably the concept *two* is learned from the context as *one and another one,* along with *both* and *a pair,* in association with plural nouns. This should be rather easy in connection with dressing since the child has two feet and two shoes to put on them, and such words are used often in many different sentences in situations where the meaning is closely related to other cues in the sentence or accompanying behavior. The abstractness of numbers is balanced by the circumstance that there are only a few small numbers and these are used with high frequency in situations where the association between term and referent is easily observed. Even such terms as *none* and *all gone* occur frequently in ordinary communication and in games, hence the association between these terms and their referents should be relatively easy to learn. The empty class may be very abstract but the distinction between a goodie, of any kind, and *nothing* is one of the salient facts of early life.

Differences between one and none and between one and two as classes or sets are salient to the young child, but above two such differences are less obvious. In the short-run activities of the young child, the instrumental value of a set of four objects does not differ much from that of a set of three objects; likewise there is usually nothing in the context of communication to differentiate sentences that refer to four peanuts from sentences that refer to three peanuts. One study of children's word usage in kindergarten (Horn, 1929) recorded sharply decreasing frequencies for the larger numbers: one 3,678, two 1,252, three 626, four 443, and five 277. Records of usage in the first grade showed a similar decrease (Rinsland, 1945). The difference between one and many objects is probably perceived before the corresponding symbols are learned; but the symbols for the largest numbers are learned by rote as a meaningless series long before they are used to refer to perceived sets of objects (Russell, 1956).

The methods of investigating the number classes of young children may be illustrated by a study by Long and Welch (1941) that deliberately avoided number terms. In their number discrimination test, one group of ten marbles was displayed in a box and another group of five marbles was displayed in another box. The child was told to choose the box with the most marbles and he would find a toy under it. If he failed, he was offered a choice between ten and four; if he succeeded, he was required to choose between ten and six, and so on, up to ten and eight. In the number matching test, two marbles were placed in front of the child. He was handed a supply of marbles and told to make a pile himself, alongside these two, that was "just as big." If he succeeded, three were placed in front of him, to be matched. In the group matching test, the child was shown four groups of marbles—two groups of two each and two groups of three each—and asked to point first to the groups containing the most marbles and then to the groups containing the smallest number. Children of four years got a mean score of 5.6 on number discrimination; they could discriminate five or six from ten. The mean score on number matching was 3.5; on group matching 2.6. By age six, these concepts had been quite well mastered up to numbers as large as seven. In general, the children who did well on one test did well on the other two tests, a correlation which points to some degree of unity in the conceptual achievement underlying performance on the three different tests.

Since "the new math" introduces sets at a tender age, the learning of set concepts by young children takes on especial interest. When the sets are not designated by numbers, they are not in fact number concepts but figure classes of the relational type. Practice with sets is often introduced as a kind of stimulus predifferentiation, however, to help the children discriminate the sets that numbers refer to. Suppes (1965) and others presented first-grade children with 2 sets, side by side, of simple designs (such as a star and a circle or 3 circles) and told them to push one button if the sets were "the same" and another button if they were "not the same." Wrong responses were corrected, according to the definition of the concept to be learned. Learning the identity of 2 ordered sets was very easy; when the elements were, for example, in the order AB and AB, about 95 percent of the responses in the first block of 8 trials were "the same." Sets that were not ordered were more difficult; when unordered sets contained the same elements, as represented by AB and BA, and "not the same" was reinforced, only about 70 percent of the responses on the first block of trials were correct. But both achievements came up to almost 100 percent in 56 trials. Perhaps concrete perception suffices for the former; some abstraction and manipulation are certainly necessary for the latter.

The concept of identity of sets, disregarding the order of the elements, was somewhat more difficult, but the most interesting outcome was that nonidentity was easier than identity. When the sets were such as AB and CD, detection of nonidentity began in the first block of trials, at about 90 percent; but when they were such as AB and BA and the identity response was reinforced, the identity response in the first block was less than 50 percent. Perhaps with these sets the nonidentity task requires less abstraction than the identity task, but in any case achievement on both tasks approached 100 percent in 56 trials.

Equipollent sets are the hardest to learn. These are, in Suppes's terminology, sets of the same number, such as ABC and BDE, regardless of the elements or their order. Nonequipollence, as between AB and CDA, was detected readily, but equipollence, without the help of identity of elements, came rather slowly. In general, set concepts differed markedly in their difficulty, depending on the definition of the set; furthermore, the amount of transfer from the learning of one set to the learning of another was surprisingly small. In fact, negative transfer was common, as in learning the identity of un-ordered sets after training on ordered sets. In general, the learning curves for such experiments fit all-or-none assumptions rather than incremental assumptions (Suppes, 1966).

There are only a few number concepts to be learned, but complex rules for grouping objects enter into mathematics as well as logic. In order to examine the strategies for achieving such rules, Dienes and Jeeves (1965) had schoolchildren and adults learn the systems of relations that mathematicians call two-groups and four-groups. These are genuine mathematical structures, but they have the advantage for experimental purposes that they are unfamiliar to most people, and adults as well as children have to start from the beginning. A two-group, for example, has two elements, such as cards A and B. The experimenter displays A or B in the window of an exposure device, then the subject plays A or B and guesses which will appear next in the window. The rules for the structure of one problem are: A followed by A yields A; $AB \rightarrow B$; $BA \rightarrow B$; $BB \rightarrow A$.

Observation of the subjects' moves and comments indicated that some tried to memorize all the combinations of events; others treated all the cards on the same level and tried to find patterns in them. The third strategy was to regard the card played as operating on the card in the window, as having the power to alter it. This was the most effective and was most often employed by the adults. Even though these mathematical structures seem rather difficult, presenting them in the complex-to-simple order, that is, from the four-group to the two-group, yielded more explicit statements of the rules than the simple-to-complex order. The latter order allows the subject to get started just by memorizing instances, but evidently delays the search for the underlying structure.

Learning names for sets of different numbers is more than a discrimination task and also more than a one-to-one naming task because the numbers are arranged in an order. Children learn to say their numbers in order by rote, as they learn to chant their ABCs: "One, two, buckle your shoe; three, four, shut the door. . . ." This is easy serial association. Enumeration or counting, which requires coordinating the verbal behavior with pointing or grouping, is more difficult; the abstract numerical properties of sets of objects become more definite through the activity of counting just as figure classes become more definite as words are applied to them. But whereas the achievement of small numbers takes place in so many contexts that it is difficult to study, counting can be studied in the laboratory.

Counting a limited number of objects requires the perceptual segregation of the counted set from the uncounted set, so Beckwith and Restle (1966) raised the question whether the principles of perceptual grouping that Gestalt psychologists have emphasized might have any function in this counting process. A line of 18 symbols printed on a page, for example, has continuity; hence if one counts from left to right, the set that has been counted is easily grouped and separated from the set to be counted. A circle has continuity but no ends; hence separation of the counted from the uncounted might be more difficult. Reading skills are involved, of course, but the counting task goes beyond mere reading.

Experiments with school children and college students disclosed that small printed figures were more easily counted when arranged in rectangles. The linear arrangement was also easy. A circle was quite difficult, and counting time was longest when the figures were scrambled. Similarities of color and shape were also important. The facility of counting the rectangular arrangements was related to the choice of numbers with fairly equal factors: 12, 15, 16, 18. The subjects, especially the college students, took short-cuts when possible, counting subgroups based on color, shape, or size of a rectangle, then multiplying.

The progression from the perceptual to the abstract is nowhere more impressive than in mathematical achievement. The first few natural numbers are learned concretely by preschool children, but achievement then moves from these small numbers to larger numbers that have less concrete significance and from number concepts to numerical operations. Children in school learn higher-order classes of numbers—such as even numbers, perfect squares, and prime numbers—but mostly they learn the relations between numbers and numerical operations like addition and long division. It is this abstractness of number classes and numerical operations that has led many teachers, from time to time, to introduce concrete construction materials to facilitate mastery, arranging them, or letting the child arrange them, in order to make the abstract properties more apparent (Bruner and Kenney, 1965). Such tricks are useful in the acquisition of figure and word classes also, but not as much as in the acquisition of numerical relations. The hardest task for schoolchildren is arithmetic problem solving, to which we shall return in later chapters.

Other Cognitive Structures

Viewed structurally, a class concept is rather simple: certain things are included, others excluded. A dimensional concept is also a simple structure. A taxonomy for classifying birds is a more complex cognitive structure, as is the structure of a university or a state government. But students do learn the more complex structures in one way or another, as is indicated by an improvement in the ability to assign an object to its proper place in the structure, to describe the structure, to communicate with others in terms of this structure, and to solve problems involving it.

The achievement of a complex structure of knowledge, in the arts and sciences, is a difficult task that requires study; it is much easier to arrange objects, especially people, in a simple linear order or hierarchy, or in simple groups, as suggested by Gestalt principles of organization. The argument for treating a simple structure as a "good figure" comes from the preference shown in ordering objects and from errors made in learning social structures of different degrees of complexity (Henley, Horsfall, and De Soto, 1969). The more difficult, complex social structures can be learned, of course, but, like disjunctive figure concepts, the learning goes slower.

Extrapolating from the research on figure classes, we can assume that achievement of classes of people will be influenced by salient features: the effects of skin color, hair styles, and clothes on the formation of stereotypes are obvious examples of this principle. We can assume too that the achievement of classes will be influenced by labeling, and the effect of labels for occupational groups on stereotyping illustrates this tendency. The weak influence of negative information as opposed to positive information also applies to stereotypes.

The self is a concept of special interest to each individual and to the psychology of personality. Each individual's concept of himself is a singular concept, as *I* and *me* are singular terms that refer to it, but the self is multidimensional. Each individual can assign himself to classes, such as nationality, sex, and religion, and can locate himself on many dimensions, such as height, age, economic status, aspiration level, and acceptance by others. Thus the concept of self defines the individual's position, as he conceives it, in various overlapping social structures.

In addition to the cognitive structures so far mentioned, which for the most part are explicitly defined and labeled, each individual's knowledge also includes cognitive structures that are implicit and unlabeled. Some of these may not be represented by words but rather by spatial images or diagrams. Such idiosyncratic structures are not very useful in communication, but some (e.g., implicit theories of personality) may be critical to the private life and thought of the individual.

Explanatory concepts and principles are cognitive structures with a specific role in problem solving; they will be given due consideration as such in a later chapter.

Major Trends and Implications

The concept ranks as one of man's most effective inventions, a multifunctional unit of abstract thought associated with a conventional concrete symbol that extends man's powers of classification, communication, and problem solving far beyond those of other animals. In accordance with its several functions, a concept may be acquired in several ways. The development, during the past few decades, of objective methods for empirical attack on the concept constituted, therefore, a victory for experimental psychology.

It was a minor victory, however, because the methods were adapted from the study of discrimination learning in nonliterate animals and were limited to the classification function. In justification of this restricted methodology the concept, as teachers, philosophers, and other scholars understood it, was redefined as a common response to diverse objects. Thus, the early experiments consisted merely of learning to make one response to positive instances of a class and another response to other objects.

The questions asked by educational, social, and developmental psychology about the class and dimensional concepts current in the culture were not answered by this limited approach; hence more varied approaches and more realistic definitions have recently appeared. Many observers have noted that children often learn the word first, then the class or dimension to which it refers. Children, and adults also, frequently acquire a concept from the context of a sentence, from an explanation, or from a dictionary definition. The diverse functions of a concept in intellectual activity suggest diverse ways of acquisition and diverse measures of achievement. Whatever unity a standard concept has for an individual, as measured by his performance on different tests of concept achievement, depends on the consistency of his experiences and ultimately on the consistency of usage within the culture. The concept is a part of the culture as well as an achievement of the individual, and concept achievement an intellectual aspect of the socialization of the individual.

A large share of recent concept research has focused on the learning of figure classes synthesized from familiar dimensions—more because of the convenience of the materials and the hope of generalizing the findings than because of the urgency of this particular problem. In spite of variations in details, some major trends are clear: unidimensional classes are easier to learn than multidimensional ones, and among the latter, conjunctive classes are easier than relational and disjunctive. Positive instances are more informative than negative for learning conjunctive classes, but negative instances are more informative for disjunctive classes. Learning is influenced by the number of irrelevant dimensions that are varied as well as the number of relevant dimensions, but it goes faster when the relevant dimension is salient. Although such effects can be stated one at a time, in complex situations interactions are common.

Stimulus-response associationism, accepting the common-response definition of a concept, can theoretically account for concept learning quite simply because the common feature of positive instances of a class is always associated with the response that is reinforced, while the irrelevant features are reinforced only randomly. The limitations of this theory in complex situations led to mediated associationism, with hypothetical verbal mediators between stimuli and responses. The reversal experiment was introduced to validate the mediation hypothesis, but interpretations have not been uniform. The results of certain kinds of verbal training support the hypothesis of verbal mediation, but these results could also come from learning to attend or from perceptual differentiation.

The principal alternative to the associationist view of concept learning sees the thinker in a more active, exploratory role, selecting promising cues and testing hypotheses. Whereas the associationist view predicts a continuous increase in frequency of correct responses, the hypothesis-testing view predicts an abrupt improvement when the correct attributes are identified. Supporting evidence of all-or-none learning has been reported in some simple situations; multidimensional concepts allow more opportunity for step-by-step acquisition.

When complex classes are to be acquired, it is fruitful to separate identification of the relevant attributes from identification of the rule of combination of the attributes. The initial difficulty in grasping complex classes and rules is reduced considerably by appropriate instructions and training. Suggestions for materials and for training procedures have come from symbolic logic, and concept learning of this type resembles logical reasoning more than discrimination learning.

The model builder is the romantic of psychology, dreaming of an elegant solution to the messy problems of psychological research. But no single model of concept achievement has consistently generated more substantial dreams, when exposed to the light of continuing empirical investigation, than the others. Determining the conditions under which associative learning and hypothesis testing occur and the contribution of each to the overall performance is a more sophisticated theoretical enterprise than arguing for one against the other. The evidence already available suggests that when the subject does not know what he is doing, associative learning is a good first approximation. When he is well informed about the task and the materials to be conceptualized or when he has had appropriate pretraining, the hypothesis-testing model accounts better for the observed activities. But even when testing hypotheses the subject does not select cues at random except under rather restricted conditions; variations in the salience of cues and in the associative strength between the correct cue and others have to be included in the model. In this theoretical context, pluralism is realism.

Experiments on the learning of word classes are especially informative because the effects of word associations can be examined. Several of the variables that influence the learning of figure classes also influence the learning of word classes in about the same way. In addition there is convincing evidence that certain strong prior associations help and others impede the formation of word classes; under some conditions these effects can be predicted in advance. Knowledge of the structure of word associations is clarifying some aspects of cognitive organization just as cognitive organization, in exchange, is clarifying some aspects of verbal learning.

Abstract concepts are acquired through relationships with previously learned concepts. It is now necessary for concept research and psycholinguistics to pool their techniques in order to describe how a reader, or listener, acquires the meaning of a word from many sentence contexts. College students, especially, are accustomed to studying concepts communicated by a variety of methods in books and lectures, and they can transfer their achievements to other situations quite flexibly.

Research on elementary number concepts is not vulnerable to some of the criticisms that have been directed toward research on figure concepts. There is no uncertainty about definition, because when a child discriminates and matches groups of objects according to an abstract numerical property, such as *threeness,* in spite of differences in other properties, and uses the conventional numerical symbol to refer to groups that have this numerical property, he is demonstrating achievement of the concept by any reasonable definition. And there is no argument about the applicability of the results because the concepts of *three, four, five,* and so on are not concepts synthesized to simulate something else; they *are* the standard concepts that children learn. In spite of their abstractness, they are acquired incidentally in ordinary domestic conversation, like the other basic concepts, probably because there are so few of them to learn. All intellectual development is cumulative, of course; but this generalization is most obvious for mathematical achievement, because elementary number concepts are prerequisite for arithmetic manipulations and arithmetic manipulations in turn are prerequisite for the abstractions of higher mathematics.

Man's perceptual operations are adapted for perceiving objects in the environment, rather than events in the sense organs that mediate the perception of objects. Analogously, man's intellectual operations are directed toward the concepts that have become significant to him, rather than the particulars through which they were acquired. The psychologist is interested in the particulars of the acquisition processes; the thinker forgets the particulars but retains the concepts as instruments for communication and problem solving in the future.

CHAPTER 3

COGNITION AND CONCEPTS CONTINUED

Individual Differences
Cognitive Development
Language and Thought
Major Trends and Implications

 f psychology were only a search for general laws, the experimental evidence assembled in the preceding chapter would serve as an introduction to our topic. But there is evidence in all experiments of individual variations in performance. These may be quantitative variations in the parameters of the general laws: some subjects learn concepts faster than others; some attain a higher terminal level of achievement than others. Experimental psychologists would be happy if all these individual differences could be explained as differences in parameters of general laws, but this is an oversimplified hope. The present chapter must consider individual differences along lines that have not entered into concept experiments, as well as those that have. The largest individual differences depend on age, of course; hence we shall compare children of various ages and try to trace the course of cognitive development. Since this is intertwined with language development, the last section will be devoted to questions about language and thought.

Individual Differences

The most interesting differences between people are those that remain stable over a period of time; and although most concept experiments are not directed toward this, evidence of stability is occasionally reported. Some consistency in concept attainment strategies from problem to problem has been found (Eifermann, 1965). There is also some consistency across problem materials, for those who worked a figure concept problem conceptually, rather than nonconceptually, did the same on a verbal concept problem (Segel and Johnson, 1969). But many of the interesting variations between subjects' activities that show up in a concept experiment are transitory, specific to the situation, and unlikely to show up again.

VARIATIONS IN RESPONSE TO OBJECT PROPERTIES

People do not approach a concept problem without bias. A property of the stimulus objects that impresses one person as an obvious basis for conceptualization may not impress another person at all. In the case of children, responses to object properties shift markedly with age.

PREFERENCES FOR DIMENSIONS

When young children are allowed to sort multidimensional objects into a few groups or categories in their own way and when they choose alternative attributes to match a model, they usually exhibit a preference for matching by color. After age five or so they prefer to match by form. One comparison of form and color, for example, found a slight preference for form (45 form choices out of 72) at age five, increasing to a strong preference (69 out of 72) at age nine (Harris, Schaller, and Mitler, 1970). The salience of the dimensions can be experimentally manipulated, of course: increasing brightness differences increases the frequency of matching by color rather than form (Corah and Gross, 1967).

The next question is whether these preferences influence performance on a concept attainment task. To answer this, the subjects must first indicate their preferences by sorting in their own way, and then learn to sort according to the dimension specified by the experimenter. When college students learned to categorize pairs of dots, their initial preferences for dimensions had no effect (Imai and Garner, 1965); but the dimensions in this experiment were the position and orientation of the dots, dimensions that do not seem to be as compelling as form and color are to children. The performance of children in nursery school and kindergarten on a simple concept task was facilitated when the critical dimension corresponded to their preferences for form or color (Suchman and Trabasso, 1966).

There are methodological difficulties with this type of experiment, however. A later experiment gave a preference test to children in kindergarten, first, and third grades, followed by the Wisconsin Card Sorting Test, which includes color, form, and number, as the concept task (Mitler and Harris, 1969). The expected results were obtained, most subjects preferring the form dimension and then learning the form concept rapidly. But when other children were given the two tasks in the reverse order, quite different results were obtained. We see again that children are impressionable, like adults: both their dimension preferences and their concept achievement were influenced by the immediately preceding activity. So the question of preferences and concept achievement has not yet been completely answered.

If we turn now to verbal materials and ask how children classify words when they are free to choose their own categories, the most interesting result is an increase in the use of classes based on grammatical attributes. In one developmental study, for example, adjectives were grouped with other adjectives 20 percent of the time in the second grade, 30 percent in the fourth grade, and 41 percent in the eighth grade (Mandler and Stephens, 1967).

REPRESENTATION OF OBJECTS

The use of more lifelike objects in concept experiments brings up the question of mode of representation. When line drawings representing trees and other familiar objects, varying in form and color, were presented to children for matching to a sample, 95 out of 120 preferred to match on the basis of meaningful representation (Bearison and Sigel, 1968). At this age, from seven to eleven, meaning dominated form and color. In fact, earlier research (Sigel, 1953) had indicated that middle-class boys of this age would categorize by meaning whether they were categorizing objects, pictures, or words. This is not the case for all children, however. Lower-class children of five and six categorized actual three-dimensional objects (such as a cup, a pencil, and a pipe) just as the middle-class children did, but they had more difficulty in categorizing photographs of these objects—even though the photographs were realistic, lifesize, and in color (Sigel, 1968). Research of this kind is beginning to specify the environmental conditions that produce conceptual deficiencies in disadvantaged children.

(A later section will take up the question of how the child acquires meaningful cognitive structures and symbols for representing the objects and events of his environment, since this pursuit of meaning is one of the main themes of the story of cognitive development.)

CATEGORICAL STYLES

When children and adults sort meaningful objects in their own way, by free classification, variations in preferences for different types of categories can be distinguished. Kagan, Moss, and Sigel (1963) were able to describe three such categorical styles as they appeared in adults' groupings of pictures of people. The analytic style tends to abstract an element of objective similarity shared by two or more figures, for example, "People with no shoes on." The inferential style involves an inference about the patterns grouped together, for example, "People who help others." And the relational style prefers to group objects on the basis of a functional relation between them, such as "A married couple." Similar studies of children showed a fair individual consistency of cognitive style over one-year intervals, although the preference for the analytic approach did increase somewhat.

Whether these are the best names for such sorting tendencies may be argued, but cognitive styles do make a difference in concept achievement

(Lee, Kagan, and Rabson, 1963). Third-grade boys characterized by the analytic approach learned analytic concepts more readily than others, and the nonanalytic boys learned relational concepts more readily. Since the category style tests and concept learning tests were given several weeks apart, the criticism noted above (that the first test may influence performance on the second) probably does not apply.

COGNITIVE ABILITIES

It has long been known that the achievement of concepts is related to age and intelligence, but to clarify these relationships requires the standardization of materials and methods. Osler and Fivel (1961) had 180 children, half in the average range of intelligence and half in the superior range, learn to choose one of a pair of pictures to match another of the same class (e.g., birds) in order to get a marble. Fig. 3.1 displays an increase with age and a consistent difference due to intelligence. By age fourteen, all the subjects of high intelligence were able to reach the criterion of ten consecutive correct choices.

Dividing the children, according to the records of their responses, into sudden and gradual learners indicated that the sudden learners were mostly in the groups of superior intelligence. Presumably the superior children understood the nature of the task and thus used a hypothesis-testing approach which caused discontinuous progress, while the other children learned by a gradual strengthening of associations. However, a similar study with children of eight and nine classifying dot figures found discontinuous acquisition for those below average IQ as well as those above (Hamilton and Saltz, 1969). These are simple classes for which discontinuous acquisition would be expected according to the general trend of the results outlined in the preceding chapter.

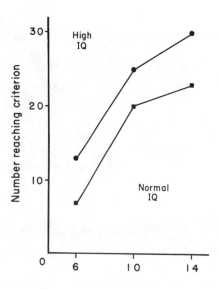

FIGURE 3.1. Concept learning in relation to age and intelligence. Six groups of 30 children each. Data from Osler and Fivel (1961).

Recalling the importance of the instructional set in earlier work with adult subjects, Osler and Weiss (1962) carried out another study, like that of Osler and Fivel, but this time they gave half the children the explicit instructions that "There is an idea that will tell you which picture will give you the marble [p. 530]." These special instructions were generally helpful, but most helpful to the subjects who needed them most, the average children aged six and ten.

Undoubtedly, general intelligence is correlated in a general way with abstract intellectual accomplishments of the past and present. To obtain more detailed information about the abilities required for success in concept acquisition under controlled conditions, tests of narrower abilities have been constructed. Tests of general reasoning ability are often put together from arithmetic reasoning problems and deductive reasoning problems, such as evaluating the validity of a syllogism. Tests of induction, or inductive reasoning, may present such items as oak, maple, pine, and birch: the subject is instructed to find out what three of these words have in common and then underline the odd one. Hence these are often called *oddity problems*. Or pictures of the four objects may be presented with the same instructions. Thus an ability test and a concept experiment might call for corresponding conceptual processes, but there are differences in the methodology that limit the correspondence.

The purpose of the test is to get useful scores representing individual differences in ability during a short testing period. The methodology of test construction sets up certain psychometric standards, such as reliability, and the items are selected and revised to meet these standards. The concept experiment, on the other hand, usually tests a hypothesis about improvement in performance involving a comparison between groups of subjects, and the materials and procedures are selected to fit this purpose. If the two assignments evoke the same intellectual process from the subjects, this process may easily be obscured by the methodological variations. The fact that similar names are given to ability tests and to experiments does not guarantee similarity of the psychological processes.

The pattern of abilities that determines which people get high scores and which get low scores on a variety of different tests is often described by a statistical procedure known as *factor analysis*. Individual differences in performance on 15 tests are probably not due to 15 different abilities; the goal of factor analysis is a simpler description of the abilities involved. After a large number of subjects have taken the tests, all the scores are correlated: if the correlation coefficients are all high, it is reasonable to assume that there is a common factor, such as general intelligence, underlying performance on all tests. But often the pattern is more complicated. A group of tests, A, B, and C, may be highly correlated, another group, D, E, and F, highly correlated, and a third group G, H, and I, also highly correlated; yet the correlations between groups are low. Inspection might reveal that one group is composed of tests of verbal content, another of numerical content, and another of geometrical figures, hence three group factors are identified. By such procedures—partly statistical and partly inferential—factor analyses of scores on batteries of diverse tests have attempted to identify the principal factors responsible for individual differences in performance. The same procedures have also been used in analyzing the abilities to be discussed in later chapters.

In a serious attempt to analyze conceptual abilities in detail, Dunham, Guilford, and Hoepfner (1969) persuaded 177 juniors and seniors in high school to spend three days taking a battery of tests and working a variety of concept problems. Factor analysis of the scores disclosed 11 abilities, some described by content (such as figures, letters, and words) and some described by operations (such as cognition, memory, divergent production, and convergent production).[1] The concept learning scores were correlated with the ability factors at several stages of learning, but these correlations were low; scores for success in verbalization of the concepts also had low correlations with the ability factors. Tasks requiring classes of figures and of letters can be transformed, at least by some subjects, into verbal tasks, so that success is correlated with verbal abilities at some times but not at others. Some agreement comes from another factor analysis of similar performance data (Lemke, Klausmeier, and Harris, 1967), which found factors of general reasoning, induction, and verbal comprehension in concept learning.

Since instructions about concepts influence performance, they might also influence the pattern of abilities required. Dunham and Bunderson (1969) therefore gave a battery of standard ability tests and concept learning tasks to high-school students with and without instructions in decision rules for discovering the concepts. The well-known induction factor contributed to concept achievement under both conditions, as one might expect. But when rule instructions were given, the general reasoning factor also contributed, and when rule instructions were not given, associative memory was involved. Such findings are consistent with the contributions of associative learning and reasoning to performance in the concept experiments of the preceding chapter.

The general drift of these results is that if anyone wishes to predict which students will achieve concepts most readily, a test of general intelligence gives a good indication. If more precise prediction is desired, tests of inductive thinking, general reasoning, and verbal comprehension are worth trying. But in order to adapt teaching procedures to individual differences by varying the instructions and materials, similar data from the specific situation in which the procedures are to be employed will be needed.

Cognitive Development

The story of intellectual growth is an intricate one, with major and minor characters, plots and subplots, which we shall start to take up now and will resume again later. This chapter will provide a synopsis and will emphasize the role of the concept, certainly a major one.

[1] In this terminology, inductive reasoning is included under cognition and deductive reasoning under convergent production.

As children grow, their intellectual performance expands in all directions. Older children have more experience, more interest in intellectual things, more understanding of what is expected of them, better memory, and better control of their attention. Higher scores on intelligence tests are an index of the general quantitative improvement. This development is influenced by biological maturation, similar in all cultures; but beyond this, development proceeds in the direction of the particular adult culture in which the children mature. With a few exceptions, development is cumulative: elementary schoolchildren build on their preschool concepts as high-school students build higher on their elementary-school achievements.

Some of our knowledge of cognitive development comes from research that makes these generalizations more precise, by comparing the achievements of children of different ages and plotting curves of their progress. The more exciting and more difficult research attempts to uncover the nature and causes of such development, the qualitative changes as well as the quantitative. All theories of development predict that older children do better than young children, hence graphs and tables that show age changes do not support any one theory. More specific descriptions of achievement and more specific hypotheses of their origins are necessary.

Methods for studying cognitive development could begin with the methods of concept learning research, as described in the preceding chapter. A few illustrations were given there to show how experimental psychologists have modified their experiments to make them suitable for children. By combining experimental and developmental methods, Kendler and Kendler (1962), as we noted in the preceding chapter, have described a transition during the early school years from single-unit association to mediated association in concept learning. More recently, after analyzing the data of a concept shift study including college students, they have suggested that with increasing age an increasing proportion of their subjects were operating in the hypothesis-testing mode (Kendler and Kendler, 1970). Experimental child psychology is a growing trend, but for the most part research styles have not been copied from experimental psychology. Observations and tests of children aimed at attaining measures of status at different ages have been more common than experimental manipulations of independent variables. Susan Isaacs (1930), for example, carefully observed young children's intellectual activities, especially their Why questions, in natural settings and then interpreted her data to show the interplay of cumulative experience and maturation.

Child psychologists often use classifying or sorting tests, not only to measure progress in learning, but to make qualitative inferences about the child's conceptual activities. A common procedure is to spread out before a child a number of blocks or other objects, with instructions to "put the ones together that belong together." The Vygotsky Test, which has been described in English by Hanfmann and Kasanin (1937) and can be found in many clinics, represents another procedure. In this test, 22 blocks of various sizes, shapes, and colors are displayed to the subject on a table. The examiner states that there are four kinds of blocks, the names being concealed on the bottom.

He turns one block over, showing the subject its name. The subject is instructed to find other blocks like this one, put them at one corner of the table, and put the other three kinds at the other three corners. The subject may begin to group the blocks on the basis of color, but then sees that there are five colors. He may begin with shape, but there are more than four shapes. The examiner can correct the subject, if his grouping is wrong, by turning over two or more blocks in a group and showing that they have different names. Overall scores may be obtained from the time required and the number of corrections given, but Vygotsky (1962) and his collaborators in Russia studied the test performance qualitatively in order to make inferences about conceptual and linguistic processes in children and adolescents.

Many observers have reported that on such sorting tasks young children group objects in collections—Vygotsky called them *complexes*—rather than classes and by concrete perceptual similarities rather than by abstract properties. The concrete syncretic language of the child has also been contrasted with the more flexible symbolic language of the adult. We have noted how children differ at different ages in their initial responses to perceived objects. Thus, while some psychologists have been following the quantitative route toward reliable measures of intelligence and smooth curves of intellectual progress, others have been following the qualitative route toward describing cognitive structures and processes at different stages of intellectual development. Much of the early qualitative work was summarized and published in English some years ago by Heinz Werner (1940).

In recent years the study of cognitive development has been dominated by the influence of Jean Piaget, of the University of Geneva. His work and the reactions to it have brought new life to research on cognitive development and a whiff of fresh air into the concept learning laboratory.

PIAGET'S STAGES AND STRUCTURES

Piaget's grand design is to chart the growth of the child from a sensorimotor animal, beginning life with some reflexes and some sensory capacities, to the abstract thinker of fourteen or so, who uses arbitrary symbols to refer to abstract classes, carries on formal logical operations, and detaches himself, so to speak, from his sensorimotor limitations to spend his life with the cognitive structures of the adult culture. Returning to the meanings of *thought* given in our introductory chapter, it is not the introspective analysis of thought as mental experience that interests Piaget, nor the objective description of problem-solving behavior, but the cognitive schemas, the structures of knowledge, which guide the observable behavior.

In the first year or two the child, according to the Geneva school, has only sensorimotor schemas—one could hardly say knowledge—of things. He knows a plaything only in terms of what he does with it, how it feels when he grasps it, how he transfers it from one hand to another, how it looks and tastes, how it drops when he lets go. Adults are likely to separate perception from action, but the child's schemas are not differentiated at this stage. One of the first actions is looking.

The assumption of coordination between sensory and motor systems in perception of the environment is not peculiar to Piaget, of course. It is the standard doctrine, although the language differs, among modern students of perception. In a discussion of "active touch," for example, Gibson (1962) has described in subtle detail how motor and sensory systems cooperate to collect information about objects in the environment.

But around age two the child develops relatively permanent schemas for objects, so that he can identify a toy whether he sees the front or the side of it, whether he is biting it or throwing it, and even after it has rolled out of sight. His actions and thoughts are controlled by the schema even though he is no longer actively handling or looking at the object. Freed from dependence on his actions and the feedback from his actions, his knowledge of the object moves from the motoric and the perceptual toward the cognitive. The child may acquire a name for the object and thus we might say, in the language of an earlier chapter, that he has acquired a singular concept. But Piaget calls this stage preconceptual because the child does not use concepts flexibly, as he will later. He has grasped the permanance of objects; he perceives relations and can choose the larger of two pieces of candy. But these accomplishments are still more perceptual than conceptual.

From age two on, his intellectual operations become more elaborate, and around age seven flexible, reversible, cognitive structures and operations can be assumed. A *reversible structure,* to the Geneva school, is one that permits the elements to change in form while overall equivalence is preserved. Like a class concept, it permits the child to grasp the abstract similarities in spite of superficial perceptual differences. In general terms, it means knowing that if AB, then BA. If $A + B = C$, it is possible in thought to reverse the act of addition to get $C - B = A$.

The celebrated demonstration of "conservation" involves the reversibility of a physical change. A lump of Plasticine or modeling clay is shown to a child, then it is squeezed flat, and the child is asked if it contains the same amount of material as before. At age five or six the child will probably say No. Influenced by one dimension or the other, the *preoperational* child will say it has more or less than before. But if it is molded back into its original shape, so that the child can *perceive* the equivalence, he will agree that it is the same as when first seen. A parallel test for conservation of liquid begins with a glass of water, which is poured into a tall, thin glass, and into a short, wide glass, each time with questions about amount. After age seven or so, the child has a cognitive structure that enables his thought processes to follow the physical processes and conserve the integrity of the material in spite of changes in form. He has a schema, albeit rather concrete, of conservation of matter that overrides the perceptual instabilities. When he sees the clay flattened, he can reverse this change in thought and thus answer questions about amount correctly.

After seven, the child performs many indirect thoughtful operations, according to this account, at least on objects that he perceives concretely. The *concrete-operational* child can put things into classes and combine classes. He can reverse some of the simpler relations, like *taller than* and *father of*. He knows that if A is the father of B, then B is the child of A. The five-year-old knows his right hand and his left hand, but not until seven or eight will he be able to point to another child's right and left hands. One way of putting this is that at this time, the latter part of the stage of concrete operations, he can do most of what adults do with complex problems of combination and physical space, but only with particular materials.

Around age twelve the third major intellectual development begins, the development of formal abstract thought. Given a rich cultural environment, a child attains mastery of many logical operations within a few years and thus completes the liberation of his thought processes from their dependence on concrete particulars.

The Geneva school does not insist on the ages at which these stages occur, but the sequence of stages is central to the theory. The child does not reach the stage of formal logical operations unless he first goes through that of concrete operations. Piaget was first a biologist, and the concept of maturation is prominent in his speculations. But this is not tissue growth or maturation in the neurophysiological sense; it is the cumulative, orderly assimilation of the normal experiences of life, which organizes schemas that liberate the mind from control by any specific experience.

The role of experience in intellectual development is not that of rewarded practice, at least not in the conventional sense of learning due to external reinforcement. Rather, the child acquires a new cognitive structure when he perceives some conflict in his experiences and forms a new equilibrium from them. It is when a child experiences the discrepancies in his perception of the lump of clay at different times that he tries to devise an atemporal cognitive structure to resolve his cognitive conflict. The learning is cognitive and the reinforcement is cognitive, though of course the Geneva school does not use such language. But when stated thus this hypothesis should not sound radical to students of psychology. In his well-known discussion of the reinforcement of perception, Woodworth (1947) invoked somewhat similar reasoning, and American social psychologists write often of cognitive conflict and balance in the modification of attitudes. But the Geneva theory of the modification of a cognitive structure is rather sketchy—and so are American reinforcement theories when applied to these subtle intellectual achievements.

FIGURE CLASSES AND DIMENSIONS
The most pertinent work of the Geneva school on concepts is that of Inhelder and Piaget (1964) on classification and seriation, which describes how children classify objects and how they arrange them in ordered series. The acquisition of general terms to refer to classes in communication (discussed in an earlier chapter as one measure of concept achievement) is not an explicit part of the Genevan program. Inhelder and Piaget are concerned rather with children's classification of perceived objects and their replies to questions about the classification; and they are willing to assume that the child's communicative skill is adequate to the task—if the examiner is experienced and astute.

Piaget establishes rather strict logical criteria for a class because of his interest in genetic epistemology. The class is characterized by extension: the set of instances that belong to the class. It is also characterized by intension: the properties of the members of the class. A child may be able to discriminate dogs as instances of one class from cats as instances of another without being able to describe the properties of either. He may be able to talk about dogs in the conventional way, but he does not really have the class *dog* until he has the superordinate class *animal* and knows about other animals that are not dogs, as well as the similarities and differences between these classes. In general terms, Piaget says that the child does not use classes correctly in cognitive operations until extension and intension are coordinated, so that the objects included in the class are consistent with the general and specific properties of the intensional definition.

It is somewhat different for an ordered series. While the child cannot perceive classes per se, he can perceive some relations: similarities; symmetries; and inequalities, such as *larger* and *farther*. But an ordered series is more than perception; it implies transitivity and other transformations within the series, based, not on the perceived objects themselves, but on the abstract dimension common to all of them. A child may perceive that A is larger than B and B is is larger than C, but he does not make the logical inference that A is larger than C until he has achieved the transitivity schema. This is the reason, according to Piaget, why even though a child can perceive directly which block is longer than another, the ability to place three or four blocks in order of length develops quite slowly.

Before classes are attained, certain preconceptual attainments are necessary. Maturation is not enough; language plays an important role but is not sufficient by itself. The chief supports are the sensorimotor schemas, built up by perception and action. When an object is presented to a child, he identifies it as if by comparing its visual, tactual, and instrumental properties with whatever schemas he has developed. These diverse properties will later become the intension of the class. (Thus Osgood's fractional-response construct, page 66, and Piaget's schema are similar in that both make the cognition of an object depend, at least in part, on response to the object.) To the Geneva school the schema constitutes a basic component of the class, not because it comes directly from perception but because it adds to perception the feedback from active manipulation.

The child's arrangements of the objects displayed and his answers to questions are interpreted by Inhelder and Piaget in relation to these idealized cognitive structures, which mark the stages of progress toward adult logic. The method of free or unconstrained classification is used, with instructions to put together the ones that are alike—though these instructions are sometimes varied in order to bring out critical differentiations between stages. The objects to be classified may be beads, geometric forms, pictures of plants, and the like, varying in color, size, shape, and other familiar attributes.

Children of three four, and five, lacking true classes that are independent of the location of the elements, often place the objects where they form spatial patterns or little aggregates of similar objects that seem to satisfy them.

One child, for example, put the objects in a straight line, each object having some attribute in common with the next, though the common attributes shifted along the line. This is what Vygotsky (1962) called a chain complex. The child at this stage seems to change his intensional definition and his basis of grouping as he looks from one part of the collection to another.

At later ages, five to eight, spatial juxtaposition is less common as a basis for grouping. Heterogeneous residues, which at younger ages are often left over from inadequate partial collections with shifting criteria of similarity, are no longer seen. Then comes an important step, building on what has gone before, when all the objects are arranged by a single criterion of classification—all the squares in one pile, all the circles in another, and so on. Inhelder and Piaget insist, however, that the development of classes is not complete until these are differentiated into subdivisions so that the child can operate by inclusion and exclusion to obtain a hierarchical classification. A class does not exist in isolation.

One study by Inhelder and Piaget on the addition of classes will illustrate their methods of observation and the inferences made from them. The materials consisted of 20 cards, 4 of which represented colored objects, the other 16 representing flowers. Eight of the flowers were primroses, 4 yellow and the other 4 other colors. The child was expected to answer such questions as: "If you make a bouquet of all the yellow primroses, will it be larger or smaller than a bouquet of all the primroses?" "If you cut all the flowers, will there be any primroses left?" By age ten such questions are most often answered correctly. For example, when the question was, "Are there more primroses or more yellow primroses in the bouquet?" the proportion of correct replies increased from 30 percent for children of five and six to 96 percent for children nine and ten. Above age eight questions such as, "If one cuts all the flowers, will any primroses remain?" are usually answered correctly: "Anyone who takes all the flowers takes all the primroses too." Thus extension is at last adjusted to intension.

We must remember that Piaget and his colleagues are not directly concerned with the use of concepts in interpersonal communication. They are more concerned with the use of concepts in the child's own reasoning. If a class A, that might be primroses, is contained in the superordinate class B, that might be flowers, logical reasoning calls attention to the complementary class A′ consisting of the Bs that are not As, in this case the flowers that are not primroses. In order to get credit for conceptual thinking from the Geneva school, the child must know, in a formal abstract way, that the class B includes the class A and also all the A′, and thus that the number of elements in the class B is necessarily larger than the number in the class A, regardless of the number of each in view. The addition of classes can be expressed formally as: $B = A + A'$. A child might, at one stage in his growth, be able to use the terms *primrose* and *flower* in ordinary conversation but be unable to perform these logical operations or answer questions about the elements in each class.

NUMBER CONCEPTS

Number classes, like others, are based on a common abstract property. All classes of two things, designated by the term *two,* have the property of *twoness* in common. But, while classes of flowers are arranged in a hierarchical system or taxonomy, classes of numbers are arranged in a series, characterized by even more abstract properties, such as asymmetry and transitivity, which permit very abstract and very efficient operations. The small number classes and their names, such as *one, two,* and *three,* are acquired by young children in ordinary domestic communication in connection with pointing, picking up, and asking for more, but they remain tied to the perception of concrete materials. The larger numbers are acquired later, in connection with counting and other serializing operations.

One of Piaget's methods (Flavell, 1963) for studying the development from perception of numerical correspondence to more abstract operations was to give the child a row of beads and ask him to take the same number from a pile of beads nearby. The method was similar to the number matching method that Long and Welch employed in 1941 (see page 83) but whereas they stressed standardized testing and quantitative treatment, Piaget stressed qualitative observations. Piaget reported that the young child is likely to make a row of about the same length as the model, with more beads or fewer, thus demonstrating perceptual rather than abstract control. Later the child is likely to make use of a one-to-one correspondence, placing one bead opposite the first one of the model, another bead opposite the next, and so on. But if the examiner destroys the correspondence by spreading the beads of the model farther apart, the child at this stage may have to add more beads to make the two lengths look the same. Only later will the numerical properties be preserved in spite of perceptual dislocations. As Flavell put it, "Once more a concept must fight its way into stable operational existence through a cobweb of illusion-producing perceptions [p. 313]."

The next step is to look at the correspondence between series of dissimilar objects. In one of Piaget's studies, the child was shown ten dolls of differing heights and ten miniature walking sticks of differing heights and told to arrange the sets so that each doll could easily find the stick that belongs to it. This seriation problem was impossible for the youngest children because it depends on such abstract properties of the series as reversibility. It requires, for example, the cognition that the second doll in the series can be taller than the first and *at the same time* shorter than the third. The older child who could seriate one set could seriate the other, however, and establish the correspondence between them—although some children lost the correspondence when the perceptual alignment was disturbed by the examiner. The Beckwith and Restle experiments (page 86) remind us that even college students make use of perceptual patterns when possible to speed up counting.

CONCEPTS AND COGNITIVE STRUCTURES

Students who approach cognitive development via the experimental psychology of concept attainment often have difficulty in understanding just what Piaget's structures are. Are they the same as the concepts of the preceding chapter?

The concepts of experimental psychology and the cognitive structures of the Geneva school are both ability constructs. People who have acquired them can do things that others cannot do. Both are general achievements, not specific responses to specific stimuli. And both are abstractions, inferred from what people do and say. But a structure may be more or less than a concept. To Piaget, classes and dimensions are just two kinds of structures. Larger cognitive structures include systems of classes, even in the minimal case of flowers, primroses, and flowers that are not primroses. The structures underlying the achievements of conservation and transitivity are more than simple classes and might be called principles or explanatory concepts. In fact, Piaget's questions, aimed at description of the structure, often ask for explanations of superficially puzzling events.

If we define a concept to include the symbol that refers to the objects or relations between them, the concept may be more than the structure because, to Piaget, the structure is used by the child in his own thinking and does not necessarily have a label for use in communication. Verbal methods as well as behavior methods are necessary for examining the child's thought structures, but a structure may be operational even though it is not verbalized. That is why, we are told, the examiner must be informed and skillful.

RESPONSES TO PIAGET

While research continues at Geneva, Genevan ideas have traveled far. Reactions, as to all new ideas, have varied (Isaacs, 1930; Kessen and Kuhlman, 1962; Lovell, 1966). Regardless of the evidence, many psychologists have an a priori distaste for the cognitive structures, the flexible methods, and the speculative style of the Geneva school. Piaget's insulation from the predominant trends in English-language psychology gave him the freedom to elaborate an original set of ideas and gave others the freedom to ignore them, as he ignored the ideas of others. To many psychologists, however, the impact of Piaget was to make the child's intellectual development as exciting as his social and sexual development. If the many evaluative essays on Piaget's influence agree on anything, it is that child psychology will not be the same again.

The most fundamental criticism of Piaget and the Geneva school is directed against their methods for inferring the existence of a cognitive structure. The demonstrations that they report assume that these structures can be directly diagnosed through the child's behavior and answers to questions by a sensitive examiner familiar with the responses of younger and older children. Others, such as Braine (1962), argue that the cognitive structure is a theoretical construct that can be validated only by specifying how it is tied to the test situation—including test materials and instructions—and to the resulting verbal and motor behavior. When other investigators get similar results with similar methods, the empirical findings are confirmed, but the possibility of an alternative interpretation is not eliminated. An inadequate reply to a question about classification of figures may be due to a lack of verbal skill or the inability to attend to the critical dimension, as well as a lack of a certain logical structure. Smedslund (1969) has listed specific examples to illustrate how an apparently inadequate response may be due to failure to understand the instructions or the information given or simply to forgetting them, rather than to lack of cognitive structure. Gelman (1970) has devised a very sensitive number test for children of 3 and 4 which gives positive results for conservation of the numbers 2 and 3 in spite of spatial rearrangements, even though other children of the same age could not pass the conventional test of conservation of these numbers. In the same way an apparently adequate response may be due to guessing, direct perception, or accidental success rather than to achievement of the structure.

Piaget, like Freud, will not be proved right or wrong. There seems to be little dispute about the major theme of development, that it proceeds from the concrete perceptual to the abstract, but questions have been asked about many of the minor variations on this theme. Some are too vague to test, but others have inspired interesting research that can be illustrated by a few examples.

DEVELOPMENTAL STAGES

One obvious question raised by the apparently casual Geneva methods is an empirical one: Will other examiners working with other children get the same results? In general, the answer is a qualified Yes. Somewhat similar stages were described in the 1930s by Vygotsky (1962) in a book on the thought and language of Russian children that has only recently become available in English, and also by Werner (1940) working with German children. The work of Smedslund (1961a) on conservation of weight and substance illustrates well-controlled, quantitative research of this type. He found that two judges agreed very well, 95 to 97 percent, in coding the children's explanations and that Oslo children were roughly similar in kinds of explanations to Geneva children. He found less consistency between tests and a somewhat different sequence of development than that reported by Piaget, however.

Another illustration of sophisticated research giving general support to Piaget is Wohlwill's (1960) application of scalogram analysis to the development of number concepts. Using a different language, Wohlwill began with the premise that "the development of a concept has its origin in an essentially discriminative function of abstraction, proceeding thence by a process of gradual elaboration of mediating structures to an eventual state in which the concept exists as a purely representational symbolic entity [p. 345]." Although scalogram techniques have been used primarily in the field of attitude measurement, they can be applied to a set of tasks presumed to develop in sequence. An analysis of the patterns of success and failure by children of different ages should then reveal whether these tasks constitute a scalable set. If they do, it may be concluded that mastery of a given task presupposes the mastery of all tasks below it in the hierarchy of difficulty, which is equivalent to the assertion of a sequential order of development of the functions tapped by these tests.

Wohlwill employed a carefully planned matching-from-sample method: choice cards containing two, three, and four dots were hung in view in the apparatus, then a sample card containing perhaps three figures was placed in front of the child to match to one of the choice cards, a chip being the reward. Some preliminary practice assured understanding of the task. The tasks were selected to test the child's ability to transfer the response to problems in which the correspondence between sample and choice cards requires symbolic mediation in a variety of forms. The tasks, in theoretical order of difficulty, follow.

A. *Abstraction*. In this task, presumed to be the easiest, the sample cards differed from the choice cards not only in number but also in form and color. Thus the child had to abstract the dimension of number from among other, irrelevant dimensions.

B. *Elimination of perceptual cues*. The sample cards for this test contained rectangles drawn in outline and divided into two, three, or four equal, adjacent squares, separated by thin lines. It was assumed that perceptual cues were thus eliminated and correct response would depend on the intervention of a symbolic process, such as counting.

C. *Memory*. The sample cards were those of the training series, but the choice cards were removed so the child had to make his choice by the position of the choice cards as he remembered them.

D. *Extension*. This test exposed choice cards of six, seven, and eight dots, and corresponding sample cards were in view. Since numbers of dots higher than five are not immediately discriminated, it was assumed that mediation of some symbolic activity would be necessary.

E. *Conservation of number*. The choice cards contained six, seven, and eight dots, but small buttons were used in place of sample cards. The buttons were first arranged in a configuration which matched that of the correct choice card; then the buttons were scrambled and the child had to match to the correct choice card without counting. This test differs from the previous ones in demanding a concept, not of a specific number, but of number in general, and more particularly of a functional property of this concept: its independence of configurational aspects of the stimulus aggregate. As noted above, Piaget postulates that the conservation of number, independent of perceptual variations, is a central step in conceptualization.

F. *Addition and subtraction*. This test was like E above except that one button was either added to the collection in view of the child or subtracted from it. Here the test seems to assume conservation of number and to go one step beyond it.

G. *Ordinal-cardinal correspondence*. The choice cards held two, three, and four dots; the sample cards showed eight solid bars, one of which was red, arranged in order of increasing length; and the ordinal position of the

TABLE 3.1. NUMBER OF CHILDREN (OUT OF 72)
PASSING EACH OF SEVEN NUMBER TESTS

B.	Elimination of perceptual cues	49
A.	Abstraction	46
C.	Memory	32
F.	Addition and subtraction	24
D.	Extension	21
E.	Conservation	14
G.	Ordinal-cardinal correspondence	6

From Wohlwill (1960).

red bar was to be matched with the number of dots on a choice card. That is, if the red bar was third in length, the card with three dots was the correct choice. This correspondence between ordinal number and cardinal number is a rather abstract attainment which is presumed to depend on the attainments measured by the previous tests.

When these tests were given to 72 children, age four to seven, the order of difficulty, shown in Table 3.1, was approximately as expected—although F was surprisingly easy compared to D and E—and the overall performance showed the expected correlation with age. More important, the scalogram analysis indicated, in Wohlwill's words,

a very substantial degree of order in the response patterns of the individual Ss, such that the mastery of any given item presupposed, in general, success on all easier items. Such a finding justifies the postulation of a single scale of conceptual complexity underlying these problems and suggests the operation of a consistent developmental process in the conceptualization of number [p. 374].

A series of studies by Dodwell gave somewhat less support to the sequence of development of number concepts assumed by Piaget. Dodwell (1960) confirmed Piaget's contention that young children do not fully understand the concept of number, even though they may be able to count, but the sequences he found, with Canadian children, were quiet different. Dodwell's results, unlike Wohlwill's, could only be fitted to a quasiscale (1961). A later study (1962) compared number development and the logic of classes but found that correlations between tests assumed to be at the same level were quite low.

Another limitation on the generality of Piaget's stage comes from research by Jahoda (1964) on Glasgow children's concepts of nationality and geography. He adopted the questions used by Inhelder and Piaget in their work on classes, asking the children whether they were Scottish, whether they were British, whether they could be both at once, and whether they lived in Glasgow or in Scotland. Certain developmental regularities appeared in the answers, but not the developmental stages of the Geneva school. The Geneva stages, worked out with classes of beads and flowers, may not be applicable to these abstract concepts of nationality.

Measures of achievement of conservation are influenced by small variations in method, as well as content, more so than one would expect of stable cognitive structures. Consider the father who is a doctor; is he still a father? An affirmative answer would be evidence of conservation of the concept of *father* in spite of additional information about a particular father's occupation. Sigel, Saltz, and Roskind (1967) asked three such questions of children aged five to eight, but introduced some variations. When the children were told that the father *was* a doctor, 69 percent gave replies indicating conservation; but when other children were told that the father *studied and became* a doctor, the proportion dropped to 39 percent. When representative cutout pictures were presented instead of verbal questions alone, the proportion of correct responses dropped from 71 percent to 42 percent, presumably because the pictures contained irrelevant, distracting information.

The consistency that showed up in this experiment should also be mentioned. The children who had three conservation tests, dealing with father, mother, and sister, under the same conditions, were very consistent. Most of those who exhibited conservation on one test exhibited it on all three; most of those who failed one failed all. Such results are evidence of consistency across variations in content, though the variations from father to sister are not as large as from beads and flowers to nationalities.

The examination of children's thinking has proceeded, with few exceptions, by the cross-sectional method, but Almy (1966) exploited the advantages of the longitudinal method also by examinations at six-month intervals, beginning in kindergarten. Although the two methods told the same story of achievement of conservation of number and quantity for overall percentages at any one time, the longitudinal data disclosed fluctuations in the progress of individual children during this transitional period. About half the children moved ahead steadily, but many who performed well on an early examination regressed on a later one. It is difficult to evaluate the magnitude of these fluctuations psychometrically; but they are probably not entirely due to unreliability of measurement because correlations between .50 and .60 with measures of intelligence set a lower limit to the reliability of the conservation measures. At present when a child gives evidence of conservation, we cannot be sure that he will do the same at another time by another method of examination with quite different content.

Despite continuing questions about methods, the cumulated evidence has established that Piaget's stages are more than epistemological speculations; they can be understood and investigated by other psychologists, with interesting empirical results. The final certificate of scientific respectability was attained when computer programs for simulation of these stages were written (Gyr, Brown, and Cafagna, 1967). Ambiguities of method were bypassed by arranging induction problems with lights and switches, hence the apparatus resembled the problem-solving apparatus of the next chapter and the problems resembled the rule-learning problems of the preceding chapter. Since the circuits that controlled the lights were not visible, of course, the subjects were free to think of the connections in terms of their own cognitive structures. Programs written to simulate preoperational, concrete-operational, and formal-operational thought turned out different sequences of responses, and when students in grade school and college worked the problems, their response sequences had some relation to the Piaget stages. For example, 65 percent of the children in the fourth grade (ages nine and ten) exhibited behavior like the model for concrete-operational thought, as expected at this age, while 22 percent exhibited behavior like the model for preoperational thought, and 13 percent like formal-operational thought. As in the concept experiments of the preceding chapter, detailed instructions raised the level of performance.

It is fair to conclude, from these few samples of recent studies, that standardized procedures and careful control of the test situation do not destroy the phenomena to be studied. Reliable multiple-choice tests of conservation of quantity and weight, additive composition of numbers and classes, and other structures have been constructed to yield scores that correlate closely with the corresponding scores obtained by more flexible interview procedures (Freyberg, 1966). For 151 schoolchildren ages five to seven, the scores correlated with intelligence .532 and with spelling .418. Furthermore, these scores predicted achievement two years later: arithmetic computation .524, arithmetic problem solving .571. Such results, which are typical of results from other correlational studies with smaller samples of children, show that achievement on Piaget's trend-setting tests and achievement on standard educational tests of similar content have much in common. In fact, items testing achievement of conservation, transitivity, and the like could be included in a test of general intelligence where their correlations with total scores would be similar to the comparable correlations for vocabulary and arithmetic items.

Thus, carefully controlled research clearly does not destroy the phenomena to be studied; on the contrary, it yields more precise description of the stages of development and illuminates inconsistencies due to variations in content and method that might otherwise escape our notice. Apparently, if a child has only a vague, unstable structure, some test questions and some materials may bring it to operational status, at least temporarily, and others may obstruct it. There is considerable evidence that all manner of task variations can facilitate or impede the child's ability to give concrete-operational responses during the transitional period between six and nine (Flavell and Hill, 1969). Hence differences in the criteria of achievement and in flexibility of probing for evidence can produce wide variations in results. Fortunately, materials and procedures for individual testing have now been standardized so that several psychometrically adequate measures of conservation can be obtained (Goldschmid and Bentler, 1968).

DEVELOPMENTAL PROCESSES

Piaget's assertions about the acquisition of a new cognitive structure by a new equilibrium are not explicit, but assertions about stages of development do have explicit negative implications. To say that the child does not perform logical operations until he has progressed gradually through several preoperational stages is to challenge the efficacy of education and the optimism of educators. It is this aspect of Piaget's writings that has stimulated critical discussion and research by educational psychologists. No one objects when Piaget states that the child constructs reality by experience with it nor when he implies that varied experience with concrete objects is good preparation for the achievement of abstractions. But those with faith in learning react against what they interpret as assertions that learning must wait on internal autonomous changes.

Piaget's equilibration theory assumes that conservation results, not from external reinforcement, but, internally, from an organization of the perceptual feedback from addition and subtraction. Adding means more, subtracting means less. If no adding or subtracting is perceived, no change is perceived; hence conservation has been achieved. Smedslund (1961b) reversed this logic and tried to extinguish conservation of weight by tricking his subjects. On the basis of tests of conservation of weight, children five to seven were divided into a group that had achieved conservation normally and a group to be given practice in this performance. The practice consisted of weighing balls on a balance before and after deformation until they were able to give correct explanations. Smedslund's test procedure was to place two balls of Plasticine on a balance showing that they weighed the same. Then he molded one into a sausage, inconspicuously removing a small piece so that one weighed more than the other, and asked for an explanation. Six of the 13 who had attained conservation in the normal course of experience resisted extinction, but none of the 11 who had received the recent training with external reinforcement did so.

Wohlwill and Lowe (1962) tried to teach kindergarten children conservation of number but did not find that ordinary reinforced practice was effective. Four conditions of training were tried out but none of the groups improved more than the control group which had only the pretests and posttests. Apparently, merely giving the pretests and posttests aroused the cognitive conflict and equilibration necessary for some subjects to achieve conservation.

Limited success in training for conservation was obtained by Beilin (1965) with an apparatus similar to that of Wohlwill and Lowe for testing for conservation of number. There were three parallel columns of corks, as in Fig. 3.2A, and the child was asked to choose the row that was like the middle row. The apparatus permitted contraction of the middle column so that the length changed perceptually while the number was conserved, as in Fig. 3.2B. Then the child was asked again to choose the column that was like the middle column. Training was given by several methods, including Smedlund's equilibration method, but the only one that was effective was a verbal explanation:

Now I am moving them. See, they are standing in a different place, but there are just as many dots as before. They only look different. See, I can put them back just the way they were, so you see, there are still the same number as

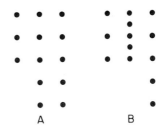

FIGURE 3.2. *Arrangement of corks used by Beilin (1965) to study conservation of number.*

before because I did not add any dots or take away any dots. I only moved them [p. 326].

This verbal training was effective in increasing conservation of number and length, on which the training was given; but there was no transfer to conservation of area, on which no training was given. Beilin suggested that the essential feature of the verbal-rule instruction was its algorithm feature: "It provides S with a model or rule for processing relevant input data [p. 337]."

In Beilin's experiment, those children who on pretest showed no conservation at all and those who showed almost complete conservation did not improve much. The training was most effective for those children who were in a transition state, a result that emphasizes the interaction between learning and maturation.

One of the most thorough experiments on the acceleration of conservation by deliberate training was carried out by Goldschmid (1968) with 110 kindergarten children, using several standardized measures of conservation and two kinds of training. *Reversibility training* consisted of repeated demonstrations that after an object's shape has been changed, it may be returned to its original form; *compensation training* showed the child that when one dimension was changed (when the ball of clay was flattened), there was a compensatory change (the ball became longer). The training was done individually for three and a half hours over a three-week period. The experimental groups that were trained on three tasks registered definite improvement on three other tasks which were similar, and the improvement also transferred to other, less similar conservation tasks. Reversibility training was more effective than compensation training. On a follow-up test two years later, the experimental groups were still superior to the control group.

One of the minor mechanisms in the Piaget machinery of thought is *centration*, the tendency of the young child to center attention on one salient attribute of an object. In a test of conservation of liquid, for example, the attention of the preoperational child may be captured by the height of the liquid in the glass to the neglect of other attributes, while the older child is able to *decenter* and check the other attributes. He might notice a decrease in width compensating for the increase in height, for instance.

These little tasks, that look so simple to an adult or an adolescent, who knows what to look for, are perceptually quite complicated to children. From the young child's point of view, it appears that he is asked to make a judgment of multidimensional stimulus objects without knowing which dimensions are critical. Evidence of this complexity comes from an experiment carried out by Kenney (Bruner, Olver, and Greenfield, 1966). This showed children pairs of glass containers of water and asked which of each pair was fuller and, later, which was emptier. In these simple comparisons there were many perceptual attributes that the child could observe, such as height of the glass, water level, water volume, and whether the water reached the top or not; some of these visible attributes supported the correct judgment while others were misleading. When all the attributes supported the correct judgments, nearly all the judgments were correct, even at age five. Less perceptual support yielded fewer correct judgments and, when all the perceptual cues were misleading, nearly all the judgments were in error, until age eleven.

The inability of the young child to decenter can be overcome by appropriate training, like so many other inabilities. The appropriate training in this case consists of practice on a variety of problems, called *oddity problems*, with distracting stimuli (Gelman, 1969). Children of five who had failed conservation tests learned not to attend to the irrelevant features of oddity problems and then became successful on conservation tests. The gain transferred to other conservation tests and was still in evidence two or three weeks later.

Does this mean that an improvement on conservation tests should be described as an improvement of attention? Not necessarily. If children achieve conservation through one of the other kinds of training described above and a test of attention is administered later as a dependent variable, it would probably appear that directing attention to the relevant attributes is an effect as well as a cause. Under ordinary conditions the cognitive structure and the control of attention develop together, but training on either one could produce improvement that would then transfer to the other.

If assessing the quantity of water in a cylinder is a multidimensional judgment, the complete conceptual achievement includes the assessment of height and breadth and the relation of these to assessment of quantity. As Halford (1970), put it, "The impediment to the adoption of a quantity criterion is removed, not when cues such as height are found to be irrelevant, but when height and breadth jointly are found to be consistent with quantity [p. 302]." Most conservation tasks do not require a precise knowledge of height and breadth but they do require knowledge of the effects of change in the system. Knowledge of the system means, for example, the knowledge that if height is increased and breadth remains constant, quantity increases; if height is increased, a compensating decrease in breadth would conserve quantity. Halford suggests that children learning to use quantity indicators alone would not be learning the quantity concept but rather a sophisticated rule which enables them to do without it.

The samples of training studies reviewed here, and many others (Elkind and Flavell, 1969), suggest some general conclusions. The developmental stages described by Piaget are susceptible to change by special training under certain conditions. The most favorable condition, to be sure, is that of the child in a transition stage, about to move into a higher stage by himself. Apparently the early training studies were not as carefully carried out as the later studies, but it is evident now that definite gains can follow from well-planned programs. There is agreement also (Brainerd and Allen, 1971; Goldschmid, 1968) that reversibility training is the most effective. One could speculate that reversibility operations facilitate the achievement of the multidimensional system and thus are a significant part of the processes by which transition occurs under natural conditions.

In general terms, this transition must depend on an interaction between the internal maturational forces and the external effects of experience in a specific environment; but apparently the optimal environmental conditions are complex and have not yet been adequately determined. It is a hopeful sign that experimental psychologists are turning their attention to cognitive development and beginning the unspectacular task of manipulating materials, instructions, and conditions (as in the preceding chapter) in order to examine cognitive achievements of genuine significance.

THE DEVELOPMENT OF REPRESENTATION

Impressed by Piaget's mapping of the development of logical structures, Bruner and his associates (Bruner, Olver, and Greenfield, 1966) undertook to map a parallel, and sometimes coincidental, development, which they call the development of representation. How does the child represent the world? How does this representation change with age and experience? How is it influenced by the development of language?

The earliest form of representation, corresponding to Piaget's sensorimotor stage, in which things are "lived rather than thought," Bruner terms *enactive*. The young child knows where an object is not only because he perceives it against a stable perceptual background but also because the reaching movements that attain it are launched from a stable background of balanced neuromuscular tensions. One might say, if one wishes to talk of representation at this age, that the cognitive task is to cast off the limitations of this internal neuromuscular representation and replace it by a more flexible, perceptual, action-free representation.

A second stage in representation, which Bruner terms *iconic*, begins to emerge in the second year when the child represents the world to himself by images or spatial schemes that are relatively independent of action. Iconic representation is egocentric in that the images are projected from the child's own point of view and colored by his likes and dislikes. By adult standards, iconic representation is superficial. The young child attempting to make sense out of a complex display may grasp at concrete details depending on the salience of the stimuli and fluctuations of attention, or at obvious global characteristics, whereas the older child is more likely to grasp the full schematic structure.

An image, like a picture, may be worth a thousand words, but it is the "unpicturable" categories associated with symbols that represent that world most effectively. This symbolic form of representation is built on enactive and iconic foundations by cultural (especially linguistic) processes. Thus Bruner's tracing of the path to symbolic thinking touches on more of the linguistic precursors than Piaget's.

The linguistic accomplishments of a child of four—the ability to understand and produce sentences according to complex rules, and the accompanying motor skills—have aroused much wonder and, recently, sophisticated research. But an even more subtle accomplishment, as Bruner points out, is the child's ability a little later to adjust his thinking to the syntactical requirements of the language and to *use* the sentence to *express* his thoughts. To differentiate words from objects and to use words instrumentally to refer to objects, even to objects not present or to their abstract properties, is to gain a powerful semantic leverage.

To examine the development of iconic representation and the transition to symbolic representation, Bruner and Kenny (Bruner, Olver, and Greenfield, 1966) gave children a double classification problem, with the matrix of nine glasses displayed in Fig. 3.3. The glasses varied by three values in height and three in diameter. To acquaint the child with the matrix, the experimenter removed a few glasses and asked the child to replace them. After the replacement task came a reproduction task: the glasses were scrambled and the child was asked to build "something like what was there before." Then came a transposition task: the glasses were scrambled again but the short thin glass in the southwest corner was now placed in the southeast corner and the child was asked to build something like what was there before, leaving the one glass where it had just been placed.

The replacement task was easy, except for the youngest children of age three; but the reproduction task seemed to require the retention of an image of the matrix and the guidance of behavior by this image (see Fig. 3.4). Few children below five succeeded. It seemed to be a copying task because virtually every successful child reproduced the matrix in its original orientation with no transposing of dimensions; in fact, the children said they were trying to remember where the glasses had been before. Transposition was much harder, for rigid image-bound representation was not sufficient. Ap-

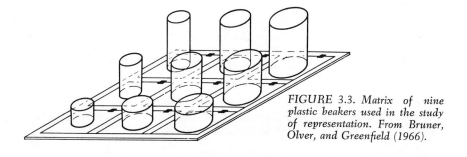

FIGURE 3.3. *Matrix of nine plastic beakers used in the study of representation. From Bruner, Olver, and Greenfield (1966).*

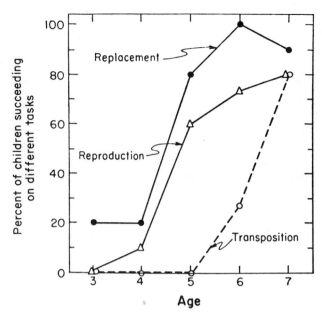

FIGURE 3.4. *Performance of children, ten at each age, on three tasks. From Bruner, Olver, and Greenfield (1966).*

parently the transposition problem required some kind of verbal formulation, and this was not common before age seven. The data gave evidence of a scale of sorts: those subjects who succeeded on transposition succeeded on the other two tasks, and those who succeeded on reproduction succeeded on replacement.

The methods for studying iconic representation are not yet well established, and the logic of the above demonstration is not altogether clear because it depends on prior knowledge of the requirement for success on each task. If the reproduction task requires imagery and imagery is not handled well before age five, this argues for imagery at age five. Likewise, success on the transposition task is taken as evidence for symbolic processes, but it is conceivable that a child with good visual imagery, unspoiled by verbal transformation, could construct an image of the matrix, tilt it over in imagination, and read the location of the glasses off the transposed image. An independent check on the imagery is much to be desired and, since imaginal representation has been reemphasized by Bruner and others, further work will probably tighten up the methodology.

Performance on this problem can be improved, both in the reproduction and the transition phases, by pretraining on each of the two dimensions separately (Darnell and Bourne, 1970). The pretraining was more helpful to children above average in verbal ability than to those below average, but the effects of superior verbal ability were not evident during pretraining since all the subjects succeeded on the simple pretraining tasks. More likely, the effect of verbal ability consisted in the application of the components acquired on the pretraining tasks to the matrix problem.

The development of representation by imagery and then by symbols appears again in an experiment by Olson (Bruner, Olver, and Greenfield, 1966) involving a matching problem with a matrix of light bulbs, some of which made a pattern—for example, a T—when lighted (see Fig. 3.5). The subject had a similar matrix of bulbs which were unlighted but could be pressed one at a time to light up the bulbs in the pattern of the model. The easiest problem presented a single pattern of lights and the subject pressed bulbs to see if he could make a pattern to match the model. On other problems, two or more models were presented and the subject had to discover, by pressing his bulbs, which one he could match. The older children did better than the young children, to be sure, but the sequences of their attempts permitted inferences about the strategies made possible by their additional mastery of images and symbols.

One strategy was a simple search; without regard to the model, the subject pressed bulbs to see what would happen. Some bulbs were preferred over others, so the search could not be called random, but it was not related to the information in the model. This inefficient strategy—if it can be called a strategy—was typical of children of three (see Fig. 3.6).

Another identifiable strategy was a successive pattern matching. The subject pressed light bulbs suggested by one of the models and tried to trace out a pattern, without considering alternative patterns in other models. This strategy, which was common at ages five and seven, was more efficient than the search, but contained many uninformative moves because the lights in different patterns overlapped; that is, turning on a light contained in two patterns or in neither does not furnish any discriminative information.

The most efficient strategy was a more deliberate information selection.

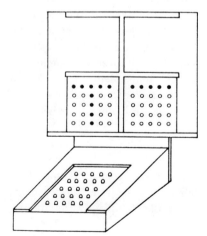

FIGURE 3.5. Apparatus presenting patterns of light bulbs for matching experiments. From Bruner, Olver, and Greenfield (1966).

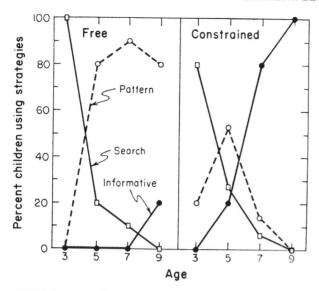

FIGURE 3.6. *Performance of children, 10 to 15 at each age, using 3 types of strategies. From Bruner, Olver, and Greenfield (1966).*

The subject chose those nonredundant light bulbs that gave discriminative information about the patterns of the models. The strategy was adopted only by subjects of nine, and only by a fifth of them.

Other children had the same problems, under a constrained condition that permitted them to press only one bulb at a time, after which the experimenter would ask, "Now do you know which of the pictures is the correct one?" This constrained condition was designed to encourage the most economic or informative strategy. The children were more deliberate under these conditions and, as Fig. 3.6 shows, the use of the information selection strategy increased considerably among seven- and nine-year-olds. The conclusion is that in pattern matching the subject has an image corresponding to the model and uses this to guide his movements. The information selection strategy requires a more abstract conceptualization of the properties that distinguish between different models, so that the subject can symbolically represent separate critical features of the patterns rather than respond to the images as wholes.

Even when children are using words fluently to represent familiar objects, they are still dominated for a while by perceptual rather than abstract attributes. A study of "equivalence" by Olver and Hornsby (Bruner, Olver, and Greenfield, 1966) illustrated this point by a simple procedure appropriate for ages six to nineteen. The subject is shown the words *banana* and *peach* and asked: "How are *banana, peach,* and *potato* all alike?" Words are added and similar questions asked until the list consists of *banana, peach, potato, meat, milk, water, air,* and *germ*. These words, and those of other lists, can be grouped by perceptual similarities ("they are both yellow"), by functional similarities ("you can eat them"), and so on, but perhaps more interesting is an analysis of the structure or syntax of the groupings. As the perceptual grouping gives way to the functional, with increasing age, the complexive structure gives way to the superordinate. A superordinate structure puts the items in a higher class. Complexive structures are tied together by associations or varying similarities but without a consistent common attribute: "Banana and peach are both yellow, peach and potato are round, potato and meat are served together, meat and milk both come from cows." The longer lists are harder to group in one superordinate class, of course, so around age twelve most subjects formed superordinate groupings for all easy lists but complexive groupings for many of the hard ones. Similar studies with pictures to be grouped tell the same story. The six-year-old sees equivalence in perceptual terms, perhaps with the aid of imagery. With the development of symbolic representation in the older child, according to this account, linguistic structures increasingly guide what and how things will be judged alike.

It is difficult, of course, to validate the exact contribution of language to this developmental process beyond the possibility of alternative interpretations. Piaget (1967), in his turn, has taken up the weapon of methodological criticism to locate errors in results that are inconsistent with the Genevan results, especially on the role of language. With all the instabilities that have turned up during the transitional period, however, and all the language that children are exposed to at this time, there is plenty of opportunity for linguistic acquisitions to slant cognitive development to a significant degree.

Language and Thought

The language-thought problem, like the mind-body problem, has changed over the centuries of controversy, but in the annals of speculative psychology certain questions persist (Carroll, 1964a; Jenkins, 1969; Révész, 1954). Is thought possible without language? Is language possible without thought? Are language and thought the same? The many philosophers and psychologists who have explored such questions agree that man's thought is closely related to his language, that is, to his use of a system of words and other symbols. But the relationship between language and thought can be viewed from several angles, hence a clarification of the question is part of any answer. In addition, the progress of psychology has produced relevant empirical evidence (some of which has been mentioned on preceding pages) and there are fresh ways of viewing the problem. However, since many of the arguments about language and thought still sound like comparisons of two reified mental faculties, the discussion needs first to be placed in a biological context, along with other psychological functions.

It is the general rule of biological organization that different functions are not completely independent nor completely redundant, but interdependent and overlapping. The nervous system and the circulatory system work together to integrate the activities of the organism, as in the control of activity level; there is some overlap in function but they are not redundant systems. Similarly in the normal person, vision and audition function interdependently to supply information about the environment; each helps the other in certain tasks, such as the localization of objects, but not in all. If one system is inoperative, the other can take over some of its duties but not all. Language and thought are more recent, highly specialized developments in the evolution of man, but by this analogy we would expect a similar overlapping organization, nonredundant, nonparallel, and nonindependent. We would look for the development of interactions between thought and language because both are functions of one living organism.

Many who have struggled with the language-thought question have complained about the shifting usage of each term. The nature of thought and its various meanings—mental experience, problem solving, mediation—were discussed in Chapter 1. The nature of language is also complex, but a few features are especially relevant to the present discussion. In the normal adult, the function of language includes communication between individuals. Content words, like nouns and verbs, that refer to objects and events are obvious features of language; but function words, like prepositions and conjunctions, that do not refer to anything but relate words to other words must also be included. Above all, language is characterized by structures, such as phrases and sentences, that are more than lists of random series of words, yet a great variety of sentences can be generated from a few basic structures by standard transformations. Thus language involves a skilled performance by the speaker (or writer) and a skilled performance by the listener (or reader), who share a competence in the standard linguistic forms underlying the specific performances.

If we consider thought in the sense of mental experience, we must trust introspection as the method of inquiry. By this method it appears that our thoughts consist often of words and other linguistic forms. But introspection also reveals nonlinguistic thoughts, such as smells, visual images, and ineffable fears, so thought and language cannot be equated by this method. Introspection is not a convincing guide. And yet, if we wish to explore mental experience at all, we must admit that both linguistic and nonlinguistic thoughts are frequently experienced and we cannot say that either class of thoughts is unthinkable.

If we consider thought as problem solving, it is obvious that many of the problems that man has to think about are verbal problems: achievement of the concepts and conceptual systems of the arts and sciences, reading and evaluation of abstract arguments, construction of effective sentences, organization of paragraphs, comparison of alternative sentences, and debates with worthy opponents. All these problems appear in verbal form; thus their solution requires the ability to read and write, to listen and talk. There are other problems, of course, that do not appear as verbal problems: the discrimination of figure classes, as well as arithmetic, spatial, construction, and interpersonal problems. In these cases, the assertion that thought depends on language involves hypotheses about verbal mediation.

Instead of the strong assertion that problem solving is not possible without language, one could make the weaker assertion that problem solving is facilitated by language. Few would object to this claim; indeed, the chapters on problem solving will supply convincing evidence of it. Evidence of occasional interference will also be presented; some reasoning problems are solved by extricating them from the language in which they appear and representing them in a nonverbal way, as by Venn diagrams.

The reverse assertion has also been made from time to time, that language depends on thought. This is quite reasonable at a gross level of analysis if language is considered as an adaptive function and speech is treated as one way of solving problems, especially interpersonal problems. Language habits can easily be interpreted as residues of previous problem-solving successes and failures. One might say that language merely puts thought on record. But many counterexamples can be offered: "How do you do?" "Please pass the salt." "Ouch!" Language is a complex performance, like driving a car, but when thoroughly learned it is performed mechanically, thoughtlessly. The grammatical structures of language coincide only occasionally with the actual course of problem solving.

Again, instead of the strong assertion that language is not possible without thought, one could make the weaker assertion that language is facilitated by thought. And few would object to this statement; certainly not teachers of speech and writing. But, assuming that language is a skilled performance directed toward communication, thought can occasionally interfere with language just as language can interfere with thought. Two obvious examples of this are reading aloud and reciting a memorized speech.

In general, when thought is treated as problem solving and language is treated as a skilled communicative performance, the two cannot be equated, nor can it be said that either depends completely on the other. The relationship can best be described as one of mutual facilitation, with occasional interference, and the analogy with listening and looking holds. But this analysis may be too gross; when thought is treated as mediation, more subtle hypotheses can be elaborated.

VERBAL MEDIATORS OF THOUGHT

In many discussions of language and thought, *thought* refers to unobservable mediators. It is possible, indeed, to restrict the meaning of *thought* to the manipulation of concepts and to restrict the meaning of *language* to terms that refer to concepts; then there is an identity by definition. But both functions are broader than concepts.

Obviously, thinking about verbal problems involves language—both overtly and covertly. The words, phrases, and sentences of a skilled speaker, though spoken effortlessly, reflect his struggle to achieve the concepts and principles of interest to him; and the standard language of the culture today embodies the creative thinking of philosophers, scientists, journalists, and other wordsmiths of yesterday. But arguments for the dependence of thought on language often include the hypothesis that verbal mediators are involved in the solution of nonverbal problems. Following ancient scholars, Benjamin Whorf (1956), an anthropologist and a linguist, is largely responsible in recent times for the claim that the language of any society determines the thinking of those who live in that society. Any individual's view of the world depends on the concepts by which he categorizes his experiences and, since the standard concepts are provided by the language, speakers of different languages code their experiences into different categories and think different thoughts. If the task is to categorize sensory data, the ready availability of a category designated by a familiar word simplifies a task which if the category did not exist might prove a difficult problem of concept formation. Familiarity with the word for a category or dimension draws attention to it. Thus the color names used by a society slant the categorizing of the colors of the visible spectrum. Whorf has also argued that the fundamental concepts of space, time, and causality are language-dependent and vary more from one society to another than a person who speaks a Western European language would suspect.

There is little empirical support for linguistic relativity in its extreme form (Diebold, 1965). An agricultural society, to be sure, is more likely to invent convenient terms for agricultural concepts and use them precisely than a fishing society, and a speaker is likely to code his experiences in the categories provided by his own language and to talk about them in these terms. But all languages are adaptable. There are no primitive languages; all have changed and continue to change as new ideas invade the language area. Hence some scholars (Jenkins, 1969) have suggested that any natural language can be considered a universal meta-language, which can comprehend, with appropriate circumlocution, any other language. The apparently untranslatable religious concepts of certain remote African tribes have, with difficulty, been described in English. Likewise, Western European science uses very special concepts that are inconceivable to many African, Indian, and Polynesian societies, yet with considerable patience some members of these societies do learn Western science. The weaker form of this assertion—that linguistic mediators influence thought one way or another, making some concepts and principles harder to learn than others—has much support, even when thought is concerned with nonverbal problems.

It would be erroneous to assume that all mediators are verbal, even in the case of verbal problems. Although sentences are constructed of words, sentence structures are not always labeled by words. Many a speaker has make skilful use of such literary devices as alliteration and synecdoche without having words to refer to them, and many a debater has detected a standard fallacy in his opponent's argument without knowing the standard label for it. The evidence for nonverbal mediators in thinking about verbal problems is no less convincing than the evidence for verbal mediators in thinking about nonverbal problems.

DEVELOPMENTAL INTERACTIONS

The interaction between thought and language must be a dynamic one. As the child grows older and more intelligent and acquires more of the adult culture, he becomes more sophisticated in both functions. The persistent language-thought problem can be raised again in the form of a question about the sequence of development: Does language develop first and influence the development of thought, or does thought develop first and influence the development of language?

As soon as the young child starts to respond to adult voices and to direct his babbling toward adults, we can say that language is developing. Some utterances at this time may be considered attempts to solve a problem, such as retrieving a fallen toy, and these attempts are not much different from a child's tug on his mother's arm or a dog barking at a closed door. If thought means problem solving, this is thought of a simple childlike kind. But there is no reason at this time to infer that the language is influenced by cognitive mediators, internal representations of the environment, or conceptual thought. Reaction to adult voices at this time is similarly direct, not mediated. This direct, interpersonal, linguistic performance might be called preconceptual language or, if thought means cognitive mediators, language without thought.

The most extraordinary phenomenon—one that has puzzled both linguists and psychologists—is that normal children acquire the basic structures of their native language by age four or five, when they are characterized by Piaget as preoperational and before they can solve simple problems like tieing their shoelaces. Even children of low intelligence, with IQs of between 50 and 75, learn the language moderately well. This is not to say that their language includes words for abstract concepts and principles, but that they construct sentences according to rules so complex that linguists have not yet worked them out satisfactorily. Nor does this mean that children can state the rules for generating sentences, only that they are capable of complex linguistic performance. Such performance gives evidence of the development of language skills without corresponding development of thought.

As we noted in the section on cognitive development, there is reason to infer that the young child acquires some simple cognitive structures for representing what he sees and feels before he learns to refer to them by name. These structures are limited in the early years to concrete, perceptual schemas, but they act as mediators in facilitating adaptive responses to different views of the same object on successive occasions and to classes of perceived objectives. The role of such mediators is difficult to evaluate, but if they are operative at this early age, this operation could be considered prelinguistic thought.

Thus, if these accounts are accurate, in the first few years of life the child develops a language facility and a repertoire of cognitive mediators to represent his world—perhaps to think about his world—but the two are distinct. As to individual differences, correlations between the conventional intelligence tests (supposed to measure cognitive accomplishments) and the conventional measures of language skill, such as length and complexity of sentences, are quite low during these early years (Furth, 1966). The next question is how the child integrates these two functions so as to develop the relatively smooth interactions that are observed in the normal adult.

VERBAL FACILITATION OF INTELLECTUAL DEVELOPMENT

The block-sorting test described on page 97 was designed by Vygotsky (1962) in the 1930s to study the intellectual progress of Russian children. Unlike conventional figure concept tasks, this task begins with a word for a block, and thus a symbol can orient the conceptualization of a class of blocks. Learning to direct one's own mental processes with the aid of words or other symbols is an integral part of the process of concept formation, according to Vygotsky.

The role played by speech in intellectual development is dramatized by the egocentric speech of the child, which has been considered the beginning of socialized speech. As Vygotsky observed the performance of children of different ages on the block test, he rejected this sequence and asserted that socialized speech comes first. Egocentric speech splits off from general social speech, and this split leads to inner speech, which now has a mediating rather than a social function. All the higher functions are mediated processes, according to this view, and language is the basic means used to direct and control them. Words are the means of actively centering attention, abstracting attributes of objects, synthesizing them, and symbolizing them.

For young children, in Vygotsky's view, the word is not an arbitrary name for a class of objects; it is an attribute of the objects, like size, shape, and color. Only later, at adolescence, is this verbal absolutism replaced by the more formal, adult type of meaning, and even then, after true concepts are formed, the elementary forms of thought are not completely abandoned. Thus the relation between words and objects is a dynamic one, changing with the child's maturity, experience, and education. Progress in thought and progress in speech are not parallel. Rather, their growth curves cross and recross. In time, the meaning of a word joins thought and language so closely that it is hard to say whether thought depends on language or language depends on thought.

The importance of language in the development of thought has been emphasized by Russian investigators since Pavlov's description of the second signal system. Pavlov considered the ordinary conditioned reflexes of the lower animals as a first signal system, not adequate to explain the complex behavior of man for whom a word can be a signal of a signal. The appearance of a light can be a signal for food, but in man the word *light* can be a signal for the light which is in turn the signal for the food. Thus as language introduces words for objects, he responds less often to the objects directly and more often to the verbal signals of objects.

Luria (1961) and his students, who have been studying this verbal control of behavior in Russia for many years, began with Vygotsky's assumption that the most important mental activities result from the child's social development, in the course of which language develops and acquires control over behavior. An adult draws attention to an object, for example, by pointing to it and this object becomes the controlling stimulus for a response. If at the same time he names the object, the name gradually acquires the power to evoke the same response. Later the child himself pronounces the name to evoke the response. Thus complex mental activities, bound up with speech, are initially carried on slowly and only by external audible communication with adults; but they gradually speed up as they are interiorized in the form of thought rather than speech.

To demonstrate this development, Luria arranged conditioning experiments with a simple hand movement, such as squeezing a rubber bulb, as the response, and lights and words as stimuli. Children in the second year can be conditioned to squeeze when a light appears, but more complex tasks require extra verbal instructions from the experimenter. If the task is to squeeze, relax, then squeeze again, the performance is facilitated by telling the child to say, "Push, Push." If the child of three or four is conditioned to react to a red light, the presentation of a yellow light may evoke a different response: "Shall I press for that one too?" Following appropriate instructions he forms a rule, such as: "I am to press for a red light and not for a yellow light." The younger children state these rules aloud while the older children usually do not, but even older children are occasionally heard to say "No, No" aloud in order to inhibit a well-practiced response. Whereas associations develop gradually in animals and very young children, by age four or five they can be formed at once, even if fairly complex, by the incorporation of the given signals into an existing verbal system.

Thus language facilitates thought as the instructions for the control of behavior are understood and acted upon, then as they are repeated aloud, and then finally as they mediate behavior soundlessly. In the third stage, Luria believes, as the control is transferred from external to internal speech, the regulatory function is transferred to the system of meaningful referents provided by speech. The analytic flexibility that derives from the abstracting and generalizing functions of language becomes the property of thought.

American behaviorists also have adapted the machinery of stimulus-response associationism to the investigation of verbal facilitation of intellectual development. According to the Kendlers' hypothesis about verbal mediation outlined in Chapter 2, children learn words in ordinary communication, then the words mediate the acquisition of class concepts. While the child of five responds directly to objects, the first response of a child of ten may be an implicit verbal response which, because it has previously been associated with classes of objects, evokes behavior appropriate to classes.

NONVERBAL COGNITIVE STRUCTURES
Those who have studied cognitive development seriously are likely to point out that the early cognitive structures influence intellectual development in general and facilitate the later acquisition of words for these structures. Piaget

in particular has reported many examples to illustrate how the young child at the sensorimotor level represents objects and events by movements of his hands and feet, sometimes even by playful imitation of actions that interest him. The sensorimotor schemas that control such behavior can be considered mediators in a sense—though cognitive theorists do not typically use this term—but they are private, idiosyncratic representations, not verbal mediators at this stage.

In Piaget's (1954) discussion of language and thought from the genetic point of view, sensorimotor schemas confer significance of a kind on objects and events but only as indicators or signals of them, just as, in the conditioned reflex, the conditioned stimulus is a signal for the unconditioned stimulus. They are the preconditions, along with images however, of the true symbolic function, which distinguishes the signifier from that which is signified and thus permits thought of an object even in its absence. Socialized language, which develops later on the basis of these early types of cognition and inter- action with adults, is only one kind of symbolic function; but it transforms thought profoundly by facilitating the attainment of thoroughly abstract schemas that can be used more flexibly. When this level of intellectual ma- turity is reached, according to Piaget, asking whether thought precedes language or language precedes thought is as hopeless as asking whether the river controls the banks or the banks the river. But earlier, before age three or so, there is supposed to be a nonverbal state of cognitive development that precedes and makes possible the later acquisition of language. Each child has to construct reality for himself, and his constructions guide his appropriation of the language that he hears.

Specific illustrations in support of this position have been supplied by Sinclair-de-Zwart (1969), working with Piaget and Inhelder at Geneva, from her experiments on the spontaneous use of quantitative terms by children who have achieved conservation of liquids and seriation and children who have not. In describing different quantities of Plasticine, the conservers used mostly comparative expressions: "The boy has more than the girl." The nonconservers used absolute terms in the same situation: "The boy has a lot. The girl has a little." Conservers were able to construct sentences that co- ordinated two dimensions of objects: "This pencil is long but thin; the other is short but thick." Most of the nonconservers referred to only one dimension in each sentence. Verbal training for the nonconservers produced some im- provement in their verbal descriptions, but this was unstable and did not help them to acquire conservation.

Bruner (Bruner, Olver, and Greenfield, 1966) follows Piaget in recent speculations on this question but adds the insights of Vygotsky and others to link cognitive development and language development more intimately. The link is the referential function, by virtue of which symbols refer to other things, for this is the basis of both language and thought. Progress beyond enactive and iconic representation requires some social training in the use of language. Not that language alone can mold the raw dough of reality; some degree of cognitive organization is necessary. But when perceptual differentiations are taking shape, words can reorder cognition by only a gentle nudge. The availability of terms like *large* and *small,* for example, can nudge cognition of magnitudes into opposing categories; at a later time the availability of a term like *length* can draw attention to the continuous dimension.

As it happens, syntactic development outruns semantic development, according to this account, so that at age five children are quite skillful at organizing sentences but less skillful at conceptualizing the things the words and sentences refer to. Their language has more potentialities than they can utilize at this time, but with experience and social interaction their sometimes empty sentences will fill up with meaning. The continuous adjustment of speech to thought and thought to speech in social interaction sharpens both and enables the older child to solve the developmental problem raised by Piaget, which can be phrased as the child's matching of his extensional classifications to his intensional sentences.

Although many scholars have stated that words slant thought, Bruner adds that the more complex structures of language, such as the sentence, slant thought in more complex ways. Once the child has mastered the language of his culture and has coded his own experience in this language, the syntactic rules may endow his sentences with a surplus meaning that he does not at first understand. It is when a child listens to what he says, as he has listened to what others say, that he reorganizes what he thinks. Bruner's position on this critical issue is revealed in the following paragraph:

Until the time that this "surplus meaning" is read off from our linguistic coding of experience, language and experience maintain an important independence from each other. A child can say of two quantities that one is greater than another, a moment later that it is less than the other, and then that they arc the same—using his words as labels for segments of experience. It is not until he inspects his *language* that he goes back to his experience to check on a mismatch between what he sees with his eyes and what he has just said. He must, in short, treat the utterance as a *sentence* and recognize contradiction at that level. He can *then* go back and reorder experience, literally *see* the world differently by virtue of symbolic processes reordering the nature of experience [pp. 51–52].

THE SPECIAL CASE OF DEAF CHILDREN

The intellectual performance of children who have been deaf since birth, or shortly thereafter, is particularly relevant to the question of language and thought since their deafness deprives them of the cumulative practice in listening and talking enjoyed by normal children during their preschool years. With special remedial training they may acquire a little language by age sixteeen, but in early childhood they adjust to the problems of this world as best they can without the aid of language. Oléron (1957) therefore made several comparisons between the accomplishments of normal children aged four to seven and deaf children of the same ages equated roughly in scores on intelligence tests. Problem-solving performance was studied by requiring the children to manipulate various combinations of latches and bolts to open a problem box and obtain a bonbon. Language might or might not be helpful on this task; in fact, the deaf children without language did as well as the normal children.

Even simple laboratory problems can be solved in more than one way; the important question is whether deaf children solve problems with mediators which normal children designate by words. To investigate this, Oléron turned to a task often employed in studies of discriminative learning: a pair of squares is presented and the child is rewarded for choosing the larger. Then, on the transposition task, another pair is presented to see if the child chooses the larger of these. Typically, young children make an absolute response, choosing the stimulus previously rewarded, while older children make a relational response, presumably because they are familiar with the word *larger*. The question is whether deaf children, who do not use such words, acquire abstract relations from a concrete situation and apply them to a different situation. Another task involved two cylinders varying in weight to determine whether children can acquire and transfer the relation of heavier when they do not know the word *heavier*. A third task involved the relation of faster. Children learned to choose the faster of two rotating discs; then the transfer tasks involved two lights of varying speeds of alternation and two miniature trucks descending an incline at varying speeds. Even though the normal children used words like *larger, heavier,* and *faster,* which the deaf children did not use, there was little difference in the performance of the normal and the deaf. The older children were superior to the younger children, of course, but there was no consistent difference in rates of development.

Another type of task in Oléron's experiments depended on mastering the rules for series of choices. The double alternation task required choosing one of two squares according to the sequence L, L, R, R, L, L, R, R, and so on; triple alternation involved the sequence L, L, L, R, R, R, L, L, L, and so on; and there was a series of eight boxes to be opened according to simple rules about spatial-temporal sequences. When children have to generate rules from experience and apply them to later tasks one would expect that language would be helpful, but in fact the deaf children again performed about as well as the normal children. There are methodological difficulties in equating groups of deaf and normal children for these comparisons, but evidently there were no large differences in performance. The results indicate that children without language can handle certain tasks that presumably involve the mediation of relations, rules, and other simple cognitive structures about as well as children with language.

The special conceptual difficulties of the deaf come to light on tasks that involve word meanings, as in an experiment requiring extension of the meaning of a word (Oléron, Gumusyan, and Moulinou, 1966). Deaf children of five, six and seven were shown common words in association with pictures of corresponding objects and events. When different pictures, representing positive and negative instances of the classes designated by the words, were presented, the deaf children were unable to generalize to the new positive instances as well as comparable children with normal hearing. At age five there was little difference in performance on this task, but at age six and seven normal children were quite successful, while the deaf children's performance was characterized by many errors of nongeneralization and a few errors of false generalization. The authors explain that what the deaf lack is not just the direct connection between a word and its referents but the complex tissue of relations between objects and their properties which language makes available to the normal child during these years. The deaf do not participate fully in the linguistic milieu.

A hopeful implication can be gleaned from these results, however. The experiment consisted of three series of instances; in the second, errors were corrected. During the course of the experiment the deaf children, even the five-year-olds, improved markedly. They did not improve as much as the normal children, to be sure, but their performance on the last series was much superior to that of the normal children on the first series. Obviously they were able to broaden their comprehension of common words by a short set of semantic exercises.

Despite their severe language handicap, the deaf do get along. According to the evidence assembled in a recent book by Furth (1966), with the provocative title *Thinking Without Language,* average achievement in silent reading at age sixteen is only at the level of normal children in the third or fourth grade; and yet adults who have been deaf all their lives do solve the routine problems of daily existence. Although they do not get into the professional occupations, as some blind people do, they hold steady jobs, typically in the low-pay, low-status classifications. Hence Furth raised the question of how they can make as good an adjustment as they do. When he compared the deaf and the normal, he found approximately the same results with American children that Oléron had found with French children. On such tasks as reversal shift and double alternation, which are presumed to require verbal mediation, the deaf children were about equal to their agemates of normal hearing. Although normal children at seven are learning words that could serve as verbal mediators on many conceptual tasks, no noticeable gap between the normal and the deaf appeared at this age. But a difference did show up on certain tasks, such as one involving the abstract relational concept of *opposition,* on which the normal children could be aided by knowledge of a specific word, *opposite,* that the deaf children did not know.

The conclusion from these comparisons is that young deaf children can acquire certain cognitive structures—specifically, spatial and temporal relations closely tied to visible objects—and apply them to the solution of other problems of the same type. If we define concepts to include the association of the cognitive structure with the standard label used in communication, these are not complete concepts, but they are cognitive structures that mediate or control behavior. As these children grow older and encounter problems that depend on more abstract relations, their handicap becomes more serious because the more abstract concepts that normal children are achieving at age ten are not tied to visible objects and cannot be learned without good verbal communication. The deaf adult must have acquired the cognitive structures that he needs for his low-level adjustment, but he acquired them slowly, with great difficulty, and without much help from verbal mediators. Furth believes that there is, in addition, a general discouragement among the deaf due to inadequate teaching methods directed toward linguistic rather than cognitive education. For educational practice, the fact that cognitive structures can be achieved with the help of verbal mediators may not be as relevant as the fact that they can also be acquired without such mediators.

The more general inference is that, if deaf children can acquire certain cognitive structures without language, normal children can also. Or they can acquire the cognitive structures first and the names for them later. The superiority of the deaf in a few comparisons suggests that some normal children may be temporarily retarded by premature attempts to use their inadequate language facility. Until language and thought are appropriately matched, the expanding potentialities for intellectual development will not be realized.

PRESENT STATUS OF THE PROBLEM

When the arguments are examined carefully, it appears that those who say thought depends on language and those who say language depends on thought are not too far apart. Both sides give illustrations to show that the dependence does not go exclusively in one direction; the differences are matters of emphasis and priority. Actually, there is only a little hard evidence; the arguments typically rest on examples and counterexamples. It has been difficult to design convincing experiments because the hypotheses are based on theoretical mediators that are not directly observable. Precise methods would be necessary to check on differences that are only matters of emphasis.

In spite of discrepant points of view and the difficulties of research it is possible to discern some agreement about the development of language and thought:

1. In the first three years of life these two functions operate independently.
2. Word meaning or, in more general terms, the referential function of symbols, is the link that joins language and thought.
3. Interpersonal communication is critical for conceptual development. Deaf children can acquire the more concrete concepts, but they are severely handicapped on abstract concepts as well as on silent reading. Similarities between objects can be emphasized for both deaf and normal children by pointing and by spatial grouping, but only normal children can profit by linguistic grouping in a sentence.
4. The contribution of syntactics to the development of thought is different from that of semantics. A word is perceived as a unit, after it has been segregated out of the flow of speech, and the class of

objects to which it refers is conceived as a unit; but a sentence is a linguistic structure that relates words to other words, restricts the meaning of words, suggests meaning, and makes assertions. As the child listens to his words, he also listens to his sentences—approximately as he listens to those of others—and the older child can agree or disagree with what he has said. Developmentally, grammar precedes logic; it supplies a framework within which the older child compares one assertion with another.

5. The development of language and thought is one of mutual facilitation, with occasional interference.

6. Since intellectual development is an interaction between language and thought, it can be retarded by suboptimal conditions for the development of either.

Thought and language are large, abstract categories and the above statements are large generalizations. Obviously, achievement of abstract concepts leans more heavily than achievement of concrete concepts on previous linguistic achievement. Depending on the specific concept and the specific environment, a child may acquire a word and use it conventionally in a sentence before he uses it efficiently in thought and he may use a concept in solving problems before he has a word for it. The specifics of the development of language and thought make large generalizations about this question especially hazardous.

Major Trends and Implications

When different people attempt to categorize the objects and events around them, they do not all start out the same way. Young children are impressed more by color than by form; older children and adults, with more interest in meaning, are impressed by representative features. Even at the same age categorical styles, such as biases toward perceptual or abstract attributes, distinguish different individuals. But the large, stable individual differences in concept achievement are correlated with abilities, either general intelligence or the more specific abilities known as general reasoning, inductive reasoning, and verbal comprehension. This intelligence difference is manifested in method as well as final performance; children of below-average ability plod along by associative learning while those above average are testing hypotheses.

As children grow, their cumulative cognitive development is manifested quantitatively by more use of abstract concepts, higher scores on vocabulary tests, and better performance in concept learning experiments. But many psychologists are also trying to chart this development qualitatively, by describing stages in the sequence of logical operations, representational functions, and language. Once the measurement wrinkles are ironed out, all idealized accounts of intellectual development are likely to be correlated with objective performance data over the years from two to twenty because any sequence that is intuitively satisfying to a well-informed observer will be reasonably accurate. No one would expect children to form abstract classes before concrete classes or to make good inferences about the relation between two concepts before they have mastered the single concepts. It is the methods of measurement, the nature of the stages, and the transitions from one to the next that have aroused interest and controversy. As in motor development, both maturation and experience are necessary, and a more mature child can profit from a small amount of experience in natural situations just as a less mature child can be pushed ahead by a heavy dose of planned experience.

Jean Piaget, leading the parade at present, has described the sensorimotor schemas of the first two years of life, the concrete-operational structures that develop from five to eight, and the formal abstract structures of the adolescent. He has stressed the orderly maturation of these structures, given adequate environmental support, while others have picked up instabilities in the hypothesized sequences and inconsistencies across structures of varying content.

The basic contrast in purpose produces a contrast in procedures. Piaget and his colleagues aim to describe cognitive structures at various levels of intellectual maturity and arrange their examination procedures to diagnose the child's natural achievements. Many American experimental psychologists, on the other hand, possessed by a genius for converting imported ideas into learning experiments, rearrange the procedures so that practice becomes the main independent variable. Systematic attempts to accelerate the development of conservation, seriation, addition of classes, and so on by planned practice are intended to clarify the nature of the stages and especially the processes by which each transition to another stage is achieved. And the encouraging results to date, obtained under optimal conditions, are beginning to stimulate changes in educational practice.

Achievement of formal operations includes the use of words and other symbols to represent reality. As Jerome Bruner tells this part of the story of cognitive development, iconic representation, making use of imagery, precedes verbal representation, and enactive or motoric representation precedes iconic. Distinguishing imaginal representation from verbal has always been troublesome, but the revival of interest in imagery (in several branches of psychology) will stimulate the invention of better methods for doing this. The methodological possibilities originate in the fundamental differences: iconic representation is extended in space and has some perceptual correspondence with reality; verbal representation is linear and has only a conventional correspondence with reality. The available evidence, from experiments with patterns of objects and lights and with words of perceptual and abstract meanings, indicates that iconic representation gives way to verbal during the transitional years six and seven.

Words start arguments. Debate continues on the question whether language depends on thought or thought depends on language. When the question refers to adult functions, however, extreme positions are untenable and moderate positions indistinguishable. Refering to intellectual development, the arguments are more empirical because abundant data can be arrayed to support intricate hypotheses about developmental interactions. The controversy over verbal facilitation of cognitive development has the same ingredients as the controversy over verbal facilitation of the learning of figure concepts in the laboratory.

During the first two or three years of life, language and thought develop independently. But evidence has been offered by Russian and American investigators to emphasize the role of language in controlling thought as well as action from these years onward. Piaget and his followers, on the other side, have published many observations and a few experiments to show that the development of the structures of thought is an autonomous development, prerequisite for the acquisition of language, which is genuinely flexible and adaptive rather than bound to superficial particulars. Bruner and his colleagues have made use of the recent insights of psycholinguistics, research on perception and language—skipping the verbal mediation evidence, however—and their own research with children to synthesize a developmental theory that unites speech to thought. When cognition is starting to take shape, the availability of words in the culture slants the organization toward certain classes of objects and relations between them. At the same time, sentences structure experience and allow the child to reflect upon his own assertions as well as the assertions of others. Thus the childish thought forms soon become embedded in the more mature forms, which are much more convenient and more efficiently represented by the language habits of the adult culture.

Research with deaf children supports the autonomous view of cognitive development, for concrete perceptual classes and relations, and at the same time underlines the severe handicap of the deaf in respect to the more abstract achievements that are normally acquired through verbal communication. Language is the best approach to the thought of another person, even though it is not the thought itself.

A distant view, from above the fields of battle, reveals parallel trends in the struggle to understand the cognitive development of children and the struggle to understand the laboratory acquisition of concepts. In both cases the simple maneuvers of the early researchers have become more complicated each year, because flexible human beings will do almost anything to achieve a stable cognition of changing objects and events. Certainly the biological maturation of the organism underlies all development. But once the child graduates from discrimination learning to the acceptance of cognitive organization as a personal problem, the psychologist's task of theory building undergoes a corresponding increase in complexity. All the individual's functional versatility can be trained on the problem: perceptual preferences, direction of attention, perceptual differentiation, verbal mediation, strategies of problem solving, and, penetrating at all levels, the linguistic offerings of the culture. This does not mean that the development is unlawful, but that the laws must be equally versatile.

CHAPTER **4**

THE SOLUTION
OF PROBLEMS

hinking characterizes human activity because problems characterize the human condition: a problem is a special kind of interaction between a person and his environment. Hence the first section provides an orientation to problem solving as a topic for psychological inquiry. Then we shall examine a few task variables, such as complexity, that have a widespread influence on the difficulty of problems in general. But what most people want to know about problem solving is the "inside story," the unseen operations by which solutions are reached. Hence the bulk of this chapter is allotted to problem-solving processes. The next chapter will take up training and individual differences in problem solving.

Orientation

As an attempt at definition, we may say that a problem arises when a person is motivated toward a goal and his first attempt to reach it is unrewarding. The motivation may be hunger, thirst, sex, achievement, fear, or any other external motive, of course, but it may also be a more subtle intellectual motivation, such as curiosity or interest in the problem for its own sake. Many people like to manipulate puzzles, words, or colors, just for the fun of it. And many creative thinkers believe that this intrinsic motivation, this love of the activity itself, is more effective than motivation toward an extrinsic goal.

Frequently the motivation for problem solving is aroused by a question. Where is Zambia? Why is intermittent reinforcement so effective? Who am I?

If the individual, motivated by the demands of the flesh or the spirit, reaches his goal on the first try, he has no problem. If he does not reach his goal but sees that he is progressing toward it, as when he is physically walking toward it or doing something that seems to be bringing it closer to him, he feels rewarded, and we may say again that he has no problem. But if his first response does not seem to do him any good and if his motivation persists, we say that he has a problem.

In what situations does this occur? Certainly not in those that are thoroughly familiar. In familiar or partially familiar situations, previously learned habits may transfer so well that the individual reaches his goal on the first try or believes that he is making progress toward it. It is in novel situations, of course, that problems arise. The individual does not know the path to the goal, the answer to the question, the computations to perform, the switch that turns on the light, or, in general, how to get what he wants. If the knowledge based on previous learning is inadequate and if the path to the goal is not directly perceived, the first response will not be rewarding; if the motivation keeps him going, we describe his activity as problem solving.

CHARACTERISTICS OF PROBLEM-SOLVING ACTIVITY

If problems and problem solving are defined in this way, then problem-solving behavior will be characterized, like other motivated behavior, by (1) goal orientation and continuity of action toward that goal; and (2) change of activity after the goal is attained. Special characteristics, in contrast to routine activity, are (3) intraindividual variability, because the individual makes diverse attempts at solution; (4) interindividual variability, because even the first attempts of different individuals are seldom the same; and (5) time required, because problem solving takes longer than the execution of a previously learned response pattern of comparable complexity. Furthermore, (6) the assumption of mediating activities is plausible. These mediating activities are assumed to be responsible for the longer time and the greater variability, and are particularly important for theoretical understanding. If we may judge from the contexts in which the words *thinking* and *thought* occur, they frequently refer to the time required ("I had to stop and think") and to the hypothesis of mediating activities. The introductory chapter noted that thought often has the meaning of mediation and often also of problem solving.

It follows from all this that the shift from routine activity to problem-solving activity may result from the individual's perception of a physical barrier between him and his goal or, in the case of an abstract problem, from knowledge that he is not progressing toward a solution. Similarly, the reverse shift from problem-solving activity back to routine activity may result from attainment of a tangible reward, like food or money, or from the knowledge that he has produced an acceptable solution. Certainly in solving many problems with well-defined solutions—such as anagrams and construction puzzles—the individual stops, not when he is given a tangible reward, but when he decides that he has reached the solution. To the individual who is inspired by intrinsic motivation, the knowledge that he has solved the problem is his reward. Until this occurs his attempts are unrewarding and, given adequate motivation, his problem-solving activity continues.

This broad definition of problem solving includes deductive reasoning, productive thinking, and judgment; but these activities show special characteristics that justify treatment in separate chapters. Concept attainment under certain conditions would also be embraced by this definition, but this class of problems too has special characteristics, noted in previous chapters.

PROBLEM SOLVING AND LEARNING

To say that problem solving differs from the performance of a previously learned response pattern is not to deny the importance of previous learning. Problem solving cannot be thoroughly understood without clarifying the contributions of such previous learning.

The old question about the relation between problem solving and learning is partly about the use of equivalent versus related but nonequivalent terms. The term *reasoning* has been used in the past as equivalent to problem solving in contrast to associative learning. This usage seems to be going out of style since *reasoning* is used today in a more technical sense (to be dealt with in Chapter 6). But in referring to tests of arithmetic achievement, it is appropriate to speak of arithmetic reasoning in contrast to computational skill, since the former partakes of the nature of genuine reasoning.

When the term *learning* is given the narrow meaning of a strengthening of associations through rewarded practice, then the question becomes one of differentiating problem solving from such associative learning. But when *learning* is broadly conceived to cover all modifications of behavior, problem solving must be included, and here the question becomes one of differentiating problem solving from all other forms of learning.

The terminological question has been avoided by referring to simple and complex behavior. This superficially peaceful answer may suffice for preliminary exploration, but it does not give problem solving the distinction it merits. Both problem solving and learning are usually involved in complex human behavior.

Actually, there is some broad agreement in the distinction between problem solving and learning. Duncan (1959) has pointed out that problem solving, and thinking when it means problem solving, differs from other forms of learning chiefly in the emphasis on the discovery of the correct response. Experiments directed toward the processes by which the correct response is produced the first time are different from experiments directed toward an increase with repetition in efficiency of performance.

Gagné's (1964) more detailed answer to this question is worth quoting here:

There is a striking difference which can perhaps best be summarized in this way: the learning situation for problem solving never includes performances which could, by simple summation, constitute the criterion performance. In conditioning and trial-and-error learning, the performance finally exhibited (blinking an eye, or tracing a path) occurs as a part of the learning situation. In verbal learning, the syllables or words to be learned are included in the learning situation. In concept learning, however, this is not always so, and there is consequently a resemblance to problem solving in this respect. . . . Although mediation experiments may present a concept during learning which is later a part of the criterion performance, many concept learning experiments do not use this procedure. Instead they require the S to respond with a performance scored in a way which was not directly given in learning (the stating of an abstraction such as "round" or "long and rectangular.") Similarly, the "solution" of the problem is not presented within the learning situation for problem solving. Concept formation and problem solving are *nonreproductive* types of learning [p. 311].

As a result of such agreement in emphasis on the first performance of the solution it is not necessary to review experiments in which the terminal performance or solution is practiced. But the dependence of a novel solution on previously learned facts, habits, concepts, skills, and other "subordinate capabilities," as Gagné calls them, is important for problem-solving research.

Problem solving depends on previous learning—and goes beyond it. The dependence on previous learning seems to be the easier part to study, and many investigators assume that the study of problem solving should therefore begin at this point. This assumption is historically understandable, but it may be the kind of historical trend that impedes progress. As one experienced researcher (T. Kendler, 1964a) has pointed out, the question whether the S-R unit, so useful in the study of simple learning, is suitable for the study of problem solving remains open. Considerable progress has been made, as we shall see, by taking previous learning for granted and concentrating on the critical variables in the present situation. And some of the investigations to be reviewed demonstrate how problem-solving research is contributing to a more thorough understanding of learning. As one would expect from the preceding chapters, it is the cognitive theorists who have insisted most strongly on differentiating problem solving, or thinking, from learning; while the association theorists maintain the hope that general principles of learning will explain problem solving also.

CLASSIFICATION OF PROBLEMS

Students of problem solving, overwhelmed by the variety of problems that man encounters, have often yearned for a tidy little classification system by which problems could be arranged and compared in orderly fashion. There is no standard system because the criteria of classification vary widely, depending on the purpose of the comparison. But there are a few differences between problems that researchers have found useful, at least in preliminary analysis.

Obviously problems differ in difficulty. The proportion of failures and the average solution time can easily be recorded, so that problems can be described as "easy," "difficult," and so on, for a specified sample of subjects.

Problems differ, at the outset, in the materials presented to the subjects. They may involve verbal, numerical, or spatial materials, that are concrete or abstract, representative or nonrepresentative, personal or impersonal, artificial or meaningful. Such distinctions are useful, but they are not permanent because the materials can often be converted to another form. Verbal problems are frequently transformed to numerical or spatial relations. Abstract problems become more concrete as algorithms or rules for solution are applied. The anagram problem, which is widely used in problem-solving research, appears to be one of rearranging a meaningless set of letters, but the research shows that the meaning of the solution word is one of the most important variables.

Problems can be described also in terms of the processes by which they are solved: judging which of two lines is longer obviously is a different process from writing a limerick. Some problems seem to depend largely on the collection of relevant information by exploratory procedures; others, such as reasoning problems, present all the information, so that the solution consists of fully grasping the information in view. Psychological processes are matters of inference, of course; all problem solving requires certain basic processes—such as a proper understanding of the instructions and full attention to the task—hence classification of problems in this way can only be tentative. But problems can be constructed so as to emphasize one process or another, as concept problems have emphasized the identification of the relevant attributes or of the rule of combination.

Factor analysis of the abilities required for solving problems offers still another method for comparing problems. This is a sophisticated statistical approach, which has resulted in abilities that represent materials and abilities that represent processes. The ideal is an equation of the form: $Y = aA + bB + cC$, showing that success on problem Y requires a certain amount, a, of ability A, plus a certain amount, b, of ability B, and so on. Some of the outcomes of this approach will be summarized at the end of Chapter 5.

DEPENDENT VARIABLES

In the analysis of problem solving many conditions have been manipulated and many theories proposed, but the basic data come from records of only a few dependent variables:

Frequency of solution is the most common dependent variable, and problems are usually chosen or manufactured so that one solution can be identified as the correct one. Occasionally, problems with two or three correct solutions have been presented and the frequency of each solution recorded. (Research on problems with many solutions that must be rated for quality is considered later, Chapter 7, under productive thinking.)

Time to solution, or latency, is also a common dependent variable. Typically, time and frequency of failure are well correlated; but there are occasional exceptions because some people emphasize accuracy, at the expense of time, more than others.

Number of moves is a feasible measure when the moves are observable and discrete.

Number of hints necessary for solution can be recorded if the problem is difficult. This is a rather unsatisfactory measure, however, because hints are not standard units and comparisons are uncertain.

Verbal statements of the subject are often recorded and are much employed by some experimenters. These consist most often of comments about difficulties, generalization of a principle, description of problem-solving methods, and explanations of phenomena.

Some complex problems permit the calculation of derived measures, such as the sequence of moves or the percentage of certain moves of theoretical interest, but the ones listed are the most common. The evidence obtained from each of these dependent variables will be illustrated in the pages to follow.

General Task Variables

If we look at the materials that face people in the form of problems, we see words, sentences, anagrams, numbers, pictures, blocks, strings, lights, switches, and many other kinds of materials. The problem content does make a difference in the problem-solving activities, as we shall see, but it is still possible to pick out a few variables that influence the difficulty of solution of many problems of varying content. These general task variables are interesting in their own right and also because they furnish the basic data needed for inferences about the problem-solving processes.

COMPLEXITY

Complex problems are more difficult, by and large, than simple problems, as anyone who has played Tick-tack-toe in three dimensions will agree. Complexity can be measured in terms of the amount of material presented, the number of specifications for the solution, the minimal number of moves to the solution, the amount of information to be processed, and probably also in other terms. We have already noted that the achievement of concepts is influenced by the number of relevant dimensions, which is a property of the solution, and also by the number of irrelevant dimensions, which is a property of the problem material presented. The difficulty of achieving disjunctive classes, as compared with conjunctive, lies in the specifications of the solution rather than in the material presented.

TABLE 4.1. NUMBER OF MOVES AND TIME OF SOLUTION
IN DISK-TRANSFER PROBLEMS

Number of Disks	Minimal Number of Moves	Mean Number of Moves	Mean Time in Seconds
2	3	3.5	7.0
3	7	24.3	93.5
4	15	182.7	557.0

From Cook (1937).

An experiment by Cook (1937) with the disk-transfer puzzle illustrates some of the relations. This task requires taking disks off one peg and putting them on another, using a third peg for storage, without putting a large disk on top of a small one. The complexity here can be stated in terms of the number of disks or the minimal number of moves, and by either measure difficulty increases at an increasing rate (see Table 4.1). As the number of disks increases, the necessity for planning moves increases, with a sharply increased possibility of mistakes and unnecessary moves. Similar results have been obtained with other problems that require planning of the moves before their outcome can be observed (Hayes, 1965).

Word problems can be constructed so that each word is a specification for the solution, in which case complexity can be measured in terms of the number of words (Johnson, Lincoln, and Hall, 1961). The example below illustrates a problem with four specifications:

flat	1. *map*
readable	2. *book*
descriptive	3. *label*
gummed	4. *paper*
	5. *globe*

The subject is asked to study the words on the left and be prepared to find a word for an object that meets all specifications. Then he turns to the list on the right and selects his answer. The time spent looking at each list is recorded separately. Fig. 4.1 shows, for problems of 3 to 11 specifications, the time spent studying the specifications, called preparation, and the time spent selecting one of the five solution words, as well as frequency of errors. Preparation time increases, almost as a linear function, as the number of specifications increases. One might expect an increasing function as more and more words must be remembered and organized, but it is likely that some of the additional specifications are redundant. The addition of words may actually add cues as well as restrictions and moderate the increase in memory load. Thus the increased complexity does not increase the difficulty as much as one might expect.

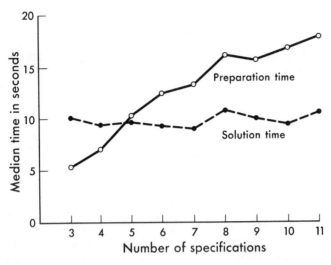

FIGURE 4.1. *Preparation time and solution time for problems with varying numbers of specifications for the solutions. From Johnson, Lincoln, and Hall (1961).*

To study the memory load more directly the experiment was repeated with unrelated digits rather than words. When 3 to 11 digits were presented in the same way, to be matched with alternative displays of digits, the time increased at an increasing rate. Log mean time was approximately linear with number of digits; since no organization was necessary and no cues were available, this logarithmic relation probably represents the memory load involved in grasping different numbers of items and retaining them long enough to match them with a display. But this is a special case. The effect of amount of material on solution of problems is generally more variable because of the intervention of other problem-solving processes.

The anagram achieved popularity as a parlor game long before psychologists borrowed it for research on problem solving. Charles IX of France, we are told, fell in love with Marie Touchet and brought her to his court because the letters of her name could be rearranged as *"Ie charme tout."* In psychological experiments the anagram consists of letters, such as *tigul*, to be rearranged to spell one word, *guilt*. From years of careful research, we know more about the anagram than about any other problem, yet only recently have the effects of the basic variable, the length of the anagram, been investigated.

One might expect that a small increase in the number of letters would produce a large increase in difficulty. Three letters can be arranged in only 6 different orders, but 4 letters can be arranged in 24, 5 letters in 120, and so on. And, in addition to the increase in number of possible letter orders, there is an increase in the numbers of letters to be held in memory and manipulated toward a solution. (Pencil and paper are usually not permitted.) Actually, it is not feasible to determine average solution time for long anagrams because some people would not finish within any reasonable time limit. Kaplan and Carvellas (1968) therefore took the approach of holding time constant and determining the number of anagrams of 3 to 10 letters solved in 100 seconds. Almost all the short anagrams, such as *gub* and *luge,* were solved within this limit, but only a fifth of the long ones, such as *ylhmcaelon.* The increase in number of letters did not produce the large increase in difficulty that one might expect from the increase in number of possible orders and the memory load, however. That is, an increase from 4 to 5 letters resulted in a drop in number solved within the time limit; but an increase from 8 to 9 letters resulted in a smaller, not a larger, drop. The relation between complexity and difficulty was more like that of the word problems described above and graphed in Fig. 4.1 than that of the disk-transfer problems shown in Table 4.1.

There are several reasons for this outcome. Longer words are more likely to include a repetition of letters, which cuts down the number of possible letter orders. But people do not solve long anagrams by rearranging letters at random, according to the laws of chance, anyway. They begin with likely hypotheses, usually with familiar combinations of three or four letters, and add others. Thus many rare letter combinations are eliminated from consideration. Also many of the longer words have familiar letter groups, such as *ness, ory,* and *tion,* that can be identified as suffixes and manipulated as units, and there are fewer long words than short words to think about as possible solutions.

If the elimination of distracting material makes some complex problems easier, the addition of unnecessary material can make certain problems more difficult. Most laboratory problems are constructed, like anagrams, so that all the items must be involved in the solution. In the case of complex verbal code puzzles, the addition of superfluous data, whether apparently relevant or irrelevant, slowed down the solution (Campbell, 1968). But the absolute amount of data was not so distracting as the probability of starting out on a wrong approach, which was increased by an increase in the amount of data in view. When the letter cues were arranged so that the probability of starting out on a wrong approach remained constant, an increase in complexity did not increase solution time.

The generalization that emerges from such experiments is that, while complex problems are usually more difficult than simple problems, the increase in difficulty is often moderated by nonrandom relations within the problem materials and by nonrandom proclivities among the people solving the problems. An increase in the amount of pertinent data may add useful cues for solution, but the probability of making a false start is increased by adding superfluous data.

FAMILIARITY

Familiarity with the materials in a problem influences the difficulty of solution as it influences rote learning and other tasks. Wilkins (1928) found that syllogisms written in familiar terms are somewhat easier for college students than syllogisms of the same logical form written in unfamiliar terms, such as *chigs* and *gorils,* or in terms of letters. Brownell and Stretch (1931) investigated this effect on the solution of arithmetic problems by writing the problems in four different versions. Form A was written in terms familiar to children—for example, children making posters. Form B used less familiar terms—for example, soldiers grooming cavalry horses. Form C used terms even less familiar. And Form D used artificial terms, for example, *shulahs* destroyed by *planti.* When problems made up in these four forms, otherwise equated, were given to fifth-grade children, the percentages of correct solutions were : A 64, B 58, C 57, D 51. These differences are not large, considering that the differences in familiarity are extreme. They indicate the same small effect of familiarity as that found by Wilkins. Such small effects are a result of familiarity with the terms of the problems, not with the problem-solving operations.

In the solution of anagrams the effect of familiarity is large, but this effect pertains to the solution word rather than to the anagram presented as a problem. We do not know, of course, which words are familiar to each individual subject; but words that appear frequently in ordinary reading matter must be more familiar on the average to a large group of subjects. Fortunately, millions of words of English text have been counted for other purposes (Thorndike and Lorge, 1944), and from these counts Mayzner and Tresselt (1958) selected words that are very frequent, such as *chair;* frequent, *beach;* infrequent, *cobra;* and very infrequent, *ghoul.* They suspected that letter order would be an important variable also, since the word *beach,* for example, can be made into an easy anagram by rearranging the letters *eachb,* and a hard one *hecba.* When they rearranged many such words as anagrams and gave them to college students to solve, the effects of the familiarity of the solution word, as well as letter order, were very large (see Table 4.2). Furthermore, if the anagrams have three solutions and the subjects must get all three, the solutions written first have the highest word frequency and those written last have the lowest (Johnson and Van Mondfrans, 1965).

This strong effect of word frequency, confirmed by other experiments, leads to intriguing theoretical speculations given later in this chapter.

TABLE 4.2. EFFECTS OF LETTER ORDER AND FREQUENCY
OF SOLUTION WORD ON MEAN ANAGRAM
SOLUTION TIME (in seconds)

	Easy Order	Hard Order
Very frequent	9.7	51.0
Frequent	7.3	55.7
Infrequent	20.5	116.5
Very infrequent	46.8	135.0

From Mayzner and Tresselt (1958).

ABSTRACTNESS

The question of abstractness in the achievement of certain concepts was discussed briefly in Chapter 2. The best examples of the effect of abstractness on the difficulty of problem solving come from mathematics. The meaning of the number 3 is more abstract than three objects in view, and an algebraic symbol, X, that refers to any number has more abstract significance than a specific number. It is generally true that problems involving highly abstract materials are harder than those that involve only concrete materials.

The abstractness, obviously, is a property of the referents of the symbols, not the symbols themselves. The letter X is no harder to perceive than the digit 3. Furthermore, as abstraction increases, we tend to use rules or algorithms for manipulating the symbols, ignoring temporarily their abstract significance. As an example, we learn an algorithm for finding the product of $X + Y$ and $X - Y$ that involves manipulating these symbols in such a way as to obtain a result that holds for the abstractions to which these terms refer. The use of the algorithm reduces, in practice, the abstractness of the problem.

We should note that abstractness and unfamiliarity often overlap: the more abstract words tend to be more unfamiliar. We should note also that when a problem is difficult, we often assert that it is abstract without considering the other task variables.

EMBEDDING

Embedding is a structural property of the material presented. It is thus most easily illustrated by visual patterns. The principle states that a pattern is hard to perceive when its outlines coincide with the outlines of another, more inclusive pattern. Two illustrations of this are given in Fig. 4.2; Fig. 4.3 contrasts complexity and embedding.

The effect of embedding on difficulty turns up also in the perception of typographical patterns. In the following line, the problem is to find an animal word:

a robe a robe a robe

FIGURE 4.2. Embedding. In each row the figure on the left is concealed in both figures on the right. After Gottschaldt (1926).

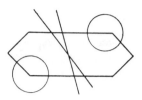 

FIGURE 4.3. *Complexity
without embedding.
From Johnson (1955).*

It is somewhat easier to find it in this line:

wofdulgibeark

and very easy to find it in this:

xyz bear stuvw.

The embedding is destroyed, of course, if the critical pattern is somehow made more salient. The effect of salience in the illustration below is analogous to the effect of salience in concept attainment.

a roBE A Robe a robe

When this principle is applied to abstract patterns, it is often confounded with familiarity and abstractness. Hence specifying the abstract pattern and the larger pattern in which it is embedded becomes a critical methodological issue. The processes by which such abstract structures are reorganized to facilitate cognition of the solution will be discussed in detail later.

SPECIFIC DIFFICULTIES

Much can be gained by identifying the general factors or conditions that influence the difficulty of problems. But nearly all research on problem solving turns up difficulties specific to a class of problems or even to a single problem. There are difficulties that are specific to anagram problems, to syllogism problems, to construction problems. The influence of anagram letter order on solution time, for example, is peculiar to the anagram problem. Anyone with experience in teaching others how to solve arithmetic problems, automobile repair problems, or personnel problems can identify specific sources of difficulty not covered by a few generalizations. This does not mean that the generalizations are not helpful; merely that they do not account for all the variations in difficulty.

Problem-Solving Processes
as Inferences from Behavior

The evidence assembled above on general task variables shows that we can learn something about problem solving by observing the input (the materials of the problem) and the output (the solutions) without speculating very much about the intervening activities. The yield from this input-output analysis soon approaches a limit, however; hence many psychologists infer problem-solving processes that mediate between input and output. The hypothetical processes vary from association of ideas to formal reasoning and complex strategies for processing information. But they are all similar in that they are attempts to answer dynamic questions: What is the subject doing? How does he solve the problem?

Problem-solving processes are dynamic constructs assumed to take place in time, in contrast to some other hypothetical constructs—such as cognitive structures, frames of reference, and abilities—that are static or latent. The aims of this type of theoretical endeavor are to describe such processes, to time them, to discover the conditions under which they occur, to determine the contribution of each to the solution of problems, and to record individual differences in their operation. Before reviewing the outcomes, we should scrutinize the methodology of this kind of theorizing.

A half century ago analysis of one's own thinking was a fashionable enterprise, based on the assumption that the thought processes would be revealed to introspection by an astute psychologist. Also fashionable was the "thinking aloud" method, which required the subject to report his thoughts while solving a problem and allowed the experimenter to classify the reports into intuitively reasonable categories labeled as thought processes. John Dewey's (1910) description of "how we think" was widely quoted. His purpose was to analyze reflective thinking for schoolteachers, before explaining how thought may be educated. It was a subjective analysis, based, he said, upon "descriptions of a number of extremely simple, but genuine, cases of reflective experience," which were turned in by students.

Upon examination, each instance reveals, more or less clearly, five logically distinct steps: (i) a felt difficulty; (ii) its location and definition; (iii) suggestion of possible solution; (iv) development by reasoning of the bearings of the suggestion; (v) further observation and experiment leading to its acceptance or rejection; that is, the conclusion of belief or disbelief [p. 72].

Another influential analysis of this kind, by Graham Wallas (1926), began with the preliminary assembly of information, called *preparation*. The second phase, called *incubation*, was described negatively. After the thinker has loaded himself up with the problem, he lays it away for a while to hatch, and, though he does not consciously notice anything, something must be going on because later, at some casual moment, new happy thoughts occur. The third phase, the occurrence of these happy thoughts or promising new leads, he named *illumination*. The final testing of the leads was called *verification*.

Such subjective analyses of thought processes succumbed in time to the increasing emphasis on objectivity. Current methodology treats such research as an attempt to demonstrate the consistency and utility of a coding system for interpreting subjective data (as in content analysis of protocols from projective tests or interviews) and seeks objective procedures as well. But the ancient fascination with "how the mind works" still persists in the modern, more critical efforts at the analysis of problem-solving activities.

The identification of one activity implies a differentation from other activities. The units of activity of interest in this theoretical endeavor—whether they are called processes, phases, operations, techniques, procedures, strategies, or methods—are smaller than the complete solution of a problem but larger than the single responses. Thus an inductive procedure is feasible if some regularities in the subject's activities can be identified and differentiated from others. If the subject begins by adjusting the light or fetching a ruler before manipulating the problem materials, we may describe the first activities as preparatory and, if desirable, time the preparatory process. In some problems, uncovering objects and looking for a malfunction has been differentiated from repair of the malfunction. When the problem is presented on paper, the reading of the problem can easily be separated from writing solutions. If the problem is a serial one, the sequence of moves may disclose regularities.

As to the temporal relations between intellectual processes, two extreme possibilities can readily be imagined: we can imagine two activities as completely different and completely separated in time so that, if we knew where to draw the line, we could divide them clearly. Alternatively, we can assume that the problem-solving episode is undifferentiated and that wherever a division is made, the activities on one side would be indistinguishable from those on the other. But everything we know about living organisms suggests that the most likely possibility is neither complete separation of the processes, illustrated visually as _____ _ _ _ _ , nor no separation (=======), but partial overlapping (————— _ _ _ _). Reading aloud, for example, includes a perceptual process and a vocalization process, and the first no doubt precedes the second, but the two overlap to the extent of the eye-voice span. Regressive eye movements, when the material is difficult, indicate an even greater overlap at times. Problem-solving processes, like physiological processes, are functionally interdependent in that the conclusion of one initiates the next; but the first does not always cease when the second commences.

In describing a factor analysis of the abilities required for solving problems, Merrifield, Guilford, Christensen, and Frick (1962) outlined five phases: preparation, analysis, production, verification, and reapplication. These are not viewed as clear-cut, successive steps; rather, "there is an approximation to temporal ordering with much overlapping of particular events [p. 2]." Preparation and analysis are the more cognitive phases; the motivation leads to mobilization and integration of stored information, examination of goal requirements, and the development of a search model, or alternative search models, for the control of production. The production of solutions involves both convergent and divergent abilities, according to this account. Verification, which has also been called evaluation and judgment, results in acceptance of a solution, or rejection followed by reapplication. But there is much variability in the solution of complex problems; evaluation, especially, may take place at any step. The purpose of this description was primarily to facilitate the construction of tests for the abilities involved in each process and to coordinate the results of factor analysis with general psychological theorizing.

The inductive procedure is best suited to activities that are at least partially observable. The deductive procedure begins with a hypothesis about covert, or mental, processes and attempts to arrange experiments to check it. The hypothesis may come from the investigator's introspection, from a mechanical analogy, from logic, from a mathematical model, from a computer model, or from principles of learning and perception. It may follow from a rational model of optimal procedure, such as a strategy of concept attainment.

Such a hypothesis leads to various facilitative and inhibitory arrangements of the conditions and training procedures, with predictions of frequency of success, time of solution, frequency of errors of different types, and other dependent measures. Occasionally, an adequate test of a hypothesis requires constructing a novel problem; for example, if we wish to isolate an information-seeking process for special study, we can devise "troubleshooting problems," in which repair is easy and the problem consists mostly of finding the trouble. For some purposes, questions about the problem have been printed on one side of a card and answers on the other side, so that as the subject turns over cards, his information-seeking activities can be recorded (Rimoldi, 1955; Rimoldi, Devane, and Haley, 1961). Several methods have been described (Johnson, 1960) for separating the preparation process from the remainder of a problem-solving episode and timing it. One of these exposes the problem materials serially by putting the illumination of different portions under the subject's control (some of the results of the serial exposure technique were mentioned earlier). Problems have also been constructed in the form of lights and switches so that all the subject's overt activities can be recorded in sequence (John, 1957).

The overall assumption behind these attempts to identify processes is that they will lead to more adequate descriptions of problem solving and more precise predictions than can be obtained from correlating observable antecedents with observable solution responses or from theories that assume only one process. A generalization that holds for one process may not hold for another, and procedures that improve one process may not improve another. All of these methods for inferring processes, and the logic behind them, will be illustrated in the experiments to be reviewed.

There is no standard catalog of problem-solving processes, but there is a large amount of experimental evidence. This can be organized and summarized around the following processes. *Associative mechanisms* have been called upon to explain problem solving as well as simple learning. But when the individual shifts from routine activity to problem solving, his activities come under the control of *problem-solving sets,* and experiments on set have considerably advanced the understanding of problem solving. From daily observation it is obvious that much of the time is spent in *seeking information,* after which the solution often necessitates *representing and transforming the data.* Experimental evidence on *organizing and reorganizing cognitive structures* is abundant and enlightening. We must also consider *the judgment process in problem solving.* A more recent endeavor which promises rich rewards but has not yet been fully integrated with the others is the generation of *problem-solving processes from computer simulation.* A review of the research under these seven headings follows.

Associative Mechanisms

The stimulus-response behaviorists avoid describing behavior in terms of logical operations as they avoid identifying psychological processes from introspective evidence. Facts that others have interpreted as evidence of the control of responses by some hypothetical higher process have been interpreted by behaviorists in terms of associations and chains of associations. Complex associative mechanisms have the same dynamic role in association theories of problem solving as problem-solving processes, in that they are intended to account for the relative difficulty of problems, sequences of problem-solving activities over time, types of errors, and so on; but the associative mechanisms are supposed to operate according to laws of association derived from simpler situations.

RESPONSE HIERARCHIES

The associative interpretation of problem solving often calls upon the principle of a *response hierarchy,* a class of responses elicited by one stimulus. This principle was originally developed to account for maze learning by rats, but its most convincing applications today are in the field of verbal performance, as in the perception of briefly exposed words and the solution of anagrams. Examining the effect of frequency on anagram solution raises a question that at first seems unanswerable: How can the time of solution of a problem be influenced by a characteristic of a solution word that is not known until the moment the problem is solved? The explanation offered by Mayzner and Tresselt (1958) invoked a hierarchy of implicit verbal responses. If the anagram is considered a stimulus, any one of the many words in the subject's response repertoire, that is, his vocabulary, could be an implicit response or attempt at solution. But words, considered as responses, do not all have the same response strength. Some words have been more thoroughly learned than others, in many situations, and thus are more readily elicited as associations to verbal stimuli in many situations. The relevant response hierarchy consists of words that are potential solutions, hypothetically ranked in order of response strength. To avoid confusion, it should be noted that the strength of the association between a response word and a specific stimulus word is not considered here because the stimulus is only an anagram.

Since response strength depends on frequency of occurrence of the words in the past, high-frequency words will be elicited first, then words of lower frequency. Thus, if the correct solution is a high-frequency word, the problem will be solved quickly. If the solution is a low-frequency word, high-frequency words will be evoked first, the correct low-frequency word will be evoked later, and solution time will be longer. This is an especially convincing explanation for the solution of anagrams because frequency tables supply independent data on frequency and generate the predictions that Mayzner and Tresselt confirmed. Note that nothing is assumed about any separate process controlling the responses; the sequence of responses is simply a consequence of variations in their strength.

The same theory about previously learned associations can be applied to pairs of letters, known as *digrams*. Some digrams occur frequently in English, so that anyone who reads has had considerable exposure to them; others, however, are rare. Digrams were first counted by cryptanalysts as an aid to deciphering coded messages, but recently psychologists have made more extensive counts as an aid to research on verbal performance. To take some examples, the digram *hi* is very common, while *ih* is uncommon; another pair of high frequency is *ca*, in contrast to the infrequent *rc*. Thus a five-letter word may consist of four digrams of high frequency while another may consist of four digrams of low frequency. Except for very easy anagrams that are reorganized wholisticly as soon as the experimenter can start and stop his watch, anagrams are usually solved by manipulating combinations of two, or perhaps three, letters. Mayzner and Tresselt (1962) assumed, according to the principle of the response hierarchy, that digrams of high frequency will be elicited first and therefore that words consisting of high-frequency digrams will be solved more rapidly than comparable words consisting of low-frequency digrams. An appropriate experiment found the expected difference in solution times, though this effect was much smaller than the effect of word frequency.

The difficulty of problems, according to the principle of the response hierarchy, is due to interference from the incorrect responses. Considering a problem as a stimulus, if incorrect responses have high associative strength to the problem, they are produced first and so delay the production of the correct response. It follows that anagrams without such interferences will be relatively easy, and Ronning (1965) applied this principle to generate a "ruleout" factor that predicts the difficulty of anagrams. There are many combinations of letters that do not appear as the beginnings of English words. Furthermore, vowels are not as common as consonants at the beginning of a word. Any well-read problem solver is likely to rule out such beginnings. It is true that the 5 letters of the anagram *higlt* can be arranged in 120 different orders, but such combinations as *hg*, *hl*, *tg*, and *thl* can be ruled out and do not delay the evocation of the correct response. In fact 90 of the 120 permutations of these 5 letters can be ruled out. Thus this particular anagram would be easy, while one with few letter combinations that can be ruled out would be harder. An experiment demonstrated that this "ruleout" factor did influence the solution of both high-frequency and low-frequency words. Obviously, the ruleout factor overlaps other factors, such as digram frequency, but when some of these complications were controlled, the ruleout effect was still substantial (Gribben, 1970).

There is a more direct way to increase the response strength of a word and make it readily available for problem solving. The frequency counts give an index of exposure to different words at unknown occasions in the past, but the experimenter can increase exposure by presenting the solution words just before presenting the anagrams. Wiggins (1956) did this by choosing anagrams with two alternative solutions, one of which was a more frequent solution than the other. As an example, under ordinary conditions 90 percent of the solutions to *irgn* were *ring* and only 10 percent were *grin*. But for subjects who studied a list of the infrequent solution words just before working the anagrams, the frequencies of the alternative solutions were reversed. This is an illustration of how a little experience can promote a word of low rank, at least temporarily, to the top of the hierarchy.

More subtle ways of altering the availability of words for use in problem solving are suggested by hypotheses about word association. Consider the anagram *irach*. Suppose, instead of the solution word, a common associate of the solution word, *table*, is presented just before problem solving. The hypothesis is that such exposure of a common associate will raise the availability of the solution word, though not as much as exposure of the solution word itself. Dominowski and Ekstrand (1967) found that the mean solution time for a series of anagrams after priming with the actual solution words was 1.95 seconds, and after priming with words frequently associated with the solution words, 7.25 seconds. These means are to be compared with a mean of 31.00 seconds for a control group lacking any priming. For other subjects, who expected that the words of the preceding list were relevant when they were not, the comparable mean was 54.35 seconds.

Since recent learning of words has such a strong influence on anagram difficulty, even the order in which the words are learned might have an effect. If the series of words is learned in a fixed order, perhaps they will be recalled in that order; then the anagrams that are solved by the first words of the series will be solved quickly and those solved by the last words slowly. Davis and Manske (1968) tried out this hypothesis with ten-letter anagrams but did not find the expected effect. What they found instead was the well-known serial position effect. When a series of words is memorized in a fixed order, the first and last sections of the series are learned quickly, and the middle section is the last to be learned. When the series of words was followed by anagram solution, the words in the middle of the series were the hardest to learn, as usual, and the anagrams constructed from these words the hardest to solve.

We have long known that previous learning contributes to problem solving in a general way, but in these experiments the facilitation, and also the interference, has been specified with some precision.

INTEGRATION OF BEHAVIOR SEGMENTS

The solution to an anagram problem is a word from the subject's response repertoire; yet the solution to many other problems is a response, or pattern of responses, that the subject has not previously performed. Years ago the classic demonstrations by Gestalt psychologists, that apes could reach a banana in a new way by putting two sticks together and that many animals

readily take a detour to a goal when necessary, challenged associative interpretations based on previous learning. Clark Hull (1935) therefore undertook to explain such novel accomplishments by postulating mediating associative mechanisms that have the role of integrating separately learned
behavior segments. Although Hull's integrative mechanisms were derived from
nonhuman behavior, they were intended to apply generally and can be illustrated most conveniently by the behavior of children solving problems.

The problem in one experiment by Kendler and Kendler (1956) was to
attain a goal, specifically an attractive toy hidden at G. If a child learns to
pull string B to get G and to pull a different string A to get a subgoal at B,
will he combine these components on a later occasion and pull A to get G?
The associative interpretation states that when B is performed to get G, B is
reinforced and in turn acquires some secondary reinforcing value. Thus
when A is performed to get B, this segment is secondarily reinforced. On a
later occasion, the stimulus A elicits implicit responses that have been indirectly associated with the goal G. In other words, the B component acts
as a mediator linking A with G.

Any child will pull a string, of course, so Kendler and Kendler introduced
another string X, tied to a subgoal Y, which was comparable to B, but had
not been associated with the major goal, the attractive toy G. The test, then,
was the frequency of choices of string A over string X. But this was not an
experiment in learning, by rewarded practice, to pull one string rather than
another. The question was whether the child, having learned two separate
habits, would put them together and pull the correct string on the first test
trial.

When this experiment was carried out with 128 children, three and four
years old, 72 percent succeeded in solving the problem, as compared with
47 percent of control groups without experience with the B-G component. As
one might expect, older children, of eight and ten, were able to make the
necessary integration of habits better than young children (Kendler and
Kendler, 1962). The weakness in this theory is the absence of a predicted
order effect. Since the primary reinforcement was at G, the theory predicts
that the optimal order would be to learn B-G first, then A-B. But in two
experiments (Kendler and Kendler, 1956; Kendler 1961), no such order effect
appeared.

Problem solving can be analyzed in terms of these associative mechanisms
and young children can integrate the separate habits in experiments suggested by the analysis. The secondary prediction suggested by the analysis
was not confirmed, however, hence there is much that the mechanisms of
associative learning leave unexplained, at least for the present. But the effects
of previous learning often show up in unexpected ways. When Anthony
(1966) attempted to discover whether adults, given difficult problems in the
form of incomplete maps resembling mazes on paper, would work forward
toward the goal or backward from the goal, he found that they would go
either way, depending on which direction had been effective on preceding
problems.

Problem-Solving Sets

Motives can be likened to general policies, varying in strength and pertinence, while the set is analogous to the executive manager, guiding an organism moment by moment. The set for a simple performance, as in a reaction time or a word association experiment, can be considered a readiness to make a specified response to a specified stimulus. Thus the set generated by reading the first half of a sentence controls the interpretation of the last half. A set to solve a problem is more complicated, to be sure, but it still can be considered a readiness for some specified activity. One side of the set is stimulus preparation, or attention; the other is response preparation, and either side may be emphasized for experimental purposes. The response may be a complex pattern prepared and performed as a unit, and the stimulus an abstract attribute picked out of a variegated display; but the essence of the concept of set is that the readiness to make the response to the stimulus anticipates the appearance of that stimulus.

The set itself may be considered an activity or process, but it is an activity of short duration, preparatory to some other activity. The set alone does not solve any problems. Hence two explanations are required: how the set is established, and how it controls subsequent activity. Most of the early introspective analyses of the thought processes included a preparatory process, often under the name of determining tendency, and most modern behavior theories include some short-term mechanism or chain of mechanisms to control the final responses, though the names for these constructs vary. Since the term *set* has been widely used in relevant experiments on problem solving and seems to be generally understood, at present this seems as good as any.

CONDITIONS AND EFFECTS OF SET

If motives supply the long-term dynamics of our lives, sets function as the short-term transmission mechanisms, geared to immediate stimuli and responses. When motives are various and the offerings of the environment exciting, whatever unity and continuity can be observed in behavior are attributed to the set. A central adjustment is prepared so that, of all the activities the organism is capable of, some are facilitated and others inhibited or delayed. Four conditions are particularly important for the activation of problem-solving sets.

In the first place, of all the motives for solving problems most do not supply much control of activity. In problem-solving experiments, for example, the subject simply agrees to cooperate with the experimenter. The social motives are the operative ones, but their effects are quite general.

Secondly, within a favorable motivational background sets are often activated by instructions. The control of one human being's activity by instructions from another human being is a remarkable effect that no theory of psychology can overlook. Instructions do more than communicate facts and request people to start and stop; they prepare them for perception and for action. These instructions may be rather general: "Your task is to construct words from these anagrams." Or they may be more specific: "Each anagram must be rearranged to form the name of a common animal." A large part of the achievements of experimental psychology is built on the ability of human beings to prepare themselves in advance, when requested, so that they can respond optimally when the anticipated event occurs.

The effects of interpersonal relations on problem solving are not limited to explicit instructions. The subject of an experiment may pick up cues from the experimenter's voice, or his gaze, or a hand movement that leads him to be prepared for speed rather than accuracy, or for one type of solution rather than another. Many findings of differences in results from different experimenters are probably due to the sets aroused by these subtle variables or by the subject's own perception of the demands of the situation (Orne, 1962). Thus taboo words are not offered as anagram solutions under ordinary social conditions, although they do emerge under more permissive conditions.

Since sets function at an intermediate level, between motives and actions, the effects of motives may override the effects of instructions. Ask someone who is nauseated to act hungry or to see food in ambiguous pictures, and he may try and fail, or he may not try. Many curious results have been obtained in the laboratory because people are loath to adopt sets that conflict with their ulterior motives.

Thirdly, sets are influenced, like other activities, by previous learning. When a person faces a problem that looks familiar, he usually reinstates a set to approach it as he approached similar problems in the past.

Fourthly, it is the short-term effects of practice—in the form of a training series of problems immediately preceding a test series—that have been most frequently studied in experiments on set. A brief series of problems can narrow the set so that, when another problem is presented, the solution will be quick and invariant.

Thus the set is influenced by several antecedent conditions. But once established, it integrates and channels the individual's efforts so that certain momentary potentialities and limitations can be observed. When the individual has been prepared, by appropriate instructions and practice, he can attend to sounds, words, or numbers optimally, but his attention span is still not unlimited. Seven items are commonly cited as the number the average adult can retain when the task is merely to listen and recall; but when the items are to be retained and related so as to solve a problem, the limit is probably lower.

The set is limited on the perceptual side in that if a subject is prepared to perceive the shapes of objects, he is less likely to perceive their colors. It is limited on the response side in that if a subject is set to add, subtraction will take him somewhat longer. Thus the effects of a set may be facilitative or inhibitory. If the experimenter tells the subject to look for shapes and the task requires finding shapes, the set instigated by the instructions will be helpful. If, however, the task requires finding colors, the shape instructions will be detrimental. Likewise, a series of arithmetic problems easily solved by addition engenders a set to add, which will be helpful if the next problem can be solved by addition but not if it must be solved by subtraction. It follows that successful problem solving often requires shifting the set.

A few representative experiments will serve to illustrate how problem-solving sets are activated and how they influence solutions.

ILLUSTRATIVE EXPERIMENTS

The classical experiments were designed by Rees and Israel (1935) to demonstrate the importance of the set in problem solving by the use of ambiguous anagrams with two solutions. They demonstrated that an appropriate set could be established by direct instructions. Subjects told to construct words of a certain category, such as nature words, solved more anagrams this way than control subjects. They also demonstrated that a set can be built up by a series of problems with solutions in the same category. Subjects who solved a block of anagrams by nature words solved more of the next block by nature words than control subjects. Rees and Israel were able to show the effect of a letter-order set as well. To take one example, *lecam* can be changed to camel by starting with the middle letter, and subjects who solved a block of anagrams by changing letters in this order readily solved the next block by the same procedure. Later experiments have verified these results, for both the category set and the letter-order set (Johnson, 1966).

Luchins (1942) went a step further to illustrate the detrimental effects of a set. He had his subjects do a series of arithmetic problems, with three imaginary jars of water, that could be easily solved by two subtraction operations, then gave them two ambiguous problems that could be solved by the same procedure or by only one subtraction. Use of the longer procedure was considered evidence that the set established on the first series of problems had persisted, and most of Luchins's subjects did in fact use the longer procedure although control groups starting with these ambiguous problems did not do so at all. Luchins also included a problem that could not be solved by the longer procedure but could be easily solved by the short one. The majority of the subjects failed to solve this critical problem in the time allowed, though there were few failures in control groups that had this problem first. Luchins also increased the amount of practice with the first procedure and

FIGURE 4.4. *Arrangement of letters for study of eye movements during solution of anagrams. The letters can be rearranged in order 34521, using the numbering system shown at the left, to form the solution word. From Kaplan and Schoenfeld (1966).*

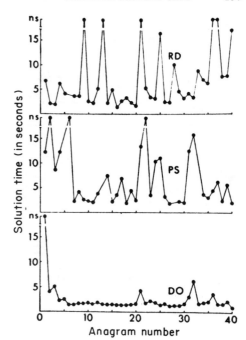

FIGURE 4.5. Solution time on successive anagrams for three subjects; ns indicates no solution. The first 20 anagrams were solvable by the rule 34521, the next 10 by the rule 31245, and the last 10 by the rule 52143. From Kaplan and Schoenfeld (1966).

found that this strengthened the set and increased the number of failures on the critical problems. Later experiments have confirmed these findings.

Other experiments to be mentioned below have allowed subjects to manipulate light switches, turn cards, remove covers, and so forth, in order that problem-solving sets and other processes can be inferred from observable information-seeking movements. The serial exposure procedure for studying concept attainment (described on page 56) was designed to time performance on a sequence of problems as the set developed and also the shift to a new set. The experiment demonstrated an inhibitory effect on the cognitive side: once the set to attend to the shape dimension was established, the texture dimension was ignored. Another outcome was the identification and timing of four problem-solving operations in sequence: the first formulation of the problem; the unsuccessful search for a solution to match this formulation; switchback and reformulation; and the unsuccessful search for a solution to match the second formulation.

An ingenious experiment by Kaplan and Schoenfeld (1966) took a more direct approach by photographing eye movements during problem solving. The letter-order set for solving anagrams is convenient here because the letters can be separated and fixation of the eyes on each letter recorded. The letters were spaced out as in Fig. 4.4. One can begin with the middle letter, move to the lower left corner, and so on, to make *brick*. The first 20 anagrams were soluble by one order, the next 10 by another order, and the next 10 by another. The lowest graph in Fig. 4.5 shows that solution time for 1 subject dropped rapidly as he did the first few anagrams and rose

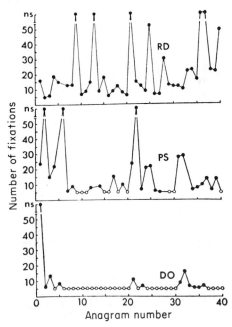

FIGURE 4.6. Number of fixations per anagram for subjects of Fig. 4.5. The open circles indicate solutions reached after only five fixations in the order of the rule. From Kaplan and Schoenfeld (1966).

temporarily when the order was changed for problems 21 and 31. The lowest graph in Fig 4.6 shows that the drop in variability of eye movements for this subject paralleled the drop in solution time as the letter-order set developed. The other 2 subjects did not adopt the set so readily. Consequently, their solution times were longer and their eye movements variable, but the same parallelism between eye movements and solution times can be seen in the records.

These experiments with various problems demonstrate that sets are easily established and have predictable consequences on solution time, errors, information-seeking movements, and eye movements. In this respect, problem solving is similar to many other activities of living organisms. Even a sneeze requires a preparatory inspiration. Thus the concept of set in problem solving illustrates the continuity between intellectual activities and simpler activities for which a preparatory adjustment can be identified. It is not surprising that set is a favorite concept of American functionalism (Woodworth, 1937).

THEORETICAL ANALYSES

Fig. 4.7 has been prepared to clarify some research designs and attempts at theoretical interpretation. The column at the left illustrates one design. Within a certain laboratory atmosphere, general instructions from experimenter to subject establish a set to solve problems, for instance, make words out of anagrams. Then, as a result of brief practice with easy Alpha problems, the subject establishes a set to use the Alpha method, that is, to arrange the letters in a certain order, so time and variability decrease. Since we are assuming that the subject has one set at a time, we do not speak of this set as different from the general set with which he began, but we say that this general set has been narrowed and made more specific. There is no incompatibility between preparing to solve anagram problems and preparing to solve anagram problems by the Alpha method.

It would not be correct to say that the subject learns new responses; he already knows how to add and subtract, to rearrange letters, and to spell words. What is carried over from the earlier problems in a series to the later ones is the adjustment; trial and error has been eliminated and the subject looks directly for the critical aspects of the materials presented. When he perceives them, he quickly makes the manipulations he is prepared to make. The observable reduction in solution time and invariability of problem-solving attempts, in comparison with a control group of the same background and the same general set who have not had the training series, is the evidence for assuming that a set has developed. The test series might also be a series of ambiguous problems, soluble by either the Alpha or Beta method, and another group would be given a training series of Beta problems. Then the dependent variable would be frequency of use of Alpha and Beta methods on the ambiguous test problems.

The column at the right of Fig. 4.7 illustrates another design. Instead of establishing a general set by instructions and narrowing it by specific training, a specific set is established at the beginning by specific instruc-

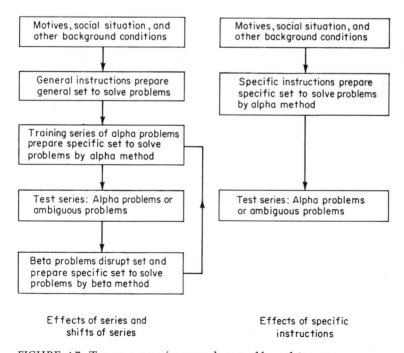

FIGURE 4.7. *Two sequences for research on problem-solving sets.*

tions. The dependent variable may be solution time or frequency of solution of ambiguous problems by the alternative methods. As far as the observable evidence indicates, it is the same set whether developed by general instructions and a training series or by specific instructions.

In order to study shifts of set, many experiments have included a different series of problems for which the first set is not appropriate. When a subject set for solving Alpha problems by the Alpha method encounters Beta problems, he fails, or he shifts to the Beta method. Typically this set, while not incompatible with the general set to solve problems, is incompatible with the previously practiced specific set. Hence development of the new set implies cancellation of the old, and questions of the interfering effects of previous training arise. The new set can be instigated also, of course, by new instructions.

EFFECTS OF THE TRAINING SERIES

Although the training series usually requires only 15 minutes or so, the acquisition of a problem-solving set is an obvious opportunity for testing various theories of learning. Maltzman and Morrisett (1952) looked at the development of a set for solving anagrams from the point of view of S-R learning theory and tried to test some quantitative predictions. The growth of habit strength as a function of practice is negatively accelerated; practice produces improvement in the lower part of the learning curve faster than in the top part. This leads to the prediction that a difference in habit strength will develop more rapidly between two weak habits, otherwise equal, than between two strong habits. In their first experiment, a strong habit strength group received 15 eating-set anagrams and 15 nature-set anagrams in random order before solving 10 test anagrams. A weak habit strength group received irrelevant anagrams, then 2 eating-set and 2 nature-set anagrams before the 10 test anagrams. The test anagrams were all eating-set anagrams for half the subjects in each group and all nature-set anagrams for the other half; and the critical measure was the frequency of appropriate set solutions. The prediction from the theory was that the weak habit strength group would learn the new set faster, and the confirmation of this prediction supported the assumption that the set can be treated as a complex habit acquired in the laboratory situation.

The effects of the experimenter's instructions cannot be separated completely from the effects of a training series because as soon as the subject begins to follow instructions, training effects begin to cumulate. Training effects cannot be completely separated from the effects of instructions either, because some general instructions always precede the training series as part of the subject's introduction to the experiment. But Maltzman and Morrisett (1953) were able to study the effects of specific instructions added to the effects of a training series. Instructions to "look for a particular order" given just before the training series did increase the frequency of letter-set solutions above that produced by the training series alone. Similar instructions given just before the test series also increased the frequency of set solutions (Maltzman, Eisman, Brooks, and Smith, 1956). Apparently, instructions have an effect on the set that cannot be replaced by the growth of habit strength during a training series; hence the experimenters had to conclude that the effects of instructions on the set are not completely explained by associative learning.

Safren (1962) applied a word association theory, coming from research on free recall, to the development of a set to solve anagrams. She began by making up lists of 6 words of maximal interitem associative strength, such as *milk, cream, sugar, coffee, sweet,* and *drink.* The hypothesis was that a series of anagrams so constructed will be easy, because when 1 solution word is attained, its associations facilitate recall of the solution word to the next anagram, and then the associations of these 2 words further facilitate recall of the solution to the next, and so on. Six such lists were used, and the same 36 anagrams were also used in 6 unorganized lists. As expected, there was a gradual reduction in median solution time for the group who did the organized anagrams but not for the group who did the same anagrams without the interitem facilitation. Overall, the median solution time for the unorganized lists was 12.2 seconds, and for the organized lists, 7.4 seconds.

Another group in the Safren experiment received special instructions giving the labels of organized lists, such as *beverages,* and for these the median solution time was 2.8 seconds. As noted above, Maltzman and Morrisett found a parallel effect of instructions in addition to the effect of a training series. The large effect of the labels suggests that each one facilitates immediate recall of a cluster or a class of solution words. This word association theory has the virtue of describing a specific mechanism for the development of a set for solving anagrams, but the specificity limits it to the category set.

The experiments on the development of problem-solving sets are parallel in some respects to experiments on the acquisition of concepts and principles. Successive problems present apparent differences and abstract similarities, and as the subject proceeds, he perceives the similarities easily and executes the common response quickly. This parallel recalls the controversy between continuous and discontinuous conceptions of concept learning discussed in a previous chapter, and suggests a methodological criticism. The experiments given above have reported group data only. The possibility of discontinuity in the individual acquisition curves, which is the most interesting alternative to incremental associative learning, is obscured by averaging. Stellwagen (1968) therefore plotted the development of a category set for anagrams by following the procedures described in Chapter 2. She gave a series of 17 anagrams, constructed from 5-letter food words, to 40 subjects in different orders. When the solution times were averaged in the usual way, the usual gradual decrease was evident, suggesting cumulative learning. But when the solution times were combined before and after each subject's last long solution time, a discontinuity was apparent, as in Fig. 4.8, suggesting that the different subjects "caught on" at different points in the series, after which they solved all problems quickly. The usual large variation in solu-

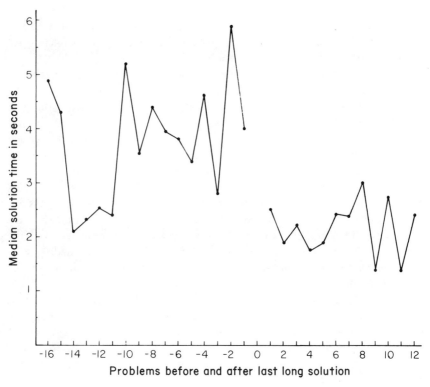

FIGURE 4.8. *Solution times for a series of anagrams arranged to show evidence of discontinuity.*

tion times before the decrease makes the demonstration of discontinuity less than completely convincing, but the results do suggest an alternative to the customary interpretation in terms of cumulative associative learning.

It is not necessarily the best start to treat the development of a set as the acquisition of something; something is lost also. Rather, the development of a problem-solving set should be regarded as a progressive sharpening of the general set communicated by the instructions. Instructions to look for a letter order or to look for a class of words sharpen the set somewhat, while instructions giving the actual letter order or the category of solution words sharpen it more specifically. This view is not incompatible with the view of a set as a complex habit if we consider it a temporary habit, easily turned on and off.

The nature of the motivation for solving problems and the reinforcement of a problem-solving set must then be examined. Whatever the motivation that initiates problem solving, when the subject succeeds by one method he is likely to continue to use that method. The problems that have been used in these experiments—anagrams, little arithmetic problems, and figure concept problems—have been chosen by the experimenters because the subjects can recognize a solution as soon as they attain one and stop work. It is not necessary to give points or toys or pieces of candy; the reinforcement is cognitive in that the subject knows he has or has not succeeded. The fact that there might be an alternative solution, even a shorter one, does not influence the subject unless he knows it.

SHIFTING SET

Since failure to solve a problem is often attributed to rigidity, shifting from one set to another has attracted considerable experimental attention. Schroder and Rotter (1952) approached this rigidity question from a social learning theory that emphasizes the subject's expectations. "Under what conditions does an individual enter a problem situation with an expectancy that a single behavior will lead to reinforcement and under what conditions will he expect that there may be more than one way of reaching the goal [p. 141]?" To study this they devised training series which, according to their hypothesis, would build up different expectancies about alternative paths to the goal. Each problem consisted of six designs to be grouped into three pairs, and the training series were arranged so that some subjects had practice in grouping by one attribute (form) and others various kinds of practice that encouraged grouping by one of two attributes alternatively (form or color). Performance of the test series, which required shifting from one method of grouping to another, showed clearly that those training sequences that forced shifting and built up expectancies for alternative routes to the goal facilitated shifting on later test problems. Similar results were obtained by Gardner and Runquist (1958) with the Luchins arithmetic problems, but they preferred the language of simple associative learning so they analyzed the situation in terms of competing responses rather than alternative expectancies.

Another variable that could influence readiness to shift is the amount of effort invested in the practiced method. Knight (1963) gave his subjects only one arithmetic problem for training, but one group had round numbers easy to add and subtract while the other group had to go through the same arithmetic operations with awkward three-place numbers. Those who worked harder on the first problem were more reluctant to shift to other feasible procedures and, when forced to do so, shifted as little as possible. This effort variable may be an alternative interpretation for the effects of differences in amount of practice.

We have seen that theoretical speculations about sets have followed the theoretical fashions of the time; hence we may next anticipate a cognitive type of theorizing. The reinforcement for acquisition of the set during a training series could be the subject's knowledge that he has attained the right solution. The problems in the experiments above have solutions that are immediately recognized as such by the subjects; no external confirmation by the experimenter is needed. When the subject encounters a different type of problem in a test series, he faces a cognitive conflict in that the problem does not fit his expectations. If he applies the practiced method, he will recognize the outcome as a failure. It could be this mismatch between what he perceives and what he is set for that forces him to change his set. Such an interpretation offers a modern alternative to the interpretation in terms of competing responses, and would predict discontinuity in solution times for a series of simple problems.

THEORETICAL DIFFERENTIATIONS

If the notion of a problem-solving set is to have any precise meaning, it must be differentiated from some other, related notions. The set is not the response, and the development of a set is not the same as the acquisition of the component response patterns, the writing, spelling, adding, and subtracting. These have been learned at some time in the past, not in five minutes of practice with seven problems. What is developed is the readiness to execute one or another of the alternative patterns when appropriate.

The set is not the same as attention. The individual does not look at the most salient or the most intense stimuli in the field of view; he may do so at first, but the concept of set implies reduction of this trial-and-error search. The property of attention that is especially relevant to problem solving is selection. One cannot attend to everything, and, once a set is established, one does not attend to as much as he can. In the experiments on figure concept problems, for example, after the subjects were set to conceptualize the figures in terms of shape, they did not attend to texture and had, in fact, to switch back to perceive texture similarities.

The essence of the set is a prepared adjustment. In the simple reaction time experiment, when perception of the signal and execution of the response are easy, it is obvious that the critical feature of the set is the neuromuscular readiness. In the word association experiment, it is obvious that the set somehow prepares memory or recall so that when the stimulus word is heard, an appropriate response word occurs quickly. In problem-solving experiments, where the problem situation is complex and several alternative response patterns are possible, establishment of the set means that the critical features of the situation have been identified (as a result of instructions and perhaps of a training series) and a response pattern integrated, so that the subject is prepared to respond quickly, without attending to other possibilities, when another problem is presented. Putting the hyphens in situation-and-goal set, as Woodworth did (1937), emphasizes the fact that the coordination between the response and the critical features of the situation is prepared in advance.

The difficulty in theorizing about set in conventional terms is that it can be established by instructions as well as by training. There are certain advantages in trying to fit problem-solving activities into the theoretical frameworks that have been useful in research on animal learning and on human learning of simple tasks, just as there are advantages in putting problem solving into the cognitive framework. But there are disadvantages also, and these show up prominently when we come to the effects of interpersonal communication on problem solving. Telling a college student how to avoid errors on a pursuit rotor task or how to memorize nonsense syllables has only limited value, but telling him the relevant attributes in a concept problem or the class of words that are solutions to anagrams reduces the solution time drastically. One sentence of instructions might be equated with 20 minutes of practice. The capacity of the literate, socialized person to prepare a complex adjustment of his perceptual and motor systems for anticipated problems merely by listening to brief instructions is a distinctly human capacity. Any theory that deals with instructions under the heading of standard conditions or as a minor methodological nuisance cannot go far.

One criticism of the concept of set is that it is vague. We have seen that sets can easily be established with predictable consequences; the vagueness does not lie in the empirical facts. What is felt to be vagueness may be the difficulty of fitting these facts into theories that are inadequate. There are many mechanical and electrical analogies, the most familiar being the gear shift on an automobile. Moving the shift lever does not move the automobile. It prepares an adjustment of the gears so that the car will go forward, or backward, when the power is applied. The gear-shift mechanism is not the same as the other parts of the drive train and automobiles have been built without gear shifts. What the changeable gears contribute is just what the set contributes: flexibility of control.

The problem-solving set will be properly interpreted only when the cognitive side is taken as seriously as the response side and when the capacity of the literate individual for immediate temporary adjustment as a result of social communication is fully appreciated.

Seeking Information

In the solution of many problems a process of information seeking can be identified without difficulty. Those concept experiments that allow the subject to choose some cards rather than others or to switch lights from one display to another and the anagram experiment that photographed eye movements all reveal something of the subjects' search for useful information. Other experiments have been designed expressly to differentiate this process from others and to study it separately. In one class of problems, called diagnostic or troubleshooting problems, finding the relevant information is the main difficulty. The information-seeking process can be viewed as an elaboration of the cognitive side of the set. The initial set is necessarily very general, but as information is uncovered, presumably the set is narrowed to a search for more specific possibilities.

DIAGNOSTIC PROBLEMS

The troubleshooter can usually find the trouble if he checks every component in the system that has broken down, but this may take some time and work, so questions about the order of checking components arise. What are the determinants of information-seeking sequences? And do troubleshooters use the optimal sequence?

To answer these questions, Detambel and Stolurow (1957) built a device with three components, each of which could be labeled "OK" or "Out of order." But these components were covered with lids that could be lifted for inspection only by removing some screws by hand: seven screws for Component A, four for Component B, and one for Component C. If we consider the number of screws, indicating the work to be done or the cost of the information, as one independent variable, the other was the probability of malfunction. Component A was defective in half the problems, B in a third, and C in a sixth. The optimal sequence depends on both probability and work. When we have all the data—as we have in Table 4.3 for one problem—we can calculate that the optimal sequence in the long run would be C, B, A.

College students were paid to find the troubles in 200 such pieces of equipment and were told that they could quit when finished. The amount of work required to lift each lid was apparent from the number of screws in view, but the probability of finding the malfunction in each component came only from cumulative experience with the problems. More than half the subjects began by minimizing work, that is, by unscrewing the lid on Component C. Then, as they learned the probabilities, they gradually shifted toward lifting A first to maximize the chances of a quick discovery. Many shifted back to a work-minimizing strategy later, but the authors concluded that the subjects generally emphasized probability more than work. It is true that the subjects were influenced by both variables in seeking information, but only 1 of the 12 adopted the optimal sequence and stayed with it.

Another experiment of this type (Goldbeck, Bernstein, Hillix, and Marx, 1957) employed two systems of electrical components, one simple and one complex, to determine if college students could learn to use an efficient troubleshooting method called the *half split*. When there is a chain of components all equally liable to malfunction, the most efficient procedure is to dichotomize or split the system in half and check one half; whichever half is defective is split again, and so on. The results of a training session showed that the half-split method was quickly mastered in simple cases when each unit in the system was easily understood. When the system was complex,

TABLE 4.3. DESCRIPTION OF A TROUBLESHOOTING TASK
OF THREE COMPONENTS

Component	Probability of Trouble	Number of Screws
A	.500	7
B	.333	4
C	.167	1

From Detambel and Stolurow (1957).

most subjects did not catch on to the optimal procedure with one hour of instruction, but some did with two hours. Those who got high scores on a reasoning test caught on quicker than the average. Ability to apply the checks at the optimal places required some skill in deductive reasoning when the relationships within the system were complicated.

Dale (1959) allowed his subjects more freedom in looking for the faults in a system in order to observe their strategies. Each subject saw a display of 19 electric sockets and was told to find the one that was defective. Plugging in a tester would show a red light if the socket was defective, otherwise a green light. Most of the subjects searched by some kind of pattern, for example, stepwise. A third searched randomly—as far as the experimenter and other judges could determine.

Then the subjects were told that the electric current was flowing by 19 stages and that the malfunction could interrupt the current at any one of these. The tester, if lighted, would show that all was functioning properly up to that point. The experimenter called this an ordered system in contrast to the others in which the items were independent. On problems involving an ordered system, only a few subjects used the optimal half-split strategy but many were more or less systematic. They did improve a little with practice on three problems. Those subjects who got high scores on an intelligence test used more systematic information-seeking strategies on both ordered and unordered problems and therefore were generally more efficient.

A special problem board with shutters that could be moved aside to disclose the information underneath was devised by Neimark (1967), who arranged information in different patterns so that certain moves would indicate a safe information-gathering strategy and others a gambling strategy. The safe strategy for this problem, like the half-split strategy for other problems, eliminates half the alternatives with each move and thus obtains complete information with the smallest average number of moves. The gambling strategy is a move that might, with good luck, uncover the needed information on the first try, and the experimenter manipulated the proportion of problems on which gambling would be successful by manipulating the information revealed. Analysis of the first moves on successive problems indicated that college students were able to profit by their experience in this situation and to formulate strategies, or rules, to guide their moves. Those who were never reinforced for gambling soon developed a safe strategy and stayed with it. Those who found that their gambling moves frequently paid off leaned toward the gambling strategy. In general, the results came closer to a theoretical model that assumed college students could make rational decisions than to other models considered.

When this task was given to 96 children (Neimark and Lewis, 1967), their information-gathering moves were random at the nine-year level, but the optimal strategy was frequently employed by those who were intellectually more mature, as shown by a correlation of .52 with mental age. This rather high correlation was attributed, not to an increase in learning rate, but to an increase in the number of children, at mental age of twelve or above, who could profit from their mistakes in an all-or-none fashion, and work out the more logical strategy.

In high school and college also there are substantial correlations between the use of an optimal strategy for seeking information and such standard measures as intelligence and average grade (Rimoldi, Fogliatto, Erdmann, and Donnelly, 1964).

GUESSING GAMES

Information-seeking strategies show up also in simple card games, as when one person tries to guess what card another person is thinking of. D. J. Davis (1967) manipulated the structure of the display of cards to see how this would influence the questions asked. He placed 16 cards before the subject, each labeled with a letter or a number, one of which was the correct card. The subject's task was to determine the correct card by asking questions, to which the experimenter answered only *Yes* or *No*. All cards had equal probability of being the correct one, hence the optimal information-seeking procedure in the long run would be successive half splits, as in the problems above.

When half the cards had letters and half had numbers, the perceived structure of the problem favored the half-split strategy and all subjects used this as an opening question. First, they arranged the cards in two rows, thus:

A B C D E F G H

1 2 3 4 5 6 7 8

With this structure in view, the obvious first question would be "Is it a letter?" or "Is it a number?" The perceived structure thus encouraged the optimal information-seeking strategy. For other subjects, more letters and fewer numbers were presented; hence questions based on the letter-number dichotomy would no longer be optimal, and such questions were actually less often asked. In the extreme case, with 15 letters and 1 number displayed, this question was not asked at all; more awkward but more efficient questions were used.

The familiar game of twenty questions is psychologically intriguing because the questions put the player's thoughts on record. In this game, one player asks questions to which the answers are only Yes and No, in order to find out what it is that the other is thinking of. Many systems or strategies are employed and experienced players are more efficient. In one experiment (Faust, 1958) covering five days, it appeared that the improvement consisted not so much of asking better questions as of eliminating poor questions that yielded little information.

Children enjoy guessing games like Twenty Questions and sharpen their information-seeking skills while playing them. We expect them to ask better questions as they mature, but we also expect the changes in their questions to fit in with what we know of cognitive development in general. Mosher and Hornsby (1966) looked for age changes by the simple procedure of showing each child pictures of 42 familiar objects and requesting him to find out "which one it is that I have in mind." *Yes* and *No* were the only answers to the children's questions. The optimal strategy, the half split, is hardly applicable to this collection of miscellaneous objects. The next best thing would be to begin with a general question that groups a large number of specific possibilities into 2 domains, in one of which the correct answer must lie. "Is it a toy?" "Does it cut things?" This strategy was called *constraint seeking*. At the opposite pole was the strategy, if it deserves the name, of *hypothesis scanning*. "Is it the hammer?" The most distinctive feature of the results was that the six-year-old children were limited to hypothesis scanning, while constraint seeking was characteristic of eleven-year-old and, to some extent, eight-year-old children. The older children began with general questions and used the information thus obtained to formulate narrower ones.

A more difficult form of this game involves a verbally described incident, such as: "A boy goes home from school in the middle of the morning." In this case, the children had to generate alternative explanations for themselves before asking questions. The eleven-year-olds established contraints and asked series of connected questions much more than the six-year-olds, but on these unbounded verbal problems the eight-year-olds were not much advanced beyond the six-year-olds. The authors, following Bruner, state that:

> as the child increasingly relies on symbolic representation rather than on representation by action and image—and thus is able to construct groupings of objects and events on the basis of characteristics they have in common—he attains the structure of information necessary to follow through a constraint seeking strategy, to guide his inquiry by cycles of questioning that narrow from the general to the specific [p. 101].

THE INFORMATION-SEEKING SET IN READING

As the information sought is narrowed to certain possibilities rather than others, a set to perceive these in the present situation or to recall them from the past is established. The close connection between information seeking and a problem-solving set can be illustrated by reading, which is, after all, the method by which most information for solving problems is gathered. Reading by older children and adults is a highly practiced skill, but it is swayed, like other intellectual activities, by the cognitive demands of the moment. A set to read for one kind of information rather than another can be established, like other sets, by successful use of the information in previous problem solving or, as Torrance and Harmon (1961) did, by instructions. They had graduate students read assignments in preparation for an examination and gave different groups different instructions. One group was told to read with a memory set: "Remember everything." Another group was instructed to read creatively: "As you read think of ways that you can use this information. Think of many uses." Another stressed evaluation: "Try to find defects in the research. Is what the author is saying really true?" When they were tested on memory, creative, and evaluative tasks, the differences came out as expected. Those who had studied with a creative set did best on the creative problems; those who had studied with an evaluative set did best on the evaluative problems. Differences on the memory tasks were small—probably because all graduate students are habitually set to remember everything.

SOME GENERALIZATIONS

Despite the diversity of materials and procedures in research on information seeking, when the results are lined up, a substantial amount of agreement appears, justifying some general conclusions: (1) A variety of very simple procedures, all requiring overt movements or questions, have been quite successful in producing objective evidence on information-seeking activities. (2) Typically, the subject is set for acquisition and retention of information, but he can also get set to make creative or evaluative use of the information obtained by reading. (3) Most subjects improve with practice, if the information is not too complex, by taking advantage of the structure of the information and eliminating inefficient moves. (4) Intelligent adults tend to approach logically ideal strategies, but they seldom reach the ideal. (5) The complex problems of this type require a series of decisions, which may be logically arrived at, hence they resemble reasoning problems and success correlates with success in reasoning tests. (6) As children develop the ability to conceptualize the information needed, they shift from guessing about concrete facts to more organized strategies that move from broad categories of information to narrow subcategories.

Representing and Transforming the Data

Let us consider a simple everyday problem. We are expecting certain people to meet in a certain room, so the problem arises of supplying a chair for each person. One procedure would be a direct physical matching of chairs and people. Let each person pick a chair and see if any chairs or people are left over. More likely, someone will count the people and count the chairs and determine arithmetically if the two counts match. In general terms, we can say that the essential elements of the problem are represented symbolically, and the problem is solved symbolically; then the symbolic solution is applied to the real problem. The first step can be likened to encoding, the last to decoding.

This representative process does not always occur. If the problem is a construction one, such as a jigsaw puzzle, it is usually solved by manipulating the pieces directly. Anagrams are solved by rearranging the given letters. But the process of representing the data of the problem in some other form is a common phase of problem solving that merits systematic consideration.

One simple type of representation is the labeling or naming of singular concepts. When the hostess solves the seating problem for a dinner by arranging name cards around the table, the function of each card is to represent the single person to whom it refers. On maps, specific cities, rivers, and other geographic features are represented by specific names. But a symbol may also represent a class of objects, as when the hostess uses square cards for male guests and round cards for female guests. The admiral solves some naval problem by letting blue markers stand for ships of one class and red markers for another, then moving the markers in accordance with his knowledge of the capabilities of each class. Mathematical symbols, of course, representing relations, operations, and higher abstractions, have the greatest utility in problem solving. We are so accustomed to the symbolic representation of objects and classes that we need to be reminded occasionally that this is a highly cultivated accomplishment. According to the preceding chapter, each of us reaches this stage of development only after years of representing reality through images and actions.

Although a problem is, by definition, a novel situation, each adult has a repertoire of symbols that are potentially applicable. One of the first steps toward solving many problems consists of representing the given facts in conventional terms, then structuring the relations between them and the specifications for the desired solution in sentences: a verbal conceptualization of the problem. Some problems can be formulated in mathematical terms: Let X represent the number of trials. Let Y represent the proportion of errors. What is required is . . . The representation of geographic conditions, human activities, economic events, and other abstract complexities in verbal or mathematical symbols so that the essentials of the problem can be put down "on paper" is a major step forward. This may identify the data that are missing and lead to more enlightened information seeking.

When problem solvers and teachers of problem solving speak of "conceptualizing," or "formulating," or "setting up the problem," they are not speaking of the words, numbers, letters, and other terms, but of a structure of terms that represents the structure of the problem. Usually the terms are familiar but the structure of terms is a novel structure, organized to fit each new problem. Errors are made by choosing a set of terms that is not appropriate to the problem and by arranging a structure of terms that does not accurately represent the structure of the problem. They also occur in the decoding operation, that is, in applying the symbolic solution to the real world, as well as in encoding.

Because of the spatially extended properties of the visual system, the relationship between elements can often be represented graphically with special clarity. Charts, maps, schematic drawings, diagrams of mathematical and logical relations, electrical circuits, musical scores, and other schemes that code the relevant relationships in visual form take advantage of these properties to show structures that are not amenable to verbal communication. In some cases, when the facts are represented visually, one can "read off" the solution directly. In addition, some thinkers report that they use their own idiosyncratic schemes for representing complex data. These may be images, vaguely formed patterns, or heuristics not easily communicated, but all representational systems existed at one time only in the minds of original thinkers.

The general adoption of a system—such as the Mercator projection and the

Linnaean classification system—depends on the thinker's ability to make it explicit and communicate it to others. Thus, while most people are acquiring standard structures for representing reality, a few are trying to exteriorize their own visions of reality. The other side of the representation process is exemplified by the scientists who puts down on paper the imaginary structures that evolved in his own fantasy. Even more inventive is the work of the novelist, who dreams of a locale, peoples it with characters, and engages them in action, then represents his private world on the printed page so that others can share it.

Many problems can be more easily solved, or perhaps can only be solved, when the information about the problem represented in one mode is transformed to another. Solution may be aided by translating a verbal description of the facts into a set of numerical statements, or by representing numerical data in graphic form. Smaller transformations are common: from Cartesian coordinates to polar coordinates, from a decimal system to a binary system, or from stimulus-response language to cognitive language. More generally, useful transformations are those in which the structure of the data is preserved through the transformation so that the solution in symbolic terms can be decoded back to the original problem. This achievement seems to require at least the level of cognitive development that Piaget calls *reversibility*.

Despite the importance of this process for problem solving, experimental evidence is meager. One unpublished study by Curt Wilson asked how psychology students represent the data of a psychological experiment and found that those who took the trouble to draw a graph formulated the best conclusions. In this case the data, presented as a series of statements on cards, included an interaction which was obvious when, and only when, the data had been converted to graphic form.

In any case there are individual differences in the ability to handle different representational systems, which appear, for example, in Guilford's (1967) structure of intellect. These may be related to problem-solving preferences because we know that some people prefer to solve problems by graphic means whenever possible, others prefer a numerical solution, and others typically substitute words for numbers. They may be related to success also, if an experiment by Gavurin (1967) with a small sample of subjects is confirmed with a larger sample. On the assumption that the letters of an anagram are visually represented and rearranged in imagination, Gavurin compared success in solving anagrams with scores on a standard test of spatial ability and found a correlation of .54. When the letters were on tiles that could be physically rearranged, the correlation was negligible, presumably because spatial representation was unnecessary.

Organizing and Reorganizing Cognitive Structures

Structure has many meanings; of those involved in problem solving we can say that a structure consists of an organization of elements which is more than the elements and which persists when the elements change. A triangle drawn in black ink on white paper, for example, could have the same structure as one drawn in white on black. As we noted earlier in the discussion of embedding, an element is hard to pick out when its outlines coincide with those of the larger structure. One may restructure what he perceives by looking at it from a different point of view, by breaking it in half, by rotating it, by coloring one part, or by reversing figure and ground. Some relations within the structure, necessary for solving a problem, are apparent only after such restructuring.

The concepts of structure and restructuring, or reorganizing, are favorites of Gestalt psychology and are usually illustrated with examples from visual perception. But abstract cognitive structures are more relevant here. If we have A and B classified under I; C and D classified under II; and I and II classified under Ω, the structure is a tri-level binary structure that is different from a list of seven elements (see Fig. 4.9). An illustration of restructuring would be the reclassification of C, putting it under I, and a more radical case would be changing the whole to a bi-level structure. Figure 4.10 represents two family structures composed of father, mother, and three children. These figures are representations; we cannot draw a family. We can, however, represent graphically the relations between the elements, that is, the structure, of an organization so that the difference between two structures, as in this figure, is obvious.

The most important structures for problem solving are dynamic structures of behavior, some of the elements of which are moves or actions. A baseball game, for example, includes not only such elements as players and balls, but a variety of plays, all of which are replaceable although the structure has been quite stable for many years. Card games supply other familiar examples. The elements of the game may be visible objects, such as bats, balls, diamonds or spades; visible moves, such as swinging a bat or playing a card; and abstract concepts, such as strike, trump, or win. An integrated series of moves, such as a forcing play, may profitably be treated as a substructure. Some complex dynamic organizations of objects and functions are called systems: a ventilating system, an accounting system, a wiring system.

The intricately structured behavior of a spider weaving a web or a bird building a nest suggests a genetic mechanism for structuring behavior and integrating substructures into the larger structure, adapted in turn to the structure of the environment. The structures of human behavior are more dependent on individual experience in adapting to the environment and on individual knowledge of the functional significance of the elements and substructures in the overall structure. An S-R association might be considered

FIGURE 4.9. *Representation of a tri-level binary taxonomic structure.*

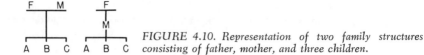

FIGURE 4.10. *Representation of two family structures consisting of father, mother, and three children.*

a simple structure, and a chain of S-Rs would be a more complex serial structure, all executed mechanically. But if an individual is to make flexible use of a cognitive structure in solving a problem, he must know the instrumental function of each component; then, if a component is missing or defective, he can replace it. Obviously, a knowledge of the elements, the substructures, and the overall structure facilitates solution of problems involving the structure and, in the case of games, the participation of the individual as an element in that structure. Thus many of the more enlightening experiments are concerned with knowledge of the components of some larger structure.

The relation of the part to the whole is an old controversy in psychology, and many of these questions have been discussed in other terms. Knowledge of the overall structure and of the functional relations of the constituent elements is often called *understanding* in contrast to a fragmentary knowledge of the elements. It makes little sense to speak about knowledge of a reflex or simple S-R association; only when behavior becomes more complicated can one ask about understanding of the components and their function in the whole. Bartlett (1958), for example, treated thinking as filling in gaps in a system. Another old term, recently used in a more precise meaning, is *plan*, which, according to Miller, Galanter, and Pribram (1960), is "any hierarchical process in the organism that can control the order in which a sequence of operations is to be performed [p. 16]." Thus plans and the integration of subplans within plans give behavior its structure. De Groot (1965), following Selz, noticed that the thinking of master chess players was characterized by the formulation of a plan and that the moves were integrated with, and realized, that plan.

The desired solution to a problem may be described, especially by writers of mystery stories, as the missing piece in the structure. In some cases, problem solving consists of organizing the known pieces into an incomplete structure or *search model*, then searching the environment or one's memory for a missing piece that fits. This notion of a search model implies that the solution must fit certain specifications, that these specifications are organized rather than just listed, and that accuracy and completeness in the search model help the solution. Unfortunately, the idea of a search model, though intuitively plausible, has not generated relevant empirical research. But recent research from the verbal learning laboratory under the name of "free recall" has documented the influence of clusters, rules, coding systems, strategies, and other organizing principles in the production of words previously learned.

A persistent methodological question arises at this point: How can we determine whether the subject knows the structure? The spider does not know the structure of the web that he spins so expertly. A beginner may play a game quite well for some time before he understands how the elements are integrated into substructures and how manipulation of these affects the whole. Structures may be inferred by an experimenter which have no significance to the subject of the experiment. One obvious method is to ask the subject of an experiment to represent a structure somehow. He may do this graphically (as in Figs. 4.9 and 4.10) or by stating the rules of the game verbally, by executing a series of gestures, or perhaps by mathematical equations. The study of the thinking of expert chess players by De Groot (1965) was made possible by standard schemes for representing moves and combinations of moves, schemes known to both the players and the experimenter. Adequate representation requires that the structure be preserved through a transformation of elements, as from pieces on the chessboard to symbols on the printed page. Just as we take a definition or a classification rule as one measure of knowledge of a class concept, we take a description of the relations between members of a family or a diagram of an electrical circuit as measures of knowledge of these structures.

It is possible also to ask which of five alternative representations of the structure is the correct one. Is the family next door represented by the left side or the right side of Fig. 4.10? The limitations of these methods are parallel to the limitations of similar methods for measuring knowledge of a class concept.

Another method is based on observation of the attempts to solve a problem which involves the structures of interest. The subject's arrangement of the materials, use of tools, search for information, sequence of arithmetic operations, and consistent errors may permit inferences about the structure he is assuming. People solving arithmetic problems, construction problems, jigsaw puzzles, and concept problems can often be seen arranging terms more conveniently or lining up some pieces in a row for comparison with others. In many card games, the cards come at random and the average player's first operation is to arrange them in a manner that he assumes will be helpful. This is a preparatory process that does not solve any problem; it merely facilitates the next step. But the subject's arrangement of the materials frequently reveals his understanding of relations within the materials and his plan of action.

When the game is played or the problem is solved by a series of moves, many observers (e.g., De Groot, 1965; Gyr, 1960) have noticed that elementary moves are often integrated into a combination of moves, a substructure, that is then executed as a unit. Likewise when the goal is a complex solution, it is often analyzed into subgoals, with the expectation of synthesis later.

More formally, the experimenter predicts certain problem-solving behavior from a hypothesis about the subject's structure of the problem, then takes the observed behavior as support, or lack of support, for this hypothesis. The limitations of this method also are parallel to the limitations of corresponding methods for assessing knowledge of a concept. Naturally the convergence of inferences from a representation of the structure and from problem-solving behavior would be more convincing than either one alone.

The question that has concerned most investigators is whether the subject knows the structure that is necessary for solving the problem. Success is more likely if the subject's structure of the elements corresponds with the objective structure. If he does not know the correct structure, we may also ask, as we do in the case of concepts, what is the idiosyncratic structure that he is assuming?

In the case of complicated structures, knowledge of the structures may be partially correct, rather than either right or wrong. One person may know enough about an electrical circuit to turn the right switch, another may know enough to make minor repairs, and another may be able to redesign the system. To put this point more generally: some problems require a higher criterion of attainment than others for solution.

In a taxonomic structure, the relations are relations of inclusion. One who knows the structure of Fig. 4.9 knows that whatever is true of I as a class is true of A. Thus a taxonomic structure, such as Inhelder and Piaget studied, is useful in solving certain problems. The important structures for the solution of most problems, however, are made up of functional, means-end, or cause-effect relations: the relation between a child's attention-seeking activities and the mother's responses (and perhaps the modulation of this by the presence of the father); the relations between the elements of a dynamic system of switches, meters, lights, and resistances; the relevance of a certain arithmetic operation to a series of arithmetic operations; the fit of a tool to a part that needs adjustment; the articulation of an administrative procedure with a system of administrative procedures. According to our definition of problem solving, if the subject knows all the parts and how they fit together, he has no problem. Problems arise from ignorance of the parts or of their organization.

PRINCIPLES, PROPOSITIONS, AND EXPLANATIONS

From the psychological point of view, a principle is an abstract achievement of special use for the solution of problems. It has the form of a proposition or statement with a subject and a predicate. Birds fly. Babies are cute. Sugar dissolves in water. Plural verbs go with the plural nouns. Work = force × distance.

Although the term *concept* is often used to include principles, a distinction can be made. In many laboratory studies of concepts, one learns a word, such as *dax,* and uses it discriminatively in classifying and pointing to objects without asserting any more about *dax* than when one says, "This is a baby." Correct classification and correct usage are the tests of achievement. In educational situations, however, one learns the standard concepts of the culture; hence to classify an object as a bird is equivalent to an assertion that it has the properties of other birds. It is in such situations that the terms *concept* and *principle* are used interchangeably.

A principle is more than an observed event. One can see a bird fly, but the statement that birds fly is an abstract generalization relating a class of activities to a class of objects. Thus we can treat the principle as the structure and the concepts as the elements. But a principle is more than a conjunction of concepts. Combining the concepts *square* and *red* to form the concept *red square* is not stating a principle. The distinctive feature of the principle is that concepts are combined in a special relation: the subject-predicate relation. Both subject and predicate may include substructures, with modifiers and exceptions, in a complicated sentence structure; but the subject-predicate relation is the kingbolt of the whole.

Principles have a close connection with explanations. Explanation may be a difficult notion technically, but in psychological and educational contexts we count a reply to a question about an event as explanatory if the applicable principle is stated. Thus thinking is often initiated by a question—posed by the thinker or someone else—and terminated when an explanatory principle is found.

The close connection between principles and problem solving has been emphasized by Gagné (1965) in the following statement:

To summarize, discovery or problem solving involves the combining of previously learned principles into a new higher-order principle that "solves" the problem and generalizes to an entire class of stimulus situations embodying other problems of the same type. Problem solving occurs when the instructions provided the learner do not include a verbally stated "solution," but require him to construct such a solution "on his own." When this happens, the individually constructed higher-order principle is effective in generalizing to many situations and is at the same time highly resistant to forgetting [pp. 165–166].

The achievement of principles, like the achievement of other standard abstractions of the culture, can be tested by several methods, five of which are listed in Table 4.4 for comparison with methods of measuring achievement of concepts. We can observe someone's use of the term for the principle in writing or speaking and note proper usage and gross errors, or we can arrange situations which call for discriminating use of the term. We can ask for a verbal statement of the principle or, if appropriate, for a mathematical or graphic representation. Or, just as we ask someone to identify objects as

TABLE 4.4. COMPARISON OF SOME MEASURES OF ACHIEVEMENT OF CONCEPTS AND PRINCIPLES

Concepts	Principles
Use of term in communication	Use of term in communication
Verbal definition on request	Verbal statement on request
Classification of positive and negative instances	Classification of situations to which principle does and does not apply
	Given in explanation of an event
	Application to solution of a problem

positive and negative instances of a class, we can ask him to identify those situations to which a certain principle is applicable, or to select that one of five principles that is applicable to a given situation.

The special functions of principles, however, are in the explanation of phenomena and in the solution of problems. So the achievement of principles is most often tested by a Why question about an observed phenomenon, or by a problem, such as a geometry problem, for which the principle is supposed to be necessary.

LEARNING PRINCIPLES

The learning of principles has not been investigated as thoroughly as the learning of concepts. It is reasonable to suppose that principles are learned somewhat as the more abstract concepts are learned, and that some of the variables emphasized by the results of concept research—such as relevant and irrelevant variables, positive and negative information, and salience of the critical dimensions—will be important here also.

Duncan (1964) studied the induction of a simple principle that paired odd numbers with certain letters and even numbers with other letters by having his subjects guess at the relations, and then informing them of their success. They were more successful—as measured by numbers of pairs required and by number of correct statements of the principle—when the experimenter permitted them to select whatever pairs they wished than when they were restricted to pairs chosen by the experimenter. This finding agrees with the comparison of the selection and reception methods of learning concepts. In this relatively simple situation, it is advantageous for the subject to be able to test his own hypotheses in his own way. In general, those subjects who succeeded were more systematic in their approach to the task, varying only one variable at a time.

The nature of the relation between the statement of a principle and the behavior that illustrates it is an important question, frequently asked but not yet thoroughly answered. Presumably, there is a mutual facilitation between the formal statement of a principle and its application to concrete situations, so that the learning of either one assists the learning of the other. But we know that verbal expressions of a principle, for example, frustration leads to aggression, are often memorized without regard to observable facts. And a tactful person in a social situation may reveal behavioral skills predictable from the frustration-aggression principle even though he cannot state such a principle formally.

No matter how the principles are acquired, it is generally agreed that they are retained better than isolated facts—although the retention of concrete isolated principles may be surprisingly small under some conditions (Gagné and Wiegand, 1968). The general question of teaching principles for use in problem solving will be taken up systematically in the next chapter.

DEVELOPMENTAL TRENDS

Games, as noted above, provide interesting illustrations of dynamic systems of objects and actions. In his well-known book, *The Moral Judgment of the Child,* Piaget (1932) described how children explained the rules of a game of marbles to him and how well their behavior corresponded with these rules. The youngest children did not talk about rules, of course, nor give any evidence of following them when they played with marbles. Children of age three or so seemed to know that the game has a structure, that some moves are right and some are wrong, and they tried to imitate the older children in these respects. As in classification at this stage, however, they were influenced more by superficial perceptual aspects than by abstract principles. They talked in terms of rigid eternal rules even though they did not describe them or follow them accurately. Children of seven and eight followed the rules quite well. But only the children of ten to twelve had mastered the complex rule structure in an abstract way so as to integrate rules and behavior systematically and to conceive of the rules in terms of mutual agreements instrumental to mutual enjoyment of the game.

It is in adolescence also that formal propositional thinking develops, according to the Geneva school. Propositions are stated and tested against observations, and specific events are explained by reference to a general proposition. The younger child, at the stage of concrete operations, is tied to specifics while the older child looks for general principles. For example, one of the tasks used by Inhelder and Piaget (1958) required the subjects to try to hit a target by bouncing a ball off a bank, as in billiards, and to explain what happened. The younger children gave concrete explanations, such as: "It hits here, then it goes there." The adolescents gave more explanations in terms of a general principle, although not always well expressed, to the effect that the angle of incidence equals the angle of reflection.

ORGANIZING THE PIECES OF A SOLUTION

In the 1930s Norman Maier, who had been exposed to Gestalt ideas at the University of Berlin, began a series of ingenious experiments that attracted considerable attention and have had a strong influence on subsequent problem-solving research. The problems were rather difficult construction problems, requiring the integration of component pieces and physical principles. Maier used the term *reasoning* to distinguish the integration of separate experiences from ordinary learning and transfer. Although this term no longer seems appropriate, the question whether ordinary principles of learning are sufficient to explain such problem-solving activity is still a live one. In fact, it was these experiments and Maier's interpretations of them that challenged Hull and his followers to work out the associationist interpretations of problem solving sketched earlier in this chapter.

One experiment (Maier, 1930) gave college students the task of constructing supports to hold two pendulums that would swing to make chalk marks at designated places on the floor. The solution of this problem requires the use of several physical principles or techniques, such as wedging and clamping, as parts of the solution pattern. And all these parts must be properly combined in the correct organization. Different groups of subjects were given (1) the problem only, (2) demonstration of the necessary parts of the solution, (3) instructions to combine the demonstrated parts of the solution, (4) a hint about hanging a pendulum on a nail in the ceiling, and (5) all of these aids. Only in the groups that were given all the aids was there an appreciable number of solutions. None of the aids was sufficient by itself.

Maier argued from these results that knowledge of the component parts was not enough; the organization of the parts was crucial. But this research has not gone unchallenged. Weaver and Madden (1949) found that they could induce relatively more solutions by a thorough explanation of the parts. Saugstad (1957) gave his subjects even better understanding of the principles, not by demonstration but by having them actually perform little tasks using these principles. Then almost all the subjects, under the most favorable conditions, were able to apply the principles to the problem.

Another experiment by Maier (1931) was done with a two-string problem that has since been widely employed by others. Two strings hanging from the ceiling are to be tied together, though they are so far apart that the subject cannot grasp both at once (see Fig. 4.11). The best solution is to tie a weight to one string and set it swinging like a pendulum, then run over to the other string and bring it to the swinging string at the right moment. Only 39 percent of Maier's subjects got this solution in 10 minutes, even though a pair of pliers, suitable for a pendulum weight, was in sight on a table. Pliers are conventionally used to hold things, so their use as a pendulum weight requires restructuring the functional significance of pliers. When the experimenter brushed one string to make it swing and handed the pliers to the subject, 38 percent more were able to solve the problem. Apparently this aid directed their attention to the unusual potential of the pliers.

A third experiment by Maier (1945) attempted to evaluate the contribution of previous experience to the problem of constructing a hatrack from

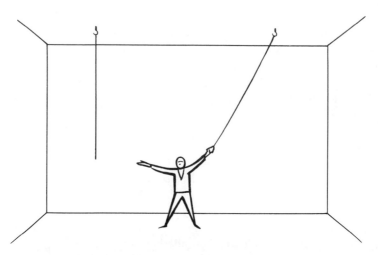

FIGURE 4.11. *Two-string problem. How can he tie the two strings together? From Johnson (1961).*

given materials. Only 6 out of 25 who tried this problem without previous experience solved it. Another group had practice on a similar problem that included the critical components, as a test of transfer, and 12 of this group of 25 succeeded. But the best results were achieved by a third group that had the initial practice with the other problem and also a view of their completed solutions while working on the hatrack problem; 18 out of this group of 25 succeeded. Evidently previous practice gives some help, and an example of a critical component in view gives more. Maier claimed that the transfer by itself was not sufficient.

The argument for an organizing or structuring process is both negative and positive. To say that knowledge of the parts of a solution is not sufficient is a negative statement, difficult to confirm. Psychological research seldom accounts for all the factors that determine results; all experiments leave a large portion of the variance unexplained. Therefore, a hypothesis which predicts that some portion of the results will be unexplained is not specific enough for us to test it. The positive side is the demonstration that certain conditions facilitate organization: instructions, practice, hints, and examples. Apparently, previous practice is effective and aids the solution to some extent by transfer of previously learned components. A second possibility is the subject's unaided restructuring of the functional significance or means-end possibilities of an object. A third effect, which Maier has emphasized under the name *direction* and others call *set,* is that instructions, hints, and an example in view all direct the thinker's attention to the problem-solving function of an object that otherwise might be overlooked.

INITIAL ORGANIZATION OF THE MATERIALS

It would not be correct to assume that solutions to problems are constructed from unrelated elements. Even if the materials in view appear to be unrelated, the thinker's associations to them, his perception of them, and the cognitive structures by which he conceptualizes them are all organized. This initial organization of the materials at hand, and the associated memories, may be a help or a hindrance, but it cannot be ignored. That is why problem-solving processes include the process of breaking up and reorganizing the initial pattern of the problem.

The old horse-trading problem offers a businesslike illustration of the influence of the initial organization and one trick for reorganizing it. "A man bought a horse for $60 and sold it for $70. Then he bought it back for $80 and sold it again for $90. How much did he make in the horse business [p. 305]?" According to Maier and Burke (1967), college students make many errors on this problem because the identity of the horse combines two transactions into one. What is needed in this case is not an overall structure but separation into two structures, and the two transactions can be separated by coloring the horses. Errors are seldom made, they say, when the problem is stated as follows: "A man bought a white horse for $60 and sold it for $70. Then he bought a black horse for $80 and sold it for $90 [p. 309]."

From analogy with perceptual and construction problems, we might expect that the initial organization of an anagram, that is, the letter order, could have an inhibitory effect on reorganization. Usually, anagrams are just strings of letters with no apparent organization; but if the anagram is a word, breaking it up and making it into another word might be delayed. This is an old controversy (Johnson, 1966), but recent research is more clear-cut because the influence of word frequency and other confusing variables can now be controlled. Beilin and Horn (1962) constructed a list of anagrams in unorganized or nonsense form—for example, *erten* (for which the solution is *enter*)—and another list, equated for word frequency and other variables, in word form—for example, *cause* (*sauce*). The results of their experiment showed that the word anagrams were much more difficult; the average solution time was 16.7 seconds, as compared with 9.4 seconds for the nonsense anagrams. They concluded that a word does resist analysis and reorganization more than a meaningless group of letters. The same difference was found again with tachistoscopic exposure of these anagrams at 1 second and also at a half-second (Beilin and Levine, 1966).

This inhibiting effect of words is due to the structure of the word, hence one might ask if it would apply to children who are not so familiar with the words. Beilin (1967) investigated this question by giving anagrams in word form and in nonsense form to children of eight, ten, twelve, and fourteen. He found the usual difference at age fourteen: 34.5 seconds for five-letter anagrams in word form, and 18.0 seconds for equated anagrams in nonsense form. Children of eight had a hard time with these problems; the average time was almost a minute, but there was no difference between word and nonsense forms. Thus Beilin's data disclosed two developmental trends. There was a general improvement in anagram-solving skill with increasing age; and there was a special inhibitory effect of word structure, which did not appear until around age ten, when the children had become quite familiar with the structures of these words (see Fig. 4.12).

Although the investigation of anagrams in word form was started to test a hypothesis derived from Gestalt principles, other hypotheses are possible. Ekstrand and Dominowski (1968) confirmed the inhibitory effect but suggested an associationist interpretation. Associations to nonword anagrams are likely to be series of letters, which would facilitate solution, while associations to words are likely to be other words, which would seldom be the correct solution words. Pronouncability is another contributing factor because anagrams in word form are easier to pronounce than nonword anagrams. But nonword anagrams vary in pronouncability also, and those that are easy to pronounce—and thus presumably tightly organized—prove more difficult to solve than the ones hard to pronounce (Dominowski, 1969; Hebert and Rogers, 1966). A little practice in pronunciation decreased reading time and, by strengthening the organization, reduced the number of solutions (Dominowski, 1969). The apparent implications of this novel line of research are that vocal processes intervene in the solution of anagrams and that the vocal organization is as important as the visual organization.

In nonword anagrams, the amount of reorganization required is a function

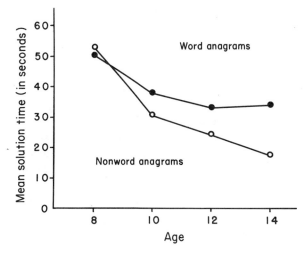

FIGURE 4.12. Solution times for five-letter anagrams by children at four age levels. Data from Beilin (1967).

of the similarity between the letter order of the anagram and the letter order of the word. We might predict that *nbtul* will be difficult because considerable rearrangement is necessary. And *bnult* should be easier, not only because fewer moves are necessary, but also because the end letters remain in place. When only two letters have to be moved, as in *blnut,* solution goes quickly. In general, anagrams are harder when the letters of the word have been highly scrambled and more reorganization is necessary to reconstruct the word (Hunter, 1961; Mayzner and Tresselt, 1958). A large difference between easy and hard letter orders is displayed in Table 4.2, both for high- and low-frequency words.

The importance of the ends of the anagram has been confirmed by separating nine-letter words into thirds of three letters each and mixing up the thirds to make alternative anagrams. Preserving either end in proper order helps in solving anagrams, as well as in the perception of words in rapid reading, more than preserving the middle (Oléron, 1961). Ends are more critical substructures than middles.

Moving now to the substructures—combinations of two or three letters— we would expect that familiar combinations would be more difficult to break up and reorganize. Mayzner and Tresselt (1959) demonstrated that this does happen, though the effect is much smaller than the effects of the whole word and of letter order.

One consequence of all this is that those who attempt to solve anagrams by a wholistic method are not very successful. The wholistic method may suffice for easy anagrams, but difficult ones require a more analytical multi-stage operation, breaking up the initial patterns and manipulating a few letters at a time (Rhine, 1959).

FUNCTIONAL FIXEDNESS: CAUSES AND CURES

Like Maier, Karl Duncker, of the University of Berlin, also designed construction problems around the Gestalt concept of structure or organization. His best-known work, published in German in 1935 and later in English (Duncker, 1945), reported several experiments illustrating how an object can be functionally concealed, or at least made unavailable for problem solving, by being included as part of an irrelevant structure. His box problem may be taken as an example. The task is to support three candles on the door at eye level, ostensibly for an experiment on vision. On a table lie many objects, including a few tacks and three small boxes of different shapes and colors. The correct solution is to tack the boxes on the door as platforms for the candles.

The experimental variable in Duncker's experiments was the initial arrangement of the materials. For an experimental group of seven subjects, the three boxes were filled with candles, tacks, and matches, respectively. For the control group of seven subjects, they were empty. The hypothesis was that perception, or cognition, of the boxes used as containers would interfere with using them as platforms. All of the control subjects solved the problem but only three of the experimental subjects. Similar results were obtained with several other problems of this kind, and Duncker's interpretation stressed heterogeneous functional fixedness. Cognition of an object used for one function fixes it to that function (or means-end relation) and hinders its cognition for another function, a special case of embedding. This generalization could also be stated as the establishment of a set for one cognition that hinders another cognition if the emphasis is placed on the cognitive rather than the executive side of the set.

In Duncker's experiments the differences between groups was in what they perceived; but others have introduced modifications to test the effect of what they learn. The independent variable is preutilization of an object, and the transfer paradigm, helpful in designing experiments on motor and verbal learning, is helpful also in visualizing the sequence of events in recent functional-fixedness experiments. Task A consists, for example, of *using* a box as a container, and Task B consists of a problem. If the box is used as the solution to the problem more often by those who have had Task A than by control group, the outcome can be called *positive transfer*. If the box is used less often by those who have had Task A, the outcome can be called *negative transfer*. Putting the functional-fixedness experiment into the transfer paradigm is helpful methodologically: it suggests appropriate controls and elaborations. It does not eliminate the difficulty of deciding whether the results are due to negative transfer of a response or of a cognition.

One carefully designed experiment (Birch and Rabinowitz, 1951) had subjects try the Maier two-string problem using either a relay or a switch as a weight for the pendulum. The test was not whether the subjects would solve the two-string problem but which of the two objects they would use to solve it with. A preliminary experiment showed that the two were used equally often to solve the problem under standard conditions. The preutilization consisted of using either the relay or the switch in constructing a simple electrical circuit. In solving the pendulum problem later, those who had used the relay now used the switch, and most of those who had used the switch now used the relay (see Table 4.5). In general, 17 out of 19 subjects avoided the object that they had just used for a different purpose and made use of the object not previously used. Other experiments by similar methods have also confirmed such functional fixedness.

Research on other problem-solving processes, especially sets, has stressed the importance of instructions, and in one of Maier's experiments the instructions directed the subjects' attention toward uses of an object that would otherwise be overlooked. Instructions were also found to influence solution of the two-string problem, by limiting or extending the range of objects to be considered (Battersby, Teuber, and Bender, 1953). One group of subjects, told to use only the five objects on the table, solved the problem in an average time of 2 minutes. Another group, told to use any object in the room, including the five objects on the table, solved it in 7 minutes. The average time for a third group, told to use any object in the room but not told specifically about the objects on the table, was 18 minutes.

We now know that functional fixedness is a genuine phenomenon that can seriously impede the solution of construction problems and we know that it is temporary (Adamson and Taylor, 1954). But do we know how to eliminate it? Attempts to do so have been planned around hypotheses about associations, including verbal associations, as well as cognitive structures. The experiments require several groups of subjects working under different conditions because it is necessary to demonstrate, first, that functional fixedness is present, and then, that it can be removed.

EFFECTS OF VARIED EXPERIENCE

One attempt, by Flavell, Cooper, and Loiselle (1958), tested the effects of more varied experience with alternative objects. They had 6 groups, each composed of 24 college women, solve the two-string problem under different

TABLE 4.5. FREQUENCY OF USE OF TWO OBJECTS FOR SOLVING THE TWO-STRING PROBLEM BY TWO GROUPS

Test Object Used	Nature of Preutilization	
	Relay in Circuit	Switch in Circuit
Switch	10	2
Relay	0	7

From Birch and Rabinowitz (1951).

conditions. In the control group, with a switch and a relay in view, as well as a few useless objects as decoys, 10 used the switch and 14 used the relay as a pendulum weight. One experimental group, E_1, used the switch in its conventional function, to make a small light bulb in a simple battery circuit go on and off, after which they did the two-string problem. Only 3 then used the switch as a pendulum weight and 21 used the relay, thus demonstrating functional fixedness clearly.

But the experimenters did not stop at this point. They gave four other groups varying amounts of experience with the switch used in novel functions, such as a container for holding pins and a straight edge for drawing a line. Different groups (see Table 4.6) got two, three, four, and five uses, one of which was the conventional use, by working problems for which these were the easy solutions—though a few hints were necessary for half the subjects. Groups that used the switch in four or five functions did not become fixated; they used the switch as a pendulum weight just as often as the control group. In fact, as the authors pointed out, Table 4.6 shows a high inverse correlation between the functional fixedness in a group and the amount of varied preproblem experience.

This experiment has been criticized by Yonge (1966), however, on the grounds of a hidden order effect. Order effects in experiments of this kind had been noticed earlier by Van de Geer (1957), and Yonge suspected that, since the familiar use of the switch is easily recognized as such, minor uses experienced later would not be very impressive. This line of reasoning led to a study of variations in the order in which the familiar use of the switch occurs.

Yonge's experiment, resembling the first in most respects, also involved college women, 23 in each of 5 groups. The control group, with no preutilization, used the switch 14 times as the solution to the two-string problem. Another group, which had used the switch as a switch in a circuit, used it for the two-string problem only 6 times (see Table 4.7). These results are the expected evidence of functional fixedness. Yonge's other groups had 5 uses of the switch, like E_5 of Flavell, Cooper, and Loiselle, but the order was varied. Those who got the familiar use of the switch first, followed by 4

TABLE 4.6. FREQUENCY OF USE OF TWO OBJECTS
FOR SOLVING THE TWO-STRING
PROBLEM BY SIX GROUPS

Test Object Used	C	Preutilization Groups				
		E_1	E_2	E_3	E_4	E_5
Switch	10	3	8	9	13	12
Relay	14	21	16	15	11	12

From Flavell, Cooper, and Loiselle (1958).

TABLE 4.7. FREQUENCY OF USE OF TWO OBJECTS FOR SOLVING THE TWO-STRING PROBLEM BY FIVE GROUPS

Test Object Used	Control	Preutilization of Switch			
		Familiar Use Only	Familiar Use First	Familiar Use Third	Familiar Use Fifth
Switch	14	6	4	12	10
Relay	9	17	19	11	13

From Yonge (1966).

other uses of the switch, used the switch only 4 times and the relay 19 times on the test, showing strong functional fixedness. As Table 4.7 shows, there was little difference on the two-string test between this group and the one that had only the familiar use of the switch. But those who had the familiar use of the switch in the third and fifth positions, following the more unusual uses, did the test problems approximately as the control group did.

These results apparently negate the assumption that the effects of varied experience with the switch summate to produce a flexible approach that reduces functional fixedness.

Yonge's phenomenological interpretation was that the use of the switch first in its conventional function is an unambiguous event that fixes the switch in its conventional meaning, unshakeable by subsequent minor uses. The same event is less powerful and does not produce functional fixedness when it comes after the minor uses have emphasized the multidimensional, or multifunctional, nature of the switch. Thus Yonge's work does not repudiate the beneficial effect of heterogeneous experience but raises questions about any simple calculation of these effects.

These experiments outline a trend toward the analysis of natural objects—potential tools for the solution of construction problems—into separate attributes or dimensions, comparable to the analysis of the artificial stimulus patterns of concept research. The separate dimensions may be called *functions, uses, response properties,* or *meanings,* depending on whether one wishes to emphasize what the subject does with the object or how he perceives it. As in the concept experiments, some functions are, or become, more salient than others, more relevant to the present problem than others, and so on. Though the details are not altogether clear, the experimental manipulations do shift the frequency of use of different functions of a single object. Hence the analysis must correspond in some way to the subjects' problem-solving processes.

VERBAL FACILITATION OF REORGANIZATION

Single words are quickly organized into verbal structures, and alternate structures furnish an opportunity to study verbal associations and organizing processes. Here are four words that Judson and Cofer (1956) presented with instructions to eliminate the one that is not related to the rest:

Sailor   *Soldier*   *Marine*   *Ship*

Two meaningful organizations are possible: a personnel class, to which *ship* does not belong; and a seagoing class, to which *soldier* does not belong. When the words are printed in the above order, 94 percent of the subjects eliminated *ship*. But only 44 percent eliminated *ship* and 55 percent eliminated *soldier* when they were printed in another order. Such results can occur if reading the first two words temporarily activates a hierarchy of responses, specifically, a class of verbal responses:

Sailor   *Ship*   *Marine*   *Soldier*

Thinking in terms of a hierarchy of uses for an object, one might ask if a verbal hierarchy will correspond to the instrumental hierarchy so that one can predict from verbal responses to problem solving. Staats (1957) investigated this question by having college students list uses for objects, including a screwdriver, and then attempt the two-string problem, then again list uses for a screwdriver. Only a few gave a verbal weight response to the screwdriver at first, yet nearly all solved the problem by tying the screwdriver to one string as a weight. After the problem had been solved, weight responses to the screwdriver were frequent. Even though the verbal response hierarchy did not predict use of an object in problem solving, the solving did alter the verbal response hierarchy.

Several attempts have been made from time to time to reduce functional fixedness by verbal facilitation, but the results have been ambiguous. More recently, Glucksberg and Weisberg (1966) tried the trick of labeling the objects in view in order to shift their frequencies of use in solving the problem. Adapted from Duncker's candle problem, this presents a candle, a book of matches, and a box of tacks on a table, with instructions to affix the candle to the wall so that it burns properly. The trick is to rescue the box from its function as a container and tack it to the wall, where it has the function of a platform to support the candle. Glucksberg (1964) had observed that blindfolded subjects struggling with such problems were aided when accidental contact with the box gave them a cue. Perhaps those subjects who look right at the box of tacks and do not see the box will be aided by a verbal cue. Glucksberg and Weisberg prepared a printed form of the candle problem and varied the labeling of the objects (see Fig. 4.13). When all four objects were labeled—*candle, tacks, box,* and *matches*—95 percent of the subjects gave the box as their first solution, as compared to 65 percent with only the tacks labeled and 54 percent with none of the objects labeled. Another experiment displayed the actual objects on a table for three small groups, each composed of eight college men, and varied the labels by projecting slides resembling Fig. 4.13 on a nearby screen. When all four objects were labeled in this way, functional fixedness of the box was almost elimi-

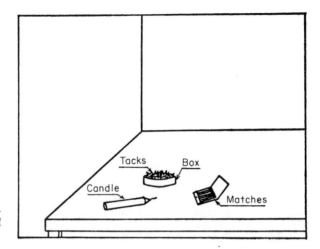

FIGURE 4.13. Printed
form of the candle prob-
lem. From Glucksberg and
Weisberg (1966).

nated; but when only the tacks were labeled, and when one of the objects
was labeled, the functional fixedness persisted.

It is important to note that labels are discrete. The subject perceives
the box of tacks as a whole, but he perceives the labels *box* and *tacks* as
separate labels and thus is more likely to perceive, or conceptualize, the
objects they label as separate. We have the same question of interpretation
here that appears in verbal facilitation of concept attainment. Does the verbal
label act as a cue to elicit the critical response, or does it facilitate perceptual
differentiation? The labeling of all four objects may draw special attention
to the instrumental value of one of the four, or it may simply distribute attention to four objects rather than three.

Glucksberg and Danks (1968) were able to adapt their labeling technique
to aid the use of a conventional object in a novel function, namely, a screwdriver to replace wire in an electrical circuit. Wire was provided, but not
enough; the solution was to use the metal blade of the screwdriver to com-
pensate for the short wire. Attempts to separate the blade (a conductor)
from the handle (a nonconductor) of the screwdriver perceptually, by
differentiating the colors, were not effective; but differential labeling (*screwdriver: handle, blade*) did increase frequency of solution. Furthermore, tools
were more often used for novel functions when the subjects had to ask for
them by nonsense labels than by their conventional names.

If one considers this verbal facilitation as a matter of word association, the
question of the dimension of association, or generalization of association, is
then raised. Glucksberg and Danks (1967) found that a metal tool labeled
pliers was used for the function of wires more often than when it was labeled
wrench. When these objects had rhyming nonsense names, no such effect
was obtained. Thus they concluded that, in this case at least, an acoustic
similarity between the labels for the two objects was not enough to mediate
the functional association; a semantic association was also necessary. This may

be a special case because pliers are actually used with wires more than wrenches are, but we know that adults are prone to semantic associations in other situations, so these results can perhaps be duplicated with other objects.

CONCEPTUAL GROUPING

Duncker's original view of functional fixedness was a cognitive one, stated in terms of the perceived functional properties of objects. Concept experiments have demonstrated how the various properties of multidimensional objects can be organized in one category or another, hence Terborg (1968) designed conceptual grouping tasks to reduce functional fixedness. The test problem was an electrical circuit problem, modeled after Glucksberg's, the critical function being the use of the metal blade of a screwdriver as a conductor to complete a circuit. According to the hypothesis, practice in grouping miscellaneous objects according to their properties as electrical conductors would emphasize this function, so that it would be more readily perceived as a property of other objects.

As listed in Table 4.8, each group of 20 college men had 10 conceptual grouping tasks which, in the two control conditions, required them to sort small common objects by a nonfunctional attribute, such as length, or a non-electrical function, such as pounding. The experimental subjects had similar training in sorting objects with conducting and insulating properties, such as paper clips and crayons. Although the results were not as clear-cut statistically as they appear in Table 4.8, because of the usual variability of solution times, the experiment does suggest a rational method for reducing functional fixedness.

Just as there are several ways of describing the essential difficulty of func-

TABLE 4.8. EFFECTS OF CONCEPTUAL GROUPING ON SOLUTION TIME (IN MINUTES) ON CIRCUIT PROBLEM

Group	Training Task	Solution Time
C_1	Attribute grouping, nonfunctional	5.23
C_2	Functional grouping, nonelectrical	5.41
E_1	Functional grouping, 2 electrical functions	3.38
E_2	Functional grouping, 4 electrical functions	2.74
E_3	Functional grouping, 4 electrical functions, 1 with screwdriver	2.75

From Terborg (1968).

tional fixedness problems, there are several ways of overcoming it. But we should note that we are discussing a special difficulty and its removal. None of the training procedures outlined raise the level of problem solving above that of control groups not held down by functional fixedness.

FROM ASSOCIATION TO STRUCTURE

Complex structures of knowledge and behavior are not the property of any one system of psychology. A cognitive structure is an explanation for certain phenomena and also a phenomenon in its own right, to be explained. The most important property of a structure is that once the elements are integrated, it functions as a unit. Mandler (1962) has collected considerable experimental evidence to show how such a structure may be constructed from associations and may be recalled and transferred to new situations as a whole. Although he maintains that some behavioral phenomena defy current associationistic interpretation, an extract from his discussion is quoted below to illustrate what this kind of interpretation may contribute to our understanding of problem solving.

Once a response sequence has been integrated and acts as a unit, it develops a structural representation, a "central" analogue of this new response unit which can function independently of the overt response sequence. . . . Analogic structures permit covert trial and error behavior, i.e., cognitive manipulation of previously established behavior. In this sense, the analogic representation of a prior behavior sequence is one possible "hypothesis" to be applied to a particular situation. Given many such structures which are relevant to a situational input, the several structures will occur seriatim and covertly until an appropriate one is expressed behaviorally. If it is incorrect, a new structure may occur, thus giving the appearance of an entirely discontinuous process, of shifting from hypothesis to hypothesis. We say "appearance" of discontinuity because a continuous process prior to the appearance of cognitive structures in fact gives rise to them. Structures are developed on the basis of associationist stimulus-response relationships but, once established, enable the organism to behave "cognitively" [pp. 417–418].

Since switches and lights are discrete units, the switch-light problem offers an opportunity to study in some detail how one attains patterns, higher units, or substructures by the integration of separately acquired associations between switches and lights and then uses these to solve problems. G. A. Davis (1967) chose the switch-light problem in order to compare covert and overt trial and error. According to Davis, if the nature of the problem permits the subject to predict the results of his moves, he solves it by covert trial and error. If, however, he cannot predict the results of his moves, he must proceed by overt trial and error—and thus his problem-solving attempts can be more easily observed. Davis therefore presented his subjects with a display of 12 lights and a panel of switches; various problems involving the relation between switches and lights were devised. The one illustrated in Fig. 4.14, for example, required lighting 2 and only 2 pairs of lights; but while some switches were *relevant* to the problem, some were *irrelevant* (they turned on lights other than the target pairs) and others were *distracting* (turning on

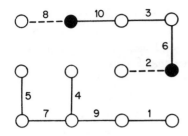

FIGURE 4.14. *Example of a problem involving 10 switches. Three switches are* relevant *(nos. 3, 6, 10); two are* distracting *(2, 8); five are* irrelevant *(1, 4, 5, 7, 9). From* G. A. Davis (1967).

only one of a target pair). As one might expect, the difficulty of a problem increased with an increase in the number of available switches, both relevant and irrelevant, and especially with an increase in the number of distracting switches. Even one distracting switch greatly retarded acquisition of the structure of relations between the switches and lights.

Davis gave one group of subjects special pretraining on the correct associations between each switch and a pair of lights; these subjects, in comparison with others, then proceeded more slowly and made fewer errors. According to the experimenter's interpretation, they could now predict the results of their moves, hence they solved by covert trial and error. There may be other interpretations for the decrease in errors, but usually a decrease in time accompanies a decrease in errors. Reversing the usual correlation between dependent measures points to a difference in problem-solving activities between groups. We might say, in the language of the quotation from Mandler, that the trained group could proceed cognitively because they knew the functional relations between switches and lights, and we might guess that they could represent these substructures graphically or verbally if necessary.

In general, we do not deny the importance of a cognitive organization when we admit that it was acquired by uncontrolled prior learning, or recent preutilization, or instructions that draw attention to new possibilities for organization. In the same sense, we do not deny the importance of prior learning when we admit that the crucial learning for solving problems is often that of grasping a cognitive structure.

The Judgment Process in Problem Solving

Psychologists who have analyzed their own problem solving and those who have observed others solving problems have usually included a process of evaluation or judgment of the solution. The thinker judges the solution acceptable and quits work, or he rejects it and recycles the problem-solving machinery. Thus, judgment of the solution is the last operation if it is affirmative; but judgment also takes place throughout the course of problem solving, as in deciding on one of several alternative plans of attack. Under productive thinking, Chapter 7 will consider problems for which multiple solutions are produced so that solution judgment can be conveniently studied.

The problems of the present chapter are supposed to have one correct solution, easily recognized as such, hence judgment goes quickly, and the judging process is easily overlooked. But the involvement of judgment in the solution of anagrams has attracted some attention since this operation, like so many others, is influenced by word frequency.

In a multi-stage procedure, the subject tries out combinations of two or three letters and matches these with the words that he knows. Presumably, words of high frequency are more available for comparison. Whether a word is found to match the solution attempt, or no match found and the attempt abandoned, the comparison would be easier if the word is familiar. This prediction was confirmed for a representative sample of five-letter words by printing anagrams beside attempts at solution, for example, *garus sug_____* , and asking college students to differentiate the true starts from the false ones (Johnson, Lynch, and Ramsay, 1967). The solution attempts were evaluated with more speed and less error for anagrams with solution words of high frequency than of low frequency. Evidently, the familiarity of the high-frequency words aids both the first stage of attempts at solution and the last stage of evaluating these attempts.

An ingenious method devised by Bremer (1968) for studying judgment as well as production of solutions to word problems assigned a special role to the judgment process. The problem was to make a four-letter word from initial and final letters, such as T __ __ K. Some subjects were instructed to make words of high frequency, such as TOOK, others words of low frequency, such as TUSK, and the subjects, who were college students, were able to solve the problem as instructed. But there are two ways of obtaining the specified solution. The subject could produce a word of the specified frequency, or he could produce several words of various frequencies then select one of the specified frequency. Bremer had chosen problems with a limited number of solution words (of any frequency) so that he could display a list of possible solutions in alphabetic order and ask the subject which words he had thought of while solving the problem. Analysis of the results of this recognition test showed that all experimental and control groups produced words of about the same frequency prior to final solution. If the recognition test was dependable —and the subjects were quite confident of their reports—the difference in the final solutions must have been due to the selection, or judgment, process.

Judgment, as we shall see in the last two chapters, may be a rather simple process of discrimination: associating one response with one type of stimulus and another response with another type. But during the solution of a problem, it often takes the form of a cognitive comparison process: comparing an irregular piece of wood with the gap in a jigsaw puzzle to see if it fits, comparing the conclusion of a syllogism with the implications of the premises and judging it valid or invalid, matching a hypothesis with a table of empirical data to evaluate the agreement. The judgment process can be temporarily neglected by oversimplified theories, but it must be considered in any full-scale account. It is explicitly included in computer programs for simulation of thought.

Problem-Solving Processes
from Computer Simulation

We might be tempted to dismiss computer simulation of problem solving as an idiographic enterprise of no general scientific significance. Why take the time to simulate in detail the particulars of the problem-solving output of one subject? Are there no generalizations to show for two decades of these digital exercises? We must admit that no new psychological principles have been advanced, nor have any of the old ones been repudiated, by such work. But it is instructive at this time to see what operations computer model builders have had to assume in order to approach the simulation endeavor. It is easy to envisage how machines can store symbols in the state of an electronic circuit or on a tape to simulate memory, and retrieve what has been stored to simulate recall. Recognition can be simulated by a systematic scanning and matching of what has been stored against new imput, after both have been converted to the same system of symbols. Combining operations, so that the output of one is the input for the next, runs off easily. There are a few characteristic features of computer programs, however, that deserve special mention as showing what has been done so far to simulate the flexibility of human thinking.

It is often possible, after a problem has been explicitly stated, to proceed logically, though perhaps at considerable length, to a solution, and computers are very good at such monotonous tasks. But most people and most simulation programs, instead of systematically exhausting all possibilities, try various tricks or strategies, called *heuristics,* to short-cut the process. The concept problem illustrates this well. Given all positive and negative instances and complete memory, a direct solution is possible. But we have seen that the human problem solver, with a limtied capacity for processing the information he gets, prefers to formulate a hypothesis, accept it, and stop; or reject it and formulate another, accept the second one, and stop; or reject it and formulate another; and so on. Most simulation programs, therefore, include a matching of the outcome of a preceding operation with a specified goal or subgoal, and the direction of the next branch of the program is conditional on this matching. In simulating concept attainment, for example, the program might select "angular" as a criterial attribute and test this against the next instance. If the match is correct, the program retains this hypothesis and proceeds to the next operation. If not, the computer routine that selects an attribute for testing recycles with another attribute. The overall flexibility of the program and the similarity to human thinking comes from the ability of the program to perform such an operation and make subsequent operations conditional on the matching of the outcome with a desired state of affairs, and to recycle the operation as often as necessary. This conditional branching and recycling can also be included as a subroutine in a larger routine that is itself recycled as necessary.

To illustrate these processes as they might occur in simulation of the wholistic strategy described by Bruner, Goodnow, and Austin, Reitman (1965) has set down the seven steps that a computer program and a human subject might perform, assuming that the first card is a positive instance. Note that Reitman has italicized the information-processing operations.

1.—*Remember* as hypothesis the value of each attribute.
2.—If there is a next instance, *get* it; if not, stop. (This is called a *conditional branch.*)
3.—*Compare* this instance against the hypothesis to determine whether it is identical, and note and *remember* any difference.
4.—If the instance is identical, do step 2 again; if it is not, do the next step (*conditional branch*).
5.—*Get* feedback indicating whether the card actually is an instance of the concept.
6.—If answer is "no," do step 2 again; if "yes," do next step (*conditional branch.*)
7.—*Forget* any values of the previous hypothesis which differ from those of this positive infirming instance. Do step 1 again with this new hypothesis [p. 66].

Another characteristic of simulation models, pointed out by Newell, Simon, and Shaw (1958) in an early paper that first opened these arcane practices to psychological scrutiny, is their hierarchical nature. The branching and recycling have a trial-and-error character, but the subroutines take place within larger routines. The little wheels are run by the big wheels and the program moves in a strictly mechanistic manner toward an insightful conclusion. Their Logic Theorist, capable of discovering proofs for theorems in elementary symbolic logic, begins with the goal (what is to be proved), transforms it into symbols similar to what is given, and then tries various heuristics to reduce the difference between the two. But the program maintains a set for the goal throughout the detailed maneuvers. One of their summary paragraphs puts this in psychological language as follows:

We postulate an information-processing system with large storage capacity that holds, among other things, complex strategies (programs) that may be evoked by stimuli. The stimulus determines what strategy or strategies will be evoked; the content of these strategies is already largely determined by the previous experience of the system. The ability of the system to respond in complex and highly selective ways to relatively simple stimuli is a consequence of this storage of programs and this "active" response to stimuli. The phenomena of set and insight . . . and the hierarchial structure of the response system are all consequences of this "active" organization of the central processes [p. 163].

Some of the elements in an information-processing model and the alternative sequences of operations are illustrated schematically in Fig. 4.15, taken from E. S. Johnson (1964).

Attempts at computer simulation favor problems in which all the information available to the subject can also be given to the computer in symbolic form. The major difficulty in writing a program for the solution of algebra problems written in ordinary English sentences was the translation of the relevant information into algebraic symbols (Paige and Simon, 1966). When the text of each problem was edited a little in advance and an English-algebra dic-

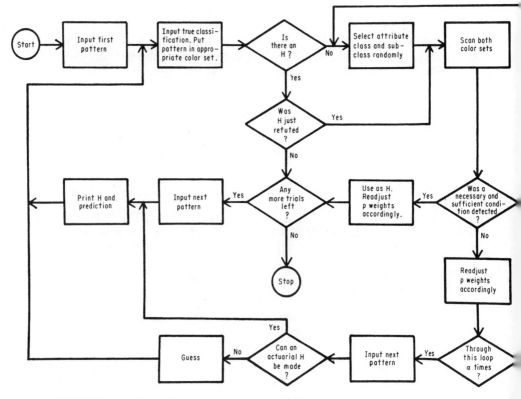

FIGURE 4.15. *Flow chart for a simple information-processing model.* H *stands for the current working hypothesis;* p *for probability;* a *is a parameter of the model. From* E. S. Johnson (1964).

tionary prepared for the computer to consult when needed, fair success was attained, and the program seemed to perform as human subjects perform. Some subjects, however, used auxiliary cues from their own experience, which the computer, with its carefully programmed experience, could not simulate.

In attempting to reduce this difference between computer performance and human performance, Reitman (1965) was impressed by the long-term persistence of human thinkers in spite of distractions from the telephone, irrelevant ideas that spring from nowhere, and internal anxieties; so he built a program, called Argus, that would operate with a gradual loss of information and with variable control over the cognitive elements of the system. He says,

Argus assumes that many cognitive processes go on at once, that all information structures change and decay away unless special circumstances intervene, and that centralized sequential control in thinking varies from almost none, in free association, to a high degree in some individuals in some forms of goal-directed problem solving [p. 225].

Argus is capable of solving simple analogy problems in word form, such as

bear : pig :: chair : (foot, table, coffee, strawberry)

as men do, but some analogies cause difficulties because human subjects possess all kinds of information about words—not altogether complete or correct—which influences their thinking but not the computer's. What is needed next, according to Reitman, is a model which, when exposed to a casual information environment, will store portions of that information, as harried human beings do, and retrieve some of it, in the peculiar ways that men do, when faced with an unanticipated problem.

Not only verbal processes but perceptual processes also impose a structure on the problem materials that appears to offer difficulties for computer simulation. When expert chess players look at the positions of two dozen pieces on a board, they quickly perceive functional groupings: pieces vulnerable to attack from other pieces, pieces that can attack others, pieces that defend others, and so on. Highly proficient players with years of experience have displayed an almost unbelievable capacity to reproduce the positions of the pieces after only a brief exposure of the board—but only if the pieces are disposed in meaningful patterns, or substructures, not if they are disposed at random (De Groot, 1965).

Fortunately, a chessboard is spatially extended so that eye movements around the board can be photographed and fixations located with moderate accuracy. Simon and Barenfeld (1969) therefore adapted their information-processing model of problem solving to the simulation of eye movements by making a few reasonable assumptions about the information, on the functional relations between pieces, obtained in one fixation and the next fixation implied by this information. Some fragmentary comparisons with tracings of actual eye movements show fair agreement; this suggests that an information-processing model can account for the preparatory organization of the problem materials that occurs in the first few seconds of exposure.

Main Trends and Implications

Most psychologists can live in peace with others' definitions of problem solving—more so than with their definitions of a concept—but the struggle between expansionist stimulus-response and cognitive forces to take over the interpretation of problem-solving behavior goes on here as elsewhere. The newest contender to enter the theoretical arena is information processing, often armed with a magic weapon, the electronic computer, for simulating problem-solving behavior. Meanwhile, by avoiding or misperceiving the contest between traditional theories, or by shamelessly embracing all contestants, many psychologists are attempting to describe the task variables that make problems difficult, and the processes by which problems are solved.

The difficulty of problems increases as complexity increases, but there are two qualifications to this obvious relationship. The more complex problems make greater demands on memory and require advance planning of moves, hence difficulty increases more sharply than one might expect. On the other hand, additional material often contributes helpful cues rather than additional demands. The familiarity of the materials of the problem has a generally helpful effect, but familiarity with potential solutions, from exposure in the past or present, has a much greater effect, facilitating judgment as well as solutions.

The old attempt at analysis of the thought processes by examining one's own thoughts or by observing other people solving problems has been brought up to date by exposure devices that allow more complete observation and timing of moves. The trend now is toward more objective methods, which necessitate choosing problems that are convenient for objective observation (often very artificial), and toward formulating and testing specific hypotheses about observable behavior. The aims of modern analyses are more modest than a description of *the* thought processes; the processes and effects examined are limited both in number and magnitude.

The associative mechanisms developed to extend theories of simple learning into the problem-solving domain lean heavily on the hypothesis of a response hierarchy, which has been quite successful in accounting for the effect of word frequency in anagram solution. Another associative mechanism, mediating responses intended to integrate separately learned behavior segments, has had only limited success as yet.

Demonstrations of the control of problem solving, for better or worse, by a problem-solving set are as old as this century, the interpretations of the demonstrations varying with the theoretical fashions of the times. The social situation and the general instructions are the basic conditions that activate the general set or adjustment to a problem-solving assignment. Given this general set, a more specific set for a specific method can be quickly established by a short series of problems that are readily solved by such a method—or even more quickly by specific instructions. Single words and their associations exert a semantic influence while the instructions exert a syntactic influence. Some of the effects of sets can be interpreted by association hypotheses derived from animal learning or from free recall. The similarities between the anagram experiment and the concept experiment are also of theoretical interest and, as in concept learning, some evidence for discontinuity under certain conditions has been presented. But evidence for a continuous, cumulative learning curve obtained by uncritical pooling of data from different subjects is suspect.

An information-seeking process can be isolated by arrangements which minimize the other processes and permit the subject to uncover the necessary information in his own way. Most ordinary adults improve somewhat by adjusting their strategies to their experience with the work required and the probabilities of finding the information. But, as in experiments on probability learning, they seldom discover the mathematically optimal strategy and stick with it.

Unlike the jigsaw puzzle that may be solved by manipulating the pieces directly, many problems are solved by representing the data symbolically and manipulating the symbols. Transforming the information from one system to another while preserving the structure is necessary for solving some problems, but these processes have not received the experimental and theoretical attention from students of problem solving that they deserve. Obviously, errors can occur in the coding of data into symbols, in the manipulation of the symbols, and in the application of the symbolic solution to the original problem situation.

The cognitive structures that are most useful in solving problems are—in addition to perceived structures of objects—behavioral structures, or plans, whose elements are simple acts. The understanding of a structure is something more than the ability to perform the elementary acts, and methods are available for differentiating achievement of the structure from achievement of the elements. Principles, which make general assertions, are particularly useful for problem solving: some problems are solved by application of a principle and some by the mere statement of one. These measures and others can be used to test achievement of a principle, and the converging results of several measures are more convincing than the results of one alone. Sequences in the development of principles and other cognitive structures parallel those in the development of concepts.

But problem solving does not start from nowhere. Speaking loosely, we can call problems stimuli, but they are often complex stimulus patterns, some of which resist analysis more than others. Anagrams in the form of words are more difficult to break up and restructure than comparable anagrams in non-word form. And anagrams that require much rearrangement of letters are especially difficult, unless the ends of the structure are preserved. Hence it is reasonable to say that problem solving consists of reorganization as well as organization.

Functional fixedness was originally conceived as a characteristic of the perceived situation—namely, the embedding of the critical function of a component in a larger structure—and investigated by manipulating the initial arrangement of the materials. It has also been conceived as a consequence of previous learning of the components and investigated by manipulating pre-utilization of the components. Functional fixedness interferes with solution, as does the problem-solving set under some conditions; but, to go one step further, such interference can be reduced by manipulation of the perceived situation, by more varied preutilization, by strategic labeling of the components, and by practice on sorting tasks.

Equally important for the future is the trend among several investigators, branching out from concept research, to treat an object as multidimensional, as if the thinker analyzes it into various dimensions, functions, uses, and other attributes. Just as the cognition of a large red triangle can emphasize size, color, or shape, making cognition of the other attributes temporarily more difficult, so does cognition of one function of an object make cognition of other functions temporarily more difficult.

Behavioral structures, like concepts, can be treated as hypothetical mediators, with either cognitive properties to be interpreted by principles of cognitive organization or response properties to be interpreted by principles of stimulus-response learning. But decades of research and argument have not brought forth results that force a choice between the two interpretations. The theoretical stalemate suggests that hypothetical properties of hypothetical mediators are not distinguishable in fact or in theory. There is a clear trend, however, toward mediators with structural properties, whether they are called stimulus-response chains, conceptual systems, cognitive schemas, or sub-routines. The most human characteristic of programs for computer simulation of problem solving is their ability to organize elementary moves into these subroutines and integrate them as units, dependent on the outcomes of previous moves, into the larger movement toward a solution.

CHAPTER *5*

THE SOLUTION OF PROBLEMS CONTINUED

Training in Solving Problems
Individual Differences in Problem Solving
Major Trends and Implications

veryone knows that the solution of a problem may be a complicated enterprise. We have related how this depends on various components—such as associations, information, skills, concepts, and principles—some of which are the achievements of previous learning and thinking, while others are achieved on the spot during solution of the present problem. Solution depends also on the appropriate organization of these components into the larger structure that fits the problem, often in spite of an initially resistant organization. In any such system of activity, composed of so many interacting processes, there are multiple possibilities for improvement because there are many points where performance can be inefficient, and many dimensions in which problem solvers differ from one another. The two main topics of this chapter are training in solving problems, and individual differences among problem solvers.

Training in Solving Problems

Some generalizations about difficulties in problem solving and how they are overcome (gleaned from hundreds of experiments) were set forth in the previous chapter. But it is one thing to establish generalizations about problem solving and another thing to teach peo-

199

ple how to do it. A theory of learning, or thinking, should not masquerade as a theory of instruction.

The controversies over methods of instruction are somewhat similar in shape and intensity, nevertheless, to controversies over theories of learning. And one of the most persistent of these, which may be phrased as rote learning versus meaningful learning, or drill versus understanding, applies with equal emphasis to problem solving. A second controversy, overlapping the first, is that between discovery and expository learning. Is it better to let a student make errors and discover the solution by himself or to explain to him how to solve a problem? This is an active topic of discussion even though there is some uncertainty about the meaning of *discovery* in this context (Shulman and Keislar, 1966). But one thing is clear. There is no magic formula for teaching people how to solve problems. Research will not prove that one method is right and the others wrong. Progress is more likely to come from a better understanding of the effects of alternative methods and their combinations.

Any comparison of instructional methods must consider the criterion of achievement, since different criteria suggest different conclusions. The criterion may be a reduction in solution time or in number of errors when solving a series of problems. More important, however, is the transfer to other problems, either immediately or later. The transfer problems may be similar to the training problems, but if we are concerned about remote transfer or general problem-solving skill, the transfer problems should be different. Some investigators have included the criterion of interest in solving problems, because it is claimed that some methods are boring while others are fun.

TEACHING CONCEPTS

Concepts are necessary equipment for the problem solver because certain problems are stated in general terms. These terms may refer to class concepts, such as deciduous trees and uninsured drivers, or to dimensional concepts, such as acidity and resistance. In other cases, solution depends on knowledge of a concept that does not appear in the statement of the problem. There the concept is a mediator. Solution may depend, for example, on arranging the elements of the problem in the form of a right triangle and knowing the properties of right triangles. In any case, achievement of the concepts involved is necessary, and the question arises how they should be taught to facilitate their use in the solution of problems.

Conventional concept research is not directed toward this question. Looking at the method of the concept experiments outlined in previous chapters from the teaching standpoint, we would describe it as learning by discovery. The experimenter does not usually tell the subject in advance that the class consists of large squares with double borders; he merely confirms correct guesses, expecting the subject to discover the class by himself. There are some instructional implications, however. It is important to note that the general set communicated by the experimenter, which is a form of instruction, has a strong effect. Few subjects discover subtle concepts in laboratory experiments without being told to look for them. It is pertinent also that negative information, telling what a concept is not, is less helpful than positive information, and that this difference can be reduced by special training.

If we are not concerned with plotting the course of this inductive type of concept learning, we can simply tell the subjects what the concept is, that is, what we mean by *dax* or *deciduous tree* or *acidity*. But we cannot assume without data that this method is better than others. College students given definitions of four concepts (page 82) did well on later tests of concept achievement but no better than subjects who learned the same concepts by other methods. The possibility of interference between concepts in this simple experiment reminds us that the greater likelihood of interference in school, on the job, and in the library, may shift the relative weights of factors found in the laboratory. One would expect, however, that the superiority of the mixed program—combining four methods of teaching concepts—would be generally applicable.

TEACHING PRINCIPLES

Many teaching procedures combine the teaching of concepts and principles. But since principles have a special place in problem solving, their teaching also has a special place in discussions of training for problem solving. Is it more efficient to teach students the basic principles for complex performances —such as making a cake, wiring a television set, and solving an algebra problem—or to let them discover the principles by themselves? What would be the optimal combination of problems for teaching principles?

One of the earliest experiments on this question used the disk-transfer problem later used by Cook (see page 139). Ewert and Lambert (1932) gave their subjects various kinds of instructions, but the most efficient performance was attained by those who were given a statement of the principle for such efficient performance.

Another classic series of experiments, which Katona (1940) called a comparison of organizing and memorizing, required college students to master complex performances, such as card tricks and matchstick puzzles. In one of these experiments, a group of students was given the exact order of arranging the cards to perform a trick, which they memorized by repetition. Another group observed a demonstration and explanation of the principle of the trick, given only once, and it was this group that was most successful in performing the tricks later. A group that received a verbal statement of the principle was intermediate between the other two.

A number of studies in the 1950s followed up these early studies, making use of Katona's problems, disk-transfer problems, arithmetic problems, word problems, and others. One by Craig (1956), with the familiar oddity problem, gives a good illustration. Each of his problems consisted of five words, four to be related by a principle, the other to be identified as the odd one. The principles for different blocks of problems were based on similarities of sound, spelling, or meaning; but one group of students was told only that there were principles, while another group could read the relevant principle printed above each block of problems. This latter group did better on an immediate transfer test of new problems involving the same principles and also on another test a month later. They were not superior in learning different principles for different types of problems however.

It appears, in general, that there is much to be said for teaching principles, especially when the problems are difficult and the criterion is the amount of transfer to new problems. But generalizations are hazardous because, as Duncan (1959) pointed out, after reviewing many of these studies, "Anything one learns probably has both positive and negative transferring effects, depending on the situation [p. 401]." These effects may vary with the specifics of the teaching procedures and materials. Recent investigations have looked more critically at these specifics.

MATHEMATICS

The concepts of mathematics, strictly speaking, are few. Most of the learning consists of the acquisition of mathematical relations, principles, rules, and operations for carrying out mathematical manipulations that are learned and recalled as higher-order units. Recently, the development of teaching machines and the demand for efficient programmed materials has accelerated the interest in optimal methods for teaching such units and their use in problem solving. Gagné and Brown (1961), therefore, tried out three programs for teaching high-school boys to derive general formulas for the sum of a number series, such as 1, 2, 4, 8, 16, —, —. If n represents the position of a term in the series and T the value of a term, it is easy to see that when n is 6, T is 32. But the problem is to find the sum of a series of n terms, the formula for which in this example is $T_{n+1} - 1$. All students had the same introductory program, after which three groups had different programs designed to teach four such formulas. The *rule-and-example program* gave each student the correct formula and required him to apply it to a few examples, then another formula and a few more examples, and so on, proceeding by small steps. The *discovery program* asked each student to try to find the formula by himself, giving hints as necessary. The *guided discovery program* asked each student what was necessary to get the sum, whether adding or subtracting would be helpful, and so on, and later asked for a general rule. The next day each student did each problem again, as before. Then all students did four new problems, getting hints as necessary, to determine how well each type of training would transfer to the solution of similar new problems.

The results were quite clear-cut. The method of guided discovery was most effective; with this method, the mean time for the four new problems was 16 minutes. Mean time for the discovery method was 20 minutes, and for the rule-and-example method 27 minutes. Certainly, other programs, better or worse than these, could be designed under the same three labels. But by looking closely at what each group of subjects did, Gagné and Brown concluded that the superiority of guided discovery in their experiment consisted in the use of previously learned concepts, as represented by such symbols as n, T and T_{n+1}, in new contexts. The discovery program made use of the same concepts, but systematic practice and guidance in their use was not given. In the rule-and-example program such symbols occurred as stimuli, in the formula provided, but the responses to these consisted merely of the writing of numbers. In comparing methods, we should look not only at the names but also at what the student learns under each method, whether, as in this case, he learns to substitute numbers for symbols or to manipulate concepts.

Mistakes can easily be made in arranging the materials for teaching principles. One characteristic to be watched is the heterogeneity of problems (Traub, 1966). A group of sixth-grade pupils, given a homogeneous series of problems in graphical addition of integers, acquired the necessary principles, in a limited way, and solved new problems better than a control group. But they skipped the harder problems and they made stereotyped errors. Another group, given a heterogeneous series of problems with more variation in numbers and algebraic signs, spent more time on the training series, but they did much better on application to the new problems than the other groups.

There is no magic in learning by discovery. If it is superior, why is this so? One possibility, put forth by Berlyne (1965), is that the discovery method causes cognitive conflict and thereby increases motivation for understanding the problem. In a study by Worthen (1968), however, use of the discovery method did not make a noticeable difference in the subjects' general attitude toward arithmetic. Roughead and Scandura (1968), on the basis of a study of college women assigned to several combinations of methods, suggested that those who learned principles by the discovery method learned, not only the relevant principles, but also something about deriving principles that can apply to transfer tests. Those who were given the rule had no special reason to learn how to derive it for themselves.

ANAGRAMS

We noted (in the preceding chapter) that a problem-solving set, acquired in the solution of a series of problems, can facilitate or impede solution of a second series. If we treat the first series as a training one and the second as a transfer one, then the various transfer designs developed in other areas (especially in experiments on verbal learning) suggest other ways to clarify the application of problem-solving principles. Di Vesta and Walls (1967) took up this kind of analysis by giving solution rules for rearranging the letters of anagrams. One rule, for example, was: "Each pair of letters in order, but the members of each pair are reversed [p. 322]." They then planned several variations in the relation between the rules on the training series and those on the transfer series. It turned out, in line with the predictions, that the most improvement occurred when the solution rules acquired on the training problems were similar to those needed for the transfer problems, and the least when the solution rules were inappropriate.

But consider the case in which the transfer problems necessitate shifting

204 # THE SOLUTION OF PROBLEMS CONTINUED

from one principle to another. Then what is the optimal sequence of training problems for developing flexibility in solving the transfer problems? Di Vesta and Walls (1968) tried out several variations in training problems, preceding transfer problems that required shifts in the rule for rearranging the letters and also in the category of the solution word. Variations in training with the letter-order solution rule had surprisingly little effect on the transfer problems, but training with anagrams that had multiple categories of solution words did aid shifting on the transfer problems. Shifting from a set for one category of solution words to another may be considered a kind of strategy, and Di Vesta and Walls point out that those who trained on multiple categories had more practice on the "win-stay," "lose-shift" strategy. Despite the difference in content, these results agree with Traub's for arithmetic problems in emphasizing the beneficial effects of variations in the training series when subjects turn to new problems.

STATING THE PRINCIPLE

"If you want to learn something, teach it." This old truism can be rephrased as the hypothesis that learning is more efficient when the learner puts the relevant information into words for communication to others, or as the saying goes, "verbalizes" it. In Chapter 2 we noted that attempts at the verbal definition of a concept facilitate the attainment of figure concepts. But attempts at the statement of a principle have more complex effects. It is not the actual enunciation of the principle that is important, of course, for a principle stated by the teacher can easily be memorized and repeated verbatim by the student; it is the generalization of the principle by the student on the basis of his experience with certain problems that is supposed to facilitate application to other problems.

Ervin (1960) approached this question by training children in the third and fourth grades to shoot a ball so that it would ricochet off a backboard and strike a target. Some of the children were able to formulate an explanation for the path taken by the ball, but others could not, even though their performance was successful. When a transfer task called for aiming a flashlight at a mirror to strike a target, the advantage of formulation of the principle showed up. But at this age, although language and thought are both fairly well developed, they are not well correlated. Ervin pointed out that the verbal statements of these children did not correspond very well with their problem-solving actions and should not be taken too seriously. "The great skill that children acquire in verbal learning is something of a hazard in that it is likely to reward both teacher and pupil so readily that the teacher overlooks the learning criterion she is most concerned with, which is not necessarily verbal learning alone [p. 553]."

The familiar disk-transfer problem described on page 139 is convenient here because the moves are easy ones that can be made without much thought, but they are discrete moves that can also be conceptualized and described verbally. Thus the subject can talk about patterns of moves and plans or rules for efficient solution of the problem. He can make some progress by planning one or two moves ahead, but he can make more progress by working out a more rational formulation.

Gagné and Smith (1962) had boys in the ninth and tenth grades work this problem with several variations in instructions in order to study the contribution of the subjects' verbal statements to overall efficiency of performance. It was the subjects who were encouraged to state why they were making a move at the time they were making it who did best after shifting to new problems of the same type, both in respect to minimal number of moves and to the adequacy of their statement of a general principle for such problems. Similar results have been obtained by other investigators (Davis, Carey, Foxman, and Tarr, 1968).

One can select cards, write numbers, and make moves without much intellectual effort and usually make some progress. But if one is expected to justify his problem-solving attempts verbally, he has to analyze the problem in sufficient depth to give names to the variables in view and the relationships between them. It is easy to believe that training in producing verbal rationales will be beneficial when the criterion of achievement is a verbal generalization, but in the experiments mentioned here the nonverbal achievements also benefited.

HIERARCHIES OF KNOWLEDGE

Consider the following analogy problem.

laconic is to *loquacious* as *hackneyed* is to ___?

The solution here can be treated as a high-level performance that integrates four low-level components. No one would be expected to get the answer if he did not know the meanings of the four words. So putting the problem aside temporarily and teaching the low-level components would presumably be an efficient start.

The notion of a hierarchy of performances, some of which, at low levels, are necessary for performance at higher levels, is implicit in much research on problem solving. Discussions of the function of concepts, principles, cognitive schemas, and other substructures generally assume that these are separate components to be organized into a larger solution pattern, but hierarchies of knowledge have been examined most explicitly by Gagné (1962). Fig. 5.1 illustrates a hierarchy of nine subordinate capabilities involved in the problem that Gagné and Brown (1961) studied (see page 202): finding a formula for the sum of n terms in a number series. Tests of each of the nine tasks were prepared and given in a fixed sequence from the top down, stopping when a task was reached that the subject could perform. It was assumed that the subject could perform tasks lower in the hierarchy, but that instruction would be necessary for those above which had been failed. Thus the subordinate capabilities, as worked out for arithmetic problems, are intellectual skills, not necessarily verbal statements of principles.

The implication of complex task hierarchies for training is that the subor-

Task

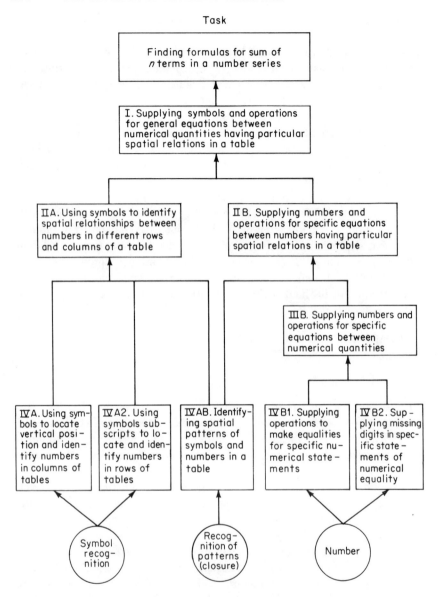

FIGURE 5.1. *Hierarchy of knowledge for the task of finding formulas for the sum of* n *terms in a number series. From Gagné (1962).*

dinate capabilities must be learned before the higher ones. By this procedure, the learner does not begin work on the terminal performance. The instructor first analyzes the complex terminal performance into the requisite subordinate capabilities and teaches these one level at a time. The learning is cumulative. The final level is practiced when all the subordinate performances have been mastered.

Some novel empirical consequences of this hierarchical approach came to light in a report by Gagné and Paradise (1961) of an experiment with 118 students in seventh-grade mathematics classes learning to solve linear equations. Task analysis by the investigators identified 22 components located at 5 levels. In the records of performance at each level before and after a teaching program, there were four contingencies for testing the theory:

Success at one level and also at a higher level. This is predicted from the theory.

Failure at one level and also at a lower level. This is predicted from the theory.

Success at one level and failure at a lower level. This is opposed to the theory.

Failure at one level and success at a lower level. This is not opposed to the theory; it just means that the subject did not learn to make the integration at the higher level.

When the data were examined in this way, more than 90 percent of the instances were predicted from the theory.

Describing a structure of capabilities in a complex problem-solving performance is probably easier than describing the optimal method for learning the structure. The improvement in the Gagné and Paradise experiment was smaller than expected. Learning from the bottom up is not necessarily better than learning from the top down; it seems to run contrary to the recommendation to learn principles rather than facts.

Of course it is easy to make up a logical hierarchy and assume, like those who make certain college courses prerequisite to others, that students must learn the first before they can go on to the next. But this cannot always be true. A recent experiment by Merrill (1965), which required university students to learn a new imaginary science constructed so that the concepts and principles were arranged in clearly distinguishable levels, found, surprisingly, that it was not necessary to master one level before going on to the next, more complex level. Many students apparently learned the allegedly essential low-level concepts while working on the higher levels. A control group that received only a summary statement of the science made many errors on the first tests but later outperformed the groups who had the benefit of the carefully designed programs. The conclusion was that in trying to ensure mastery at lower levels the experimental program had actually slowed down the subjects' progress. Other experiments (e.g., Payne, Krathwohl, and Gordon, 1967) also have shown that the order is not too important, that adults can acquire the necessary components even though the presentation does not proceed up the hierarchy in a logically engineered progression.

Evidently, analysis of a hierarchy of capabilities tells us more about individual differences at the moment and reasons for failures than about the optimal sequence of study. To return to our verbal analogy, we can teach the meaning of *laconic* by its relation to *loquacious*; or, in general, we can teach the components by teaching their functions in a larger structure. The evidence suggests that we can err by spending too much time on the low-level components, and also by jumping up a level too quickly.

TEACHING REPRESENTATION AND TRANSFORMATION

Max Wertheimer's (1945) well-known book *Productive Thinking* did not contain any empirical evaluation of alternative methods for solving problems. His contribution was rather to analyze the difficulty of certain arithmetic and geometric problems by describing their structure and to suggest methods that would reveal the structure more clearly to the student. Although Wertheimer did not emphasize the transformation process, many of his suggestions consisted of transforming a symbolic representation of the problem into a graphic representation. Consider his hypothesis of the difficulty involved in the problem of vertical angles: the assignment is to prove that angles a and c of Fig. 5.2 are equal. One can proceed algebraically, as follows:

$$a + b = 180 \text{ degrees}$$
$$c + b = 180 \text{ degrees}$$

Subtracting	$a - c = 0$
Therefore	$a = c$

According to Wertheimer, this demonstration is hard to follow. Students may learn it mechanically, but the occurrence of mechanical errors in repeating the proof shows that it has not been genuinely understood. The principal reason for the difficulty is that it is hard to perceive angle b as part of $a + b$, which equals 180 degrees, and also as part of $b + c$, which equals 180 degrees. It is the structure, including the relation of the parts to the whole, that must be grasped rather than any particular equation or sequence of equations. Wertheimer recommends graphic representations of the problem, as in Fig. 5.3, as successful devices for revealing the structure to the student. At the same time, Wertheimer's discussion includes considerable verbal analysis and many transformations of numerical equations into ordinary sentences.

Solid objects, or construction materials, permit more flexibility in the representation of mathematical and physical principles, and many teachers have used such materials for this purpose. But a child's understanding of the principles may be limited to the specific materials or apparatus from which the illustration was contrived—as the ancient Egyptian surveyors were

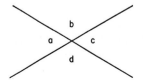

FIGURE 5.2. The vertical angles problem.

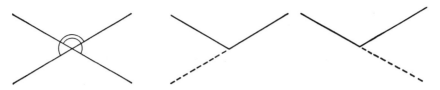

FIGURE 5.3. *Alternative ways of restructuring the vertical angles problem. After Wertheimer (1945).*

limited to specific applications. The teacher's task, of course, is to conduct the child beyond specific imaginable examples to general principles. Bruner and Kenney (1965) have shown how to represent the multiplication table with blocks that children can manipulate in order to multiply and divide perceptually and thus *see* the equality between $(x + 2)^2$ and $x^2 + 4x + 4$. An appropriate notation for representing the mathematical quantities and relations, the heterogeneity of the examples, and considerable explanation in ordinary English seem to be the critical ingredients for the effectiveness of such learning. But Bruner and Kenney believe that even after older children have acquired the formal properties of the mathematical expressions and a systematic symbolic notation, they still utilize their imagery to explore problems and relate them to problems already mastered.

The apparent advantages of the manual-visual mode of representation can easily be combined with those of discovery learning. For example, Anderson and Johnson (1966) gave one group of college girls a short, barebones statement of the forces operating on balls rotating about a standard and then asked about its application to a somewhat similar test situation. Another group was told to experiment with the apparatus until they understood it and then was asked about the test situation. Both groups gave better explanations of the test situation than a control group, but the perceptual form of presentation was superior, and those who were successful reported more visual imagery. The results of this experiment and other similar ones have obvious implications for training in problem solving; but we do not know whether to attribute them to the difference between the perceptual and verbal modes of representation or to the difference between discovery and expository learning.

Scandura (1967) evaluated alternative representation systems in more detail by writing the rules for certain mathematical operations in ordinary English and also in mathematical form, with summation signs, parentheses, exponents, and other symbols. The subjects, mostly college women, learned the symbolic statements more rapidly than the English statements, probably because the latter were longer. Mathematical expressions that are used repeatedly are often recoded into more compact symbols, which, though less familiar, are more efficient representations of the information to be retained. But when these subjects were faced with applications to new problems, they applied the rules written in English just as readily as the rules written in mathematical symbolism. Incidentally, those who were given symbolic problems applied the symbolic rules successfully if, and only if, they had previously been taught the meaning of the symbols and the underlying grammar, such as the order of operations signified by parentheses. These results are evidence, in general, of cumulative or hierarchical learning. The high-level accomplishments depend on the low-level ones, yet the subjects were able to benefit from some of the advantages of mathematical representation, relative to ordinary English, without realizing all its potentialities.

There is much still to be learned about alternative modes of representation. The graphic mode is most appropriate for representing the structure of some problems, and for these instruction in drawing graphs and in transforming data from other forms into graphic form will no doubt be helpful. The verbal definition of a class of figures and the verbal statement of a physical principle, which may be treated as transformation operations, are helpful in other cases. Hence we may suggest the hypothesis that, aside from the appropriateness of a specific mode of representation, *any* transformation from one mode—verbal, numerical, algebraic, graphic, gestural, cinematic— to another affords the student a further avenue for penetration to the structure of the problem and increases his depth of understanding. Any transformation that the teacher makes would be instructive, and any transformation by the student would presumably be even more helpful.

TEACHING PROBLEM-SOLVING STRATEGIES

There is some ambiguity in the psychological usage of such terms as *principle*, *rule*, and *strategy*, but most often a *strategy* is a general approach. As in the terminology of concept research, a strategy is not a method for solution of the problem, but a method for collecting and retaining relevant information, for formulating and testing hypotheses, for representing and transforming the data, for detecting errors, or, in short, a method for finding a method for solution. Thus many of the procedures outlined above may be considered as the teaching of strategies when they are taught with general implications for a broad class of problems. Examples are the half-split strategy for information seeking, breaking up a problem into subproblems, and the explicit verbal statement of a principle.

The most generally effective strategy is to stop and think: several experiments on a variety of problems have shown that when the subjects are told not to start immediately to solve the problem, but just to sit and think about it for a while, their performance is improved (Cohen, 1954; Duncan, 1963; Ray, 1957). Unless the subject starts out right, which raises the suspicion that the task is not a genuine problem for him, or makes a lucky guess, which is unlikely in complex situations, the immediate production of solutions interferes with the chances of cognitive reorganization and of identifying alternative response patterns.

Everyone knows that children like to ask questions, yet many observers of classroom behavior have been impressed by the passivity of the children, and many teachers would like to increase the number and quality of the questions asked, even to the extent of isolating and cultivating this art by itself. It is possible that the strategies most in need of improvement are in-formation-seeking strategies, especially since these preparatory activities are easily overlooked. As a first step in what he calls Inquiry Training, Suchman (1964) showed films of a physics demonstration to schoolchildren and ar-ranged the conditions so that they had freedom to ask questions and received prompt, reasonable answers. Taped records of the children's questions were analyzed by the investigators and also played back to the children so they could learn some of the consequences of the various strategies of data gather-ing. In comparison with control groups, those with Inquiry Training asked more questions, and classification of the questions indicated that they were generally of a higher quality. Questions that merely asked the teacher to do the thinking became less frequent after this type of training, and those aimed at identifying the parameters of the problems more frequent.

The type of questions asked by children is influenced also by the ques-tions asked by others, especially by a prestigious model. Rosenthal, Zim-merman, and Durning (1970) displayed pictures of 12 familiar objects to a group of disadvantaged sixth-grade children while an adult experimenter asked questions about physical attributes of the objects (e.g., shape) as criteria of classification. In other groups the model asked questions about the function of the objects, about relations between objects, or about their value. Later, when the children were encouraged to ask questions about the objects, the most frequent questions in each group were of the same type as those asked by the model in that group—though exact mimicry was not frequent. Then new pictures were presented, and the effect of the model on type of questions asked generalized to these also. The success of such social learning experiments, which have already shown how a model in-fluences moral judgments, aggressive behavior, and the like in slanting in-formation-seeking tendencies, suggests how parents and teachers slant the child's attempt to categorize the objects around him.

The effects of giving information about strategies and principles were evaluated in one comprehensive experiment by Corman (1957). He had high-school seniors work matchstick problems like those used by Katona and gave three degrees of information—much, some, and none—about a method for solving the problems and the same three degrees of information about a rule for solution. The information about the method was helpful in solv-ing the problems, while the information about the rule was more helpful later when the students were asked to state a general principle. In this experiment, the improvement was specific to the criterion that corresponded to the kind of information given, but in some other experiments (e.g., Gagné and Smith, 1962) the benefits of teaching principles were not always limited in this way.

Can young children be taught to solve problems? Previous chapters have noted the limitations implied by Piaget's stages of intellectual development and some attempts to teach children to overcome these implied limitations. Moderate success was reported. An attempt by Anderson (1965) to teach young children rather complex problem-solving skills is more encouraging.

He gave first-grade children a variety of complicated problems involving concepts and principles, such as determining which kind of cowboy is a friend of the sheriff and why one pendulum swings faster than others. He taught one group the strategy of varying each factor in succession while holding other factors constant and found that their success on transfer tasks of the same type, while far from perfect, was distinctly better than that of a control group. The operations the successful children used were, according to Anderson, those that Piaget and Inhelder restricted to age fourteen. It is true that these were superior children, with a mental age around nine, and that they had the benefit of individual training sessions of 20 minutes three times a week for 27 sessions; but still the results shows what concentrated training can do to stages presumed to depend on age and cumulative experience. As to verbal statements of the relations, the results of the training were less encouraging; the trained group gave somewhat more invalid explanations than the control group.

Comparable results were obtained by Stern (1967), who was able to teach a simple problem-solving strategy to third-grade children, about nine years old, in six lessons. Keislar and Stern (1970) were also successful in teaching two problem-solving strategies, a complex hypothesis-testing strategy and a simple gambling strategy, to children of very high intelligence in second and third grades. The experiment was planned as an examination of differentiated instruction, and the results demonstrated that the most superior children, of sixth-grade ability, profited more from the complex strategy while other children, of fourth-grade ability, profited more from the simple strategy.

There are a few very general—perhaps too general—strategies, such as "Stop and think" and "Think about what you are doing while you are doing it." The strategies that have interested psychologists seem to be those at a middle level of generality, related to psychological principles, some of which, as we have seen, can be taught to others with fair success. In addition, many strategies are restricted to specific problems, as in football, chess, merchandising, politics, and administration. They are utilized by experts in these fields and may even be taught to others, usually without firm knowledge of the psychological basis for their success.

SOME LIMITATIONS

The evidence reviewed here should make it clear that improvement in problem solving can be obtained by several methods. The critical question is not whether a certain type of training is effective but which method or combination of methods is more effective under specified conditions.

One of the conditions that limit generalization is the nature of the problem, whether verbal, numerical, spatial, behavioral, or other. The principles that apply to some problems are rather easily comprehended and utilized by the subject to guide his efforts, and we might suppose that these are composed of familiar concepts designated by familiar words. If the elements and the relations between them are conspicuous, the principles will be easily grasped and applied. But the essential principle for some problems is more subtle, and considerable manipulation of the elements is required before it is comprehended—thus the problem may be solved by trial and error or by memorizing single moves before any overall principle is grasped, even if given by the instructor. This seems to be the case in many mathematics problems, and some principles of linguistic usage are notoriously difficult to state, even though children follow them quite well. The obvious implication is that generalizations about training for problem solving should be limited to problems of the type on which the generalizations were found.

Another condition that limits our generalizations about teaching methods is the intellectual level of the students. The more intelligent students will do better, of course, but there is more to it than that. For example, in the study of matchstick problems mentioned above, Corman gave his subjects a test of general intelligence and found, as expected, that those above average did better. But, to be more specific, the results suggested that those above average were able to integrate information about the principle and about the strategy, while a little information about the principle seemed to distract those below average from doing their best to solve the problem at hand. Likewise, although the stages of cognitive development described by Piaget may not be immutable, they cannot be ignored in any comparison of training methods. Again, in general, statements about training for solving problems should be limited to subjects similar to those on whom the results were obtained.

A comparison between two methods of teaching problem solving, as between verbal and graphic representations of a principle, implies that each is an equally potent representative of its class. But it has often happened that an excellent specimen of one method is pitted against a mediocre specimen of another. The results must therefore be discounted, to an unknown degree. A comparison of methods that are both optimal and both feasible would be the most informative.

Individual Differences in Problem Solving

Whenever two or more people struggle with a complicated problem, the observer will notice differences in intellectual proficiency and, if he looks closely, in intellectual style as well. These individual differences are hidden when scores are averaged for comparisons between conditions, but any attempt at a thorough understanding must bring them out into the open.

PROBLEM-SOLVING ABILITIES

Differential psychology and experimental psychology have both developed sophisticated methodologies and, while there is no real incompatability between them, emphasis on one to the exclusion of the other is the rule, in spite of efforts (Gagné, 1967) to bring the two disciplines together. In the study of individual differences, the dependent variables of problem solving (such as number of problems solved, time to solution, and type of strategy employed) are analogous to test items, hence the terminology and techniques of test construction and analysis are appropriate here.

The first question, of course, is the ubiquitous criterion question: What problems shall we accept as measures of problem-solving proficiency? There is no standard catalog of problems from which a representative sample can be drawn. Most of the problems selected for the experiments reported earlier in this chapter were selected for methodological reasons, that is, because certain experimental manipulations were feasible, discrete moves could be observed, or some other research requirements could be met. Such problems may be suitable, secondarily, for disclosing differences between means of two sex groups or three or four age groups, but they do not necessarily yield satisfactory scores for individuals, whether performance is measured in terms of success and failure or solution time. It is in the nature of problem solving, by definition, that a subject may hit immediately on a successful approach to one problem and then get stuck on several unsuccessful approaches to the next. Because of this large variability, performance on a single problem is not a stable index of a subject's average performance. When 2 or more problems are attempted, this variability is reduced, proportionately, but correlations between scores for 2 problems are generally rather low. The sum of the 2 scores corresponds, in psychometric terms, to the score on a 2-item test, whereas most reliable tests consist of 20 or more items.

The variability between problems can be reduced also, at least for grouping problems of the Vygotsky type (see Chapter 3), by a careful control of conditions and optimal spacing of the clues that aid the elimination of incorrect hypotheses (Brunk, Collister, Swift, and Stayton, 1958). Under optimal conditions of administration, the correlation (phi) between performance on two problems was .77; under nonoptimal conditions, the corresponding correlation was .10.

The obvious way to get scores of satisfactory reliability is to increase the number of problems, and this usually means the use of short problems. Furthermore, since large samples are required for stable correlations, a printed format is desirable. Thus, it turns out that the problem-solving criterion is often a printed test that looks more like another printed test than like the problems of the controlled experiments described above. This is not necessarily inappropriate. Some problems are corrupted when put into paper-and-pencil form; some are not. After all, much of the important intellectual work that anyone does is paperwork. Seldom does anyone suspend pieces of string from the ceiling and tie them together with the aid of a pair of pliers.

The critical question concerns the nature of the difficulty in the various problems. When laboratory problems constructed for experimental manipulation of set or functional fixedness are converted to printed format, there is a danger that the original content will be destroyed. An illustration is the case of the water-jar problem for studying set. Frick and Guilford (1957) devised a group form of the water-jar test as a measure of flexibility, but its loading on the factor—measured by the correlation of the test with the factor—which they called Adaptive Flexibility was quite low. A high loading would further the understanding of both the water-jar test and the Adaptive Flexibility factor, but a low loading of a modified test cannot be clearly interpreted.

Even the relatively simple matter of level of difficulty raises questions of interpretation. A correlation between the time scores for a test of easy anagrams and one of hard anagrams was rather low even though each test had satisfactory reliability (Sargent, 1940).

The ideal criterion of success in solving problems in general could be constructed by following the procedures for constructing a test of general intelligence. That is, one could begin with a large variety of items that clearly fit the definition of a problem, refine the test by eliminating those that do not correlate with the rest, and thus maximize the general factor. An early investigation by Billings (1934) gives some evidence for generality. He gave 60-minute tests of problem solving in eight academic areas: geometry, arithmetic, physics, mechanics, economics, sociology, geography, and history. Since he wanted to test problem solving separately from a mastery of the material involved, he gave his subjects instruction in the materials in advance of the problem solving itself. The average intercorrelation of the scores obtained by this technique was .67. The problem-solving criterion scores had high correlations, as one might expect, with general intelligence as measured by the Army Alpha.

Actually, we will have to admit that the choice of problems for a study of individual differences is a decision made by each investigator in the light of his own interests and hypotheses just as it is in laboratory experiments on problem solving. The results apply to a restricted sample of problems rather than to problem solving in general.

SEX DIFFERENCES

If various kinds of difficult problems, demanding concentrated effort, are given to students in high school or college, the male students usually succeed more often than the female students (Bedell, 1934; Billings, 1934; Maier and Burke, 1967; McNemar, 1955; Staats, 1957; Sweeney, 1953). Since the girls' grades and general intelligence are at least as good as the boys', the resources that they bring to the problems from previous learning are not deficient; the search for an interpretation of this sex difference therefore turns to their motivation or attitude toward problem solving.

When college students were given a test of masculinity of interests, those who made more masculine scores, whether men or women, solved more difficult problems (Milton, 1957). Furthermore, students who scored high on a projective measure of achievement motivation worked longer on difficult problems and got more right (French and Thomas, 1958). The obvious next step would be to try to increase the motivation of the reluctant women, and one attempt (Carey, 1958) took the form of a group discussion of attitudes toward achievement after a problem-solving session. The fact that the women did register some improvement on a second session while the men did not supports the hypothesis of a sex difference in motivation. Another attempt (Milton, 1959) took the form of a modification of the wording of the problems to make them more appropriate to the feminine role. For example, a problem that began: "Snuffy, the tramp, rolls his own cigarettes from butts . . ." was changed to: "Sally, the cook, cuts cookies from batter . . . [p. 705]." Such changes in the problem materials did reduce the sex difference somewhat.

These inquiries do not settle the question of sex differences in problem solving, which have been reduced but not eliminated; and there may be stable sex differences in specific intellectual abilities. But the results to date suggest that this question belongs in the area of the social psychology of motivation. The methodological implication is that a sex difference may obscure the results of other variables in problem solving. If a sex difference sometimes appears and sometimes does not, this transitory character also points to subtle motivational aspects of the experimental situation, such as the nature of the relationship with the experimenter.

CONTRASTING GROUPS OF GOOD AND POOR PROBLEM SOLVERS

If we could identify a group of good problem solvers and a contrasting group of poor ones, it would be enlightening to compare them on other variables. Acting on this plan, McNemar (1955) selected four tests, judged best for her purpose by several psychologists, from previous research on reasoning. These were tests that had "the type and level of reasoning involved in problem solving . . . and low variances on verbal, numerical, and perceptual factors [p. 21]." From a sample of 488 college sophomores who took these tests, she selected 73 with high scores and 73 with low scores for comparison on other tests. (The significant sex differences necessitated different cutting scores.) The important findings were that the good problem solvers were superior on word fluency, especially fluency in supplying words to fit a meaningful criterion; on induction and deduction; and on overcoming a set on the well-known water-jar problems.

High and low groups were contrasted also by Tate, Stanier, and Harootunian (1959), who gave tests of verbal and abstract reasoning, problem-solving games, and thought problems to 500 pupils in grades 7 and 8, mean age about thirteen. The correlation of the composite score on these tests and IQ was .645, hence it is clear that general intelligence predicts problem-solving success moderately well. But the prediction was far from complete, so the analysis was carried further. Those subjects whose problem-solving scores were higher than predicted from IQ were designated as good problem solvers and those whose scores were lower as poor problem solvers. This procedure identified 117 good and 117 poor problem solvers of the same average IQ.

When these extreme groups were compared on a variety of tests of more specific intellectual functions, the good problem solvers were significantly superior on nearly all tests where quality of response, accuracy, or judgment was required; and, without exception, the more complex the task or the more restricted the requirements, the greater their superiority.

We have noted that large-scale investigations of individual differences typically employ test items adapted to the requirements of group testing, but Tate, Stanier, and Harootunian gave problems of the type employed in controlled laboratory experiments, such as water-jar problems, functional fixedness problems, and disk-transfer problems, to random samples of 50 of the good and 48 of the poor problem solvers—in 3 hours of individual experimentation. The good problem solvers were generally superior on these also, especially the more complex problems.

A more conventional correlation analysis of the large sample of 500 was also performed (Harootunian and Tate, 1960). The correlations of predictor tests with the composite problem-solving criterion were: reading .732, judgment .707, and problem recognition .624. The results, taken as a whole, give some support to the hypothesis of a general problem-solving ability which has much in common with scores on a conventional measure of general intelligence but which remains when general intelligence is statistically removed. The tests with the largest independent weights in predicting problem-solving scores were tests of judgment and of problem recognition.

GENERAL INTELLIGENCE, REASONING, AND PROBLEM-SOLVING ABILITY

A good argument could be put up for considering general intelligence as the ability to solve the general run of life's problems. Ordinary intelligence tests are composed in large part of minor problems to be solved and of abilities, such as attention span, that contribute pervasively to the solution of problems. If we take success in life as an index of the ability to solve the general problems that emerge, the evidence of the importance of general intelligence is impressive. Life does not offer everyone a standardized set of problems, to be sure, but even so it is undeniable that those who score very low on intelligence tests, the mentally retarded, do not solve their problems very well, even if born with a silver spoon. Those who score very high run far ahead, in almost any contest, of the mentally retarded, and even of average citizens. The remarkable group of 1,500 boys and girls that Terman followed for several decades must be considered good problem solvers by any reasonable standard that could be applied (Terman and Oden, 1958). It is true that most of them started their careers with middle-class advantages, but it is also true that they were picked out of the large middle class by scores on the intelligence test. The many limitations and misuses of the general intelligence test should not obscure its general predictive validity—which none of its rivals have demonstrated (McNemar, 1964).

The same statements could be made for other tests that are closely related to general intelligence, such as verbal comprehension and reasoning ability. Reasoning items have been included in tests of general intelligence since the start. The fact that reasoning problems appear often among the criteria of problem-solving ability reflects a common understanding among psychologists of the nature of problem solving and of the contrast with simpler processes. The fact that reasoning tests correlate with success on various types of problems, including those that consist mostly of seeking information, reflects the generality of this ability.

AN ILLUSTRATIVE FACTOR ANALYSIS

But we can admit the usefulness of such broad measures as general intelligence and general reasoning and still seek a more detailed description of the contributions of narrower abilities. It is possible that some interesting relations are obscured by the use of such general measures. The procedure typically is some kind of factor analysis of the correlations between scores on tests designed to measure single functions.

Guilford and his associates have carried out factor analyses of planning, evaluation, creative thinking, concept achievement, and reasoning, any of which might be called problem solving. But the advantages and disadvantages of this approach are well illustrated in an analysis by Merrifield, Guilford, Christensen, and Frick (1962) explicitly labeled *The Role of Intellectual Factors in Problem Solving*. Instead of studying all problem-solving processes, they limited their study to the production process, which requires the completion format.

Three problem-solving tests were used, all including problems in which the initial information and the goal or desired situations were clearly stated. The instructions were to indicate the necessary steps in proceeding from the initial to the final events. In Missing Links, the subject was required to think of three words to complete a chain of associations, the first and fifth words being given. There were two parts, each consisting of six items, and 6 minutes were allowed. In Predicaments, a problem situation was described and a solution required, with the restriction that only some combination of two or more of four given objects could be used. There were two parts, of three items each, and 10 minutes were allowed. In Transitions, the beginning and ending of a very short story were presented, and the subject was asked to compose the middle part, making the total as complete and logical as he could. There were two parts, of one item each, and 19 minutes were allowed. A large number of other tests of known factor content were also given for reference.

When these tests were given to 200 naval cadets and officer candidates, the reliability coefficients, computed by correlating the two parts of each test, were, respectively, .58, .55, and .46. These reliabilities are good, considering that total time was short and that the scores represent ratings of the solutions by one or two judges. Nevertheless, most of the variance between individuals in solution of these problems escaped the analysis. The variance that was analyzed was quite well accounted for by combinations of the 16 known intellectual factors, and thus no new problem-solving factors were identified. For example, scores on Missing Links, with a reliability of .58, were related to the familiar *verbal comprehension factor* (also called *cognition of semantic units*) by a factor loading of .39. Scores on Transitions, with a reliability of

.55, were analyzed into two factors: *conceptual foresight* (also called *cognition of semantic implications*), with a factor loading of .32, and *sensitivity to problems* (also called *evaluation of semantic implications*), with a factor loading of .31.

Factor analyses of this type describe the relationships between problems and systems for classifying them so far as individual differences in successful solution are concerned. The results obtained reflect, of course, the range of ability of the subjects, the problems included in the test battery, and the type of factor analysis chosen. (There are other types of factor analysis, starting from different assumptions, that would disclose a common factor in test batteries like the one above, which would then be given a general designation, such as General Reasoning). To anyone who understands this methodology and the nature of the previously identified reference factors, the obtained factor loadings help to describe the abilities required for success on the new tests.

The principal limitation on this illustrative factor analysis is the nature of the three problems chosen as a criterion of problem solving. Many other problems could have been chosen, including some in the test battery, such as verbal analogies and logical reasoning problems. Those chosen for investigation slant the results of a factor analysis of individual differences just as they do the results of an experiment directed toward general principles of problem solving.

LEARNING AND PROBLEM SOLVING AGAIN

The question of the dependence of problem solving on previous learning can be asked in various ways, and the experimental research reviewed earlier gives some of the various answers. Analogous questions can be asked of individual differences also, and such questions were often investigated in the 1930s and 1940s, when achievement tests were new and exciting and factor analysis was not yet in common use (Johnson, 1955).

When scores on a test of arithmetic problem solving, also called arithmetic reasoning, were correlated with scores on a test of arithmetic computation assumed to represent the results of past learning, moderate correlations were obtained, usually in the .40's. When tests that require reading and interpreting difficult paragraphs, called verbal inference or problem solving, were correlated with vocabulary tests assumed to represent past learning, the correlations were also moderate, usually in the .50's.

Another way to approach this is to have students study facts and principles and then work problems based on these. The scores for recall of material just learned and for solution of problems based on such material also correlated in the middle range (Bedell, 1934; Billings, 1934). Boys were generally superior to girls on the problem-solving tasks, in agreement with more recent evidence noted above, but not on the recall tasks.

Within any limited area of knowledge, it is safe to conclude that the more successful problem solvers bring more to the problem from their previous learning. The conventional correlations between ability test scores and problem-solving success reflect the contributions of aptitude and remote learning. Task analysis of success on specific problems shows up the contribution of more specific subordinate capabilities to success on tasks at a higher level in the hierarchy. We can say, in terms of sampling, that ordinary ability tests achieve some predictive validity by sampling widely but sparsely. To predict success on a specific set of arithmetic problems, we would have to sample the requisite component capabilities more thoroughly. All of this does not mean, however, that individual differences are completely determined by previous learning or that the individual does not learn anything while engaged in solving the immediate problem.

The relation between learning and problem solving goes both ways. Does the sex difference imply that the optimal method for teaching women would be different from the optimal method for men? Sex differences in solving problems are usually small, but Anderson (1967) has raised the question whether the results of factor analysis suggest differential training methods. Those individuals who are high on certain factors might learn by one method while those high on other factors would learn best by other methods.

As Anderson pointed out, however, the factor loadings do not necessarily describe the skills involved in the solution of the problem because of the possibility of alternative abilities. For example, although the factor analysis presented above gave equal weight to conceptual foresight and sensitivity to problems in solving the Transitions problem, it is possible that some subjects were successful because of high ability on one factor and other subjects because of high ability on the other. The obtained factor loadings, therefore, might not be a good guide to the construction of an optimal training program.

The other difficulty in the use of factor loadings to guide training is the possibility of transformation. As noted earlier, some people solve numerical problems by transforming the data into verbal form. Some transform verbal data into numerical or spatial form. We know that success in solving difficult numerical problems correlates with verbal ability. The discussion of functional fixedness listed a variety of tricks by which organization of a solution out of its components can be facilitated. When problems get difficult the possibility of transformations and of alternative abilities must certainly be considered in the design of a training program. In fact, the good problem solver is just the one who shifts, rearranges, transforms, and reformulates when the going gets hard, and training programs must encourage such versatility of approach.

Since the factor analysts, especially Guilford and his associates, have constructed many problems to meet the specifications of factor analysis and have described their factorial content, it is possible that controlled laboratory experiments with these problems would be more generally enlightening than similar experiments with the traditional problems. Experimental manipulations applied to problems predominantly loaded on one factor might have different effects from the same manipulations applied to problems loaded on another. If evidence for the efficiency of differential training methods suggested by factor loadings could be obtained, it would have practical value and would validate the factor analysis.

At present, from the results of tests given only once, it appears that general intelligence is a rough-and-ready guide to problem-solving ability, but that reasoning ability, which can be analyzed out of general intelligence, is better. This reasoning ability, as identified by psychological research, does not differ greatly from reasoning as understood by educated people in general. It appears in tests of arithmetic problem solving, syllogisms, sensitivity to problems, estimation and evaluation from incomplete data, logical judgment, and the like, and can be further analyzed into narrower components if necessary. To sum it up for the present, the general reasoning factor found by factor analysis "is best defined as the ability to comprehend or to structure problems in preparation for solving them [p. 17]" (Kettner, Guilford, and Christensen, 1959). However, the importance of individual differences in reasoning ability and the experimental evidence on reasoning justify a separate chapter later.

PROBLEM-SOLVING METHODS AND STYLES

It is customary to differentiate ability traits, indicated by responses that are easily graded as right or wrong, from consistencies in responses that reflect individual differences in motivation, style, social habits, work methods, and other aspects of personality. This has been a useful distinction, by and large. But the difference between ability traits and personality traits is not as conspicuous as it once was, and an adequate understanding of the production of correct solutions may involve clarifying the role of other response consistencies.

The methodology of this research follows that of research on ability traits. The basic question is one of consistency over time and consistency, or generality, across problems. Relations with other traits, especially familiar ability traits, have been investigated, usually later, and developmental trends plotted.

Cognitive styles are frequently woven into an intricate embroidery of ideas about personality differences. Pulling out single threads for inspection does not display the fabric to advantage, but a few illustrations will serve as an introduction to the current styles that are most relevant.

FLEXIBILITY OF ACTION AND THOUGHT

Individual differences in some of the problem-solving processes described in the preceding chapter have attracted attention. The research on set led, in the 1940s and 1950s, to studies of individual differences in rigidity, or flexibility in shifting set, and some promising relations were reported in small samples. Little evidence for generality of this trait across problems appeared, however, and the common variance seemed to be shared with general reasoning rather than with a general flexibility factor (Frick and Guilford, 1957; Johnson, 1955; Levitt and Zuckerman, 1959).

The essential psychometric difficulty is the difficulty of fooling people twice. If the sequence of problems traps the subject into adopting a set and then shifting from it, he is not likely to be trapped again. It is probably for this reason that a factor of flexibility in shifting set on a variety of problems, independent of general ability or general reasoning, has not yet been demonstrated.

Cognitive flexibility is a much more substantial factor, as demonstrated by the influential work of Rokeach (1960) on open and closed minds. Scores on a printed test of dogmatism, devised to compare individuals in this respect, correlate with scores on printed tests of attitudes, values, and changes in belief systems, but also with individual differences in certain observable aspects of problem solving. The open-minded, who get low scores on the Dogmatism Test, are more capable of dealing with a new belief system that is at odds with a previously held belief system and of synthesizing new information into an integrated whole.

INFORMATION-SEEKING STYLES

The methods by which different individuals collect information for the solution of a problem can be observed without much difficulty, and various aspects of this information-seeking process can be treated as individual differences. We noted earlier that different troubleshooting strategies could be observed and that those subjects who adopted the more systematic logical strategies scored higher on tests of general reasoning.

The printed test format has also been adapted to the study of information-seeking preferences (Cross and Gaier, 1955). Pulling a tab disclosed either a principle or some facts pertinent to a set of balance problems. The tendency to seek facts was negatively correlated with the tendency to seek principles; a preference for the latter was related to mathematical ability and predicted achievement in an Air Force mechanics course as well as conventional predictors (Gaier, 1955).

Rather large differences can be observed in the amount of information that different people collect to solve a problem. Give some people a little information and they jump to a conclusion—intuitive thinkers. Others wait until the data are all in. In order to study these "intuitive leaps," Westcott (1961) prepared problems with five clues hidden under tabs and presented the clues by allowing the subject to lift one tab at a time. One simple example follows:

4:2, 9:3, 25:5, 100:10, 64:8 Complete the analog 16:___.

Verbal analogies and series problems were given to college students, who were instructed to work the problems with as few clues as possible. The principal results were the rather high reliability coefficients, which indicated that the demand for a lot of information or a little was a stable aspect of each subject's problem-solving style. The information demand for verbal problems was moderately correlated with the corresponding score for numerical problems. For the group as a whole, more problems were solved correctly when more information was exposed; but for individuals, there were negligible correlations between information-demand scores and problem-solving success.

More recently, Westcott (1968) has constructed corresponding problems from pictures that begin very sketchily and progress toward greater completeness. Corresponding scores for information demand can be obtained, and these too are quite reliable. But the correlation between information-demand scores on the two types of problems are negligible, hence it appears that these are rather narrow cognitive traits.

Rokeach's theory of dogmatism has implications for information seeking, which Long and Ziller (1965) tested by similar techniques. On a series of speculative questions the frequency of "Don't know" replies and dogmatism scores correlated −.32. Delay in making a decision also correlated negatively with dogmatism. The open-minded, nondogmatic person is likely to seek more information, according to the authors, while the dogmatic person protects the information he has in order to maintain his belief system.

The in-basket technique, which has been used in studies of administrative performance, has also been adapted to the study of the information-seeking styles of teachers in training. Shulman, Loupe, and Piper (1968) placed a variety of realistic pieces of information in the in-basket to simulate the problems facing an elementary teacher on the first day in a new school and the resources available for dealing with them. They were able to identify a group of dialectical teachers (in contrast to the didactic) who were more sensitive to problems and spent more time on inquiry, during which they juxtaposed different sources of information and shifted their attention among them.

CONCEPTUAL DIFFERENTIATION

Early studies with free sorting tests and other techniques that allowed the subject to choose his own categories showed that 1 subject might use 30 categories to sort a pile of objects that another would sort into 4 categories. Those who used many categories were said to have a narrow equivalence range for each. Gardner and Schoen (1962) questioned whether those who exhibited a broad equivalence range by this technique were actually conceptualizing all the items included in the large group. Hence, in their studies on conceptual differentiation they required the subject to define the relations among all items in a group. To some subjects a large grouping of objects turned out to be a wastebasket category, while to others it was based on a genuine conceptual differentiation of comprehensive similarities and differences. This procedure disclosed a fairly stable style of cognitive control, that was best measured by conceptual differentiation as opposed to other differentiations (such as merely listing concrete particulars) and was apparently independent of general intelligence and ability to abstract.

THE REFLECTIVE STYLE

Variations in rapidity of attack on a problem have been noticed in children as well as adults, and in solving problems as well as in motor performance. Kagan, Rosman, Day, Albert, and Phillips (1964) attributed some of the variation among children in grades 1 and 2 on conceptual grouping problems to control over impulsivity which allowed for inhibition of incorrect solutions and reflection over alternative possibilities. Response times were consistent over tasks and consistent also with response times on similar tasks given later when these children were in grades 3 and 4.

The development of control over impulsivity between grades 1 and 6 led to the production of more concepts of an analytic type, and more such concepts could also be produced by instructions to slow down and reflect on the alternative possibilities. This is probably the same as the analytical style of categorization outlined in Chapter 3. The benefits of reflection are consonant with the benefits of the stop-and-think strategy for adults.

COGNITIVE COMPLEXITY

Individual differences in concept learning measure achievement when everyone is trying for the same cognitive achievement. How can we measure individual differences in cognitive structures when different individuals have different structures? One stylistically prominent attribute of cognitive structures is complexity, which is a property of the structure rather than the content and therefore is applicable to many different structures. When comparing two countries, for example, one person may compare them on one dimension, standard of living, while another compares them on three dimensions, standard of living, birth rate, and area. Number of dimensions is a simple measure that has been applied to the cognition of countries, foods, persons, and even motherhood.

A variety of procedures have been invented in order to get people to reveal the complexity of their cognitions of objects of interest. Some of these procedures are quite complicated, but in general they ask the subject to write about an object or to evaluate several on alternative dimensions, or to categorize them in groups. Then the traits or dimensions of evaluations that the subject has used to differentiate them are counted. The subject who uses several dimensions to characterize an object presumably has a more complex cognition of that object than the subject who needs only one or the black-and-white thinker who uses only two extremes. In a complex problem-solving situation, for example, the more cognitively complex people ask more questions (Karlins and Lamm, 1967).

Some psychologists have implied that cognitive complexity is a general trait, but most of the evidence points toward several narrow factors. Vannoy (1965) administered a variety of tests of complexity of cognition of persons to 110 college men and found no single unitary factor that could account for the correlations. Several small factors were extracted. He concluded that what has been termed cognitive complexity may consist of several relatively independent conceptual dispositions. Apparently, cognitive complexity is not the same as conceptual differentiation (Gardner and Schoen, 1962).

ANALYTICAL FIELD APPROACH

Witkin and his associates (Witkin, et al., 1962) observed that some people tend toward an analytical approach to perceptual tasks and thus can overcome an embedding context, as on the rod-and-frame test and the embedded figures test, while others, unable to analyze the elements, take a more global approach. This dimension—extending from field independence to field dependence—is not limited to perception, however, but characterizes problem-solving activities as well. So the more general term is *analytical field approach*, at one end of the continuum, as opposed to *global field approach*.

Children of ten and twelve who got high scores for field independence did particularly well on the problems of the Picture Completion, Block Design, and Object Assembly tests of the Wechsler Intelligence Scale for Children. Among college students, the analytical field approach was associated with good performance on problems of the type devised by Duncker and Maier and described in the preceding chapter. High school boys who got high scores on the embedded figures test achieved figure concepts much faster than those who got low scores (Davis and Klausmeier, 1970).

THE ABSTRACT APPROACH

Sorting tests have been given to neuropsychiatric patients as diagnostic instruments for several decades. The patient may group a variety of objects on the basis of color, putting the green objects in one pile, the red in another, and so on. Then he is asked to group them in some other way, or the arrangements may be such that the first grouping is obviously inadequate. Thus he has to shift the cognitive side of his set and group according to size, shape, function, or some other attribute of the perceived objects. Most patients with cerebral lesions do not perform as well as normal subjects on these tests, and many schizophrenics are also handicapped (Fey, 1951; Hunt and Cofer, 1944). The pathology apparently results in a fixed concrete approach, or set, to the test materials. The normal person has the capacity to view the task more abstractly, his first approach being only one example of several possible approaches, so that he can shift to another when necessary.

Like many other dichotomies between the normal and the abnormal, this one can also be treated as a dimension—extending continuously from the abstract to the concrete—to permit more refined measurements. Harvey, Hunt, and Schroeder (1961) have gone beyond the clinical interest in abstract thinking to incorporate it as part of a general theory of personality. The abstract thinker is said to have a more complex, differentiated system of concepts for categorizing the data of his experience. Thus he is not so prone to absolute evaluations as the more concrete thinker.

Incomplete sentences provide a method for obtaining a statement that can be rated on the concrete-abstract continuum by such criteria as absolutism, evaluativeness, and simplicity. One study (Ware and Harvey, 1967) with a small number of subjects, whose statements had been rated by these criteria, found that, when processing information about people, the more "concrete" subjects made up their minds more quickly and with greater certainty than the "abstract" subjects. The more concrete subjects manifested a greater need for cognitive consistency, presumably because they could not generate superordinate concepts to encompass superficially conflicting data.

The early work on abstractness in sorting tests used perceived blocks and other objects. The more recent concept, going by the same name, may have more in common with cognitive complexity than with the early notion of abstract attitude.

It appears, finally, that many interesting cognitive styles and problem-solving methods have been described but, as yet, not well analyzed. Traits that are grouped under one broad term may be analyzed into narrower traits, and some that go by different names may turn out to be the same. The relations with ability traits also have not yet been well analyzed. It is possible that a cognitive style that does not correlate with general intelligence will correlate with the more specific tests of abilities pertaining to classes and the learning of concepts devised by Dunham, Guilford, and Hoepfner (1969). It is also possible that the construction of ability tests has advanced to the point where the injection of new ideas, coming perhaps from problem-solving methods and cognitive styles, is needed for further advance.

Major Trends and Implications

Problem solving has been distinguished from learning for theoretical clarity; but experiments on training in problem solving have both theoretical and practical implications. Problem solving is seldom taught as an undifferentiated whole. Typically, the enterprise is conceptually divided into the achievement of certain components, such as concepts and principles, that are the constituents of the solution, and the integration of these into a solution. In relation to the structure of the solution, the components are substructures; in relation to the elements of the problem, they are higher units organized from the elements and manipulated as unitary patterns.

When the components have been achieved in the past, their integration into a solution is the principal difficulty. But when they have not been previously learned, the learner's task and the teacher's task are even more complicated. Analysis of a complex intellectual performance into levels of component capabilities appears to be useful to the teacher in clarifying the hierarchy of knowledge required and in planning training procedures. Teaching the components is generally helpful, and teaching problem-solving strategies is also helpful. The evidence at hand does not certify the necessity of teaching the components first, because the subordinate capabilities can often be achieved *during* problem solving. Students can learn from the top down as well as from the bottom up.

Discovery procedures are not the most efficient for the communication of large amounts of information, but they seem to have special advantages for teaching principles and strategies that apply to problem solving. The best discovery procedures require the student to manipulate the constituent concepts and to derive principles and state them explicitly. The rigidity that often occurs when rules are learned mechanically can be overcome by training on heterogeneous sets of problems that necessitate shifting from one rule to another.

The use of manually manipulable construction materials in arithmetic problem solving often confounds the representation and transformation of data with the opportunity for discovery of relations. Personal discovery of the relevant relations is useful, but so is practice in transforming mathematical relations to a spatial mode of representation. Direct comparison indicates that the representation of rules for arithmetic operations in ordinary English has the advantage of familiarity; but representation in mathematical notation has its own efficiency, not always completely realized by college students. This is another area in which training on low-level components facilitates the high-level performance. Aside from the advantages of a specific mode of representation, practice in transforming data from one mode to another, while preserving the structure, may be expected to be generally facilitative.

Instructions about very general strategies, such as "Stop and think," have some value for the unsophisticated. But the strategies that have been most helpful are directed toward specific problem-solving operations, such as seeking information, stating generalizations, and testing hypotheses.

The teaching of problem solving at present is much like prescientific farming. Some teachers are more successful than others; and much good advice can be had for the asking. But the determination of optimal procedures for a specific situation requires measures of the critical factors in the situation and in the students and a consequent adjustment of the training procedures. If problem solving is a complex system of interacting processes, as seems likely, success requires at least a minimal level of achievement on the constituent processes. The system often includes alternative paths to the solution, however, and suboptimal achievement at certain points can be compensated by superior achievement at other points or corrected during the general effort. In other words, problem-solving systems are quite tolerant of deviations from optimal procedures.

Measures of individual differences in problem-solving abilities require a different methodology from that of problem-solving experiments. There is no catalog of problems that can be taken as the domain to be sampled. But when printed tests are constructed of a variety of problems, some evidence is found for generality of problem-solving ability, correlated with general intelligence and other broad abilities. The problems that appear on printed tests are not usually the ones that appear in problem-solving experiments, but students who score high on the former also score high on the latter. If there is a general problem-solving ability, the reasoning factor contributes importantly to it. Large-scale factor analysis with printed tests yields somewhat similar results, identifying such factors as verbal comprehension, conceptual foresight, and sensitivity to problems.

Aside from abilities, a number of interesting cognitive styles have been described, often in connection with a theory of personality. From the psychometric point of view, cognitive styles have not been analyzed as thoroughly as cognitive abilities. As far as we know, most of them are rather narrow traits, limited to certain materials and testing methods, but further work may demonstrate more generality.

Teaching methods interact with developmental level: the optimal method for teaching concepts in the third grade would not be optimal for the eighth grade. Teaching methods interact also with specific educational achievements: the optimal procedures for teaching the solution of mathematical problems would not be the same for those who have had algebra as for those who have not. Some efforts have been made to demonstrate similar interactions for cognitive abilities and styles. Perhaps those who get high scores on adaptive flexibility, or on cognitive complexity, or on some other intellectual trait, would learn to solve problems best by one procedure and those who get low scores would learn best by some other procedure. The results to date have not been very encouraging, but this is a promising design that may someday justify such differentiated training procedures. Thus we arrive at the not very startling conclusion that the contribution of individual differences to problem solving looks much like the contribution, outlined in Chapter 3, of individual differences to concept achievement.

CHAPTER 6

DEDUCTIVE REASONING AS PROBLEM SOLVING

ogic and psychology grew up together, sharing a common interest in rational thought; but as they matured, they specialized and drifted apart. Logic, once concerned with the laws of thought, became an abstract science concerned with formal relations between propositions, rather than the thinking of them, and found much in common with mathematics. Psychology, pushed by the doctrine of evolution, moved in with the biological and social sciences, relinquishing the study of idealized thought for the study of actual behavior and treating both rational and irrational thought as natural human activities open to empirical investigation.

Today, the psychological study of logical thought is part of the study of problem solving, but the problems to be solved are logic problems or problems in which logical relations are assumed to be critical. This variety of prob-

229

lem solving has certain distinctive characteristics, as we shall see. Since the psychological investigation of such problems began, around the beginning of this century (see Burt, 1919; Wheeler, 1958; Woodworth, 1938), the term *reasoning* has therefore been used to distinguish this topic from trial-and-error problem solving, creative thinking, and other varieties. The term *reasoning* was used at one time for the integration of isolated experience by infrahuman animals, such as the laboratory rat; but such a special meaning is far removed from the conventional one and need not be considered here.

Some aspects of inductive reasoning were considered in the chapters on concepts; deductive reasoning is the topic of this chapter. Like other complex activities, the two types of reasoning overlap. The achievement of a concept may include testing deductions from a hypothesis, and deductive reasoning may include evaluation of the validity of a rule generalized from a series of statements. But the empirical psychological research summarized in this chapter is quite different from that of previous chapters.

Logic and the Psychology of Reasoning

A psychologist may need to know a little logic just as he may, at times, need to know a little chemistry or a little anthropology. The distinction between logic and psychology must be respected, but logic is helpful here in defining the problems of this chapter and making a start on their investigation.

THE NATURE OF REASONING

From the psychological point of view, we can say that reasoning is problem-solving enlightened by logic. Thus reasoning can occur in the solution of many of the problems described in previous chapters, but it can be identified most unambiguously in the solution of problems of formal logic, such as a syllogism. Is the following argument valid?

Some Y is Z;
All X is Y.
Therefore, some X is Z.

To anyone who has recently studied logic this will not be a problem. If he has memorized the rules for evaluating such syllogisms and has practiced their application to particular cases, he will be able to judge the validity of the conclusion with no difficulty. This easy task is deductive reasoning from the logical point of view, that is, it consists of an inference from given premises to a conclusion; but from our point of view it would not be problem solving. To anyone without logical training, however, this will be a problem, and his activities when faced with such a problem conform to our definition of problem solving. Deductive reasoning, then, is the solution of problems about the validity of inferences. This chapter will also consider information-processing tasks involving very easy inferences, performed very rapidly, for the understanding they contribute to the processes involved in genuine reasoning problems.

The distinctive feature of logic problems is that they are based on formal propositions. When we speak of "formal logic" or a "logical form," we are referring to the structure or form of an argument rather than the content. The syllogism printed above, unlike anagrams, light switch, and two-string problems, is not concerned with any particular materials. Replacing X, Y, and Z by S, M, and P, or by animals, vegetables, and minerals, would not change the logical form of the argument or the validity of the conclusion. The two premises are general statements without particular content, and the question is not whether the conclusion corresponds to any material state of affairs but whether it is a logical deduction from the premises.

In this respect, logical reasoning is like mathematical reasoning. We can say that $3a \times 4a = 12a^2$ without consideration of the referents designated by these symbols. The distinctive characteristic of reasoning, both inductive and deductive, that gives it its tremendous power and engages every chapter in this book consists of letting symbols stand for reality and then manipulating them to solve problems that cannot be solved by manipulating the concrete reality. Just as the use of a symbol to refer to a class of objects is not true or false except in respect to standard usage, the conclusion to a logical discussion is not true or false except in a formal sense, as a logical consequence of the premises.

Deductive reasoning may be a part of the solution of many problems, especially in science, after the empirical data have been represented symbolically. In such cases, the success of the whole enterprise depends on appropriate symbolization of the data and later application of the symbolic solution to concrete data, as well as on the deductive reasoning per se. Thus, in respect to efficiency of performance, formal reasoning has great potentialities for transfer. But, precisely because deductive reasoning is formal, similarities between relevant logical patterns are not easily perceived, and the transfer to concrete data may be difficult.

Logic grew out of the resources of the general language, in India as in Greece, probably as a technique for winning arguments (Bocheński, 1961). The celebrated syllogism, *All men are mortal; Socrates is a man; therefore, Socrates is mortal,* appears in the form of sentences, and anyone with ordinary ability can read it. But, as logical systems have developed, they have elaborated special concepts and symbols that are not in the general language, rules for evaluation of arguments that are not rules of grammar, and a metalanguage for making statements about statements. Like many other intellectual accomplishments, these logical achievements depend on the general language but add to it. When someone uses letters to designate standard propositions, or rearranges the verbal expressions of ordinary language into a standard logical form, he has explicitly gone beyond the general language. The average citizen, untrained in logic, may not go this far, but when he departs from ordinary listening or reading to look for an inconsistency or to examine the validity of a statement as an inference from other statements, we say he is reasoning.

Many problems that do not look like logic problems are solved with the aid of logical reasoning, but in such cases the contribution of reasoning is obscured. The most clear-cut research on conditions that influence reasoning has been done on problems that are frankly logic problems rather than those in which the logical operations are hidden.

ARE PEOPLE LOGICAL?

A popular question in the last century, when man's kinship with other species was being both proclaimed and denied, was whether man is a rational animal. Are people logical? In past centuries, when logic was closer to the general language, it was part of the general culture. An educated man was expected to be logical just as he was expected to be able to ride a horse, cast up sums, and make a creditable speech.

This old question can be put in its proper context by asking a parallel question: Are people astronomical? When astronomy was part of the general culture, an educated man was expected to be able to tell time by the sun, plot his course by the stars, and foretell which phase of the moon would be right for an amorous adventure.

Today, when knowledge has diversified into so many areas, we do not expect all educated people to be masters of logic, or astronomy, or any other specialty. But, avoiding the erudite developments of modern logic, it is a fair question to ask how well ordinary adults, such as college students without training in logic, can do on the more elementary aspects of logical reasoning. It is particularly informative to classify the errors that they make and to try to account for them psychologically.

The motivation for reasoning should be considered briefly. If we take a functional view, logical reasoning is one way, a particularly effective way, of reaching a goal. In addition, logical consistency may be a goal in itself, or a snare to be avoided. Some people worship logical consistency, regardless of long-term goals, just as others enjoy the absurdities of their actions, as if inconsistency had a value also. The famous inventor, Charles F. Kettering, once warned his colleagues: "Beware of logic. It is an organized way of going wrong with confidence." A complete treatment of the motivation for thought would include esthetic valuations of spontaneity and asymmetry, religious preferences for direct, nonlogical grasp of truth, and the appeals of magical symbols and rituals, all of which may, if nothing more, diminish the appeal of logical consistency. It is safe to assume, however, that the ambience of the psychological laboratory and classroom encourages rationality and that most departures from logical consistency under these conditions can be interpreted as errors rather than as the products of an alternative value system. Elsewhere, the dynamics of nonlogical outcomes may deserve more subtle exploration.

MATERIALS

Logic supplies the materials for experiments on reasoning just as chemistry supplies the materials for experiments on smell and the dictionary materials for experiments on anagrams. Logic also supplies a standard terminology for referring to these materials.

Most research has been concerned with propositions, or statements with subjects and predicates; hence it is convenient for analysis to let S refer to the subject of a statement and P to the predicate. Conventionally, the four standard propositions are designated by vowels, as follows:

A. Universal affirmative: *All S is P*
E. Universal negative: *No S is P*
I. Particular affirmative: *Some S is P*
O. Particular negative: *Some S is not P.*

These are called *categorical propositions* because they are statements about categories or classes, and the copula *is* refers to the relation of inclusion. Thus the statement *All S is P* means that the class designated by S is included in the class designated by P.

Simple problems can be constructed from such propositions around the operation of conversion. Knowing that *All S is P*, can we conclude that *All P is S*? This question is put in true-false format, but the open-end format is also used. What can we say about P, given that *Some S is P*? (The direct converse of an E or an I proposition is valid, but the direct converse of an A or an O proposition is not.)

Conditional reasoning has been investigated with conditional statements of the *If . . . then* form. *If it rains tomorrow, I shall stay home.* These are symbolized *If P, then Q*, and a variety of problems can be constructed, given that P is true, or not true, and so on.

There are problems involved also in reasoning from inequalities, such as *A is larger than B*. Linear syllogisms or three-term series problems can be assembled from two premises: *Mary is shorter than Sophia*, and *Mary is taller than Rachel*. Who is the tallest?

The 4 categorical propositions, A, E, I, O, can easily be combined as 2 premises and a conclusion so as to construct a variety of syllogisms. The number of syllogisms thus constructed is not large, hence the universe of syllogisms can be explicitly defined. When such syllogisms are used as problems to be solved, this universe of problems can be sampled more systematically than most others, and the complete universe can be studied if desirable. The number of three-term series problems and conditional reasoning problems is even smaller. While the results obtained from a study of a sample of 20 arithmetic, anagram, or construction problems might not be duplicated from a study of another sample of 20 such problems, this sampling question does not arise in the study of logic problems. And there is no question of apparatus differences. Moreover, there are rules in the logic books for ascertaining the right answers to all problems.

Another advantage that logic problems enjoy, in comparison with other problems, is the information that can be obtained from analysis of errors. Although general discussions of test item writing usually point out that wrong options in multiple-choice items can yield useful information about the causes of the errors, this opportunity is seldom realized. Logic problems written systematically, however, permit the subject to make the same logical error on different problems so that error tendencies above chance levels can be diagnosed. Many of the experiments to be discussed have therefore employed the multiple-choice format and have systematically tabulated the different types of errors made.

METHODS

Some of the early inquiries had subjects think about the conclusion to a reasoning problem and report their thoughts. Since the difficulties of this method are now recognized, recent research takes advantage of the objective methods of modern experimental psychology. Generally, the subject's response, whether valid or invalid, is treated as the consequence of multiple antecedent conditions. The aim is to identify these various conditions one by one.

Certainly, the form of the argument, the combination of propositions, is a likely possibility, and this is investigated by varying the logical form while holding the content constant. Typically, this is done by using letters, such as X, Y, and Z, or A, B, and C, as the terms of the propositions. The frequency of valid and invalid reasoning for each logical form can thus be studied and, more important, the logical forms that lead to invalid reasoning can be specified.

The content of the argument is another likely influence on reasoning and this is studied by varying the content while holding the logical form constant. The content may be letters, nonsense terms, such as *planti* and *glubs*, or meaningful words, such as *angels* and *zinnias*. When the terms are words or resemble words, the statements need not be printed formally, as above, but can be printed as ordinary sentences embedded in continuous text. From the standpoint of formal logic, which is independent of content, variations in outcome that are correlated with variations in content are nonlogical.

Most questions about reasoning are not questions about the effects of a course in logic. They are stated rather in respect to the ordinary intelligent adult, hence subjects with training in logic are usually eliminated. Similarly, errors are more psychologically revealing than correct judgments, hence many investigations of syllogistic reasoning have been based on indeterminate syllogisms, the correct response to which is *None of these*. Determinate syllogisms are often interspersed, however, to retard the development of a response set and also to supply a measure of general reasoning ability.

General Task Variables

Some of the difficulties that arise in the solution of reasoning problems are the same as in other kinds of problems, and the methods of studying them have been about the same. Complex arguments composed of several propositions are harder to evaluate than simple arguments composed of one or two (Anderson, 1957). Syllogisms written in familiar terms are somewhat easier than syllogisms of the same form written in letters or unfamiliar terms (Wilkins, 1928). Abstractness is probably also important, but all general propositions are intrinsically abstract, and this circumstance makes all formal reasoning difficult.

Boredom is a general factor in reasoning problems, as in other problems. Exciting arguments about politics, religion, and sex may be sustained for hours, but several investigators have noted that experiments involving formal arguments written in terms of A, B, and C, and repeated in terms of D, E, and F, are monotonous. Those subjects who have a special interest in such abstract materials and those who can force themselves to analyze each proposition will be more successful; environmental conditions that maintain alertness will also be helpful.

The Difficulties of Syllogistic Reasoning

Syllogisms are assembled from two propositions as premises and another as a conclusion. Three universal affirmative propositions would form the following syllogism, M being the customary symbol for the middle term:

All S are M;
All M are P.
Therefore, all S are P.

These syllogisms, taken as they are, can be considered problems in the true-false format; the subject can simply be asked to evaluate each conclusion as *valid* or *invalid*. The principal disadvantage of the true-false format is the possible operation of a response set. When syllogisms are manufactured systematically, from the various combinations of propositions, many more are invalid than valid. Thus anyone who responds *invalid* to more than half the problems, either because he has a general negative set in such situations or because a smattering of logic has made him wary of logical tricksters, will get more right answers. Likewise, any experimental condition that increases undifferentiated caution will increase the proportion of right answers.

Alternatively, syllogisms can be turned into problems in the familiar multiple-choice format by writing A, E, I, and O propositions as possible conclusions. Read the two premises that follow, then select the logical conclusion:

Some S is M;
All M is P.
Therefore,
1. All S is P
2. All S is not P
3. Some S is P
4. Some S is not P
5. None of these conclusions is valid.

In comparison with the true-false format, the multiple-choice format looks like a giveaway since all conclusions, valid and invalid, are explicitly stated. But these problems are difficult for educated adults without formal training in logic; the number of errors is large. And it is in fact the opportunity for analysis of these errors—that is, the invalid conclusions that are accepted as valid—that constitutes the principal advantage of this format. The aim is to tabulate and describe such errors and to explain, in psychological terms, why they occur.

EFFECTS OF CONTENT

In addition to general task variables that make some arguments hard to follow and thus increase errors in judging the soundness of the conclusions, there are more specific and powerful effects that arise out of the content of the argument. As we noted in Chapter 2, the introduction of thematic content into concept formation experiments disrupts the logical information-processing strategies observed with meaningless geometric figures. Although this lead has not been followed up in inductive reasoning, content effects in deductive reasoning have been studied in relation to attitude toward the conclusion and cognitive inconsistency.

ATTITUDE TOWARD THE CONCLUSION

When the course through an argument to its conclusion is hard to follow, the reader or listener is tempted to rely on his attitude toward the conclusion itself rather than evaluate the validity of the whole argument. In order to demonstrate this effect, Janis and Frick (1943) resorted to syllogisms with familiar terms printed in short paragraphs like ordinary text. The instructions to the subjects, particularly important in these experiments, and the first two of their syllogisms follow.

Instructions: This is a test in reasoning. You are to check each of the following arguments as "sound" or "unsound." A sound argument is one in which the conclusion follows logically from the premises. (Note: "All" in logic means *each and every case.* "Some" means *at least one* and perhaps *all* cases.)
No Bolsheviks are idealists and all Bolsheviks are Russian. Therefore some Russians are not idealists.
The Eskimos are the only people who eat nothing but meat and it is found that all Eskimos have good teeth. So we may conclude that no people who eat only meat have bad teeth [p. 74].

After judging 16 of these syllogisms, each subject reread the conclusions and was asked whether he agreed or disagreed with each one. Thus the judgments of the conclusions could be sorted into four types: *agree-valid, disagree-invalid, agree-invalid, disagree-valid.* The effect of the subject's bias would be expected to make him judge the conclusion valid when he agreed with it and invalid when he disagreed with it, and thus to increase the proportion of judgments in the first two of the above types and decrease the proportion in the last two. Even though the subjects, who were graduate students with no formal training in logical analysis, had only two alternatives to choose from, they made errors on 23 percent of the judgments and, as expected, these errors were preponderantly of the agree-valid and disagree-invalid types. With subjects of less education and interest in abstract things, the difference would probably be even greater.

One interpretation of this experiment is that the emotional content of the syllogism interferes with logical evaluation, so Lefford (1946) deliberately manipulated this feature. He asked several groups of college students to judge the validity of syllogisms, instructing them "to judge whether the conclusions arrived at in these passages are warranted by the statements given in support of them [p. 129]." Half the syllogisms were concerned with controversial issues, as in the two examples below:

War times are prosperous times, and prosperity is highly desirable, therefore, wars are much to be desired.
All communists have radical ideas. All CIO leaders have radical ideas, therefore, all CIO leaders are agents for communism [p. 131].

The instructions called for judgments of the validity of the conclusions from the premises. Such judgments are difficult, even for college students, and the scores were quite low.

The other half of the syllogisms were matched for form, but the content was noncontroversial:

Philosophers are all human, and all human beings are fallible; therefore, philosophers are fallible too.
All whales live in water, and all fish live in water too; therefore, all fish must be whales [p. 130].

These syllogisms, of the same form as the others and approximately the same length, were evaluated correctly much more often by college students. Apparently, the difficulty of the reasoning is compounded by the intrusion of the controversial material, which makes it even more difficult for the untrained person to play the syllogism game straight and evaluate the argument on purely formal grounds.

The terms used in these early studies were not carefully standardized. We have only the experimenter's assumption that some were controversial or emotional, and such factors may have been confounded with unfamiliarity, incongruity, and the like. Parrott (1967) reexamined the Lefford syllogisms in this light by having college students rate each premise on a scale of truth-falsity, and found that the emotional premises were rated significantly closer to the false end of the scale than the nonemotional premises. Hence, the effect that Lefford attributed to emotionality must have been confounded with the effect of cognitive inconsistency, to be discussed below.

This approach to deductive reasoning began with attempts to show how wishes "distort" beliefs or emotions "bias" reason; and several experiments, as well as public opinion polls, have shown that educated people and citizens at large are susceptible to this effect. The more recent approach admits that both personal desires and logical reason influence acceptance of a conclusion and studies the interaction of these two influences. An example of the more inclusive approach, the "logic model" of McGuire (1960) moved away from the classical two-valued logic, which considers only propositions that are either true or false, to study ratings of the probability that a proposition is true. McGuire began by asking people to estimate the probabilities of premises and conclusions, and also to rate the desirabilities of each. Good reasoning, according to this model, requires that the probability of a conclusion be quantitatively related to the combination of the probabilities of the premises. Research with high-school and college students disclosed a moderate relation; even on controversial issues these people were somewhat logical. A moderate relation was also found between acceptance of conclusions and ratings of desirability of premises, which can be interpreted either as the influence of desires on beliefs (wishful thinking) or of beliefs on desires.

A more subtle logical influence was demonstrated by McGuire when new information raising the probabilities of minor premises resulted in higher estimates of probabilities of logically related but not explicitly mentioned conclusions. Then a test of McGuire's logic model with more advanced college students (Dillehay, Insko, and Smith, 1966) confirmed the usefulness of this approach in general but found somewhat less wishful thinking. Logical consistency was demonstrated in that, following changes in beliefs due to a persuasive communication, significant changes occurred in logically related but unmentioned beliefs.

But consistency, like other abstract criteria, means different things to different people. College students today do not know the technical meanings of such logical terms as *contradiction* and *contrary*, and when evaluating pairs of statements on a single topic, they often justify apparent inconsistencies by mentioning the virtue of being democratic and open-minded (Luchins and Luchins, 1965).

A glance back at trends of research on attitudes and acceptance of conclusions—only illustrated here by a few examples—brings into view a curious historical twist. The early research was designed to show how emotions, attitudes, and prejudices can bias the acceptance of a conclusion to a logical discussion. Then more quantitative studies show that both the logical structure of the discussion and biases toward the content of the conclusion must be considered. In fact, it is those who score high on an ordinary test of reasoning ability, with noncontroversial conclusions, who are most able to discount their own biases when judging the validity of controversial conclusions (Feather, 1964). Recently, as social psychologists have elaborated cognitive theories of attitude change, it appears that acceptance of one proposition can come from acceptance of another logically related but unmentioned proposition. This phenomenon, which might, by analogy with covert S-R association, be called *covert deductive reasoning*, usually goes by such terms as *cognitive consistency* or *cognitive congruity*. No one claims that beliefs are accepted, rejected, and modified by rational processes alone, but any model of man which hopes for completeness must take these processes into account.

COGNITIVE INCONSISTENCY

Regardless of bias, the terms of a proposition may be consistent or inconsistent. We do not call a person biased if he likes the good and dislikes the evil, but the proposition *All good things are fine* may be easier to deal with than the formally equivalent *All evil things are fine*. Frase (1966a) approached this question by having college students rate a number of adjectives on the evaluative scales of the Semantic Differential. With the aid of these ratings, he assembled propositions in which subject and predicate were compatible in that the difference between evaluative ratings was small. A syllogism made up of three such propositions follows:

All sinful things are cruel,
and all disgusting things are sinful.
Therefore, all disgusting things are cruel.

Equally compatible negative propositions were constructed from two terms with large differences. Moderately and highly incompatible syllogisms were also constructed in this way; an illustration of the latter follows:

No natural things are creative,
and no natural things are successful.
Therefore, no successful things are creative.

This semantic inconsistency did increase time and errors in judging the validity of conclusions to syllogisms.

The Frase procedure was an improvement in that the terms were standardized by students' ratings, but the effect of a statement constructed from a combination of subject and predicate terms may not be accurately measured by combining ratings of the component terms. In fact, a later study (Frase, 1966b) found only moderate correlations between the incompatibility index and belief in a proposition. The question of additivity of judgments of terms will be taken up more systematically in Chapter 8.

Turning to a more direct procedure, Parrott (1967) had college students rate the truth of complete statements of varying content on a scale of 1 to 7. He then assembled these in 3 tests of 15 syllogisms each, equated for logical structure, 1 composed of true premises (ratings of 1 to 3), 1 of false premises (ratings of 5 to 7), and 1 of mixed premises. Each syllogism was followed by 5 statements, one of which was a valid conclusion to the syllogism. The results showed that, in relation to syllogisms with true or mixed premises, those with false premises required more time and were evaluated more accurately. Furthermore, subjects given syllogisms with false premises first, then true premises, reduced solution time on the second test; but subjects given the two types of syllogisms in the reverse order did not show this reduction. One plausible interpretation was that the cognitive inconsistency of the false premises operated as a challenge and a reminder of the formal logical problem.

To test the cognitive inconsistency interpretation, and others, Parrott

(1969) analyzed reasoning time in more detail and included symbolic or content-free syllogisms, written in terms of letters such as X, Y, and Z. As an additional control, some subjects were required merely to read the syllogisms, and, as Table 6.1 shows, the time spent reading two premises and five alternative conclusions was about the same whether the premises were true or false. But reasoning, directed toward selection of the valid conclusion, took more time when the premises were false. In comparison to syllogisms with true premises, those written in symbolic terms required much less time for reading but only slightly less time for reasoning. Exposure of premises and conclusions was under the subject's control, so it was possible to record that syllogisms with false premises necessitated much more switching back from conclusions to premises than the other two types.

It is apparent from these results that reasoning is more than just reading: that the thinker processes the information somehow after he reads it, and that the information processing is influenced by the nature of the content. When transfer experiments were arranged, by shifting the subjects from syllogisms with one type of content to syllogisms of another type, some positive and some negative transfer effects were obtained, but the hypothesis that the cognitive inconsistency of the false premises would improve later syllogistic reasoning was not supported. The clearest transfer effect followed reasoning with the symbolic syllogisms, which Parrott regarded as evidence for a structural insight interpretation. That is, the content-free syllogisms gave the subjects the best opportunity to master the syllogistic structures and apply them quickly to other syllogistic problems.

PSYCHOLOGICAL ANALYSIS OF LOGICAL ERRORS

Wallonians dance the polka. My worthy opponent dances the polka. Therefore, it is obvious that my worthy opponent is a Wallonian.
Some Republicans have inherited oil wells. Some Wallonians are Republicans. Hence we know that some Wallonians have inherited oil wells.

Logic books identify, label, and expose many types of logical error, and debaters are fond of detecting these in the other side's arguments. Among the most notorious are the first one above, which is the fallacy of the undistributed middle term, and the second, which bases a conclusion on two particular premises. The actual frequency of logical errors in the syllogistic reasoning of educated people is, of course, a question for quantitative re-

TABLE 6.1. READING AND REASONING TIMES (IN SECONDS)
FOR THREE TYPES OF SYLLOGISMS

Task	Symbolic	True	False
Reading	10.3	15.7	14.5
Reasoning	21.9	24.2	29.4

From Parrott (1969).

search; we know that college students are quite susceptible to the fallacy of the undistributed middle term and that they often draw invalid conclusions from two particular premises (Wilkins, 1928). Such errors are of general extralaboratory concern to all educated people. The analysis of the errors is complicated, as in other kinds of problem solving, because different errors occur together, but several years of research have achieved some degree of clarification.

THE ATMOSPHERE EFFECT

All S is M;
All P is M.
Therefore, all S is P.

Labeling this *the fallacy of the undistributed middle* is not an explanation of why intelligent adults are so susceptible to it, but a psychological hypothesis has been offered by Woodworth and Sells (1935) under the name of *atmosphere effect.* The untrained reader who does not know the rules and cannot follow through the abstract implications seizes on nonlogical verbal cues. The word *All* in the premises suggests a universal affirmative atmosphere, so when the reader sees the same word in the conclusion, he accepts it. Similarly, the word *Some* in particular premises wafts a favorable atmosphere around a *Some* conclusion, making it easy to accept the conclusion that *Some Wallonians have inherited oil wells.* In general, *AA* premises create a favorable atmosphere for acceptance of an *A* conclusion, *EE* premises an *E* conclusion, *II* premises an *I* conclusion, and *OO* premises an *O* conclusion, whether logically valid or not. To take care of mixed premise combinations, Woodworth and Sells added two supplementary hypotheses: (1) A negative premise creates a negative atmosphere, even when the other premise is affirmative; (2) a particular premise creates a particular atmosphere, even when the other premise is universal. When Sells (1936) presented syllogisms written in terms of *X, Y,* and *Z* to college students and tabulated their errors, the results agreed with the predictions fairly well. Similar research using syllogisms written in familiar words as well as letters— with the valid conclusion to be chosen from five alternative conclusions—also confirmed most of the predictions from atmosphere effect (Morgan and Morton, 1944).

INVALID CONVERSION

The error of *invalid conversion* is a common one. Knowing that *All X is Y,* it is easy to say that *All Y is X.* Knowing that *Some X is not Y,* it is easy to say that *Some Y is not X.* Both of these inferences are illogical, yet ordinary adults who solve their daily problems adequately succumb frequently to this fallacy. For example, when French adults were asked to convert the statement *All men are rational,* only a few gave a valid conversion, such as *The class of rational beings includes man,* but many wrote statements like *Rationality is the property of man* (Oléron, 1964). Woodworth and Sells (1935) considered the error of invalid conversion as a special case of atmosphere effect. Inferring from *All X is Y* that *All Y is X* was attributed to the *All* atmosphere.

The plausibility of the invalid conversion arises partly from the confusion between the reading of conventional sentences and formal categorical propositions. To say that *All right angles are 90° angles* is equivalent to saying that *All 90° angles are right angles.* But this is not exactly what the verb in a categorical proposition means. When the statement *All S is P* is rewritten as S ⊂ P and read as S *is included in the class P,* invalid conversions can be expected less frequently.

This insidious error of invalid conversion, whatever its basic origin, has been invoked by Chapman and Chapman (1959) as an alternative explanation for errors in syllogistic reasoning previously explained by the atmosphere effect. Acceptance of the invalid conclusion to the syllogism printed above, for example, might be due to the atmosphere generated by the repetition of *All,* but it might also be due to conversion of the second premise. If *All P is M* is converted to *All M is P,* the conclusion would follow logically. Conversion of *E* and *I* propositions is valid, but conversion of *A* and *O* propositions could explain the acceptance of many invalid conclusions. Chapman and Chapman tried out this hypothesis by giving syllogisms in multiple-choice form to college students and found that they could thus account for a large proportion of the errors. While the atmosphere effect is completely nonlogical, invalid conversion seems to be an attempt at logical reasoning that goes awry.

DIFFERENTIAL ANALYSIS AND TRAINING

Three independent investigations of syllogistic reasoning (Chapman and Chapman, 1959; Morgan and Morton, 1944; Sells, 1936) agreed fairly well in identifying the invalid conclusions that were most frequently accepted by educated adults. The explanations of these errors were different, but the procedure of tabulating errors does not by itself furnish the data for a choice between the alternative explanations. One possibility for separating the two explanations would be to use separate training procedures for reducing errors designed around each explanation.

To explore this possibility, Simpson and Johnson (1966) first constructed two separate scales of syllogism problems written with letters, (such as X, Y, and Z) in multiple-choice form, one for testing atmosphere errors only and one for testing conversion errors only. The atmosphere effect was simplified and restated as follows: "When both premises of a syllogism contain the same qualifier, *are* or *are not,* or the same quantifier, *all* or *some,* many subjects will accept a conclusion which also contains the common term [p. 197]." A short scale of syllogisms made up on this basis was fairly adequate in that about 70 percent of the errors were the predicted atmosphere errors. Another scale, made of *AO* syllogisms to test invalid conversion, was also fairly adequate in that about 60 percent of the errors were the predicted conversion errors. Reliability coefficients were .64 for the atmosphere scale and .80 for the conversion scale. Justification for treating the two errors separately came from the correlation between scores on the two scales, which was only −.12.

Brief training was arranged for different groups of college students: training specifically directed against the atmosphere error, training specifically directed against the error of invalid conversion, and general training as a control. The results showed that atmosphere errors were significantly reduced by anti-atmosphere training but not by anticonversion training. The results for conversion errors were not so specific. These errors were correlated with errors in general reasoning, and they were reduced by general training as well as by anticonversion training. Thus, this experiment demonstrated that both errors could be identified and that neither hypothesis alone would account for all the results.

Since atmosphere and conversion errors occur so frequently in the evaluation of syllogisms written in terms of letters, it is an interesting question whether these errors can be identified when the same syllogisms are written as ordinary continuous text. To approach this, Stratton (1967) wrote syllogisms in paragraph form with novel terms similar to those a student might find in a science textbook. Atmosphere and conversion scales were built in, as well as a scale of determinate syllogisms. Two examples follow, acceptance of No. 3 in the first indicating an atmosphere error, and acceptance of No. 4 in the second an error of invalid conversion.

As technology advances and natural petroleum resources become more depleted, the securing of petroleum from unconventional sources becomes more imperative. One such source is the Athabasca tar sands of northern Alberta, Canada. Since some tar sands are sources of refinable hydrocarbons, these deposits are worthy of commercial investigation. Some kerogen deposits are also sources of refinable hydrocarbons,
Therefore:
1. All kerogen deposits are tar sands.
2. No kerogen deposits are tar sands.
3. Some kerogen deposits are tar sands.
4. Some kerogen deposits are not tar sands.
5. None of the above [p. 59].

. . .

The delicate Glorias of Argentina, which open only in cool weather, are all Sassoids. Some of the equally delicate Fragilas, found only in damp areas, are not Glorias.
What can you infer from these statements?
1. All Fragilas are Sassoids.
2. No Fragilas are Sassoids.
3. Some Fragilas are Sassoids.
4. Some Fragilas are not Sassoids.
5. None of the above [p. 53].

These scales for atmosphere and conversion errors were fairly adequate; reliability coefficients were .65 and .73 respectively. Most of the errors were the predicted ones, 62 percent on each scale.

Such paragraphs, with new terms and irrelevant information, appear to be harder to follow than syllogisms of the same logical form written in letter terms, and more errors might be expected. On the other hand, they are more interesting, more challenging; verifying the truth of the conclusion seems to be more worthwhile. Actually, the errors were similar, both in frequency and in kind. On paragraphs that included an atmosphere error about 75 percent of the responses were errors, mostly atmosphere errors. On paragraphs that included a conversion error about 90 percent of the responses were errors, mostly conversion errors. We should not jump to the conclusion that these college students were especially irrational because only 25 percent of their judgments of the determinate arguments were errors. The error frequencies were no higher, perhaps a little lower, than those reported by Simpson and Johnson for syllogisms of the same form but less meaningful content. But, unlike the former study which reported a correlation of −.12 between the two kinds of error, this study found a correlation of .38. Brief training intended to reduce the two errors differentially produced only negligible improvement.

A STEP TOWARD RECONCILIATION

Recently, Begg and Denny (1969) attempted a reconciliation of the opposing hypotheses by restating the atmophere hypothesis—but retaining the two supplementary principles of Woodworth and Sells—in the form of two inclusive principles which summarize the errors more completely than previous statements. Their first principle states that whenever at least one premise is negative, the most frequently accepted conclusion will be negative; when neither premise is negative, the conclusion will be affirmative. Their second principle states that whenever at least one premise is particular, the most frequently accepted conclusion will be particular; when neither premise is particular, the conclusion will be universal.

The frequencies of errors made by 33 college students on the 14 critical syllogisms—which differed slightly from the frequencies reported by others—demonstrated that the most frequent error was the one predicted by these 2 principles in all 14 cases. The principles evidently describe the data on errors quite succinctly, eliminating the need for the hypothesis of invalid conversion. Thus this is reconciliation by envelopment, but the authors were careful to point out that the agreement of the principles with the error frequencies does not support any specific hypothesis about reasoning processes.

In general, when these half-dozen studies are brought together, it appears that atmosphere errors and conversion errors can be separated if necessary, but the atmosphere hypothesis can be stated to include the conversion errors. Perhaps the conversion hypothesis could be similarly expanded to include all atmosphere errors, but this would be more difficult. Yet it is still true that errors of illogical conversion are common in the evaluation of single propositions. Does this mean that when propositions are combined as syllogisms, the tendency toward acceptance of an invalid conversion evaporates? Or does it mean that the invalid conversion is basically an atmosphere effect, as

Woodworth and Sells suggested long ago? The fact that brief anticonversion training by Simpson and Johnson (1966) failed to reduce conversion errors offers some indirect support for the atmosphere hypothesis, but more direct evidence would be desirable.

When propositions are combined to form syllogisms, the order of the propositions might be a factor in judgment of the conclusions. Premises in the AO order, for example, might not have the same psychological effect as the same premises in the OA order. Although this order effect has not been seriously investigated by itself, the data from the investigations mentioned above suggest that it is negligible. The sequence of the terms of the proposition is another matter.

THE SEQUENCE OF TERMS

The terms of a syllogism can be arranged in four sequences, known as figures, which are logically equivalent but may vary in difficulty. The four figures of a syllogism—all invalid—constructed from particular affirmative, or I, propositions, are as follows:

First   Some X are Y.
           Some Z are X.
           Therefore, some Z are Y.
Second Some Y are X.
           Some Z are X.
           Therefore, some Z are Y.
Third   Some X are Y.
           Some X are Z.
           Therefore, some Z are Y.
Fourth Some Y are X.
           Some X are Z.
           Therefore, some Z are Y.

According to Frase (1968), these figures correspond to the mediational paradigms of paired-associate learning which are known to vary in difficulty. A syllogism of the first figure, for example, is analogous to a paired-associate task in which the subject is required to associate X-Y, then Z-X, and finally, in the test condition, to learn the association Z-Y. Thus, this syllogism corresponds to a forward chain of associations, Z-X-Y, which should be relatively easy to evaluate. Syllogisms of the fourth figure correspond to a backward chain, which should be difficult. Experiments requiring judgments of the validity of 11 syllogisms, written in X, Y, and Z and arranged in these 4 figures, revealed small differences in time and errors that gave some borderline support to the hypothesis.

More convincing support for the mediated association interpretation came from a comparison of the second and third figures by Pezzoli and Frase (1968). If we think of the middle term, which in the above illustration is X, as a mediator, the second figure is a stimulus-equivalent syllogism in that both subject and predicate of the conclusion precede the mediator in the premises, thus: $\underset{Z}{\overset{Y}{>}}X$. The third figure is a response-equivalent type in that mediator precedes both subject and predicate terms, thus: $X\underset{Z}{\overset{Y}{<}}$. Since the third figure requires different responses to the same mediator, it can produce interference and hence more errors in reasoning. To test this hypothesis, syllogisms were written in ordinary English, such as:

> No grass is red.
> All grass are plants.
> Some plants are red.

As predicted, college students made significantly more errors in judging the validity of syllogisms in the third figure than the second. Even more convincing was the interaction with associative strength. While there was no difference between second and third figures for syllogisms written in terms of nonsense syllables or in English words of low associative values, there was a large difference between the two figures for syllogisms with premises in which the second term was closely associated with the first.

This effect of the sequence of terms is stated in respect to frequency of total errors, rather than frequency of specific errors, as in the research on atmosphere and conversion effects; but predictions about the acceptance of specific conclusions can probably be stated and tested. As it is, we have another factor that influences the difficulty of reasoning for syllogisms written with closely associated terms.

The Solution of Three-Term Series Problems

Three-term series problems, also called *linear syllogisms*, have been included in intelligence tests for half a century, but the recent interest in these little problems has been directed toward the processes by which they are solved. The terms are usually first names, like *John* and *Mary*, and the relation between them is an inequality, such as *taller than* or *happier than*, or some other asymmetric relation, such as *below* or *in front of*. When the 3 terms are arranged in 2 sentences, or premises, as a problem, with a conclusion to be evaluated, there are 8 such problems, or, if negative premises are included, there are 16 (see Table 6.2). Comparisons of time and errors when terms, relations, and sequences of these are systematically varied have disclosed unexpected facts, in explanation of which ingenious hypotheses about rearrangement of premises, spatial imagery, and psycholinguistics have been elaborated. Consider the following:

> John is taller than Mary;
> Mary is taller than David.
> Is John taller than David?

Many people solving such problems can be observed drawing little charts on paper, as at the right, or making gestures with their hands to indicate relative heights. Many report that they utilize some   John
imaginary spatial representation, resembling the chart. Thus, |
problems stated in a relation that is easily visualized, such as   Mary
taller than, were easier for English schoolchildren at age eleven |
than problems stated in *warmer than* or *happier than.* This differ-   David
ence in difficulty was not found at age sixteen when symbolic
skills have presumably replaced visualization (Hunter, 1957).

Now consider another example:

John is taller than Mary;
David is shorter than Mary.

Unlike the first problem, which is so straightforward that the thinker can almost read the conclusion directly from the premises, this one requires conversion of the second premise before the logical implications are evident.

Here is a third example:

Mary is shorter than John;
David is shorter than Mary.

This one seems to require, not conversion of terms, but reordering of premises, placing the second premise in front of the first. According to Hunter (1957), the problems that require conversion take longer than the straightforward ones, and problems that require reordering of premises take even longer. Problems that require both are the most difficult.

SPATIAL PARALOGIC

If the solution of such problems involves representing abstract relations by a spatial ordering, more specific predictions of the relative difficulty of different problems should be possible. De Soto, London, and Handel (1965) formulated two principles to account for difficulty and compared problems by the number solved correctly in 10 seconds. The directionality principle states that an ordering from *better* to *worse* is easier than one from *worse* to *better.* Problems were constructed in terms of men's first names, the question being the relation between A and C. In accord with the directionality principle, problems of the form *A is better than B and B is better than C* were solved by 61 percent of college students in the time limit, while those in the form of *C is worse than B and B is worse than A* were solved by only 43 percent. The principle of end anchoring—which has something in common with the end anchoring of judgments, to be discussed in Chapter 9—states that it is helpful to the subject if the first term is an end term, the best or the worst, so that the premise proceeds from an end toward the middle rather than from the middle toward an end. Thus *A is better than B and C is worse than B* was solved correctly by 62 percent while *B is better than C and B is worse than A* was solved correctly by only 38 percent. The percentages of success for other problems in which one principle helped while the other hindered fell between these extremes. These two principles of spatial paralogic therefore seemed to agree quite well with the data from problems written in *better* and *worse,* even though the subjects were college students capable of symbolic operations.

To get more direct evidence of the spatial representation in cognitive space, De Soto, London, and Handel had their subjects locate the elements of comparative statements on paper, in boxes printed horizontally and vertically. As expected, *better* was consistently represented above *worse,* while the representations of *lighter* and *darker* were spatially inconsistent.

Such findings lead to predictions about the difficulty of different relations, so De Soto, et al., compared problems written in *better* and *worse* with problems of the same forms written in *above* and *below.* As expected, the percentages of success were similar because these problems are represented similarly in cognitive space and so the difficulty of aligning premises and conclusion is about the same. For example, problems written in *better* were easier than those written in *worse,* and problems written in *above* were easier than those written in *below* because, according to the authors' interpretation, the natural tendency is to represent these relations spatially and proceed from above downward. "Worseward *is* downward [p. 518]." The pattern of percentage correct was not the same for problems written in *lighter* and *darker,* however. The problem *A is better than B and C is worse than B* was much easier than the parallel problem *A has lighter hair than B and C has darker hair than B.* Apparently the clear spatial representation of *better, worse, above,* and *below*—especially when the ends are anchored—eliminated the presumed difficulty of the reversal of one proposition. Introspectively, it appears that the third term to be read is simply added to an already structured image. Problems written in terms not conducive to spatial imagery must be handled indirectly, presumably linguistically, hence a reversal increases the difficulty.

Problems written in *left* and *right* did not conform very well to the authors' predictions about difficulty. One might guess that in these cases the confusion between a spatial representation and reading habits could introduce inconsistencies.

There are other abstract relations that can be represented spatially, with the expected effects on reasoning. A follow-up experiment by Handel, London, and De Soto (1968) found that the relations *father-son* and *more-less* were represented on paper vertically, as the *better-worse* relation was. Some others, such as *earlier-later,* had a horizontal representation, and others again, as *cause-effect* and *farther-nearer,* were inconsistent. As expected, the pattern of difficulty of linear syllogisms written in *father* and *son, better* and *worse,* and *more* and *less* were all about the same. In the authors' words, "People have the ability to order elements in a cognitive space, of at least two dimensions, which has properties not found in geometric space [p. 357]." The difficulty of problems involving relations that are naturally represented in this cognitive space can be predicted from their spatial representation, while those involving other relations apparently depend more on linguistic complexities.

GRAMMATICAL-SPATIAL CORRESPONDENCE

A different, but overlapping, interpretation of such findings by Hutten-locher (1968) was based on her previous observation of children's difficulties in arranging blocks on shelves, a concrete form of the three-term series problem. If blocks A_1 and A_2 are in place and block B is to be placed in the middle, the descriptions can be stated with B as the subject (B is above A_1; B is below A_2) or as the object (A_1 is below B; A_2 is above B). It seems to be more natural to think of the mobile block, B, as the subject; and, in fact, when B was described as the object, there were many more errors and correct placements took longer. When a toy truck pushed or pulled another toy truck, it was easier to place the mobile truck if it was described as the subject. But for passive statements, as when the truck was pushed by an-other, it was easier to place the mobile truck if it was described as the object. Huttenlocher's generalization is worth serious consideration: "Com-prehension requires a correspondence between the form of a linguistic expression and the situation it describes [p. 553]."

To apply this interpretation to college students reasoning about three-term series problems, Huttenlocher arranged series which compared people by height: *Tom is taller than John; Sam is shorter than John.* Assuming that the first premise establishes the relation between the first two terms, *Tom* and *John*, the hypothesis was that the third term, *Sam*, is more readily located when it is the subject of the second premise, as in the above example, than when it is the object, as in the following example: *Tom is taller than John, John is taller than Sam.* Various combinations of premises with boys' and girls' names were given to students, followed by the question *Who is taller?* or *Who is shorter?* These are very easy tasks, of course, and the response times were brief, but the results do show some differences. When the third term was the subject of the second premise, errors were fewer and times shorter than when it was the object. These problems, written in *taller* and *shorter*, would be ordered in cognitive space by spatial imagery, according to De Soto, et al., and generally the two sets of data on relative difficulty of problems are in agreement. But the end-anchoring interpreta-tion for certain comparisons is replaced by the linguistic interpretation.

Three-term series were also arranged by Huttenlocher with verbs that have an active form, *Tom is leading John*, and a passive form, *John is led by Tom*, the question being *Who is first?* or *Who is last?* This new vari-able doubled the number of series to be compared, but by and large the difficulty, in terms of errors, depended on the grammatical status of the mobile third term and the grammatical form of the premise. As in the above experiment, active premises were easier when the mobile term was described as the subject than when it was described as the object. Passive premises—

which take longer in general—were easier when the mobile term was described as the logical subject even though it was the grammatical object. An illustration of the most difficult type, in which the mobile third term, *Sam*, is the grammatical subject but the logical object, follows: *Tom is leading John, Sam is led by John.*

Huttenlocher's experiments and interpretations were guided by her subjects' introspections, revealing spatial imagery, but it was the linguistic forms that were experimentally manipulated. Evidence of spatial imagery was not directly obtained in these experiments, but the evidence for the influence of grammatical structure is quite convincing.

LINGUISTIC PROCESSES

Three principles derived from linguistic theory were applied to these problems by Clark (1969a). The principle of the primacy of functional relations asserts that the conceptual relations out of which sentences are constructed are stored, immediately after comprehension, in a more readily available form than other kinds of information, such as the superficial grammatical structure of the sentence. Underlying *John is better than Dick,* for example, are the base strings, *John is good* and *Dick is good,* which may be transformed to *John is more good than Dick is good,* or *John is better than Dick is,* and so on. Comparative sentences, then, include the functional relations, such as *John is good* or *John is bad,* as well as the *more than* information; but the first kind of information is more available. Hearing *John is worse than Pete,* the listener realizes that John and Pete are bad more readily than that John is more extreme than Pete in badness.

The principle of lexical marking separates two senses of certain adjectives, like *good. Good* and *bad* are used in an evaluative sense, as contrasting adjectives, but *good* is also used in a nominative sense, to refer to goodness in general. The *good* underlying the sentence *John is better than Pete* can be interpreted either nominally or contrastively, but since the lexically marked contrastive sense takes longer to store and retrieve, this *good* will usually be interpreted in the nominative sense. The *bad* underlying *Dick is worse than Jack* can only be interpreted contrastively. Although Clark was concerned with adult reasoning, it is interesting to note that Donaldson and Wales (1970) have reported that children of three-and-a-half do not make a distinction between *more* and *less.* When asked to make various choices of objects, they treat *less* as a synonym of *more,* apparently because the nominative sense is acquired before the contrastive.

Clark's principle of congruence simply asserts what others have asserted in other language, namely, that answering a question requires more than understanding the surface question. It requires information that is congruent, at the level of functional relations, with the information asked for.

To check out these principles, Clark constructed 32 problem types, of 16 premise combinations and 2 question forms, as listed in Table 6.2. An example of negative premises, not covered in previous research on three-term series, illustrates the format:

If John isn't as good as Pete,
And John isn't as bad as Dick,
Then who is best?
Dick   Pete   John

The principles of primacy of functional relations and lexical marking predict that Problem Types I and II′ will be solved more rapidly than II and I′ respectively. Table 6.2 shows that, when college students did these little tasks, the predictions were confirmed. The principles of primacy of functional relations and congruence predict that III and IV′ will be solved more quickly than IV and III′. These two principles also predict that solutions will be faster for I and II′ when the question is *Who is best?* and for II and I′ when the question is *Who is worst?* The data of Table 6.2

TABLE 6.2. GEOMETRIC MEAN TIMES (IN SECONDS) FOR SOLVING THREE-TERM
SERIES PROBLEMS

Form of Problem		Form of Question		M	Overall M
		Best?	Worst?		
I	(a) A better than B; B better than C	5.42	6.10	5.75	5.49
	(b) B better than C; A better than B	4.98	5.52	5.25	
II	(a) C worse than B; B worse than A	6.27	6.53	6.40	5.91
	(b) B worse than A; C worse than B	5.93	5.04	5.47	
III	(a) A better than B; C worse than B	5.35	5.34	5.34	5.33
	(b) C worse than B; A better than B	4.84	5.84	5.32	
IV	(a) B worse than A; B better than C	5.00	6.02	5.49	5.63
	(b) B better than C; B worse than A	6.12	5.45	5.77	
I′	(a) A not as bad as B; B not as bad as C	6.77	5.95	6.34	6.59
	(b) B not as bad as C; A not as bad as B	7.16	6.56	6.85	
II′	(a) C not as good as B; B not as good as A	5.58	6.63	6.08	6.22
	(b) B not as good as A; C not as good as B	6.11	6.60	6.35	
III′	(a) A not as bad as B; C not as good as B	6.34	6.66	6.50	6.52
	(b) C not as good as B; A not as bad as B	6.73	6.34	6.53	
IV′	(a) B not as good as A; B not as bad as C	6.10	6.18	6.14	6.19
	(b) B not as bad as C; B not as good as A	5.48	7.12	6.25	

From Clark (1969a).

are in general agreement. Linguistically negative statements require one more transformation than logically equivalent positive statements, and a comparison of the upper and lower halves of the table indicates that additional time was required. Clark's three linguistic principles do not account for all the differences in Table 6.2, such as those between the *a* and *b* variations in I, II, I', and II', but the interpretation is more complete than previous ones had been. And a similar pattern of difficulty values was obtained when difficulty was measured in terms of proportion of solutions within a 10-second time limit (Clark, 1969b).

Clark's data agree with those of De Soto, et al., in most respects, but the interpretations differ. The relations that seem, according to spatial paralogic, to be easily visualized in a vertical direction are the ones that Clark believes are unmarked, hence the principle of lexical marking and the principle of directionality would make the same predictions. The special case of *deep-shallow* is critical because *deep* is represented spatially as below *shallow;* thus, according to spatial paralogic, problems written in *deeper* should be harder than problems written in *shallower.* But Clark's data indicate the reverse and, since *deeper* would be unmarked, his principle of lexical marking would be in agreement with this.

Clark's data agree with Huttenlocher's in most respects, but Clark's interpretation, unlike those of Huttenlocher and De Soto, et al., includes the negative statements. Introspectively, the spatial assignment of negative statements is confusing; on the other hand, statements written in passive form may be more adequately handled by Huttenlocher's principles than by Clark's.

With Clark's analysis, the interpretation of three-term series problems has moved from spatial representation to grammatical-spatial correspondence, to a linguistic interpretation that makes spatial representation unnecessary. It is still possible, of course, that spatial representation is involved under some especially favorable conditions but is abandoned for linguistic reasoning when conditions are not favorable. As in the case of syllogistic reasoning, differential training may assist the choice between alternative theories when a mere tabulation of errors and times does not suffice.

The Strange Case of the Awkward Negative

The special difficulties that negative information brings to inductive reasoning (Chapter 2) cause trouble in deductive reasoning also, as we have seen in the solution of syllogistic and three-term series problems. Although negative instances do have a special value in the case of disjunctive classes, in the more common cases they are troublesome and therefore deserve examination. Suppose we are concerned with a closed system in which we know that an event is determined by either X or Y, and we have a hypothesis that it is due to X. This hypothesis can be evaluated directly, by trying X to see if the outcome is positive, or indirectly, by trying Y to see if the outcome is negative. But negative information is not used in the same way as positive information, even when the two are logically equivalent.

There are analogies in other areas of psychology. The effects of punishment are not equal, in the opposite direction, to the effects of reward. Unpleasantness is not merely the other end of a scale of pleasantness. In the case of deductive reasoning, the important factors to be considered in analyzing the function of negatives are the logical propositions, the language in which they are stated, and the nature of the logical system or universe that is assumed. Some ingenious experiments have been designed, mostly in Great Britain, to isolate the effects of these factors. The first mentioned here are based on single problems that require 15 minutes or more, and the others on a series of short tasks in which speed of processing information is emphasized.

PROBLEM SOLVING

An experiment by Donaldson (1959) is a good illustration here. Grade-school students were required to construct a system of statements that would give sufficient information to match five objects (A, B, C, D, E) to five other objects (1, 2, 3, 4, 5). In one problem, for example, boys named Arthur, Bob, etc., were to be assigned to schools numbered 1, 2, etc. The subjects were told to construct an economical system with a small number of statements and, furthermore, that positive statements, such as *A goes with 1*, cost five points while negative statements, such as *A does not go with 2*, cost only one point. Thus in the best solutions, negative statements would be explicit and the positive matches would be derived from these.

In general, the subjects avoided positive statements, as instructed, though they wrote more than the optimal negative statements. The introduction of one or two positive statements, in spite of their high cost, made later use of negative statements much easier. More than half the subjects were able gradually to eliminate all the positive statements and eventually write a set of negative statements only. Similar results were obtained with college students under somewhat different conditions.

An interesting difficulty showed up in second-order derivation. Stating that A is not 2, 3, 4, or 5 determines indirectly that A is 1. Furthermore, from the positive derivation that A is 1 can be derived secondarily the negative statement that B is not 1. However, this sequence of transformations was generally avoided. While the instructions emphasized deriving positive statements from negative, a positive match, once derived, was treated with finality, as an end in itself, rather than as a step to further reasoning.

The problem that Wason (1960) employed to study this further required generating a rule from particular examples and therefore included inductive reasoning, but the important question was the subjects' utilization of negative examples that could eliminate a hypothesis. The instructions were simple: "You will be given three numbers which conform to a simple rule that I have in mind. . . . Your aim is to discover this rule by writing down sets of three numbers, together with reasons for your choice [p. 131]." A positive instance, 2, 4, 6, was displayed as a starter.

The rule that the experimenter had in mind was "three numbers of increasing order of magnitude." The triviality of this rule for college students may have some bearing on the results, since they wrote many sets exemplifying more complex rules that were positive instances, but such confirmation was not helpful in narrowing down the possibilities. Most subjects seemed to avoid negative examples that could eliminate a hypothesis, but those who were most efficient wrote more negative examples and thus eliminated alternative hypotheses quicker.

Campbell (1965) followed up these experiments by one with word problems which were to be solved by replacing the letters of the words with other letters. Problems in which the substitutions could be reasoned out directly were easier than others, involving the same words, in which the substitutions could only be made indirectly, by the elimination of alternatives. The difference was found even in groups given brief instruction in indirect procedures.

Campbell attributes part of the difficulty to the necessity for dealing with complementary classes, since the reasoning required consideration of *A* not only as *A* but also as *not B, not C,* etc. Piaget's children had trouble (see Chapter 3) in understanding that *primroses* and *not primroses* were included in the supraordinate class *flowers,* and Campbell's college students had to do this incidentally while solving a problem. Another factor in the difficulty, according to Campbell, was the change of logical subject. To infer from *A is 1* to *B is not 1* involves not only going beyond the finality of a positive statement, but also shifting to a statement on another subject.

All the above evidence on the sequence of terms and the role of the negative is compatible with the assumption that there is an upper limit to the amount of information that the individual can handle and that as he approaches this limit, he makes errors. Presumably, he retains the information that first comes to him while taking in new information to be related to it. If he can relate the new information directly to what is being retained, solution is easy. But if he must transform the new information, as from negative to affirmative, or reverse the order, or change the subject, the total load may approach his capacity and errors may occur. Transforming one bit of infomation may, as a guess, be as much work as retaining two bits, and many problems require simultaneous retention and transformation.

INFORMATION-PROCESSING TIME

The processing of affirmative and negative information can also be compared by timing performance on simple tasks which require little else. These are not full-scale reasoning problems, but the results clarify some of the difficulties in handling the information in the more complex problems described above. Wason (1959), for example, exposed simple displays of information together with four types of statements to be aligned with them. The time required for true affirmatives was 8.99 seconds, for false affirmatives 11.09, for true negatives 12.58, and for false negatives 15.17 seconds. Possible explanations, according to Wason, are a habitual set for positive statements, the inferential nature of the negative information, and an emotional response to negatives. One subject said: "I don't like 'not'— it's a horrid word."

Following up these possibilities, Wason (1961) made use of odd and even numbers to construct binary statements in which the probabilities are equal *Seventy-eight is an odd number. Fifty-seven is not an even number.* There were four types of statements: true affirmative, false affirmative, true negative, and false negative. The subjects, students at London University, needed only a few seconds to verify these statements as true or false, but they verified the affirmative statements more quickly.

Such tasks can also be written in completion form, with the same four types of statements. "Complete this statement with a number that will make the statement true: __ *is an even number.*" "Complete this statement with a number that will make the statement false: __ *is not an odd number.*" On the construction task, like the verification task, response was faster to affirmative than to negative statements, and, in addition, response was faster under "true" than "false" instructions.

In a binary task, the negative can easily be changed to the affirmative, just as the false can easily be changed to the true. But the results showed that the negative introduces more difficulty than falsity. Instructions to make a statement true are superfluous, since this is the habitual thing to do, but instructions to make it false must be retained in memory. And the completion of a negative statement as true seems to require also thinking of the contrary of the whole statement. Completion of a negative statement as false could easily be done by canceling the negative and the false components, but the subjects apparently preferred to perform two separate, time-consuming operations. There is a curious inconsistency, perhaps only superficial, between these effects and the atmosphere effect which makes a negative conclusion more acceptable than an affirmative one.

Results such as these led Wason and Jones (1963) to draw a distinction between the denotative function of the word *not* in reversing the truth value of an affirmative statement and the possible associated meanings or connotations of this familiar English word—which may be different in other languages. The methodological problem was to eliminate the connotations of *not*, and once again the valiant nonsense syllable rescued psychology from the coils of meaning. One syllable was assigned as a symbol for affirmation and another for negation. Statements such as the four below were shown to the subjects, with a tick indicating *true* and a cross indicating *false* on the first four only.

7 MED an even number ✔
4 MED an even number ✕
8 DAX an even number ✔
3 DAX an even number ✕

Some subjects checked a large number of such implicit statements, while others checked corresponding statements containing the explicit *is* and *is not*. Although a few subjects reported that they translated the nonsense syllables into explicit meaningful language, the overall results showed that the difference between responses to affirmative and negative statements was smaller for the implicit than for the explicit format. Wason and Jones suggest, on the basis of such data, that the purely logical function of denial, when symbolized by an innocent nonsense syllable, makes little difference in time of response to affirmative and negative statements; but conventional verbal interpretation of the negative does make a significant difference, and the specific effect of the stimulus *not* makes an additional difference. These data can also be explained by Clark's (1969a) principles of congruence and lexical marking, assuming that *false* is marked and *true* is not.

A related logical effect turns up as a consequence of instructions to make exceptions. If we have 2 classes of items, A and B, we can ask subjects to mark the As directly or we can ask them to mark all except the Bs. Jones (1966a) compared these instructions by having students, aged twelve to fourteen, perform a canceling task with rows of 8 digits, specifically, the digits 1 to 8. The instructions were stated by inclusion, such as: "Mark the numbers 3, 4, 7, 8," or by exclusion, such as: "Mark all numbers except 1, 2, 5, 6." Performance under exclusion instructions was considerably slower. The errors were not much different in total numbers, but they tended to be errors of omission under inclusion instructions and false positives under exclusion instructions. To be sure, such instructions, though symmetrical, are rather unlikely; the excluded class is usually smaller than the included class, as in "The library is open evenings except Saturday." When Jones compared instructions to mark 5 digits with instructions to mark all except 3, smaller differences of the same kind were obtained.

The awkwardness of making exceptions suggests that the instructions might be transformed at the outset. Jones (1966b) told other students, of the same age, that they should mark all numbers except 3, 4, 6, 8, etc., emphasizing that there were only 8 numbers, and then, after thorough instructions and a demonstration, asked the students: "Tell me what you are going to do." About half the students given the exclusion instructions merely repeated them, but half decoded them into the more efficient inclusion form and then performed the cancelation task almost as quickly as students given the inclusion instructions directly. Those who were given exclusion instructions but did not report decoding them performed much more slowly. Surely instructions are important; there are other variations to be tried out. There must be a point at which the exclusion instructions are more efficient. Perhaps with such ratios, transformation of inclusion instructions to exclusion instructions would be an efficient strategy.

Since these simple tasks require only a few operations and the timing can be quite precise, it is possible to estimate the times of specific operations and combinations of operations. Trabasso (1967) gave one subject 32 rules about figures that varied in size (large or small) and color (orange or green) to verify. The rules were made by pairing 1 value of 1 attribute from each figure with a logical connective. The connectives were either conjunctive (orange and small) or disjunctive (orange or small). Each rule was transformed by negating the first, the second, or both attributes. For example, the conjunctive statement *orange and orange* underwent 3 logically equivalent transformations: *Not-green and orange, orange and not-green,* and *not-green and not-green.* The times required to verify such conjunctive rules by comparing them with the figures in view were, respectively: 0.634, 0.736, 0.736, and 0.824 seconds. Thus these results are similar, in principle, to those obtained by Wason (1959). But Trabasso went further and assumed that the difference between 0.736 and 0.634 was the time required for one transformation. Adding this difference to 0.736 would estimate the time for 2 transformations, 0.838 seconds, which is very close to the obtained 0.824 seconds. Other calculations of this type, all with the data of one well-practiced subject, working in 2 sessions a day for 32 days, indicate that storage of a rule requires more time than verification and that, as Wason reported, confirmation is easier than disconfirmation.

OPEN AND CLOSED SYSTEMS

One error that is emphasized in the above research is the failure to make a positive inference when the alternatives are negated. It is a curious comment on trends in psychological research that a quarter-century ago Morgan (1945) was warning psychologists against a prevalent error in the opposite direction, under the title: *The Credence Given to One Hypothesis Because of the Overthrow of Its Rivals.* The error that Morgan emphasized is based on the distinction between a system in which the possible alternatives are known to be limited and a system that is not so limited.

Morgan's first problem, illustrating a closed system, informed the subjects about five buttons, one of which would ring a bell, then gave them a series of questions:

How many chances are there in a 100 that the bell will ring if you press button C?
Suppose you press button A and the bell does not ring; now how many chances are there in a 100 that the bell will ring if you press button C [p. 56]?

Similar series of questions, written around a murder and five men who had been rounded up as suspects, and two other examples illustrating open systems, were given to college students following the bell problem.

Two-thirds of the students raised their probability estimates on the bell problem as four of the five alternatives were successively eliminated, but half of them did the same in the case of the five murder suspects also. The design of this study is open to several criticisms, to be sure, but more careful research would probably confirm the general trend, that intelligent adults often assume a closed system of alternatives, whether warranted or not, and reason from the negation of one to the affirmation of another. The circumstances under which this type of error occurs have not been analyzed in such detail as the complementary error described above.

258 ⅔ DEDUCTIVE REASONING AS PROBLEM SOLVING

Implications of Conditional Statements

Conditional sentences, common in scientific reasoning, do not make categorical assertions but describe hypothetical relations. *If X is a fish, X can swim. If Henry passes the aptitude test, he gets the job. If Janellen is studying problem solving, she is studying psychology.* Reasoning of this sort is an extraordinary, unworldly venture: describing hypothetical relations, talking about them in conditional terms, and proceeding, on the basis of consistency, to logical consequences that would be true if . . . It is not surprising that errors occur. Actually, some of the implications of conditional statements are quite straightforward and easy; others give rise to several identifiable logical mistakes that demand psychological interpretation.

To clarify conditional sentences and to separate the formal structure from the content, logic books often represent statements of the form, *If P, then Q*, as $P \rightarrow Q$ (Ehlers, 1968). *P* is the antecedent proposition, while *Q* is the consequent, and the negation of these can be represented by $\bar{P}$ and $\bar{Q}$. Here is a valid argument, affirming the antecedent, written in English and in logical symbols:

If *X* is a fish, then *X* can swim.	$P \rightarrow Q$
X is a fish.	P
Therefore, *X* can swim.	$\therefore Q$

A valid argument that denies the consequent:

If *X* is a fish, then *X* can swim.	$P \rightarrow Q$
But *X* cannot swim.	$\bar{Q}$
Therefore, *X* is not a fish.	$\therefore \bar{P}$

A common argument, which is fallacious because it depends on denial of the antecedent:

If *X* is a fish, then *X* can swim.	$P \rightarrow Q$
But *X* is not a fish.	$\bar{P}$
Therefore, *X* cannot swim.	$\therefore \bar{Q}$

And another fallacious argument, called affirmation of the consequent:

If *X* is a fish, then *X* can swim.	$P \rightarrow Q$
X can swim.	Q
Therefore, *X* is a fish.	$\therefore P$

When the conditional statement $P \rightarrow Q$ is taken as a major premise, a minor premise, P, Q, $\bar{P}$, or $\bar{Q}$, can be added and a conclusion can be deduced, as in the first two examples above. Reasoning also proceeds in the other direction. Various combinations of P, Q, $\bar{P}$, and $\bar{Q}$ can be used to affirm or to falsify the conditional statement. But, although there are only four cases —$P\ Q$, $\bar{P}\ Q$, $P\ \bar{Q}$, and $\bar{P}\ \bar{Q}$—to be considered, evaluating the truth or falsity of the rule is quite difficult for intelligent adults without training in logic. One device that logicians have found to be helpful in evaluation, a truth table, is shown in Table 6.3. This table is to be read as follows: in the first case, when P is true and Q is true, the statement $P \rightarrow Q$ can be affirmed. In the second case, when P is true and Q is false, the statement $P \rightarrow Q$ is false. The third and fourth cases are consistent with the truth of the conditional statement.

With this little excursion into the logic of conditionals, we are now in a position to look at the empirical evidence. The fallacies of denial of the antecedent and affirmation of the consequent have long been recognized, and we know that college students are moderately vulnerable to the former and very vulnerable to the latter (Wason, 1964). When we look for a psychological explanation of such difficulties, we see several possibilities. The intrinsic nature of the logical structure is not understood by all reasonable men and women. The sentence $P \rightarrow Q$ may be read as a statement of temporal or causal relations although only logical relations are intended. As we have noted earlier, logical forms grew out of the general language but they have acquired formal constraints of their own. Another hypothesis for the difficulties of conditional reasoning involves the semantics of the enigmatic If. The temporal flavor of then can be misleading. Even such terms as antecedent and consequent have temporal connotations that may be logically confusing, which is one reason why logicians prefer their astringent symbolic language: $P \rightarrow Q$. Still another hypothesis is the difficulty, noted above, of negation and falsity. A general set for truth seems to be more regular. Hence P. C. Wason, P. N. Johnson-Laird, and associates at University College, London, undertook a series of analytical experiments to tease out the various psychological factors that produce these logical difficulties.

The materials of several experiments were cards with numbers on one side and letters on the other, and the procedure was a variation of the selection procedures used in studies of concept attainment (Wason, 1968). Four cards, showing D, 3, B, and 7, were placed before each college student, with instructions to evaluate the validity of the rule that if there is a D on one side of any card, there is a 3 on the other side. (In logical symbols, the cards were P, Q, $\bar{P}$, and $\bar{Q}$ respectively.) The subject was then asked which cards he would turn over to determine whether the rule was

TABLE 6.3. A SIMPLE TRUTH TABLE

Case	P	Q	$P \rightarrow Q$
1	T	T	T
2	T	F	F
3	F	T	T
4	F	F	T

true or false. Every subject selected D, of course, because it was obvious that a 3 on the other side would confirm the rule. Selecting 7 would be an equally informative selection because a D on the other side would falsify the rule by denying the consequent. In fact, Table 6.3 shows that the joint occurrence of $\bar{Q}$ and P, in this case 7 and D, is the only contingency that falsifies the conditional. But few subjects made this selection. Knowing from the research summarized above that negatives are awkward, Wason suspected that most people are more accustomed to truth than to falsity and therefore find it awkward to falsify a rule by denial of the consequent. This appears to be a promising interpretation, even though experimental emphasis on falsity did not improve performance, compared to that of a control group.

Denial of the consequent implies denial of the antecedent, or $\bar{Q} \rightarrow \bar{P}$, but to many people denial of the antecedent appears irrelevant to the argument. *If X is a fish, X can swim,* but one could say that *If X is not a fish,* all bets are off. This is an ancient way of interpreting conditional sentences, out of place in a two-valued logic which insists that propositions be true or false, but it may explain what many people actually do. Therefore, Johnson-Laird and Tagart (1969) asked how college students would evaluate conditional statements, given letters and numbers on cards as in the Wason experiment above, when judgments of *true, false,* and *irrelevant* were allowed. When P Q cards were presented, the conditional was judged *true;* when P $\bar{Q}$ cards were presented, the conditional was judged *false*— both valid inferences. But when $\bar{P}$ Q or $\bar{P}$ $\bar{Q}$ cards were presented, the judgment was usually *irrelevant.* The data were consistent with the assumption that the subjects were operating with an incomplete truth table, like Table 6.3, but with the "truth value" of cases 3 and 4 considered irrelevant. In other words, the subjects did not grasp the intrinsic nature of the conditional argument and missed the information contained in half the instances.

The experiment included, for comparison, the disjunctive form: *Either there isn't P, or there is Q.* This expression has the same implication as denial of the antecedent in the conditional form, but the disjunctive form seldom led to the judgment of *irrelevant.* The disjunctive form was the one on which the most time was spent, hence it is possible that the awkwardness of this expression slowed down the subjects and made them approach the logical task more analytically. Following up such leads, Wason and Johnson-Laird (1969) studied disjunctive rules systematically, asking college students to select instances to show that a rule was false and, in other examples, to show that a rule was true. These expressions, like others, were difficult to reason with when negated but, more important, reasoning with disjunctive expressions was more efficient than reasoning with denial of the conditional. The *Either . . . or* sentence itself creates uncertainty and demands more analysis than the conditional *If . . . then* sentence. Say the authors:

With a conditional the individual is likely to be confident but wrong; with a disjunction he is more likely to be unconfident but right. The meaning of a conditional gives no hint of the negation or falsity which underlies its logic. The disjunctive expression makes this element explicit, but this seems to weaken the grounds upon which any inference can be made [p. 20].

Johnson-Laird and Wason (1970) have offered a tentative but plausible description of reasoning processes in these cases, based on the above inquiries and several others. It is necessary to differentiate the selection process, which is turning over a card to seek information, from the evaluation process, which is a judgment about the effect of the information on the truth or falsity of the rule. The naïve subject, who has not memorized the truth tables of the logic books, has a kind of incomplete truth table derived from his implicit knowledge of the language, which contains information only about those contingencies that make the rule true. He has to infer from this information which contingencies would falsify the rule when his incomplete truth table creates a bias toward verification. Thus he considers only cards mentioned in the rule, namely, P and Q, and tests only whether they could verify the rule. Those subjects with partial insight are likely to ask whether any cards, other than those which could verify the rule, could falsify the rule. Those subjects with complete insight ask whether any cards could falsify the rule. According to these authors, as insight into the logical structure of the conditional sentence is acquired, more reliance is placed upon tests of falsification.

In general, then, the difficulty of reasoning about conditional sentences arises out of their hypothetical nature. The thinker has to process propositions that are not only abstract, like all general propositions, but are also *iffy*. Even propositions that appear irrelevant to the uninitiated have logical consequences. This hypothetical characteristic is complicated by linguistic factors because *If . . . then* constructions, being common in ordinary discourse, appear more straightforward than they logically are. And, although information that falsifies a statement is logically valuable, the processing of such information is especially difficult because most people are set for truth—in this situation as in others. Thus, grasping the logical structure of conditionals consists largely of attaining insight into the consequences of falsification.

Learning to Reason Logically

Reasoning is a cultivated performance that requires practice. A sound mind in a sound body is not drawn irresistibly to sound conclusions. Learning to reason depends on, and goes beyond, the learning of concepts. But logical connectives—such as *if, then, and, or,* and *except*—are not learned as class concepts—such as *tree, sonnet,* and *green triangle with double borders*—are learned. Rather, they are learned in the context of sentences, as functional parts of statements. Learning to reason also depends on, and goes beyond, learning the general language in which statements are made. Part of the training in reasoning consists of practice in using familiar concepts and language structures more critically; but a large part consists also of learning new terminology (e.g., conversion), new formal structures (e.g., syllogisms), and new procedures (e.g., mapping statements into truth tables, and falsification).

Such training is effective even in small amounts. It is not surprising that a college course in logic improves skill in handling logic problems, but average young men have acquired some facility in the calculus of propositions in only two hours of instruction (Moore and Anderson, 1954). A game played with logic cubes is said to change the drudgery of learning the calculus of propositions into an enjoyable pastime even for schoolchildren (Allen, 1965). Special instructions with diagrams and examples helped a group of adults to reach a high degree of accuracy in syllogistic reasoning in a short time and to demonstrate that the distorting effects of bias can be minimized (Henle and Michael, 1956). In Hunter's (1957) study of three-term series problems, an improvement appeared between the first and last halves of a set of 16 problems. Such improvement would not occur, of course, if formal reasoning were a routine performance that everyone practiced daily. Nevertheless, some people do learn such skills by themselves, and some make better use of what they have been formally taught than others. Hence, when intelligent adults who have not studied logic are compared on reasoning tests with those who have, the averages differ as expected, but there is considerable overlap between the groups (Morgan and Morgan, 1953).

From the psychological point of view, education in logical reasoning resembles education in other systematic disciplines. It takes off from the general language and consists of learning special concepts, operations, and purposes. Practice in putting verbal patterns into classes, such as conditional propositions, and naming them facilitates mastery of the concepts and skill in manipulating the classes as units in further reasoning. Rules for operations, such as conversion, are memorized and practiced. Ordinary discourse is analyzed and the arguments rearranged into formal patterns. The purposes and restrictions of formal logic are distinguished from those of ordinary communication much as, in other disciplines, fine art is distinguished from applied art and pure science from technology.

Many of the difficulties described in this chapter can be reduced by techniques that make abstract relations more concrete. Euler's circles offer one example of a visual aid that displays relations of inclusion and exclusion involved in syllogistic reasoning. In the illustration below, the proposition *All S is P* is shown by placing the S circle inside the P circle and $\bar{P}$ outside the circle to indicate the not-P space. Venn diagrams, another graphic system, are more complex and more generally useful; and truth tables (illustrated by Table 6.3) are widely exploited as an aid in analysis of logical relations.

Psychologically, all these schemes may be considered alternative representation systems for illustrating abstract logical structures on a two-dimensional surface. Teachers use these, as they use maps and models, to demonstrate relations between elements, and such demonstrations have been helpful to third-grade children working three-term reasoning problems (Morgan and Carrington, 1944). But the most improvement occurs when students are given practice in transforming or recoding the information from one representation system to another. Many of the exercises in logic books consist of practice in representation and transformation. Whimbey and Ryan (1969) have interpreted the results of a training experiment with college students by assuming that syllogistic reasoning depends on a good short-term memory, as tested by a modified digit span test, and that practice in representing the logical structures by Venn diagrams reduces this dependence. When the logical structure of a given problem is appropriately represented and matched to a familiar pattern, conclusions can be tested almost mechanically—much as complex algebraic manipulations are carried out by the mechanical application of a memorized algorithm. When all instances to be considered and all logical consequences are represented exhaustively, by any representation system, the difficulties of negative information and of falsification are minimized.

Since logical analysis of an argument has a critical purpose, the detection of fallacies is a prominent feature of training in reasoning. Training often includes the classification and naming of fallacies, along with exposition of the logical flaws. The procedures of Simpson and Johnson (1966), aimed specifically at atmosphere errors, were fairly successful. Wason (1964), however, has worked out an ingenious procedure for getting the student to discover and correct his own fallacies without the mediation of any technical terminology. The reasoning tasks were conditional statements of the form *If P, then Q*. One task, called the *antecedent task,* consisted of using the information given in a series of ten statements to complete the following rule: "Any employee aged 34 years, or more, will receive a salary of at least _____ a year [p. 30]." For example, one statement asserted that a particular employee aged twenty-four received £1,800. It is tempting to infer that if this is so, the critical salary must be more than £1,800. But the next statement asserted that another employee aged thirty-seven received £1,600. The order of the statements was arranged so that a statement suggesting a valid inference was followed by a statement suggesting an invalid inference consistent with the one before, then a statement suggesting a valid inference inconsistent with the preceding fallacy, and so on. Thus college students who drew invalid inferences were able to detect their own logical errors and correct them.

Another task, called the *consequent task,* required completing the following incomplete rule: "Any employee aged _____, or more, will receive a salary of at least £1,900 a year [p. 30]." A corresponding series of statements leading to alternate valid and invalid inferences was arranged. This task was more deceptive. Fallacious reasoning from the consequent to the antecedent was twice as common as from the antecedent to the consequent. But on both tasks, experimental programs produced more recognition of errors than control programs in which successive valid and invalid inferences were not contradictory. It is interesting to note also that the improvement in the experimental groups occurred in an all-or-none manner. Those students who eliminated their errors did so quickly when the contradiction became apparent and did not err again. The small improvement in the control groups was more variable. Teachers of reasoning, as far back as Socrates, have confronted students with their inconsistencies, but this procedure, which might by analogy with programmed learning be called programmed reasoning, is a systematic teaching procedure that allows the student to confront his own inconsistencies and correct them.

Self-contradiction was included also in a training procedure devised by Wason (1969) for teaching the best information-seeking strategy on the conditional reasoning tasks used by the London group in the research mentioned above. We should bear in mind here that insight consisted mainly of grasping the logical value of falsification and that mere emphasis on falsification was not helpful. The training procedure first familiarized the subjects with all four combinations of instances: $P \, Q$, $\bar{P} \, Q$, $P \, \bar{Q}$, and $\bar{P} \, \bar{Q}$. Then the experimenter chose cards and asked questions that confronted each subject with increasingly obvious contradictions until he realized that $\bar{Q}$ was relevant. The success of such "discovery" procedures points to one way in which intelligent adults without training in logic may have learned to reason logically.

Reasoning Abilities

It is relatively easy to construct a reliable test of deductive reasoning, as Burt (1919) did in England a half-century ago, simply by assembling a number of logic problems, like the problems in this chapter, of difficulty appropriate to the subjects. Such tests predict academic success at all levels and success in solving various kinds of problems. Good reasoners, in this sense, are less susceptible to emotional bias in evaluating arguments than poor reasoners (Feather, 1964). Scores on these tests correlate well with intelligence tests, and reasoning has long been considered an important component of general intelligence.

One of the common difficulties in test construction is that of defining the domain of interest and sampling it fairly. But the number of logical forms is rather small; hence sampling of this domain is not hard to do, and tests of deductive reasoning can be constructed more systematically than tests of most other abilities. Furthermore, it is possible, as we have seen, to construct separate tests of specific logical errors in a systematic fashion. Atmosphere and conversion errors are rather independent, and there may be others also that can be similarly isolated.

Inductive reasoning, as well as deductive, is included. Analogies composed of words, numbers, and shapes have been used. The series-completion item, based on numbers or shapes, is a favorite. Arithmetic reasoning has long been distinguished from facility in arithmetic computation and treated as a component of general reasoning. Scores on tests of general reasoning correlate with general intelligence, of course, and predict success in solving problems, as we noted in the preceding chapter.

Several attempts have been made to analyze such reasoning tests, but the results vary, depending on the kind of analysis, the tests, and the range of ability in the sample of subjects. The conclusion reached by Guilford, Kettner, and Christensen (1956) after a careful factor analysis may be taken as representing the results of one sophisticated attempt. They say that general reasoning is not general intelligence, though it is undoubtedly one of the important intellectual abilities. It is not a broad ability to manipulate symbols, but there seems to be a narrow ability of this sort. It is not a generic ability to solve problems, though it undoubtedly plays a role in solving problems of certain types. It is neither the familiar deductive reasoning nor arithmetic reasoning. "By elimination and by consistent indications of a positive nature, the best we can say is that general reasoning has something to do with comprehending or structuring problems of certain kinds in preparation for solving them. . . . It may be a general ability to formulate complex conceptions of many kinds [pp. 171–172]." Performance on reasoning tests can also be interpreted as convergent production, in line with Guilford's (1967) general treatment of the nature of intelligence.

Attempts to separate inductive reasoning ability from deductive reasoning ability by factor analysis have not yielded convincing results; Guilford (1967) does not include this distinction in his structure of intellect. On the other hand, when students in fifth and sixth grades were taught elementary set concepts by inductive or deductive procedures, tests of inductive and deductive abilities did yield differential predictions of criterion performance (King, Robert, and Kropp, 1969). This is one teaching experiment—there are not many—in which an interaction between aptitude test scores and teaching methods was demonstrated.

The Development of Reasoning

If reasoning is such a sophisticated accomplishment, how does it develop? After collecting considerable data on children of different ages, Burt (1919) selected reasoning problems which were passed by 40 to 60 percent of the children of each age and arranged them in age levels. Two of these follow, the first at the seven-year level, the second at the nine-year level.

> All wall flowers have four petals; this flower has three petals.
> Is it a wall flower?
> Three boys are sitting in a row. Harry is to the left of Willie;
> George is to the left of Harry. Which boy is in the middle [p. 73]?

Burt also varied the form of the problems and asked the children to give the reasons for their answers to each. The results led him to the conclusion that by age seven children can avoid most fallacies if obvious and by age fourteen they will be caught by the same fallacies if well disguised. The formal character of the fallacy was not as important as the amount and kind of material. The picture presented is one of a continuous quantitative development in general breadth of comprehension and in experience with the important concepts. Burt believed that when the child has a mental age of seven, he has all the "mental mechanisms essential to reasoning." Subsequent development consists of an increase in the complexity of the processes which the child can perform.

In the Paris laboratory of Binet and Simon at about this time, Jean Piaget was given the assignment of standardizing Burt's tests for French school-children. He was more intrigued by the children's comments, however, than by the quantitative data, so he turned to a question-and-answer procedure, less rigid but more subtle, directed toward the role of reasoning in the child's social and intellectual progress. Piaget (1926, 1928) collected records of children's spontaneous questions in natural situations, and, in the interview situation, he asked Why questions (*Why does the wind blow?*) and gave the children incomplete sentences to complete (*The man fell off his bicycle because . . . The pebble sank although . . .*).

Piaget's interpretation of his material emphasized the young child's egocentrism and its consequences for thinking. Unlike the older child, the young child of six or less does not communicate well. When a girl of four was asked: "Have you got a sister?" she replied: "Yes." But the next question was: "And has she got a sister?" to which the reply was: "No. I am the sister." The difficulty of communication in this situation is not so much a language difficulty as the difficulty of seeing herself from her sister's position. The presence of another child may encourage speech, but it is not give-and-take conversation because at this age the child cannot appreciate the other child's point of view and adapt his language to the requirements of communication. When he makes a statement he has no need to justify it, and for this reason the young child, before seven, seldom uses words having the function of *because* spontaneously. When asked to finish a sentence that includes *because,* he misses the logical connection. This does not mean that the young child is not curious; it means that his search for reasons has not yet been socialized. A personally satisfying answer will suffice.

The use of such logical connectives as *because, therefore,* and *although* increases with the child's socialization, according to Piaget, not because language molds thought, but because of the child's increasing interest in communication and his increasing ability to take another's point of view. Even so, the first efforts at logical justification, like the first efforts at classification at this age, are characterized by juxtaposition of superficialities and accidental connection. It is as if *because* means no more than *and* or *and then.*

Piaget adapted one of Burt's tests to his purpose as follows:

Edith is fairer than Suzanne; Edith is darker than Lili. Which is the darkest, Edith, Suzanne, or Lili?

The young child can put these girls in obvious classes, composed of fair girls or dark girls, but the problem depends on the relation *darker than*. The difficulty, according to Piaget, is that Edith can have one relation to Suzanne and simultaneously another relation to Lili.

As the child accommodates his playing, talking, and thinking to Suzanne's point of view and also to Lili's, and his mother's, and his brother's, he moves toward thinking from everyone's point of view, or no one's. Thus children's answers to questions begin, after age eight, to look to impersonal principles, at first quite limited and concrete, for explanation. This development requires the accumulation of experience with specific objects and situations, and facility with certain concepts, as well as language skill. As we would expect, knowing the difficulty of disjunctive concepts, the use of *although* to express discordance or exception to a rule, occurs later than the use of *because*. After fourteen or so most youngsters, having reached the stage of formal operations, know about general principles and try to explain an event by stating one. They are also competent, at minimal levels, in *If . . . then* arguments. Thus reasoning, which started as a social technique, becomes an impersonal operation directed toward abstract generalizations.

Some other developmental treatments of reasoning are at variance with the Geneva account, either in data or interpretation. The training study by Anderson (1965), as noted earlier, demonstrated that children of ten could be trained to use a strategy for finding a generalization that Inhelder and Piaget restrict to age fourteen. Wheeler (1958) reached a similar conclusion from factor analysis of reasoning tests of the Burt type given to children of different ages. Her data showed that children are capable of logical reasoning at a much earlier age than usually assumed and that there was a steady improvement throughout the school period. She also found, like Burt, that the calculus of classes was achieved before the calculus of relations and propositions. The British interpretation assumes that operations with propositions come later than operations with classes, not because a transition from one stage to another is involved, but simply because there are more complex operations to be performed.

Clark (1969a) has an alternative interpretation for the development of success on the three-term series problem. Instead of emphasizing the differences between classes and relations, he asserts that children develop the semantically prior nominal sense of adjectives before the contrastive senses. That is why a young child can take the sentence *Betty is older than May* to mean that *Betty is younger than May*. Both *young* and *old* are interpreted in a nominal sense, so that both sentences can mean *Betty is different in age from May*. This interpretation follows from Clark's work with the reasoning of college students, but it is not consistent with the usual assumption that children acquire contrastive adjectives, like *old* and *young*, before they acquire the continuous dimension.

If the development of reasoning appears to be incompletely described and explained, it should be noted that there seems to be no disagreement with the assumption that this development depends on the socialization of thinking and especially on moving from one's own point of view to that of another and to that of everyone. The linguistic forms provided by the culture may play a larger role in this development (see Chapter 3) than the Geneva school allows, however. As to the question of stages, since reasoning involves operations with propositions (which are more complex than classes), testing hypotheses about discontinuities in the development of reasoning will run into methodological difficulties at least as serious as those involving classes (see Chapter 2).

Certainly, much will be learned as the carefully written problems, the terminology, and the research designs of the experiments described in this chapter are applied to developmental questions. Probably all would agree that the growth of the child's capacity for immediate or short-term memory is a gradual, quantitative development; and, if we assume that the processing of the information in a problem takes place within the limits of short-term memory (Miller, 1962), that the upper limit is continuously rising during the growth period. Thus, at a certain age a child may be able to perform operations involving classes but not operations involving propositions, simply because the complexity of the latter approaches the limit of his capacity for handling information. By the same assumptions, problems that involve transformation of a proposition—for example, from *Edith is fairer than Suzanne* to *Suzanne is darker than Edith*—will be solved even later. We also know, however, that specific concepts become easier to manipulate as they are learned more thoroughly, or overlearned. The meaning of negative terms and the procedure of falsification are again rather specific acquisitions. So it appears probable that a general continuous growth in capacity for memory, retrieval, and information processing goes along with discontinuous jumps in specific acquisitions, depending on the contingencies of schooling and experience.

Major Trends and Implications

Logic is formal and timeless, but reasoning is a human enterprise that proceeds step by step in measurable periods of time. Deductive reasoning, specifically, was considered in this chapter as the solution of problems concerned with the validity of inferences. These are not problems of inventive or productive thought, for alternative conclusions to deductive arguments are usually obvious. They are problems of evaluation of conclusions according to the criteria of formal validity. Hence the productive thinking that occurs consists of reorganization of the structure of the argument to facilitate evaluation of the alternative conclusions. The purely formal nature of logical validity is a cultivated notion that evolved historically through centuries of debate and is achieved by each individual through social interaction and education.

Deductive reasoning enters into the solution of all kinds of problems, but the reasoning processes are exhibited most prominently in the solution of logic problems, especially those systematically constructed by the manipulation of content or structural variables. Experimental investigations have varied the content from purely symbolic, content-free arguments written in X, Y, and Z to arguments of the same structure written in continuous, meaningful sentences. The content of the meaningful arguments has varied from neutral to controversial and from patently true statements to patently false. The logical structures that have been studied most thoroughly are syllogisms, three-term series, and conditional statements.

Thus, in the 1940s, research focused on man's irrationality was able, by manipulation of the content of syllogisms, to obtain objective evidence of the biases that psychologists observed in their neighbors. Later, when cognitive theorizing became fashionable, more comprehensive research designs were able to quantify the effects of the cognitive consistency of an argument as well as the emotional bias toward the content. When the content of the premises makes them clearly false or inconsistent, reasoning is slowed but, under certain conditions, is more accurate. There is some evidence from experiments on attitude change that "covert deductive reasoning" accounts for the acceptance of conclusions not explicitly mentioned in the message.

Even an unbiased thinker confronts many obstacles as he works his way through a logical discussion to a valid inference. Most of the terms that appear in a logical statement—such as *some, is, or, If . . . then,* and *not*—have previously appeared in the context of ordinary language. The logicians prune away the lively meanings, leaving the idealized structure, but the ordinary person retains the conversational connotations. Errors related to the logical structure of syllogisms and identified in logical terms were given a psychological explanation in terms of atmosphere effects in the 1930s and in terms of invalid conversion in the 1950s. In the 1960s, differential training reduced atmosphere errors but not conversion errors, and a broader interpretation of atmosphere effects encompassed the most frequent error tendencies, leaving the error of invalid conversion with an ambiguous status. At the same time, variations in the difficulty of certain syllogistic figures, previously lumped together, were interpreted according to principles derived from paired-associate learning.

Unlike syllogisms, three-term series problems are solved by adults in a few seconds, but even so variations in time and errors throw some light on the reasoning processes. The hypothesis that the terms are spatially represented in visual imagery has long been intuitively attractive, and objective data in agreement with this hypothesis have recently been obtained. Those problems that are easily visualized are more easily solved than those that are not. Problems stated so that one premise must be rearranged to be aligned with the representation of the other in cognitive space are more difficult. But much of the empirical evidence on variations in difficulty between problems can also be explained by assuming that the second premise is easier to line up with the first if the initial term of the second premise is the subject of the sentence. And much of the evidence can also be explained by linguistic principles, particularly by assuming that the nominative sense of common adjectives is more readily processed than the contrastive senses.

Hence, this is one example of how psycholinguistics is beginning to contribute to progress in general psychology.

The plausibility of each of the hypotheses for three-term series and the successful predictions of each suggest that there are several sources of difficulty and that no single hypothesis will suffice. The agreement of one hypothesis with the data on time and errors does not dispose of the others. Furthermore, if these diverse and subtle hypotheses are plausible for such modest little reasoning tasks, we should not expect simple explanations for more complex problems. The hypotheses offered for syllogisms and for three-term series problems have surprisingly little in common, but this might stem from the research interests of psychologists rather than from complete disparity among the reasoning processes.

In deductive as in inductive reasoning, negative information causes more trouble than positive because an additional transformation is required and because the word *not* has avoidant connotations beyond its logical significance. Furthermore, the logical significance of a negative statement, or of an exception to a statement, depends on the assumption of a closed universe of discourse, which many have been taught to question.

Inferences from conditional statements are also difficult, partly because of their hypothetical nature, partly because statements that appear irrelevant have logical implications, partly because of the pervasive awkwardness of negative information, but above all because reasoning with conditionals depends largely on falsification of the consequent, which runs counter to the normal propensity to describe things as they are.

Research on deductive reasoning converges with recent research on inductive reasoning, especially on attribute and rule learning, to emphasize the psychological difficulty, as well as the logical efficiency, of falsifying a statement. The difficulty of negative information also applies generally, and so does the difficulty of switching from ordinary discourse to formal reasoning. But, aside from these few generalities, most of the difficulties of deductive reasoning are specific to the various logical forms.

Education in logical reasoning resembles education in other systematic disciplines. Beginning with the general language, the student learns the special aims and limitations of formal reasoning, standard logical structures, common fallacies, and methods of verifying inferences. He practices logical manipulations, logical analysis of ordinary statements, and alternative systems for representing relations between statements. Methods of "programmed reasoning" have been devised that permit the thinker to observe the contradictions in his own inferences. Such training is quite effective, even in small amounts, when evaluated by performance on reasoning tests, probably because most people do not get such practice in their routine activities. But some people do apparently teach themselves to reason clearly because in all comparisons there are some without logical training who exceed the average performance of groups with such training.

We have seen that concept learning, information seeking, and other intellectual tasks take on the character of reasoning tasks as artificial laboratory materials are presented and as the subjects acquire skill in converting interesting content into content-free, formal statements. But this does not mean that content is unimportant or that the results thus obtained can be directly applied to real-life activities with meaningful content. Transfer from training in formal logic to reasoning about events headlined in the evening paper has typically been minimal. Yet it is possible to teach any topic with an emphasis on reasoning, or critical thinking as it is often called, rather than on the accumulation of facts. The reasoning tests constructed for factor analyses of reasoning supply models for tests of achievement in academic subjects.

Children acquire simple reasoning skills in the normal course of development, but whether this development occurs gradually or by stages is a matter of controversy. Age differences are obvious, but it is questionable whether they are peculiar to logical operations or to general intellectual growth, whether they can only be acquired according to nature's plan or can be advanced by special schooling. It is not inconsistent to expect a continuous growth in the basic intellectual functions along with discontinuities resulting from experience with specific logical structures.

CHAPTER 7

PRODUCTIVE THINKING

nlike the problems dealt with in previous chapters, there are also problems with solutions that cannot easily be categorized as successes and failures but rather are evaluated on continuous dimensions, such as appropriateness and originality. Productive thinking, conceived as constructing, writing, or otherwise producing solutions, can be contrasted with finding the correct solution or reaching the goal. The distinction drawn by Guilford (1956) between *convergent thinking,* which zeros in on the right answer, and *divergent thinking,* which moves outward, is now generally recognized. The distinction is blurred, to be sure, because traditional problem-solving experiments have often reported solutions that did not fall neatly into either success or failure categories. Although thinking is not well described by calling it creative, divergent, productive, original, or imaginative, all these refer to intellectual activities with certain distinctive characteristics.

In this division of the psychology of problem solving, the defining characteristics reside in the solutions rather than in the processes involved. Whereas in previous chapters the correct solution was easily differentiated from the others, in the present chapter this will not be so easy. Here we must consider problems each of which has multiple solutions that vary on several dimensions. Judgment of the solution plays an important part in the experimental methodology, and, if the thinker produces more than one solution, judgment is part of his problem also. The most interesting solutions psychologically, and the most influential historically, are those that are judged creative. In the previous chapter, the cold formal reasoning of the logician was the ideal; in the present chapter, it is the ardent thought of the creative genius.

Creative Thinking

The most dependable criterion of creative accomplishment is the judgment of history. The names of Beethoven, El Greco, Goethe, Einstein, and Freud are celebrated in the arts and sciences, not for feats of memory, prolonged errorless performance, nor efficiency on routine assignments, but for outstanding creative contributions that exemplify man at his intellectual best. In attracting disciples and making intellectual history, creative geniuses have also raised questions that mark out an area of sociological and psychological investigation.

Creative thinking of such a high order is not common. Even the geniuses of history reached their creative heights rarely and spent much of their time elaborating the brilliant ideas that came in their most creative moments. Most of them made a few mistakes, in their less creative moments, that embarrass their disciples and their biographers. But reknown as a creative genius is built on one or more outstanding achievements, not on freedom from mistakes, nor on average level of performance.

Any intellectual achievement that is recorded in the pages of history must have been the joint consequence of a creative individual and favorable conditions in the intellectual environment. In some instances, historians and biographers have been able to describe the intellectual conditions in an art or science that gave a favorable welcome to a particular innovation. They tell us that the general illiteracy of the medieval ages encouraged the development of realistic painting and sculpture which tells a story. We know, for example, that many of the bas-reliefs that ornament medieval cathedrals, admired and imitated today, were put there to illustrate some now obscure conflict between clergy and laity. Students of the history of psychology usually try to describe these factors of the *Zeitgeist* that stimulated new developments, and the contemporary sociology of invention and innovation is a necessary complement to any account, like the present one, that emphasizes psychological factors.

There is a large literature (Ghiselin, 1952; Koestler, 1964) of personal testimony about the conditions that influence creative output. This introspective literature supplies background information and suggests some intriguing hypotheses, but the psychology of thinking has not lacked for intriguing hypotheses as much as for objective data. If one approaches these ruminative accounts inductively, one is impressed by the frequency with which great thinkers, at an honorary banquet or the unveiling of a portrait, compare themselves with other great thinkers. Helmholtz recognized his own thought processes in the reports of Goethe and Gauss, and many scientists have invoked the image of Archimedes. Fascinating as these anecdotes may be, especially to readers who also can recognize similarities to the workings of great minds in their own thinking, the difficulties with such evidence are obvious.

There are, however, some solid biographical data on creative individuals of the past, so we shall begin with some individual differences. Previous chapters opened with the conditions that facilitate and retard performance and came to individual differences secondarily. But in dealing with creative thinking, information about creative individuals, identified by the criteria of outstanding accomplishment, is more definitive, and a more secure starting point than information about conditions or processes. The preoccupation with great thinkers is caused partly by an intrinsic fascination with them as personalities—it is true, as far as such people are concerned, that there are no dull biographies—and partly by the hope of finding some generally useful information about the personal characteristics and environmental conditions that promote creative thinking.

THE GENIUSES OF HISTORY

The creative geniuses that we know about from records of the past came predominantly from middle-class families and had the benefits of a good education, although in some cases a rather irregular education. Biographical data give evidence of strong motivation toward intellectual goals in spite of frustration, indeed, often in spite of strong opposition from family, friends, and social norms. There are many more portraits of men than women adorning the pages and histories of the arts and sciences, probably because of the cultural expectations and psychological reasons discussed in Chapter 4.

Records of intellectual development in childhood are available for some eminent thinkers of the past and can be used in an indirect way to estimate intelligence on our present IQ scale. We know, for example, that the average child learns to read at seven or eight, so we can assume that a mental age of six is necessary for this accomplishment. We also know that John Stuart Mill was reading at age three, so we can divide mental age by chronological age and get an IQ estimate of 200 for young John. A mental age of about fourteen is necessary for algebra and he learned algebra at eight, so another IQ estimate would be 175. In Mill's case there are several such facts that permit estimates, the average of which is 190 for his childhood and 170 for his youth. The records of 300 eminent men and women have been evaluated in this way by three psychologists working independently, and in cases for which the records were adequate and the psychologists agreed, the average estimate can be taken as the minimum IQ that will account for the recorded achievements (Terman, 1926).

Estimates of intelligence for those with adequate records suggest very high IQs. Goethe, who wrote poetry in Latin when he was eight, was scored 185 for his childhood and 200 for his youth. Others of interest are Pascal, the mathematician, 180; Voltaire, the French writer, 175; Mozart, the composer, 155. In general, those who made their reputations as philosophers averaged 170, the poets, novelists, and dramatists 160, and the scientists 155.

The other important fact that has turned up in the old records is that these eminent thinkers did their most distinguished work when they were young. There are exceptions, like William James, but a study of many histories of art, science, architecture, medicine, and other specialties by Lehman (1953) demonstrated that the age of creative achievement is lower than most people suspect (see Figs. 7.1 and 7.2). A study of the hundred most important inventions since 1800 (Alexander, 1945) disclosed that the average age of the inventors at the time was thirty-seven. This type of analysis has been criticized for several reasons, but Lehman's generalization about creative accomplishments of very high quality seems to hold up on further examination (Botwinick, 1967). The grey-bearded gentlemen in the fading portraits on museum walls were not painted while they were achieving fame but after they had it made.

The comparison between young and old is more unbalanced than the cold figures indicate because the young men usually created their masterpieces when they were burdened with occupational and domestic problems. Eminent thinkers of fifty have arrived. They are generally established—with facilities, assistants, and the prestige that smooths away many difficulties. These same thinkers at thirty had to find and hold jobs, perhaps to move several times, and to compete with their peers for support and a place to work. Most had wives to entertain and children who wanted to play with them. But the abundant energy of the young and their enthusiasm for new ideas enabled some of them to surmount the typical hurdles of this stage of the life cycle. Their intellectual capacities show up, moreover, in learning as well as thinking. An eager young scientist, for example, will often absorb and synthesize two ideas that seem incompatible to older scientists. Such open-minded learning will be harder for him later when his ideas are well organized into cognitive systems that resist penetration by new ideas.

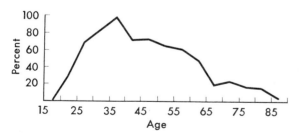

FIGURE 7.1. Age and creative achievement. Study of 60 histories of art disclosed that 650 oil paintings were mentioned at least twice. More of these masterpieces were painted when the artist was thirty-five and forty than in any other 5-year interval, but an appreciable number were painted before twenty-five and after seventy. From Lehman (1942).

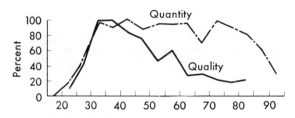

FIGURE 7.2. *Quantity and quality of creative achievement at different ages. The solid line shows the ages at which 182 famous philosophers first published their best treatise, i.e., the one most frequently mentioned in the histories of philosophy. The broken line was constructed by tabulating the ages at which all the philosophical works of these 182 philosophers were first published. From Lehman and Gamertsfelder (1942).*

When we ask about the personalities of great thinkers, the evidence is limited, but something can be learned from careful study of their lives and works. R. B. Cattell (1963), who has analyzed much of the variance of personality into 16 standard factors, read many biographies and autobiographies of scientists and inventors to work out a generalized description of them on these standard factors. They were much like other people in most respects, of course, but there were some interesting differences. On the average, these scientists were schizothymic, that is, withdrawn, skeptical, internally preoccupied, precise, and critical. Despite this internal preoccupation, they were frequently dominant men, especially on intellectual matters. When Pasteur was director of a laboratory, he was much criticized for his authoritarian methods. The great scientists of the past, according to Cattell, were desurgent, that is, introspective, restrained, brooding, and solemn, but this is not incompatible with a high level of resourcefulness and adaptability.

As to the old question of genius and madness, Cattell's study did not indicate any special relation; in fact, his estimates gave the scientists and inventors more ego strength and emotional stability than the average. But similar studies (Juda, 1953; Raskin, 1936; White, 1930) are consistent in uncovering more signs of psychopathology among artistic and literary geniuses than among scientists.

DIMENSIONS OF CREATIVE ACHIEVEMENT

The concept of creative achievement comes from the idealization of great men and their works. After their praises have been sung, investigation begins with the identification of a few dimensions that embody these ideals so that we can set up criteria for evaluating contemporary achievements. The dimensions that psychologists apply to creative achievement today are the ones that others, as far back as Plutarch, applied, but the present methods are more systematic.

INTELLECTUAL LEADERSHIP

Many of the great thinkers of the past are honored today, not only for their own creative output, but for their influence on other thinkers. When a new method of analysis, a promising theory, or an exciting art form inspires some bright young men and women of the next generation to continue this work, a trend has started. A master has found disciples. The creative scientist may sit back and wait for the judgment of history, but more often he tries to convince his peers of the value of his innovations. The radical philosopher, composer, or film maker who succeeds in cultivating an audience for his message is the one who is likely to acquire a reputation.

Investigation of this dimension of creative achievement must wait, of course, for the trend to take shape. Critics, reviewers, and other judges may attempt to predict the life span of the intellectual flurries set in motion by the novel ideas of the present decade, but most do so with great caution. Style of communication, for one thing, can easily confound the evaluation. Objective data begin to accumulate, however, as soon as one person's work is cited or imitated by someone else.

SENSITIVITY TO PROBLEMS

A reputation for creative thinking can be made, at least in part, by asking questions, by identifying problems, and thus opening up a new area of thought. The creative thinker is a problem finder as well as a problem solver —he often perceives a challenging inconsistency where others perceive a satisfying order. On this dimension, intellectual leadership is much like political leadership: one has a fortunate start if the problems that challenge him and arouse his creative efforts are latent problems that arouse others also as soon as they are made explicit.

ORIGINALITY

This dimension is often included in instructions to judges of creative achievements. An original solution to a problem is a novel one, not a copy of some other solution. In principle, this is an unambiguous dimension, but judges need experience with the other solutions in order to evaluate originality. Arguments about originality have often followed applications for patents.

INGENUITY

Ingenuity is often included or implied in the discussion of creativity, but it has been explicitly described by Flanagan (1963) as the invention or discovery of a solution to a problem in an unusually neat or surprising way. The solution should be practically useful, more than just satisfactory, according to Flanagan. It should be clever, not a solution that could be arrived at by a logical routine. In the research context, cleverness is a synonym for ingenuity.

USEFULNESS

The practicality of a solution to a problem can be ignored for some purposes, as in pure science and fine art, but in applied research organizations it may be the most important dimension. Usefulness is not always obvious; expert judgment may be necessary here also.

APPROPRIATENESS
A solution may be unusual without being appropriate to the situation. Hence this dimension is often included in instructions to judges of creative products. Even artistic products, for which usefulness may be an irrelevant dimension, are often criticized if the form is not appropriate to the content, but *Alice in Wonderland,* for example, is convincing as well as imaginative.

BREADTH
Literary critics contrast novels that sweep wide over human experience with those of smaller scope. Studies of scientific research often request the judges to consider the breadth of an invention or a theory, the area of possible application. Achievements commonly mentioned as illustrative of breadth are Tolstoi's *War and Peace,* Newton's laws, and Darwin's theory of evolution.

UNUSUALNESS
When word association tests were first given to mental hospital patients, it was noticed that the patients gave more unusual responses than normal. This was the incentive for compilation of frequency tables, which record that *table* is a more common response to *chair* and therefore presumably more normal than *octopus.* Poets, for example, avoid the old clichés, and even when saying something said before, try to say it in an uncommon way. One psychologist, having administered a word association test to Amy Lowell, reported that she gave "a higher proportion of unique responses than those of any one outside a mental institution [p. 491]" (MacKinnon, 1962).

Early studies of imagination collected work samples from children (Andrews, 1930) and adults (Hargreaves, 1927) and scored them as the inverse of frequency, and this procedure is still used today. It can be done objectively, with the aid of frequency tables, or as an impressionistic rating by experienced judges.

Each of these dimensions is inadequate in itself. Genuine creative accomplishment would be high on more than one dimension; intellectual leadership is compounded of sensitivity to problems and ingenuity in solving them; originality needs to be supplemented by usefulness or appropriateness. But some of these dimensions are easier to catch hold of than others. Evaluation of intellectual leadership has to await the judgment of history, of course, at least for a few years, while the unusualness of simple products produced on demand in the laboratory can be evaluated immediately. The research summarized below has most often evaluated output on such dimensions as unusualness (or uncommonness), originality, appropriateness, usefulness, and cleverness (or ingenuity).

Since most of those certified by history as creative geniuses are dead and information about them is scanty, the inquiry turns to creative thinkers of today. They may be lesser men than the geniuses of the past and their achievements may be more modest, but the difference is a quantitative one; there is no divine dichotomy between geniuses and ordinary mortals. One or two of those thought of as eminent today may be called creative geniuses by historians of the next century.

Although discussions of creativity are usually focused on high-level achievements, and the dimensions listed above are most clearly defined in reference to the high end of each, it is reasonable to assume that the dimensions are continuous, and that all products and all individuals can be located somewhere along them. Thus, it is true that everyone is creative, but the truism does not flatter everyone. Everyone has some creativity just as everyone has some height and some intelligence; high, medium, or low.

CRITERIA OF CREATIVE ACHIEVEMENT

The study of creative thinking requires a group of creative individuals, called a *criterion group,* for contrast with other groups which are comparable in some respects but not creative. To identify the creative individuals, psychologists have collected product records, peer judgments, and work samples.

PRODUCT RECORDS

Some creative achievements are matters of public record: patents granted, books published, paintings hung, musical compositions performed, and the like. These products have been evaluated by specialists, on whatever dimensions they consider important, in competition with other products of the same kind, following the normal mechanisms of the arts and sciences—the same social mechanisms that evaluated Beethoven and Einstein and differentiated them from Jones and Smith. Anyone may quarrel with a single decision of editors and official commitees, but when large numbers are considered, most will agree that the products accepted are more creative, on the average, than those rejected. The painting that remains covered in the artist's studio and the manuscript that lies in the writer's bottom drawer contribute nothing to the arts and sciences nor to the psychology of creative achievement.

Fortunately for present purposes, psychologists themselves are both introspective and quantitative. A survey of the productivity of psychologists, conducted for the American Psychological Association (Clark, 1957), illustrates the information available in product records. The survey was limited to those members of the association who received doctoral degrees between 1930 and 1944. From these names, a list of 150 "high producers" was obtained simply by counting publications noted in the *Psychological Abstracts,* a fairly complete record of publications of interest to psychologists. Other names were added to make a list of 624 "highly visible" psychologists, and later a group of 601 randomly selected "psychologists in general" was included for comparison. The publication records of these 1,225 psychologists over a four-year period are shown in Fig. 7.3.

The most obvious fact about the distribution of production records for psychology is that it is highly skewed. A few contributed 40 or more publications during this time, while most contributed few if any. The picture would be the same in other arts and sciences if comparable data were plotted.

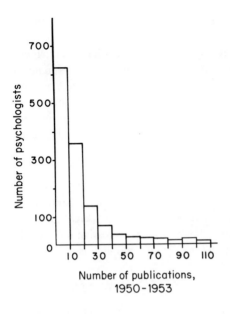

FIGURE 7.3. *Publication records over a four-year interval of 1,225 psychologists who received doctoral degrees between 1930 and 1944. Data from Clark (1957).*

PEER JUDGMENTS

It is a common assumption that a work of art or science "speaks for itself," but none of the geniuses of history got his name in the history books unless someone put it there. A man's reputation for creative accomplishment rests on a series of social evaluations, first by his peers, later by his followers. A writer sends a poem or a short story to an editor, and the editor decides that it is or is not worth publication. If it is published, reviewers praise it or ignore it. If it is widely praised, another editor may decide to include it in an anthology. Teachers tell their students to read it or skip it. Most important, other writers detect special meaning in it for themselves and attempt to write as their idol did. Later, perhaps, when a history of the period is written, it is included; a masterpiece has been created.

The serial evaluation in other arts and sciences is much the same. No one becomes a saint even, unless a committee of church officials rates him at the high end of the "saintliness" dimension. Thus, when researchers ask a panel of artists, scientists, editors, professors, and literary or music critics to judge the creative accomplishments of a list of names, these judgments reflect prior judgments by others as well as direct judgments of the products. At best the judging processes of the panel parallel the processes by which judgments are made in the ordinary course of serial social evaluation. The question is not whether to depend on human judgments, but whether there is agreement between judgments made by different judges at different times.

The use of peer judgments to assemble a criterion group is illustrated by MacKinnon's (1962) study of architects. He began by asking 5 professors of architecture, working independently, to nominate the 40 most creative architects in the United States. If the nominators did not agree at all, 200 names would have been submitted, but there were only 86. Of these 86, 13 were nominated by all 5 professors, and 40 were single nominations each proposed by one member of the panel. Later, MacKinnon asked 11 editors of the major American architectural journals to rate the creativity of the 64 architects invited to participate in the study. Still later, he asked the 40 who accepted the invitation to rate these 64 and found that the architects' ratings and the editors' ratings were in close agreement, as indicated by a correlation of .88. A group of comparable, but less creative, architects was also assembled for contrast. One of the determinants of these peer judgments is suggested by the fact that during the 8-year period under consideration 97 articles were written by or about the creative architects, and only two by or about the others.

It is not the purpose of this procedure to obtain a rating that will be fair to each individual; that must wait for his obituary. The purpose is to develop a criterion group for research purposes, and a small amount of error can be tolerated, as in any research. A history of architecture written 50 years from now will record more creative accomplishment from 40 architects selected as creative by their peers today than from a control group, even though the reputations of a few individuals may shift up or down.

Systematic errors are more serious. These occur when the judges nominate individuals who conform to a common stereotype of the creative thinker, or those who belong to a temporarily popular local movement or in-group. Established men of prestige may be preferred over younger men, or vice versa, or products that represent a certain trend or school may be systematically preferred over others.

Some specific data on the determinants of peer judgments emerge from the survey of America's psychologists mentioned above (Clark, 1957). Lists of the names of 624 "highly visible" psychologists were sent to all persons whose names appeared on them, with instructions to vote for the 25 who had made "the most significant contributions to psychology as a science." The number of votes that an individual received was related, as one might expect, to the number of publications produced; the correlation was .43. But publication is only the first step up the ladder; the next step is recognition by others. Those who deplore emphasis on quantity of publications will be glad to know that quantity was not enough. The number of times that a psychologists' work was cited by another psychologist correlated only .36 with the number of publications, whereas the number of votes received correlated .67 with the number of citations by others. Evidently quality, as reflected in recognition by one's peers, was considered more important here than quantity.

An index of organizational advancement—number of offices held—was also included. Election to an APA office is based on diverse considerations, such as administrative competence and social "visibility," as in other large scientific and professional organizations. This index correlated only .19 with number of publications during the four-year interval but correlated .38 with number of citations by others. Apparently, the characteristics of an individual that favor election to office overlap those that favor nomination for "the most significant contributions to psychology as a science," because the correlation between number of offices held and number of votes received was .64.

The close relation between scientific reputation and citations by others was revealed again in a more recent analysis of psychologists' achievements (Meyers, 1970). A correlation of .68 between a citation index and ratings by peers was found, and a check of names of psychologists who had received medals, awards, and other tokens of scientific eminence in the past few years disclosed that practically all had very high citation counts. This close relation is direct, in that scientists cite publications they have personally read and consider important, and indirect, in that they tend to cite publications that have been frequently cited by others and to give high ratings to those whose names they see and hear frequently (intellectual leadership).

WORK SAMPLES
Some of the difficulties of other criteria can be avoided by the use of work samples, intended to be representative of the work under consideration. An applicant for a typing job, for example, may be asked to type a letter since that is typical of the regular work to be done. The logical status of work samples should be clarified because they are also used for other purposes. When we use a work sample as a criterion, we are not aiming at a theoretical analysis of performance, nor a prediction for future performance. We are simply evaluating present performance on a sample of the regular work required. As to creative work, we can ask people to write a short story, paint a picture, put sticks and blocks together, or design a research project. Creativity can be manifested on almost any assignment, but appears most clearly when the situation calls for originality and the problem allows many possible solutions.

The advantage of the work sample as a criterion is that the investigator has some control over production; variations in opportunities and working conditions are minimized. The work sample is not entirely typical, however, since it is done in a short time, and persistence of involvement in creative work, a point that has been stressed in many biographies of creative thinkers, is not sampled. A high level of creative achievement is not to be expected.

Work samples must be evaluated, of course, like other complex products, but this is not as difficult as it may appear. When students write short stories or design research projects in an hour on request, the range of originality is wide, and two judges with some experience can rate the products for this with good agreement. Performance on such assignments can then be treated as a criterion of creative achievement against which other measures can be compared.

RELATIONS BETWEEN CRITERIA
The complexity of the criterion problem emerges when it is studied seriously. It is a general truth of intellectual progress that anything which looks simple at first glance becomes more complex on close examination, and the criterion of creativity is no exception. Taylor, Smith, and Ghiselin (1963)

collected data on 56 variables characteristic of 166 scientists—mostly physicists, mathematicians, electronic engineers, and chemists—in a large laboratory at a government basic research center. The variables included research products; ratings made by laboratory chiefs, immediate supervisors, and peers on the same level in the organization; and indices of organizational status. No unitary criterion of scientific creativity resulted from any type of analysis, but several interesting factors emerged from factor analysis.

One factor represented originality of work and thought, carried through to the stage where it appeared in patents and in research reports, judged by expert scientists in the same field to be original and significant. Another factor, coming from ratings by laboratory chiefs, represented the contribution of each scientist as viewed from higher levels in the organization. And a third factor, coming from ratings by supervisors, represented effectiveness in meeting immediate goals of a lower level. The negative loading of number of publications on this third factor illustrates the conflicts that a scientist faces as he tries to satisfy the supervisory level of the organization and, at the same time, to make a contribution to the scientific community outside the organization.

The criterion arrived at in the survey of psychologists summarized above was more unitary because the demands and conflicts within a large laboratory did not enter into it. Over half the psychologists worked in universities and colleges, but data on effectiveness in meeting the immediate goals of the local institution were not collected. No one asked whether the psychologists were good teachers or good committeemen or whether they turned in their grades on time. Judgments by peers at other institutions are based on evidence that goes beyond the intramural demands and probably represent a cleaner criterion of creative accomplishment. But even in the data on psychologists, there was a suspicion of two factors in that the number of offices held showed only a low correlation with publication records. Psychologists play dual roles as professional persons in the Association and as research psychologists according to Clark (1957). Similar low correlations between publication records and ratings of usefulness to the organization have been reported by Pelz and Andrews (1966) from a large-scale survey of scientists in diverse organizations.

Unfortunately, despite the apparent advantages of the work sample as a criterion, there seems to be no evidence on the relation between this criterion and the others mentioned above. Students can be asked to sit down and plan the landscaping for a new building or design an original psychological experiment, but established artists and scientists are usually too busy to undertake such things.

It is useful at this point to compare the treatment of the criterion question in the case of creativity with that of intelligence. Many intelligence tests were tried out in the early days of research, but the one devised by Binet was related to a social criterion, success in school. Further study with intelligence tests clarified the nature of intelligence, and further correlations with social criteria clarified the predictive validity of intelligence tests. We now have considerable objective knowledge of what criteria intelligence tests do and do not predict. We know enough about intelligence to be willing to say that if success on a job does not correlate with intelligence test scores, this job does not need much intelligence. In the same way, we can expect that the criteria of creative achievement and the creative abilities that predict the criteria will be progressively clarified.

DISTINCTIVE CHARACTERISTICS OF CREATIVE THINKERS

When creative thinkers are identified by the methods outlined above and compared with others, a fairly consistent description emerges. The study of architects by MacKinnon (1962) disclosed that the highly creative were inclined to have good opinions of themselves, as evidenced by their use of favorable adjectives to describe themselves. They claimed to be inventive, determined, independent, individualistic, enthusiastic, and industrious more often than the others, who described themselves as responsible, sincere, reliable, clear thinking, and understanding. The more creative architects—all male— revealed an openness to their own feelings and emotions, a sensitive intellect, and wide-ranging interests, including many which in the American culture are considered feminine. In fact, scores for femininity taken from personality tests correlated .49 with scores for creativity.

On a figure preference scale, the creative architects preferred complex, asymmetrical designs, which they called vital and dynamic; the correlation with creativity ratings was .48. On a word association test, the score for unusualness of associations correlated .50 with creativity. Each of the creative group had shown an early interest in drawing and painting, and had one or both parents of artistic temperament and considerable skill.

This kind of research is difficult to carry out. Only 40 of the 64 who were invited agreed to participate. The most serious criticism is that the creative architects were successful and distinguished men when the study was done, and they knew it. Anyone who acquires a reputation as a distinguished thinker develops independence and confidence in his own opinions. People listen to him. He will probably feel secure enough to mention some little weaknesses; many great men have permitted themselves this kind of upside-down egotism. Tolstoi, in his old age, said that all he tried to do in *War and Peace* was to amuse his readers. Those who have lived uncreative lives have little to offer except reliability and sincerity. This criticism does not question the obtained differences, only the time and mode of their acquisition.

The most distinctive characteristic of creative writers, according to a limited study of a small sample (Barron, 1965), is, to no one's surprise, their verbal intelligence. This was manifested in very high scores on the Terman Concept Mastery Test, devised to test high-level achievement of abstract verbal concepts, and in ratings by psychologists of concern for philosophical matters and skill in self-expression. The creative writers made high scores for psychopathology on personality inventories, as compared with ordinary writers. The psychological interviewers noted their unusual ideas and unconventional thought processes, but did not rate them at all pathological. On the contrary, the creative writers impressed the psychologists as effective, productive persons, and they made high scores for ego strength on personality inventories. They were unusual, thoughtful characters who got things done, things that they themselves wanted to do. In other respects, such as independence, high aspiration level, and nonconformity, they were similar to other creative thinkers.

Another study of this type is more limited but has certain methodological advantages. Cattell and Drevdahl (1955) gave a personality test to three categories of successful men: successful administrators, successful teachers (including textbook writers), and creative scientists, 300 in all. As compared with the other groups, the eminent scientists were more schizothyme, self-sufficient, emotionally unstable (but no more than the norm for the general population), bohemian, radical, dominant, and paranoid. The self-sufficiency and avoidance of social contact that is characteristic of distinguished scientists appears in boyhood and thus cannot be a result of prestige acquired later in life (Terman, 1954). Although the Cattell and Drevdahl study included biologists, physicists, and psychologists, the results agree in many respects with the MacKinnon study of architects.

A companion study (Drevdahl and Cattell, 1958) compared eminent artists and writers with the general norm group. The creative ones were more intelligent, emotionally mature, dominant, adventurous, emotionally sensitive, bohemian, radical, self-sufficient, and energetic. These data refer to means of the creative group which probably differed from the general norms in education, income, and other respects; but still the results agree roughly with the results of the first study, which included better control groups.

Both of these studies were done by mail, and thus they raise the question whether the returns were representative. Only half the artists and writers returned their tests, and one might suspect that those who agreed to expose themselves to the psychologist's scrutiny would be dominant, adventurous, and self-sufficient.

The survey of America's psychologists (Clark, 1957) was directed at background factors more than personality and motivation, but it does confirm other data on early interests and productive contributions. Of the significant contributors to scientific psychology who received doctoral degrees between 1930 and 1944, more than half had undergraduate majors in psychology, as compared with only a third of the control group. And a large proportion of the significant contributors, but hardly any of the control group, had published at least one paper before age thirty.

Unfortunately the research on artists is scanty, but the research on scientists, in spite of the methodological weaknesses typical of studies of substantial intellectual phenomena in the real world, reveals a consistent picture. A good summary has been written by Taylor and Barron (1963), after reviewing several years of research, in the form of a list of traits found in study after study as characteristic of productive scientists.

1. A high degree of autonomy, self-sufficiency, self-direction.
2. A preference for mental manipulations involving things rather than people: a somewhat distant or detached attitude in interpersonal relations, and a preference for intellectually challenging situations rather than socially challenging ones.
3. High ego strength and emotional stability.
4. A liking for method, precision, exactness.
5. A preference for such defense mechanisms as repression and isolation in dealing with affect and instinctual energies.
6. A high degree of personal dominance but a dislike of personally toned controversy.
7. A high degree of control of impulse, amounting almost to over-control: relatively little talkativeness, gregariousness, impulsiveness.
8. A liking for abstract thinking, with considerable tolerance of cognitive ambiguity.
9. Marked independence of judgment, rejection of group pressures toward conformity in thinking.
10. Superior general intelligence.
11. An early, very broad interest in intellectual activities.
12. A drive toward comprehensiveness and elegance in explanation.
13. A special interest in the kind of "wagering" which involves pitting oneself against uncertain circumstances in which one's own effort can be the deciding factor [pp. 385–386].

A more recent summary, including some additional data, by Cattell and Butcher (1968) agrees essentially with the above. These investigators, after comparing personality profiles of those who had achieved eminence in the sciences and in the arts and noting the rather small differences, went on to comment: "It would almost seem as if the differences between science, art, and literature are differences of particular skills and interests only, and that the fundamental characteristic of the creative, original person is a type of personality [p. 294]."

Lest the traits of creative thinkers seem like a universal catalog of virtues, it should be noted that creative thinkers are not, as far as we know, any more agreeable, friendly, considerate, or tolerant than other people. They are seldom described as happy and well-rounded, nor are they accused, any more than others, of excessive modesty. Their errors of judgment in matters outside their own specialties, though no more common than the errors of ordinary citizens, are pointed out with glee by these ordinary citizens.

It is unfortunate that so much of the research has been limited to scientists. The intellectual preference for things rather than people illustrates this limitation because it is the socially challenging situations that have had an analogous appeal for novelists and dramatists, and for another class of innovators: political, economic, and religious reformers.

Nevertheless, this list of traits offers a reasonably consistent profile of the typical adjustment of the creative individual to his society. There are many exceptions to this generalized description, of course. It would not be logical to convert these generalizations and infer, for example, that self-sufficient people of high ego strength are unusually creative or to assume that practice on the signs of creativity will improve the substance.

Creativity Tests

A very different approach to individual differences in creativity begins in the testing laboratory. Many tests of abilities relevant to productive thinking have been devised, but the most sophisticated and sustained research has been carried out by J. P. Guilford and his colleagues with tests of the open-end or completion type. Since the tests were designed for the production of uncommon, remote, and clever responses, many of them must be scored by expert judges, but this can be done with satisfactory reliability after brief training. The Guilford group has been concerned with the construction of tests and the analysis of their interrelations; the task of correlating the tests with other variables has been taken up by others.

TESTS AND FACTORS

A factor analysis of 46 tests, including many of the open-end, divergent-thinking type, by Wilson, Guilford, and Christensen (1953), extracted 16 factors, one of which was identified as an originality factor. Some of the best tests of this factor will be briefly described because they have had a dominant influence on subsequent research and have often been called tests of creativity.

Plot Titles presented the plot of a story and asked the subject to write titles for it. The rating of these titles for cleverness was the best test of originality, in terms of factor loadings.

Quick Responses was a word association test scored for uncommonness. Objectively derived weights gave low scores to common responses and high scores to uncommon responses.

Figure Concepts consisted of 20 simple drawings of objects and individuals. The subject's task was to find qualities or features suggested by 2 or more drawings; these also were scored for uncommonness.

Unusual Uses listed familiar objects, such as a newspaper, with instructions to write uses for them other than the usual ones. The more unusual uses received higher scores.

Remote Associations presented two words separated by a blank space, such as *Indian* _____ *money,* with instructions to write on the line between them a word that associates the two. The words were selected so that the right answer, which might be *penny,* was a remote associate of both.

Remote Consequences required the subject to list the consequences of certain unexpected events, such as the sudden abolition of all national and local laws. The number of remote consequences was counted for one score and the number of immediate consequences for another.

Several of these tests were scored for sheer number of words produced so that the originality factor could be differentiated from the well-known factor of simple word fluency.

A more recent factor analysis of the contribution of productive thinking abilities to problem solving (Merrifield, Guilford, Christensen, and Frick,

1962) identified four divergent production factors and described them in a revised terminology: ideational fluency, the production of many semantic units or ideas appropriate in meaning in response to a given idea; spontaneous flexibility, the production of many categories of ideas or semantic classes; associational fluency, the production of many related ideas; and originality, the production of a variety of changes of interpretation, neither immediate or obvious, that are appropriate to a general requirement. Approximately the same factors have been identified at the junior-high-school level (Guilford, Merrifield, and Cox, 1961), and, with specially adapted tests, at the sixth-grade level (Merrifield, Guilford, and Gershon, 1963). A further systematic development of this program (Hendricks, Guilford, and Hoepfner, 1969) is the construction of many tests of creative social intelligence and the analysis of these into six divergent-thinking abilities involving the generation of behavioral ideas in quantity and variety.

Another test of this type, developed by Mednick (1962) and called the Remote Associates Test, has also been used in recent research. Three words were given, such as *surprise, line, birthday,* and the subject was asked to find a fourth word associated with these three. This is very similar to Guilford's test of remote associations except for the theory behind its construction. Whereas most people have a strong association between a stimulus word and the common stereotyped response word associated with it and only weak associations with the more uncommon response words, Mednick assumed that the more creative people have flatter associative distributions, that is, less strong associations with the common response words, and stronger associations with uncommon response words. This flat distribution of associates theoretically enables the more creative individuals to produce the relatively unusual associates necessary for success on these test items.

The Torrance Tests of Creative Thinking (Torrance, 1965) employ similar procedures to get measures of fluency, flexibility, and originality with verbal and figural materials from kindergarten to university levels. Some ideas of the nature of these tests is indictated by the names of a few: Asking Questions, Guessing Causes, Guessing Consequences, Product Improvement, Unusual Uses, Picture Construction, and Figure Completion. A large share of the research in educational situations has made use of these tests.

Use of the name *creativity* for tests of this nature has led to considerable misunderstanding. They are not samples of work that is obviously creative, hence performance cannot be taken as a self-evident criterion of creative achievement. Nor can test performance be taken, without proof, as predicting creative achievement, since validity for this purpose is a troublesome empirical question. The tests were devised for the study of productive abilities not well represented in conventional intelligence tests, and, despite misunderstanding and mislabeling, performance on tasks such as these deserves serious examination. Individual differences in performance on these tests have been analyzed in some detail; the scores have been used as predictor variables and as dependent variables, measuring the effects of experimental manipulations. It is true that some of the tasks seem rather trivial, especially when the dimension of breadth is recalled, but the hope here, as in other areas of psychology, is that general principles will be found which will be applicable to more substantial problems.

CORRELATES OF CREATIVITY TEST SCORES

Aside from definitions, labels, and good intentions, the meaning of scores on creativity tests will be progressively clarified as their relations with other scores are examined. The data at hand include comparisons with conventional measures of intelligence and achievement, personality, and specially constructed laboratory tasks.

INTELLIGENCE

If creativity tests are to be useful, they must be different from intelligence tests. It is not just that intelligence tests have a well-worn place in the psychologist's bag of tricks. Intelligence test scores are fairly stable, administration is standardized, and norms are available. Their uses and limitations are fairly well understood, especially in educational situations. When creativity tests are used as intelligence tests are used, do they supply additional information?

The correlations between scores on tests of intelligence and tests of creativity vary considerably, depending on the specific tests used, the methods of testing, and the samples tested. The range of ability in the sample tested is most important because the correlation between any two abilities is reduced when the variation of either is restricted, as in special schools for superior children and in college samples. Low correlations have been reported for restricted samples of above-average children (Cicirelli, 1965; Flescher, 1963; Getzels and Jackson, 1962), but correlations of between .55 and .77 have been obtained in a broader sample of 175 Scottish children with mean IQ of 102 (Hasan and Butcher, 1966). Correlations from −.40 to above .60, with a median of .20, have been obtained with the Torrance Tests (Torrance, 1967).

In samples of college students, Mednick and Andrews (1967) obtained correlations in the .30's and .40's between various intelligence tests and the Remote Associates Test, and the correlation of .48 between the same test and the Terman Concept Mastery Test reported by Laughlin (1967) is similar. In the general population of college age, somewhat larger correlations would be expected.

Although it is commonly asserted in discussions of creative thinking that intelligence is important only up to a point, there seems to be no empirical support with large samples for assuming that the relation between intelligence and performance on creativity tests is anything but linear. Scores for creativity, IQ, and academic achievement obtained from 609 pupils in a suburban sixth grade (Cicirelli, 1965) indicated mostly linear relations, with little evidence for interactions or threshold effects. Since Mednick and Andrews had a large sample of 1,211 college freshmen, they were able to examine this question by dividing their sample into 5 levels in respect to scores on the Scholas-

tic Aptitude Test. They found that the correlations with the Remote
Associates Test were about the same at all levels of intelligence. Low correlations are easily confused with nonlinear correlations, both conceptually
and empirically.

Guilford's factor analyses have been directed, not at separating creative
ability from general intelligence, but at analyzing both of these into narrower
factors. Nevertheless, it would be logical to assume that tests of divergent
thinking would be grouped on one factor and tests of convergent thinking,
which constitute a large part of general intelligence, on another factor. To
check this assumption, Cropley (1966) gave tests of both types to an un-
selected sample of children, and, though the analysis identified the divergent
and convergent factors, the correlation between them was .51. As Cropley
concluded, divergent and convergent abilities can be factorially differentiated,
but they are not independent.

In addition to the questions which these findings pose for factor analysis as
a method, they suggest that some of the variance attributed to creativity scores
could just as well be attributed to intelligence. Tests of creativity are relatively
new. The objective tests may not be pure, and the scoring of the open-end
tests requires time and training. Hence correlations between tests of creativity
are often as low as the correlations with intelligence (Barron, 1955, 1957;
Cline, Richards, and Abe, 1962; Cline, Richards, and Needham, 1963;
Flesher, 1963; Getzels and Jackson, 1962). On the other hand, a study of 53
scientists in several South African research institutes found moderately high
intercorrelations among creativity tests and quite low correlations with a
conventional intelligence test (Shapiro, 1968). Evidently, a general statement of the relation between intelligence and creativity test scores is not
possible at this time. Improvements in reliability will raise correlations;
purification by elimination of noncreativity variance will lower them.

Wallach and Kogan (1965) tried to take account of all these methodological
considerations when designing new creativity tests for children. They gave
their tests individually, in a gamelike situation with plenty of time. "Tell
me all the ways in which a potato and a carrot are alike." The tests were scored
for unusualness, with good reliability. For a sample of 151 fifth-grade children
from professional and managerial families, the average intercorrelation among
the creativity measures was .40, among the intelligence measures, .51, and
between a composite score—derived from an intelligence test and standard
tests of educational achievement—and creativity only .09. Wallach and Wing
(1969) got similar results with 500 high-school graduates. As a measure of
intelligence, they used scores for verbal and mathematical achievement on
the Scholastic Aptitude Test. These scores were practically independent of
scores for fluency of ideas and uniqueness of ideas in working with verbal
and figural materials.

EDUCATIONAL ACHIEVEMENT

Historically, conceptually, and empirically, intelligence has been closely
related to educational achievement, and the recent emphasis in some quarters
on creative thinking is intended to broaden both. The argument is that intel-

ligence tests should be supplemented by creativity tests, and that the conventional learning of right answers should be supplemented by learning to produce original ideas. If all goes well, school grades will someday include a just measure of creative accomplishment and therefore will be predictable by creativity test scores as well as by intelligence test scores. At present, creativity tests cannot be expected to predict scores on standard achievement tests unless such achievement is somehow facilitated by productive thinking or the creativity scores are impure measures containing some noncreative convergent abilities. Both explanations are tenable, since the data are sparse.

In a special secondary school with average IQ of 132, Getzels and Jackson (1962) selected a group of students with high scores on creativity tests but relatively low scores on intelligence (mean IQ of 127) for contrast with a group with very high scores on intelligence (mean IQ of 150) but low scores on creativity. The educational achievements of those called high-creatives, as well as those with high IQ, were definitely superior to the school average. The teachers enjoyed working with the high-IQ children but not the high-creatives. Similar results were reported for some other schools by Torrance (1962, 1967), and Cline, Richards, and Abe (1962) also reported rather high correlations with grades. But the corresponding correlations reported by other investigators (Cicirelli, 1965; Edwards and Tyler, 1965; Flescher, 1963; Wallach and Kogan, 1965; Wallach and Wing, 1969) have been low. There are also contradictions between the published reports which may clear up when separate school subjects are studied. Cline, Richards, and Needham (1963), for example, treated science grades separately and found that IQ had the highest correlation, but that the creativity tests also contributed a little to the multiple correlation. In this school, incidentally, science teachers did not dislike those who got high scores on creativity tests.

Since teachers have been accused of disliking creative children, the results obtained by Hasan and Butcher (1966) are particularly enlightening. Their Scottish children of high IQ and low creativity were liked by the teachers more than the children of low IQ and high creativity, as Getzels and Jackson had reported, but the best-liked group were those high on both measures. The simple explanation of all the data, according to Hasan and Butcher, is that teachers dislike children of low IQ.

PERSONALITY AND COGNITIVE STYLE

When individuals have been scored on the basis of performance on creativity tests, it is instructive to see how they rate in other respects that may disclose their intellectual habits, motivation, and interests. A study of 100 Air Force captains by Barron (1957) is especially informative because the men were given a composite score for creativity, primarily based on Guilford's tests; then the component due to verbal intelligence was statistically eliminated by partial correlation. The high-creatives, as thus identified, were characterized by several groups of traits, which may be summarized as follows:

Disposition toward integration of diverse stimuli
Energy, fluent output, involvement
Personal dominance and self-assertion

Responsiveness to impulse and emotion
General effectiveness of performance
Expressed femininity of interests

Since the correlation between creativity scores and intelligence scores in the Wallach and Kogan (1965) research was low, they were able to group their 151 fifth-grade children into 4 groups: high on both; high on intelligence and relatively low on creativity; high on creativity and relatively low on intelligence; and relatively low on both. Without regard to any creative achievements, they found rich variations in modes of thinking and adjustment to the school situation. The results for girls and boys were different in many respects and had to be analyzed separately; a few selections from the abundance of detailed comparisons will illustrate the trends of the results.

The girls high on both variables were self-confident, sociable, and interested in academic work. In a boring classroom they were eager to propose novel, divergent possibilities; hence, from the teacher's side of the desk, they were noticeable for their disruptive, attention-seeking behavior.

Girls high on creativity but low on intelligence were at a disadvantage in the classroom; not confident in themselves, they did not seek the companionship of others, nor did others seek them. They too were often disruptive, not so much from enthusiasm as from protest against their plight.

The low-low group seemed to get along better. They were more confident and outgoing in social relations, perhaps in compensation for poor academic achievement.

The girls high in intelligence but low in creativity were oriented toward academic achievement, not distracted by new ideas, and quite suited to the usual school situation. They were cool and cautious in social behavior, but were liked by others anyway.

The same analysis for the boys yielded less clear-cut differences.

The cognitive styles for categorizing strategies of these children were disclosed by sorting tests. Pictures of 50 objects—such as a rake, a screwdriver, a telephone, a lamppost, and a candle—were displayed with instructions to put together what seemed to belong together. The important contrast here was between thematic reasons for grouping and reasons based on abstracted similarities among the objects. Wallach and Kogan give the example of a comb, a watch, a pocketbook, and a door grouped thematically under the label "getting ready to go out." Conceptual groupings were based on abstracted similarities, with labels such as "hard objects" and "objects used for eating." It has usually been assumed, as noted in Chapter 2, that sorting on a thematic basis represents an intellectually inferior level of development, and the boys of high intelligence and low creativity avoided this kind of grouping in favor of conceptual grouping. The highly creative boys, however, made use of both thematic and conceptual grouping; they seemed to be able to switch flexibly from one to the other, while those of high intelligence and low creativity seemed to be locked in conceptual categorizing. These contrasts were much less clear for the girls.

These studies of psychometric creativity, which started out to differentiate an exciting new variable from general intelligence, have not yet progressed very far. In the Wallach and Kogan study, as in most others, the correlations of other variables with creativity scores were low in comparison to the correlations with intelligence. In the words of one reviewer (Shulman, 1966): "Whether due to lower reliability or less relevance, the newly defined creativity variable is far less productive than the old workhorse, intelligence [p. 307]."

SPECIFIC LABORATORY TASKS

Perhaps more research by the same methods will clear up the present rather diffuse picture of the correlates of creativity test performance, but the sharper methods of controlled experimentation may also be necessary. For example, the information yield from laboratory experiments can often be augmented if the subjects are grouped first into two or three levels according to their scores on an ability test. When the levels effect is significant, the results give more specific meaning to the test scores.

The Remote Associates Test correlates with measures of verbal productivity (Mednick, Mednick, and Jung, 1964), as one would expect; but Mendelsohn and Griswold (1964) went further and used scores on this test to divide college students into three levels of creativity for comparison with their performance in solving anagrams, after focal and peripheral exposure to the solution words. A list of words that included solutions to some of the anagrams was read and memorized in advance while a tape recorder was playing another list. The subjects of high-creativity level solved more anagrams with solution words previously exposed (peripherally as well as focally), as compared with another list not previously exposed, than those of lower-creativity level. The best interpretation seems to be that the high scorers deploy their attention more widely and thus receive a broader range of information; they screen out less of the incidental material. This breadth of the high scorers in attention to, and recall of, seen and heard words corresponds with their production of remote associates on the creativity test.

A similar design was employed by Laughlin (1967) in an experiment, like those described in Chapter 2, on the formation of word classes from relevant and irrelevant words. College students were given lists of 6 words and asked to "figure out the concept or way in which four of the six words go together." Later, they were asked to recall the other two words and the concept they exemplified. For example, given the list: globe, vinegar, wheel, spool, sauerkraut, and baseball, learning the 4 that are round would be intentional learning, and learning the 2 that are sour would be incidental learning. In order to discover the 4 relevant words, the subject had to inspect the 2 irrelevant words, but he could then forget them. However, when the 148 subjects were divided into 3 levels according to their scores on the Remote Associates Test, those who scored high did better on the incidental task, both in recalling the words and in stating the concept, than those who scored low. A parallel division by levels of verbal intelligence did not separate performance on the incidental task so sharply. The words were all familiar, so vocabulary size was not important. What was important was the ability to form, retain, and utilize remote associations—the ability that is involved in the Remote Associates Test. Overall, performance on incidental concept formation correlated .35 with scores on this test and .20 with scores on the Terman Concept Mastery Test. But, as in most of the correlation studies mentioned earlier, the correlation between the 2 tests was larger, in this case .48, than the correlation with other performances.

Corresponding results came from an experiment (Riegel, Riegel, and Levine, 1966) which divided people up according to composite scores from a creative personality test and the Remote Associates Test. Those who scored high produced more different responses on logical tasks, such as naming superordinate and subordinate classes, but fewer different responses on infralogical associations and simple grammatical tasks, than those who scored low. In producing words from semantic classes, the more creative had better control of their production or better adaptation to the task, in that they separated their restricted associations from their free associations more clearly.

These recent studies of the intellectual processes related to creativity test performance are limited in scope and the obtained differences are small. They point, however, to a common ability—in a verbal creativity test, in anagram solution, and in the formation and utilization of word classes—to make intentional use of words and associations originally acquired incidentally and to adapt them to the requirements of the present task. This ability does not coincide with the theoretical assumptions on which the Remote Associates Test was developed, but recent research (Jacobson, et al., 1968; Olczak and Kaplan, 1969) has failed to support these assumptions. This test seems to measure convergent production more than divergent (Guilford, 1967).

Predicting Creative Achievement

Predictions of behavior are notoriously inaccurate, especially predictions of socially significant behavior, and in the case of creative achievement, the criteria to be predicted appear to be complex. We have noted, however, that one trait, high general intelligence, characterizes creative thinkers of past and present, hence it should be enlightening to follow the adult careers of highly intelligent children. Such a long-term study was started in 1922 by Terman (Terman and Oden, 1958) with about 1,500 boys and girls who had IQs of 140 or higher; the average IQ at ten was 152. Now that these children have grown up, records of books, poems, patents, and similar achievements show that their creative output has been far above average. It is true, as some critics have noted, that they came mostly from middle-class families and started life with middle-class advantages. But it is also true that these children were picked out of the vast middle class by their scores on the intelligence test. Even in this select group, most individuals had little creative accomplishment to boast of; many intelligent people lead happy, worthwhile lives and attain success by achievements that would not be called creative.

Although there is abundant evidence for a relation between intelligence and creativity, intelligence is not so useful a predictor as one might expect. Since a college education, and often additional graduate or professional training, is a prerequisite for entrance into most of the occupations that have been examined, the prediction question arises only for samples of individuals with intelligence enough to complete considerable formal education. Even so, a small sample of creative women mathematicians scored significantly higher on the Terman Concept Mastery Test than representative women mathematicians, all well educated (Barron, 1965). In most studies, however, when advanced education is the first selection device, the predictive value of scores on a test of general intelligence is not large.

Completion of the necessary formal education is one predictor of creative achievement, especially in the sciences; and it is effective, not only because of the contribution of intelligence but because of the special interest in the materials. Few people go to art school unless they enjoy art. No one can endure graduate training in chemistry or psychology unless he enjoys at least a portion of it. A psychological study of the successful dropouts, those who made significant creative achievements without the customary formal education, would be particularly informative, but the small number of such cases prevents it. For the same reason, a study of those individuals who have made creative contributions to new fields for which formal educational preparation has not been widely available, such as directing films, would be informative. In the common fields of work, completion of formal education means that the whole sample is characterized by adequate intelligence, education, and interest in the field. Hence three potentially good predictors have already been used as selection devices. The problem now is to improve prediction among individuals who are already well screened.

If we are willing to take work samples as a criterion, some validity coefficients reported by Jacobsen and Asher (1963) seem quite promising. The work samples consisted of four 15-minute problems, such as improving office desks and encouraging foreigners to visit the United States. The authors' neofield theory of problem solving emphasizes cognitive flexibility, hence their tests include perceptual materials (such as a series of pictures in which a cat changes to a dog) and a good score represents readiness to shift from one perception to the other. The scores on these tests yielded surprisingly high correlations with performances on the work samples, although the predictors were perceptual and the criteria verbal.

Since tests of creativity seem to have something in common with creative achievement, many attempts have been made to predict creative achievement from performance on creativity tests. The results have not been impressive except in a few small samples (Taylor and Holland, 1964). The most encouraging results with creativity tests come from a recent study by Wallach and Wing (1969) conducted by mail. About 500 high-school graduates, who had been admitted to college and were willing to participate in the research, reported their high-school extracurricular accomplishments in several categories: leadership, art, social service, writing, dramatic arts, music, and science. At the same time, they took tests of productivity of ideas and unique-ness of ideas. The creativity tests differentiated quite well between groups of high and low nonacademic achievement in art, writing, science, and surpris-ingly, leadership. The test of productivity rather than the test of uniqueness separated those of high achievement outside the classroom from those of low achievement. Thus the authors' interpretation emphasized ideational activity or "cognitive vitality" rather than novelty as such.

Some success in prediction has been achieved also in exploratory studies with printed personality tests (Cattell and Butcher, 1968).

The most consistently successful predictors are biographical data, probably because interests, work habits, and other requirements for creative achieve-ment develop early and remain fairly stable over time. Schaefer and Anastasi (1968) demonstrated this stability by constructing a biographical inventory for identifying creative high-school boys, using as a criterion teachers' nomin-ations supported by actual creative products. With large samples, after cross-validation, they were able to attain validity coefficients of .64 for artistic achievement and .35 for scientific achievements. Intelligence was not directly controlled, but criterion and control groups were matched on school grades and socioeconomic levels. A companion study (Anastasi and Schaefer, 1969) of high school girls yielded coefficients of .34 for artistic achievement and .55 for literary achievement.

Looking back at the discriminating items of the inventory, it is evident that the creative students came from families of intellectual interests and activities, oriented more toward reading than sports. Even as children they had become absorbed in their hobbies, to the extent of skipping meals and staying up late in pursuit of their own intellectual goals. The creative students, more than the controls, had been exposed to environmental diversity, having traveled more often and enjoyed more unusual experiences. Like the geniuses of history, the creative students showed more unconventionality, less social participation, and more daydreaming than the other students. In general, the biographical correlates of creativity are quite similar for boys and girls, for potential scientists, artists, and writers. But the creative boys were closer to their mothers than to their fathers, while the creative girls were closer to their fathers.

The life styles developed in grade school and high school persist into col-lege. Richards, Holland, and Lutz (1967) have demonstrated, with large samples, that extracurricular achievements in college can be predicted from extracurricular achievements in high school. Their measures of creative scien-tific achievement consisted of self-reports, such as: did an independent scientific experiment, won a prize or award for scientific work, had paper published in a scientific journal. The correlations from high school to college were .31 and .22 for male and female college freshmen and .40 and .24 for male and female college sophomores. Corresponding predictive correlations for artistic achievements and writing achievements were in the .40's and .50's. These correlations were quite specific to the different fields of achievement, indicating an early channeling of productive interests and efforts. Academic grades did not correlate well with these extracurricular college achievements. However, a printed test, called the Preconscious Activity Scale, made up of items such as "I often daydream about unsolved problems," was related to achievement in art, writing, speech, and drama in high school, but not in science (Holland and Baird, 1968).

The next step, prediction of achievement in adult jobs, is the big one. Certainly there is some stability of interests and abilities, but the predictive value of these may be lost if the sample includes only college graduates or graduates from special training programs. Nevertheless, predictions of scientific achievement are approaching the accuracy necessary for practical application in large research organizations where the competition for scientists and the commercial value of their output justifies the statistical work necessary to develop a specific inventory. Smith, Albright, Glennon, and Owens (1961), for example, developed an inventory of personal history items for the identification of petroleum scientists, using patents and ratings as criteria, and succeeded in getting coefficients of concurrent validity, with large samples, above .50, even among these highly selected personnel. The most creative in this large oil company laboratory had what the authors called an "academic orientation," in that they resembled their university colleagues in intellectual interests and working habits.

Similar biographical inventories have been constructed for large samples of pharmaceutical scientists, yielding validity coefficients, after cross-validation, in the .30's (Buel, 1965; Tucker, Cline, and Schmitt, 1967). The discriminating inventory items sketch a personality profile not unlike that of the creative people who appeared earlier in this chapter.

Although biographical inventories have been developed for specific practical purposes in the selection of high-level personnel, some generality has been reported. The keys constructed for petroleum scientists have reasonably good validity for pharmaceutical scientists also (Buel, Albright, and Glennon, 1966). The profile of the industrial research scientist in British laboratories, outlined by biographical data, resembles that of their American counterparts in general, though there are some differences in the particulars (Chaney, 1966).

After reviewing many of the attempts to predict creative achievement, Taylor and Holland (1964) wrote the following summary:

If we look at predictors by class rather than by specific scales or inventories, we get a crude ordering. The biographical items and past achievements are our most efficient predictors. Self-ratings and direct expressions of goals and aspirations are next. Originality and personality inventories run a very poor third. Aptitude and intelligence measures rank fourth (except where restriction-of-range corrections are really applicable), followed finally by parental attitudes [p. 41].

Biographical data inventories do not explain creative achievement. By a strict definition they do not even predict, since the measures reported are measures of concurrent validity, of success in identifying scientists already productive, and some traits, such as a positive self-image, may be a consequence as well as a predictor. But they do give evidence of intellectual orientations, working habits, and life styles acquired rather early in life, which distinguish the more creative from others of similar ability and education.

Favorable Environments for Creative Work

Every employer knows that arranging favorable working conditions is just as important as selecting capable individuals, but in the case of creative work less effort has been expended in this direction. The available evidence comes mostly from surveys of accomplishments and complaints of scientists, often contrasting the university setting with the large research organization (Meltzer, 1956; Pelz and Andrews, 1966; Taylor, Smith, and Ghiselin, 1963). The optimal condition, in general terms, is one which the individual's goals and working habits match the goals and working conditions of the organization that pays his salary. Scientists working in governmental and commercial laboratories typically complain of the pressure of the immediate goals of the organization, inability to pick their own problems and follow the leads that turn up, and lack of recognition for their work. They would prefer to publish under their own names so that their colleagues and children will recognize their accomplishments. Some large laboratories are organized, either by accident or design, to conflict with the working habits and demands of individualistic creative thinkers.

In medical research also these conflicts between the investigator's desire for intellectual freedom and the goals of the organization appear more severe in large hospitals and health organizations than they are in medical schools and universities (Gordon, Marquis, and Anderson, 1962). The critical feature is the specificity and immediacy of an organization's research goals in contrast to the creative thinker's long-term, inner-directed motivation.

In the universities, the scientists' complaints usually stress the lack of facilities and technical support that they might enjoy in a large industrial laboratory and the daily pressure of other organizational goals.

Complaints are not good data on which to base psychological generalizations; but scientists, like other people, tend to inhabit the environments where they feel most comfortable. Thus scientists highly motivated for productive research prefer the university setting, and more creative scientific research does come out of university laboratories, by and large.

The survey of psychologists referred to earlier (Clark, 1957) discovered that the significant contributors care more about the opinions of top people in their field, while "psychologists in general" care more about the opinions of local colleagues than their immediate supervisors. When psychologists were asked about an ideal setting, the significant contributors were quite explicit in what they wanted. The paradise of creative psychologists' fantasies, as sketched by Clark, follows:

The setting is in a university or is at least a place with stimulating co-workers where there is an opportunity to consult experts in other fields and where the researcher is free to choose his own kind of research problem; the researcher wants enough time, that is, he wants to be released from other activities and he wants to have enough money to do the sorts of things he chooses to do. Much more popular than a group setting is a setting where one has freedom to choose one's own work and where he has independence [p. 89].

By contrast, dependable information about the conditions of artistic production is meager; painters, composers, writers, and other creative artists do not gather in large organizations where their output can be rated by supervisors. Many flee when an inquisitive psychologist approaches. And unfortunately, the reminiscences of artists and writers, after they have become eminent, have more literary than psychological value. We do know, however, that there is a great variation in "ideal" settings. Painters and sculptors have often constructed their own environments, to meet their own requirements. Scholarly writing, linked to library facilities, has frequently come out of the universities, but imaginative writing, linked to the writer's personal dreams and frustrations, has been produced in stimulating cities, in pastoral retreats, and even in suburban homes after a hard day at the office.

Genuine creative achievements are not usually produced on demand under controlled conditions, so empirical investigations of favorable and unfavorable environments have had to turn to creativity tests, or similar tasks—which for this purpose are dependent variables rather than predictor variables. Pieper (1965), for example, looked into the effects of the physical environment of office workers on creativity test performance. One setting was a semidark, monotonously furnished office, in which the subject had no stimulation but his memories; another was a typical everyday office. The third was an enriched, stimulating setting, with pictures on the walls (including objects similar to but not identical with those of the test), pleasant furniture, and pleasant lighting; the subject was encouraged to walk around or break away from the typical chair-bound posture and enjoy the delights of the environment as he worked. The experiment, conducted in a furniture factory with management personnel as the subjects, found a significant difference between these situations, presumably because the richness of the surroundings and the freedom of movement aided the imagination. Similarly, at the kindergarten level children who were allowed to handle objects as simple as a paper clip produced more unusual uses than children who could only look at them (Goodnow, 1969).

The university setting, despite its general advantages, arouses its own special stresses, which stimulate some individuals and frustrate others. Hinton (1968) studied the effects of these frustrations by asking students in a graduate school of business to estimate their frustration level immediately after entrance, when most were enthusiastically anticipating the best, and a few months later, after they had taken their first examinations. On the second occasion, three creativity tests were given and, as expected, those students who reported the most increase in frustration made the lowest scores. The differential effects on the consequences test were especially convincing since frustration seemed to reduce the production of remote consequences, which are the creative ones, but had no effect on the production of immediate consequences.

A classroom environment that discourages creative thinking is another of the many things teachers are blamed for, and it appears that this environment can be analyzed more readily than most others. Torrance (1964) has collected considerable evidence from questionnaires and checklists of classroom activities to show that the atmosphere in most classrooms is inimical to creative thinking and that many teachers can, although with some difficulty, shift toward more encouraging practices. This is an important factor, as we shall see, in the outcome of training programs for creative thinking.

Such environmental variables deserve more serious attention than they have received so far; some at least can be experimentally manipulated. The results of the experiments outlined above, if duplicated in other settings, would have important theoretical and practical consequences.

Processes and Conditions of Productive Thinking

This chapter began with the assertion that the processes by which creative accomplishments are produced are matters for research rather than definition. Now we must try to describe these processes and the conditions that influence them, making some use of our knowledge of creative thinkers and their environments but depending chiefly on laboratory manipulations. Although no one believes that solutions produced in the laboratory at the request of an experimenter deserve to be called creative, it is the achievements of creative thinkers and the fascination of hypothetical creative processes that have stimulated laboratory experiments. The principal ingredient that the subjects of the laboratory experiments lack is, of course, the persistent personal involvement that appears so prominently in the biographies of creative thinkers. The two dimensions of creative achievement that laboratory measures conspicuously lack are breadth of achievement and intellectual leadership. Within these limitations, the aim of laboratory research is to derive some general principles that will apply broadly to the more intellectual aspects of creative thinking. Admitting that the achievements of the Nobel prize winner are far from those of the average taxpayer, we can still assume that the differences in thought processes are quantitative rather than qualitative.

Simple verbal assignments illustrate man's ability to produce words to a variety of specifications. Any literate adult can easily produce words from a given class when requested: "Write down the names of some automobiles." "List some vegetables." The results give evidence for achievement of the class as well as ability to limit output to this class in response to instruction. When more complex products are required, productive thinking is a special kind of problem solving, and all the processes described in Chapter 4 may occur before the thinker is satisfied with his efforts. But the attempts at analyzing productive thinking have concentrated on the production process, presenting problems that encourage abundant production of solutions and varying the conditions of production. Alcohol in the bloodstream, for example, sets up a condition that has differential effects on production processes and thus offers a method of analysis. In one experiment (Hartocollis and Johnson, 1956), the production of simple responses (Name words that begin with M) declined after alcohol, and so did convergent thinking on a vocabulary test of the completion type; but the production of words from a fairly large class of words (Name trees) increased slightly. Examination of the words produced, such as *shoetree* and *family tree,* suggested that the experimental subjects did not adhere to the specifications for the responses as strictly as the control subjects. This relaxation of standards encouraged moderately restricted responses but not fluent production of unrestricted responses nor production of the one right answer.

In order to study production processes per se, some experiments have eliminated any judgment or evaluation of the solutions produced; others, however, have included the judgment process in order to describe the overall enterprise more completely. When the problems are not too complex, production and judgment can be separately identified and timed. An experiment with three plot title problems in which preparation, production, and judgment were separated illustrates this method of analysis (Johnson and Jennings, 1963). The time spent reading the plot, projected on a screen, was considered preparation time. When the subject was ready, he wrote five titles to the plot, and the time spent on this operation was called production time. The time spent in selecting the best of these five titles as the final solution was considered judgment time. Some of the data for college students are shown in Table 7.1. The production of five solutions consumed the most time, as one might expect, but the important point is that those who spent a long time supplying solutions to one problem did the same with another problem. And the same consistency is apparent for preparation and judgment. In general, correlations between times spent on the same process in different problems were fairly high, while the cross-correlations between different processes were lower.

These processes are differentiated by individual differences in time spent on each and by function in the whole enterprise, but they are interdependent.

TABLE 7.1. MEAN TIME (IN SECONDS) FOR THREE PROCESSES INVOLVED IN SOLVING PLOT TITLE PROBLEMS, AND CORRELATIONS BETWEEN TIMES

Process	Mean Time	Mean Correlation		
		Prep.	Prod.	Judg.
Preparation	48	.69		
Production	198	.40	.85	
Judgment	45	.40	.47	.62

From Johnson and Jennings (1963).

Preparation does not just mean reading the problem; it consists of integrating the information and getting ready to produce solutions to specifications. In this experiment, the reading time was longer for preparing to produce plot titles than preparing to judge titles that others had produced. The production process is the most obvious one; it appears to be the central component of productive thinking and thus has received the most experimental attention. Judgment, although it has usually been treated in experimental psychology as a separate topic related to psychophysics, consists, in these experiments, of evaluating the products just produced.

PREPARATION FOR PRODUCTIVE THINKING

The results of experiments on the preparation process and on information seeking summarized in previous chapters apply also to the present topic. But there is a special question about optimal information for productive thinking. Some eminent thinkers have recommended a thorough study of the problem and of previous attempts to solve it; others, equally eminent, have recommended that we ignore past failures and maintain a fresh approach. This old question was reexamined by Hyman (1961), but he emphasized what may be more important, the attitude—or set—toward information about a problem.

Working in a large electrical manufacturing plant, Hyman asked engineers to study attempts already made to design a system for recognizing boxes in an automatic warehouse. One group studied these previous attempts critically, in order to make up a list of faults; another group studied them constructively, in order to make up a list of useful features. Later, when all subjects were asked to propose their own solutions to this problem, and to another problem involving practical uses of the pyro-electric effect, those who had studied constructively produced better solutions to both.

A parallel study by Torrance (1964) reached a parallel conclusion. He asked psychology students to read two articles in psychological journals, either critically or imaginatively, before the middle of the term. Then they had to develop an original idea, theory, or hypothesis and turn it in on the last day of the term. Here again, the products of those who had read imaginatively received superior ratings for originality. The implications of these two experiments for teaching are obvious.

QUALITY AND QUANTITY OF SOLUTIONS

Much of the interest among psychologists in the quality-quantity relation can be traced to the brainstorming procedure described by Osborn (1953) in a book with the auspicious title *Applied Imagination*. He advised people (partly on the basis of the psychological research then available) to think up ideas enthusiastically, as many as possible, without criticism, and to do this in a group so that each member could build on the ideas of others. Checklists and other suggestions to get thought moving were provided. Although brainstorming was promoted as a practical technique for the solution of merchandising and industrial problems, it has spread to other areas, as distant as educational and military problem solving, and has led to significant psychological research on productive thinking.

The brainstorming procedure has two essential components, which may be stated as psychological hypotheses, each worthy of serious investigation. The first is that avoidance of criticism improves the production of ideas. The second, that group thinking is more productive than individual thinking, has a long and controversial history. Since we cannot stray far into social psychology here, we can only note that careful research (Dunnette, Campbell, and Jaasted, 1963; Taylor, Berry, and Block, 1958) has cast considerable doubt on the social side of the brainstorming procedure. When individuals working alone and in groups have been equated, those working alone have produced as many different ideas as those working in groups.

The other side of brainstorming, the hypothesis that production of ideas goes better without criticism, is more plausible. Courses in creative problem solving, built around brainstorming, emphasize quantity rather than quality and advocate the postponement of judgment so as to free the thinker from the curse of premature self-criticism. The outcomes of brainstorming will be discussed systematically in a later section, along with other training procedures. But, aside from the results of training, investigation of the relation between quality and quantity of solutions is beginning to throw some light on the processes by which the solutions are produced and on the conditions that affect these processes.

As dependent variables, three measures must be considered: the number of solutions, the mean quality of these, and the number of superior solutions. All solutions are rated by trained judges or scored objectively; those above an arbitrary level are called high-quality or superior products. These three measures overlap, as we shall see, but each may be an appropriate answer to a different question.

ONE SOLUTION OR MANY?

Experiments on problem solving typically require the subject to give one solution to a problem; experiments on productive thinking, in a different tradition, require many solutions. A series of experiments by Johnson, Parrott, and Stratton (1968), directed toward analysis of processes as well as improvement of outcomes, included the basic comparison between writing one solution—called the *standard condition*—and writing many. Since tasks as simple as writing uses for a brick have been criticized as trivial and vulnerable to variations in instructions, more substantial problems that could offer some challenge to college students were preferred. The plot title problem—which is a good test of the originality factor according to Wilson, Guilford, and Christensen (1953)—was taken as a model and four others of the same type were constructed in the hope of finding general trends as well as differences between problems.

Plot Titles. A paragraph, giving the plot of a story or movie, was presented with instructions to write alternative titles for it.

Table Titles. A table of agricultural statistics was presented with instructions to write titles for it.

Conclusions. A chart, with column diagrams representing expenditures for social welfare, was presented with instructions to write conclusions that may be drawn from the chart.

Sentences. Four words, *happy, expensive, horse, lake,* were printed with instructions to write sentences containing these words.

Cartoon Captions. A cartoon in four squares, with the printing removed from the last square, was presented with instructions to write alternative quotes for the last square [p. 4].

The solutions, about 1,000 for each problem, were rated independently by 2 judges with close agreement, and those above the 90th percentile were considered superior solutions.

As compared to the standard single-solution condition, the multiple-solution condition resulted in two distinct differences: a decrease in the mean quality of the solutions, and an increase in the number of superior solutions. These results are not contradictory. Subjects instructed to write many solutions wrote about seven, on the average, of a wide range of quality, and thus the increase in quantity included an increase in superior solutions as well as mediocre and inferior solutions. This is obvious when the complete distribution of solutions is scrutinized, as in Fig. 7.4. The increase in number of superior solutions can be attributed to a pure quantity effect, since the instructions made no reference to criticism, quality, or postponement of judgment.

INTRAINDIVIDUAL VARIABILITY IN QUALITY OF SOLUTIONS

A fundamental characteristic of productive thinking under multiple-solution instructions is the variation in quality of the solutions produced by each subject. It is conceivable that some subjects write mostly inferior solutions, some mostly mediocre solutions, and others mostly superior solutions. If this were true, the superior solutions would come predominantly from a small number of subjects; but this assumption is contradicted by individual production records in the experiment above. Almost every subject, whatever the mean quality of his solutions, wrote some solutions of higher quality and some of lower quality than the group mean. About 2 percent of the production records actually extended through the whole scale of quality, from 2 to 14, shown in Fig. 7.4. The median range was about 7 points on this scale. One important consequence of this intraindividual variability was that almost *any* subject who was encouraged to write many solutions had a good chance of writing one or two superior ones.

Although comparable production records for simpler tasks (such as unusual uses) have not been made public, it is a fair assumption that the same large intraindividual variability will be observed, and that the same consequences will follow.

VARIATIONS IN INSTRUCTIONS

The emphasis that the thinker puts on quality relative to quantity depends, in an unknown degree, on previous training; but it is also vulnerable to instructions and working conditions. Meadow, Parnes, and Rees (1959)

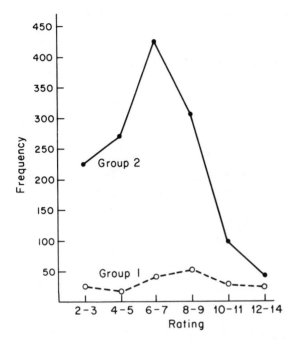

FIGURE 7.4. *Complete distributions of ratings of solutions to 5 problems by 40 subjects who wrote one solution (Group 1) and 40 subjects who wrote many solutions (Group 2). The base line represents the sum of 2 independent ratings on a scale of 1–7. Odd and even sums have been combined to remove irregularities, except that the highest ratings, 12, 13, and 14, have been placed in 1 interval. From Johnson, Parrott, and Stratton (1968).*

examined the effect of instructions by giving alternate sets to students during a course in creative problem solving. The task was to produce unusual uses, and the brainstorming instructions were: "Brainstorm to your fullest ability; forget about quality entirely. We are going to count only quantity on this test. . . . Quality is of no concern at all." The other instructions were: "Forget all about brainstorming. Strive completely for quality. We want to see how many good ideas you can produce in a certain amount of time. You are going to be penalized for any bad ideas [p. 414]." When the responses were rated and the superior solutions identified, it was the group with the brain-storming instructions that had produced the most. And this effect is not limited to a restricted range of ability, for brainstorming instructions improved the performance of the top third of a distribution of subjects (identified by scores on a pretest of creativity), as well as the bottom third (Turner and Rains, 1965).

Weisskopf-Joelson and Eliseo (1961) also compared two types of instruc-tions, but their method of analysis led to a different conclusion. The subjects' task was to think of attractive names for a new deodorant, and other mer-chandise, which were then rated for quality. The data showed that under instructions emphasizing quantity the quantity increased, but most of the increase was in the low-quality responses, not the high-quality ones. Mean quality was higher under instructions to be critical.

Specific instructions about solutions are not the only factor that makes a difference; the social atmosphere generated by the examiner's instructions and demeanor also influence production. Without varying the instructions about the solutions, Dentler and Mackler (1964) arranged a relaxed, "safe" condition (the examiner was friendly and said he knew the subjects would do well on the test) for comparison with an "unsafe" condition (the examiner was serious and distant while stressing the challenge and competitiveness of the test). As expected, more unusual uses were produced under the safe conditions. The results of the Hartocollis and Johnson (1956) study mentioned above suggest that alcohol dissolves the "unsafe" constraints and allows the subjects to produce ideas as if they were "safe." Similar instructional effects have been obtained in a ninth-grade classroom with tests of unusual uses and consequences (Adams, 1968). Instructions emphasizing competition depressed performance compared to that of a control group, while instructions emphasizing freedom from competition and open receptivity to ideas elevated performance. It is because they appreciate these effects of an insecure competitive atmosphere that careful experimenters, like Wallach and Kogan (1965), have administered their tests in an informal, gamelike situation.

The most complete investigation of the effects of specific instructions about solutions to be produced comes from Gerlach, Schutz, Baker, and Mazer (1964), with six sets of instructions, including penalty for bad responses, brainstorming, nonbrainstorming, and what they called "criteria-cued" instructions. The task was to list uses for a coat hanger. Their hunch was that the improvement attributed to brainstorming was really due to learning a criterion of quality, so they spelled out the criterion in the criteria-cued instructions: "The more *imaginative* or *creative* your ideas, the *higher* your score will be. Each idea will be scored in terms of how *unique* it is . . . how *valuable* it is . . . the more *original* and *creative* the better [p. 80]." As the results turned out, the criteria-cued instructions did yield the largest number of superior responses, slightly more than the regular brainstorming instructions.

The instructional effects revealed by Manske and Davis (1968) with three tests of unusual uses were even more clearly distinguished, since they rated responses on "practicality" as well as "originality" dimensions. When instructed to "be original," the subjects gave uses that were more original but less practical; when instructed to "be practical," they gave uses that were more practical but less original. However, they were unable to give uses that were both original *and* practical. In fact, over all conditions there was a strong negative correlation, −.80, between the ratings on originality and practicality dimensions. This negative correlation depends, of course, on the judges as well as the responses. But it does suggest that in these rather unstructured situations the subjects trade off one dimension for another as, in other situations, they trade off accuracy for speed.

The experiment by Johnson, Parrott, and Stratton (1968) verified the effects of information about the criteria of good solutions with more substantial problems. The information given was as follows.

Plot Titles. By clever we mean an imaginative, creative, or unusual title for this plot.

Table Titles. A good title is a comprehensive one that includes the important points concisely.

Conclusions. A good conclusion would be a valid generalization which integrates the chart as a whole.

Sentences. A good sentence reads smoothly; the four words fit unobtrusively into the structure of the sentence.

Cartoon Captions. A clever quote is an imaginative idea that fits the cartoon [p. 4].

The results gave definite evidence of the effects of criteria-cued instructions on solutions to the 5 problems. Those who were given the information about the criteria of good solutions wrote fewer solutions, but of higher mean quality, and contributed a larger number of superior solutions than those who did not have the benefits of this information. To be specific, 80 subjects with criteria cues wrote 281 superior solutions, which was 12 percent of their total output of solutions; while 80 subjects without such cues wrote 226 superior solutions, which was 8 percent of their output.

Even with information about the criteria of good solutions, however, those who wrote many solutions did not produce solutions that were as good, in respect to mean ratings, as those who wrote only one. (They produced a larger number of superior solutions, of course, because of the quantity effect). But if criteria information improves the quality of solutions in the multiple-solution condition, why not let subjects in the single-solution condition have the benefit of criteria information also? An experiment (Johnson, 1968) which allowed 4 minutes to write one solution to a problem yielded solutions of greater mean quality on three out of four problems for those who had criteria information (see Table 7.2).

We must conclude that instructions are very important in experiments on productive thinking, as in experiments on flicker fusion, operant conditioning, and other performances by human beings. Apparently, relaxed conditions and instructions not to evaluate are sometimes helpful; better yet are instructions that imply evaluation but are specific about the criteria. Although some of these experiments were designed to refute certain claims for the efficacy of brainstorming, on the positive side they demonstrate the intellectual flexibility of educated young adults, and their ability to adjust their output to the apparent demands of the situation.

TABLE 7.2. EFFECTS OF INSTRUCTIONS ON MEAN QUALITY OF SOLUTIONS TO FOUR PROBLEMS WHEN EACH SUBJECT WRITES ONE SOLUTION

Instructions	Plot Titles	Conclusions	Sentences	Cartoons
Standard	7.7	7.0	8.4	6.0
Criteria	7.7	9.8	9.7	6.9

From Johnson (1968).

PROBLEM DIFFERENCES IN THE QUALITY-QUANTITY RELATION

The relation between quality and quantity was investigated in more detail (Johnson, 1968) by having different groups of subjects write 1, 2, 4, or 6 solutions with the benefit of criteria information. Two problems, Conclusions and Sentences, were chosen for this study because in previous research the difference between single-solution and multiple-solution conditions in mean quality of solutions had been large for Conclusions and small for Sentences. The data for groups of 25 to 30 subjects are shown in Fig. 7.5, and a logarithmic curve has been drawn to each set of points. The equation of this form that best fits the data for Sentences is $Y = 8.3 - 1.60 \log X$, and for Conclusions $Y = 9.4 - 4.78 \log X$.

Both the general decline in quality and the difference between problems in rate of decline need explanation here. It is reasonable to assume that the subjects take instructions to write more than one solution as permission to lower their standards, but instructions to write four would not be twice as permissive as instructions to write two. The standard-lowering effect of the

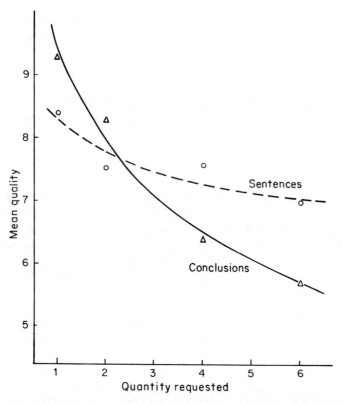

FIGURE 7.5. Quality and quantity of solutions to 2 problems. Groups of 25 to 30 subjects were requested to write 1, 2, 4, or 6 solutions. Logarithmic curves describe the decline in mean quality as quantity increases. From Johnson (1968).

number requested would probably be curvilinear. An explanation of the difference between the two curves must take account of the quantity and quality of available solutions. The number of good sentences that can be constructed from the four given words is almost unlimited, hence the decline with quantity would be small. The number of good conclusions to the chart is distinctly limited, however, hence the curve falls sharply with an increase in quantity requested. Those who tried to write many conclusions frequently wrote conclusions to only one aspect of the chart, and such fragmentary solutions got low ratings. The high mean quality of the single conclusions suggests that one good solution is easily constructed and differentiated from others of lower quality. Thus the quality-quantity relation depends in part on the shape of the frequency distribution of available solutions as a function of quality.

Neither problem had only one right answer, but on the continuum from divergent to convergent thinking Conclusions would be located toward the convergent and Sentences toward the divergent end. Thus this analysis offers a preliminary differentiation of solution processes at different locations on the convergent-divergent continuum.

INDIVIDUAL DIFFERENCES

In groups instructed to write many solutions, it is possible to examine the relation between individual differences in quantity and quality. When quantity is emphasized, some write more than others, probably because the instructions are somewhat ambiguous and the subject can choose whether to emphasize quantity or quality. Parnes and Meadow (1959) reported correlations of .64 and .81 between number of solutions written and number of high-quality solutions written. Parnes (1961) and Gerlach, et al. (1964) reported similar correlations for simple production tasks. Johnson, Parrott, and Stratton (1968) computed correlations between the quantity score and two quality scores, namely, mean quality and number of superior solutions, for several groups on five problems. On these more substantial problems, mean quality of all solutions showed consistent negative correlations with quantity; those who wrote more solutions wrote solutions of lower mean quality. The corresponding correlations between quantity and number of superior solutions were near zero.

Such correlations are probably secondary effects of the relations described above. Those who take the instructions to emphasize quantity at the expense of quality act accordingly and thus their mean quality is low. If quantity is emphasized, the number of superior solutions is increased; but this increase due to the quantity effect apparently is not sufficient, in the case of substantial problems, to overcome the general reduction in mean quality.

REORGANIZATION OF ELEMENTS

Reorganization occurs in divergent thinking as it does in the solution of anagrams, arithmetic problems, and other instances of convergent thinking. When the task is to produce single words or short phrases, the production process can easily be conceived as the retrieval of previously learned information, perhaps even as the sampling of a specified class of words. When the task is more complex, as in writing a sentence or paragraph, such a simple conception is less plausible. Previously learned elements reappear, of course, but not typically in the form in which they were originally learned.

To see what happens to information acquired immediately before a production task, Maier, Julius, and Thurber (1967) gave college students 12 pairs of words to memorize, then asked them to write a story about a prisoner, using as many of the words as possible. Later, they were asked to write a second story on a topic of their own choosing. Under these conditions, pairs of words that fit together and could easily be used in proximity, such as *damp-weather* and *hot-soup,* often reappeared as pairs in the stories. Pairs of words that could not easily be used in proximity, such as *steal-prison,* seldom appeared in the original form as word pairs, but single-word fragments of the original pairs often appeared alone. Many of the words from both types of word pairs appeared in the stories paired with other words as new pairs (e.g., *damp-prison*). As to individual differences, the subjects tended to be somewhat consistent from the first story to the second in frequency of use of old pairs, of single words, or of new pairs.

Stratton (1970) applied similar methods to study of the Sentences problem described earlier, which requires the construction of sentences from the words *happy, expensive, horse,* and *lake.* A group of subjects who had memorized sentences that included the pairs *happy horse* and *expensive lake* wrote sentences that contained these clichés and thus got lower quality ratings than the control subjects. Another group of subjects who had memorized sentences that included several unusual meanings for *horse* and *lake* wrote sentences that reorganized these nouns into more unusual constructions, such as *horse around* and *Happy Lake Resort,* and thus got higher-quality ratings.

Although creative thinking has often been viewed as the reorganization of experience, empirical investigation from this point of view is not common. Reorganization will not show up unless the methods permit it; the experiments above, together with others now being used in the study of verbal meaning, can disclose how words acquired just before a production task are, or are not, reorganized. But study of the reorganization of information acquired at other times in other places in the more remote past for use in the present production task will be more difficult.

PRODUCTION SEQUENCES

When someone writes many solutions to a problem, a record of the sequence of solutions offers an opportunity for testing hypotheses about the processes by which they are produced. It is reasonable to suppose that the thinker produces his best solution first, then his next best, and so on, in descending order of quality. The opposite sequence also seems reasonable: the best ones come later. The number of solutions and their quality must be considered, as well as the complexity of the task.

SIMPLE RESPONSES

Some years ago, Bousfield and Sedgewick (1944) published cumulative curves—two of which appear in Fig. 7.6—showing that the production of single words of the same class decreases with time. When the number of words emitted over a period of 10 minutes or so is plotted cumulatively, the production curve can be represented by an exponential equation, $n = c(1 - e^{-mt})$, in which n is the cumulative frequency, c represents an upper limit, e is the base of the natural logarithms, m is the rate of approach to the limit, and t is the elapsed time.

The general shape of the production curve has been confirmed by other experiments, but there is some question about the reason for the decrease in production rate. Bousfield and Sedgewick suggested that the upper limit represents a supply of words which is sampled without replacement. As the supply is depleted, the production rate decreases. Indow and Togano (1970) described one scanning model for scanning all items in the supply in order to reject those already produced and a second model that moves the scanning process to regions of lower density. The upper limit implied by these models, and by extrapolation of the empirical curves, cannot, however, represent the total supply of words in the subject's vocabulary but more likely the supply under specific experimental conditions. When Merrill (1950) asked college students to write words beginning with S, the above equation, applied to the data of one subject, yielded a value for c of 132. But 12 percent of the words in the dictionary begin with S, so if 132 is 12 percent of this student's vocabulary, his vocabulary would be 1,095 words, an absurd value. Furthermore, this equation gave larger estimates for words beginning with V, which constitute only about 2 percent of the dictionary, than for words beginning

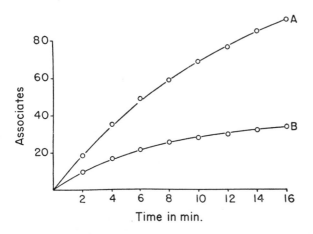

FIGURE 7.6. *Continuous production of words. College students were asked, in one experiment (A), to think of names of fellow students, and in the other (B), to think of animal names with two or more syllables. From Bousfield and Sedgewick (1944).*

with S, which constitute 12 percent. There must be some task-related limit on the availability of the words, perhaps an associative interference whereby some words get in the way of others during copious production. Another possibility is a general work decrement or simple boredom with the task. When increments per minute are plotted, the curve looks like a fatigue curve; a short rest is followed by partial recovery (Hall, 1960). All in all, if we ask about the number of simple responses produced in a short time, the hypothesis of sampling without replacement is still tenable, but there are questions about the class of responses sampled and about performance factors.

Turning now to the quality of the responses, it is clear that the production of simple responses is characterized by the early appearance of the more common ones. Bousfield and Barclay (1950) found that words of high frequency of usage were produced early. Christensen, Guilford, and Wilson (1957), reversing the proposition and calling uncommon responses creative, found that more creative responses were produced late: more unusual uses of a pencil or a button, more uncommon figure concepts, more uncommon number associations. The occurrence of more unusual uses late in the production sequence has been confirmed for 5-minute and 15-minute periods (Parnes, 1961) and for 10-minute periods (Manske and Davis, 1968).

Such results match the hypothesis of a response hierarchy, derived from association theory. For convergent thinking (as in the anagram problems of Chapter 4), the hypothesis is stated in respect to problem difficulty; for divergent thinking with multiple solutions, it is stated in respect to order: the common responses occur first, followed by the more uncommon responses. And the uncommon responses are of higher quality, on one dimension of creativity, than the common ones.

COMPLEX RESPONSES

The production of complex solutions to problems differs in some respects from the production of simple responses. A complex response, produced on demand, resembles a multidimensional class concept in that the specifications of the product are analogous to the attributes of the concept. Instead of requesting names of birds, we can request two-syllable names of birds (a conjunctive class), and college students can produce these quite readily. College students can readily produce relational classes also, such as pairs of words that are synonyms, or antonyms, or books and their authors. The attributes may, of course, be abstract dimensions: "Name women who are intelligent as well as virtuous." It is probable also that many thinkers supplement the specifications of the task with a few of their own, such as brevity, conformity, or avoidance of the obvious. Although some of the elements of complex responses may be drawn from a reservoir of experience—and this portion of the operation resembles recall—a large portion comes from reorganization of the elements, from integration, construction, or invention.

Thus complex solutions usually vary on several dimensions pertinent to creative achievement—such as cleverness, originality, and appropriateness— as well as on statistical uncommonness. If we speculate about a class from which the solutions are drawn, it must be smaller than a comparable class of simple responses. The number of solutions produced is usually less over equal periods of time. As a specific illustration, in the Manske and Davis (1968) experiment, instructions to be original led to the production of 11.4 uses, and instructions to be practical to 18.4 uses; but instruction to be original and practical led to 10.2 uses. In contrast with the decreasing production curves for simple responses, the curves exhibited by Christensen, Guilford, and Wilson (1957) for writing plot titles and listing impossibilities are linear over working periods of 12 minutes. The slow initial rate of production is caused by the small supply of suitable words. The linearity of the production curve could be due to the weakness of the factors hypothesized for a decreasing rate of production. When solutions are complex, avoidance of repetition is less difficult and the task less boring.

As to the quality of the solutions to complex problems, the number of superior solutions increases, in agreement with a response hierarchy interpretation, for some problems but not for others (Christensen, Guilford, and Wilson, 1957). Similar inconsistencies appeared in the results for the 5 problems studied by Johnson, Parrott, and Stratton (1968), but much of this inconsistency has been cleared up by Stratton's reanalysis of the data, shown in Table 7.3. In this experiment, 40 college students were instructed simply to write many solutions in 7 minutes. Another group of 40 had instructions to write many solutions, then to judge these solutions and select their best. Others were given the criteria of good solutions, and others again had both the criteria information and the request to select their best. As to number of superior solutions, the totals for all problems show that the largest difference between first and last halves occurred under the simplest condition. When judgment was requested or criteria information given, the difference was smaller; and when both complications were added, the difference disappeared. It is noteworthy also that the increase under simple instructions,

TABLE 7.3. NUMBER OF SUPERIOR SOLUTIONS IN FIRST AND LAST HALVES OF PRODUCTION SEQUENCE FOR FIVE PROBLEMS UNDER FOUR PRODUCTION CONDITIONS

Conditions	Plot Titles First Half	Plot Titles Last Half	Table Titles First Half	Table Titles Last Half	Conclusions First Half	Conclusions Last Half	Sentences First Half	Sentences Last Half	Cartoons First Half	Cartoons Last Half	Totals First Half	Totals Last Half
Many solutions	9	19	4	5	7	9	6	16	7	13	33	62
Many solutions with judgment	12	12	7	4	6	11	11	13	19	19	55	59
Many solutions with criteria	9	8	7	10	14	16	13	17	12	14	55	65
Many solutions with judgment and criteria	10	16	7	9	17	10	13	18	21	12	68	65
Totals	40	55	25	28	44	46	43	64	59	58	211	251

from 33 to 62, did not bring this group up to the initial level of 68 superior solutions produced under the more complicated instructions. Obviously, the more specific instructions increased the number of superior solutions produced at the beginning, after which improvement was small.

A later study by Stratton (1970) analyzed production sequences from the Sentences problem in more detail, for sequences of five solutions and ten solutions. Mean quality increased over five solutions with and without criteria information, but over sequences of ten solutions mean quality increased only without criteria information. Stratton went further and analyzed the separate dimensions of the solutions as they varied over production sequences. The length of the sentences increased, and in general so did the number of times the four given words were used with unusual meanings. The number of times that the given words were paired in a sentence (e.g., *expensive horse*) declined over a sequence of five solutions, but, surprisingly, some other dimensions, such as the complexity of the sentences, did not change as expected. When the solutions to be produced are complex, it is not reasonable to expect that all the dimensions will change in the same way, and this analysis shows that in fact they did not.

In Table 7.3 the differences between problems, over all conditions, were of the same order of magnitude as the differences between first and last halves. For Sentences and Plot Titles, the increase was large; for Table Titles, Conclusions, and Cartoon Captions, it was negligible. The comparison of Sentences and Conclusions is particularly enlightening because these two problems have already been compared in respect to the quality-quantity relation. Fig. 7.5 displayed how the mean quality of the solutions to the Conclusions problem decreased sharply as a function of the quantity of solutions requested while the mean quality of Sentences decreased slightly. And this difference was apparently due to the smaller number of good solutions to the Conclusions problem. Putting these data together with those of Table 7.3, we can say that for any problem the improvement from first half to last half of a production sequence is related to the number of potential superior solutions to the problem. In the Unusual Uses problem, when superior solutions are defined as uncommon responses, substantial improvement can be expected.

In general, two factors determine the difference between the quality of solutions in the first and last halves of a production sequence. Improvement is maximal when the instructions are general and therefore the quality in the first half is low. Improvement is maximal for problems with many good solutions. Thus in the case of Sentences with general instructions, almost three times as many superior solutions were produced in the last half as in the first. In the case of Conclusions and Cartoon Captions under specific instructions, almost twice as many were produced in the first half.

CONTINUOUS AND DISCONTINUOUS PRODUCTION

The concept of *incubation* implies that after the thinker has struggled with a problem and then abandoned it, the solution often comes to him later while he is attending to other things. Many eminent writers, scientists, and inventors have testified that such sequences of events have happened to them, and psychologists have tried to explain this phenomenon by hypotheses about unconscious work and the reduction of interferences (see Johnson, 1955). Such matters are difficult to study objectively, but two experiments have manipulated the most obvious variable by comparing output during a continuous working period with output during discontinuous periods of the same total time.

In one experiment of this design, Gall and Mendelsohn (1967) gave college students 2 minutes to work as many items of the Remote Associates Test as they could. Then each subject was given 25 minutes to do five problems that he had been unable to solve, but half the subjects first had a period of 25 minutes of unrelated activity which was supposed to facilitate incubation. Most thinkers who have claimed benefits from incubation refer to concentration on a single problem, so this may not be a fair test; in any event, those who worked continuously did considerably better than those who worked discontinuously. On the other hand, when Fulgosi and Guilford (1968) had college students produce solutions to two items of the Consequences Test, they found a small increase in number of immediate consequences following a 10-minute interruption (with no interpolated activity) and a large increase following a 20-minute interruption. There was no increase in the number of remote consequences; in other words, there was an improvement in quantity but not in quality. So far as objective evidence from these rather superficial experiments is concerned, the status of incubation therefore remains uncertain.

JUDGMENT OF THE SOLUTIONS

When anyone produces many solutions to a problem, the question of identification of the best arises. There is no advantage to producing a superior solution unless it is identified as such; like making clothes without trying them on, producing solutions without evaluating them is an unfinished performance. For experimental purposes, superior solutions can be identified by the experimenter, but surely this is an atypical situation. Generally speaking, the thinker selects the one he considers the best for submission to a journal, a museum, or a patent office, or to keep for his own use. We have seen that instructions emphasizing quantity increase the number of superior solutions, but increase the number of inferior solutions even more. If the thinker chooses at random among the solutions he has produced, the proper measure of overall performance would be the mean quality, and this is likely to be lowered by the quantity emphasis. But of course a thinker does not choose at random. Hence we must look carefully at judgment of the solutions as a separate process that makes its own contribution to the overall enterprise.

A small-scale study (Johnson and Jennings, 1963) demonstrated that college students could judge solutions to the Plot Title problem—both their own solutions and those written by others—with fair accuracy when their choices were compared with the choices of expert judges. In respect to individual differences in the time spent on each process, judgment and production were somewhat independent. Johnson, Parrott, and Stratton (1968) therefore examined this judgment operation more thoroughly by requesting some subjects in the experiment described above to select their best solutions to five problems. Such a request is feasible because of the large intraindividual variability in quality of solutions produced by each individual. In general, the solutions preferred by the subjects as their best were better than the others; when given the criteria of good solutions, the difference between their preferred and nonpreferred solutions was even larger. Nevertheless, their judgments were not as good as they might be. For example, a subject who wrote seven solutions might pick the best of the seven, as measured by the ratings of expert judges, but he might pick the second best instead, or the third best. The third best would be better than the average of the other six but not much better. Hence, when the subjects who wrote many solutions were given the criteria of good solutions and asked to select their best solutions to each problem, their preferred solutions were about the same, in mean quality and number of superior solutions, as those of the subjects who wrote only one solution. In fact, when the proper comparisons are made, it appears that the standard condition of asking the subject to write one solution to a problem is a hard one to beat. Such findings indicate that multiple-solution experiments, which ignore the judgment process and do not include a single-solution condition as a baseline, are incomplete. They suggest, furthermore, that attempting to improve judgment of the solutions might be worthwhile.

The introduction to this chapter made passing reference to the dependence of extraordinary creative achievement on favorable intellectual conditions at the time. Similarly, productive achievement in the classroom depends on the teacher's recognition of a student's achievement. The student whose novel contribution matches the teacher's criterion of productive achievement is more fortunate than the student whose productive efforts go off in another direction. And in the small world of the psychology laboratory, the subject whose productive efforts match the criteria used by the expert judges is again the fortunate one. It is true that careful experimenters have used two or more judges who have worked together until they reach satisfactory inter-judge agreement, but this is not the end of the matter. If the solutions are at all complex, we need to ask which dimensions of the solutions determine the judges' ratings and, eventually, the outcome of the experiment.

Stratton (1970) made a beginning of this kind by correlation analysis of judgments of solutions to the Sentences problem. In one condition, for example, the overall rating of quality of the sentences was correlated .65 with number of unusual meanings attached to the four given words, .45 with number of times the given nouns were used other than as the subject or direct object of the sentence, and .26 with sentence length. This analysis is mentioned, not just to prove that judges are human, but to underline the importance of the judgment process and of the match between the dimensions that the producer emphasizes and those that the judges—whether literary critics, museum directors, or editors of scientific journals—emphasize.

PRODUCTIVE THINKING IN THE PSYCHOLOGY CLASSROOM

Most research on productive thinking has avoided problems from any specific course of study, presumably for methodological reasons, but the introduction of productive thinking into a college course is not at all difficult. At Michigan State University problems have been constructed in formats similar to those described above and in content that samples standard introductory psychology textbooks. The instructions and three examples are printed below. Reliability of scoring is indicated by the correlation between the ratings of two judges.

> This part of the examination emphasizes creative thinking. You can use the knowledge you have acquired from the textbook and the lectures but you should go beyond this to produce an original solution to each problem. Short answers, never more than one sentence.
> Suppose television had been invented and had become popular before books. What would be the consequences for the learning processes of children? ($r = .88$)
> Suppose you want to train an animal in a new, unique way. Invent a reinforcement schedule different from those used by others. ($r = .93$)
> Write an original sentence that includes the words: easy, performance, motivation. ($r = .87$)

It will be interesting to see how performance on these tests is influenced by variations in instructions, classroom atmosphere, and teaching procedure.

Training for Productive Thinking

Library shelves abound in books telling us how to train our minds to think creatively, and there are some paragraphs of good advice in all of them. The training procedures that have been subjected to empirical evaluation are of most interest here, of course. Such procedures have been developed around hypotheses about productive thinking, and the outcomes of evaluation studies are relevant to these hypotheses.

BRAINSTORMING

Training in creative problem solving, by the brainstorming techniques of Osborn (1953), is grounded on one hypothesis about the exchange and enrichment of ideas in group interaction and another about increasing the quality of ideas by postponing criticism and emphasizing quantity. The evidence related to the second hypothesis was reviewed earlier; it is time now to estimate the overall value of such training.

As a check on outcomes, Meadow and Parnes (1959) administered several tests of the Guilford creative thinking type before and after a 30-hour course in creative problem solving and before and after unrelated courses.

They found increases in quantity of production of unusual uses and plot titles, as one might expect; but they also found increases in high-quality products, as indicated by scores for uniqueness and value of responses on three tests of unusual uses. The difference on the plot title test scored for high quality was small. The tests were somewhat like the practice materials, but not identical; the authors concluded that the course in creative problem solving had been effective.

Somewhat similar results were obtained by Parnes and Meadow (1959) comparing performance on unusual uses by subjects with and without a course in creative problem solving. The most convincing results came from a follow-up study (Parnes and Meadow, 1960) eight months after a course in creative problem solving. As compared with control groups matched for verbal ability, the trained subjects showed improvement on all tests, including plot titles rated for high quality.

Even a brief training period seems to be effective, at least temporarily. Comparing individual production before and after 10 minutes of group training, Lindgren and Lindgren ·(1965a) found an improvement in the creativity level of captions written for cartoons by California students and also (1965b) by Lebanese students. The same type of experiment disclosed a gain in ratings of sketches for a postage stamp after 10 minutes of brainstorming (Lindgren, 1967). In these three studies, the critical measure was the mean quality of all productions, not the number of superior productions. Hence the gain could not be merely a consequence of an increase in quantity.

The emphasis of brainstorming on quantity instead of quality is a general content-free technique, intended to aid the production of ideas on any topic. It is also a negative technique, intended to remove barriers that prevent the thinker from making fluent use of the ideas he already has. These two features limit its effectiveness for more specific positive training programs. As distinct from the immediate effects of instructions, the gains that have been reported are rather small and hard to interpret. On the positive side, however, there is the possibility, noted by several investigators, that practice with this novel techinque stimulates an enduring interest in the production of ideas. Brainstorming is more fun than most parlor games and, when dignified by an organization's official stamp of approval, it makes thought as respectable within the organization as action. Certainly, brainstorming can claim legitimate status as a promising psychological technique and cannot just be dismissed as a Madison Avenue merchandising stunt.

ASSOCIATIVE TRAINING

"We are assuming that originality can be learned and that the same principles of conditioning hold as in other forms of operant behavior. . . . By originality, or original thinking, we mean behavior that occurs relatively infrequently, is uncommon under given conditions, and is relevant to those conditions." This quotation from Maltzman, Simon, Raskin, and Licht (1960, p. 1) outlines the basis for another attempt to improve productive thinking.

One experiment (Maltzman, Bogartz, and Breger, 1958) began with ordinary word associations: 25 words, like *pencil,* to which the subject gave another word in response. Then the subject went through the list again 5 times altogether, with instructions to give different responses, after which he was tested on another list of 25 words. In comparison with a control group, the training groups gave somewhat more unusual responses. Ambiguous results were obtained from a test of unusual uses for a button, included as a test of transfer. The instructions were varied also, and those who were instructed to be original on the test list gave more unusual responses. In fact, the difference due to instructions was about 5 times as large as the difference due to training.

Since these results were promising but inconclusive, Maltzman, Simon, Raskin, and Licht (1960) undertook an extensive series of further experiments along the same line, varying the conditions to tease out the important factors in this associative approach to originality training, but depending on the same two tests: uncommonness of word associations and unusual uses. The best training was to give one list of stimulus words twice and ask for different response words the second time. This procedure increased both uncommon word associations and originality of uses. Repeating the task five or ten times increased uncommonness of the word associations but not originality of the test of unusual uses.

So far, associative training looks promising, but some criticisms of the results and interpretations have arisen. When Gallup (1963) tried to duplicate these results, he found improvement from one test to another in all groups, even in those that had unrelated training in arithmetic, for example. Hence he suggested that the results of the training might be due to self-instructions or to a shift in the set for such tasks rather than to the associative training itself.

The criticism of Caron, Unger, and Parloff (1963) dealt with the scoring standards. They repeated the word association training with a strict criterion of relevance of the responses and got no improvement at all. They therefore concluded that the associative training "may enrich one's fantasy life but without benefit to ingenuity of output [p. 422]."

Some of these discrepancies have been partly clarified by Rosenbaum, Arenson, and Panman (1964). In their experiment, the effects of instructions to be original were small and temporary; but training in word association, with six lists, following Maltzman's procedure, did increase unique responses on the unusual uses test. Since common responses were increased, as well as unique responses, they stated that the increase in unique responses was a consquence of the general increase in productivity—an interpretation that is consonant with the general quantity effect mentioned above.

The Remote Associates Test can also be used as a criterion of the success of originality training. Maltzman, Belloni, and Fishbein (1964) tried out their associative procedure on this criterion but were successful only when the stimulus words, or words closely associated with them, also appeared on the test. They concluded that "performance on the problems employed which have only one correct solution can not be facilitated by the originality-training procedures successfully employed with tasks having no one correct solution [p. 20]."

Since it had been shown that those who obtain high scores on the Remote Associates Test produce more words in continuous production, Freedman (1965) tried a somewhat different kind of practice. He encouraged fluency of production simply by having the subjects practice giving rapid associations to ten stimulus words. Such practice did increase scores on the Remote Associates Test, although equivalent practice in defining words did not. Apparently the demand for greater productivity during training leads to greater productivity on the transfer task, with increased originality as a secondary effect of productivity. Ray (1966) also has suggested, from the results of a training experiment, that it was the subjects' expectancy of many solutions rather than the training that increased the number of solutions.

The original assumption about the effects of associative training has not been entirely negated by later experiments. More associations with the practiced words and closely related words apparently are acquired. But this rather narrow effect must be evaluated in relation to two more general effects: the establishment of an adaptive set for such tasks as a result of instructions and self-instructions, and the general increase in productivity which, depending on the scoring standards, can include an increase in high-quality responses.

TRAINING FOR THE ROLE OF ORIGINAL THINKER

The influence of instructions from one person on the productive thinking of another person has already been well documented here. In many laboratory and classroom experiments this has been the strongest influence. Levy (1968) has pushed the interpersonal interpretation a step farther by proposing "that originality is better conceived as a form of role-defined behavior than as a form of operant behavior, and that the effects of originality training may be understood as due to changes in the person's criterion for an appropriate response rather than to increases in the associative strength of original responses [p. 72]."

To compare these different conceptions of originality training, Levy asked college students to take on the characteristics of another person's personality, Mr. (or Miss) S.J. One group was given a word association test, with instructions to respond with the first word that would come to S.J.'s mind, and the experimenter gave verbal reinforcement by saying "good" or something similar after each uncommon response. Each subject of another group was shown a list of uncommon responses attributed to a role model, S.J., and told to study it in order to be able to put himself in S.J.'s role. A third group was given a description of S.J. and instructions to play S.J.'s role: "S.J. enjoys doing things in a unique or novel way; his whole personality portrays him as creative, imaginative, and always full of new and interesting ideas [p. 74]." A fourth had both the reinforcement and the role instructions.

All groups improved in the number of uncommon responses after training, but the role-instruction training was slightly more effective than the reinforcement training or the role-model training. The combination of reinforcement and instructions was the best, of course. Transfer effects were tested by giving each subject the Holtzman inkblots, with printed alternative responses, choice of the uncommon responses being the measure of originality. All training groups registered some transfer compared to a control group, but on this test also the role-instruction training was more effective than reinforcement or role-model training.

The unusual feature of this experiment was that after the training all subjects were asked to fill out rating scales to describe their impression of S.J. It is not surprising that those with role instructions rated S.J. as original, but it is critical to the role interpretation that the subjects in the reinforcement group made the obvious inferences and also rated S.J. as original. Such results support the suspicions of many experimenters that verbal reinforcement in this and similar experiments is not limited to strengthening the responses but has the cognitive effect of informing the subject also of their appropriateness. According to Levy, the instructions provide the subjects with a general definition of their role, thereby supplying the criterion to be applied in judging response appropriateness. Then the reinforcement makes the role more specific.

It will be difficult to establish that the subjects were adopting the role of a model rather than following instructions or trying to infer the experimenter's expectations. Actually, the role-model training was the least efficient of the four procedures. But much of the evidence on instructions, criteria information, and associative training in this chapter and on set in Chapter 4 requires an interpretation that takes account of the personal relationship between experimenter and subject. Levy believes that his "cognitive role theoretical explanation" permits more explicit definitions and more precise experimental manipulations than the complex mediated generalizations that are necessary for an associative interpretation of the effects of originality training.

TRAINING IN PRODUCTION STRATEGIES

The more lyrical descriptions of creative thinking conceive it as a loose, undisciplined activity, to be left free from control so that fervent ideas can bubble up from the depths of the unconscious. Others conceive it as a rational systematic process and thus generate positive recommendations. Instructions to "stop and think" are generally beneficial, and so is a set to be original, whether communicated by instruction from others or adopted as a self-instruction by the thinker. Specific information about the criteria for good solutions also improves performance.

As to working methods, artists are typically more systematic than nonartists and display more control over their creative efforts (Eindhoven and Vinacke, (1952). Writers also speak of control over their medium; certainly, they do not write novels or poems one word at a time, by continuous association. From what distinguished poets tell us (Arnheim, Auden, Shapiro, and Stauffer, 1948), the initial ideas may come from anywhere, perhaps by association, but soon a structure is outlined, at least tentatively, and then filled in with the right words. Hence it is not unreasonable to design programs of explicit recommendations about strategies for divergent as well as convergent thinking.

Since the phenomenon of incubation has been reported by many successful thinkers, and disregarding for now the uncertain evidence from one-shot experiments, an *alternation strategy* can be proposed. The hypothesis suggested by the testimony of eminent thinkers is that, when one is stuck on a difficult problem, it is better to stop a while and then return to it, rather than plod on without interruption. This does not exclude the possibility of going over the facts or of daydreaming about the solution during nonwork periods because reports of incubation have explicitly referred to such activities. Nor is it stated in terms of efficiency per unit of time because productive thinkers seldom mention this measure.

Many training programs have been designed for advertising men and for engineers engaged in research and development (Allen, 1962; Arnold, 1962; Gordon, 1961; Lincoln, 1962). Typically, these begin with a few inspiring anecdotes, then recommend an open mind, sensitivity to problems, and other general requirements for effective thinking. The specific aids often consist of checklists—or even matrices and more elaborate diagrams—to facilitate a systematic approach to the development of new products and projects. One such list, abridged by Arnold from the book by Osborn (1953), consists simply of verbs: Adapt, Modify, Magnify, Minify, Substitute, Rearrange, Reverse, Combine. Helpful examples of improvements coming from the actions listed are also supplied.

LABORATORY EVALUATION WITH ADULT SUBJECTS

To evaluate such procedures, Ridley and Birney (1967) gave their subjects a booklet of strategies for the unusual uses test containing, for example, the following suggestions. "Transform the object: burn it, cut it, paint it, etc. What uses of your object do these transformations suggest [p. 159]?" An illustration is a brick, with a hole in it, to be used as a pencil holder. In this experiment, word association training and instructions to be original were helpful, but training in strategies, or heuristics, produced much larger gains in terms of unique uses. Similar heuristics training, as well as word association training, yielded improvement on the plot title problem also.

Long checklists of suggestions for improving a product, although they may contain useful information, are not as effective as one might expect, according to a recent study by Warren and Davis (1969). Given the assignment of writing ideas for improving a doorknob, college students with a long checklist of 73 hints actually produced fewer ideas than a control group, but those with a short list produced more. The most productive technique in this experiment, however, was one called morphological synthesis (Allen, 1962), which requires analysis of the dimensions of the problem followed by a new synthesis. Ideas for improving one feature of the product are listed along one axis of a two-dimensional diagram and ideas for another feature are listed on another axis so that novel combinations appear at the intersections. It was this technique, along with the short checklist of hints, that stimulated the largest output of ideas. These two techniques also generated more ideas that were superior in respect to the experimenters' ratings of originality and practicality—because of the general quantity effect. Mean ratings of originality and practicality were not improved, however. Klein, Frederiksen, and Evans (1969) also found an increase in the quantity but not the quality of hypotheses written by college students to explain research data as a result of having a list of acceptable hypotheses.

CONFLICTING VALUES IN THE SCHOOL ENVIRONMENT

The conflict in universities and research organizations between pressure for creative achievement and pressure for more immediate practical achievement has often been described. The demands on the adult come partly from his own motivation, since he does have options for adjusting his own life style to the demands of different environments. Children, on the other hand, are much more vulnerable to the demands of the school environment. Pressures from parents, teachers, and peers, some explicit and some implicit, can operate to strengthen or weaken the effects of deliberately planned training programs. There is considerable agreement about the value of reading, writing, and arithmetic, but less about encouraging children to turn out fanciful ideas of their own before they have mastered the sound ideas of their elders.

After unsuccessful attempts at improving children's creative performance in the classroom, Torrance (1965) turned to an examination of the teachers' attitudes since some seemed to enjoy the opportunity to encourage creative activities while others seemed to be threatened by wild ideas and irritated by irrelevant questions. From his observation of teachers' responses to children's imaginative activities and questions, Torrance then constructed an attitude inventory for creative motivation—reflecting an inquiring, searching, reaching-out, and courageous attitude—as contrasted with critical motivation—reflecting a controlling, censoring, and inhibiting attitude. Tests of creative thinking were given in 20 elementary-school classes and again, with alternate forms, five months later, so that the gains in different classes could be related to the attitudes of the teachers in these classes. For the pupils, the training program stressed quantity rather than quality, avoidance of criticism, combination of ideas, reading constructively, word games, and challenging assignments. For the teachers, it stressed respect for children's questions and imaginative ideas, and encouragement of self-initiated learning without evaluation. A comparison of scores before and after training showed that more children in the primary and intermediate grades improved than in the kindergarten, as one might expect; but it was in the kindergarten that the favorable influence of teachers with creative attitudes was most evident. In a similar way, Torrance compared stories written by children over a four-month period and found more improvement (in terms of ratings of sensitivity, originality, and richness) in stories from children taught by teachers with favorable attitudes toward creativity.

Variations in instructions (illustrated earlier) were applied by Torrance to a regular classroom assignment in four sixth-grade classes and amplified by a monetary reward. The pupils were asked to write stories around one of several suggested titles and were offered a prize for the best story. In two classes, they were told that the stories would be judged "on the basis of how interesting, exciting, unusual, and original they are"; in the other two classes, the stories were to be judged "on correctness of spelling, punctuation, grammar, and sentence structure [p. 134]." Substantial differences were found in the expected directions. The emphasis on originality allowed more than twice as many errors but led to higher ratings for originality and interest. Depending on the environmental reward, children of this age can trade off grammar for originality just as college students can trade off practicality for originality.

EVALUATION OF CLASSROOM TRAINING PROGRAMS

Very encouraging results have followed a broad but carefully conceived and executed program described by Crutchfield (1966) for fifth and sixth grades. He used a loose style of programming, in large chunks rather than small steps, that encourages the children to think about the complex materials presented and directs the reinforcement, not toward right answers to simple questions, but toward the production of original and relevant ideas. Each lesson consists of a problem in story form, illustrated with cartoons, in a 40-page booklet requiring about 30 minutes to do. The readers can identify with boy and girl characters solving a series of detective problems and other mysterious occurrences, but the lessons are written and sequenced to instruct the reader in helpful procedures for creative problem solving: the formulation of the problem, the asking of relevant questions, the laying out of a plan of attack, the generation of many ideas, the search for uncommon ideas, the transformation of the problem in new ways, the evaluation of hypotheses, the sensitivity to odd and discrepant facts, and the openness to metaphorical and analogical hints leading to solutions. The program was planned for practice on component processes but these were integrated into a coherent attack on a concrete problem. Sixteen such lessons, one a day in regular classes, required three or four weeks.

Two evaluation studies, conducted in regular classes, followed the training with new problems of the complex open-end type calling for multiple solutions. As compared with matched control groups of 214 children in the same classes, trained groups of 267 children asked more questions, and generated more ideas, which got higher ratings for creative quality. In fact, the superiority of the trained children was greatest on the most critical measure, percentage of creative solutions. As one might expect, the difference on those problems most unlike the training problems was smaller, but even the transfer to such problems was substantial. The usual correlation of test performance with intelligence appeared; but when the children were divided into 3 IQ levels, the superiority of the trained children over the untrained was about the same at all levels. And a follow-up test 5 months later, when the children were in different classes, disclosed a reduced but still definite superiority for the trained children.

Another evaluation of these procedures and materials (Olton and Crutchfield, 1969) went beyond previous studies by extending the training period from 4 to 8 weeks, by bringing the teacher into an active role in stimulating and guiding class discussion of the materials, and by adding supplementary exercises on diversified topics in social studies, science, human relations, and current affairs. Although 280 students in fifth and sixth grades were involved, the clearest comparison was between 25 fifth-grade students in an instruction group and 25 matched students in a control group. At the end of the 8 weeks, the instruction group was distinctly superior to the control group on a composite score representing the various productive thinking skills. And on a follow-up test of different problems of the same type 6 months later, the instruction group was still distinctly superior.

Others have not obtained such encouraging results. Treffinger and Ripple (1969) used the same training materials in grades 4, 5, 6, and 7, but their measures of achievement after training were the Torrance tests of creative thinking and tests of arithmetic problem solving. By these measures, there was no evidence for superiority of the instruction group. They used only the programmed materials and concluded that the lack of improvement, even on tests of divergent thinking, indicates the importance of the classroom environment and of active involvement by the teacher. Transfer to convergent thinking, as in arithmetic problem solving, is perhaps too much to expect.

A training program designed by Davis and Houtman (1968) for grades 6, 7, and 8 incorporates checklists of attributes of objects in order to encourage feature analysis and synthesis, and a simplified kind of morphological synthesis in the form of an illustrated story about a boy, a girl, a backyard scientist, and a pet bear. A preliminary field test (Davis, Houtman, Warren, and Roweton, 1969) compared 21 students who volunteered for the creative thinking course with 32 students who volunteered for a creative writing course. After 10 weeks of training 3 tests were administered, asking the students to change or improve a hot dog, a doorknob, and a coat hanger. On each problem, the students with creativity training produced many more ideas and more that were rated as original. These results could be due to a general quantity effect, but, in addition, the mean ratings of all ideas for originality were higher in the experimental group. As in the Manske and Davis (1968) experiment, ratings of practicality were inversely correlated with ratings of originality; mean ratings of practicality of ideas were slightly lower for the experimental group on each of the three problems. Nevertheless, because of the quantity effect, more ideas that were rated as practical were produced by the experimental group. An extreme example of the quantity effect is the finding that, even though originality and practicality were inversely correlated, the experimental group produced more ideas rated both original and practical on two of the three problems than the group without creativity training.

The contribution of the teacher showed up again when an evaluation of performance gains on creativity tests compared a printed program with regular instructors in 6 high schools (Reese and Parnes, 1970). The program consisted of practice on 28 booklets, two 40-minute sessions a week, for 13 weeks; the teachers used the same materials but also interacted with the students. The students who had the program improved more (from pre-test to posttest performance) than students in control groups, but the ones who improved most were those who had the additional benefits of the teachers' instruction.

All in all, these programs for training creative thinking seem to be most effective under two conditions: (1) when the posttests are similar to the training materials, and (2) when the printed materials are supported by the influence of the teacher. As usual, the question of transfer has arisen, but how far should we expect the benefits of the training to transfer? Certainly, the improvement will transfer most completely to new problems similar in content and format to the training materials. A teacher of writing would not expect to find much help in a list of hints for solving engineering problems. Attempts to improve creative thinking in other areas will have to use appropriate training materials—though the format and materials of the present programs may suggest possibilities.

These programs are multiple programs, teaching cognitive skills of various kinds, problem-solving strategies, information about creative thinking, and favorable attitudes toward new ideals. For deeper understanding, it would be desirable also if the various components of the training were studied separately so that the reasons for the gains could be specified more distinctly. The effectiveness of the Purdue Creativity Program, for example, appears to be due to different components or combinations of components at different grade levels (Feldhusen, Treffinger, and Bahlke, 1970). The effects of the printed program and of the environment generated by the teacher have not yet been clearly differentiated. Nevertheless, from the magnitude of the gains reported under the best conditions we can infer that these skills had not been practiced previously, in school or at home, and that well-planned practice is worthwhile. The recent development of tests of divergent production of behavioral ideas (Hendricks, Guilford, and Hoepfner, 1969) may shift the emphasis away from the improvement of gadgets and the solution of physical problems toward creative thinking about social and environmental problems. The fifth grade is not too early to start.

JUDGMENT TRAINING

Judgment of the solutions, the conclusive phase of thought, should ideally be a cool deliberative process, but there seems, at first glance, to be an inconsistency between training for this and for the ideal of enthusiastic imaginative thought. The inconsistency vanishes, of course, if production and judgment are different processes, separated in time, hence the superordinate assumption of thought control is implicit in such training programs. We do not expect that training directed toward a judicious choice among tentative solutions will interfere with training directed toward copious production of solutions because we assume that the thinker can turn these complementary processes on and off adaptively under appropriate conditions. It is not likely that any kind of training will make the thinker produce more deliberately and choose more enthusiastically.

This separation of production and judgment in time does not mean, however, that improvement in one process cannot affect the other. Some improvement in the judgment of plot titles as a result of producing plot titles has been obtained (Johnson and Zerbolio, 1964), probably because in their effort to produce clever titles the subjects clarified their criteria of cleverness, which benefited their subsequent judgments of the titles.

Several types of judgment practice were arranged by Johnson, Parrott and Stratton (1968) for training in judging solutions to the five problems described above. The training included study of a rating guide which the expert judges had developed, practice in selecting the best one of several triads of solutions—with knowledge of results and explanations for the official selections—and practice in contrasting superior and inferior solutions. Some subjects had the practice individually, others worked cooperatively in pairs, and others again had the benefit of tutorial practice with an experimenter; but the sequence of activities was the same for all: production of many solutions, practice in judging solutions written by others, selection of the best of those produced by the subject himself.

There are two questions about the value of such judgment training: Will it increase the difference between the solutions selected as best and the remainder, and will the ones selected as best be better than single solutions written under standard conditions? For the first question, the judgment training generally was successful. Among subjects who wrote many solutions, the difference between the quality of any one subject's preferred solution and the mean quality of his nonpreferred solutions was larger for groups with judgment training than for comparable groups without it. For the second question also the judgment training was successful, but there were exceptions. The quality of the solutions selected as best is the joint consequence of quality of solutions produced and accuracy of judgment. When instructions to produce many solutions debased the quality of the solutions severely, even the ones selected as best were no better than the single solutions produced under standard conditions. Otherwise, however, this brief training in judgment appears to be a useful technique for raising the quality of the best single solution.

What the subjects learn during this practice appears to be the criterion of judgment: the conceptualized dimension of quality, what features of the solutions are relevant to this dimension, and what features are irrelevant. In certain circumstances, it may be more practical to obtain improvement in the final solution by training in judgment than by training in production.

If judgment training is really helpful, it should transfer to a second problem, and such transfer was obtained in a study of the Sentences problem (Stratton, Parrott, and Johnson, 1970). One effect of the judgment training was an improvement in mean quality of the sentences written around a second set of four words, as compared with control groups without judgment training. Relatively few low-quality sentences were produced on the second occasion, so the comparison of preferred and nonpreferred sentences did not give impressive evidence of the effects of the judgment training. But a group of subjects who had a multiple-choice test of judgment of sentences, without producing any, registered substantial gains on a second sentence problem, as compared with control groups. Probably the best sign of the effects of the judgment training was that the quality of the preferred solutions on the second problem was significantly higher for those who had the benefit of judgment training.

Since judgment training helps subjects to write high-quality solutions and select the best of these, the obvious next step was to give the benefit of judgment training to those subjects who write only one solution. When this was done, the performance on a second problem was substantially superior to that of control groups writing one and to that of control groups writing many. To sum up, the optimal condition among the many that have been investigated (Johnson, 1968), was to ask the subject to write one solution to a problem, with the benefit of information about the criteria for good solutions and with training in the judgment of solutions.

Production and judgment training have both been effective, in different ways, so Stratton and Brown (1972) designed a comprehensive experiment on writing plot titles, as many as possible in seven minutes, that included production training, adapted from Allen's (1962) morphological synthesis, judgment training as described above, and a combination of the two. The production training resulted in a large increase in the number of solutions written but no increase in the mean quality of these solutions. The judgment training resulted in a significant increase in mean quality of the solutions produced and, of course, in accuracy of judgment. As to the number of superior solutions, plot titles rated above the 90th percentile in quality, both kinds of training were effective, and detailed analysis implied, as the authors put it, that the subjects with production training generated superior solutions by virtue of their fluency and those with judgment training by virtue of their selectivity. The combination of the two types of training was not a simple addition, but those who had both types combined produced solutions of higher mean quality than those with only production training and a larger number of solutions than those with only judgment training. We may hope that combined training increases flexibility of thought control, leading to high productivity under appropriate conditions and critical judgment under other appropriate conditions, but this is only a hope at present.

Production Controls

Having identified the processes by which ideas are produced, we should next describe the controls on these processes: what turns them on and off, what directs and limits them, and how they are affected by training and individual differences. The description is necessarily speculative, but the research outlined above supplies an empirical foundation. We can discuss controls on production with reference to the three processes—preparation, production, and judgment—around which much of the research has revolved. The discussion would not differ greatly if other names were given to the processes which account for the empirical results.

The preparation process is turned on and the preceding routine activity turned off by an environmental obstacle which impedes routine activity, by cognition of an unexplained event, or by questions or instructions from another person. There are large individual differences in willingness to stop and think, which go by such names as interest in abstract thought and sensitivity to problems. If the individual accepts the problem, then the preparation process continues until he feels that he is ready to produce a solution. This readiness for production, which involves a personal parameter as well as the objective conditions and the instructions, controls both the duration of the preparation period and its adequacy.

The production process, once started, is controlled by the preparation and several other factors identified by the above research and discussed below. The duration of production is controlled by the criterion of achievement, feelings of boredom, and the like. If more than one solution has been produced and only one is to be submitted, conclusion of production triggers a judgment process, which typically continues until one solution has been chosen.

Thus it appears that one process continues until it reaches some criterion or threshold, then the next begins. Overlap is also possible: production may begin before the preparation is finished, as when one reads to get ideas for a solution. Presumably, the criterion of readiness for the second operation is approached asymptotically, hence it is reasonable to expect that the second operation may begin before the first ceases completely. Judgment often begins before many solutions have been produced, and the judgment of solutions often leads to a retroflex shift in the criterion that controls production. If all solutions are judged inadequate and motivation persists, the judgment process initiates another try at production, or even another preparation.

CLASSES AND MODELS

Much research and discussion suggest that the production of words and other items can be viewed as sampling from a class of items, as in writing down the names of cities—given the usual instructions, the subject names cities rather than automobiles or prime numbers, and the output is controlled by his knowledge of the class and of instances of the class. This is a point at which the psychology of thought joins the psychology of memory, and an explanation of the retrieval of previously learned items to fit specific instructions will advance an explanation of productive thinking also. The class may be diminished in size and the control increased by additional restrictions, such as a request to produce cities that have symphony orchestras or uses for a coat hanger that are both original and practical. When several such restrictions are added, the assignment approaches memory for a single item.

It would be a mistake, however, to assume that sampling from a class is typical of productive thought. Suppose the assignment is to name cities of medium size. The adult subject has a dimensional concept (size of cities) but it is not likely that the interval called *medium* on this dimension has definite boundaries. It is more likely that the subject has a conceptualized point, albiet rather indefinite, on the size dimension and that production is biased by proximity to this point. Thus, if someone wrote down the names of 50 cities of medium size, a distribution of these plotted on the actual size dimension would be unimodal rather than U-shape, and the subject's concept of *medium* would be better represented by computation of the mean and standard deviation than by computation of the boundaries between *medium* and *small* on the one side and between *medium* and *large* on the other. The lesson to be learned from this example is that production may be controlled by a conceptualized ideal or model as well as by a conceptualized class. It may be convenient to talk about multidimensional classes and the intersection of sets of solutions, but more often production is controlled by a conceptualized model, defined by the intersection of dimensions or attributes. Production of solutions to the Sentences problem, for example, is controlled, first of all, by the class. That is, the product is supposed to be a sentence, not a single word or an unstructured list of words. Within this class, production is biased toward the high end of the cleverness dimension and the high end of the smoothness dimension. The obtrusiveness of the given words is supposed to be low. No doubt there are other dimensions, not made explicit by experimenter or subject, which also influence production. The records show that some subjects produce mostly short sentences, others mostly long sentences. None of the records contained obscene words. Hence the subject's production of solutions is guided by the conceptualized model which he has formulated: what he puts in, what he leaves out, which dimensions he considers primary, which he considers secondary, and so on.

RESPONSE HIERARCHIES FROM THE PAST
AND ANTICIPATIONS FOR THE FUTURE

A naïve reader of research on productive thinking could easily get the impression that the researchers are opposed to thought; they want their subjects to respond immediately. But serious thinkers often contemplate a problem for a while, analyzing the relevant features and anticipating what a good solution might be. Observation of a child playing with blocks will often justify the inference that he has a preview of his end product—he wants it to be big or to look like a truck—even before he has learned the responses necessary for attaining his goal. Production is for a purpose. Just as a sentence is produced in order to communicate, a solution is produced in order to fit some specifications, to perform some function. The control of production by a response hierarchy is control by the past; the control by a conceptualized model constructed to meet certain specifications for a solution is control by anticipation of future achievement.

Analysis of the requirements for a solution often begins by listening and reading, which are preparatory information-seeking processes, and it often involves a feature analysis. Feature analysis in the perception of a complex pattern, as described by Neisser (1967), probably has something in common with feature analysis in preparation for production of solutions, although the former proceeds much faster. Listening to the instructions for a word association test, for example, the subject figures out what the experimenter expects, what role he himself is supposed to play, what attributes of words are important, and so on. Studying the chart for the Conclusions problem, the thinker sees a time dimension, a program dimension, and probably more abstract features. He ignores many other features of the objective situation. Records of the production of plot titles illustrate how many different features of a plot can be picked out as the basis for construction of a title. The thinker then tries to construct a solution to match the requirements as he understands them. Hence his production is controlled by his preview of the solution to be produced at the same time that it is controlled by the strength of the responses that have been produced.

When the subject knows little about the solutions required, as in writing unusual uses and word associations under standard conditions, the influence of the response hierarchy is strong. But when he is told, or infers, that the solutions should have certain properties, the relative influence of the response hierarchy decreases and the influence of the model increases. This conceptualized model should not be treated merely as a search model, controlling exploration of the physical environment and search through the recesses of memory to find the needed item; it should rather be treated as a construction model, controlling the assembly of old parts and the invention of new patterns to fit the pattern of requirements anticipated. As production proceeds, the thinker may, of course, reanalyze the problem, may shift the emphasis on different dimensions of the solution, and may reorganize the dimensions into a quite different model, but this is likely to be a multidimensional model composed of several dimensions and classes.

THE PRODUCTION CONCEPT

The conceptualized model of the desired solution can be called a production concept since it has many of the properties of other concepts and can be investigated by the methods of concept research. Consider first the task of drawing a tree. In the field, the artist's activity is guided by perception of a specific tree. In the studio, his activity is guided by a memory image of a specific tree or perhaps by a general concept of a tree. Or he modifies the general concept to include more abstract, imaginary dimensions: a stunted tree representing despair, a flourishing tree representing hope. Next, consider the construction of a sentence to communicate a complex thought. It is reasonable to assume that the speaker's vocal output is guided by a prior conception of what he wishes to communicate. Such examples suggest that the production concept operates positively, as a target or goal toward which production is directed. The thinker's satisfaction with his achievement is evaluated subjectively in terms of the agreement of the output with the conceptualized goal. Discrepancies from that conceptualized goal are rejected, as when the artist erases a line that does not give the effect he wants and when the speaker interrupts himself to revise his sentence. Thus the control includes a feedback component, a recurrent evaluation of progress toward the goal.

In the solution of a more abstract problem, a production concept has much in common with a class concept, such as the concept of *sonnet* or *aggression*. A production concept is a general conceptualization of the solution, not a specific solution, just as a class concept is a generalization, not a specific instance of the class. Like a class concept, a production concept is a cognitive achievement, based on previous experience, present circumstances, and social communication. Unlike a class concept, which is standard in the culture and associated with a standard label, a production concept is usually a transient, idiosyncratic, unlabeled achievement of the individual, instrumental only to solution of the present problem. Thus the class concept guides classification of objects and communication about objects, while the production concept guides production of solutions and, to a limited degree, communication about solutions.

The production concepts that different individuals construct for the solution of a complex problem vary in many attributes, some of which are discrete features or classes, while others are continuous dimensions. More important, some attributes are explicitly included in the task assignment as requirements of the desired solution while others are not. If the problem has many good solutions, those attributes included in the instructions are easily incorporated into the production concept and normally appear in all solutions. Students asked to write plot titles write plot titles and those asked to draw trees draw trees. The variations in output are due to variations in ability, to be sure, and also to variations in additional attributes included in the conceptualization of the desired solution. Thus it happens that most solutions are acceptable in that they include the explicitly stated criteria, but they vary on other dimensions that can be treated as additional criteria of evaluation. It is these additional unspecified, or imprecisely specified, dimensions—such as practicality, style, and scope—that make the production assignment somewhat ambiguous and permit production concepts to vary widely between individuals and conditions.

The idea of a production concept is not altogether new. The "anticipatory schema" was discussed long ago in the context of experimental introspection (see Chapter 1), and more recently the "plan" was discussed in the context of computer simulation (Miller, Galanter, and Pribram, 1960). The research reviewed in this chapter ties the old idea more directly to empirical data on productive thinking. The hypothesis of the control of thought by a production concept cannot be validated by production records alone, however, because there are alternative explanations for the records. But if the thinker has constructed a concept that controls his production of solutions, it will also influence his judgment of solutions—both his own and those produced by others—and his verbal description of his production concept. Let us say that past experience and working conditions lead an individual to construct a production concept for a given problem with practicality as an important dimension. He will therefore produce practical solutions, within the limits of his ability; and, if asked to judge solutions produced by others, he will give high ratings to practical solutions. If he is asked to describe his production concept by ranking several relevant dimensions of the solutions, he will rank practicality high. Other conditions that lead to production concepts emphasizing other dimensions (such as originality or comprehensiveness) will have corresponding effects on production, judgment, and verbal description.

INTERNALIZATION OF CONTROLS

It is often assumed that, when asked to write a solution to a problem of the type considered here, the subject thinks of several solutions before writing down his best one. If so, the process can perhaps be laid open for inspection by asking the subject to write these several solutions as he produces them. But we cannot assume without evidence that production of many solutions is a slowed-down version of production of one solution. There is a possible fallacy here, comparable to the fallacy of assuming that perception of a figure under repeated tachistoscopic exposures is a slowed-down version of perception under normal exposure. It is especially hazardous to assume that what happens in an effective condition, the single-solution condition, is a condensed version of what happens in a less effective condition, the multiple-solution condition.

Evidently, multiple-solution production has some value as training for single-solution production; the two procedures must have something in common. But the research summarized in this chapter demonstrates that the controls on single-solution production are more restrictive than the controls on multiple-solution production and suggests how these controls are developed. When someone is asked to write many solutions, we have seen that he usually takes this as permission to relax his standards and write solutions of lower quality. When instructions about the criteria of good solutions are given, the number of solutions is smaller and the quality higher. Does this mean that production continues as before and that solutions which do not meet the criteria are then rejected? Probably not. As compared with ordinary multiple-solution groups, multiple-solution groups with criteria information write solutions of higher mean quality but the standard deviations are not smaller. The effect of the criteria information is to improve quality evenly along the quality scale. Hence it seems likely that the criteria information is used by the subject to formulate a more adequate model for production, not that it is applied after production has occurred. The checklists, hints about strategies, and other materials of the training programs, along with the rewards from a supportive environment, may in effect supply criteria information. They may aid judgment as well as production, but, if the program is successful, the subjects probably build these features into the controls on the production process.

The same argument is relevant to simpler responses, as in discrimination experiments of the signal-detection type. The subject could make responses and later, by a separate process, judge each response right or wrong. In fact, he is more likely to control his activity in advance, establishing a strict criterion of accuracy and achieving a low error rate, or a weak criterion, depending on the instructions about the payoff or his previous experience with it.

Practice in judgment of solutions has a similar effect on the control of production. It appears that the criteria of judgment, once learned, are internalized and so control the production of solutions as well as the judgment after they are produced.

The beneficial effects of criteria information and practice in judgment are not properly described merely as a tightening of controls. It is true that the number of solutions is reduced, but the more important effect is a positive one: the construction of a more specific model for production.

Major Trends and Implications

The intellectual glow that radiates from the great thinkers of yesterday lighting up goals for ambitious young men and women today also outlines a field of study, a division of the psychology of problem solving. The creative achievements of the geniuses of history—and those of eminent living artists and scientists as well—have been characterized, in varying amounts, on such dimensions as intellectual leadership, sensitivity to problems, originality, and unusualness of output. The criteria by which these have been evaluated are product records, peer judgments, and work samples. Distinction is rare, the consequence jointly of favorable circumstances and a creative individual.

Creative thinkers, identified by these criteria and contrasted with comparable men and women, are distinguished on the average by high intelligence, good education in their own field, a strong preference for choosing their own goals, and an equally strong drive toward achieving these goals. Scientists, particularly, prefer intellectually challenging situations and tend to avoid distracting social situations. There are differences between fields, but creative thinkers in general seem to be independent individuals, capable of resisting pressures toward conformity from their families and teachers when they are young and, later, from peers and supervisors. They start early and do their best work when relatively young. Since creative individuals are usually studied after they have become eminent and adjusted to the public role of deep thinker, some of the distinctive traits may be results of this role. But others, such as high intelligence, an interest in abstract thought rather than social interaction, and independence, are manifested early in life.

Creativity test scores have been obtained from tasks as simple as the association of one word with another, objectively scored for unusualness, and as complex as the writing of plot titles, rated for cleverness by trained judges. Scores on different tests have enough in common to identify an originality factor by the techniques of factor analysis, but it must be a weak, poorly defined factor because in many studies the correlations between tests of creativity are as low as the correlations of these with intelligence. When a battery of creativity tests is administered and the total scores correlated with intelligence tests, the correlations are in the low and medium ranges for the most part, although influenced by the nature of the sample and the circumstances of testing. Scores on standard measures of educational achievement can be predicted better by intelligence tests than by creativity tests. But if creativity tests are purified and if the current emphasis on creativity actually has an effect on measures of school achievement, correlations with intelligence will decrease and correlations with creativity scores increase.

Attempts to describe the personality traits and adjustment of high scorers on creativity tests, in spite of many inconsistencies, have yielded some agreement with the distinctive traits of the creative thinkers of history. Laboratory tests of more specific intellectual traits, constructed according to a hypothesis about associations, suggest that the high scorers deploy their attention broadly and thus receive a broad range of information which they can later use adaptively.

Predictions of creative achievement, like other predictions, are difficult, and the criteria of creative achievement, like other criteria, complex. Nevertheless, some success has been reported in identifying productive scientists in large laboratories, by a variety of predictors, especially the biographical data bank. The usefulness of intelligence and education as predictors is limited by the conditions of employment; but work habits, family interests and activities, and personal orientations that take shape early in life and can be investigated through the collection of biographical data, are all useful.

While many organizations dependent on research and scholarly production are attempting to progress by identifying and attracting creative thinkers, others are attempting to better the working conditions of the personnel they have. The two policies are not independent; surveys of scientists' likes and dislikes indicate that the optimal conditions for creative work are the conditions that attract and hold creative thinkers: financial support, laboratory facilities and technical assistance, communication with colleagues, and free choice of research problems, methods, and deadlines.

The problems solved in laboratory research on conditions and processes of creative thought can be criticized as trivial, but the intent is to discover general principles that will apply also to problems of more substance. A separation of the processes is worthwhile, perhaps necessary, because the principles may be specific to processes. Three candidates, with some support for their independence, are preparation, production, and judgment. Preparation most often consists of collecting information by reading, integrating the relevant material, and getting set for the next process. The information thus collected is more useful for productive thinking if the reading is done with a constructive rather than a critical emphasis.

As to the old question of the relation between quality and quantity, it is clear that subjects instructed to write one solution write solutions of higher mean quality than those instructed to write many, but the latter write more superior solutions because of a general quantity effect. Among those who write many solutions, instructions not to evaluate seem to be helpful but even more helpful are instructions that are specific about the criteria of evaluation. Instructions shift the emphasis from quality to quantity, or the reverse, but information about criteria of good solutions makes a more positive contribution to the production process—both for those who write many solutions and for those who write one. The quality-quantity relation varies between problems also. Problems at the convergent end of the convergent-divergent continuum have only one good solution, so attempts to produce many solutions result in many low-quality solutions; problems at the divergent end of this continuum have many good solutions, so attempts to produce many solutions result in only a slight drop in quality. For similar reasons, studies of individual differences with simple tasks show positive correlations between quantity produced and number of superior solutions, but the corresponding correlations for more substantial problems are near zero. Correlations between quantity and mean quality are generally negative.

Records of production sequences afford an opportunity to test the current hypotheses about production processes, but no single hypothesis accounts for all the data. On simple tasks the common responses occur early, followed by the uncommon responses, which are considered of higher quality. But there are differences due both to conditions and to problems. Typically, instructions to write many solutions are taken as permission to lower quality, after which improvement can easily occur. When instructions specify evaluation and include the criteria for good solutions, no such improvement occurs. When the problems involve convergent thinking, better solutions are produced in the first half.

Producing solutions without judging them is incomplete—like mixing drinks without tasting them. When college students select one solution from several produced by them, the one selected is better than the average of the others not selected, but this difference is not large. The solutions selected under such conditions are no better, on the average, than comparable solutions produced by subjects who write only one. Even in the case of minor laboratory problems, analysis of the thinker's judging operations along with his producing operations generates a more complete description of intellectual activity and suggests possibilities for improvement. But the judging operations of reviewers, editors, and others who evaluate someone else's products also deserve psychological analysis. It is possible to determine the relative weights which reviewers attach to the various dimensions of complex solutions and perhaps to train the producers accordingly. These possibilities illustrate again, in more detail than usual, the dependence of the productive thinker on the social environment in which he attempts to make his mark.

Although serious attempts to train productive thinking in industry and in school have been carried on for only a decade or so, encouraging progress has been reported. The brainstorming techniques taught in courses in creative problem solving have resulted in some improvement on tests of creative thinking. And so has associative practice in giving uncommon responses. The favorable outcomes do not unequivocally support the hypotheses that generated the training programs, however. Improvement in performance on these simple tasks may not indicate any increase in intellectual skill but may result from a temporary shift of set—as from an emphasis on quality to an emphasis on quantity—which under some conditions can raise scores. The social side of the training must also be considered in the interpretation because in most training situations the alert subject can easily figure out the criteria of a good solution so as to give the experimenter what he expects and can even learn to play the role of original thinker.

Training in strategies of production has used more substantial problems, involving the explanation of mysterious occurrences, as training materials and as tests of achievement. This training has included a variety of thought processes as well as class discussions, so the success that has been obtained does not clearly specify the nature of the improvement. It does offer considerable promise for educational practice. The training transfers to other problems of the same type, perhaps not to problems of a different type.

These programs generate an increased interest in productive thinking and encourage a more playful attitude toward problem solving. Hence, critics have suggested that the favorable interest and attitude may explain the training's success, especially in school and industry where conformity to institutional norms can easily spread to conformity of thought. This is a convincing criticism of the theoretical basis of the training, but is it a criticism of the practice? Any procedure, in school or in industry, that bestows institutional respectability on original thinking cannot be all bad.

The realization that solutions to a problem have to be screened by someone leads to attempts to train the judgment phase of productive thought. Reasonable gains have been obtained on several substantial problems and, as with training procedures, these gains then transfer to other problems of the same type, but the extent of the transfer has not yet been determined.

The central question of productive thinking is one of thought control. Although production may be conceived as association of ideas, or as sampling from a class of objects, more often it is controlled by an ideal or model of the required solution, constructed from the relevant dimensions of the problem situation. While the flow of ideas is biased by response hierarchies from the past, it is at the same time controlled by anticipation of the future achievement. As knowledge of the specifications of the solution increases, the influence of response hierarchies is replaced by the influence of the conceptualized model.

While it may appear that the production of many solutions is an expansion of the production of one, the evidence indicates that the controls are different. Instructions to write many solutions reduce standards and lower the quality of output, though some improvement may follow. More specific instructions, giving the criteria of good solutions and requiring judgment of the solutions, raise the quality of output not, negatively, by more restrictions but, positively, by facilitating construction of a more specific production model. The controls could be applied to the rejection and selection of solutions after they are produced, but the data suggest, on the contrary, that the controls are built into the conceptualized construction model and influence production from the outset.

CHAPTER 8

JUDGMENT: STIMULUS DIMENSIONS AND COMBINATIONS

Unidimensional Judgments ·
Multidimensional Judgments in Discrete Categories
Multidimensional Judgments on Continuous Scales
Some Characteristics of Judges
Major Trends and Implications

udgment has been defined as the assignment of an object to a small number of specified categories (Bieri, et al., 1966; Johnson, 1955). The object may be assigned to one of two complementary classes or to one of several intervals on a scale, but in either case the terms used by one person to describe an object to another, as well as the effect on his own behavior, depend on the outcome of the judgment. The categories are specified and the judgments are communicated by various sets of category names: *guilty* and *not guilty; strongly approve, approve, neutral, disapprove* and *strongly disapprove;* 1, 2, 3, 4, 5, 6, and 7. This assignment of objects to categories is not random, to be sure, nor is judgment simply the discrimination of a difference between objects. Logically, judgment has the function of settling an uncertain state of affairs—in contrast to productive thought, which may be quite unsettling—and in judgment experiments the final state is more orderly than the initial state. The order may be achieved by assigning a hundred objects to seven categories or by stating priorities for choices and actions; but, in general, the state of affairs that impeded routine activity and instigated the judging process becomes less confusing, less obstructive to further activity.

The critical dimensions to which attention is directed and responses are related are determined by the situation in which the judgment occurs. When judgment occurs as the conclusive phase of a complex problem-solving enterprise in which the thinker halts his productive activity to evaluate his productions, the critical dimensions are consequences of the conditions (such as motivation and previous experience) that started all this. When judgment involves the comparison of alternative courses of action, the critical dimensions may be as varied as financial gain, intellectual enjoyment or bodily comfort. In psychophysical judgment, the critical dimension is usually a simple one, implicit in the set of category names, such as *long, medium,* and *short.* In general, the thinker tries to match the response categories, or output, with certain dimensions of the objects of judgment, or input. As Stevens (1966a) put it, after extensive experience with psychophysical judgments by several procedures, "the core of the act of judgment is a process of matching [p. 385]." Hence a more complete statement would be that *judgment begins with unordered objects, events, or persons, assigns them to specified response categories so as to maximize the correspondence between the responses and the critical dimension of the stimulus objects, and thus ends with a more orderly situation.*

In psychological terminology *judgment* seems to be the general term, probably because interest in these processes grew out of psychophysical judgment, but other terms are applied in special situations. The word *rating* appears frequently when judgments are made on a scale of numbered categories. If the critical dimension is one of value, as when the judgment follows productive thinking, the term *evaluation* may be used and the categories are likely to have value-laden names, such as *acceptable* and *unacceptable.* If the judgment involves the outcomes of alternative courses of action, it is often called a *decision* and then the categories have such names as *buy* and *don't buy.* The term *preference* is used to emphasize personal taste or individuality, and the term *choice* seems to embrace both preferences and decisions.

A judgment can be considered the solution of a special kind of problem, in accordance with the discussion of problem solving in Chapter 4. The first tentative response is not the final response. Judgment involves some delay, some uncertainty, and some variability within and between subjects. And the response may be mediated by a conceptualized dimension, such as cleverness, guilt, or length. In distinction to other problems, however, judgment is conclusive, not productive. New solutions are not produced, but alternatives are decided. These matters of judgment, as we call them, are not always settled completely, however; variations in ·confidence in the judgment may be expected.

It is the dimension mediating the judgments that distinguishes this process from discrimination. If the task is to compare two lines and say which is longer, this could be called discrimination as well as judgment. But if the task is to rate ten lines by length, then each separate response is mediated by the common dimension of length. This is more than a terminological nicety; many animals can make sharp discriminations but no one expects them to make judgments. The distinctively human capacity is an ability to use the common dimension in judging separate objects. Piaget has noted that seriation develops later than classification (see Chapter 3), and the next chapter will show that accuracy of judgment is not the same as accuracy of discrimination.

Judgments made about an abstract dimension that is a common attribute of superficially different objects point up the dependence of judgment on concept formation. A judge cannot follow instructions to rate drinks for sweetness or children for defensiveness unless he knows the meanings of these dimensional concepts. Analogy with the results of concept experiments suggests that if a subject is presented a set of ten objects that vary in several dimensions and instructed only to rank them, he will rank in respect to their most salient dimension. But the ability to make consistent judgments of a particular dimension is not the same as the ability to name or to define the dimension. As in the case of a class concept, different measures of achievement of a dimensional concept are usually correlated but they are not identical.

The preparation for judgment may be instituted in several ways, most often by verbal instructions. "You are to judge the defendant guilty or not guilty solely on the basis of the evidence presented in this court." "Lift these weights one at a time and tell me if the second is lighter than, heavier than, or the same as the first." "Rate these children in respect to friendliness on a scale of 1 to 7." However it may be organized, the preparation accomplishes two things. It alerts the thinker, or directs his attention, to the relevant attributes of the stimulus objects and it specifies the alternative response categories. Thus the instructions, along with the stimulus materials, are the independent variables of experiments on judgment, relatively easy to manipulate.

Yet although the instructions may be simple, if the objects in view vary in more than one dimension, maintenance of a set for one dimension rather than another is difficult. Postman and Page (1947) demonstrated the effects of retroactive inhibition in psychophysical judgments of this kind by having their subjects judge rectangles for height, then for width, and then again for height. The precision of the second series of height judgments was disturbed by the interpolated activity, because of the interference of the set to judge width on the set to judge height.

When judgment occurs as the terminal operation of productive thinking, the preparation follows from the dynamics that initiated the thinking, and the thinker himself supplies the materials to be judged. In this case, manipulation of the conditions of judgment is more difficult but, as noted in the preceding chapter, not impossible.

Here we are concerned with stimulus variables, or the input side of judgment, moving from unidimensional to multidimensional judgments; the next chapter will deal with response variables, or the output side.

Unidimensional Judgments

In referring to the stimulus variables, judgments can be treated as simple and complex, or unidimensional and multidimensional—though this distinction turns out to be less clear-cut than it sounds. Unidimensional judgments are those in which the objects of judgment vary mainly along the one dimension on which they are to be judged. When the objects vary in several dimensions, it often becomes an empirical question which dimension or combination of dimensions determines the judgments. There are three kinds of stimulus dimensions, and different procedures have been elaborated for the study of each, but some general principles of judgment have emerged.

THREE KINDS OF STIMULUS DIMENSIONS

PERCEPTUAL JUDGMENTS
The psychology of judgment started with psychophysics. Methods were invented to standardize judging operations so that thresholds could be determined and perceptual functions studied precisely. But certain constant errors—such as series effects, errors of central tendency, and anchor effects —turned up regularly. At first, these were treated as distorting influences, to be eliminated by a more careful methodology; but to some observers the constant errors were interesting in their own right. When the emphasis shifted from attempts to eliminate these effects to attempts to understand them, the psychology of judgment began to take shape.

AFFECTIVE JUDGMENTS AND CHOICES
A century ago Fechner, the father of psychophysics, tried to start an empirical science of esthetics by collecting data from hundreds of observers on their preferences for rectangles of different proportions. Studies of affective, or hedonic, judgment ask the observer how an object or event affects him, how pleasant or unpleasant it seems, which of several he would choose. Such judgments may be considered extensions and refinements of primitive approach and avoidance reactions, coded into communicable response categories. Most people adopt a set for these personal judgments easily because they enjoy directing their attention to the affective dimensions of their experiences. We all know that casual conversation is made up largely of exchanges of likes and dislikes. As an illustration, Fig. 8.1 plots some results of an early quantitative investigation by Saidullah (1927) of the pleasantness of salt solutions of different concentrations.

It is noteworthy that the stimulus materials, whether salt solutions, rectangles, or sounds, may be the same as for an experiment on perceptual

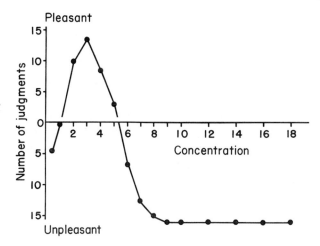

FIGURE 8.1. *Affective judgments of salt solutions. The ordinate indicates the number of pleasant judgments by several observers minus the number of unpleasant judgments, 16 being the maximum in either direction. Data from Saidullah (1927).*

judgment. The difference is in the instructions. The observers are not asked to judge the size of the rectangles or the concentration of the salt solutions but the pleasantness of each.

When someone chooses between alternative courses of action, as between going to a movie and reading a book, the basis for comparison is not so clear. The actions are apparently unrelated and the affect is anticipated rather than immediate. Although there is no obvious dimension common to the actions, the fact that choices are made suggests the hypothesis that the judge can compare the alternatives on a dimension of enjoyment or value to be expected from each. This dimension is called *expected value,* and under some conditions tabulation of choices permits calculation of the scale value of each alternative and prediction of subsequent choices.

ABSTRACT JUDGMENTS
Many educated people base their judgments on highly abstract attributes. An editor decides to publish one manuscript and to reject another; a teacher gives a term paper a grade of B; a psychologist states that a client's defenses are extremely weak; a merchant estimates the probability of increased sales following installation of air conditioning. All common dimensions on which diverse objects are judged are abstract, but some, such as defensiveness and probability, are more abstract than others, such as length and saltiness. Naturally, individual differences due to education and experience are more prominent in the more abstract areas.

Good evidence on the judging process also comes from research on economic and social attitudes, because attitude statements often have the form of affective judgments of abstract symbols and statements. "I am opposed to a state income tax." "A state income tax may be necessary under some conditions." "A state income tax distributes the wealth." Judges who aid in the construction of an attitude test have the task of assigning each statement of opinion to a position on a dimension (e.g., from antitax to protax), and the consistency of the judgments indicates the influence of this abstract dimension. Such dimensional concepts are properties of the culture as well as the individual judges.

Logicians commonly speak of a judgment as a proposition, or statement, and judgments of the logical validity of propositions are perhaps the most abstract of all. But from the psychological point of view, the judging process is a small part of formal reasoning in comparison with other processes, hence these matters were discussed in a previous chapter.

CONSISTENCY AND ACCURACY

SCALE CONSTRUCTION
It is not surprising that stable discriminations can be made and that objects can be consistently scaled on dimensions for which man has specialized sensory mechanisms. Consistencies that are obtained in scaling abstract objects, such as statements of opinion, are more relevant here because they are dependent on an acquired dimension, a property of the culture. If different judges agree in scaling statements for conservatism, whether they agree on the definition of conservatism or not, the agreement indicates a shared cultural dimension, in reference to which the statements are judged. Scaling methods are described elsewhere, but it should be noted here that the analysis of consistencies and inconsistencies in scaling contributes to knowledge of the judging process and, in exchange, knowledge of common phenomena of judgment improves scaling methodology. Furthermore, scaling procedures make possible the construction of stimulus materials to specifications for research.

INDIVIDUAL PREFERENCES
When someone in a cafeteria chooses apple pie rather than something else, he makes a decision that has interested businessmen and theoretical economists for many years and should be integrated with other judgments. Such a decision cannot be scored right or wrong so there is no measure of accuracy, but this does not mean that all is chaos. Man may not be a completely rational animal, but some consistency appears in his preferences; the story of research in this area is largely the story of a search for a model that will account for whatever consistencies are found in the choices.

One type of consistency that argues for rationality is *transitivity* of preferences. In a rational world, if A is preferred to B, and B is preferred to C, then A is preferred to C. Certainly, if you choose X dollars rather than Y dollars and Y dollars rather than Z dollars, you would choose X dollars rather than Z dollars. If you like apple pie more than blueberry pie and blueberry pie more than custard pie, consistency requires that you like apple pie more than custard pie. The relevant experiments have been conducted by offering an adult subject sets of alternatives, such as tickets to a concert, a tennis tournament, and a play. When choices of single individuals made from many sets of such alternatives are examined, considerable evidence for transitivity has been found (Edwards, 1954). Conditions can be arranged that disclose intransitivity of choices, especially when the alternatives are multidimensional, but even in such cases some order or "semiorder" can usually be discovered (Tversky, 1969).

The high frequency of transitive choices, among simple alternatives, suggests that in making his choices the subject is expecting to get more of something good or, in general psychological terms, is maximizing expected value. Going to a tennis match may be independent of going to a concert, but when one is forced to choose between them, the relative position of each on the judge's scale of values is critical. Choices made as in the example above indicate that the judge has a scale of values on which B lies between A and C. It is only an ordinal scale, of course; the order from low to high value is C, B, A, but the facts do not show that the intervals between them are equal. We do not know whether B is closer to C or to A.

Even with a scale composed of equal intervals, such as a scale of dollars on which $7 is equidistant between $6 and $8, the relation to choices is probably not linear. Fechner pointed out that as the magnitude of a stimulus, such as a sound or a light, increases arithmetically, the magnitude of the sensation increases only logarithmically, and, long before that, Bernoulli made a parallel suggestion about the value of money. If you have no money at all, the offer of $10 will strongly influence your decisions. But if you have $1,000, the offer of $10 more will have a weaker influence. In worldly units $10 dollars is $10; the unit of value is constant. But in human terms, the utility declines with the amount at one's disposal. Hence decision theorists differentiate between *value*, in objective terms, and *utility*, which represents the goal value or the influence on the individual's judgments.

The relation between utility and value, though curvilinear, is still a relatively simple, monotonic relation. In the case of money, the more the better on either scale. Preferences on some other dimensions, such as environmental temperature, give evidence of the operation of an optimal value which is preferred to temperatures either higher or lower. Fig. 8.1 illustrates another nonmonotonic relation, also related to physiological mechanisms, and the next chapter will include similar graphs for attitude data.

INTERJUDGE AGREEMENT

Judgments are frequently made in a systematic manner for many practical and scientific purposes even though no measure of accuracy is available, and justified by the agreement between judges. The test of agreement is some measure of correlation between judges working independently or a count of the number of agreements relative to occasions for agreement. If the judges do not reach adequate agreement, the project may be abandoned; but many studies of personality have demonstrated that, after judges have practiced making ratings with the aid of a code book or rating system, good interjudge agreement can be attained. Most reports of such projects merely give the measure of interjudge agreement after training, when a satisfactory level of agreement has been demonstrated, but the progress toward agreement can also be examined in more detail.

In order to plot a learning curve, two graduate students in clinical psychology (King, Ehrmann, and Johnson, 1952) rated nursery-school children, one at a time, for about an hour each, on such dimensions as sociability, aggression, and forwardness. Interjudge agreement was low. Then they worked together briefly, defining these dimensions and differentiating them from irrelevant behavior, and went back to judging independently. After several practice sessions together, they were able to rate independently with high agreement (see Fig. 8.2). The improvement was due to common definition of each dimension to be judged and of the meaning of each category of the rating scale, and it did not decline after the training ceased.

One reason for such high agreement is that both judges observed the same behavior and maintained a set for the same dimensions. When the judges supplemented their observations of the children with background data from the children's records, the agreement was lower, presumably because the judges then made divergent inferences about the significance of the observed behavior.

In many training situations—for example, in medical and psychological clinics—the important consideration is the agreement between student and

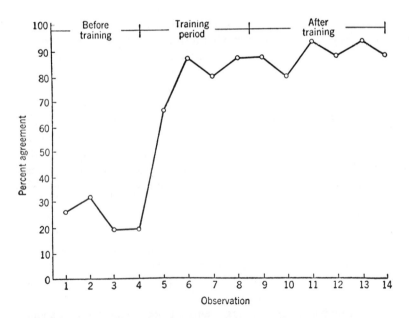

FIGURE 8.2. *Consistency of judgment and learning. The agreement between two observers rating nursery-school children on several classes of social behavior before and after training. From King, Ehrmann, and Johnson (1952).*

teacher or between subject and experimenter. To improve means to emphasize the dimensions the expert emphasizes and to use the scale categories as the expert does. Some experiments on the judgment of solutions to problems in the preceding chapter demonstrated how information about the critical dimensions of evaluation and practice in using such information brought the subjects' judgments closer to the official ones made by the experimenters.

An increase in agreement between judges usually indicates an increase in accuracy; raising reliability raises validity. But there are exceptions. The increase may come from reduction of errors peculiar to each judge, to be sure, but it may also come from agreement on a bias or stereotype, from domination of one judge by another, and from nonjudicial group processes currently under investigation by social psychologists. If four judges practice as two pairs and within-pair agreement increases, will between-pair agreement increase likewise? Fragmentary research indicates that the between-pair increase is much smaller than the within-pair increase, but the conditions that influence the outcome have not been thoroughly explored.

STIMULUS INFORMATION AND ACCURACY OF JUDGMENT

For some purposes errors of judgment can be counted, but this measure fluctuates widely with the conditions of judgment. In the past two decades, many experiments have employed a more stable measure, the amount of information transmitted by a judgment. The measure of information is the *bit*, abbreviated from binary digit, which is the logarithm to the base 2 of the information in the system. Suppose, for example, that the stimuli are red and green cards, presented equally often, and they are to be assigned to categories R and G. The uncertainty as to which of the two will appear is one bit, since $\log_2$ of 2 is 1. Now if the judgments are correctly made, this uncertainty is reduced, and information transmitted is defined as uncertainty reduced, which in this case is one bit. If the stimuli are red, yellow, blue, and green cards, presented equally often, the information in the set is two bits, and for a set of eight objects of judgment the information is three bits. But as the input information is increased, the information transmitted by the judgments approaches a limit in the information-processing capacity of the judge.

One experiment requiring judgments of pitch (Pollack, 1952) got perfect transmission for 2 pitches (i.e., 1 bit), 3 pitches, and 4 pitches (i.e., 2 bits), but above 5 pitches accuracy fell off. The upper limit was about 2.3 bits—which corresponds to perfect discrimination of five items—whether the number of stimuli presented was 6, 7, 8, 10, or 12. For judgments of loudness, the upper limit found by Garner (1953) was 2.1 bits. Apparently the limit for judgment of hues is larger, about 8 hues or 3 bits (Eriksen and Hake, 1955). Several conditions shift this limit over the range from 5 to 9 items, but it is fairly constant for physical stimuli that vary on 1 dimension and may be symbolized by the magical number 7, plus or minus 2 (Miller, 1956). Recent calculations suggest, however, that when the number of stimuli is increased beyond the number that can be processed with only a few errors, the amount of information transmitted may actually decrease (MacRae, 1970).

It is possible to increase accuracy in categorizing a set of blocks of different sizes by coding them, as by painting them different colors. In one experiment (Eriksen and Hake, 1955), use of any 1 of 3 dimensions (hue, size, or brightness) to code 20 stimuli resulted in the transmisson of 2.75 bits, but when each stimulus was coded redundantly by 2 of these dimensions, the value was 3.43, and when each was coded by 3 dimensions, it was 4.11 —although the stimulus information in the 20 stimuli remained constant.

The same kind of analysis has been applied to social judgments by having clinicians rate the behavior described in short paragraphs on separate dimensions such as aggressiveness and dependency. Several values for the information transmitted by these judgments, assembled by Bieri, et al. (1966), vary from 1.71 bits to 2.12 bits, somewhat lower than for physical stimuli. Attempts to increase information transmitted by redundantly combining two types of behavioral information have not yet succeeded.

The general principle under investigation in these experiments is that when a set of objects varies on several dimensions, accuracy of judgment is increased by redundancy of coding. Most objects of commerce and industry vary in size and color, for example, and sorting errors are less frequent if objects of the largest size are all red, the medium ones all yellow, the smallest all green, and so on. But this principle is too simple because redundancy can take several forms. If we imagine size and color defining a two-dimensional space, the coding can be arranged so that the stimuli are scattered throughout this space and the distances between neighboring stimuli can be increased or decreased even though each size is still redundantly associated with a single color. Lockhead (1970) has shown that stimuli manufactured to maximize distances in this two-dimensional cognitive space were identified more accurately than comparable stimuli that minimized distances. The subjects of his experiments apparently did not judge separate dimensions and combine them; rather, they acquired knowledge of the two-dimensional space through experience with the stimuli and then judged them as if they were locating each in the cognitive space.

Furthermore, the redundancy principle applies only to integral dimensions. Typically, an object has an intrinsic hue, size, and brightness; that is, these dimensions are perceived as properties of one object. In such cases, redundancy of coding increases accuracy, but when extra dimensions are added on, the effect may be different (Garner, 1970). Coding a set of objects by redundantly adding separate features (such as letters or arrows) may have an interfering effect, probably because instead of making unitary judgments of the objects, the subjects make separate judgments of the dimensions. This seems to be the case for abstract social judgments in which adding redundancy is not effective.

As Garner points out, one person may make separate judgments of stimuli that another person organizes into unitary objects; the flexibility of human intellectual capacities must be considered along with general principles of information processing. Highly practiced musicians, artists, and winetasters generate new dimensions and treat them as unitary while novices get confused by the separate elements. The principles that influence accuracy of judgment are of limited generality, but specific data on stimulus information and accuracy of judgments under specific conditions have accumulated (Bieri, et al., 1966; Garner, 1962). Accuracy of judgment is also influenced by the scale on which the judgments are expressed, as we shall see in the next chapter.

CORRELATION OF RESPONSE SCALE WITH STIMULUS SERIES

Under some conditions, the association of judgments with stimuli can conveniently be measured by the correlation coefficient. Whereas the information-processing model treats judgment nonmetrically as the coding of discrete stimuli into discrete categories, the correlation model treats judgment as the adjustment of an ordered scale of response categories to an ordered series of stimuli. The judge attempts to correlate the response scale as a whole with the stimulus series. And, if the stimuli are measured in objective units such as inches or grams, and the responses are numbered, as from 1 to 9, the conventional correlation coefficient measures the accuracy of the overall performance. As an illustration of this approach, Fig. 8.3, taken from Johnson and Mullally (1969), shows how the correlation between judgments and stimuli varies as a function of time of exposure of the stimuli.

Multidimensional Judgments in Discrete Categories

Most judgments are complex. The objects to be judged vary in several dimensions, none of which has a unique claim on the judge's attention. And ostensibly simple judgments are not always unidimensional when

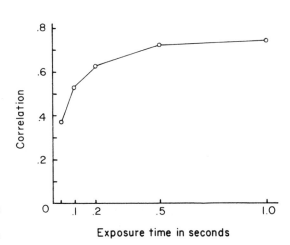

FIGURE 8.3. Correlation between judgments and stimulus patterns as a function of exposure time. From Johnson and Mullally (1969).

Exposure time in seconds

studied empirically. Judgments of the heights of blocks are influenced by their widths. The affective dimension biases judgments of formal propositions (as noted in the chapter on reasoning) and even judgments of the size of coins. The complexity of judgments of people, often technically called *person perception,* is matched only by the fascination they hold for biographers and psychologists. What appears to be a simple judgment on a prominent dimension, when taken seriously often turns into a comparison of the weights of different dimensions.

In this diversified world that we are continuously evaluating, the correlation between stimulus dimensions is a basic condition of the evaluation. The experiments on stimulus information mentioned above used stimulus objects with perfectly correlated dimensions, so that judgments made on the basis of hue would be identical with judgments made on the basis of size. But that is a very special case. The judge is more often faced with situations in which the dimensions are moderately correlated, such as height and weight in judgments of persons, and with situations in which the correlation between dimensions is negligible.

There are three general questions about multidimensional judgments: (1) What are the dimensions that influence the judgments? (2) How much weight does the judge give to each? Weighting dimensions differentially implies refined quantitative judgment, as compared to the concept experiment, in which the distinction between relevant and irrelevant dimensions is more clear-cut. And (3) How are these effects combined in the judging process? Individual differences between judges can be expected in the answer to the third question as well as the others, and a judge may shift in any respect as his experience accumulates.

When the judgments are simple and the data imprecise, a crude empirical approach, such as the tabulation of judgments of various stimuli under various conditions, may be the most suitable for a preliminary description of the principal features of the operation. But in recent years, as multidimensional judgments have attracted more research attention and the data have become both more abundant and more interdependent, many psychologists have preferred to begin with a hypothetical model of the judge's activities. Prescriptive or normative models prescribe, like the norms of logic, what the judge should do, while descriptive models attempt to describe what the judge actually does—and some models have both functions. Most models have been stated in mathematical form, and judgment data (more often than problem-solving data, for example) have the precision necessary for evaluating a mathematical model.

The elaboration of judgment models has not taken over and certainly has not unified the field of judgment. Most models are applicable only to those situations in which they were developed. Furthermore, models for judgment are not often comparable because they lead to different experimental arrangements and compute different measures. They all have in common, however, some respect for the rationality of the judge in that they assume he can analyze, and attend to, different attributes of the stimulus objects and that he tries to fit these to the response categories in some consistent fashion within the restrictions specified by the instructions.

Although the grand psychological theories took shape in other areas, the field of multidimensional judgments is an excellent arena for psychological controversies. All the classical antinomies are here: the subjective versus the objective, rationality versus mechanism, the accumulation of empirical facts versus model building, addition versus configuration. The experiments involve adult human subjects thinking about matters of some significance, yet the data can be collected with considerable precision.

It will be convenient to discuss judgments in discrete categories first, then judgments on a continuum.

SERIAL PROCEDURES

The serial nature of many judgments should be mentioned first because this is a common way of organizing heterogeneous data into a final decision. Consider the case of a grocer debating whether to expand his business. He may first raise the question: Can I increase sales volume? If his best guess is No, the matter is settled. If he can say Yes, he goes on to the next hurdle: Can I acquire more space? If the answer is No, the matter is settled at this point. If this second hurdle is surmounted, he goes on to the third: Can I finance the addition? And so on. The overall enterprise may be viewed as a decision tree made up of branches leading to other branches.

When the data are all available at once, the judge has a choice between a simultaneous and a serial strategy, but in some situations the data are collected serially as a consequence of prior decisions. The evaluation of applicants for a job or a scholarship, as well as medical and psychological diagnosis, often proceed by a succession of decisions, each of which influences the collection of more information for the next decision. The employment official reads a letter of application and tosses it in the wastebasket or requests the applicant to take a test. If the test score is below a critical point, the application is finished; but if it is above the critical point, he is invited for an interview.

To call this procedure a series of categorical decisions assumes that the data are in discrete categories or that critical scores divide the data into favorable and unfavorable categories. It is true that at the final summing up the judge may examine all the data on hand and that distance above any critical score may enter into the final evaluation. But it is also true that the information available depends on prior decisions. In medical diagnosis, the number of possible tests is so large and the information resulting from them so variable that the decision which to recommend is as critical as the evaluation of the test results. The rationale is one of efficiency; but the most efficient sequence in these cases, as in information seeking in general, is a joint function of information and cost. Thus, computer models for diagnosis include recommendation of tests to be given as well as evaluation of the results. In other areas also, the optimal linkage between the human judge and the computer is a serial one (Shelly and Bryan, 1964).

This description of serial judgment does not explain how any one decision is made, but it does show where each fits into the larger enterprise.

JUDGMENT MODELS FOR CLINICAL DIAGNOSIS

A SYLLOGISTIC MODEL

Since clinical psychologists often assign patients to diagnostic categories and make categorical statements about them on the basis of multiple cues, they have a special interest in multidimensional judgments. In discussing the problem of clinical inference, Sarbin, Taft, and Bailey (1960) suggest a syllogistic model.

All fulminating schizophrenics are dangerous;
This man is a fulminating schizophrenic;
Therefore, this man is dangerous [p. 52].

The major premise is a generalization derived from reading, experience, and implicit theories, while the minor premise comes from examination of the individual. Within this structure the familiar logical fallacies can be identified, as well as valid conclusions.

Probabilities may be included in the major premise, such as: The frequency of association between improvement in psychotherapy and intact ego, mild anxiety, and high motivation is six in ten. If the clinician assumes that this statement applies to present conditions, he operates with it as his major premise. Then, having examined Jones, he states a minor premise, such as: Jones is a member of the class of persons characterized by intact ego, mild anxiety, and high motivation. In formal logic there is no valid conclusion to this syllogism because it is not known whether Jones belongs to the 60 percent who improve or the 40 percent who do not. But if a decision must be made, it can be stated in two ways. The probability that Jones will improve in therapy is six in ten, or the statement "Jones will improve in therapy" has a credibility of 0.6.

CONFIGURAL JUDGMENT OF PROJECTIVE TEST RESPONSES

For some time, projective test experts have recommended configural interpretation of the Rorschach and other projective tests (Rabin, 1950) and have taught the meaning of specific patterns. The proportion of poorly formed percepts, for example, makes a different contribution to the diagnosis when the number of percepts is large than when it is small. Configural interpretation is more difficult to master, of course, than simple counts of Rorschach signs.

DECISION RULES

The information-processing approach to clinical judgment is exemplified in a preliminary study by Kleinmuntz (1968) of an expert clinician's use of information from the Minnesota Multiphasic Personality Inventory. The expert was given the task of sorting the test profiles of 126 college students into 2 categories, *adjusted* and *maladjusted,* a task that consumed 60 hours, and to "think aloud" into a tape recorder while doing so. From records of the classifications and accompanying comments, Kleinmuntz was able to formulate 16 decision rules that the judge had apparently been using. One rule consisted simply of addition of signs of maladjustment: If the scores on 4 or more clinical scales exceed 70, call the student maladjusted. Other decision rules were more complex, including interactions between signs: Call the student maladjusted if Pa exceeds 70, unless Mt is less than 6 and K is more than 65. Clinicians often generalize such rules for themselves and, if they are explicitly stated, they can be communicated to others. In fact, Kleinmuntz undertook this search for explicit decision rules as a first step toward programming a computer to make the diagnoses.

Do clinical psychologists actually make clinical judgments according to the sophisticated models that the experts advocate? This is a case in which thinking makes it so; a psychologist is likely to adopt a model that he accepted when he was exposed to it as a student. Students follow their leaders, as a rule; but if the leader's path is not well marked or if it seems unnecessarily circuitous, the student may take an easier path—perhaps additive rather than configural. The question whether clinical signs are combined by additive or configural rules will come up again later in this chapter for judgments made on continuous scales.

THE DISCRIMINANT FUNCTION

The judge's task is somewhat different when he is required to classify people into two categories—such as *admit* and *don't admit* or *hire* and *don't hire*—on the basis of multiple dimensions, with only the restriction that the same number be assigned to each. People differ in many dimensions but they do not come in two types. This task is not like the concept attainment task that requires discovery of the critical binary attributes, therefore, but more like the sorting task that requires the subject to "put those objects together that belong together." As on the sorting task, different subjects may be expected to emphasize different dimensions. There will be some overlap between the categories since certain individuals could be assigned to either, but it is reasonable to assume that each judge will try to maximize the difference between the two categories.

The discriminant function was devised to solve statistical problems of this kind, so Rodwan and Hake (1964) raised the question whether this statistical model would describe what serious judges actually do when they combine the information on several dimensions to make two-category judgments. The discriminant function resembles the multiple regression equation. Whereas the latter maximizes the correlation between the weighted sum of the predictor variables and the criterion, the discriminant function is a weighted sum that maximizes the discrimination between the two classes. Both procedures yield a set of optimal weights.

To test this model, Rodwan and Hake used 81 photographs of schematic faces that varied in 4 dimensions: length of nose, X_1; length of chin, X_2; distance between eyes, X_3; and length of forehead, X_4. There were 3 values of each dimension, but other lines in the faces were constant. (The resemblance between these materials and those used in conventional experiments on synthetic concepts should be apparent.) The subject's task was to judge each face *intelligent* or *not intelligent*. For the data of one subject, told that half the faces were supposed to be intelligent, the discriminant function yielded these weights: $-.21X_1 +.62X_2 -.07X_3 +.76X_4$; that is, this subject gave a small negative weight to length of nose, a strong positive weight to length of chin, and an even stronger positive weight to length of forehead, while practically ignoring distance between the eyes. For another subject, the weights were: $+.09X_1 +.31X_2 -.22X_3 +.92X_4$. Three men and 1 woman weighted length of forehead, X_4, positively, but 2 women weighted this dimension negatively, perhaps as a reaction against the common stereotype.

Evidence for the validity of the model is that the equations reproduce the obtained judgments with small error. Another test varied the restrictions on the number in each category. The judges were told, when given a third of the faces to judge, that 25 percent were supposed to be intelligent; then, when given the next third to judge, that 50 percent were supposed to be intelligent; and for the other third, 75 percent. The model requires that each subject weight each dimension the same regardless of these percentages, and the data indicated that they did so, within narrow limts. Furthermore, the weights were stable over a three-week period.

A realistic feature of this model is that it allows for differences between judges in the weights given to the four dimensions—some actually were near zero—but they were stable under different conditions. The model assumes that the contributions of the different dimensions to the categorizations were linear and additive, and the fit to the data indicates that the judges operated approximately in this fashion.

DECISIONS ABOUT ACTIONS WITH UNCERTAIN OUTCOMES

It is reasonable to assume that when a person makes a choice between apple pie and custard pie, he is simply choosing the one that has more subjective value, or utility, to him. Risky choices, which force the person to decide between alternative actions when he is not certain of the outcome of each, require a more complex decision model. Consider the decision, before going out, whether to wear a raincoat or not when the weather man has given the probability of rain as .3. The four outcomes to be considered are arranged two by two in Table 8.1. Since the model requires estimates of utility (positive or negative) for all outcomes, we begin with the worst outcome, the disaster of being caught in the rain without a raincoat, and give it a utility of -100 (lower left cell). On this scale, wearing a raincoat when it does not rain would be a minor nuisance, with a utility of -20 (upper right cell). Wearing a raincoat when it does rain might be considered a small triumph of good planning, worth brief mention at lunch, so we give it a utility of 10. Not wearing a raincoat when it does not rain is the routine state of affairs, neither positive or negative.

A virtue of this model is that it takes into account the probabilities and the utilities of all four outcomes. Since the probability of rain is .3 and the

TABLE 8.1. MATRIX OF ALTERNATIVE ACTIONS AND OUTCOMES TO ILLUSTRATE A DECISION MODEL. THE PROBABILITY OF RAIN IS ASSUMED TO BE .3; THE CELL ENTRIES ARE SUBJECTIVE UTILITIES.

		Outcomes	
		Rain $p=.3$	No rain $p=.7$
Actions	Wear raincoat	10	-20
	No raincoat	-100	0

utility of wearing a raincoat in this event is 10, the expected utility of this outcome is .3(10) or 3. To this must be added the expected utility of wearing a raincoat if it does not rain, which is .7(-20) or -14. Therefore, if the decision is to wear a raincoat, the sum of the expected utilities is -11. Symbolically: $EU = p_1U_1 + p_2U_2$. The same computations for the decision not to wear a raincoat yield an expected utility of -30. All things considered, the model says that not wearing a raincoat is probably worse than wearing one. Wearing one would be the judicious thing to do. There may be more alternative actions to choose from and more probable outcomes to consider, but this simplified illustration outlines the structure of the model.

Actually, it is difficult to get good quantitative estimates of the utility of outcomes, other than money outcomes, which is why many of the investigations of the psychology of decision making are concerned with a simpler model of expected value: $EV = pV$—the expected value of an event is the monetary value of the event multiplied by the probability that it will occur. Suppose you are offered the following gamble: Toss a half-dollar coin in the air and if it comes down heads you win the coin. The value of the coin is 50 cents, and the probability that it will come down heads is .5, hence the expected value of the gamble is 25 cents. If you are asked to pay 30 cents to play this game, the price is too high. Now suppose you are offered another gamble: Pick a card from an ordinary deck of playing cards and if it is a spade you win $2. Compute the expected value of the gamble. If the two alternative gambles were offered to you at the same price, which would you prefer? The expected-value model states that the gamble with the highest expected value will be preferred. In cases where a loss (symbolized by L) as well as a win (W) is probable, the decision model states that the optimal strategy is to maximize the quantity: $p_WV_W - p_LV_L$.

Decision models of this nature are being used to organize the voluminous data involved in high-level economic and military decisions. The question for psychology is how well the model describes the decision-making processes of ordinary educated adults. From a broad perspective this question is analogous to the question raised in a previous chapter, how well the norms of logic describe the reasoning of ordinary educated adults. It seems clear, thus far, that the fit to human decision making is close enough that the model is a good starting place from which to examine the discrepancies from it and to try to improve it. At least it is better than the assumption that decisions are determined by random behavior, or nonrational associations, or naïve wish fulfillment.

From the psychological point of view, decisions under uncertainty are multidimensional judgments involving at least two dimensions—probability and utility (or subjective value). The basic assumption that these are joined in a multiplicative combination is a reasonable one, as a starter. But many people do not understand probabilities very well, and the utilities of outcomes are personal, affective magnitudes. Hence, theoretical analysis and empirical research have been directed toward the quantification of these two dimensions as people actually employ them (Becker and McClintock, 1967).

ESTIMATING PROBABILITIES

Most adults estimate probabilities from a logical analysis of the alternative events or from observation of frequencies of past events of the same class tolerably well, but certain constant errors have been observed both in analyses of bets at racetracks and in laboratory experiments. Low probabilities are often overestimated and high probabilities underestimated, perhaps because of a regression effect that will be discussed in the next chapter. Another common error is the so-called Monte Carlo fallacy, the tendency after a run of independent events of one kind (e.g., girl babies) to estimate a low probability for a recurrence of that event and higher probability for an alternative (e.g., a boy baby). This fallacy probably has its origin in card games. Withdrawing a red card from a deck of 26 red and 26 black cards, without replacement, decreases the number of red cards and increases the probability of drawing a black card next time. The Monte Carlo error is probably due to the transfer of experience from a closed system of dependent events to an open system of independent events—which occurs also in reasoning. Cohen (1960) traced the development of such predictions in schoolchildren and concluded that "no one guesses in a manner without rhyme or reason. From the youngster of 6 to the very bright adolescent of 16, predictions follow a complex system of pattern-seeking, associated with preferences for aesthetic symmetry or balance, fairness, and beliefs in magic [p. 36]."

The negative implication is awkward in making decisions under risk, as in making inferences from categorical propositions; the probability that an event will occur and that its complement will not occur do not always sum to unity, as conventional probability theories require. Sums different from unity are even more common when there are more than two probable events to consider. It is true that many otherwise intelligent people concentrate on single cases and are not impressed by statistical notions of long-run probability. In general, however, subjective probability is roughly related to objective probability—though the relation is usually not linear and is somewhat dependent on the decision situation.

After reviewing a large number of experiments which presented college students with samples of data and required them to estimate probabilities, proportions, means, variances, correlations, and other parameters, Peterson and Beach (1967) concluded that man is a fairly good "intuitive statistician." The most frequent discrepancy from the statistical model was in the conservative direction. The subjects failed to extract all the information in the samples that they observed and thus hesitated to make extreme estimates. But by and large their inferences approximated those that would be made by the appropriate statistical model. Hence the students would be entitled to a grade of A— for making reasonably optimal decisions, and the statistical models would also be entitled to a good grade for moderate success in describing human behavior under the uncertainties of a probabilistic environment.

BETTING PREFERENCES

The utilities of such outcomes as going to a concert, getting caught in the rain, and having baby girls are difficult to quantify, hence much of the research has dealt with the utility of money. One procedure is to give the subject a choice of bets, or gambles, as in the example above. A simpler procedure, like a lottery, has the subject purchase a gamble: "You can win three dollars if you draw a spade from a pack of playing cards. What will you pay for this chance?" Following this procedure, instead of the two-category decision, Komorita (1964) had college students buy many gambles and found that power functions—characteristic of many psychological magnitudes—for both probability and utility accounted for the data quite well. The subjective distance, which is what counts in making these judgments, from a probability of .25 to one of .50 was much greater than from .50 to .75. For the boys, the utility function of money was practically linear with dollar value, but for the girls the utility of the larger sums was relatively smaller. The good fit to the data indicated that the subjects were reasonable, each in his or her own way, in basing their decisions on the objective probabilities and the money values.

Since decision experiments need an adequate sample of bets, they extend over considerable time; yet the shifts in preference for bets during an experiment have been surprisingly small. Stable strategies of evaluating the situation and choosing bets presumably reflect previous learning and thinking in similar situations. The experimenter can manipulate the payoff to the players, however, if he has sufficient capital. By this maneuver, Greenberg and Weiner (1966) found that the preferences of the bettors changed with the number of wins and losses. Those who had as many wins as losses became more conservative in their betting than those who had either high or low reward ratios. This is understandable when we remember that repetitive betting, like anything else, can become an impersonal, even boring, task. When the player wins or loses and money changes hands, this adds not only information about the system but a motivational increment as well (Meyer, 1967). When college students are overworked by repetitive decisions about gambles, they often descend to a simple strategy such as always choosing the gamble with the higher probability of winning or always minimizing the maximum loss, even though they are capable of following a more complex strategy under better working conditions (Slovic, Lichtenstein, and Edwards, 1965).

DEVIATIONS FROM THE DECISION MODEL

Since the expected utility, or the expected value, model describes fairly well what the average adult does under certain conditions, the conditions under which the model does not fit are particularly instructive for the psychology of judgment. For one thing, the average adult does not always maximize expected utility by considering all possible outcomes. Everyone knows when buying insurance that the insurance company takes a percentage for expenses and profit—though the magnitude of this percentage is not generally appreciated—so the expected value to the buyer, if properly calculated, must be negative. But people do buy insurance, following what is called a *minimax strategy*. The buyer considers only the maximum loss from a single catastrophe and tries to minimize it.

Like the insurance buyer, the average amateur gambler knows that the house takes its cut but he also does not maximize expected utility in the predicted way. Either he focuses on one outcome and ignores the others or gambling has a utility of its own that should be entered in the equations. When Cohen (1960) offered English schoolchildren a choice of a small prize or a chance of winning a large one, the majority preferred to take a chance. At age nine about 94 percent preferred to gamble, at age fifteen only 54 percent. Perhaps shopping has a utility of its own for some people; at least, many merchandising schemes operate on the assumption that the customer wants entertainment in the form of a raffle or a plus value outside the money value and is willing to pay extra for it. Even rational decision making may have a utility of its own; practical businessmen have accused decision theorists of this particular deviation from rationality.

The complexity of the situation is an important factor here as in other problem situations. College students choosing between alternative bets are more likely to make choices that fit the expected value model, and thus are optimal choices, if the bets are simple ones that are easily understood. The expected value model does not fit so well when the bets are complicated. Choices between hypothetical gambles are not the same as choices between gambles that must be played (Slovic, 1969b). And the frequency of winning makes a difference even when expected value is held constant (Miller, Meyer, and Lanzetta, 1969). Even though the expected value model is a fairly good first approximation, the discrepancies are too large and too frequent to ignore.

If we treat the gamble as a multidimensional judgment, four dimensions must be considered: the value of a win, the probability of a win, the value of a loss, and the probability of a loss. It is mathematically reasonable to assume that values are multiplied by probabilities; but instead of beginning with this normative assumption, one can, in a more empirical way, ask how these four dimensions enter into the overall judgment. Slovic and Lichtenstein (1969) approached this question, not by asking their subjects to choose between gambles, but by asking them to rate the attractiveness of each. Then they used correlation procedures to determine the weight attached to each dimension. This correlation model of decisions under uncertainty will be discussed along with other such models in the next section, but the large individual differences that turned up should be mentioned here. Some subjects put the heaviest weight on the probability of winning, others on the probability of losing, and others again on the amount that could be lost.

That some individuals like to gamble more than others can be readily observed, but laboratory arrangements make it possible to observe and analyze the differences between individuals in more specific aspects of decision making. Kogan and Wallach (1964), for example, have analyzed the choices of 200 men and women for various strategies—such as maximizing gain and minimizing loss, their preferences for long odds or even bets, and postdecision satisfaction—both in hypothetical situations and with actual payoffs. These individual aspects of risk taking are interrelated, as one might expect, and are also related to personality measures, such as defensiveness and anxiety.

How rational is the ordinary intelligent adult in dealing with the uncertainties of the future? The question, as such, is too vague. We can inquire, however, for specific conditions, how closely his choices approach an explicit model of rational decision making under uncertainty. The research summarized above indicates that the expected utility model is difficult to test not only because the measurement of utilities is technically difficult but also because of the variety of utilities that people expect. In experiments on gambling (where expected utility is expected monetary value), it appears that college students follow the rational model and make optimal decisions fairly well within the limits of their comprehension of the gambles. When the gambles are complicated and especially when they are also boring, students are unable or unwilling to follow the details. They adopt some simpler, more congenial strategy, which makes their decisions appear less optimal— from the experimenter's point of view if not from the subject's. Why work so hard just to appear rational?

In general, the deviations from the optimal expected value model involve weighting and strategy. The model assumes that the value of a win is weighted (i.e., multiplied) by its probability, that the value of a loss is weighted by its probability, and that the intelligent adult follows a single-minded strategy of maximizing $p_W V_W - p_L V_L$. But the data show that the value of a win, or a loss, is often rated higher or lower than its probability and that the probability of a win, or a loss, may have a utility that is more than just as a multiplier of value. The strategy may be simply to minimize the big loss, or to maximize the number of wins, or even to choose the gamble that is easiest to understand. The subject oversimplifies the cognitive structure by focusing on one or two elements. Thus, the question of rationality in the case of decisions under uncertainty has some parallels with the same question in the case of logical reasoning with categorical propositions.

Multidimensional Judgments on Continuous Scales

When judgments of multidimensional objects are made on continuous scales, as from 1 to 7 or from *extremely favorable* to *extremely unfavorable,* hypotheses about combinatory processes can be examined with some precision. There is no single normative model that prescribes how a rational man should proceed in this situation—except in the general sense that his judgments should be adapted to reality—but the research has been guided by the pervasive psychological controversy between addition and configuration, and the models have been designed and revised in close contact with empirical data. Those cognitive models that include the organization and consistency of motives, beliefs, and actions depart from the main concern of this book and have been well reviewed in books on social psychology. The emphasis here is on attempts to describe the judging process in general, and some generalizations have emerged from judgments of people, words, photographs, behavior symptoms, occupations, foods, and other worthwhile objects of study.

THE SUMMATION MODEL: BREAKDOWN AND REPAIR

One of the earliest quantitative studies of the additivity question illustrates a method that was widely adopted in subsequent decades and anticipated the trend of more recent results. Washburn, Haight, and Regensburg (1921) presented cards with single colors and cards combining two colors for their subjects to rate as to pleasantness on a seven-point scale. They obtained a correlation of .75 between the ratings of the combinations and the sums of the ratings of the single colors. Thus the experimenters suggested that in rating the combinations, the subjects added their ratings of the constituent single colors. But 15 percent of the disagreeable colors made pairs that were judged agreeable. Hence something more than simple addition must also be considered. When Beebe-Center (1932) reviewed the early evidence on this question, under the name of *hedonic summation,* he noted the frequency of simple algebraic summation and noted also that in some cases the result of juxtaposing the separate stimuli was not merely a combination, but a new configuration.

A favorite illustration of Gestalt psychologists is that when one perceives a face, even briefly, he gets a distinct impression of the whole which comprises many separable features but also perceives the features as part of the whole. Faces are difficult to manipulate experimentally, except in the synthetic manner (see page 353) of Rodwan and Hake (1964), but Asch (1946) arranged adjectives referring to personality traits in different lists in order to illustrate how the reader organizes a unified impression of an individual and how the whole list influences the contributions of the constitutent words. What this has to do with the perception of warm, moist people is disputable, and words may not be the best medium for demonstration of Gestalt principles of perception. But lists of words can easily be assembled for judgment separately and in combination. Thus this type of experiment, under the name of *impression formation,* has supplied considerable evidence on combinatory processes in judgment. The question of generality will come up in connection with judgments of other materials.

When discrete words, or other items, are judged separately and in combination, on a prominent dimension like attractiveness, a hypothetical process of algebraic summation of pros and cons is intuitively reasonable. Or, if the judge does not add his ratings of the components, he may average them. The summation model and its variant, the averaging model, are similar in that they both assume that the judge operates additively and they both make the same predictions about correlations between ratings of components and ratings of combinations. The data from many experiments of the past fifteen years agree that one or the other accounts for a large share of the variance. More recent experiments have attempted to distinguish averaging from adding, to diagnose the weaknesses of such models, and to supplement them with corrections that will account for a larger proportion of the variance.

WEIGHTING OF COMPONENTS

One obvious possibility is that the judge attaches more importance to one component than to others, hence the model should weight the components correspondingly. The congruity model of Osgood, Suci, and Tannenbaum (1957), in order to account for ratings of combinations of adjectives and nouns such as *hairy scientists,* added the separate ratings of each weighted in accordance with their deviations from neutrality on a bipolar dimension. But when Triandis and Fishbein (1963) got ratings of individuals described by four characteristics (race, occupation, nationality, and religion), the sums of the ratings of the components, without differential weighting, correlated more closely with the ratings of the composites.

To gain more precise prediction, Rokeach and Rothman (1965) asked each judge how much weight he attached to the adjective and to the noun in rating combinations of these, and then weighted the components of their additive model correspondingly. Thus they could predict the ratings of combinations quite well for those judges who were able to follow the detailed instructions. When items of the same type, such as a set of foods constituting a meal, are rated, the first items have somewhat more influence on the rating of the whole, and appropriate weighting for this primacy effect improves the predictions (Anderson, 1965a; Anderson and Norman, 1964). This is not an unusual situation because the final judgment of a complex object is often integrated from serial judgments of the components. Differential weighting is indicated also when the separate items of information come from sources that differ in credibility (Rosenbaum and Levin, 1969). Regardless of the model chosen to reproduce the judge's operations, the possibility of differential weighting specific to the situation and even to the individual judge cannot be overlooked.

CONTRAST AND EXTREMENESS

A curious discrepancy in the averaging model turned up in a careful analysis by Willis (1960) of judgments of college students' photographs, arranged in contrasting sets of two or three extremely attractive and two or three extremely unattractive individuals. The important finding was the extremeness of the judgments of the mean attractiveness of the sets relative to the mean of the scale values of the components. Overall, the mean scale values of the components, on a scale of nine categories, were 2.15 and 4.15; but the judgments of the sets were 2.02 and 4.58. The differences may look small but they were consistent in several variations of the sets.

The enhancement of contrast discovered by Willis could be due to a tendency on the part of the judges to stereotype the two groups, but Weiss (1963b) uncovered the same effect at less extreme positions. He assembled many sets of 3 opinion statements, spaced along an 11-category scale, and instructed the judges that each set represented one person's opinion, to be judged as a whole. For triplets with mean scale values of 2.87, 4.27, 8.42, and 9.68, the judgments of the composites were 1.15, 3.80, 9.62, and 10.83. Similar extremeness has also appeared in judgments of persons described by excerpts from letters of recommendation in sets of 1, 2, and 4 (Brewer, 1968).

The interpretation of extreme ratings is awkward because of the possibility of unequal scale intervals at the extremes, especially if the ratings of the component items and of the combinations are made by different judges. Therefore, Manis, Gleason, and Dawes (1966) had the same judges rate single statements about fraternities and pairs of statements (attributed to one person), and used a simple ordinal measure of extremeness: the number of judgments of the pairs that were more extreme than their components. The pairs could be judged more extreme or more neutral than their components, but the preponderant deviation was toward the extremes. Another simple procedure used by these experimenters presented three statements attributed to one person and asked the judge to select the one that best represented the person's attitude. The hypothesis of extremeness predicts that the most extreme statement would be selected more often than the least extreme, or most neutral, statements, and this prediction also was confirmed.

The extremeness effect is embarrassing for a simple averaging model. A summation model would not be challenged by this effect, but ratings of combinations are seldom as extreme as simple summation predicts, especially when three or four components are summed. Apparently, the judges strike a compromise between the mean and the sum of all components. Manis, Gleason, and Dawes suggest a weighted average in which all components are included but the effect of the number of components diminishes as the logarithm of the number.

AVERAGING AND ADDING

Mathematically, an adding model becomes an averaging model if the weights attached to the components sum to unity. Since the data at hand offered some support for both, Anderson (1965b) designed an experiment to differentiate the two models. He used an unbounded scale since a bounded scale, such as 1 to 7, could restrict the range and thus be unfair to the adding model. Beginning with a standardized list of adjectives rated in advance, he drew some rated *highly favorable* (H) (e.g., reasonable and truthful), some rated *moderately favorable* (M+) (e.g., painstaking and persuasive), some rated *moderately unfavorable* (M−) (e.g., unpopular and dependent), and some rated *highly unfavorable* (L) (e.g., spiteful and abusive). These were presented in sets of two and sets of four to college students, with instructions to rate the person described by these sets of adjectives on an unbounded scale centered at 50. They were told to use 50 for a person they would neither like nor dislike, to use lower numbers for persons they would dislike, and higher numbers for persons they would like. Means are shown in Table 8.2.

The argument for averaging is the fact that the mean for HHM+M+ falls between the means for HH and M+M+ and the mean for LLM−M− falls between LL and M−M−. The argument for additivity is that the mean for HHHH is higher than the mean for HH and that LLLL is lower than LL. But the mean for HHHH is not twice that for HH and the subjects had preliminary practice with the scale so that they could space out their ratings if they wished. Anderson therefore accounts for this discrepancy from the averaging model by invoking an initial impression, assumed to be at the middle of the scale. If the overall impression is the average of all these, HHHH plus 50 will average out to a value somewhat higher than HH plus 50; likewise, LLLL plus 50 will average a little lower than LL plus 50.

Podell and Amster (1966) also found, when they used one, three, and six adjectives, that the composite judgment deviated more from the neutral point as the number of adjectives increased. To explore this effect further, Anderson (1967) made up sets of one, two, three, four, six, and nine adjectives. An averaging model which includes the initial impression (assumed to be at the neutral point of the scale) and the scale value of each component, with diminishing weight as the number increases, predicted the composite judgments quite well. One system of weights, computed for each judge individually, was sufficient for all set sizes.

At this point there seems to be some agreement that, in these situations where the components are discrete and independent, the judge does combine the information from each component in a weighted average, not as ex-

TABLE 8.2. MEAN RATINGS OF SETS OF TWO AND FOUR ADJECTIVES

Set Type	Response	Set Type	Response
HH	72.85	HHHH	79.39
M+M+	57.56	M+M+M+M+	63.20
M−M−	42.18	M−M−M−M−	39.50
LL	23.70	LLLL	17.64
		HHM+M+	71.11
		LLM−M−	25.67

From Anderson (1965b).

treme as the sum of all components nor as neutral as the simple mean of all. Judges are influenced by the number of items of information, but this influence is a decreasing function of the number. The nature of the components must also be considered, perhaps by an adjustment of the weights, because when similar experiments were conducted with sets of gifts, traffic violations, and behavioral symptoms, the data for gifts came closest to the characteristics of a summation model, as one might expect, while the data for traffic violations came closest to an averaging model (Hicks and Campbell, 1965). Judgments of the social class of various individuals, based on three components (occupation, income, and education), fit an averagaing model quite well (Himmelfarb and Senn, 1969), and so did evaluative judgments of "little-known" groups of people described by taped travelogues containing positive and negative adjectives (Bossart and Di Vesta, 1966).

INTERACTION EFFECTS

Interaction effects are embarrassing to adding and averaging models, and such effects do show up occasionally in analysis of the variance of the judgments. When students expressed their preferences for working in four occupations in four cities, most composite judgments could be attributed to an additive combination; but the attractiveness of teaching interacted with the attractiveness of cities (Sidowski and Anderson, 1967). This means that the attractiveness of teaching in Cleveland, for example, depended on the attractiveness of teaching in general and of Cleveland in general but that the addition of these two main effects did not account for all the variance. Teaching in Cleveland might be judged as unusually enjoyable, as if the attractiveness of these two dimensions were multiplied rather than added. And, as another example, when adjectives and photographs of college students were combined and judged as to desirability on a date, interaction effects were strong (Lampel and Anderson, 1968).

Moving from the familiar psychological laboratory to an arena that psychologists seldom enter, Slovic (1969a) found intriguing signs of interaction effects in the stock market. He persuaded 2 experienced stockbrokers to rate the growth potential of 128 companies on the basis of 11 factors—such as dividend yield for the past year, prospects for the coming year, and profit margin trend—taken from standard financial reports. The information in each dimension was reduced to 2 values, such as down and up, in order to facilitate the analysis of variance, and the brokers' judgments were made on a nine-category scale, from *strong recommendation not to buy* through *neutral* to *strong recommendation to buy*. Most of the 11 factors influenced the judgments of growth potential as expected, but definite interaction effects also turned up. High dividend yield, for example, was considered a more favorable indicator than low yield when the profit margin trend was down, while the reverse was true when the profit margin was up. Five of these interaction effects were found in the data of 1 of these expert judges and 6 in the other, demonstrating that substantial configural processing of the information on the separate dimensions did occur. Most investigators who have studied multidimensional judgments quantitatively have reported, often with some surprise, that the judges are seldom as complex as they think they are; but unless there is something peculiar about the binary information that was furnished to these stockbrokers, more evidence of nonadditive combinations can be expected in further research.

CORRELATED COMPONENTS

Since Wishner (1960) demonstrated the importance of correlations within lists of adjectives in studies of impression formation, careful investigators have tried to combine adjectives that are independent in meaning. But suppose the judge is asked to rate the attractivenes of someone described by three adjectives, one of which is inconsistent with the others, such as *honest, gloomy,* and *deceitful?* When Anderson and Jacobson (1965) gave lists of this nature to their subjects, with the instruction that each adjective was equally important, they found that the averaging model predicted the composite judgments fairly well. Then they varied the instructions, telling other subjects that those who had described the people did not know them equally well and one adjective might not really apply. With these discounting instructions, the averaging procedure yielded some discrepancies, which could be removed by weighting. Thus the results agreed with the hypothesis that the subjects identified the inconsistent one of three and gave it less weight in their overall judgments. *Discounting* in this sense is the same as giving less weight to information from a source of low credibility, as the judges of the Rosenbaum and Levin (1969) experiment did.

Dustin and Baldwin (1966) tried to take care of such relations in the input by a model that specified the correlations between the meanings of pairs of adjectives, including those with positive correlations, which can be called *redundant,* and those with negative correlations, which can be called *inconsistent.* Further evidence for the importance of the relatedness of the items was provided by Schmidt (1969). Two sentences containing redundant information about a person (*Mr. A is intelligent. Mr. A does his work intelligently.*) did not contribute as much to the judged attractiveness of Mr. A as two sentences, otherwise equated, containing different information (*Mr. A is intelligent. Mr. A is frank with Mr. Y.*). Thus the possibility of correlated components indicates another adjustment that should be included, either by weighting or by a correlation term.

The familiar context effect, to be discussed in the next chapter, is a further complication that influences these judgments, like most others (Hicks and Campbell, 1965; Wishner, 1960; Wyer and Dermer, 1968), and must be considered in a complete account of combinatory principles.

There is a certain built-in bias in the above experiments. In order to check on additivity, they begin with components that are familiar as independent items, like adjectives, and test how they are combined. Conceivably, the experiments could proceed in the opposite direction, beginning with a cognitive unity and testing whether independent additive components can be isolated. Is the fact that this has not been done an argument against additivity? The adverb-adjective combination, to be considered next, is perhaps an exception to this criticism, since intensive adverbs have little meaning when isolated from adjectives.

All in all, this vintage model, constructed on the additivity principle and leaning, as circumstances require, toward a weighted sum or a weighted average, has performed tolerably well. Weighted down with accessories to adjust for special conditions, however, it has lost the elegance of its early years. And if more interactions crop up in the years ahead, it may no longer be able to make the grade.

LINGUISTIC STRUCTURES

Experiments on impression formation have combined adjectives without regard to structure; but adverbs and adjectives are combined in a definite grammatical structure, such as *slightly wicked* or *very charming*. Any writer or speaker would expect that if *charming* is rated as a good word, putting *very* in front of it would make it better; if *wicked* is a bad word, putting *very* in front of it would make it worse. Intuitively, abverbs and adjectives seem to combine by multiplication rather than addition. To test this intuition, Cliff (1959) scaled 15 evaluative adjectives (such as *disgusting* and *charming*) and all combinations of these with 9 intensive adverbs (such as *slightly* and *very*), by having students at 3 colleges rate them on the *favorable-unfavorable* dimension. Then analysis of the judgments yielded evaluative scale values for the adverbs as well as the adjectives. The model accounted for the judgments very well, in that the scale value of a combination could be predicted by multiplying the scale value of the adjective by the scale value of the adverb. The scale value of *extremely*, for example, was 1.5, so the model says that *extremely good* is one-and-a-half times as good as *good*, and the results for large groups of subjects indicated that the judging process did, in fact, proceed along these lines.

The multiplicative model was checked again by Stilson and Maroney (1966), who found that it reproduced the judgments accurately, for single individuals as well as groups. They reported a few interesting exceptions, such as that ambiguous adjective *tolerable*, the meaning of which interacts with the adverbs that modify it.

Obviously, this multiplicative type of combination is a property of the linguistic structure, specifically the adverb-adjective structure. The adjectives refer to abstract dimensions that describe people and events, but the adverbs do not refer to anything in the same way; their function in a sentence is to modify the adjectives, to increase or decrease their effects. Hence it is not surprising that judgments of the linguistic combinations do not add or average like judgments of two adjectives.

Although sentences are longer, the components do not depend on the other components as much as an intensive adverb depends on an adjective. Sentences about men can be synthetically constructed by combining adjectives, verbs, and noun objects, thus: "The *vicious* man *harms beggars*." Gollub (1968) constructed many of these and tried to account for evaluative ratings of the men described by such sentences from evaluative ratings of the three components. First treating the verb and the object together as the predicate, a simple model that assumed additive combination of adjective and predicate accounted for 98 percent of the variance of the ratings. But the contribution of the predicate was best explained as a multiplicative interaction of verb and object. Overall, the adjective accounted for 37 percent, the verb 37 percent, and the verb-object interaction 22 percent of the variance of the ratings. In these sentences, the object of the man's behavior had little influence; it was the adjective applied to the man and the verb describing his behavior that had the most influence on the multidimensional rating.

The lesson to be learned from these studies of linguistic structures is clear. Evaluative judgments of syntactic combinations cannot be predicted from evaluative judgments of their components as well as lists of independent words. The reader not only adds the effects of the components, he often multiplies one by another.

THE CORRELATION MODEL

The correlation model, which has been mentioned above as a measure of the accuracy of unidimensional judgments, is particularly appropriate for the analysis of multidimensional judgments. A clinician, for example, is given several items of information that might be found in a person's folder and asked to make a summary judgment about him, and that judgment is then taken as a criterion to be predicted from the separate items. In the preceding chapter, judgment of the quality of solutions to a problem was correlated with separate components of quality, such as unusual word meanings. Thus the statistical model is the same as that used to predict average school grade or job success from several test variables. Standard procedures of multiple correlation and regression yield a correlation coefficient for each predictor variable, measuring its linear contribution to the summary judgment, and a multiple correlation coefficient, measuring the predictive efficiency of the optimal additive combination. This model does not differentiate between adding and averaging, but weights have been computed for each component, as in the studies of impression formation, and the possibilities of nonlinearity and interaction have been examined.

CUE UTILIZATION

As an illustration of the correlation approach, Hoffman (1960) had two judges estimate, on a 9-point scale, the intelligence of 100 persons from a set of 9 possible cues or predictors, such as high-school rating, effective use of English, mother's education, and credit hours attempted, all expressed in percentiles. The best linear combination of the predictor variables correlated .948 with the judgments of one judge. Hence, the assumption that the judge operated in a linear additive fashion seems reasonable because any deviation from this assumption would reduce the multiple correlation. For the other judge, the corresponding correlation was .829. Similar results were obtained when 2 judges rated 150 persons as to sociability from knowledge of the 8 scores each had made on a printed personality test. For the first judge, the multiple correlation was .901, for the other .770. Thus the linear additive model accounted very well for the overall judgments of 2 judges, not so well for 2 others.

Hoffman went further and asked the judges how they weighted each source of information in arriving at the overall judgment. In both analyses, the subjective weights reported by one judge agreed quite well with the weights computed by the multiple regression procedure, while those reported by the other judge did not. One judge in the first study, for example, said that he had weighted high-school rating, effective use of English and study habits strongly and equally; but his judgments were actually correlated very closely with high-school rating and negligibly with the other variables.

There are some technical questions about the computation of a set of weights to represent the independent contribution of each component (Hoffman, 1962; Ward, 1962), but it is methodologically more important here to consider the relation between weights objectively computed from the judgments and the judge's verbal statements about weights. As in concept research, when verbal statements do not agree with response-based statistics, some investigators assume that the verbal statements are misleading while others assume that the statistics are misleading. We must return to this controversy, but it should be noted here that in the Hoffman experiment, as in most others, the comparison is hardly fair, because the objective measures were carefully derived from many responses while the verbal statements were made only once, with no training.

One of the abilities claimed for the sensitive, experienced clinician is the ability to go beyond the linear additive model, to use nonlinear information and to combine information configurally rather than additively. Without entering into the contest between clinician and formula, we can raise the question whether clinicians and others do actually integrate information in these more complex combinations. The conventional multiple correlation model can be expanded to include curvilinearity and configural interaction (Goldberg, 1968), and analysis of variance has been used (as noted above) for the estimation of interaction effects when the information is categorical. It is clear from these reports and others (Hammond and Summers, 1965) that such complexities can be found if one looks for them, but after removing the main effects the variance they account for is usually small.

Like adjectives describing persons, however, the information in different components that enter into a clinical judgment may be inconsistent, and when this situation is arranged experimentally, the linear multiple correlation model is less adequate (Hoffman, Slovic, and Rorer, 1968; Slovic, 1966). As noted earlier, Anderson and Jacobson (1965) try to take care of such cases by adjustment of the weights. But Hoffman argues that evidence of change in the weight of a component due to the context of other components is evidence for a configural—as opposed to linear—utilization of cues. What is consistent or inconsistent is an individual matter; hence, models of cognitive processes will have better descriptive and predictive power, according to

Hoffman, when they include the structure of the data as perceived by each judge.

CUE VALIDITY

It is one task to describe how the judge utilizes several cues to make one judgment, and quite another to analyze the determinants of the accuracy of the judgment. The second task is not only an important practical one, as in the training of clinical psychologists, but has broader implications for judgment in general. Hammond, Hursch, and Todd (1964) have developed a lens model for this problem, which represents, in the manner of Egon Brunswik, not only the relations between the cues and the judgment, but also the relation between these cues and the distal variable to be judged. Fig. 8.4, taken from Hammond and Summers (1965), illustrates how the judge utilizes the available cues as mediators through which he attempts to focus on the distal variable.

As an example, consider judgments of the intelligence of persons whose IQs are known to the investigator but not to the judge. A clinician is asked to estimate the IQs from Rorschach signs, which are called *cues* because they are used as mediators for the judgment of the distal variable, intelligence. The correlation between the judgments and the objectively measured IQs, called the *achievement correlation*, depends on the correlations between the judgments and the cues, called *cue utilization correlations*, but also on the correlations between the cues and the objectively measured IQs, called the *ecological validity* of the cues. Obviously, if the dimensions that are utilized are not related to the objects of judgment, the judgments cannot be accurate. Although the models previously discussed have been

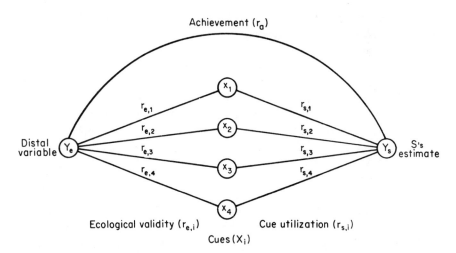

FIGURE 8.4. *Brunswik's lens model. The achievement correlation, r_a, is the correlation between the subject's estimate and the variable estimated. The correlation, r_e, between any cue, X, and the variable estimates is the ecological validity of the cue. The correlation, r_s, between any cue, X, and the estimate represents cue utilization. From Hammond and Summers (1965).*

concerned with the cue utilization side of the lens, the ecological validity of the cues is critical to the analysis of the judging process and to training of judgment.

In one study (Grebstein, 1963) of estimations of Wechsler-Bellevue IQs from Rorschach signs, a correlation of .50 was achieved by naïve judges (graduate students with one course in the Rorschach), a correlation of .65 by semisophisticated judges (second-year VA trainees) and .68 by sophisticated judges (with the Ph.D and five years of experience). The cue utilization correlations were about the same—.90 to .95—for the three groups, which means that they were all making linear use of the cues. Since the multiple correlation on the ecological side was only .79, the semisophisticated and the sophisticated judges were almost as accurate as they could be. The errors in the beginners' judgments were due to a mismatch between cue validity and cue utilization. For example, one Rorschach cue, said to indicate intellectual energy, had an ecological validity correlation of .18; but the naïve judges' data showed a cue utilization correlation of .63, as compared with .38 and .27 for the more sophisticated. Evidently, the naïve clinicians were relying on a textbook rule, while the sophisticated clinicians were depending on a rule developed from their experience. In general, the sophisticated clinicians must have been using a set of weights for the different cues that were about the same as the cue validities, because they were getting practically all the predictability they could out of the system.

Training for such abstract judgments must include conceptualization of the separate dimensions, but the evidence above raises the question whether appropriate weighting of the dimensions could be learned directly from practice with immediate feedback rather than only from prolonged experience. A partial answer to this comes from a study of judgment in a quasi-clinical situation by Newton (1965). He gave his judges four kinds of information about college students—such as test scores and personality ratings by high-school principals—and asked them to predict average grades during the first term in college. Then he calculated the statistics described above from the lens model and brought the judges back for more judgments with various kinds of feedback. Judges given their achievement and utilization correlations from the first series of judgments did not improve. Those given their achievement, utilization, and validity correlations did show some improvement in their predictions, from .58 to .65. The gains, according to the above analysis, were due to better match between the cue utilization and cue validity correlations.

This outline of the lens model is oversimplified, but it illustrates one of the few approaches to take into account the accuracy of multidimensional judgments. It is a normative model in the sense that it recommends matching the utilization to the validity correlations. Since objective measurement of the distal dimension is necessary for computing the achievement and the cue validity correlations, this model has been applied only to a few special situations such as estimations of intelligence and grades, but it teaches a lesson of wider significance. Without much difficulty, students can adjust their judgments to correspond with those of peers and teachers; it is encouraging to know that under some conditions they can also bring their judgments into closer correspondence with the objective situation.

LEARNING TO CORRELATE JUDGMENTS WITH MULTIPLE CUES

Some of the questions raised above have been investigated in more detail by laboratory experiments with artificial materials; these require the subject to make a single judgment of objects that vary on several dimensions and then give feedback about accuracy. The correlation between each cue and the criterion response to be learned can be varied from zero to unity and can be linear or nonlinear. Thus these are experiments about learning but they are about learning of a complex, cognitive type. The conditions that are manipulated by the experimenter are not the ones manipulated in conventional learning experiments, but correlations among cues and between cues and feedback. The correct combination of cues as defined by the experimenter governs the informational feedback given to the subject, and the improvement in accuracy of judgment is measured by the increase in the correlation between the subject's judgments and the experimenter's definition of correct judgments.

One of the earliest experiments of this type, by Smedslund (1955), manipulated the correlation between the cues and the correct response, giving each cue a different validity, and came to the conclusion that the subjects could learn to utilize many probabilistic cues simultaneously. A convenient experiment to illustrate the procedure is one by Summers (1962), who constructed 384 slides projecting triangles that varied in 3 dimensions (position, color, and extent of color), 8 values of each. The subject indicated his judgment graphically, by marking a line, and was allowed to see the correct line length immediately thereafter. Each of the 3 dimensions, or cues, was independent of the others; but the criterion, the correct line length, was dependent on all 3. Letting Y represent the criterion of judgment to be learned and X the cues, the relation to be learned in this experiment was: $Y = 2X_1 + 1.5X_2 + X_3$. Otherwise expressed, the correlation between criterion and cue for X_1 was .74; for X_2, .56; and for X_3, .37. To eliminate effects specific to the cues, these values were rotated among the 3 cues; but for any condition, the subject was provided all the information necessary to make a correct judgment.

When these slides were shown to 30 ninth-grade students, the results demonstrated that they did make use of all 3 cues. Their overall accuracy—as measured by the correlation between students' estimates and correct line lengths in blocks of 64 judgments—increased with practice. More than that, they learned to use the 3 cues differentially. As practice continued, they learned to put the most weight on the most important cue, that is, the cue with the highest correlation with the correct line length, and the least weight on the least important cue.

Improvement in using nonlinear information can be investigated by the experimental construction of a nonlinear dimension. Hammond and Summers

(1965) simplified the judging task by printing numbers, supposed to be test scores, on one side of a series of cards and the criterion to be estimated from these numbers on the reverse side. Half the variance of the criterion, Y, was determined by one set of numbers, X_1, and half by the other set, X_2; but one was related to the criterion in a linear manner, while the other had the form of a sine curve, and the criterion combined the two: $Y = X_1 + \sin X_2$. The subjects practiced estimating the criterion and got immediate confirmation by turning over the card. In general, they improved in accuracy of judging the criterion, but the improvement was dependent on the instructions. One group of subjects, told simply to make inferences on the basis of the test scores, made little use of the nonlinear cue; another group, told that both linear and nonlinear relations were involved, did somewhat better. But only a third group, told which was the linear and which the nonlinear cue, learned to make good use of the nonlinear information.

These findings were verified and extended in another experiment of this type by Summers and Hammond (1966), in which the stimuli were two vertical lines of varying lengths on a card and the criterion to be estimated was printed on the reverse side. When the instructions identified the linear and nonlinear cues, the subjects soon learned to make appropriate use of both and attained achievement correlations in the .80's and .90's. Summers and Hammond also called attention to the resemblance between such judgment tasks and concept attainment tasks. Asking the subject to predict a criterion from given cues is analogous to the concept task that identifies the relevant attributes and asks the subject to find the rule relating these to the class defined by the experimenter. In the other conditions, the experimenter supplies more information about the rule or rules. The analogy should not be pushed too far, however, because the rules considered in judgment experiments with continuous dimensions are not quite like those of combination of discrete attributes.

Chapter 2 noted the similarities and differences between class concepts and dimensional concepts. The attainment of a class concept is demonstrated by the correct use of two responses, one indicating class inclusion and the other exclusion, for a collection of stimulus objects. When the responses are made on a scale of eight to ten intervals, the activity is usually called *judging*, *rating*, or *scaling*, and consistency implies attainment of a dimensional concept even though, as in the case of class concepts, the concept may not be explicitly defined. An experiment by Azuma and Cronbach (1966) investigated the intermediate case, between the class concept and the dimensional concept, by requiring one of four responses, A, B, C, D, for each object. They described the task as the attainment of a *scalar concept*. Each stimulus consisted of a square frame containing a circle and a cross, the positions of which varied horizontally and vertically. Thus there were four dimensions or cues in the stimulus situation, two of which the experimenters defined as irrelevant; the criterion to be learned was a weighted average of the two relevant dimensions, thus: $Y = (2X_1 + X_2)/3$. The task was to combine the two relevant dimensions, weighting one twice as much as the other, and use the four-interval scale consistently for the composite.

Information about right and wrong responses was given, and most subjects improved (as shown by increases over several blocks of trials) in the mean correlation between responses given and correct responses. This mean correlation eventually reached .90. More analytically, the correlations between responses and relevant cues increased although the correlations with irrelevant cues did not, and the correlations with X_1 were larger than the correlations with X_2. But these are all mean correlations. The experimenters were impressed by the differences between subjects in judging tendencies. One subject, for example, did not improve at all in his matches to the weightings defined by the experimenter, nor was he consistent with himself from block to block in the way he weighted the stimulus dimensions. From the comments of their subjects, which many other experimenters do not trust, Azuma and Cronbach concluded that the overall achievement correlations may be misleading. As in experiments with complex classes, the subjects can divide the problem into subproblems to be solved in turn, although the statistics measure only overall performance. Some of these criticisms of the correlation method of analysis may be peculiar to the four-interval scale, which can be treated by the subjects as four categories; but the variations between individuals can be observed in all experiments.

College students can learn to make judgments on the basis of rather complex interactions between cues when the patterns to be judged are slides designed to simulate highly magnified blood cells (Summers, Summers, and Karkau, 1969). Cue 1 was based on the amount of crushed dark glass scattered across the background; Cue 2 was the size of the rough gray disks that appeared in each slide. Both of these relevant cues had eight possible values, and irrelevant variations also appeared in the slides. The subjects were asked to estimate the age of the cells in each slide and were then given the correct information. In one condition, the criterion was a simple additive function of the two cues; in another it was a multiplicative function. In a third condition, the value of Cue 1 was the exponent of the value of Cue 2; and in the fourth, Cue 2 was the exponent of Cue 1.

Over 2 days of practice, about 3 hours altogether, definite improvement occurred, reaching achievement correlations of .60 or above for each condition. Some of this improvement could have been due to the use of the linear component in the stimulus patterns, but the analysis demonstrated that there was an improvement in the use of the nonlinear information also. Although there was an initial tendency for all subjects to rely on a linear function, they learned, over 640 judgments, to use the relationship to which they were exposed. The specific nature of the perceptual patterns must have been important because one exponential function was considerably more difficult than the other.

CORRELATION ANALYSIS OF GAMBLING

Let us return briefly to the psychometrics of gambling. This decision situation has usually been analyzed with the aid of the expected value model, which weights the value of a win, or a loss, by its subjective probability. Slovic and Lichtenstein (1968) abandoned this model and switched to correlation analysis to describe how the dimensions of a gamble are weighted and combined. They offered their subjects duplex gambles and informed them of the probabilities of wins and losses. One gamble, for example, offered a .8 probability of winning $2 and a .8 probability of losing $1. Another offered a .2 probability of winning $1 and a .4 probability of losing $2. The subjects were asked to judge the attractiveness of each duplex gamble and bid an appropriate amount of money for it. The bids for some gambles would, of course, be negative amounts; the subject would expect to be paid to play them.

The expected value model assumes that values and probabilities are combined multiplicatively, but Slovic and Lichtenstein used a simple correlation model, which assumes that the judgment is linearly related to the four dimensions of a gamble and that these dimensions are combined additively. In one experiment, the predictions from this model correlated .86 with the actual bids. But the most striking outcome was the extent of the individual differences in the weights attached to the four dimensions. The correlations between risk dimensions and bids for one subject were: for the probability of winning .81; for the value of the win .13; for the probability of losing $-.27$; and for the value of the loss $-.30$. The corresponding correlations for another subject were: .19, .10, $-.23$, and $-.91$. Although the experiment did not compare this model with others, the data show once again that a linear additive model can account for a large share of the variance of the judgments if different weights are fitted to the data. More important psychologically, the data suggest that the subjects did not regard probabilities merely as multipliers of values, as illustrated in the expression pV, or as adverbs intensifying adjectives, as illustrated by *very charming*. They seemed to give the probability of a win, or a loss, some weight of its own, as in some of the experiments mentioned in the earlier discussion of decision models. And, as illustrated by the correlations listed above, the importance attached to a loss is not necessarily the mathematical opposite of that attached to a win.

JUDGMENT MODELS AND JUDGMENT PROCESSES

This chapter, like the others, is concerned with man's intellectual processes and relies on analysis of objective data more than the subject's statements. Several mathematical models for the integration of information have been discussed because each embodies a hypothesis about judging processes and suggests objective measures to be computed as tests of the hypothesis. But model building and testing is only one phase of the search for psychological understanding. The appeal of an elegant model capable of embracing most of the variance of judgments should not distract us from our main concern with judgment processes. Attempts to fit a linear model to judgment data are psychologically enlightening because they assume that the judge simply adds his judgment of one constituent dimension to his judgment of another. The experiments reviewed here indicate that, with a few interesting exceptions, the linear model can account for most of the data. When analysis of variance is carried out, the main effects are large and interaction effects typically small.

When correlations are computed, the linear multiple correlation is usually large. This is the evidence for the common assertion that judges are simpler than they think they are.

Although it is customary to speak of predicting the summary judgment or criterion from the separate dimensions, these are not predictions in a temporal sense. *After* the data are collected, weights are calculated, by one method or another, for each dimension. This is a mathematical trick to make the model work better, but the obtained weights can give us valuable psychological information about the importance of each dimension to the judge. The information is dependable, however, only if the model is appropriate. Calculation of a few weighting parameters *ex post facto*, like a few adjustments in a ready-made suit, can give an inappropriate model the appearance of good fit and thus yield spurious information about what the judge considers important.

Furthermore, changes in weights are often open to more than one interpretation. As noted above, Anderson (1965a) was able to account for the primacy effect in impression formation by serial adjustment of the weights attached to the adjectives. But Chalmers (1969) has offered a change-of-meaning model to account for such effects. He assumes that the meaning of a trait adjective, as it applies to the person described by a sequence of adjectives, "depends on the degree of *interference* or *facilitation* undergone by the trait as a result of the antecedent traits in the sequence [p. 453]." Although the processes assumed are different, these alternative formulations are mathematically similar and lead to the same predictions.

The general difficulty with this approach is that predictions from alternative mathematical formulations, like predictions from alternative verbal formulations, are not easily distinguished, especially when the hypothesized functional relations are monotonic, the range restricted, the data fallible, and when individuals are grouped. Wiggins and Hoffman (1968), after a careful study that separated two types of judges (summarized below), pointed out that the differences between linear and configural judges were not large. "The judgments of even the most seemingly configural clinicians can often be estimated with good precision by a linear model [p. 77]." And this statement could equally well be reversed.

Critics have often warned us in other contexts that the negation of one hypothesis does not prove another. Thus, under the usual conditions of judgment experiments, the negative statement that deviations from linearity are not significant is not equivalent to the positive statement that the linear model fairly represents what the judges are doing. As Green (1968) has put it, "the perverse pervasiveness of linearity" is due largely to methods of analysis that begin with the assumption of a linear function, compute the variance that can be attributed to linearity, and find small residuals to be attributed to nonlinearity. It may turn out by this method that 90 percent of the variance is attributable to linearity and 10 percent of nonlinearity; whereas a parabolic function, or some other, might account for all the variance in curvilinear terms. One is more likely to find evidence for configural judgment if, instead of fishing for nonlinear residuals, one begins with an explicit hypothesis about a judgment process that involves curvilinear use of the information or interactions between components and tests this hypothesis directly. The studies of adverbs as multipliers supply a good illustration of this more explicit procedure, and that by Kleinmuntz (1968) takes a step in this direction by describing configural decision rules in advance. The more recent research and reinterpretations of older research suggest that judges are not as simple as the early judgment models were.

Mathematical models of judgment tend to be applied to judgment situations that are easily quantified, as when the information on several dimensions is homogeneous or can be homogenized by conversation to standard units. But in many situations, the information to be integrated is quite diverse and the possibility of summation seems remote. To take one illustration, when you apply for a loan, your friendly banker will collect many diverse bits of information from you, usually by filling in a standard information blank. Aside from the monetary information on assets and liabilities, his treatment of the data is likely to be a serial one: he inspects each item as a possible reason for rejection. Serial procedures must be more frequent than current research indicates. In many complex situations, the data are not integrated by one multidimensional judgment but the decision is made by serial elimination of alternatives. A search for one general combinatory rule will be as disappointing as the search for one psychophysical law or one learning curve. Individual differences in combinatory strategies are as enlightening as general principles.

JUDGING PERSONS ON SEVERAL TRAITS

When someone has multidimensional information to communicate, he may (depending on the conventions of the situation and his own cognitive style) write a descriptive paragraph in the form of connected discourse, or go to the other extreme and wrap it all up in an either-or judgment. Between these extremes, he may summarize the information in one rating on a continuous scale, as just discussed above; or he may preserve the multidimensional information by making separate ratings on separate scales. The output as well as the input may be multidimensional.

Analysis of this judgment situation has been stimulated by the question whether the dimensions of information are really kept separate. The venerable hypothesis of a halo effect (i.e., that people rated high on one desirable trait are rated high on other desirable traits) is equivalent to the assertion that the output is less multidimensional than the input. The experiments reviewed above ask how the judge combines the dimensions when he is required to make a summary judgment; now the question is whether the judge does so when he is not required to.

ANALYSIS OF THE VARIANCE IN MULTITRAIT RATINGS

The early research that led to the hypothesis of a halo effect relied on correlation coefficients. When a foreman, for example, rates the individuals in his crew on several traits, the correlations between trait ratings are often quite high—as if the separate ratings were dominated by one global impression of overall effectiveness. Actually, correlation analysis is cumbersome, because of the number of correlations required, hence Guilford (1954) adapted the analysis of variance to trait ratings. The main effects—due to raters, traits, and individuals—are interesting; but the special advantage of this analysis comes from the interaction effects, which are psychologically meaningful and often quite large. Guilford distinguished two components of the halo effect: the main effect common to all raters, which is the more general component; and that varying between raters, a relative halo effect which is computed as an interaction between raters and individuals being rated. But another interaction, that between individuals and traits, is inversely related to the older measure of halo, the intertrait correlation, and can be considered a measure of differential discrimination since it measures the raters' agreement in assigning certain traits to certain individuals (Willingham and Jones, 1958).

An application of this modern analysis to the old question of the halo effect (Johnson, 1963; Johnson and Vidulich, 1956) began with ratings by college students of five individuals—Queen Elizabeth II, Senator Joseph McCarthy, Sir Winston Churchill, Mrs. Eleanor Roosevelt, and Pope Pius XII—all in the public eye at the time, on five traits. The general halo effect appeared clearly. Pope Pius, for example, was generally rated high and Senator McCarthy low. To put this effect in terms of the old method of measuring halo, it was estimated (Stanley, 1961) as equivalent to a mean interjudge correlation of about .40. The relative halo effect, the interaction between raters and individuals, was also significant. But the largest interaction was that between individuals and traits, which means that the judges did make analytical, discriminating judgments. They rated Sir Winston Churchill high on intelligence, Senator Joseph McCarthy very low on kindliness, and Queen Elizabeth high on personal appearance.

This analysis does not differentiate between correlations which develop during the judging process and those which are in the information that the judges have received. Hence the experiment tried to separate these by manipulation of the judging procedure. To minimize halo, one group judged all five individuals on one trait a day for five days, while another group, expected to maximize halo, judged one individual a day on all five traits. But the expected differences did not appear. So there is still no clear-cut evidence for halo effect, when that term means a bias introduced by judging operations. The general halo effect could be due to mass communication, which brings standard information about the individuals to all judges, and the relative halo effect could be due to selective communication.

The basic difficulty with these analyses is that the information received by the judges is not controlled, as it is in the impression formation studies. The judges are given the names of public figures or, in the industrial situation, of employees and asked to sort out their impressions of these people on several dimensions. Or, if the judges are asked to supply names of relatives and acquaintances whom they can rate, the trait ratings are generally correlated (Koltuv, 1962). But, in any case, the correlations within the information available to the judges, which have been experimentally manipulated in some impression formation studies, are unknown; hence the correlations between the dimensions of judgment cannot be clearly interpreted. Ideally, the output correlations would be isomorphic with the input correlations; to determine how the actual judgments deviate from this ideal would require a more complex analysis.

STEREOTYPES

Stereotypes and halo effects are similar in that they are intended to account for oversimplified judgments of persons, but the halo effect is supposed to develop in the judging process as a failure of analysis, while stereotypes are described as previously acquired beliefs about types of people that influence present judgments. Stereotypes had a bad reputation for many years because of their role, both as cause and effect, in prejudice against minority groups. Recent research has rehabilitated this old concept because, in competition with other effects, it is the stereotypes, especially of occupational groups, that make the highest contribution to accuracy of judgment and the teaching of stereotypes that offers the most promise for the training of judges (Smith, 1966).

The importance of stereotypes here is that they illustrate another deviation from the additivity assumption. If a woman is characterized by four adjectives, the judge may add these somehow; but if she is first introduced as an ophthalmologist, or as an exotic dancer, a classifying or stereotyping operation will precede the adding.

Some Characteristics of Judges

When the abilities that distinguish man at his best are under discussion, we often hear the phrase "good judgment." This is commonly cited among the requirements for success, whether as an executive or motorist, quarterback or parent. And good judgment is indeed complex; the research reviewed in this chapter, together with previous analyses, calls attention to the abilities involved in:

1. abstracting the relevant facts from a complex situation,
2. adopting and maintaining a set for multiple relevant facts,
3. weighting each appropriately,
4. integrating all this information to fit one of the response alternatives rather than the others, and
5. communicating the judgment with due caution.

Judgment tests devised to differentiate good and poor executives contain a large measure of general intelligence, and such tests do discriminate between those who are generally good or generally poor in problem solving

(Harootunian and Tate, 1960). Judgment tests used in the selection of personnel often include questions on information specific to the job also, because the good judge in some situations is the one who knows the relevant facts. In addition, the good judge knows which facts are important and how they should be organized.

Many differences between judges have already been mentioned in passing. Substantial differences in preferences and in accuracy appear in the data on unidimensional judgments; in multidimensional judgments, differences in the weights attached to the dimensions have been computed, and some models distinguish judges by their combinatory operations. For example, when 28 clinicians—psychologists with the Ph.D. degree and clinical trainees—made summary judgments of persons from their scores on a personality inventory, Wiggins and Hoffman (1968) were able to categorize them according to the judgment models that matched their judgments. The judges were given the personality test scores of a large number of individuals and asked to rate each on an 11-point scale extending from *neurotic* to *neutral* to *psychotic*. The judgments indicated that 12 of the judges were best described by a linear model, 3 by a nonlinear model (more precisely, a quadratic model), and 13 by a sign model. The signs in this case were certain diagnostic indicators acquired from empirical clinical literature or from clinical folklore, such as a score on a single scale or a linear or configural combination of scores on several scales. Thus 12 of the judges were considered linear and 16 configural.

Wiggins, Hoffman, and Taber (1969) followed up this approach by paying 145 subjects (heterogeneous in age and education) to make ratings of intelligence from 9 cues, such as high-school grade, study habits, and effective use of English, supposed to represent standard information on 199 individuals applying for admission to college. Factor analysis divided the subjects into 8 groups, which differed in the way they made their ratings of intelligence. When correlations between each cue and the intelligence rating were computed for each group separately, the multiple correlations were .93 or above, indicating that the linear model was reasonably appropriate for these judgments. But the weights attached to the cues by these different groups of judges varied considerably. One group, of 45 judges, rated intelligence mostly on the basis of high-school grade, as indicated by a cue correlation of .97. Another group, of 28 judges, put most of the emphasis on effective use of English, as indicated by a cue correlation of .90. The largest group, of 53 judges, made use of these same 2 cues but also of the information on study habits and responsibility, as indicated by correlations of .46 for each of these cues.

The judges also took a battery of personality inventories, from which it appeared that the group of judges who stressed responsibility and study habits were the ones who got the highest scores for authoritarianism and religious conservatism. Thus there seems to be some connection between what judges consider important in others and their own personalities; but in most other such studies, relationships between judges' personalities and their judgments have been weak.

An analysis of the variance in multitrait ratings reveals interactions between raters and individuals, which probably reflect differences in information or in the acceptance of it, but also between raters and traits, which more probably arise in the individual's judging processes. Furthermore, some judges are more inclined than others to stereotyped thinking, and even unprejudiced thinkers seem to have implicit theories which lead them to make judgments as if certain dimensions of personality were assumed by some judges to be correlated and other dimensions by other judges.

Another characteristic that could produce pervasive individual differences in multidimensional judgments is a judge's cognitive complexity or dimensionality. How many dimensions does he use? One approach to this has the judge list the dimensions that he proposes to use in judging persons; a second provides the dimensions for him. Cognitive complexity is studied by comparing the judge's ratings of a person on one dimension with his ratings of this person on other dimensions. The complex judge makes more differentiated use of the dimensions; the simpler judge makes the same ratings on different dimensions, or, in effect, uses fewer dimensions (Bieri et al., 1966). This differentiation or complexity in a judge's ratings can be measured by a count of differences between ratings on the different dimensions, by factor analysis of the correlations between dimensions, or by analysis of variance.

In different experiments, the judgments of complex judges have varied in many ways from those of judges with simpler cognitive structures, but the difference most pertinent here is that the complex judges handle inconsistent information more adequately (Bieri, et al., 1966). The simpler judges blur the distinctions between dimensions—as if they were more susceptible to halo effects—or fluctuate with the most recent information, while the complex judges preserve the distinctions and try to make sense out of all the data. In this respect older children are presumably more complex than younger children. The discussion of the development of conservation in Chapter 3 noted that a judgment of quantity can be treated as an integration of judgments of height and breadth, with older children using both dimensions while younger children discount one as inconsistent with the other. But experiments on judgment have thus far seldom taken advantage of the developmental approach.

These various characteristics of judges have, with few exceptions, been computed only once and only for judgments of persons. The methodology developed as a by-product of experimental and social psychology so that the usual psychometric questions about the stability and generality of these individual differences have not yet been answered. On the other hand, the intellectual abilities of symbolic and semantic judgment identified by a psychometrically sophisticated program of factor analysis (Guilford, 1967), though interesting by themselves, have not yet been related to the judgment processes discussed in this chapter.

Major Trends and Implications

Judgment begins, from the psychological point of view, with a disorderly situation, confused by alternatives, that interrupts the individual's course of action; it ends with a more orderly one, that permits him to move on with less uncertainty. The end in view is an ordering of the alternative responses to correspond with some physical dimension of perceived stimulus objects, or with some abstract cultural dimension of words and other symbols, or with the attractiveness of the objects at hand and of expected consequences of alternative actions. It is experimentally convenient to study judgment by itself, isolated from other intellectual operations such as productive thinking, but everyone knows that judgments are involved at critical points throughout a complicated problem-solving project, as in the initial choice of a strategy and the final choice of one of the alternative solutions. The decision to begin is itself a risky decision because, as John Dewey put it, "If we once start thinking no one can guarantee where we shall come out."

One test of unidimensional judgments is consistency within the judgments of one individual, which, in the case of preferences or affective judgments, is a measure of that elusive desideratum called rationality. Another is agreement between independent judges, which depends on a common conceptualization of the stimulus dimension and can be considerably improved by appropriate training. When an external criterion is available, objective measures of accuracy can be computed, which indicate that human limitations in the judge's capacity for processing information restrict the amount of stimulus input that he can transform into categorical output. When forced to shift from judgment of one dimension to judgment of another, his accuracy is reduced by difficulty in control of his set.

Multidimensional judgments are also subject to limitations, at a second level of complexity, in the combinatory operations. Different analyses of multidimensional judgments compute different measures and use different languages, but all agree that, by comparison with the stimulus dimensions, the amount of information in most judgments is reduced and the structure simplified. The implication of this limitation can be appreciated in contrast to analogous perceptual tasks. When we consider how man integrates sensory data into patterns—as in the perception of speech and of objects in space—we are impressed by his remarkable ability to combine sensory inputs according to complex nonlinear functions. But the research reviewed in this chapter indicates that when the data are in the form of abstract dimensions, most of the output variance can be attributed to three or four dimensions. Concept research, in earlier chapters, came to a similar conclusion: increasing the number of dimensions decreases the information extracted from each.

Simplification of the structure of the judgments is also revealed in judges' inclinations—shown by the judgment data, not the judges' statements—toward linear rather than nonlinear relations, additive combinations rather than interactions, and in multitrait ratings, correlations between traits rather than sharp differentiations. There is a tendency to put the objects of judgment into classes or, if they are people, into stereotypes, a move that may be effective or not, depending on the accuracy of the stereotypes. In either case, it simplifies the structure of the input information. The ultimate simplification is attained, of course, when people or ideas are divided into two categories—the good and the bad, or those on our side and those on the other side—and the information received is adjusted to permit two-category judgments of all instances. At the other extreme, high fidelity to the structure of the data could best be attained by graphic or mathematical representation of complex relations—usually not allowed in judgment experiments.

The linear additive model, in one form or another, has been a useful first step in describing how the judge combines multidimensional information into a summary judgment. But it has been necessary to add weights, to compromise between adding and averaging, and to recognize the occasional occurrence of configural combinations. In linguistic structures adjectives are multiplied by certain adverbs, and in risky decisions outcome values are often multiplied by probabilities. The environment contains a diversity of objects to be evaluated, some independent, some correlated, and the various models of judgment have each staked out a little territory within which they perform moderately well. Today the linear additive model is one among many.

The contribution of learning to judgment parallels the contribution of learning to the solution of other types of problems. Dimensions, values, probabilities, and such cognitive structures as stereotypes and implicit personality theories are learned. And, since we know so little about the accuracy of most judgments, we cannot offhand deny the claim that the accuracy of most judgments depends as much on previous learning as on the details of the judging operations described in this chapter. Cognitive learning experiments have demonstrated also that the intelligent adult can learn to make configural judgments with suitable instructions and information about errors. It is not surprising that a man who can shift back and forth, as the terrain requires, from activities as different as swimming and climbing, can shift also from additive to multiplicative integration of information. Judges can learn to make judgments as their peers and teachers do and thus to increase reliability of a sort, but only in a few cases has an increase in ecological validity been demonstrated. Because of a philosophical commitment or a supervisor's encouragement, a judge may also practice an intuitive approach, immersing himself in the raw data and trying to make empathic global judgments, but progress in this type of training is not usually subjected to quantitative analysis.

Trends in psychological research, like revolutions, often betray the spirit that set them going. What happened to the Gestalt emphasis on configuration? In a negative sense, Gestalt claims about the structure of the combining operations have been accepted because no one now defends a simple summation model. The positive side of the Gestalt contribution was not so explicit;

configuration is a general notion about multidimensional judgment rather than a testable hypothesis. The explicit hypotheses have been stated in mathematical terms, such as nonlinearity, multiplication, and interaction, which in some intuitive sense seem to be more structured than additive combinations. The ideal that the structure of the judgments should mirror the structure of the data has a Gestalt quality, but the tests will come from mathematical analysis.

The overlap between the judgment experiment and the concept experiment, which ties the last chapters of this book to the first, is manifested, not only in the language and the explanatory principles but also in the research trends. Both have shifted from concrete to more abstract materials, from synthetic to more realistic ecological objects of thought, from regularities to probabilities, from simple to complex combinations, from single to multiple measures of achievement, and from an exclusive concern with general laws to a concomitant concern with individual differences.

JUDGMENT: RESPONSE VARIABLES AND SCALES

he dependent variable of most interest is the actual response, the judgment; but confidence and speed of judgment also have attracted some attention. The judgment is a social response by which one person communicates to someone else that he has assigned a stimulus object or event to a certain response category. Since the function of the response is communicative, it may be made by pressing a button, making a pencil mark on paper, saying a word, or gesturing. In any case the judgment is expressed by one of a small number of responses, the meaning of which is established in advance. In a court of law, for example, the jury is instructed at the outset what categories to use in reporting the verdict. The choices open to players in most games are stated in the rule book. In the psychology laboratory, the experimenter tells the subject what responses he can make and what they mean. Thus when the judge makes a judgment, he is set, not only for certain stimulus dimensions, as noted in the previous chapter, but also for certain responses.

Judgments are collected in many psychological experiments, but the judging conditions are standardized so that some other function, such as vision, is emphasized. Judgment experiments, on the other hand, manipulate conditions that emphasize the judgment function, with the aim of discovering general principles that apply to all objects of judgment. While the previous chapter focused on the stimulus side of the judgment, the input, this chapter will focus on the response side, the output.

Scales of Judgment

Judgments are frequently passed on from one person to another in terms of standard scales (such as weight in ounces and length in inches) that are learned in school and used in ordinary communication according to standard usage. The ability to look at an object and estimate its length in inches involves achievement of a dimensional concept, length, and a unit, the inch. Uniformity of usage of these standard scales develops through comparing judgments with readings of standard measuring instruments, such as the footrule. Whatever the mode of acquisition may be, these are important cognitive achievements by which the individual knows the environment and communicates with others about it.

Contrasted with these are temporary rating scales, such as *short, medium, long,* and 1, 2, 3, 4, 5, that are acquired in specific situations, have communicative significance only in these situations, and are quickly forgotten. Temporary scales are used in many practical situations where standard scales do not apply; they appear in judgment research more often than standard scales because their development can be experimentally manipulated.

There is an interesting analogy between the judgment experiment and the concept experiment. In a conventional concept experiment, when subjects achieve the class of red squares, they are not learning the concepts *red* and *square,* but they are attaining a temporary conjunction of two familiar concepts. Likewise, when the subjects of a judgment experiment rate squares as *small, medium,* and *large,* they are not learning the concept length nor the meaning of the three adjectives; they are working out a temporary adjustment of the three-category scale to the objects in view.

SCALES AS COGNITIVE STRUCTURES

Considerable progress in judgment research has been made by study of the association between responses, such as *short, medium,* and *long,* or 1, 2, 3, 4, and 5, and objects of various lengths, just as considerable progress in concept research has been made by studying the association between common responses and dissimilar objects. Most of the research summarized in this chapter follows this approach. But there are conditions for which such a direct approach is not sufficient. Guilford (1954) has pointed out how classical psychophysics assumed a direct linear relation between responses to sensory stimuli and overt judgment and that, while this assumption is often justified there are exceptions which necessitate discussion of the "judgment continuum" as separate from the immediate response to stimuli.

Furthermore, the direct approach misses another important kind of behavior. Sophisticated people talk about scales as they talk about concepts, and this kind of behavior is as important for a theoretical understanding of judgment as any other. It would not be unrealistic to ask a college student: On what scale is 5 degrees a little above freezing? What is the meaning of a score of 90, or 125, on an IQ scale? Just as one who has thoroughly learned to classify objects can also describe the class, one who has accurately judged objects on a scale can also describe the scale. One who can judge the lengths of lines in inches can also draw lines to specifications in inches. College students can describe scales by an adjustment method as by locating the boundaries between scale categories. Investigations of the context effect, to be mentioned later, show that scales organized from judgment of objects influence production of objects, and production of objects influences judgment of objects. Such behavior can best be understood by treating the scale, like the concept, as a cognitive structure, manifested under different conditions by different behavioral achievements. The reason for calling the scale a structure, of course, is that the categories are ordered.

Suppose, by way of illustration, that someone is asked to judge a series of lines as *short, medium,* and *long.* After he has judged all lines two or three times, the three-category scale will be adjusted to the series of lines, as shown in Fig. 9.1, and later judgments of these lines will be consistent. The stimuli (i.e., the lines) and the responses (i.e., the words *short, medium,* and *long*) are observable, but the scale is a theoretical cognitive structure hypothesized as a mediator between the stimuli and the responses. It might not be necessary to hypothesize this cognitive structure just to account for the judgments. But once the subject has organized the scale, he can, if asked, draw a line that is of medium length according to this scale, or one that is at the boundary between *short* and *medium.* He may or may not have an

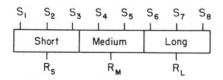

FIGURE 9.1. *Illustration of a temporary scale adjusted to a series of stimuli. The stimuli and the responses are observable; the scale is a hypothetical cognitive structure assumed to mediate communicative responses.*

image of the scale, but nearly any subject, if asked, could represent the scale graphically, by a drawing like Fig. 9.1.

In the experiments to be described in this chapter, the association between the stimuli and the responses is a temporary one, dependent on the temporary scale. A different series of stimuli may lead to the organization of a different scale and the responses mediated by this scale will be associated with different stimuli. But for the time being, the objects of the world are known and communication takes place through the medium of these scales.

Standard scales of inches and ounces are more permanent achievements, learned in school and retained throughout life, but their theoretical status and their influence on judgment are the same. In many cases, as in the judgment of attitude statements for the construction of attitude tests, there are no standard scales, only ad hoc scales.

One might expect that the development of a temporary scale for judging lengths of lines would be inhibited by the permanent scale of inches; actually, the subjects in judgment experiments do not confuse temporary scales and permanent scales any more than playgoers confuse the temporary and permanent names of actors. The subjects seem to follow the experimenter's instructions at least as well as the experimenter's theories follow the subjects' behavior.

The implication of this discussion of the nature of scales is that for many purposes judgments can be simply tabulated and directly related to the stimulus objects, but, when difficulties of interpretation arise, the hypothesis of a scale as a cognitive mediator should be considered. Some of the experimental manipulations to be described influence the relation between the stimuli and the scale; others influence the relation between the scale and the judgments.

JUDGMENTS AND SCALES

Scales may be bounded or unbounded. Many standard scales, such as scales of length and weight, are bounded by zero at one end but extend indefinitely at the other. Most temporary scales are bounded at both ends, as when the response categories are restricted to *very unsociable, unsociable, sociable, very sociable,* or 1, 2, 3, 4, 5, 6, 7, and some of the interesting phenomena of judgment occur at the ends. But under some conditions, bounded scales are undesirable. If the judge has used the most extreme category for the most extreme stimulus he has encountered, and then encounters an even more extreme stimulus, he cannot report his judgment properly because he has exhausted the available categories. To avoid this difficulty, Stevens (1956) introduced the unbounded or open-end scale, which permits the judge to choose his own categories of judgment; he called this procedure *magnitude estimation.* The instructions usually specify the middle category as 10 or 100, to be used for a specified standard stimulus, leaving the judge free to communicate his judgments of other stimuli with numbers such as 2, 5, 10, 20, 40, or 80, 90, 100, 110, 120. An alternative term, *numerical matching* (Stevens 1966a), describes the actual judging operations more clearly.

Unbounded scales have certain advantages for the study of context and anchor effects because they reduce end effects; they are not appropriate, of course, for studying end effects. Since the response categories used are variable, these scales are not suitable for the study of the amount of information transmitted by judgments nor for the study of judgment phenomena around category boundaries.

Occasionally, judgments are communicated by assigning stimulus objects to a two-category scale, such as *short* and *long* or *approve* and *disapprove*, and by ranking all objects in order of magnitude. In any case, the instructions specify the stimulus dimension to be judged, whether length, attractiveness, or conservatism, and the terms in which the judgments are to be reported—exhaustively for bounded scales, illustratively for unbounded scales. The terms, whether words or numbers, are chosen so that they are familiar to the judges, and thus the order is specified in advance. *Unsociable* is more sociable than *very unsociable; sociable* is more sociable than *unsociable;* and so on. In other words, the judge begins with an ordered scale. The terms or responses in which the judgments are expressed, such as *sociable* and 4, are names of categories of the scale to which the stimulus objects are assigned. They are not unrelated categories, but adjacent intervals of a continuous scale. Hence the word *interval* might be more appropriate, but *category* has the sanction of usage.

When comparative judgments are made, each stimulus being compared with a standard stimulus in terms of two categories such as *lighter* and *heavier,* the limen between the categories is known as the point of subjective equality and the difference between this point and the standard stimulus is a well-known systematic error. Judgments of single stimuli have also been complicated by the introduction of a standard or anchoring stimulus—sometimes before each stimulus to be judged, sometimes only once at the beginning of an experiment—and experiments of this type demonstrate the importance of the relevance of the standard, or the attention directed to it, for the organization of the scale of judgment.

Many scales appear to be bipolar in nature. Although a scale of -2, -1, 0, $+1$, $+2$ is readily translated to a scale of 1, 2, 3, 4, 5, in some cases it appears that the scale extends both ways from the zero or neutral point and that the former version is more easily used. On scales of affective value, the positive or pleasant side seems to be qualitatively different from the negative or unpleasant side and the neutral region feels different from either extreme. The cold region of the temperature scale seems to be more than a downward extension of the warm region. But when we look for quantitative evidence in support of these statements, it is not obvious what kind of evidence we want, and we shall see that different kinds of supporting evidence have been offered.

When judgments are made by the ranking method, bipolarity appears in the order in which the judge works. Tresselt (1965) asked subjects to rank 15 colors, and observed that they began by ranking the first, second, third, and so on, to about the eighth, then moved to the fifteenth, the fourteenth, and so on in the other direction. Certainly the first position is definite, the last perhaps less so, and both act as poles or anchors for adjacent positions. If the subjects were to repeat the rankings, the first and last ranks would no doubt be less variable than the middle ones.

The variety of judging operations which the intelligent cooperative human subject can perform with some consistency has led to many arguments about the validity of the results obtained. The most generally valid statement that can be made is that human judges are extremely flexible: they can abstract a single dimension from multidimensional stimulus materials, conceptualize a scale of gradations along this dimension, and utilize many systems of verbal, numerical, or manual responses to communicate about stimuli in terms of this scale or, indeed, about the conceptualized scale.

Arguments about the validity of scales and about the superiority of one over another should not obscure the fact, based on many comparisons, that scale values obtained by one method usually are closely correlated with those obtained by another. The differences are in the absolute values, in the variabilities at different regions of the scale, and in the shape of the functions relating judgments to physical magnitudes.

There are no absolutes in absolute judgment or magnitude estimation and no necessary connections between the judgment output and the sensory input. But the intelligent, cooperative subject can deliver consistent results under various conditions, even under changing conditions, and he can, to some extent, as Poulton (1968) put it, "calibrate and recalibrate himself." In presenting his theory of adaptation level, Helson (1947, 1948) has argued that the changes in the observed judgments reflect changes in perception, and a fair share of the research to be reviewed has been stimulated by adaptation level theory. Hence we must return later to some theoretical questions about the meaning of judgment data and especially of shifts of judgment.

METHODS FOR DESCRIBING SCALES OF JUDGMENT

A set of numbers from 1 to 7 and a set of words like *short* and *tall* is often loosely called a *scale of judgment*, but these are more properly called *responses*, or a *response system*. To describe a scale of judgment is not to describe such responses but how they are related to the stimuli being judged.

Three classes of methods are frequently employed to describe the scale the judge uses in making his judgments. The observed data are the judgments given in response to the stimuli and the instructions; the scale is a hypothetical construct derived from these data. But judgment data are often quite stable, hence this hypothetical construct can be described with more quantitative precision than most constructs of psychological interest.

To avoid confusion, a distinction should be drawn between the study of judgment for its own sake and the technology of scale construction from judgments. The former is concerned with description and explanation of the judgment process while the latter uses judgments for other purposes. The two enterprises interact and profit from each other, however. Knowledge of errors of judgment has reduced some errors of scale construction; and research on scale construction has enlightened the psychology of judgment.

CATEGORY BOUNDARIES IN STIMULUS UNITS

If the stimulus dimension is a quantitative one, the boundaries between adjacent categories can be calculated in units of the stimulus dimension by the method of successive intervals (Guilford, 1954; Torgerson, 1958). The transition from one category to the next is tabulated as a cumulative frequency distribution, then the average of this distribution is taken as the limen or boundary between the categories. Fig. 9.2 illustrates an application of this method to a two-category scale developed by one subject for judging a series of weights, and Fig. 9.3 a four-category scale. Fig 9.4 represents an application to children's use of semiquantitative terms referring to various numbers of printed characters. The number of category boundaries is one less than the number of categories, and the widths of only the internal categories are quantitatively described. Some of the important phenomena of judgment are boundary effects that can be understood only in relation to the location of the category boundaries.

Judgments in only two categories permit computation of only one boundary. The scale thus described is the simplest possible, but the single category boundary is a neutral level or indifference point of considerable theoretical significance, like the point of subjective equality obtained from comparative judgments with a standard stimulus.

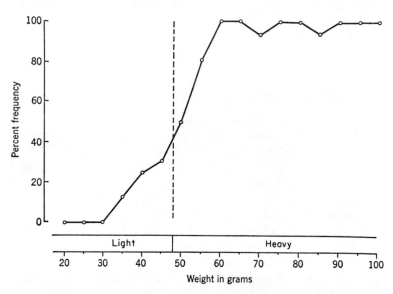

FIGURE 9.2. *Transition zone and category limen for a two-category scale adjusted to a series of 17 stimulus weights. One subject judged each weight 16 times. The limen between* light *and* heavy *was computed as 48 grams. From Johnson (1944).*

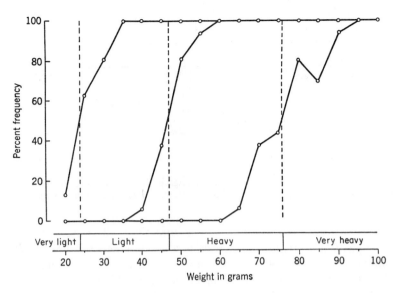

FIGURE 9.3. Transition zones and category limens for a four-category scale. The limens between adjacent categories were computed as 24, 47, and 76 grams. From Johnson (1944).

Many hypotheses about judgment are stated in relation to the center of the scale, and the central value of a two-category scale is, of course, the boundary between the two categories. Generally, the middle category boundary has been taken as a central value for scales of an even number of categories. Other, more elaborate procedures, to be described, have also been used.

NUMERICAL RATING SCALES

Many judgments are expressed on a rating scale, such as 1, 2, 3, 4, 5, 6, 7. These have often been called *absolute judgments* to differentiate them from judgments made in comparison with standard; otherwise the term is misleading since most of the research on absolute judgments has been directed toward their relativity. Another familiar term is *judgment of single stimuli*. For some purposes, it is convenient if the rating scale has as many categories as there are stimuli. Unbounded scales also have their peculiar advantages.

Numerical ratings are widely employed for practical and experimental purposes. Frequently, the numbers given to the categories are assumed to refer to equal intervals on the scale and are then used for regular arithmetical manipulations. Thus the above method describes the scale categories in stimulus units and this method describes the stimuli in rating-scale units. The effect of unequal intervals on the data obtained in this way has been emphasized and minimized elsewhere, but in judgment research the width of the scale intervals has been studied directly, for example, in relation to latitudes of acceptance and rejection of attitude statements. Naturally, the most precise quantitative information comes from temporary numerical rating

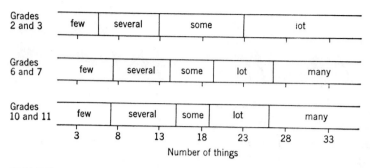

FIGURE 9.4. *Quantitative representation of scales used by children to designate various numbers of printed characters. Data from Brotherton, Read, and Pratt (1948).*

scales organized around stimuli that are quantitatively described; ideally, when the relation between judgment scale and stimulus series is linear and the intervals are equal, the scale can be simply specified as to origin and unit in terms of the stimulus dimension (Torgerson, 1958). Helson and Himelstein (1955) have outlined a least-squares procedure for computing a central value, or adaptation level, and other parameters for the case in which a logarithmic relation is assumed.

ADJUSTMENT OR PRODUCTION METHODS

Under some conditions, the subject represents his response scale by adjusting a pointer, by reproducing a line, or by some other manual adjustment. Almost anyone can describe his scale of heights of people by holding his hand at a height above which he would call people *tall* and below which he would call them *short*. In one experiment (Johnson, 1946), the subject pitched pennies as close to a wall as he could, then later placed a penny on the floor to indicate the boundary between the categories *worse than usual* and *better than usual*. Fig. 9.5 shows relations between a response scale computed from adjustments of a line to a requested angle and the objective stimulus variable. This method indicates, for example, that at 20 degrees and 70 degrees the scale corresponds closely to the objective stimuli, while at 30 degrees and 60 degrees the discrepancies are relatively large. A recent ingenious variation of the old lifted-weight experiment (von Wright and Mikkonen, 1964) requires the subject to adjust a weight to correspond to the medium category. In experiments on attitude scales, college students have been asked to write statements that fit Category 1 and Category 11 (Ostrum, 1966). Production methods are not always convenient, but when they can be used, they demonstrate the varieties of behavior that are related to the cognitive structure known as a scale of judgment.

Response Category Bias

It has long been known that people prefer to make judgments in some categories rather than others. Census reports show a preference for multiples of five and for even numbers in reports of age. When sentencing criminals, judges prefer round numbers, as do psychologists and other scientists reading laboratory instruments. The effect of a preference for any category is to increase the width of that category. In reporting age to the nearest birthday, for example, if the response scale were uniform, the category 49 would be used for ages between 48.5 and 49.5, the category 50 for ages between 49.5 and 50.5, and so on, each response category being one year wide. But if there is a preference for 50, this category will be used by some people of age 49 and some of age 51. Hence the category 50 might extend from 49.2 to 50.8, thereby attaining a width of 1.6 years, while the 49 and 51 categories shrink. Response preferences are particularly noticeable when the categories are designated by semiquantitative terms, such as *very* and *medium*. When the witness tells the jury that the man who stole the money was of medium height, what does the label *medium* mean?

Some quantitative evidence on this question was collected in an attack

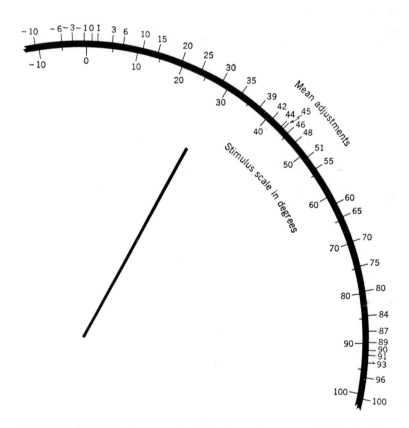

FIGURE 9.5. *Relation between stimulus series and response scale described by a reproduction method. The subjects were asked to adjust a line of light to an angle of, e.g., 30° from the vertical. Mean adjustment was 28.6°, as shown on outside scale. When 3° was called for, the mean adjustment was 4.5°. There were 6 subjects and 2,870 judgments. Data from Kaufman, Reese, Volkmann, and Rogers (1947).*

on an old question of psychophysical methodology. In comparative judgments, should the subject be restricted to two categories, such as *shorter* and *longer,* or should he be permitted to use a middle category also, such as *equal* or *doubtful?* Early discussions of this question dealt with the validity of introspective reports of the impression of equality. But when this criterion was put aside and the *equal* response was treated as the middle category of a three-category scale, the question became amenable to objective investigation. In a weight-lifting experiment, Fernberger (1930) showed that when the instructions emphasized finding a difference between the standard and variable weights, the width of the middle category was reduced to 2 grams; but when the instructions permitted free use of the *equal* response, the middle category attained a width of 10 grams.

Response bias appears also in judgments of single stimuli. A class experiment in a laboratory course at Michigan State University requires judgments of a graded series of eight gray papers as *light, medium,* and *dark.* The group data from one group of ten students gave evidence of a middle category from 3.1 to 6.4, a width of 3.3 in the units of the stimulus series. For another group of ten, told that *medium* was a nondiscriminating response to be avoided, the middle category extended from 4.0 to 5.4, a width of 1.4.

Either end category of a three-category scale can also be widened by a response bias resulting from differential reinforcement. Le Furgy (1966) had a series of circles judged *positive, neutral,* and *negative,* according to the reward expected. But whether one end of the stimulus series or the other was reinforced, the *positive* category was the widest.

Unplanned category biases are not always as large as in these three illustrations, but the effects often interact with other effects to make interpretation difficult. Individual differences in the use of a scale are often due to habitual tendencies to stress or to avoid certain categories. Instructions may lead one judge, whether deliberately or incidentally, to attempt to use each category of the response scale equally often, while another may not consider this requirement.

Context Effects

In many situations, when political, educational, industrial, and esthetic decisions are made, the series of objects or events under consideration constitutes the context within each object is evaluated. The effect can be seen most clearly in judgments of physical stimuli in two categories, such as *large* and *small,* because, whatever the physical size of the stimuli, simple calculations will usually show that the boundary between the two categories occurs near the middle of the stimulus series. When a numerical rating scale is used, the larger numbers are assigned to the larger stimuli and the smaller numbers to the smaller stimuli, so that the judgment scale corresponds approximately with the stimulus series. Thus the stimulus series can be called a frame of reference for the judgments.

DIVERSE ILLUSTRATIONS

The *context effect*, like many others, was discussed under one name or another on the basis of subjective observations before objective data became available. Around the turn of the century, according to Woodworth (1938), German investigators reported that after a series of weight judgments the observer was no longer comparing the lifted weight with the image of the standard weight but with some absolute impression of the whole series. Similar phenomena were noted in studies of pleasantness and unpleasantness in the 1920s and summarized by Beebe-Center (1932) as "mass contrast" rather than contrast between individual stimuli. Later, Hunt and Volkmann (1937) made use of such results on affective judgment to state a general principle of judgment.

The context effect showed up in another form when aviation psychologists found that a cadet has a better chance of passing the primary flight test if he is grouped and checked out on the same day with cadets of low aptitude than with cadets of high aptitude (Krumboltz and Christal, 1957). The effect has turned up also in ratings of foods by a panel of housewives (Fine and Haggard, 1958), in judgments of photographs of applicants for admission to graduate school in psychology (Levy, 1960), in judgments of the intensity of electric shocks (Bevan and Adamson, 1960), in judgments of short descriptions of aggressive behavior (Miller and Bieri, 1965), and in the scaling of social objects by several methods (Hicks and Campbell, 1965). Judgments of the pleasantness of a standard series of photographs of faces expressing emotions were shifted toward the pleasant end of the scale when judged within the context of unpleasant verbal descriptions and toward the unpleasant end within the context of pleasant descriptions (Manis, 1967).

The context effect is not just a matter of repeating judgments already made; it extends beyond the typical judgment situation. When children were asked to take *a few* beads from a tray, or *some of them* or *a lot of them,* the number they took under each instruction was influenced by the context of the number of beads in the tray (Cohen, Dearnley, and Hansel, 1958) (see Fig. 9.6). A series of angles presented for judgment as *large* or *small* determined the size of the angles drawn later, just as, in another experiment, the size of the angles drawn determined later judgment of angles (Jennings and Johnson, 1963). A reproduction method, modifying the familiar lifted-weight experiment, turned up the usual effects (von Wright and Mikkonen, 1964). The series of attitude statements judged also influenced production of statements written to describe the ends of the attitude scale (Ostrum, 1966). Apparently the scale can be organized from the context of either production or judgment and, once organized, it influences subsequent production and judgment.

The context may also be effective when the judgment occurs within a larger sequence of behavior, as when one judges his own achievements with reference to the achievements of others and then raises or lowers his level of aspiration. The consequences of one's behavior are not always immediately

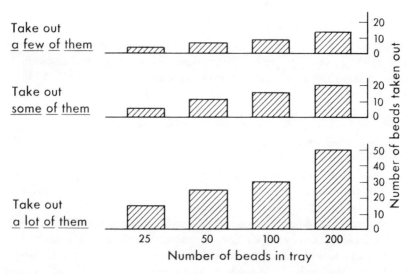

FIGURE 9.6. Context effect and number concepts. When children were asked to take beads out of a tray, the meaning of concepts such as some of them depended in part on the context furnished by the number of beads in view. Data from Cohen, Dearnley, and Hansel (1958).

obvious; an act of judgment often precedes the planning of the next action, and such judgments also are subject to context effects.

QUANTITATIVE ANALYSIS

There is no doubt about the generality of the context effect, but if we ask more detailed questions, quantitative research is necessary, for which the simple two-category judgment is a convenient introduction. As an illustration, when a series of 17 weights ranging from 20 to 100 grams by 5-gram steps was judged repeatedly in two categories, light and heavy, the category limen was 48 grams (Johnson, 1944). This value is near the middle of the stimulus series, to be sure; but the exact middle is 60 grams if it is defined as the midpoint between the two ends or as the mean or median of all weights, hence the obtained value is lower than any simple prediction. This is a general result of several such experiments, which suggests that the scale is organized from some decreasing function of the stimulus magnitudes. A logarithmic function is commonly assumed for weights, leading to computation of a geometric mean, which in this case would be 54 grams, a somewhat better prediction. Linear functions fit the data of some experiments of this kind, and in others logarithmic functions or power functions are better, depending on the stimulus objects and the receptor system.

The typical judgment experiment presents each stimulus equally often, so that the context of judgment is a rectangular distribution of stimuli. Distributions with the same range, but of positive or negative skew, provide different contexts. When the above series of weights was skewed positively, by presenting the lighter weights more often, the category limen was 30 grams, and with a negative skew it was 70 grams. This effect of skew is a general one, but distributions of other shapes have also been arranged, as we shall see later, in order to analyze the details of context effects.

When the stimuli are sounds of various frequencies to be judged for pitch, a logarithmic receptor function is commonly assumed. One experiment with seven series of sounds covering much of the audible range included skewed distributions of stimuli and computed the geometric means of the frequencies to predict the boundaries between the judgment categories *low* and *high* (Johnson, 1949a). Fig. 9.7 shows that the values predicted in this way come close to the obtained values. This figure also displays the large magnitude of the context effect; the frequencies of Series F and G, judged *low,* were objectively much higher than those of Series A and B, judged *high.*

Comparative judgments, as when stimuli are judged *lighter* or *heavier* than a standard stimulus, are not immune to the context effect. Data obtained by the method of constant stimuli indicate that the reference for the judgments is not the standard stimulus alone but the whole series of stimuli as well. The data can be predicted under some conditions by computations that weight the standard stimulus one-half as much as the series stimuli (Johnson, 1945) or one-third as much (Helson, 1947). The effective weight of the standard is presumably a consequence of the attention it receives and may reflect subtleties of the instructions and experimental arrangements.

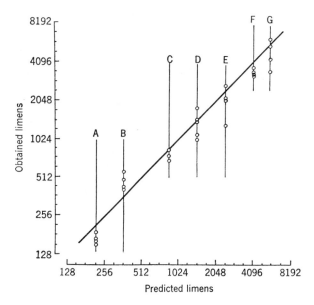

FIGURE 9.7. *Predicted and obtained category limens for two-category judgments of pitch. The vertical lines represent the range of frequencies in a series, some of which were skewed, and the circles represent the obtained category limens. The diagonal line graphs the prediction that limens will be at the geometric mean of each series. From Johnson (1949).*

COMPLICATIONS AND LIMITATIONS

The context effect can be quantified most accurately when judgments of different series are made by independent groups. If the same subjects judge different series, the change in the scale of judgment indicates the direction of the shift of context; but the effect is complicated because the adjustment to the second series is retarded by experience with the first. The effects of such shifts in the stimulus series deserve careful study in their own right in later pages.

The context effect depends on the segregation of the stimulus series from other stimuli. The context does not include all the similar stimuli that the judge can remember, and if his previous memories are strong and relevant, a simple calculation of the context effect will not be adequate. Helson's (1964) quantitative formulation of these phenomena, which explicitly provides for the residual influence of previous experience, will be discussed later. But as a general observation, Helson has stated that "sensory processes are usually less subject to the influence of residuals from past experience and imagination than are affective and cognitive processes [p. 371]."

If someone judges lengths of lines on a well-learned scale of inches that extends from zero to infinity, there is no reason to expect a strong context effect because there is no limited scale to be matched to a segregated stimulus series. Even so, when the series of lines is limited, some evidence of context effect can be obtained (Krantz and Campbell, 1961). Judgments of words on the semantic differential seem to be particularly resistant to the context effect (Sommer, 1965), and other exceptions will be noted in the section on attitude judgments.

The response system by which the judgments are communicated also introduces variations. The context effects that show up when unbounded scales are used (Hicks and Campbell, 1965; Ross and Di Lollo, 1968a) are apparently smaller than when category scales are used—although, since the scales differ, comparisons are difficult. In one experiment on weight judgments (Ross and Di Lollo, 1968b), the use of a two-category scale showed rather complete context effects in that the judgments were closely adjusted to the series presented, whether it was from 100 to 300 grams or 400 to 600 grams. But the use of a six-category scale disclosed some separation between the two series because, as the authors put it, the "locations of the five boundaries defining the six categories are determined partly on relative (or discriminative) considerations and partly to convey absolute judgments of the series as a whole [p. 550]."

In a general way, since the scale of judgment is anchored to all the stimuli, the context effect could be considered a comprehensive anchoring effect. But the term *anchoring* is typically reserved for the effects of special stimuli and for the effects of experience with a series of stimuli in retarding the shift of the scale of judgment, effects that will be systematically considered later. Although the phenomena outlined above have been manifested in several ways and have gone by several names, the name *context effect,* in current use, is the name of choice. It is not easily confused with other terms and is descriptive rather than interpretive.

The Central Tendency of Judgment

The early work by Hollingworth (1909) on inaccuracy of movement employed a reproduction method. His subjects had the task of reproducing the extent of a guided hand movement by drawing a line on paper. Three series were used and it turned out that in each the reproductions of the larger distances were too short and the reproductions of the shorter distances too long. Hollingworth spoke of a "central tendency," by which he meant that the constant error of adjustment was toward the center of any series. The same tendency appears in reproductions of short temporal intervals (Turchoie, 1948). In tracking tasks also there is a tendency, called a *range effect*, to overshoot small inputs and undershoot large inputs (Slack, 1953; Weiss, 1955).

The central tendency can be observed equally often in judgments or ratings: the larger stimuli in any series are underestimated and the smaller ones overestimated. This has been demonstrated for judgments of areas (Hollingworth, 1910), of lines (Ipsen, 1926), and of weights (Noizet, 1967; Woodrow, 1933). The effect can be illustrated most clearly when the rating scale has the same number of categories as there are stimuli, as in Philip's (1947) study of judgments of cards with green and blue dots exposed briefly in a tachistoscope. All cards had 36 dots, but Stimulus No. 1 had 13 green dots and 23 blue, No. 2 had 14 green and 22 blue, No. 11 had 23 green and 13 blue. When this series of 11 stimuli was presented repeatedly for judgment of greenness (or of blueness) on a scale of 1 to 11, a central tendency appeared systematically at both ends (see Table 9.1). Median judgment of the stimulus at the low end was 2.9 rather than 1, and median judgment of the stimulus at the high end was 9.5 rather than 11. The judgments could not go lower than 1 nor higher than 11, hence the distributions of judgments near each end were skewed toward the center and means show more central tendency than medians. The category boundaries at the extremes of the scale of judgment were indeterminate because the extreme ratings were used less frequently than the middle categories. Thus the standard deviation computed for the entire distribution of 11,550 judgments was 2.89, as compared with 3.16 for the stimuli. Central tendency is not limited to this

TABLE 9.1. MEAN AND MEDIAN JUDGMENTS OF CARDS CONTAINING GREEN AND BLUE DOTS

Stimulus number	1	2	3	4	5	6	7	8	9	10	11
Mean rating	3.3	3.7	4.3	4.7	4.8	6.3	7.0	7.4	7.8	8.3	9.0
Median rating	2.9	3.4	4.1	4.5	4.7	6.3	7.1	7.7	8.1	8.6	9.5

Data from Philip (1947).

type of rating scale, however; it has also been reported for esthetic judgments obtained by the method of paired comparisons (Kennedy, 1961).

Central tendency depends, of course, on the context effect. It is only when the stimulus series is the context of judgment that the ends and center of the judgment scale can be expected to line up with the ends and center of the stimulus series and, therefore, that overestimation and underestimation have any meaning. In Table 9.1 context effect shows in that the scale of judgment corresponds quite well with the series of stimuli. The middle stimulus, No. 6, gets a mean rating of 6.3, and central tendency is roughly the same at both ends. When such correspondence occurs, central tendency usually occurs.

Anchoring Effects of Special Stimuli

The context effect gives evidence that the scale of judgment is tied in a generalized way to all stimuli presented for judgment. In addition, a special category of the scale may be tied to a special stimulus, which is then defined as an anchor stimulus. For example, the smallest stimulus may be easily identified as such and always judged a *one,* thus anchoring the judgment scale to the stimulus series at the small end. Both ends are often anchored because the smallest and largest stimuli are identifiable. If a standard stimulus is presented with instructions that it is to be called a *one,* it will have the same anchoring effect. Similarly, if a standard stimulus is presented with instructions that it is to be called a *ten* and is to be the origin from which magnitude estimations are made, this standard also is an anchor in that it ties a special category of the judgment scale to a special stimulus.

The most unambiguous evidence for anchoring is that the anchor stimulus is judged with less variability than other stimuli. If the experimental arrangements permit a measure of error, the anchor stimulus will be judged with less error than other stimuli. But when anchor effects are strong, they spread to adjacent stimuli. Variability and errors decrease as the anchor is approached, verifying the special role of the anchor in the organization of the scale.

Anchoring effects occur when the anchor stimulus is within the stimulus series and also when it is extended beyond the end of the stimulus series.

INTERNAL ANCHORS

A good illustration of internal anchoring comes from a study of the inclinations of lines (Kaufman, Reese, Volkmann, and Rogers, 1947) from which Fig. 9.8 was drawn. The graph shows that the variability of the adjustments was especially small at and near inclinations of 0 and 90 degrees from the vertical. The same effect has been demonstrated by Chapanis by the method of reproduction (1951a) and the method of estimation (1951b). The vertical and the horizontal are natural anchors.

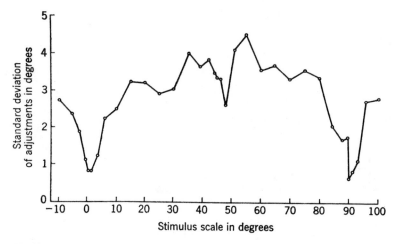

FIGURE 9.8. *Effects of natural anchors at the vertical and horizontal. Variability of adjustments is small at 0° and 90° because the response scale is tied to the stimulus series at these points. Same data as for Fig. 9.5 from Kaufman, Reese, Volkmann, and Rogers (1947).*

MIDDLE ANCHORS

In order to demonstrate how the vertical can anchor the middle of a temporary rating scale, Bourassa (1961) had 21 lines, inclined at angles of 85 to 95 degrees from the horizontal, judged 5 times each on a scale of 0 to 20. Taking the reduction of variability as evidence of anchoring, Fig. 9.9 drawn from the data of 1 subject, shows negligible end anchoring but definite middle anchoring. In judgments of loudness by the method of magnitude estimation, the standard acts as an anchoring stimulus for the middle of the scale and the variability of judgment increases gradually on both sides of this standard (Stevens, 1956, Fig. 1).

END ANCHORS

The anchoring effect most frequently reported is end anchoring. The ends of the judgment scale are linked to the ends of the stimulus, with the result that judgments of the end stimuli are made with fewer errors and less variability than judgments of the middle stimuli (Volkmann, 1951). The effects spread inward, hence it is reasonable to assume that the stimuli near each end are judged in relation to the end stimuli, and that the scale as a whole is organized from both ends toward the middle. End anchoring is most noticeable in judgments made on a rating scale of fixed categories, such as 1 to 7 or −3 to +3, and negligible in judgments on unbounded scales, when the standard is at the middle of the stimulus series and the scale is organized from the middle outward (Weiss, 1963a). Something similar to end anchoring occurs in rankings, however, as noted above, if we take the order in which the judgments are made as evidence of the order of organizing the scale.

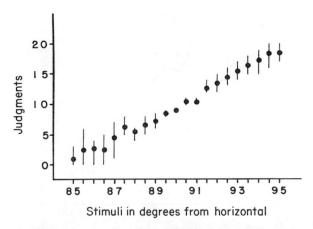

FIGURE 9.9. *Middle anchoring without end anchoring. One subject judged the inclinations of 21 lines, 5 times each, on a scale of 0 to 20. The vertical lines show the range of judgments, and the dots show the means. Middle anchoring appears in the reduction of variability near 90°. Data from Bourassa (1961).*

End anchoring appears clearly in judgments of linear proportions by a reproduction method also. Nash (1964) presented his subjects a vertical line, about 8 inches long, and asked them to mark the deciles, as by putting an X at the 90 percent point. The results showed that the scales were anchored at both ends, because the 10 percent and the 90 percent points were marked with high accuracy, and also the middle, because the 50 percent point was marked with high accuracy. The greatest variability was at 30 and 70 percent.

SALIENCE OF ANCHORS

Why do the ends exert such special effects? Is it because they are ends as such or because they are salient? Eriksen and Hake (1957) eliminated ends by the use of colored papers in an endless continuum and found that their subjects then selected other salient features, such as the end of the response scale, as anchors. After considering alternative explanations, they argued for the hypothesis that the subject selects any salient feature that helps him to stabilize his judgments and interpreted end anchoring as a special case of this.

End anchoring, though common, does not occur at the ends of all stimulus series. Although the subject is told the stimulus dimension to be judged and probably assumes that the stimulus series is a limited segment of this dimension with two definite ends, the identification of these ends comes from experience with the series and some ends are more easily identified than others. One systematic study of end anchoring (Johnson and King, 1964) used slides of 36 green and blue dots, ranging from 0 green (36 blue) to 36 green (0 blue), projected on a screen, because this combination of dimensions yields linear data. Seven sets of 11 slides each were drawn from this range to form different stimulus series and were judged on a scale of 0 to 10. The results, in Fig. 9.10, show that each monochromatic end acted as a strong anchor, but in Set 4, with ends far from the monochromatic ends, no anchor effect appeared. Strong end anchoring may be expected when and only when the end stimulus has some salient property that identifies it as an end beyond which there are no other stimuli. Weaker effects may be expected when the ends are less salient. Fig. 9.10 also shows the central tendency of judgment (Set 4) and the reduction of central tendency by end anchoring, with a concomitant increase in overall accuracy.

Adding value to a stimulus object may have several consequences, but one of interest here is that it makes that stimulus more salient. Tajfel (1959) had a series of weights judged on a ten-category scale, but when he gave a bonus for judging the weight at one end or the other, he found that adjacent stimuli were separated more clearly throughout the series and the overall range of judgments was extended. This was not due to a general increase in motivation, because the effect did not occur when bonuses were given for stimuli at random. According to Tajfel, value at one end of the series made both ends more salient.

The salience of an end stimulus depends also on the spacing of the series stimuli. End stimuli in series of lengths and in series of descriptions of aggressive behavior were judged with lower variability when they were the ends of a widely spaced series of eight stimuli than when the same stimuli were the ends of series of eight stimuli of half the range (Miller and Bieri, 1965). And if the judges are led to believe that the ends may change, the

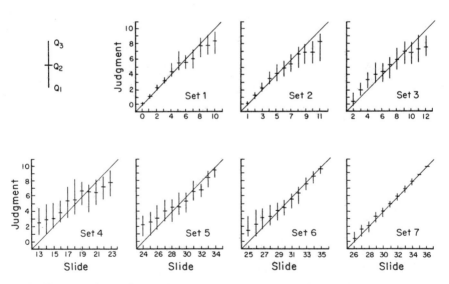

FIGURE 9.10. *The conditions of end anchoring. Seven sets of 11 stimuli each were judged on a scale of 0 to 10. Medians and quartiles are shown for each distribution of 60 judgments. Sets 1, 2, 6, and 7, with a salient stimulus at one end of the stimulus series, show definite end anchoring. Set 4, without identifiable end stimuli, shows no anchoring. From Johnson and King (1964).*

anchoring effect of the ends of series of frequencies judged for pitch is reduced and variability of judgment is increased (Tabory and Thurlow, 1959).

SUPPLIED ANCHORS

In addition to anchors that are part of the regular stimulus series, an anchor
can be supplied by the experimenter. Fig. 9.11 illustrates the influence of
such a supplied anchor. A line like the one adjusted by the subjects was
presented and the subjects were told that this line was at an angle of 30
degrees. With such help, the variability of the adjustments at and near 30
degrees was drastically reduced. Supplied anchors are particularly important
for the design of instruments and of rating scales—they will be discussed
more thoroughly in a later section on accuracy of judgment.

An ingenious experiment was arranged by Mostofsky and Green (1966)
so that the subject could supply the anchor stimuli to himself. The stimuli
were nine pulsating tones, ranging from two to ten pulses per second, for
judgment in two categories, *slow* and *fast*. In addition, the subjects had access
to two switches, which permitted them to hear the slowest and fastest stimuli,
the end anchors, whenever they wished. Aside from the help this procedure
gives the subject, it helps the experimenter to determine when the subject
is uncertain of his judgment; as one would expect, the anchors were demanded
most often when the subjects were judging stimuli near the middle of the
series, rather than at either end.

Anchors outside the regular stimulus series can also be supplied by the
experimenter, with interesting consequences to be summarized below. It
seems clear from these experiments on internal anchors that the alignment of
the scale of judgment with the stimulus series depends on the nature of the
stimuli, especially the salient stimuli, and on the activity of the subject in looking for salient features around which to stabilize his judgments and organize
an unordered situation.

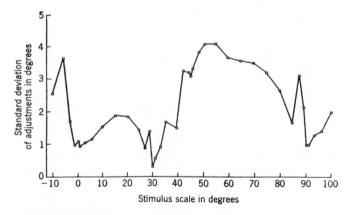

FIGURE 9.11. *Effects of a supplied anchor. In comparison with Fig. 9.8, an anchor
stimulus introduced at 30° reduced variability near this point sharply. Data from
Kaufman, Reese, Volkmann, and Rogers (1947).*

EXTERNAL ANCHORS

Dramatic anchoring effects can be obtained by the addition of an anchor stimulus outside the series of stimuli originally presented for judgment. The stimuli that produce the effects have been referred to by several names, such as *external, extended, remote,* and *extra-range* anchors, but the facts can be simply illustrated by an experiment of Rogers (1941), which set the pattern for many others. Several lines were displayed at various inclinations from the vertical, to be judged repeatedly on a scale from *one* to *six.* After the subject had stabilized his judgments, an anchor stimulus of greater inclination was presented with instructions that this one was a *six.* The subject's scale of judgment shifted upward to include the anchor, and judgments of the other stimuli shifted correspondingly downward. As more remote anchor stimuli were included, the effects on judgment of the original series stimuli increased. Similar effects have been reported for judgments of weights (Heintz, 1950; Rogers, 1941) and for judgments of the prestige of occupations and the seriousness of social offenses (McGarvey, 1943). This is a standard merchandising technique also, illustrated gorgeously in fashion magazines. An outrageous hair style, an extremely long skirt, or an extravagant eye make-up is displayed in the expectation that such stimulation will shift the scale in this direction and thus that less extreme style changes will be readily accepted.

Laboratory experiments of this kind have demonstrated substantial effects, but they are more complex than at first appeared. Clarification requires two types of experiment because there are two questions to be answered. The first is a static question: What are the differences between the scale values of stimuli when judged as part of one series and when judged as part of another, extended series? This can best be answered by a comparison of judgments made by independent groups of subjects. The second is a dynamic question: How is the adjustment to the new series influenced by experience with the old series? This can best be answered by repeated measures on the same subjects, and the controls used in experiments on learning are helpful. A separate section, Realignment of the Scale of Judgment, will be devoted to the second question.

A graphic illustration of the effects of remote anchors above and below a series of stimuli is supplied by Fig. 9.12, taken from Helson's (1964) work on adaptation level. This figure shows clearly how the mean judgments or scale values of the five weights are elevated when judged with a light anchor and depressed when judged with a heavy anchor. The judgments were made by three different groups of subjects; the anchor stimuli were not judged, but were presented as standards before each judgment of a series stimulus. Obviously, however, they acted as salient stimuli.

Striking illustrations of the effects of anchors on the operation of Gestalt principles of perceptual organization have recently been reported by Bell and Bevan (1968). The effect on the principle of proximity was demonstrated when a square matrix of dots distinctly organized as rows functioned as an anchor to increase the frequency with which ambiguous matrices were

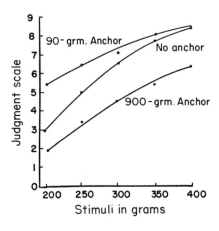

FIGURE 9.12. *Effects of remote anchors on weight judgments. In relation to the control condition with no anchor, a 90-gram anchor raises all judgments, but especially at the low end. A 900-gram anchor lowers all judgments, but especially at the high end. The curves represent equations derived from adaptation-level theory. From Helson (1964).*

perceived as columns; the matrices were perceived as rows when a column anchor was presented. Other experiments of the same design demonstrated similar effects on the Gestalt principles of similarity, good continuation, and closure.

If the anchor stimulus is extended too far beyond the series stimuli, its influence breaks down (Helson and Masters, 1966; Sarris, 1967), either because it does not receive much attention, or because it is not perceived as a part of the series, perhaps not even as relevant to the task. When Sarris had his subjects judge weights from 200 to 400 grams, with anchors ranging from 12.4 to 4,500 grams, he obtained the usual anchoring effects, increasing with distance from the series stimuli, for anchors between 90 and 3,000 grams. But outside these limits the effects of the anchors decreased.

The most extensive data on variations in anchor effects come from experiments on pitch judgments by Sarris (1969), using rather narrow series of frequencies and a wide range of anchors. For the middle curve of Fig. 9.13, for example, the stimulus series extended from 500 to 600 Hertz, or cycles per second. Anchors as low as 200 pulled the scale down—as measured by the adaptation level or central value of the scale—and anchors as high as 700 pulled the scale up. Hence within these limits the relation between adaptation level and anchor is linear. But beyond these limits anchor effects decrease at both ends, so that the effects of anchors below 50 and above 3,000 cycles per second were negligible. Similar inflections are apparent in the other two curves of Fig. 9.13.

The pure effect of an external anchor, uncomplicated by other effects, comes out when all stimuli, including the anchor stimulus, are judged in the same way and the scale adjusted to include the anchor. For the experiment illustrated in Fig. 9.14, the stimulus materials were chosen (as for Fig. 9.10) so that the relation between response scale and stimulus series would be linear. The judgments made by five independent groups show that the scale is adjusted as a whole to a series that includes a remote anchor, just as it is adjusted to a shorter standard, or unanchored, series. As in Fig. 9.12

from Helson, the difference between the judgments is greater at the end of the standard series which is closer to the anchor stimulus.

The effect of an external anchor can be called a contrast effect, since the end stimulus might be small relative to the standard series and large in contrast to the anchor stimulus. Or, to describe the effect more generally, when the scale of judgment is adjusted to the standard series, the end stimulus is at the end of the scale. But when the scale is adjusted to include a remote anchor stimulus, the end of the standard series is no longer at the end of the scale and receives a less extreme scale value.

When the anchoring experiment is simplified in this way, it is apparent that one function of the anchor is to extend the context of judgment; if the anchor stimulus is judged, the anchoring effect is a special manifestation of the context effect. But an extended anchor is also a very salient stimulus, precisely because it is extended beyond the others. Hence variability of judgment of the anchor stimulus is usually negligible.

Since the effect of an unjudged anchor breaks down at extreme distances from the other stimuli, will the effect of a judged anchor also break down? One can only speculate, but requiring the subject to judge the anchor may make it seem less remote, perhaps uniting it with the other stimuli that are the objects of the same judging operation.

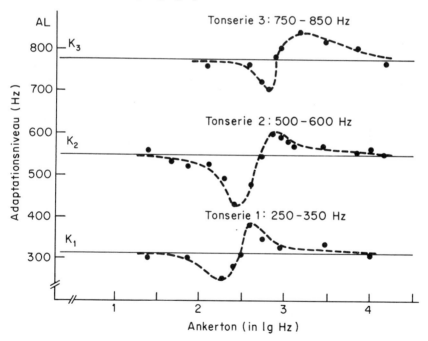

FIGURE 9.13. *Effects of remote anchors on pitch judgments with a wide range of anchors. Adaptation level is scaled on the ordinate in Hertz or cycles per second and the anchor stimulus in log Hertz on the baseline. The middle portion of each curve, roughly linear, exhibits the familiar anchor effects; but as the anchor stimulus is extended in either direction, an inflection appears and the anchor effects are reduced to zero. From Sarris (1966), permission Verlag für Psychologie.*

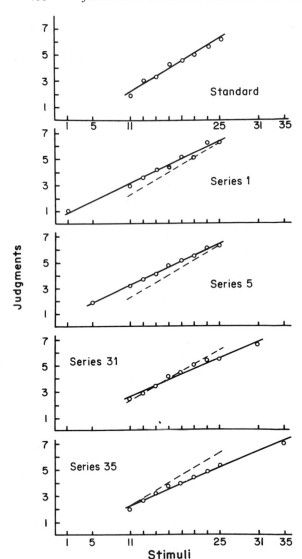

FIGURE 9.14. Judgments of a standard series of weights and 4 anchored series. Each point represents the mean of 64 judgments. The solid line in each graph shows the linear regression equation computed from all judgments. The regression line of the standard series is reproduced as a broken line on the other graphs. From Johnson and Mullally (1969).

IMAGINARY ANCHORS

The anchor stimulus need not be a stimulus that the judge perceives; this has been demonstrated incidentally by many experiments directed toward other principles. When Blumenfeld (1931), in one of the earliest experiments on anchoring, had his subjects judge the irregularity of scattered dots on a card, the judgments indicated that the subjects took zero scattering (all dots lying in a straight line) as an anchor even though they did not see such a card. Hunt and Volkmann (1937) observed that judgments of the pleasantness of colors can be influenced by reference to an anchor in the form of the most pleasant color one can think of. The vertical and the horizontal act as anchors for judgment of lines even though no vertical or horizontal line is presented. And in the Johnson and King experiment (page 402), the anchoring effect of a monochromatic slide was apparent even when this slide was not included in the series to be judged. It is easy for anyone who sees a slide with two green dots or one green dot to imagine a slide with no green dots and use that imaginary slide to anchor his scale.

Realignment of the Scale of Judgment

We have seen that the alignment of the scale of judgment with the series of stimuli is influenced by the stimulus context and by special anchor stimuli. It follows that the scale can be shifted up and down, or realigned, by manipulation of these stimuli; such shifts have also been called *context effects* and *anchoring effects*. The term *contrast* is used in addition because a stimulus that is judged small in contrast to the first series may be judged large in contrast to the second. The resemblance of experiments of this kind to experiments on learning is obvious.

JUDGMENT AND LEARNING

Judgments are learned. This is one feature that distinguishes judgments from reflexes and changes in a scale of judgment from sensory adaptation. Unlearned components are involved in perceptual and affective judgments, but the judgments are communicated from one person to another by a system of response categories the meaning of which has been learned in other social situations. The communicative significance of each response category of a temporary scale of judgment develops quickly, and the typical judgment experiment, in the psychophysical tradition, presents the stimulus series a few times for practice, then discards the practice data. The judge is expected to achieve a stable adjustment to the situation and to the stimulus series rapidly, so that the data from subsequent series can be combined. The adjustment does occur quickly if the stimulus series is constant, but it does depend on practice in judging the first few series.

To say that judgments are learned is a very general statement—as general as the definition of learning itself—that is not as helpful as one might expect. Research and discussion of learning has usually ignored the learning of scales. Since the subject's task is ambiguous, the definition of correct response, or of confirmation, is also ambiguous, especially when the stimulus series is shifted. But treating the adjustment of a scale of judgment to a series of stimuli as learning, while it does not explain anything, does suggest variables that can be examined, hypotheses that can be tested, and control conditions that can be included. The possibilities of improvement with practice will be considered later under the heading of accuracy of judgment.

The basic question is how anyone, having adjusted his judgments to one stimulus context, readjusts to another. It is not a question of learning a new dimension but of a quantitative shift along a familiar dimension. If someone is accustomed to thinking of $1 as the limen between an expensive lunch and an inexpensive lunch, how does he realign his scale of values with each inflationary rise? What will happen to a student's scale of the seriousness of offenses if he loses contact with the peccadilloes of college life and goes to work in a state prison?

The most complete picture of a realignment comes from examining judgments of all stimuli. But when comparisons are made between pre- and postshift judgments, the picture becomes complicated; hence several simplifications, depending on the feature of most interest, have been introduced.

The shift can be followed continuously and plotted with some precision if the stimuli are judged on a two-category scale, so that the limen between the categories can be computed as the central value that locates the scale and tracks its movements in stimulus units. When the scale has three or five categories, the mean of the stimuli assigned to the middle category, often labeled *medium,* can be treated as a central value.

When judgments are made on a numerical rating scale, least-squares procedures provide a central value or scale origin for each block of judgments. For some purposes, it is not necessary to analyze the judgments of all stimuli. Shifts of a rating scale can often be studied merely by following the ratings of what Krantz and Campbell called a *tracer stimulus,* that is, a stimulus that is included in all series but may be, as the series change, at the high end of one and at the low end of another.

It is a reasonable hypothesis that the lag in adjusting to a new series is related to the amount of experience with the old series, and in one of the earliest experiments of this type Tresselt (1947) was able to confirm this hypothesis for weight judgments. Since that time, most of the research has been directed toward those variations of the preshift series that impede adjustment to the postshift series.

LEARNING CURVES

When the stimuli of the old and the new series are judged in two categories, so that one category limen locates the scale, the shift can be described in terms of movement from the old limen toward the new. In the case of judgments of the pitch of sounds, we know from the research plotted in Fig. 9.7 that these limens are approximately at the geometric means of the stimulus series. If we designate these two limens as L_1 and L_2, the simplest expression describing the shift would be a weighted average of the two limens (Johnson, 1949b).

$$L_n = \frac{wL_1 + nL_2}{w + n}$$

In this equation, n represents the number of times the second series of stimuli has been presented for judgment. L_2 is weighted by n, therefore, and L_1 by w, an empirical constant indicating the weight of the preshift series in impeding adjustments to the postshift series. L_n is the category limen at the time of the nth practice trial, that is, the nth presentation of the new series.

The expression could be considered a moving weighted average. It begins at L_1 and takes the form of a hyperbola with L_2 as an asymptote.

When experiments were arranged to test this equation, the curves drawn in Fig. 9.15 were obtained. They show that a hyperbolic function is not inconsistent with the facts, although the data are not sufficiently regular to rule out other similar functions that approach an asymptote. More important, these graphs show that w, the constant representing the weight of the first series in retarding adjustment to the second, increases directly with an increase in the number of preshift trials. Similar effects of number of preshift trials have been reported by Di Lollo and Casseday (1965) for weight judgments.

The union of the judgment tradition and the learning tradition raises questions about the proper name and treatment of their offspring. Is a trial the judgment of a stimulus or is it the judgment of a series of stimuli? Only

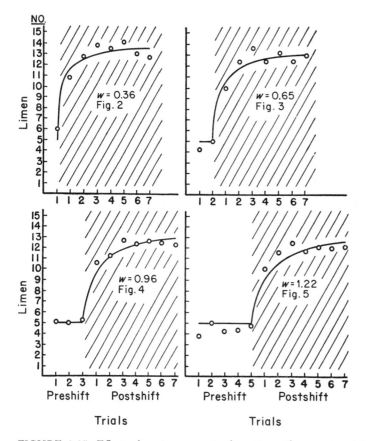

FIGURE 9.15. *Effects of varying amounts of practice with one series of frequencies on rate of shifting to a second series. The ordinate is a logarithmic scale of frequency which may be read as quarter octaves. Each point represents the limen between the categories of a two-category scale: low and high. From Johnson (1949b).*

judgments of complete series are comparable, but considerable learning can occur during judgments of a series of five stimuli. Rambo and Johnson (1964) therefore defined a trial as the judgment of a single stimulus and presented the stimuli in different orders to different subjects so that each stimulus was judged first by some subjects. Thus a central value of the scale could be computed for each trial, beginning with judgment of the first stimulus. In two experiments on judgments of dots by this more precise procedure, they found that a hyperbolic equation described the course of stabilization of the scale quite well.

VARIABLES THAT INFLUENCE LEARNING

The familiar question, What is learned? can be raised in this connection also; Parducci (1954) began with the hypothesis that it is mainly the distribution, and redistribution, of stimuli that is learned. In an experiment on judgment of distances, one group judged a block of short distances, then long distances, and finally the block of short distances again. The experimental group judged the same distances in the same order, but they were informed in advance about the range of distances to be presented. Consequently, as expected, the experimental group showed less shift between the first and last judgment of the short distances.

Another effect familiar in learning research, the effect of recency, turned up in Parducci's experiments on anchoring of judgments of the size of squares and the height of cardboard men; judgments of standard series were influenced more by immediately preceding anchors than by anchors judged earlier.

Most experiments on series shifts have added stimuli at one end and subtracted an equal number at the other end. But addition is more salient than subtraction: when Parducci (1956a) dropped the larger cards from a series to be judged for size, many subjects did not readjust their scales to the narrower range. Parducci (1956b) has also demonstrated that it is possible to learn something about the range of the stimuli, the frequency of each—as some series were skewed—and the middle of the series, by incidental learning while judging another dimension. The effects on the dimension observed incidentally were not as large, of course, as the effects on the dimension judged.

These trends were confirmed and additional controls were included by Di Lollo (1964) in a systematic experiment on weight judgments with four groups. One group shifted from a heavy series of weights to a light series. Another group continued judging the heavy series in both training and test phases. A third group shifted from a light series to a heavy series. And a fourth group continued judging the light series. The first postshift judgments, for both groups that shifted, showed considerable contrast as compared with the appropriate control groups. These differences gradually decreased but did not vanish; the convergence can be attributed to recency and the lack of complete convergence to primacy.

As interest in shifts of judgments has grown, more and more conditions influencing such shifts have been reported. Subliminal anchors seem to influence judgments of the intensity of electric shocks (Black and Bevan, 1960) and of the loudness of tones (Bevan and Pritchard, 1963a). In judgments of the size of circles, imaginary anchor stimuli are about as effective as anchors actually seen (Magaro, 1966). A two-hour lecture about contrast effects in judgments reduced anchoring effects in weight judgments, as did hypnotic suggestion to ignore the anchor (White, Alter, Snow, and Thorne, 1968). Although several narrow hypotheses have been offered for the effects of such anchors in retarding adjustment to a new series of stimuli, the diversity of the conditions investigated suggests that any condition that influences perception of a stimulus can influence the effectiveness of that stimulus as an anchor.

VARIATIONS IN THE RESPONSE SYSTEM

Campbell, Lewis, and Hunt (1958) observed that experiments on realignment of the scale of judgment utilized temporary rating scales specific to the laboratory and bounded at both ends. They therefore displayed a simulated piano keyboard, well labeled, for their subjects to use in making pitch judgments of series of musical notes. The diagrammatic keyboard represented the full range of the piano, while the stimulus series were located in the middle range; hence the subjects' choice of response language was not restricted at either end. Under these conditions, the mean judgments of a tracer stimulus included in the first series of stimuli, in transitional series, and in the last series showed the usual shift due to shift of context. It was thus demonstrated that these shifts are not peculiar to the temporary bounded scales previously used.

Krantz and Campbell (1961) then tried to get shifts in judgment of lengths of lines with two other response systems: a temporary rating scale with a center at 100 and undefined ends, and a well-learned standard scale, the scale of inches. One series consisted of lines from 6 to 20 inches and another of lines from 20 to 36 inches; for different groups of subjects the context was shifted in opposite directions. The results demonstrated that judgments of a tracer stimulus (of 20 inches) in terms of the rating scale were strongly influenced by the preshift context and shifted considerably as the context was shifted, in either direction. Judgments of the tracer stimulus in inches were less influenced by the preshift context, and this small effect was reversed after the shift. Apparently, the brief laboratory experience has a greater effect on the temporary rating scale than on the thoroughly practiced scale of inches.

Several other systems of response categories have been tried out and found to be vulnerable to shifts from one series of stimuli to another, some, of course, being more vulnerable than others (Fillenbaum, 1961; Harvey and Campbell, 1963; Ross and Di Lollo, 1968b; White, 1964). There are no absolute scales of judgment. Any correspondence between judgment categories and stimuli that can be learned can be relearned, and the same conditions that influence the original learning presumably influence the relearning. Thus the safest generalization at present is that temporary scales learned in the laboratory are more easily shifted than thoroughly learned scales, such as the standard scales of inches, ounces, and degrees. In any particular case, the amount of shift will be moderated by internal anchors, imaginary anchors, and other effects mentioned above.

Although the consequences of shifting the series of stimuli have been analyzed in some detail, little work has been done on shifting the system of response categories in which the judgments are expressed. If it is true that the learning consists mostly of grasping the series of stimuli, a switch to an alternative response system would go smoothly. That is, if a subject learns to judge a series of stimuli on a scale of 1 to 5, he should be able to judge it on a scale of 1 to 9, or −3 to +3, or by the method of magnitude estimation with little difficulty. Apparently such shifts have not been studied, but Weiss and Ten Eyck (1960) demonstrated that numerical and verbal response systems were indistinguishable and that (in its influence on the later use of a five-category scale) experience with a three-category scale was not different from experience with a seven-category scale.

INDIVIDUAL DIFFERENCES

Many investigators have commented on individual differences in readiness to shift, and some have attempted to relate these to other individual differences. The measures may not have the reliability necessary for correlations between scores for individuals, but groups can be compared. There is one case, the judgment of pitch, in which subjects with considerable experience can be separated from other subjects, and here it is clear that musically trained subjects are not as susceptible to shifts of context as untrained subjects (Campbell, Lewis, and Hunt, 1958; Schneider, 1963).

Attention and Relevance

The purest context and anchor effects are obtained when all stimuli vary along one dimension and all are judged in the same way. This standard condition is convenient for many experimental purposes, but it is a very special case that suggests a spuriously passive description of the judge's behavior. Recent modifications of the standard condition have raised interesting questions and have turned up new information on the judging process. The judge may direct his attention evenly to all stimuli, or he may focus on some to the neglect of others. He may group all stimuli together as relevant to the context of judgment, or he may exclude some as irrelevant. These factors of attention and relevance interact, to be sure; the judge is likely to attend to stimuli that are relevant to the task, and stimuli that he is instructed to attend to will appear relevant. But it is possible to achieve some clarification by examining the experimenter's operations. Without varying the stimuli, the subject's attention can be manipulated by instructions: some stimuli are to be judged while others are not. Without varying the instructions, the relevance of the stimuli can be manipulated by stimulus arrangements.

TASK INSTRUCTIONS

It is reasonable to suppose that the attention directed to stimuli that are judged is different from the attention directed to standard and anchor stimuli not judged. This question arose early, since quantitative models of comparative judgment have to make some assumption about the relative weight of stimuli and standard. Data on comparative judgments have been matched by assigning the standard stimulus one-third to one-half the weight of the variable stimuli that are judged (see page 397). The data for remote anchors are not so clear, and, of course, such estimates of relative weights cannot be detached from the other assumptions of the model. It is evident, however, from more direct comparisons, that an anchor stimulus that the subjects are instructed to judge has more influence on the organization of a scale of judgment than one they perceive but do not judge (Brown, 1953; Magaro, 1966).

Task instructions also influence the learning of a distribution of objects of judgments, especially the differentiation between incidental and intentional learning. An experiment (Parducci, 1956b) on this point mentioned on page 412 involved judgments of dot-filled squares varying in size of squares and number of dots. Instructions from the experimenter directed attention to one of these dimensions and whatever was learned about the other was learned incidentally. The subjects did learn something of the nature of the distribution of the objects on the incidentally observed dimension but, as expected, not as much as on the intentionally judged dimension.

STIMULUS RELATIONS

An early discussion of affective judgments by Beebe-Center (1932) restricted what is here called *context effect* to those stimuli that constitute a unitary temporal group, and subsequent investigations have tried to make this phrase more explicit for both context and anchor effects in perceptual judgment. It is not surprising that two important factors are factors of perceptual organization that have been emphasized by Gestalt psychologists: distance and similarity.

As to the importance of distance, the section on external anchors noted that when anchors are too remote, their influence as anchors decreases (see Fig. 9.13). Extremely remote anchors apparently are not grouped with, or perceived as part of, the series stimuli at all.

As to the importance of similarity, several experimenters have observed that during an experiment on weight judgments the subject may pick up a pencil or move his chair without noticeable influence on his judgment of the experimental weights. Brown (1953) checked on this matter of similarity by having his subjects lift metal trays as well as the usual laboratory weights. The metal trays did have an anchoring effect, but it was smaller than the anchoring effect of weights homogeneous with the stimulus series. Likewise,

Parducci (1954) found that anchor stimuli of the same color as the series stimuli had more influence on size judgments than anchor stimuli of a different color. Bevan and Pritchard (1963b) introduced several more variations in a study of shape judgments. When black rectangles were judged, the usual anchor effects appeared if black rectangles of approximately the same size were used as anchors. But no anchor effects appeared from circular figures, ellipses, rectangles much larger or smaller, or rectangles that differed considerably in lightness. Then Tresselt (1965) raised the question whether similarity of the stimuli or similarity of the task is more influential. Before judging a standard series of laboratory weights, four groups had different preshift experience with five heavier laboratory weights identified by letters and with five books of the same weight. The effect on postshift judgment of the standard weights was greater for preshift experience with the weights than the books, but the difference between preshift experience in alphabetizing and in ranking was negligible. All in all, these results justify the generalization that the most effective anchor stimuli are those that are similar to the series stimuli except for variation along the stimulus dimension. Departure from this ideal condition reduces and perhaps eliminates the anchor effect.

Another approach to the question of similarity is through the investigation of intermodal anchor effects. Judgments of temporal intervals are especially convenient for this purpose because the intervals can be marked off by stimuli of different modalities. Intermodal anchor effects have been reported for auditory and visual intervals, but they are smaller than intramodal effects (Behar and Bevan, 1961). When auditory intensities are subjectively equated to visual intensities, preliminary experience with auditory anchoring intensities, either higher or lower, has substantial effects on the equation (Smith and Hardy, 1961); but in this kind of judgment also the intermodal anchor effects are smaller than the intramodal (Bevan and Pritchard, 1964). And these intermodal effects are extended by the possibility of intermanual effects, for Dinnerstein (1965) has reported that lifting an anchor weight with the left hand influences judgment of weights lifted with the right hand.

If Gestalt factors of distance and similarity influence anchor effects, one might expect that the background of the stimuli would also be important. The background of the series stimuli is a factor in judgments of the size of squares (Engel and Parducci, 1961), and the background of the anchor is a factor in judgments of lightness (Bevan and Turner, 1965). But the effect of the background is not automatic; it is influenced, like other effects discussed here, by variations in instructions. When an effort was made to demonstrate middle anchoring of a series of 16 papers graded from white to black, displayed on a medium gray background, to be judged on a scale of 1 to 16, the usual end anchoring appeared, since white and black are salient, but the background had no effect. When instructions were given that the background was a No. 9, however, clear evidence of anchoring was obtained. The standard deviation of the judgments of Stimulus No. 8 decreased from 2.51 to .90, No. 9 from 2.26 to .23, and No. 10 from 2.74 to .67 (Johnson, 1960).

STIMULUS COVARIATIONS

When squares varying in size contain dots varying in number, attention can be directed by instructions to either dimension. In the experiment by Parducci (1956b) mentioned above, the variations in the two dimensions were unrelated; but Rambo (1962) arranged stimulus cards on which these variations were positively correlated, negatively correlated, and unrelated. On the preshift task, a control group was instructed to judge the size of the squares; other groups were instructed to judge the numerousness of the dots. The postshift task consisted of judgment of size of a smaller series of squares without dots. The largest effect on postshift judgments followed preshift experience in judging the size dimension, of course. But preshift experience in judging numerousness (both positively and negatively correlated with size) also influenced postshift judgment, more so than preshift experience with un-correlated dimensions. Rambo's interpretation, which was phrased in terms of mediated associations and response competition, stressed the consistency of stimulus covariation, whether positive or negative.

When the stimulus materials become complicated, or multidimensional, the subject's attention can vary, not only from maximal to minimal or from intentional to incidental, but by intermediate degrees. So Winters arranged a similar experiment (Winters and Johnson, 1969) with the hypothesis that the effect on postshift judgments of size would depend on the amount of attention directed toward size in the preshift task. Squares varying in size, containing dots varying in number and brightness, were presented in the pre-shift task; the postshift task consisted of judging square size. Judging square size in the preshift task had a large effect on the judgment of square size in the postshift task, as would be predicted by any hypothesis; but the effect of judgment of dot numerousness depended on the correlation in the stimulus materials. When the two dimensions were not correlated, preshift experience in judging dots had a large effect, presumably because the subjects had to attend to square size enough to discount that dimension and judge numerousness accurately. But when these two dimensions were positively correlated, the effect was smaller, presumably because the task required little attention to the redundant dimension of size. The effect of preshift experience in judging the brightness of the dots was negligible, as predicted, because this task did not require any attention to square size.

In these experiments, all dimensions of the stimulus cards were visible; the difference in effects on postshift judgment were produced by variations in the instructions for the task and in the relations between the dimensions. Although alternative interpretations are possible, the attention hypothesis is parsimonious if we merely assume that the subject attends directly to the dimension he is told to judge while attending to the other dimensions in proportion to their aid in performance of the central task.

In general, from the array of evidence presented here it appears that all variables that influence perception, even quite indirectly, can influence con-text and anchor effects. In fact, such experiments offer good techniques for studying such indirect perceptual effects; but effects that appear in affective and abstract judgments as well can be treated as due to general principles of judgment.

The introduction of intermodal variations and stimulus covariations into experiments on context and anchor effects brings us back to the multidimensional judgments of the preceding chapter. Judgments intended to be unidimensional often are multidimensional. The methodological difference is that in the research summarized in the preceding chapter, the subjects were instructed to judge the composite; while in judgments that are ostensibly unidimensional, the subjects are instructed to judge one dimension—the effects of the other dimensions are incidental or indirect. Nevertheless, we shall see that the most serious attempt to account for these indirect effects, Helson's assumption of pooling, has some similarities to the adding and averaging assumptions of Chapter 8. These two traditions will probably merge in due time.

Contrast and Assimilation

The effect of an external anchor may be called a contrast effect since an end stimulus that is judged *very large* in the context of the regular series may be judged *moderately large* in contrast to a larger remote anchor stimulus. Judgments of the stimuli at the anchored end are most strongly affected, of course (see Figs. 9.12 and 9.14), but there is a general effect that is manifested by the mean judgment of all series stimuli. Within limits, the mean judgment varies inversely with the value of the anchor stimulus. The effect also appears in frequency of use of each category of judgment, tabulated without regard to the stimuli. The end categories of judgment, normally used for the end stimuli, are less frequently used when the scale is displaced by the external anchor. The contrast due to anchoring has been demonstrated when the end of the scale is tied to the anchor stimulus by special instructions (Rogers, 1941; Sherif, Taub, and Hovland, 1958) and also when the anchor stimulus is included for judgment without special instructions (Parducci, 1954; Postman and Miller, 1945).

The contrast effect, by one name or another, is well established, but Sherif, Taub, and Hovland (1958) also reported evidence for an *assimilation effect,* which is smaller and less stable. In an experiment on weight judgments, they presented an anchor stimulus before each series stimulus with instructions to call the anchor a *six.* When this anchor was a heavy anchor, outside the regular series of stimuli, it produced the usual contrast effect, that is, the median judgment of the series stimuli was lower than without the anchor. But when the anchor was the same as the heaviest stimulus of the series, the median judgment of the series stimuli was somewhat higher than without the anchor. It is this effect, opposite to the usual contrast effect from external anchors, that is called *assimilation.* These authors investigated assimilation in weight judgments with the hope of explaining the more complex assimilation reported in judgments of social objects, as when the subject's own attitude may act as an anchor. Assimilation in weight judgments is questionable, however; for, when Bravo and Mayzner (1961) repeated the experiment, they found the usual contrast effect but no assimilation. Parducci and Marshall (1962) did find assimilation in weight judgments under certain conditions—for heavy anchors but not for light ones—and interpreted assimilation as an indirect effect of the more familiar contrast, with the anchor serving as a standard for a comparative judgment. Bevan and Turner (1964) found evidence for assimilation as well as contrast in judgments of dots enclosed in square frames. The materials and experimental manipulations were arranged so as to apply Gestalt principles of perception, and the results could be due to these perceptual principles rather than to variations in the scale of judgment. We must admit that assimilation effects are transitory phenomena, not well understood at present. These effects are not exactly the opposite of contrast effects and certainly they are not as predictable.

Theoretical Formulations

Judgment data have been treated quantitatively from the outset, for descriptive purposes at least. But quantitative formulations of more theoretical intent have also been elaborated—from different points of view, with varied strengths and weaknesses. The models outlined below are not alternative formulations of the same data; they overlap only in part. But all attempt to explain some of the results already summarized above in a more empirical manner.

ADAPTATION LEVEL

The well-known concept of *adaptation level* was introduced by Helson (1947, 1948) to account for complex data on color vision and was later extended to a wide range of data on judgment and other topics (1964). In fact, an appreciable share of the research reported in this chapter grew out of the interest aroused by AL theory. Although adaptation is treated as a general psychological characteristic, not restricted to sensory adaptation, and includes the pooling of diverse influences on the organism, the term *level* has more precise meaning. It represents the zero point or origin to which gradients of stimulation are referred. Thus scales of judgment are treated as fundamentally bipolar, the neutral category being the level to which the organism is adapted and stimuli on either side being evaluated in reference to this level.

NEUTRAL POINTS

When several stimuli, X_i, are judged one at a time, the adaptation level, or AL, approaches the geometric mean of the stimulus series, according to adaptation-level theory.

$$\log(AL + .75d) = \frac{\log X_i}{n}$$

The geometric mean is used rather than the arithmetic because Helson, following Fechner, assumes a curvilinear function relating stimulus intensity and magnitude of effect. The second term, $.75d$, which is introduced to take account of spacing of stimuli and order effects, varies with the stimulus dimension and the experimental conditions.

For the simple case of two-category judgments, the limen between the categories, the value of the stimulus that is judged equally often in both categories, is taken as a measure of the neutral point to which the organism is adapted. The theory predicts that this value will coincide with the adaptation level computed as above from the stimulus series.

When judgments are made on a rating scale of several categories, the middle or medium category is taken as the neutral region, and stimuli that are rated in this category are presumed to be at the level to which the organism is adapted. Thus, if the rating scale extends from 1 to 9, the values of the stimuli that get ratings of 5 are the obtained values which are expected to coincide with the theoretical AL.

SCALE VALUES OF STIMULI

According to the theory of adaptation level, the judgment of each stimulus is a function of its distance from the AL, which is more conveniently symbolized by A in some expressions. This distance in physical units is $X_i - A$, but the psychological unit is the just noticeable difference, the size of which depends on both the stimulus being judged and the adaptation level. Hence the judgment, J, is predicted by the following equation:

$$J = \frac{K(X_i - A)}{X_i + A}$$

K is a constant, related to the Weber constant. The judgment, J, is expressed on a bipolar scale, such as -2, -1, 0, $+1$, $+2$; hence, according to this equation, when the stimulus coincides with the adaptation level, the numerator will be zero and the judgment will be zero, or neutral. When the stimulus is lower or higher than the AL, the judgment will be lower or higher than zero, but the relation is not linear because the magnitude of the just noticeable difference varies with the magnitude of the physical stimulus. This equation is easily modified for use with the more common scales without a zero point, such as 1, 2, 3, 4, 5. The theoretical AL is estimated and the equation is fit to obtained judgment data by a least-squares procedure. An application to judgments of five weights on a scale of 1 to 9 is shown in the middle curve of Fig. 9.12, taken from Helson (1964). The AL for these data was computed as 248 grams.

APPLICATIONS

Adaptation-level theory is particularly appropriate to the quantitative formulation of context effects, and many of the phenomena described above have been interpreted by AL theory under the assumption that the organism becomes adapted to a level or point on the stimulus dimension by the pooling of the effects of the separate stimuli. Since this pooling of stimulus effects is represented mathematically by the averaging of stimulus values, the quantitative formulation has been applied without special difficulty to the results of experiments on judgments of skewed distributions of stimuli also.

If the *AL* is represented by an average, the stimulus values that are pooled can be differentially weighted on the assumption that some contribute more strongly to the adaptation than others. In the early work on judgments of visual stimuli, for example, the background was given three times as much weight as the figure, or focal stimulus. Likewise, when *AL* theory was applied to experiments with external anchors, anchor stimuli were included in the averaging, but with different weight from the series stimuli, and thus the theory accounted for the usual contrast effects without additional assumptions (see Fig. 9.12). Whenever the series stimuli, or background stimuli, or any other stimuli that may affect the judgments even indirectly, can be given quantitative values, they can be pooled in a weighted average, and *AL* theory has been applied to a variety of such stimulus arrangements (Helson, 1964).

One of the strongest arguments for the pooling assumption comes from a recent experiment by Helson and Kozaki (1968), in which the scale for judging size of squares was influenced by the differential duration of exposure to large and small squares. The stimuli were seven squares from 30 to 110 mm. on a side. For one group these were all exposed for .55 seconds; for another, the larger squares were exposed longer, up to one second; and for a third group the smaller squares were exposed longer, although the average of all three exposure conditions was the same. The results showed that duration pooled with size: that is, long exposure of the large squares pulled the *AL* upward and thus reduced the judgments of all stimuli compared to the standard constant exposure; and long exposure of the small squares pulled the *AL* downward and thus increased the judgments of all stimuli compared to the standard condition. The judgments in the three conditions were evenly separated throughout the range of stimuli, hence the pooling effect applied, not just to certain stimuli but to the entire scale of judgment.

Furthermore, a second experiment with large and small anchors, exposed for short and long durations, confirmed the pooling assumption. Long duration of the large anchor resulted in higher *AL* and lower judgments, while long duration of the small anchor resulted in lower *AL* and higher judgments of the series stimuli.

AL theory has been applied by Helson (1964) to motivation, performance, and other topics beyond the scope of this book, and the term has been used by others in a very general way as a synonym for context effect or frame of reference, with no testable quantitative implications.

PRESENT STATUS AND FUTURE PROSPECTS

In quantitative applications to psychophysical judgment, the agreement between predictions from *AL* theory and obtained data have frequently been impressive (Helson, 1964, Chapter 4). Inevitably, in two decades, criticisms have also arisen, directed at both data and interpretations.

Several investigators who have tried to apply *AL* theory under different conditions have not been able to fit the obtained results. The differences between a wide and a narrow range of stimuli are not matched by *AL* computations (Harvey and Campbell, 1963). *AL* theory does not account for the weights of standards varied in frequency of presentation (Rambo, 1964). Attempts by Parducci and others (Parducci, Calfee, Marshall, and Davidson, 1960; Parducci and Marshall, 1961) to apply *AL* theory to stimulus distributions of different shapes uncovered discrepancies that led Parducci to a different model, to be outlined below.

Much of the difficulty with *AL* computations comes from the assumption of a logarithmic relation between physical magnitudes and scale values, which leads to the use of the geometric mean, with adjustments, for the *AL*. The assumption of a linear function and the consequent use of the arithmetic mean yields better fit in some cases, as in length judgments (Rambo and Watson, 1962), and Stevens (1958) has supplied many illustrations of the superiority of power functions. The demonstration that another average may be more appropriate than the geometric mean does not by itself invalidate the concept of an adaptation level, as Helson (1964, p. 60) has pointed out, but it does complicate quantitative tests of the predictions.

Another modification in *AL* theory, as applied to the effects of an external anchor, will be required to account for data reported by Sarris (see page 406). The present *AL* formulation gives constant weight to the anchor stimulus and thus accounts only for small portions of the curves of Fig. 9.13; but the recent data require that the weight of the anchor be reduced with distance from the series stimuli. There is nothing illogical about this, but it is another complication.

As to interpretation, the first part of the term, *adaptation,* has been criticized as misleading, but many scientists, since Darwin's time, have used this in a broad sense. The adaptation of adaptation-level theory is not always sensory adaptation, to be sure, but this term is no vaguer than most psychological terms, such as *perception, learning,* and *judgment.* A more serious objection applies to the second part, *level,* because, although a central value of the stimulus series can always be aligned with the center of the response scale by least-squares procedures, there is no evidence that this statistic has any psychological significance. One might suppose from discussions of adaptation level that the *AL* could act as an internal anchor to reduce variability and errors of judgment but, as Rambo (1964) has pointed out, *AL* theory has no place for natural internal anchors. This theory is concerned with mean judgments or scale values, not with variability of judgment.

At best, psychological theories are not very satisfactory. If, in the spirit of this chapter, we put adaptation-level theory in the same context with other quantitative psychological theories, its accomplishments look as impressive as the accomplishments of the others. It is true, as Stevens (1966a) has noted, that the *AL* formulation contains several constants to be evaluated ad hoc and consequently that a decisive test is rather elusive, but this is true of the theories of the preceding chapter and most other theories as well. When a theory, like an automobile, starts to break down, it is seldom immediately discarded. More often, it is repaired and continued in operation; at worst, parts of it are salvaged and reused.

The most salvageable contribution then, one which has contributed to a reorientation in psychophysics, is the idea of pooling, the idea that the effects of various classes of stimuli—focal, background, series, anchor, and incidental—are somehow pooled, or combined, to determine judgment of the stimuli. It is no longer necessary to treat judgments of single stimuli isolated from other stimuli. The future will probably see some integration between the combinatory models of the previous chapter and the pooling feature of the *AL* model.

LINEAR CORRELATION AND REGRESSION

The complexities of judgment data documented here suggest separating the study of scales of judgment from questions about the shape of the receptor function. The most efficient designs for determining psychophysical functions are not the most efficient for the study of context effects, central tendency, anchoring, multidimensional combinations, etc. In the interests of clarity, some investigators have deliberately chosen stimulus materials that yield linear data and others have spaced the stimuli so as to achieve linearity. Thus, once linearity is achieved in a standard condition, it is possible to vary the conditions and study judgment effects in a relatively pure form. This two-step procedure illustrates the advantages of experimental standardization as compared to statistical adjustment and, at the same time, permits the use of familiar linear correlations.

From the many experiments on context effects, it is reasonable to assume that when the subject is judging a single stimulus, he is simultaneously correlating the whole scale of judgment with the whole series of stimuli. He knows the scale he has been instructed to use (e.g., the numbers 1 to 7), and the dimension he has been instructed to attend to (e.g., length). He is told, or he infers from the laboratory environment, that the stimulus series is limited to some manageable range. Hence his task can be treated as the matching or correlating of a known segment of a number system to a partially known segment of a stimulus dimension. This assumption leads to the use of the conventional correlation coefficient to measure the overall accuracy of the judgments and the conventional regression equation to estimate the scale values of the stimuli.

When ordered stimuli are judged in ordered categories, the judgments can be arranged as a rectangular table of judgments-by-stimuli data which is convenient for correlation analysis. But when the correlation coefficient is computed to get a regression equation for estimation of the scale values of the stimuli, it is obvious that the scale values depend on the magnitude of the correlation coefficient. When the correlation approaches unity, judgments and stimuli are closely matched, with little variability. High ratings go with large stimuli and low ratings with small stimuli. But when the correlation is low and the regression line approaches the horizontal, large stimuli are

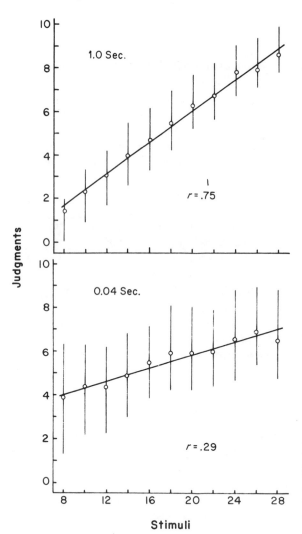

FIGURE 9.16. Regression of judgments on stimuli for two exposure times. The data points are mean judgments; the vertical lines extend from Q_1 to Q_3. The heavy line is the linear regression line. From Johnson and Mullally (1969).

underestimated and small stimuli overestimated. Thus, treating category judgment as a matching task leads to a simple explanation of the central tendency of judgment. It is a consequence of the variability of the judgments and is inversely related to the magnitude of the correlation coefficient.

The correlation-and-regression model was illustrated with reference to central tendency by Guilford (1954), with fictitious data, and by Johnson (1952, 1955), with category judgments collected for another purpose. The same relations appear in matching data obtained by adjustment methods—in fact, Hollingworth's first illustration was taken from an adjustment experiment—and Stevens and Greenbaum (1966) have reported several examples of central tendency in the matching of values on one perceptual continuum to those on another. They interpreted the constriction of the obtained scale values in terms of the regression that occurs "whenever the results of the matching judgments yield less than a perfect correlation."

Recently, to examine the implications of this approach more thoroughly, Johnson and Mullally (1969) held stimulus conditions constant and used exposure time as an independent variable. They found that a decrease in exposure time decreased the accuracy of judgment of each stimulus (slides containing green and blue dots, as described on page 402) and therefore the judgment-stimulus correlation. Fig. 9.16 shows regression lines computed from the judgments at two extreme exposure times: at 1.00 seconds when the correlation was .75, and at .04 seconds when the correlation was .29. The central tendency of judgment that appears in the graphs is also manifested in the standard deviation of the scale values which, in units of the 11-point rating scale, was 2.27 for the long exposure and .97 for the short exposure. Fig. 9.17 charts these relations by comparing the two sets of obtained scale values with those to be expected in the hypothetical condition of perfect correlation between judgments and stimuli.

The correlation-and-regression model is easily applied to the effects of an external anchor if the anchor is judged as the other stimuli are. The data graphed in Fig. 9.14 to illustrate anchoring effects are pertinent here: the anchor was a salient stimulus that tied down one end of the scale, but in each case the judgment scale as a whole was adjusted to the extended stimulus series as a whole. Hence, the assumption of linearity holds for each regression line. The usual contrast effects can be seen, but the conventional

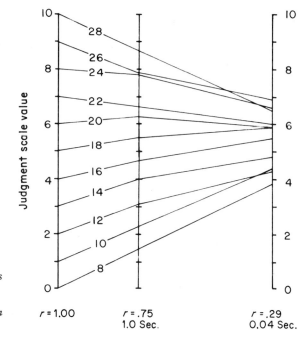

FIGURE 9.17. Regression toward the mean illustrated by scale values of 11 stimuli judged under 3 conditions. The values graphed on the left ordinate are for the hypothetical case of perfect correlation between judgments and stimuli. The other ordinates show the obtained values for exposures of 1.00 second, when r = .75, and 0.04 second, when r = .29. From Johnson and Mullally (1969).

regression equations account very well for all scale values, without additional assumptions. The linearity may break down, of course, if the anchor stimulus is extended too far (as noted above in the section on anchoring), but it is possible that judgment of the anchor stimulus reduces this danger by making the anchor a part of the regular stimulus series.

This model accounts not only for contrast but also for assimilation under certain conditions. The data graphed in Fig. 9.14 show that in the standard condition the mean judgment of Stimulus No. 11 was about 2. Stimulus No. 1, a remote anchor, produced the usual contrast effect, such that No. 11 was judged about 3. Now suppose a near anchor had been included, Stimulus No. 10. This would presumably be judged a 1 and would tie down that end of the scale so that, if linearity obtained, No. 11 would be judged about 1.5. In comparison to the judgment of 2 under standard conditions, this represents movement toward the anchor, or assimilation. Generalization of the illustration leads to the prediction that when judgments are made with less than complete accuracy and central tendency is present, the introduction of a near anchor ties down the near end of the scale, reduces central tendency, and produces assimilation.

Regression toward the mean is not just a conjecture; it occurs whenever the correlation between two variables is less than unity. But when the data are not suitable for correlation analysis, the regression may be obscured or confounded with ad hoc statistics. Correlation and regression are descriptions, to be sure, rather than explanations; the model attributes the magnitude of the correlation and consequently the scale values of the stimuli to the variability of the single judgments. Any condition that influences variability will influence the dependent statistics.

Once the regression equation has been computed, it is possible to describe the scale of judgment in terms of limens between adjacent categories. The limen between the third and fourth categories, for example, can be determined by substituting in the regression equation to find the stimulus value that predicts a rating of 3.5. As the correlation decreases and the regression toward the mean increases, the middle categories of the scale become wider and the extreme categories vanish.

Regression effects apply also to judgments made by the ranking method if mean ranks are obtained from repeated rankings by the same judge or from single rankings by different judges. Mean ranks regress toward the center of the scale in inverse relation to the average correlation between the ranks. The correlation model is presumably applicable to judgments on unbounded scales, as by the method of magnitude estimation, and the usual regression effects may be expected, but no data are available at present.

The limitations of this model are, first, those that apply to all correlation procedures. In addition, there is no provision for differential weighting of stimuli, as there is in the *AL* model, and this model is probably not applicable to the asymmetrical distribution of stimuli handled by the range-frequency model, to be considered next.

The adaptation-level model and the correlation-and-regression model are similar in that both involve a least-squares fit to obtained data. The former, however, assumes a logarithmic relation between judgments and stimuli, while the latter assumes a linear relation. But the distinctive characteristic of the correlation approach is the assumption that the statistic does what the judge does, namely, correlate judgments with stimuli. *AL* theory states that the stimuli are scaled in relation to psychological distance from the *AL*. The correlation model states that the scale as a whole is adjusted to the stimulus series as a whole, even though the judgments are made one by one.

RANGE-FREQUENCY COMPROMISE

Parducci's extensive experiments with many different distributions of numerals (Parducci, Calfee, Marshall, and Davidson, 1960) and lengths (Parducci and Marshall, 1961) disclosed discrepancies in predictions of the central value, or adaptation level, of a scale of judgment from the mean of the stimulus distribution. The obtained central values seemed to depend on two characteristics of the various distributions: the midpoint and the median. According to Parducci, the predictive usefulness of the midpoint comes from the judge's tendency to divide the range of stimuli into two equal subranges; and the predictive usefulness of the median comes from his tendency to divide the distribution into two equal frequency distributions and thus to use both sides of the response scale with equal frequency. The predictive useful-ness of the mean, either arithmetic or logarithmic, is an accidental conse-quence of the fact that it often falls between the midpoint and the median, and for that reason is often a good first approximation.

The method devised by Parducci (1963, 1965) for applying this model to the whole scale and predicting mean judgments for each stimulus makes use of the limens between adjacent categories and asserts that each limen results from a compromise between two principles. The range principle states that the judge divides his psychological range into as many subranges as there are categories for him to use. If told to judge in four categories, he would divide the range into four equal subranges. The frequency principle states that the judge puts the same number of stimuli in each category. If told to judge in four categories, he would divide the stimulus distribution into four quarters. When the distribution is not rectangular, these two principles con-flict, and the range-frequency model asserts that the judge gives each equal weight. Thus the empirical limens will be means of the corresponding range limens and frequency limens.

Tests of the model begin with a standardization experiment using a rec-tangular distribution of stimuli, 9 squares judged on a 6-category scale, to get empirical limens and theoretical limens. Since the empirical limens are the means of both the frequency and the range limens, the range limens are obtained algebraically from the other two. This procedure gives hypothetical range limens that may be outside the actual stimulus series, presumably be-cause the judge's expectations may not be limited by the stimulus series. These range limens are then used for other distributions of the same stimuli—positively skewed, negatively skewed, U-shaped, etc.—but new frequency limens are computed for each distribution. The model asserts that the new empirical limens will be the means of these two sets of theoretical limens, and the predictions are tested by comparing the judgments predicted from the compromise limens with obtained mean judgments of each stimulus. For 12 distributions of various shapes, the agreement was quite good. When the stimulus series consisted of bursts of random noise (constructed with positive and negative skew), the range-frequency model accounted for the judgments very well, though the averaging model of the preceding chapter and an intensity-summation model were inadequate (Parducci, Thaler, and Anderson, 1968). And this model can be applied also to the interpretation of anchor and postanchor effects (Parducci, Perrett, and Marsh, 1969).

Because it is a compromise, the range-frequency model will not be considered either parsimonious or elegant. But if judges do compromise between these two principles, a compromise model is necessary. And this one seems to account better than any other for the wide variety of distributions Parducci has investigated. In contrast to the adaptation-level model, which assumes that each stimulus is judged in relation to the *AL*, the range-frequency model states that each stimulus is judged in relation to the compromise limens. This is the reason given by Parducci for the failure of adaptation-level theory to account for category judgments of these widely varied distributions. Like the adaptation-level model, the range-frequency model is concerned only with mean scale values; it ignores accuracy of judgment, although accuracy may be involved in the values obtained for the hypothetical range limens.

Since compromises are not as exciting as monoideic explanations, the implications of this model have not been thoroughly explored. One would expect that variations in instructions could shift the emphasis from one side of the compromise toward the other and yield predictable consequences.

A VECTOR MODEL FOR PSYCHOPHYSICAL JUDGMENT

There is plenty of evidence in the preceding pages that judgments of one dimension of a series of objects are biased by other dimensions of the objects. Ross and Di Lollo (1968a) were concerned about the effects of such bias on psychophysical functions relating psychological magnitudes to physical magnitudes; but, when they looked into this question seriously, their studies of weight judgments led them to a vector model that relates the judgments to a collection of stimulus values, in this case, of weight and density. An important assumption is that "the different attributes assume greater salience, or contribute more strongly to discrimination, at different ranges of physical stimulus values [p. 2]." For example, if a set of stimuli lies within a range where density differences are readily discriminable, but weight differences are not, density will count more heavily in the magnitude judgments than weight. This variable-basis model implies that there is no single psychophysical function for lifted weights. More pertinent here, the model was tested by shifts in the stimulus series that resulted in realignment of the scale of judgment to the new series.

The tests of the model were indirect for the most part, but one that is convenient for illustration involved shifts of series with the same weights while density was varied. This was done by making some weights of high-density plastic and some of low-density tin. All subjects had a standard weight of 200 grams, presented once at the beginning, with instructions to call it 100 and to judge other weights as proportional to this. The preshift series consisted of five weights from 100 to 300 grams and the postshift series of five weights from 700 to 900 grams. Thus the shift in weight for all conditions was the same, but the mean shift in density, expressed in grams per cubic centimeter, varied with the materials: from plastic to tin, −.64; from tin to tin, .45; from plastic to plastic, 3.75; from tin to plastic, 4.82. The results clearly demonstrated large separations in the postshift judgments, related to the density shifts.

Unfortunately, all the judgments drifted upward, as if the weights became heavier or the subjects became weaker as the experiment continued, even in the preshift phase and in control groups that did not shift. One would expect that the judgment scales would be symmetrical around 100, but very few judgments below 100 were reported. This does not invalidate all the conclusions, but it raises questions about the meaning of magnitude estimates for weight and confuses the evaluation of the trends. The meaning of density is also unclear, since size was varied as well. A sharper test of the theory can be made, the authors tell us, when it is possible to estimate the representation of stimuli by individual subjects. Nevertheless, the results of several experiments—including judgment-stimulus correlations and regression lines—though limited to weight judgments, strengthen the case for a variable-basis model and may show the way through the complexities of judgments of multidimensional stimuli.

THEORETICAL DEVELOPMENTS AND UNANSWERED QUESTIONS

To a critical reviewer, the methodological sophistication of most experiments on psychophysical judgment is illusory. With one hand the experimenter displays graceful curves that demonstrate how beautifully his magic formula comprehends natural phenomena, while his other hand surreptitiously removes the conditions that would disturb the demonstration.

The reasons are historical. Psychophysics began by seeing single dimensions in complex natural objects and then constructing experimental objects that were more nearly unidimensional. Though such standardization of stimuli has obvious advantages for psychophysics, in the study of judgment it is an oversimplification that has been at least partly corrected by the recent interest in multidimensional psychophysics.

The fundamental questions about the part and the whole that Gestalt psychologists insisted on asking are being posed once again in the context of judgment research, though perhaps in a more researchable form. These two chapters have shown the flexibility of judgment experiments and their capacity to pick up subtle effects. Clarification of the relation of parts to wholes may prove to be one of the main contributions of the psychology of judgment to general psychological theory.

Everyone knows that the unidimensionality of a set of stimulus objects is largely due to control of the subject's attention by instructions from the experimenter, but this control was long considered a standard condition, necessary for scientific investigation. Recently, however, the subject's attention has been experimentally varied, by variations in the stimulus materials, and by instructions. Many more such variations can be expected in the future. Perhaps the role of attention in these judgments can be studied more directly, by asking the subject to distribute his attention evenly to two dimensions, for example, or to concentrate on one rather than the other.

As to the relation between parts and wholes over time, or the integration of events by learning, the parallel between the judgment experiment and the concept experiment is most instructive. Knowledge of the class is built up from experience with single instances and response to single instances in turn depends on knowledge of the class. Similarly, the scale of judgment is aligned with the stimulus series by experience with single stimuli and then response to the single stimuli depends on the alignment of the judgment scale to the stimulus series. In either case, the subject can just make responses or he can, if asked, talk about the concept or the scale of judgment. The chief difference is that concept experiments typically are concerned with combinations of familiar discrete attributes, while judgment experiments are concerned with combinations of values along one or more dimensions.

The previous chapter defined judgment, in an abstract way, as a special kind of problem, and the recent experiments make this definition more attractive. It appears that the subject who tries, as in concept experiments, to do what he thinks the experimenter wants him to do uses whatever information is available—from perception, from memory, from the context, from salient anchor stimuli, and from the instructions. When the stimuli are multidimensional and the stimulus series is shifted up or down, the problematic nature of the task becomes even more apparent. In these more modern experiments the situation is less standardized, less oversimplified, more realistic. But the problem is an ill-defined one with no clear feedback, hence the only confirmation the subject gets is from observation of the consistency of his own judgments.

To the disenchanted critic, experiments on shift of stimulus series must be ambiguous to the subject, like experiments on shift of problem-solving set. Does the subject try to hold on to the old context, or to shift to the new? Does he try to continue to use the scale categories or the magnitude estimates with equal frequency, or not? Or does he compromise, as in many other ambiguous situations? When subjects in informal class experiments at Michigan State University were asked to make category judgments of *low* and *high* following a shift in a series of auditory frequencies, the usual shift of scale was obtained. But when the subjects, who were students of experimental psychology, were asked to judge the stimuli in cycles per second, they gave

rather realistic judgments. Though their accuracy was not high, their judgments gave clear evidence that they knew the stimuli had shifted. It might be
reasonable, when the situation is complex, to speak of judgment strategies
and to try to identify them. Instructing the subjects to use two different
response systems may allow them to tell the experimenter more clearly what
he wants to know; an experiment with a definite criterion of accuracy known
to the subject might indeed clear up the ambiguities. In any event, the
problem is solved from the subject's point of view when he makes judgments
that seem consistent to him.

From this perspective, the question whether anchoring effects and realignment of judgment scales involve changes in perception seems less than
crucial. Recent experiments by Helson and Kozaki (1968) and by Bell
and Bevan (1968) offer strong evidence of perceptual changes—whether
related to adaptation level or not. And experiments on abstract judgments
(in the section below on attitude items) demonstrate similar effects with no
special relevance to perception. As in a court of law, where judgments are
based on both substantive and procedural considerations, laboratory judgments are based on perceptual variables and judgment scale variables, but
neither has any more inherent validity or psychological interest than the
other.

Regardless of the procedures and logical implications, there are inconsistencies in the published data that are probably due to differences in stimulus materials. Some experiments are more conveniently done with auditory
stimuli and others with visual stimuli. A cautionary note is required for
judgment experiments as for problem-solving experiments and concept experiments: conclusions drawn from an experiment on one kind of stimulus
material are hazardous. The difference between the judging process on one
task and another may be only in a parameter, but it may also consist in an
additional operation.

Judging Attitude Statements
and Other Social Objects

Both affective and abstract judgments are involved in the testing of attitudes. The subject taking the test makes affective judgments when he
approves or disapproves such statements as "Birth control is immoral." The
judges who aid in the construction of the scale make abstract judgments
when they rate such statements on a scale of 1 to 11 to indicate the position
of each on an abstract attitude continuum. As attitude statements have been
scaled with the help of different sets of judges, questions have arisen, especially about the effects of context and of the judge's own attitude, that are
relevant for the psychology of thinking in general as well as for psychometric methodology.

Many influential variables (such as degree of emotional involvement) that
interest the social psychologists constructing attitude scales cannot be con-

sidered here—as many variables influencing perceptual judgments were not considered. It is the cognitive variables related to the use of the scale of judgment that are most relevant to the psychology of judgment.

When a judge is asked to rate attitude statements, it is assumed that he has conceptualized the relevant dimension from previous experience with such statements. Presumably, abstract dimensions are learned as abstract concepts are learned. Scaling experiments are not concerned with the definition of the attitude dimension except as it affects variability of judgment, but more directly with the position of statements on the dimension. Most of the research has used category scales, but magnitude estimation has also been used for scaling social objects (Stevens, 1966b). Both types of scale were found useful in an extensive project on the measurement of delinquency (Sellin and Wolfgang, 1964).

THE RANGE OF OPINION

Typically, a series of statements covering a wide range of opinion is presented to the judges and the scale is aligned with the series so that extremely favorable statements get high scale values and extremely unfavorable statements low scale values. This correspondence does not necessarily illustrate the effect of the immediate context on the development of a temporary scale, as in the other examples considered in this chapter. The range of opinion on the issue may be known to the judges in advance, hence if this range is presented to them for scaling, the correspondence that results may be a consequence of considerable experience in the past rather than ad hoc laboratory experience. Attitude statements may be peculiar in this respect since the statement of an extreme opinion often suggests—to the impartial, informed reader at least—the contrary opinion, somewhat as the stimulus word *left* suggests the response word *right*.

When attempts are made to examine the effect of context, or adaptation level, by presenting different subranges of the attitude continuum to different judges, the results do not show a systematic alignment of scale and subrange. Some statements, but not all, get different scale values when judged in different subranges. In a study by Fehrer (1952), for example, extremely pacifistic and extremely militaristic statements were firmly associated with the extremes of the scale of judgment and were quite resistant to context effects; but mildly pacifistic statements were judged more pacifistic in a militaristic context than in a pacifistic one. The statements that differed most in mean scale value from one context to another were the nonspecific or ambiguous, middling statements such as "It is good judgment to sacrifice certain rights in order to prevent war."

It is not true, however, that all middling statements get variable scale values. In Fehrer's study, specifically neutral items such as "War brings out both the good and bad qualities in men" were consistently given neutral ratings. Intermediate statements can be carefully written to express a middle position, and these are consistently rated in the middle, but intermediate statements that are ambiguously written are more vulnerable to various instabilities (Zimbardo, 1960).

A study of college students' attitudes toward fraternities failed to find a context effect of the usual kind but did find a contrast effect. Segall (1959) divided a series of statements into an unfavorable range (with previously determined scale values of 1 to 4) and a favorable range (with scale values of 4 to 7). The unfavorable range was rated 1.2 to 4, and the favorable range 4 to 6.6, showing considerable resistance to the context effect. However, when the group that rated the favorable statements before the unfavorable statements was compared with a group that rated them in the reverse order, evidence of contrast appeared. Subjects exposed first to favorable statements judged the unfavorable statements more unfavorably than those who judged the unfavorable statements first. Conversely, those exposed first to unfavourable statements judged the favorable statements more favorably than those exposed to favorable statements first. And this contrast effect appeared throughout the whole range of attitude toward fraternities.

If the context can be thus alternated once, it can be alternated several times. Atkins (1966) tried this repeated-measurements design in studying college students' attitudes toward fraternities and found contrast at first, then assimilation. The interpretation is unclear, as Atkins has pointed out, but similar trends had previously been found in judgments of maladjustment in brief descriptions of behavior (Bieri, Orcutt, and Leaman, 1963), so the trends are not accidental. Whatever the interpretation, it appears to be easier to demonstrate assimilation with social judgments and a repeated-measurements design than with perceptual judgments and independent groups.

The discussion of context effects earlier in this chapter noted that the context of judgment can influence production as well as judgment, and a similar effect has been reported by Ostrum (1966) for attitude statements. Three ranges of statements about Negroes were rated by different subjects and, after rating, each subject wrote a statement describing Category 11, the pro-Negro end, and a statement describing Category 1, the anti-Negro end. When these statements were scaled by other judges, it became evident that the descriptions of the end of the scales were dependent on the ranges judged.

THE JUDGE'S OWN ATTITUDE

The judge's own attitude also deserves scrutiny in respect to the use of a scale of judgment. The scaling technique rests on the assumption that judges are able to conceive an abstract attitude continuum and give major weight to the relevant abstract implications of each statement, even though this task requires thinking in abstract, impartial quantitative terms about emotional topics. Their job resembles that of the judge and jury in a court of law, who are supposed to make impartial judgments by assigning violent events to quiet legal categories, and it is not idle to ask whether anyone can do this.

This is not a question of random error. Scaling projects use many judges so that random errors will cancel. The danger is that judges with different attitudes will systematically slant the judgments one way or another. The research here has been directed toward the practical question of whether the assumptions of the scaling technique are violated, and also toward people's reactions to persuasive communications intended to modify their attitudes.

Hovland, Harvey, and Sherif (1957) applied the assimilation-contrast model to this problem by treating the judge's own attitude as an anchor. They did not measure the anchor effect directly, as by a reduction in variability of judgment. Rather, they assumed that the judge's own attitude would act as a standard and that opinions at other points on the scale would be evaluated in reference to this standard. *Contrast* means that a statement expressing an attitude far from the judge's own attitude is judged even farther and therefore rejected; *assimilation* means that a statement close to the judge's is judged even closer. When they had subjects of different positions on the scale of attitude toward alcohol evaluate statements about alcohol, they found evidence for contrast in that the *drys* judged a *moderately wet* communication as more *wet* than those of other attitudes did. The evidence for assimilation was slight. Similar results were obtained by Manis (1960) in responses to pro- and antifraternity messages. The committed subjects at each end of the scale judged the communciations as more extreme than did the neutral subjects, but again the evidence for assimilation was slight. The effects of the subjects' own attitudes are not limited to the extremists, however, but have been found in the judgments of subjects whose own attitudes located them at five positions along the scale (Zavalloni and Cook, 1965).

A later study by Sherif and Hovland (1961) considered the involvement of the judges in more detail. When certain statements about Negroes were rated by Negro judges and by anti-Negro white judges, the two groups agreed quite well on the more extreme statements at both ends of the attitude continuum, as in Fehrer's results. But statements that anti-Negro judges considered neutral were judged anti-Negro by the Negroes. Extreme statements express salient opinions that are easily tied to the extreme categories of the judgment scale, while the middle statements are less clear and more susceptible to differences in interpretation. Such differences do not always appear and, when they do, it is not necessarily a matter of judgment. Members of a minority group have undergone specific experiences which give special meaning to statements that others consider neutral.

When attitude statements have been arranged in a series from *unfavorable* to *favorable,* it is worthwhile observing an individual's response to each one. He may divide the series in two, and accept those at one end while rejecting those at the other. More commonly, if the series includes a full range of opinion, the pattern of approvals and rejections will show that he has divided the series into three ranges, or subranges: a range of statements at one end rejected as too unfavorable, a range of statements that are approved, and a range of statements at the other end rejected as too favorable. These ranges may be called *latitudes of acceptance and rejection* (Sherif and Hovland, 1961). Typically, the extreme statements at both ends are rejected by almost everyone: the differences are in the range of acceptance between these extremes. Fig. 9.18 illustrates ranges of acceptance and rejection of statements spaced along a continuum extending from A (extreme Republican partisanship) to I (extreme Democratic partisanship). The E graph shows the pattern of acceptance and rejection for subjects whose own attitude was at E. They approved statements at D, E, and F, and rejected the extreme statements at both ends. The other graphs show latitudes of acceptance and rejection for subjects whose own attitudes were at B and H. There are transition zones between ranges of acceptance and rejection, of course, where noncommitment or uncertainty is the more common response. The E people, in the middle of the road, were most uncertain about statements at C and G. Usually, the subject in the middle finds relatively few statements that he can reject; the larger number of rejections come from the judges at the extremes.

Likewise, when statements are judged on a scale of 1 to 11 as to truth or falsity, the extreme statements, *extremely dry* or *extremely wet*, are rated most false. Naturally, the *drys* rate the *extremely wet* statements false, but they also rate the *extremely dry* statements more false than the *moderately dry* statements. In the same way, the *wets* rate the *extremely dry* statements false, but they rate the *wet* statements more false than the *moderately dry* statements (Sherif, Sherif, and Nebergall, 1965).

When Segall (1959) asked college students to rate statements about fraternities, he did not find a difference due to the students' own attitudes, possibly because the range of opinion was small. He did find, however, that these students—when explicitly asked to judge the statements in relation to their own attitudes—were able to use their own positions as standards and give different scale values as expected. This is another illustration of the ability of sophisticated subjects to adopt a flexible approach to the judgment task; certainly, the meaning of the results depends on the subjects' understanding of the task.

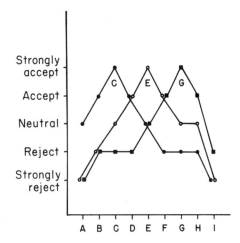

FIGURE 9.18. *Latitudes of acceptance and rejection. Modal responses to statements spaced along attitude continuum by subjects whose own attitudes were at C, E, and G. Data from Sherif and Hovland (1961).*

INTERACTION BETWEEN JUDGE'S ATTITUDE
AND RANGE OF OPINION

Because both the range of statements to be judged and the judge's own attitude have had significant effects in some experiments, Upshaw (1962) formulated a model that includes these effects and their interaction. The important addition is an interaction hypothesis, which states that the judge's attitude is critical when it is outside the range of statements presented. When the judge's position is within the range of statements presented, it is assumed that he adopts a reference scale defined by the statements. But when his position is outside the range, the judge extends the range to include his own position and adjusts his reference scale to this wider range. A consequence of this extension is that the middle of the scale moves in the direction of the judge's position and produces a contrast effect, like the effect of a remote anchor, so that a statement judged a neutral *six* by in-range judges would be judged more favorable, perhaps *seven,* by the judges outside the range on the unfavorable side and less favorable, perhaps *five,* by judges outside the range on the favorable side. Another consequence of the extension of the scale is that out-of-range judges necessarily use a scale of wider units than in-range judges.

To test this model, a series of statements covering a wide range of attitudes toward the Negro (one without the extremely *anti* statements, and one without the extremely *pro* statements) were given to *anti, neutral,* and *pro* judges for rating. The results demonstrated that the judge's own position is especially important when it is outside the range of statements presented and that in this condition the judge extends the scale to include this position.

Indirect evidence for assimilation can be uncovered in Upshaw's data (Manis, 1964). But the assimilation hypothesis requires that scale values of statements near the judge's position be displaced toward his position, and this implies some departure from linearity in the relation between scale values obtained from judges of different attitudes. Upshaw's (1964) reanalysis yielded linear correlation coefficients near unity, which appears to be direct evidence against any serious displacement of scale values. Other recent investigations have reported very high correlations between scale values obtained from groups of different attitudes (Ostrum, 1966) and by different scaling techniques (Hicks and Campbell, 1965). The importance of the judge's own attitude in determining a range of acceptance and ranges of uncertainty and in locating the statements that will be rejected is clear; but the evidence for a shift in scale values due to assimilation is disputable.

Departing somewhat from the method of judgment in given categories, Sherif (1963) allowed her subjects to choose their own categories to indicate ranges of acceptance and rejection. White and Indian high-school students considering the purchase of a warm coat simply sorted price tags—from $5 to $54 in one series and from $5 to $104 in another—to designate those that were *too cheap* to consider, within a range of *acceptable values,* and *prohibitive* in price. The context effect showed up as usual in that the range deemed acceptable varied with the values presented. For the white students, the upper boundary of the acceptable range was $49 for the short series and $80 for the long series. But the context was not the only determinant of the categorizations. These boundaries for Navaho Indian students, accustomed to lower living standards, were $38 and $70. Although the effect of the attitudes of the two groups was not as large as the context effect, it was clearly significant. And this must be called an effect of their own attitudes because a parallel experiment with the same numerals but with no reference to price tags disclosed the same context effect but no difference between whites and Indians.

ATTITUDE METHODOLOGY AND JUDGING OPERATIONS

From the standpoint of the psychology of judgment, this discussion exhibits the generality of certain principles of judgment—they apply to categories spaced along highly abstract social dimensions as well as more concrete perceptual dimensions—and clarifies some limitations. From the standpoint of social psychology, these are methodological considerations. The social psychologist has to know the consequences of variations in judging operations in order to control for them and to obtain evidence of genuine attitude differences and changes. Despite the inconsistencies, a few useful generalizations can now be gleaned from the research reviewed in this section.

1. The test constructor, who wants to get scale values of attitude statements and assemble a test for use in attitude research, can stay out of trouble unless he is looking for it. The differences between judges are of two types: differences in level or reference scale origin, and in dispersion or scale unit. But absolute scale values are not necessary (Upshaw, 1965). If the test constructor avoids extreme judges, discards ambiguous items, and, in general, follows good psychometric methodology, the scale values derived from one group of judges by one procedure will be linear with scale values derived from others.

2. Context effects sometimes do occur in the production and judgment of attitude items, but they are not as large or as consistent as in judgment of physical objects. Most demonstrations of context effects consist only of differences in scale values of a few statements when judged in different attitude ranges.

This does not imply that the context is unimportant but, more likely, that the important context is the range of opinion previously encountered in the mass media, in reference groups, and in one's own direct experience. Against these familiar and easily remembered ranges, the range of statements presented in the laboratory can yield only a recency effect. Thus Segall (1959) did not find the conventional context effect from judgments of two ranges but did find a recency effect due to the order in which the two ranges were presented. As Sherif, Sherif, and Nebergall (1965) have pointed out, shifts of this kind can easily be confused with true attitude changes.

Studies of context effects on the judgment of opinion statements have not applied the quantitative models described earlier in this chapter. Hence whatever context effects occur can equally well be interpreted in terms of adaptation level, linear correlation and regression, range-frequency compromise, variable perspective, or some other model. The special logarithmic feature of the adaptation-level model has not been used when the term has been applied to social judgments. Distribution effects, which the range-frequency compromise handles well, have not been studied, and might not show up because of the variable frequencies of previous exposure. The linear correlation-and-regression model has the advantages of simplicity and wide applicability, although correlation coefficients should perhaps be calculated for individual judges because subtle effects, such as assimilation, obscured in group data, might be manifest in individual data.

3. The judge's own position on the scale may not have much practical significance for test construction, but his division of the scale into subranges or latitudes of acceptance and rejection, which is dependent on his own attitude, is an important part of the judging process and must be included in any comprehensive theory. A statement rejected by one judge for one reason may be rejected by another judge for another reason, just as a middle-of-the-road candidate may be rejected by some as too liberal and by others as too conservative.

These latitudes of acceptance and rejection have another significance beyond dispute. It is at the boundary between one range and another that uncertainty reaches a maximum. The effect of distance from a category boundary on confidence and speed of judgment will be discussed later; statements near a boundary are also particularly susceptible to change from rejection to acceptance, and the reverse.

4. Anchoring effects are frequently reported for end stimuli, and occasionally for middle stimuli. The best measure of such anchoring effects is a reduction in variability and error of judgment. Though anchoring effects are mentioned in many discussions of social judgment, data on variability are seldom reported. Some theories emphasize the ends of a series of statements and others emphasize the middle, but no one has presented any evidence that these points have special anchoring effects beyond their general contribution to the context. Nor is the judge's own position an anchor in this respect, as far as we know.

Accuracy of Judgment

The preceding chapter considered the influence of stimulus variables on accuracy of judgment. Much of the research reviewed in this chapter has been concerned with principles of judgment that influence stability of scale values over variations in conditions and judges rather than with accuracy per se, although the correlation-and-regression approach is an exception in treating scales values as dependent on accuracy. Accuracy for its own sake can be estimated by measures of association between judgments and stimuli—

such as the correlation coefficient, the contingency coefficient, and amount of information transmitted or uncertainty reduced—as well as by direct counts of errors, when the data permit.

Many people complain, when asked to commit themselves to precise judgments of complex objects or events, that the task is "too subjective." It is subjective, of course, just as the assertion that the sky is blue is subjective. And it is true that many human judgments are full of error. But it is also true that accurate judgments of complex materials, in the sense of agreement between independent judges, can be obtained under good conditions, as in some of the investigations described in previous chapters (e.g., Johnson, Parrott, and Stratton, 1968). Under good conditions, judgments of students' English compositions are accurate also, in the sense of correlation with more objective scores (Godshalk, Swineford, and Coffman, 1966). The emphasis in this chapter on variability and error tendencies should not obscure the fact that high accuracy can also be obtained with reasonable effort.

NUMBER OF CATEGORIES

Foods, personality traits, and other complex objects of judgment are often rated, for research or practical purposes, on scales of 5 or 7 categories, but what is the optimal number? In this situation psychologists seem to admire odd numbers, especially that enchanting number 7, but it is safe to say that most ratings scales have been too short. Guilford's (1954) broad discussion of rating scales, based mostly on correlation studies, came to this conclusion. Several experiments (Bendig, 1954; Eriksen and Hake, 1955; Garner, 1960) have shown that more information is transmitted by longer rating scales, even up to 20 or more categories. In general, the response scale should allow the judge to communicate all the discriminability he is capable of, although this recommendation may include some circularity because the discriminability is not independent of the method of measuring it. Differences reported in published research, though small, favor the longer scales.

Judges often complain that they cannot make the fine distinctions required by scales of many categories, but this complaint reflects the subjective difficulty and doubt associated with judgments near category boundaries rather than objective data. One can argue in the other direction that the scale should be chosen so that all judgments are difficult, since otherwise the judge's ability will not be used to the best possible extent.

It is possible that unbounded scales of unspecified categories will turn out to be either more or less accurate than the more conventional scales of fixed categories, but there seems to be no evidence on this point as yet.

ANCHORS AND ACCURACY

The common practice of defining the ends of a scale by short phrases may be called *anchoring* the scale, and it does seem to increase accuracy, though the differences are small (Bendig, 1955; Bendig and Hughes, 1953). Recently, somewhat different results were reported by Noizet (1967), who introduced a variation in weight judgments by having one group of subjects sort the weights into unlabeled boxes. With 5 weights and 5 boxes this response system yielded better accuracy (counting systematic and variable errors) than the conventional verbal system, *very light, light, medium, heavy, very heavy,* used by another group; and the author suggested that the verbal labels may have produced asymmetrical anchoring. The sorting responses were apparently more difficult to learn than the familiar verbal system, however, because 9 out of 42 subjects switched boxes during the experiment and had to be dropped from the analysis.

Anchoring stimuli can also be spaced along the stimulus dimension to improve judgment. Wegryn (1964) selected 5 salient colors out of a series of 25 by a standardization experiment and then had another group of judges use these as reference points for category judgments. With these salient anchors strategically located, the second group was able to transmit 4.4 bits of information, much more than usual with unanchored scales. (The effects on accuracy of natural anchors—such as the vertical and the horizontal—and of supplied anchors were mentioned earlier, pp. 400–404).

IMPROVEMENT WITH PRACTICE

Improvement in accuracy of judgment as a result of practice has been demonstrated in many situations. For example, the accuracy of a panel of housewives judging ground beef for the proportion of rancid beef included, improved from the first to the third week of training, as measured by the variance of the judgments and the slope of the regression line (Bennett, Spahr, and Dodds, 1956). Accuracy could improve with learning of the distribution of stimuli (as suggested earlier), with identification of single stimuli, with mastery of the response system, or with adjustment of the response system to the distribution of stimuli. The improvement in one experiment on judgments of distance in an open field (Gibson, Bergman, and Purdy, 1955) was attributed to the development of a scale which could be transferred to a different field. Eriksen (1958) looked into the value of a correction procedure in judgments of sizes and brightnesses, but the gain from correction was rather small in terms of information transmitted. He concluded that "what S learns on this task is not to recognize individual stimuli as such, but instead to establish a frame of reference for the series of stimuli as a whole [p. 358]." As these experiments are usually carried out, the subject can correct himself by observing whether he has used the categories uniformly, so correction from the experimenter may not add much. Practice in the production of physical magnitudes also can improve accuracy of judgment of physical magnitudes (Howat, 1962).

Terborg (1966) began at this point and raised the question of the optimal order for learning to judge a series of 11 dots on a scale of 1 to 11. It seemed reasonable to expect that early presentation of the extreme stimuli would be helpful in defining the ends of the distribution and linking them to the ends of the response scale. The matter is complicated, however, by the cautiousness of the subjects. Most subjects avoid extreme judgments at first, as Wever and Zener (1928) suggested long ago, hence the early judgments will be less accurate when extreme stimuli are presented first than when middle stimuli are presented first. Thus there are two opposing tendencies to be disentangled. Performance on the first series of stimuli was facilitated by an early presentation of the middle stimuli because of the subjects' guessing habits. Learning was facilitated by an early presentation of the extreme stimuli, and this order improved accuracy on later series. After five series the differences had vanished. As a check on the methodology, Terborg used three measures of accuracy—information transmitted, correlation between judgments and stimuli, and magnitude of error. Although all three measures agreed, it was the simple error measure that seemed to be most useful as a measure of improvement in accuracy.

Even anchoring effects are influenced by practice, especially rewarded practice, as Larimer and White (1964) discovered by manipulating judgment conditions before the introduction of an anchor. As compared with a group of subjects with no knowledge of results, a group that received a monetary reward for correct judgments made more correct judgments before the introduction of the anchor and were less influenced by the anchor.

If this effect of monetary reward is a general one, the ambiguity of the subject's task in judgment experiments, especially when the series is shifted, could be cleared up by rewarding shift to the new series or adherence to the old; the interpretation of contrast effects and such phenomena would be clarified also.

Confidence in Judgment

Confidence in a judgment, reported after the judgment has been made, is a subjective dimension that is interesting in its own right and also helpful in analyzing judging operations. Confidence can be reported in conversational terms, such as *very confident* and *quite certain*, or on a rating scale. Most subjects will readily utilize a numerical or graphic scale from 0 to 100 because it seems natural. They know the meaning of zero confidence or *a pure guess* and complete confidence or *100 percent certainty*, and they use these points readily as end anchors. Distributions of confidence ratings are often J-shaped or U-shaped because the end points are used most frequently; but average values are systematically related to stimulus dimensions, and scores representing individual differences have satisfactory internal consistency (Johnson, 1939).

Psychophysical investigations occasionally require confidence ratings following comparative judgments, and the data show that confidence increases with an increase in the difference between the variable stimulus and the standard (Festinger, 1943; Johnson, 1939). Generalizing to judgments of single stimuli, one would expect that confidence would be lowest at the boundary between any two categories, and it is apparent from Fig. 9.19 that this generalization holds for scales of two, three, and four categories (Johnson, 1955).

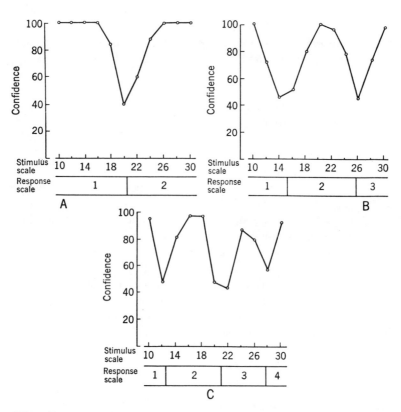

FIGURE 9.19. *Confidence and category boundaries. The stimuli were 11 cards bearing rows of 40 symbols: 10 to 30 x's and the remainder o's. The subject judged each card as to preponderance of x's, in 1 of 2 categories (A), 3 categories (B), or 4 categories (C). Mean confidence is lowest at the category boundaries, shown at the bottom of each graph. From Johnson (1955).*

In many situations, unlike the psychophysical one, the information on which the judgment is based comes serially and partially. The voter hears something about Candidate Smith, then something about Candidate Jones, then picks up a little more about Smith, a little more about Jones, and so on. Under these conditions, one would expect confidence to increase with an increase in the amount of pertinent information as well as the difference be-tween the two objects of judgment. To investigate this question, Irwin, Smith, and Mayfield (1956) arranged what they called an *expanded-judg-ment situation,* by giving their subjects two packs of numbered cards and asking them to judge which pack had the larger mean number. The question was whether college students who had not studied statistics would operate as intuitive statisticians, increasing their confidence as justified by the data.

When the difference between the numbers on the two packs of cards was 1.5, average confidence (on the scale from 0 to 100) was 30 after 10 pairs of cards had been seen. When the differences were 2.5 and 4.0, average confidence was 42 and 52, respectively. This is parallel to the 2-category

level of aspiration, is more complicated and the outcome may be unrealistic in some situations.

REALISM OF CONFIDENCE

The confidence scale is anchored at 0 and 100, but the other numbers are not often given explicit meaning. Adams and Adams (1958), however, have drawn attention to the ideal relation in which judgments made with 100 percent confidence would be 100 percent correct, judgments made with 50 percent confidence would be 50 percent correct, and so on. They explained this ideal relation to their subjects and then had them judge word meanings and report confidence after each judgment. The discrepancies from the ideal were large at first, but those subjects who were shown their percentage correct at each confidence level made significant improvement in a realistic use of the scale over five days of practice. A later experiment (Adams and Adams, 1961) reported some evidence of transfer from judging dots and weights to judging word meanings, indicating general improvement in realism of confidence. This research is another illustration of how a judge can shift his scale of judgment to correspond with varying task requirements.

CONFIDENCE IN EXPRESSING OPINIONS

Allport and Hartman (1925), in one of the earliest attempts to measure attitudes, collected opinions on controversial topics and confidence in these opinions. Their results indicated that those who held either extremely radical or extremely conservative opinions were more confident, and they attributed the extremist's overconfidence to compensation for a feeling of insecurity in his position.

Similar results were obtained later from students with extremely antiwar and anticensorship opinions (Johnson, 1940), but the interpretation was based on principles of judgment rather than compensation. Fig. 9.20 shows one student's confidence in acceptance and rejection of 84 statements about war; apparently the subject divided the attitude continuum into three categories, or subranges, or, in the terms of Sherif and Hovland (see page 435), latitudes of acceptance and rejection. Confidence was minimal at the two category boundaries, according to a general principle of judgment, and increased with distance from a category boundary. Thus the most confident judgments were rejections of statements that were far removed from the judge's own position. Applying these principles to differences between judges leads to the hypothesis that judges whose own position is at either extreme will find many statements that they can reject with high confidence and will in general appear more confident.

Judgment Time

Under some conditions, as when a standard stimulus and a variable stimulus are exposed simultaneously or when single stimuli are judged, judgment

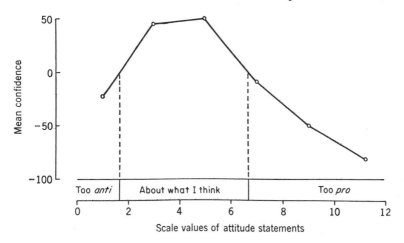

FIGURE 9.20. *Confidence and extremeness of attitude. The subject judged 84 statements about war and reported his confidence in each judgment. The highest confidence comes from rejection of statements far from a category boundary. Data from Johnson (1940).*

time or latency is easily recorded. Thus judgment times are formally similar to reaction times, but typically they are considerably longer since the tasks are more difficult and accuracy rather than speed is emphasized. It has long been known that in the comparative judgment, the judgment time increases as the difference between the variable stimulus and the standard decreases (Cartwright, 1941; Festinger, 1943; Reed, 1951). The curve rises toward a peak as stimulus difference decreases and would apparently reach infinity at zero stimulus difference, but actually all published curves round off before reaching that point. People do not deliberate forever, even when two stimuli appear exactly equal. They make a choice after a while, even if only an arbitrary one. If we approach this phenomenon by asking, as in the preceding chapter, about the utility of the decision, it is reasonable to assume that the decision maker will terminate his struggle, one way or another, when the effort exceeds the expected utility of the outcome. A quantitative model built around this assumption can be applied to a variety of difficult decision situations (Pollay, 1970).

When judgments are made by the method of single stimuli, there are several category boundaries. The generalization can then be made that judgment time decreases as a function of distance from a category boundary (see Johnson, 1955). Fig. 9.21, taken from Cartwright (1941), displays the two peaks of judgment time at the two boundaries of 3-category scale. It is not surprising that when the number of scale categories is increased, from 2 to 64, there is a regular increase in overall judgment time (Bevan and Avant, 1968).

The same relation between judgment time and category boundary was demonstrated in a very different experiment by Cohen, Hansel, and Walker (1960). They asked twelve-year-old children to attempt to hit a ball through

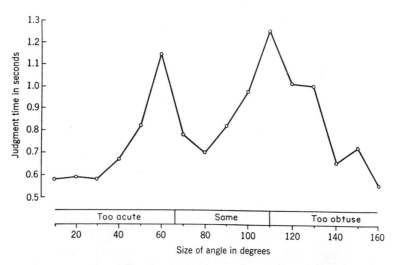

FIGURE 9.21. *Judgment time for recognition. Five angles, from 60° to 100°, were presented for learning; then 16 angles, 10° to 160°, were presented for recognition. Tabulation of the judgments permitted the inference that the subject had divided the series of angles into three categories, the boundaries of which were computed as 60° and 105°. Judgment time was maximal at these two boundaries. From Cartwright (1941).*

gaps of various widths. One group was to estimate probability of success for each width on a scale from 0 to 1.0; another group of children had to make a two-category decision whether to try or not, and the decision time for this group was maximal at the boundary between anticipated success and failure, that is, at the width that had a subjective probability of 0.5.

In the *expanded judgment* situation described a few pages back, it was noted that confidence in judgments about numbers in a pack of cards depends in part on the amount of information, that is, on the number of cards seen. The same task can be used to study the time spent in arriving at a decision if the subject is allowed to proceed at his own pace, making a decision whenever he is ready, and the number of cards required is the dependent variable. Irwin and Smith (1956) gave their subjects one pack of cards with positive and negative numbers and asked them to look at one card at a time and decide as soon as they could whether the average was greater or less than zero. On this task also, college students were reasonably good intuitive statisticians because the number of cards required decreased with the deviation from the zero condition and increased with the variability.

It is instructive to apply this type of analysis, looking at the distance of stimuli from category boundaries, to experiments in which the subjects choose their own categories. Tajfel and Bruner (1966) asked children aged eleven and twelve to decide whether each of a series of 44 lines was five inches long or not. They then divided the children into a group of broad categorizers, who said *yes* to 34–39 lines; a group of medium categorizers, who said *yes* to 22–33 lines; and a group of narrow categorizers, who said *yes* to 14–21 lines. The principal finding was that the medium categorizers made their judgments more slowly, on the average, than the other two groups.

Although category boundaries were not reported, it is a reasonable conjecture that all subjects divided the series of 44 lines into 3 categories: *less than 5 inches,* to which the response would be *no; about 5 inches,* to which the response would be *yes;* and *more than 5 inches,* to which the response would be *no.* The broad categorizers, according to the present analysis, would make their *yes* responses faster than their *no* responses because some of the lines judged *yes* were in the middle of the large middle category, far from either category boundary, while the few lines judged *no* were close to one or the other boundary. The narrow categorizers would make their *yes* responses slower than their *no* responses because all lines within the narrow middle category were close to a category boundary; fast *no* responses could be judgments of extremely short and extremely long lines. The data reported agree with these speculations. It follows also that the judgment times of the medium categorizers would be generally slow because they could find few lines that were far from a category boundary.

In general, it is well established that judgment time decreases and confidence of judgment increases with distance from a category boundary. Regardless of the stimuli being judged, the two dependent variables are understandably related. On the confidence scale from 0 to 100, as confidence increases (or doubt decreases) arithmetically, judgment time decreases geometrically (Johnson, 1939).

Individual Differences in Judgment

The variations between individuals in the activities discussed in this chapter, usually obscured by the use of averages, are often striking, and some of them have been studied directly (Johnson, 1955, pp. 382–384). Individual differences in confidence and speed of judgment can be measured with good reliability, and these traits exhibit some generality over variations in the objects of judgment. In the special case of judgment of attitude statements, individual differences in confidence depend, as noted above, on the subject's own attitude. When children and adults make estimates of various objects on familiar scales, the width of the categories used can be measured with good reliability; this trait also exhibits some generality and can be related to other characteristics of the judges (Bruner and Tajfel, 1961; Pettigrew, 1958; Tajfel and Bruner, 1966). Extremity of judgment—the tendency to use the end categories of a scale rather than the middle—is also a rather general trait, but its relation with personality variables is not clear (Warr and Coffman, 1970).

The shift experiment, which requires the subject to judge one series of stimuli, then another, on the same scale of judgment, also discloses large variations between individuals in the rate of adjusting to the new series. A cognitive style that goes by the name *leveling-sharpening* has been measured by having the subject judge a series of squares, then another series formed by subtracting a few at one end and adding a few at the other end, then another series, and so on, recording changes in the judgments. Gardner, Jackson, and Messick (1960) consider the Squares Test a measure of the degree to which new stimuli and relevant memory traces assimilate to each other. "Subjects at the leveling end of score distributions formed relatively undifferentiated memory schemata in a variety of situations involving temporal sequences of stimuli. Subjects at the sharpening extreme seemed to register discrete memories of successive stimulation [p. 67]." In a factor analysis with other measures of cognitive style (such as those described at the end of Chapter 4), leveling-sharpening scores came out on a single factor, rather distinct from the others. From Rokeach's (1960) work, one would expect that dogmatic persons would have difficulty in shifting judgments to adjust to new conditions, and in fact White and Alter (1965) found, in a study of weight judgments before and after the introduction of an anchor weight, that subjects who got high scores for dogmatism and authoritarianism were more resistant to change with changing stimuli than those who got low scores.

Individual differences in adapting to shifts in series of weights were compared with perceptual abilities and cognitive styles by Hettema (1968). A series of weights was shifted twice, either upward or downward, and judged on a scale of nine categories, the weights judged in the neutral category *five* in the last series being taken as a measure of terminal adaptation level. On the last series, a kind of anchor or reference weights, either 90 grams or 900 grams, was lifted with the other hand. Although the aim was to study leveling-sharpening, scores on the Squares Test were not related to other scores, and this test was abandoned. It is another sign of the narrowness of cognitive style factors (noted in Chapter 4) that most of the prediction came from ability factors, namely, Thurstone's perceptual factors. A factor called *flexibility of closure* (Gottschaldt Hidden Figures) requires the subject to discriminate between stimuli in the focus of attention, rather than background or series stimuli; and those who got high scores on this factor were more sensitive to differences in the reference weights and to the sequences of shifts of series than those who got low scores. A factor called *speed of closure* (Street Gestalt Test) requires the subject to unify a fluctuating perceptual field, and those who got high scores on this factor were less vulnerable to the sequence of shifts. Those who got superior scores on tests of optical illusions were less influenced by the reference weights lifted with the other hand. These differences between contrasting groups obtained by Hettema were interaction effects, which are notoriously difficult to replicate and to interpret, but they demonstrate the intriguing individual differences that have fascinated students of cognitive style.

The discussion of cognitive styles at the end of Chapter 4 noted that cognitively complex persons use more dimensions to describe an object and ask more questions in a problem-solving situation than cognitively simple persons. Sieber and Lanzetta (1966) discovered that cognitively complex persons also require more information before making decisions about ambiguous pictures and express greater uncertainty about their decisions. A hypothesis developed from the information-processing approach states that the complex persons have more associations to the stimuli and carry on more differentiation and encoding. This hypothesis was supported when training in the mediating cognitive activities made the judging processes of the simple subjects more like those of the complex subjects.

We must conclude that research on individual differences in judging activities, as in problem-solving methods and styles, has been characterized more by versatility of theoretical interpretation than by uniformity of results. Clear outlines have not yet emerged, but occasional flashes of illumination, from different quarters, continue to encourage hope for more consistent enlightenment.

Major Trends and Implications

Thought and communication are carried forward, not only by putting some stimulus objects rather than others into various unrelated categories, but also by putting all the objects under consideration into categories ordered along a scale. The stimulus objects are observable, the names of the categories constitute a system of observable responses, and it is conceivable that the judging process consists of direct association of specific responses with specific stimuli; but no one seems to argue for this. Most investigators seem to assume—though the explicitness of this assumption varies—that the scale of judgment is a construct, mediating between the stimuli and the responses, and the quantitative precision of many judgment experiments makes this construct more convincing than most. Boundaries between categories, context effects, the central tendency of judgment, anchor effects, and variations of speed and confidence of judgment near category boundaries are all properties of scales of judgment, not of the stimulus series or the response system. Scales of judgment are cognitive constructs, or schemas, in that the objects of the world are known, discussed, and evaluated in reference to scales. It is unfortunate that research on cognitive consistency and research on scales of judgment have proceeded independently, but some steps toward synthesis are being taken.

The question of the organization of a scale of judgment is one of adjusting the response system given by instructions to the series of stimuli. Scales are likely to be organized from the middle outward when there is a standard or salient anchor at the middle of the series and from the ends inward when the ends are salient. When no stimulus or response category is salient, the scale is not anchored at any special point and variability is uniform throughout the series.

When a scale of judgment is adjusted to a series of physical stimuli or attitude statements and then the series is shifted, the scale is usually realigned.

But the amount of realignment varies considerably, depending on the response system, the instructions, the amount and recency of experiences with the old series, the nature of the objects of judgment, their range, and the presence of anchor stimuli. The question whether the shift in judgment of an object constitutes a "genuine" shift in perception or a change in attitude probably cannot be clearly answered by recording only one kind of response; convergence or divergence of inferences from different measures will be more enlightening. The importance of the subject's approach to the task is documented by the results of complex experiments in which attention is manipulated, either by instructions or by variation of relations between stimulus dimensions. Under some conditions, perhaps, the subject's response may be treated as a direct measure of the effects of a stimulus, but this must be a rare situation. As judgment experiments become more complex, they resemble experiments on concept achievement and problem solving, so that the subject's understanding of his task becomes a critical factor. It is meaningful today to talk about strategies of judgment.

In psychophysical and social judgment, contrast effects are common. A stimulus may be judged large in contrast to one series and small in contrast to another or to an extreme anchor stimulus. Assimilation, however, is not common and, when it occurs, not well understood.

The well-known theory of adaptation level (AL) has stimulated much of the research reviewed in this chapter, has been applied to a variety of experimental situations, and seems to account, in a rough way, for much of the data. The criticisms revolve around the assumption of a logarithmic function, the idea of a level to which other stimuli are referred, the weight of anchor stimuli, and ad hoc statistical adjustments. The most enduring feature of AL theory is probably the pooling feature, the hypothesis that the effects of diverse classes of stimuli can be quantitatively weighted and pooled to predict single judgments.

When judgments are linearly related to stimuli, computation of the conventional correlation coefficients and regression equations accounts for scale values of stimuli, including the effects of external anchors and of the central tendency of judgment. This simple model, unlike the others, pays attention to the variability of the single judgments. The range-frequency compromise states that the judge tends to divide his psychological range into as many subranges as there are categories on the scale and to put the same number of stimuli into each category. When the distribution of stimuli is irregular, these principles conflict and compromise the results. Thus, this model accounts best for irregular distributions. A vector model—which assumes that the basis of judgment varies, depending on the salience of different stimulus attributes—promises further complications and more attention to multidimensional judgments in the future.

The judgment of attitude statements resembles the judgment of physical stimuli in many respects, but one difference is that the judge often knows the complete range of opinions on current issues. He knows the extreme opinions at both ends, anyhow; context effects are usually limited to intermediate statements ambiguously written. Some contrast due to order of presentation has also been found, but the large context and contrast effects typical of perceptual judgments do not appear in these judgments of easily remembered social objects.

Studies of the judge's own attitude indicate that each judge divides the attitude continuum into a range of opinions that he rejects as too *anti*, a range that he *accepts*, and a range that he rejects as too *pro*. Judgments of opinions in the transition regions are variable and uncertain. If the judge's opinion is outside the range of opinions presented, he extends the scale to include his own position. These effects of the range of opinion and of the judge's attitude illuminate the psychology of judgment and help to explain some of the effects found in perceptual judgment, but they do not negate the fact that high linear correlations are usually reported between scale values from different methods and different groups of judges.

Most judgment research has unfortunately been limited to accounting for mean scale values rather than single judgments, but it is evident that the accuracy of the single judgments is increased somewhat by increasing the number of scale categories, by adding anchors, and of course by practice. The judge learns the distribution of stimuli and adjusts his scale to this distribution, rewarded probably by noting observation of consistency in his judgments. Since the judge's task in many judgment experiments is ambiguous, a better definition of the task and instructions emphasizing accuracy might clarify some of the ambiguous results.

Confidence in a judgment varies up and down in predictable ways, being lowest when the difference between two stimuli to be discriminated is small, when a single stimulus or attitude statement to be categorized is near a boundary between two scale categories, and when the information for categorization is, in a statistical sense, nonsignificant. Confidence is related, in one way or another, to accuracy, and this relation can be improved by practice, so that the confidence reports become more realistic.

By the same principles, judgment time is longest when the difference between two stimuli to be discriminated is small, and when a single stimulus to be categorized is near a category boundary. Data on the time spent by college students in collecting information for decisions, like the data on confidence, indicate that they are fairly good intuitive statisticians. These principles relating to confidence and time around category boundaries offer rather simple explanations for some apparently complex phenomena of judgment.

These two chapters on judgment have integrated data on tasks as varied as brightness estimation, impression formation, and the scaling of attitude statements, and performance on these tasks is supposed to be related to perception, personality, and social psychology. But looking naïvely, behavioristically, at the subject's activities we see him assigning various objects to categories. One may hope that these performances are indirectly dependent on other psychological functions, but the fact that the subjects are making judgments is undeniable.

REFERENCES

Adams, J. C., Jr. The relative effects of various testing atmospheres on spontaneous flexibility, a factor of divergent thinking. *J. creative Behav.*, 1968, 2, 187–194.

Adams, J. K., and Adams, P. A. Realism of confidence judgments. *Psychol. Rev.*, 1961, 68, 33–45.

Adams, P. A., and Adams, J. K. Training in confidence-judgments. *Amer. J. Psychol.*, 1958, 71, 747–751.

Adamson, R. E., and Taylor, D. W. Functional fixedness as related to elapsed time and to set. *J. exp. Psychol.*, 1954, 47, 122–126.

Alexander, C. Youth and progress. *J. soc. Psychol.*, 1945, 22, 209–213.

Allen, L. E. Toward autotelic learning of mathematical logic by the WFF'N PROOF games. In L. N. Morrisett and J. Vinsonhaler (Eds.), Mathematical learning. *Monogr. Soc. Res. Child Develop.*, 1965, 30, 29–41.

Allen, M. S. *Morphological creativity*. Englewood Cliffs, N.J.: Prentice-Hall, 1962.

Allport, F. H., and Hartman, D. A. The measurement and motivation of atypical opinion in a certain group. *Amer. Polit. Sci. Rev.* 1925, 19, 753–763.

Almy, M. (with E. Chittenden and P. Miller). *Young children's thinking*. New York: Teachers College Press, Teachers College, Columbia Univ., 1966.

Anastasi, A., and Schaefer, C. E. Biographical correlates of artistic and literary creativity in adolescent girls. *J. applied Psychol.*, 1969, 53, 267–273.

Anderson, B., and Johnson, W. Two methods of presenting information and the effects on problem-solving. *Percept. mot. Skills*, 1966, 23, 851–856.

Anderson, N. H. Primacy effects in personality impression formation using a generalized order effect paradigm. *J. pers. soc. Psychol.*, 1965a, 2, 1–9.

Anderson, N. H. Averaging versus adding as a stimulus-combination rule in impression formation. *J. exp. Psychol.*, 1965b, 70, 394–400.

Anderson, N. H. Averaging model analysis of set-size effect in impression formation. *J. exp. Psychol.*, 1967, 75, 158–165.

Anderson, N. H., and Jacobson, A. Effect of stimulus inconsistency and discounting instructions in personality impression formation. *J. pers. soc. Psychol.*, 1965, 2, 531–539.

Anderson, N. H., and Norman, A. Order effects in impression formation in four classes of stimuli. *J. abnorm. soc. Psychol.*, 1964, 69, 467–471.

Anderson, R. C. Can first graders learn an advanced problem-solving skill? *J. educ. Psychol.*, 1965, 56, 283–294.

Anderson, R. C. Individual differences and problem solving. In R. M. Gagné (Ed.), *Learning and individual differences*. Columbus, Ohio: Merrill, 1967.

Anderson, S. B. Problem solving in multiple-goal situations. *J. exp. Psychol.*, 1957, 54, 297–303.

Andrews, E. G. The development of imagination in the preschool child. Iowa City, Iowa: *Univ. Iowa Studies in Character*, 1930, 3, No. 4.

Anthony, W. S. Working backward and working forward in problem-solving. *British J. Psychol.*, 1966, 57, 53–59.

Archer, E. J. Concept identification as a function of obviousness of relevant and irrelevant information. *J. exp. Psychol.*, 1962, 63, 616–620.

Arnheim, R., Auden, W. H., Shapiro, K., and Stauffer, E. A. *Poets at work*. New York: Harcourt, Brace, Jovanovich, 1948.

Arnold, J. E. Useful creative techniques. In S. J. Parnes and H. F. Harding (Eds.), *A source book for creative thinking*. New York: Scribners, 1962.

Asch, S. E. Forming impressions of personality. *J. abnorm. soc. Psychol.*, 1946, *41*, 258–290.

Asch, S. E. A reformulation of the problem of associations. *Amer. Psychol.*, 1969, *24*, 92–102.

Atkins, A. L. Own attitude and discriminability in relation to anchoring effects in judgment. *J. pers. soc. Psychol.*, 1966, *4*, 497–507.

Ausubel, D. P. Introduction. In R. C. Anderson and D. P. Ausubel (Eds.), *Readings in the psychology of cognition*. New York: Holt, Rinehart and Winston, 1965.

Ausubel, D. P. Meaningful reception learning and the acquisition of concepts. In H. J. Klausmeier and C. H. Harris (Eds.), *Analysis of concept learning*. New York: Academic Press, 1966.

Azuma, H., and Cronbach, L. J. Cue-response correlations in the attainment of a scalar concept. *Amer. J. Psychol.*, 1966, *79*, 38–49.

Barron, F. The disposition toward originality. *J. abnorm. soc. Psychol.*, 1955, *51*, 478–485.

Barron, F. Originality in relation to personality and intellect. *J. Pers.*, 1957, *25*, 730–742.

Barron, F. The psychology of creativity. In *New Directions in psychology, II*. New York: Holt, Rinehart and Winston, 1965.

Bartlett, F. *Thinking: An experimental and social study*. London: Allen & Unwin, 1958.

Battersby, W. S., Teuber, H. L., and Bender, M. Problem-solving behavior in men with frontal or occipital brain injuries. *J. Psychol.*, 1953, *35*, 329–351.

Bearison, D. J., and Sigel, I. E. Hierarchical attributes for categorization. *Percept. mot. Skills*, 1968, *27*, 147–153.

Becker, G. W., and McClintock, C. G. Value: Behavioral decision theory. *Ann. Rev. Psychol.*, 1967, *18*, 239–286.

Beckwith, M., and Restle, F. Process of enumeration. *Psychol. Rev.*, 1966, *73*, 437–444.

Bedell, R. C. The relationship between the ability to recall and the ability to infer in specific learning situations. Kirksville, Mo.: *Bulletin of the Northeast Missouri State Teachers College*, 1934, *34*, No. 9.

Beebe-Center, J. G. *Pleasantness and unpleasantness*. New York: Van Nostrand, 1932.

Begg, I., and Denny, J. P. Empirical reconciliation of atmosphere and conversion interpretations of syllogistic reasoning errors. *J. exp. Psychol.*, 1969, *81*, 351–354.

Behar, I., and Bevan, W. The perceived duration of auditory and visual intervals: Cross-modal comparison and interaction. *Amer. J. Psychol.*, 1961, *74*, 17–26.

Beilin, H. Learning and operational convergence in logical thought development. *J. exp. child Psychol.*, 1965, *2*, 317–339.

Beilin, H. Developmental determinants of word and nonsense anagram solution. *J. verb. Learn. & verb. Behav.*, 1967, *6*, 523–527.

Beilin, H., and Horn, R. Transition probability effects in anagram problem solving. *J. exp. Psychol.*, 1962, *63*, 514–518.

Beilin, H., and Levine, H. L. Word and nonsense anagram solution with tachistoscopic stimulus presentation. *Psychon. Sci.*, 1966, *6*, 171–172.

Bell, R. A., and Bevan, W. Influence of anchors upon the operation of certain Gestalt organizing principles. *J. exp. Psychol.*, 1968, *78*, 670–678.

Bendig, A. W. Reliability and the number of rating-scale categories. *J. applied Psychol.*, 1954, *38*, 38–40.

Bendig, A. W. Rater reliability and the heterogeneity of scale anchors. *J. applied Psychol.*, 1955, *39*, 37–39.

Bendig, A. W., and Hughes, H. B. The effect of amount of verbal anchoring and number of rating-scale categories upon transmitted information. *J. exp. Psychol.*, 1953, *46*, 87–90.

Bennett, G., Spahr, B. M., and Dodds, M. L. The value of training a sensory test panel. *Food Technol.*, 1956, *10*, 205–208.

Berlyne, D. E. *Structure and direction in thinking*. New York: Wiley, 1965.

Bevan, W., and Adamson, R. Reinforcers and reinforcement: Their relation to maze performance. *J. exp. Psychol.*, 1960, *59*, 226–232.

Bevan, W., and Avant, L. L. Response latency, response uncertainty, information transmitted and the number of available judgmental categories. *J. exp. Psychol.*, 1968, *76*, 394–397.

Bevan, W., and Pritchard, J. F. Effect of "subliminal" tones upon the judgment of loudness *J. exp. Psychol.*, 1963a, *66*, 23–29.

Bevan, W., and Pritchard, J. F. The anchor effect and the problem of relevance in the judgment of shape. *J. gen. Psychol.*, 1963b, *69*, 147–161.

Bevan, W., and Pritchard, J. F. The effect of visual intensities upon the judgments of loudness. *Amer. J. Psychol.*, 1964, *77*, 93–98.

Bevan, W., and Turner, E. D. Assimilation and contrast in the estimation of number. *J. exp. Psychol.*, 1964, *67*, 458–462.

Bevan, W., and Turner, E. D. The potency of a lightness-anchor as a function of the reflectance of its background. *Amer. J. Psychol.*, 1965, *78*, 645–650.

Bieri, J., Atkins, A. L., Briar, S., Leaman, R. L., Miller, H., and Tripodi, T. *Clinical and social judgment*. New York: Wiley, 1966.

Bieri, J., Orcutt, B., and Leaman, R. Anchoring effects in sequential clinical judgments. *J. abnorm. soc. Psychol.*, 1963, *67*, 616–623.

Billings, M. L. Problem-solving in different fields of behavior. *Amer. J. Psychol.*, 1934, *46*, 259–292.

Birch, H. G., and Rabinowitz, H. S. The negative effect of previous experience on productive thinking. *J. exp. Psychol.*, 1951, *41*, 121–125.

Black, R. W., and Bevan, W. The effect of subliminal shock upon judged intensity of weak shock. *Amer. J. Psychol.*, 1960, *73*, 262–267.

Blumenfeld, W. Urteil und Beurteilung. *Arch. f. d. ges. Psychol.*, 1931, Ergänzungsband 3.

Bocheński, I. M. *A history of formal logic* (Translated and edited by Ivo Thomas). South Bend, Ind.: Univ. Notre Dame Press, 1961.

Boring, E. G. *A history of experimental psychology*. New York: Appleton-Century-Crofts, 1950.

Bossart, P., and Di Vesta, F. J. Effects of content, frequency, and order of presentation of evaluative assertions on impression formation. *J. pers. soc. Psychol.*, 1966, *4*, 538–544.

Botwinick, J. *Cognitive processes in maturity and old age*. New York: Springer, 1967.

Bourassa, C. Unpublished report. Michigan State University, 1961.

Bourne, L. E., Jr. Factors affecting strategies used in problems of concept-formation. *Amer. J. Psychol.*, 1963, *76*, 229–238.

Bourne, L. E., Jr. Learning and utilization of conceptual rules. In B. Kleinmuntz (Ed.), *Concepts and the structure of memory*. New York: Wiley, 1967.

Bourne, L. E., Jr., Dodd, D. H., Guy, D. E., and Justesen, D. R. Response-contingent intertrial intervals in concept identification. *J. exp. Psychol.*, 1968, *76*, 601–608.

Bourne, L. E., Jr., and Guy, D. E. Learning conceptual rules. II. The role of positive and negative instances. *J. exp. Psychol.*, 1968, *77*, 448–494.

Bousfield, W. A., and Barclay, W. D. The relationship between order and frequency of occurrence of restricted associative responses. *J. exp. Psychol.*, 1950, *40*, 643–647.

Bousfield, W. A., and Sedgewick, C. H. W. An analysis of sequences of restricted associative responses. *J. gen. Psychol.*, 1944, *30*, 149–165.

Bower, G., and Trabasso, T. Concept identification. In R. C. Atkinson (Ed.), *Studies in mathematical psychology*. Stanford, Calif.: Stanford Univ. Press, 1964.

Braine, M. D. S. Piaget on reasoning: A methodological critique and alternative proposals. In W. Kessen and C. Kuhlman (Eds.), Thought in the young child. *Monogr. Soc. Res. Child Develop.*, 1962, *27*, 41–63.

Brainerd, C. J., and Allen, T. W. Experimental inductions of the conservation of "first-order" quantitative invariants. *Psychol. Bull.*, 1971, 75, 128–144.

Bravo, L., and Mayzner, M. S. Assimilation and contrast effects of anchoring stimuli on judgments. *J. Psychol.*, 1961, 52, 333–334.

Bremer, B. A. Inhibitory effects of positive transfer in problem solving. Unpublished Master's thesis, Michigan State University, 1963.

Bremer, B. A. Production and judgment processes in a word problem. Unpublished Ph.D. dissertation, Michigan State University, 1968.

Brewer, M. B. Averaging versus summation in composite ratings of complex social stimuli. *J. pers. soc. Psychol.*, 1968, 8, 20–26.

Brotherton, D. A., Read, J. M., and Pratt, K. C. Indeterminate number concepts: II. Application by children to determinate number groups. *J. genetic Psychol.*, 1948, 73, 209–236.

Brown, D. R. Stimulus-similarity and the anchoring of subjective scales. *Amer. J. Psychol.*, 1953, 66, 199–214.

Brownell, W. R., and Stretch, L. B. The effect of unfamiliar settings on problem-solving. Durham, N.C.: *Duke Univ. Res. Stud. in Educ.*, 1931, No. 1.

Bruner, J. S., Goodnow, J. J., and Austin, G. A. *A study of thinking*. New York: Wiley, 1956.

Bruner, J. S., and Kenney, H. J. Representation and mathematics learning. In L. N. Morrisett and J. Vinsonhaler (Eds.), Mathematical learning. *Monogr. Soc. Res. Child Develop.*, 1965, 30, 50–59.

Bruner, J. S., Olver, R. R., and Greenfield, P. M. *Studies in cognitive growth*. New York: Wiley, 1966.

Bruner, J. S., and Tajfel, H. Cognitive risk and environmental change. *J. abnorm. soc. Psychol.*, 1961, 62, 231–241.

Brunk, L., Collister, E. G., Swift, C., and Stayton, S. A correlational study of two reasoning problems. *J. exp. Psychol.*, 1958, 55, 236–241.

Buell, W. D. Biographical data and the identification of creative research personnel. *J. applied Psychol.*, 1965, 49, 318–321.

Buell, W. D., Albright, L. E., and Glennon, J. P. A note on generality and cross-validity of personal history for identifying creative research scientists. *J. applied Psychol.*, 1966, 50, 217–219.

Bulgarella, R. G., and Archer, E. J. Concept identification of auditory stimuli as a function of amount of relevant and irrelevant information. *J. exp. Psychol.*, 1962, 63, 254–257.

Burt, C. The development of reasoning in school children. *J. exp. Pedagogy*, 1919, 5, 68–77, 121–127.

Byers, J. L. Hypothesis behavior in concept attainment. *J. educ. Psychol.*, 1965, 56, 337–342.

Byers, J. L., and Davidson, R. E. The role of hypothesizing in the facilitation of concept attainment behavior. *J. verb. Learn. & verb. Behav.*, 1967, 6, 595–600.

Cahill, H. E., and Hovland, C. I. The role of memory in the acquisition of concepts. *J. exp. Psychol.*, 1960, 59, 137–144.

Campbell, A. C. On the solving of code items demanding the use of indirect procedures. *British J. Psychol.*, 1965, 56, 45–51.

Campbell, A. C. Selectivity in problem-solving. *Amer. J. Psychol.*, 1968, 81, 543–550.

Campbell, D. T. Blind variation and selective retention in creative thought as in other knowledge processes. *Psychol. Rev.*, 1960, 67, 380–400.

Campbell, D. T., Lewis, N. A., and Hunt, W. A. Context effects with judgment language that is absolute, extensive, and extra-experimentally anchored. *J. exp. Psychol.*, 1958, 55, 220–228.

Carey, G. L. Sex differences in problem-solving performance as a function of attitude differences. *J. abnorm. soc. Psychol.*, 1958, 56, 256–260.

Caron, J., Unger, S. M., and Parloff, M. B. A test of Maltzman's theory of originality training. *J. verb. Learn. & verb. Behav.*, 1963, *1*, 436–442.

Carroll, J. B. *The study of language.* Cambridge, Mass.: Harvard Univ. Press, 1955.

Carroll, J. B. *Language and thought.* Englewood Cliffs, N.J.: Prentice-Hall, 1964a.

Carroll, J. B. Words, meanings and concepts. *Harvard Educational Rev.*, 1964b, *34*, 179–202.

Cartwright, D. Relation of decision-time to the categories of response. *Amer. J. Psychol.*, 1941, *54*, 174–196.

Cattell, R. B. The personality and motivation of the researcher from measurements of contemporaries and from biography. In C. W. Taylor and F. Barron (Eds.), *Scientific creativity: Its recognition and development.* New York: Wiley, 1963.

Cattell, R. B., and Butcher, H. J. *The prediction of achievement and creativity.* New York: Bobbs-Merrill, 1968.

Cattell, R. B., and Drevdahl, J. E. A comparison of the personality profile (16 P.F.) of eminent researchers with that of eminent teachers and administrators, and of the general population. *British J. Psychol.*, 1955, *46*, 248–261.

Chalmers, D. K. Meanings, impressions and attitudes: A model of the evaluation process. *Psychol. Rev.*, 1969, *76*, 450–460.

Chaney, F. B. A cross-cultural study of industrial research performance. *J. applied Psychol.*, 1966, *50*, 206–210.

Chapanis, A. Studies of manual rotary positioning movements: I. The precision of setting an indicator knob to various angular positions. *J. Psychol.*, 1951a, *31*, 51–64.

Chapanis, A. Studies of manual rotary positioning movements: II. The accuracy of estimating the position of an indicator knob. *J. Psychol.*, 1951b, *31*, 65–71.

Chapman, L. J., and Chapman, J. P. Atmosphere effect reexamined. *J. exp. Psychol.*, 1959, *58*, 220–226.

Chlebek, J., and Dominowski, R. L. The effect of practice on utilization of information from positive and negative instances in identifying disjunctive concepts. *Canad. J. Psychol.*, 1970, *24*, 64–69.

Christensen, P. R., Guilford, J. R., and Wilson, R. C. Relations of creative responses to working time and instructions. *J. exp. Psychol.*, 1957, *53*, 82–88.

Cicirelli, V. G. Form of the relationship between creativity, IQ, and academic achievement. *J. educ. Psychol.*, 1965, *56*, 303–308.

Clark, H. H. Linguistic processes in deductive reasoning. *Psychol. Rev.*, 1969a, *76*, 387–404.

Clark, H. H. The influence of language in solving three-term series problems. *J. exp. Psychol.*, 1969b, *82*, 205–215.

Clark, K. E. *America's psychologists.* Washington, D.C.: Amer. Psychol. Assoc., Inc., 1957.

Cliff, N. Adverbs as multipliers. *Psychol. Rev.*, 1959, *66*, 27–44.

Cline, V. B., Richards, J. M., Jr., and Abe, C. The validity of a battery of creativity tests in a high school sample. *Educ. Psychol. Meas.*, 1962, *22*, 781–784.

Cline, V. B., Richards, J. M., Jr., and Needham, W. E. Creativity tests and achievement in high school science. *J. applied Psychol.*, 1963, *47*, 184–189.

Cohen, J. A preliminary study of the effect of delayed recording on the quality of thought. In G. Revesz (Ed.), Thinking and speaking: A symposium. *Acta Psychologica*, 1954, *10*, 111–124.

Cohen, J. *Chance, skill and luck.* Baltimore, Md.: Penguin, 1960.

Cohen, J., Dearnley, E. J., and Hansel, C. E. M. A quantitative study of meaning. *British J. educ. Psychol.*, 1958, *28*, 141–148.

Cohen, J., Hansel, C. E. M., and Walker, D. B. The time taken to decide as a measure of subjective probability. *Acta Psychologica*, 1960, *17*, 177–183.

Cook, T. W. Amount of material and difficulty of problem solving: II. The disc transfer problem. *J. exp. Psychol.*, 1937, *20*, 288–296.

Corah, N. L., and Gross, J. B. Hue, brightness and saturation variables in color-form matching. *Child Develop.*, 1967, 38, 137–142.

Corman, B. R. The effect of varying amounts and kinds of information as guidance in problem solving. *Psychol. Monogr.*, 1957, 71, No. 431.

Craig, R. C. Directed versus independent discovery of established relations. *J. educ. Psychol.*, 1956, 47, 223–234.

Cropley, A. J. Creativity and intelligence. *British J. educ. Psychol.*, 1966, 36, 259–266.

Cross, K. P., and Gaier, E. Technique in problem solving as a predictor of educational achievement. *J. educ. Psychol.*, 1955, 46, 193–206.

Crutchfield, R. S. Creative thinking in children: Its teaching and testing. In O. G. Brim, R. S. Crutchfield, and W. H. Holtzman (Eds.), *Intelligence: Perspectives 1965.* New York: Harcourt, Brace, Jovanovich, 1966.

Dale, H. C. A. Strategies of searching in two simple systems. *Amer. J. Psychol.*, 1959, 72, 539–546.

Darnell, C. D., and Bourne, L. E., Jr. Effects of age, verbal ability, and pretraining with component concepts on the performance of children in a bidimensional classification task. *J. educ. Psychol.*, 1970, 61, 66–71.

Davidon, R. S. The effects of symbols, shift, and manipulation upon the number of concepts attained. *J. exp. Psychol.*, 1952, 44, 70–79.

Davidson, M. Positive versus negative instances in concept identification problems matched for logical complexity of solution procedures. *J. exp. Psychol.*, 1969, 80, 369–373.

Davis, D. J. Structure of the environment and strategies for acquiring information. *J. exp. Psychol.*, 1967, 73, 227–231.

Davis, G. A. Detrimental effects of distraction, additional response alternatives, and longer response chains in solving switch-light problems. *J. exp. Psychol.*, 1967, 73, 45–55.

Davis, G. A., and Houtman, S. E. *Thinking creatively: A guide to training imagination.* Wisconsin Research and Development Center for Cognitive Learning and the Department of Educational Psychology, University of Wisconsin, 1968.

Davis, G. A., Houtman, S. E., Warren, T. F., and Roweton, W. E. *A program for training creative thinking: I. Preliminary field test.* Wisconsin Research and Development Center for Cognitive Learning and the Department of Educational Psychology, University of Wisconsin, 1969.

Davis, G. A., and Manske, M. E. Effects of prior serial learning of solution words upon anagram problem solving: II. A serial position effect. *J. exp. Psychol.*, 1968, 77, 101–104.

Davis, J. H., Carey, M. H., Foxman, P. N., and Tarr, D. B. Verbalization, experimenter presence, and problem solving. *J. pers. soc. Psychol.*, 1968, 8, 299–302.

Davis, J. K., and Klausmeier, H. J. Cognitive style and concept identification as a function of complexity and training procedures. *J. educ. Psychol.*, 1970, 61, 423–430.

De Groot, A. D. *Thought and choice in chess.* The Hague: Mouton, 1965.

Dentler, R. A., and Mackler, B. Originality: Some social and personal determinants. *Behav. Sci.*, 1964, 9, 1–7.

De Soto, C., London, M., and Handel, S. Social reasoning and spatial paralogic. *J. pers. soc. Psychol.*, 1965, 2, 513–521.

Detambel, M. H., and Stolurow, L. M. Probability and work as determiners of multi-choice behavior. *J. exp. Psychol.*, 1957, 53, 73–81.

Dewey, J. *How we think.* Boston: Heath, 1910.

Diebold, A. R. A survey of psycholinguistic research, 1954–1964. In C. E. Osgood and T. A. Seboek (Eds.), *Psycholinguistics.* Bloomington, Ind.: Indiana Univ. Press, 1965.

Dienes, Z. P., and Jeeves, M. *Thinking in structures.* London: Hutchinson Educational Ltd., 1965.

Dillehay, R. C., Insko, C. A., and Smith, M. B. Logical consistency and attitude change. *J. pers. soc. Psychol.*, 1966, 3, 646–654.

Di Lollo, V. Contrast effects in the judgment of lifted weights. *J. exp. Psychol.*, 1964, 68, 383–387.

Di Lollo, V., and Casseday, J. H. Graded contrast effects in the judgment of lifted weights. *J. exp. Psychol.*, 1965, 70, 234–235.

Dinnerstein, D. Intermanual effects of anchors on zones of maximal sensitivity in weight-discrimination. *Amer. J. Psychol.*, 1965, 78, 66–74.

Di Vesta, F. J., and Ingersoll, G. M. Effect of semantic redundancy on children's identification of verbal concepts. *J. exp. Psychol.*, 1969, 82, 360–365.

Di Vesta, F. J., and Walls, R. T. Transfer of solution rules in problem solving. *J. educ. Psychol.*, 1967, 58, 319–326.

Di Vesta, F. J., and Walls, R. T. Multiple- versus single-problem training and variations of solution rules in the formation of learning sets. *J. educ. Psychol.*, 1968, 59, 191–196.

Di Vesta, F. J., and Walls, R. T. Rule and attribute identification in childrens attainment of disjunctive and conjunctive concepts. *J. exp. Psychol.*, 1969, 80, 498–504.

Dodd, D. H., and Bourne, L. E., Jr. Test of some assumptions of a hypothesis-testing model of concept identification. *J. exp. Psychol.*, 1969, 80, 69–72.

Dodwell, P. C. Children's understanding of number and related concepts. *Canad. J. Psychol.*, 1960, 14, 191–205.

Dodwell, P. C. Children's understanding of number concepts: Characteristics of an individual and of a group test. *Canad. J. Psychol.*, 1961, 15, 29–36.

Dodwell, P. C. Relations between the understanding of the logic of classes and of cardinal number in children. *Canad. J. Psychol.*, 1962, 16, 152–160.

Dominowski, R. L. The effect of pronunciation practice on anagram difficulty. *Psychon. Sci.*, 1969, 16, 99–100.

Dominowski, R. L., and Ekstrand, B. R. Direct and associative priming in anagram solving. *J. exp. Psychol.*, 1967, 74, 84–86.

Donaldson, M. C. Positive and negative information in matching problems. *British J. Psychol.*, 1959, 50, 253–262.

Donaldson, M., and Wales, R. On the acquisition of some relational terms. In J. R. Hayes (Ed.), *Cognition and the development of language*. New York: Wiley, 1970.

Drevdahl, J. E., and Cattell, R. B. Personality and creativity in artists and writers. *J. clin. Psychol.*, 1958, 14, 108–111.

Duncan, C. P. Recent research on human problem solving. *Psychol. Bull.*, 1959, 56, 397–429.

Duncan, C. P. Effect of instructions and information on problem solving. *J. exp. Psychol.*, 1963, 65, 321–327.

Duncan, C. P. Induction of a principle. *Quart. J. exp. Psychol.*, 1964, 16, 373–377.

Duncan, C. P. Meditation in verbal concept learning. *J. verb. Learn. & verb. Behav.*, 1965, 4, 1–6.

Duncan, C. P. Effect of word frequency on thinking of a word. *J. verb. Learn. & verb. Behav.*, 1966, 5, 434–440.

Duncker, K. On problem-solving (Translated by L. S. Lees). *Psychol. Monogr.*, 1945, 58, No. 270.

Dunham, J. L., and Bunderson, C. V. Effect of decision-rule instruction upon the relationship of cognitive abilities to performance in multiple-concept problems. *J. educ. Psychol.*, 1969, 60, 121–125.

Dunham, J. L., Guilford, J. P., and Hoepfner, R. The cognition, production and memory of class concepts. *Educ. Psychol. Meas.*, 1969, 29, 615–638.

Dunnette, M. D., Campbell, J., and Jaasted, L. The effect of group participation on brainstorming effectiveness for two industrial samples. *J. applied Psychol.*, 1963, 47, 30–37.

Dustin, D. S., and Baldwin, P. M. Redundancy in impression formation. *J. pers. soc. Psychol.*, 1966, 3, 500–506.

Edwards, M. P., and Tyler, L. E. Intelligence, creativity, and achievement in a nonselective public junior high school. *J. educ. Psychol.*, 1965, 56, 96–99.

Edwards, W. The theory of decision making. *Psychol. Bull.*, 1954, *51*, 380–417.

Ehlers, H. *Logic by way of set theory.* New York: Holt. Rinehart and Winston, 1968.

Eifermann, R. R. Response patterns and strategies in the dynamics of concept attainment behaviour. *British J. Psychol.*, 1965, *56*, 217–222.

Eindhoven, J. E., and Vinacke, W. E. Creative processes in painting. *J. gen. Psychol.*, 1952, *47*, 139–164.

Ekstrand, B. R., and Dominowski, R. L. Solving words as anagrams: II. A clarification. *J. exp. Psychol.*, 1968, *77*, 552–558.

Elkind, D., and Flavell, J. H. *Studies in cognitive development.* New York: Oxford Univ. Press, 1969.

Engle, G., and Parducci, A. Value of background in the specification of the stimulus for judgment. *Amer. J. Psychol.*, 1961, *74*, 569–575.

Erickson, J. R. Problem shifts and hypothesis behavior in concept identification. *Amer. J. Psychol.*, 1971, *84*, 100–111.

Erickson, J. R., and Zajkowski, M. M. Learning several concept-identification problems concurrently: A test of the sampling-with-replacement assumption. *J. exp. Psychol.*, 1967, *74*, 212–218.

Eriksen, C. W. Effects of practice with or without correction on discriminative learning. *Amer. J. Psychol.*, 1958, *71*, 350–358.

Eriksen, C. W., and Hake, H. W. Absolute judgments as a function of stimulus range and response categories. *J. exp. Psychol.*, 1955, *49*, 323–333.

Eriksen, C. W., and Hake, H. W. Multidimensional stimulus differences and accuracy of discrimination. *J. exp. Psychol.*, 1955, *50*, 153–160.

Eriksen, C. W., and Hake, H. W. Anchor effects in absolute judgments. *J. exp. Psychol.*, 1957, *53*, 132–138.

Ervin, S. Transfer effects of learning a verbal generalization. *Child Develop.*, 1960, *31*, 537–554.

Ervin, S. M., and Foster, G. The development of meaning in children's descriptive terms. *J. abnorm. soc. Psychol.*, 1960, *61*, 271–275.

Eustace, B. W. Learning a complex concept at differing hierarchial levels. *J. educ. Psychol.*, 1969, *60*, 449–452.

Ewert, P. H., and Lambert, J. F. The effect of verbal instructions upon the formation of a concept. *J. gen. Psychol.*, 1932, *6*, 400–413.

Faust, W. L. Factors in individual improvement in solving twenty-questions problems. *J. exp. Psychol.*, 1958, *55*, 39–44.

Feather, N. T. Acceptance and rejection of arguments in relation to attitude strength, critical ability, and intolerance of inconsistency. *J. abnorm. soc. Psychol.*, 1964, *69*, 127–136.

Fehrer, E. Shifts in scale values of attitude statements as a function of the composition of the scale. *J. exp. Psychol.*, 1952, *44*, 179–188.

Feldhusen, J. F., Treffinger, D. J., and Bahlke, S. J. Developing creative thinking: The Purdue creativity program. *J. creative Behav.*, 1970, *4*, 85–90.

Fernberger, S. W. The use of equality judgments in psychophysical procedures. *Psychol. Rev.*, 1930, *37*, 107–112.

Festinger, L. Studies in decision: I. Decision-time, relative frequency of judgment and subjective confidence as related to physical stimulus difference. *J. exp. Psychol.*, 1943, *32*, 291–306.

Fey, E. T. The performance of young schizophrenics and young normals on the Wisconsin Card Sorting Test. *J. consult. Psychol.*, 1951, *15*, 311–319.

Fillenbaum, S. The effect of a remote anchor upon judgment with a salient within-series stimulus-object and with a free choice of scale. *Amer. J. Psychol.*, 1961, *74*, 602–606.

Fine, B. J., and Haggard, D. F. Contextual effects in scaling. *J. applied Psychol.*, 1958, *42*, 247–251.

Fishbein, H. D., Haygood, R. C., and Frieson, D. Relevant and irrelevant saliency in concept learning. *Amer. J. Psychol.*, 1970, 83, 544–553.

Flanagan, J. C. The definition and measurement of ingenuity. In C. W. Taylor and F. Barron (Eds.), *Scientific creativity: Its recognition and development.* New York: Wiley, 1963.

Flavell, J. H. *The developmental psychology of Jean Piaget.* New York: Van Nostrand, 1963.

Flavell, J. H., Cooper, A., and Loiselle, R. H. Effect of the number of pre-utilization functions on functional fixedness in problem solving. *Psychol. Rep.*, 1958, 4, 343–350.

Flavell, J. H., and Hill J. P. Developmental psychology. *Ann. Rev. Psychol.*, 1969, 20, 1–56.

Flescher, I. Anxiety and achievement of intellectually gifted and creatively gifted children. *J. Psychol.*, 1963, 56, 251–268.

Fodor, J. A. Could meaning be an rm? *J. verb. Learn. & verb Behav.*, 1965, 4, 73–81.

Frase, L. T. Validity judgments of syllogisms in relation to two sets of terms. *J. educ. Psychol.*, 1966a, 57, 239–245.

Frase, L. T. Belief, incongruity, and syllogistic reasoning. *Psychol. Rep.*, 1966b, 18, 982.

Frase, L. T. Associative factors in syllogistic reasoning. *J. exp. Psychol.*, 1968, 76, 407–412.

Freedman, J. L. Increasing creativity by free association training. *J. exp. Psychol.*, 1965, 69, 89–91.

Freedman, J. L.,. and Mednick, S. A. Ease of attainment of concepts as a function of response dominance variance. *J. exp. Psychol.*, 1958, 55, 463–466.

Freibergs, V., and Tulving, E. The effect of practice on utilization of information from positive and negative instances in concept identification. *Canad. J. Psychol.*, 1961, 15, 101–106.

French, E. G., and Thomas, F. H. The relation of achievement motivation to problem-solving effectiveness. *J. abnorm. soc. Psychol.*, 1958, 56, 45–48.

Freyburg, P. S. Concept development in Piagetian terms in relation to school achievement. *J. educ. Psychol.*, 1966, 57, 164–168.

Frick, J. W., and Guilford, J. P. An analysis of a form of the water-jar test. *Amer. J. Psychol.*, 1957, 70, 427–431.

Fulgosi, A., and Guilford, J. P. Short-term incubation in divergent production. *Amer. J. Psychol.*, 1968, 81, 241–246.

Furth, H. G. *Thinking without language: Psychological implications of deafness.* New York: Free Press, 1966.

Furth, H. G., and Milgram, N. A. The influence of language on classification: A theoretical model applied to normal, retarded and deaf children. *Genetic psychol. Monogr.*, 1965, 72, 317–351.

Gagné, R. M. The acquisition of knowledge. *Psychol. Rev.*, 1962, 69, 355–365.

Gagné, R. M. Problem solving. In A. W. Melton (Ed.), *Categories of human learning.* New York: Academic Press, 1964.

Gagné, R. M. *The conditions of learning.* New York: Holt, Rinehart and Winston, 1965.

Gagné, R. M. The learning of principles. In H. J. Klausmeier and C. W. Harris (Eds.), *Analysis of concept learning.* New York: Academic Press, 1966.

Gagné, R. M. *Learning and individual differences.* Columbus, Ohio: Merrill, 1967.

Gagné, R. M., and Brown, L. T. Some factors in the programming of conceptual learning. *J. exp. Psychol.*, 1961, 62, 313–321.

Gagné, R. M., and Paradise, N. E. Abilities and learning sets in knowledge acquisition. *Psychol. Monogr.*, 1961, 75, No. 518.

Gagné, R. M., and Smith, E. C. A study of the effects of verbalization on problem solving. *J. exp. Psychol.*, 1962, 63, 12–18.

Gagné, R. M., and Wiegand, V. K. Some factors in children's learning and retention of concrete rules. *J. educ. Psychol.*, 1968, 59, 355–361.

Gaier, E. L. Technique of problem solving as a predictor of achievement in a mechanics course. *J. applied Psychol.*, 1955, 39, 416–418.

Gall, M., and Mendelsohn, G. A. Effects of facilitating techniques and subject-experimenter interaction on creative problem solving. *J. pers. soc. Psychol.*, 1967, 5, 211–216.

Gallup, H. Originality in free and controlled association responses. *Psychol. Rep.*, 1963, 13, 923–929.

Gardner, R. A., and Runquist, W. N. Acquisition and extinction of a problem-solving set. *J. exp. Psychol.*, 1958, 55, 274–277.

Gardner, R. W., Jackson, D. N., and Messick, S. J. Personality organization in cognitive controls and intellectual abilities. *Psychol. Issues*, 1960, 2, No. 4.

Gardner, R. W., and Schoen, R. A. Differentiation and abstraction in concept formation. *Psychol. Monogr.*, 1962, 76, No. 560.

Garner, W. R. An informational analysis of absolute judgments of loudness. *J. exp. Psychol.*, 1953, 46, 373–380.

Garner, W. R. Rating scales, discriminability, and information transmission. *Psychol. Rev.*, 1960, 67, 343–352.

Garner, W. R. *Uncertainty and structure as psychological concepts.* New York: Wiley, 1962.

Garner, W. R. The stimulus in information processing. *Amer. Psychol.*, 1970, 25, 350–358.

Gavurin, E. I. Anagram solving and spatial aptitude. *J. Psychol.*, 1967, 65, 65–68.

Gelman, R. Conservative acquisition: A problem of learning to attend to relevant attributes. *J. exp. child Psychol.*, 1969, 7, 167–187.

Gelman, R. Logical capacity of very young children: Number invariance rules. Unpublished paper, University of Pennsylvania, 1970.

Gerlach, V. S., Schutz, R. E., Baker, R. L., and Mazer, G. E. Effects of variations in directions on originality test response. *J. educ. Psychol.*, 1964, 55, 79–83.

Getzels, J. W., and Jackson, P. W. *Creativity and intelligence: Explorations with gifted students.* New York: Wiley, 1962.

Ghiselin, B. *The creative process.* Berkeley, Calif.: Univ. Calif. Press, 1952.

Gibbons, H. The ability of college freshmen to construct the meaning of a strange word from the context in which it appears. *J. exp. Educ.*, 1940, 9, 29–33.

Gibson, E. J., Bergman, R., and Purdy, J. The effect of prior training with a scale of distance on absolute and relative judgment of distance over ground. *J. exp. Psychol.*, 1955, 50, 97–105.

Gibson, J. J. Observations on active touch. *Psychol. Rev.*, 1962, 69, 477–491.

Glucksburg, S., and Danks, J. H. Functional fixedness: Stimulus equivalence mediated by semantic-acoustic similarity. *J. exp. Psychol.*, 1967, 74, 400–405.

Glucksburg, S., and Danks, J. H. Effects of discriminative labels and of nonsense labels upon availability of novel function. *J. verb. Learn. & verb. Behav.*, 1968, 7, 72–76.

Glucksburg, S., and Weisberg, R. W. Verbal behavior and problem solving: Some effects of labeling in a functional fixedness problem. *J. exp. Psychol.*, 1966, 71, 659–664.

Godshalk, F. I., Swineford, F., and Coffman, W. E. *The measurement of writing ability.* New York: College Entrance Examination Board, 1966.

Goldbeck, R. A., Bernstein, B. B., Hillix, W. A., and Marx M. H. Application of the half-split technique to problem-solving tasks. *J. exp. Psychol.*, 1957, 53, 330–338.

Goldberg, L. R. Simple models or simple processes? Some research on clinical judgments. *Amer. Psychol.*, 1968, 23, 483–496.

Goldschmid, M. L. Role of experience in the acquisition of conservation. *Proc. 76th Ann. Convention Amer. Psychol. Assoc.*, 1968, 361–362.

Goldschmid, M. L., and Bentler, P. M. The dimensions and measurement of conservation. *Child Develop.*, 1968, 39, 787–802.

Gollub, H. F. Impression formation and word combination in sentences. *J. pers. soc. Psychol.*, 1968, 10, 341–353.

Goodnow, J. J. Effects of active handling, illustrated by uses for objects. *Child Develop.*, 1969, 40, 201–212.

Gordon, G., Marquis, S., and Anderson, O. W. Freedom and control in four types of scientific settings. *Amer. Behav. Scientist*, 1962, 6, 39–42.

Gordon, W. J. J. *Synectics: The development of creative capacity.* New York: Harper & Row, 1961.

Goss, A. E. Verbal mediating responses and concept formation. *Psychol. Rev.*, 1961, 68, 248–274.

Gottschaldt, K. Über den Einfluss der Erfahrung auf die Wahrnehmung von Figuren: I: Uber den Einfluss gehaufter Einprägung von Figuren auf ihre Sichtbarkeit in umfassenden Konfigurationen. *Psychol. Forsch.*, 1926, 8, 261–317.

Grant, D. A., Jones, O. R., and Tallantis, B. The relative difficulty of number, form and color concepts of a Weigl-type problem. *J. exp. Psychol.*, 1949, 39, 552–557.

Grebstein, L. Relative accuracy of actuarial prediction, experienced clinicians, and graduate students in a clinical judgment task. *J. consult. Psychol.*, 1963, 37, 127–132.

Green, B. F. Descriptions and explanations: A comment on paper by Hoffman and Edwards. In B. Kleinmuntz (Ed.), *Formal representation of human judgment.* New York: Wiley, 1968.

Greenberg, M. G., and Weiner, B. Effects of reinforcement history upon risk-taking behavior. *J. exp. Psychol.*, 1966, 71, 587–592.

Gribben, J. A. Solution-word letter sequences in anagram solving. *J. exp. Psych.*, 1970, 85, 192–197.

Guilford, J. P. *Psychometric methods.* New York: McGraw-Hill, 1954.

Guilford, J. P. The structure of intellect. *Psychol. Bull.*, 1956, 53, 267–293.

Guilford, J. P. *The nature of human intelligence.* New York: McGraw-Hill, 1967.

Guilford, J. P., Kettner, N. W., and Christensen, P. R. The nature of the general reasoning factor. *Psychol. Rev.*, 1956, 63, 169–172.

Guilford, J. P., Merrifield, P. R., and Cox, A. B. Creative thinking in children at the junior high school levels. Reports from the Psychological Laboratory, University of Southern California, 1961, No. 26.

Guy, D. E. Developmental study of performance on conceptual problems involving a rule shift. *J. exp. Psychol.*, 1969, 82, 242–249.

Gyr, J. W. An investigation into, and speculations about, the formal nature of a problem-solving process. *Behav. Sci.*, 1960, 5, 39–59.

Gyr, J. W., Brown, J. S., and Cafagna, A. C. Quasi-formal models of inductive behavior and their relation to Piaget's theory of cognitive stages. *Psychol. Rev.*, 1967, 74, 272–289.

Halford, G. S. A theory of the acquisition of conservation. *Psychol. Rev.*, 1970, 77, 302–316.

Hall, E. R. Verbal response production following rest. Unpublished paper, Michigan State University, 1960.

Hamilton, H. W., and Saltz, E. Role of intelligence in precriterion concept attainment by children. *J. exp. Psychol.*, 1969, 81, 191–192.

Hammond, K. R., Hursch, C. J., and Todd, F. J. Analyzing the components of clinical inference. *Psychol. Rev.*, 1964, 71, 438–456.

Hammond, K. R., and Summers, D. A. Cognitive dependence on linear and non-linear cues. *Psychol. Rev.*, 1965, 72, 215–224.

Handel, S., London, M., and DeSoto, C. Reasoning and spatial representations. *J. verb. Learn. & verb. Behav.*, 1968, 7, 351–357.

Hanfmann, E., and Kasanin, J. A method for the study of concept formation. *J. Psychol.*, 1937, 3, 521–640.

Hargreaves, H. L. The "faculty" of imagination. *British J. Psychol.*, 1927, 3, Monogr. Suppl. No. 10.

Harootunian, B., and Tate, M. W. The relationship of certain selected variables to problem solving ability. *J. educ. Psychol.*, 1960, 51, 326–333.

Harris, L., Schaller, M. J., and Mitler, M. M. The effects of stimulus type on performance in a color-form sorting task with preschool, kindergarten, first-grade, and third-grade children. *Child Develop.*, 1970, *41*, 177–191.

Hartocollis, P., and Johnson, D. M. Differential effects of alcohol on word fluency. *Quart. J. Stud. Alcohol*, 1956, *17*, 183–189.

Harvey, O. J., and Campbell, D. T. Judgments of weight as affected by adaptation range, adaptation duration, magnitude of unlabeled anchor, and judgmental language. *J. exp. Psychol.*, 1963, *65*, 12–21.

Harvey, O. J., Hunt, D. E., and Schroder, H. M. *Conceptual systems and personality organization.* New York: Wiley, 1961.

Hasan, P., and Butcher, H. J. Creativity and intelligence: A partial replication with Scottish children of Getzel's and Jackson's study. *British J. Psychol.*, 1966, *57*, 129–135.

Hayes, J. R. Problem topology and the solution process. *J. verb. Learn. & verb. Behav.*, 1965, *4*, 371–379.

Haygood, R. C. Use of semantic differential dimensions in concept learning. *Psychon. Sci.*, 1966, *5*, 305–306.

Haygood, R. C., and Bourne, L. E., Jr. Attribute- and rule-learning aspects of conceptual behavior. *Psychol. Rev.*, 1965, *72*, 175–195.

Haygood, R. C., and Bourne, L. E., Jr. Conceptual behavior. In A. R. Meetham (Ed.), *Encyclopedia of linguistics, information and control.* London: Pergamon Press, 1969.

Haygood, R. C., and Stevenson, M. Effects of number of irrelevant dimensions in nonconjunctive concept learning. *J. exp. Psychol.*, 1967, *74*, 302–304.

Hebert, J. A., and Rogers, C. A., Jr. Anagram solution as a function of pronounceability and difficulty. *Psychon. Sci.*, 1966, *4*, 359–360.

Heidbreder, E. An experimental study of thinking. *Arch. Psychol.*, 1924, No. 73.

Heidbreder, E. The attainment of concepts: III. The process. *J. Psychol.*, 1947, *24*, 93–108.

Heidbreder, E. The attainment of concepts: VI. Exploratory experiments on conceptualization at perceptual levels. *J. Psychol.*, 1948, *26*, 193–216.

Heidbreder, E., and Overstreet, P. The attainment of concepts: V. Critical features and contexts. *J. Psychol.*, 1948, *26*, 45–69.

Heintz, R. K. The effect of remote anchoring points upon the judgment of lifted weights. *J. exp. Psychol.*, 1950, *40*, 584–591.

Helson, H. Adaptation-level as frame of reference for prediction of psychophysical data. *Amer. J. Psychol.*, 1947, *60*, 1–29.

Helson, H. Adaptation-level as a basis for a quantitative theory of frames of reference. *Psychol. Rev.*, 1948, *55*, 297–313.

Helson, H. *Adaptation-level theory.* New York: Harper & Row, 1964.

Helson, H., and Himelstein, P. A short method for calculating the adaptation-level for absolute and comparative rating judgments. *Amer. J. Psychol.*, 1955, *68*, 631–637.

Helson, H., and Kozaki, T. Effects of duration of series and anchor-stimuli on judgments of perceived size. *Amer. J. Psychol.*, 1968, *81*, 291–302.

Helson, H., and Masters, H. G. A study of inflection-points in the locus of adaptation-levels as a function of anchor-stimuli. *Amer. J. Psychol.*, 1966, *79*, 400–408.

Hendricks, M., Guilford, J. P., and Hoepfner, R. Measuring creative social intelligence. Reports from the Psychological Laboratory, University of Southern California, 1969, No. 42.

Henle, M., and Michael, M. The influence of attitudes on syllogistic reasoning. *J. soc. Psychol.*, 1956, *44*, 115–127.

Henley, N. M., Horsfall, R. B., and DeSoto, C. B. Goodness of figure and social structure. *Psychol. Rev.*, 1969, *76*, 194–204.

Hettema, J. Cognitive abilities as process variables. *J. pers. soc. Psychol.*, 1968, *10*, 461–471.

Hicks, J. M., and Campbell, D. T. Zero-point scaling as affected by social object, scaling method, and context. *J. pers. soc. Psychol.*, 1965, *2*, 793–808.

Hilgard, E. R. *Theories of learning.* New York: Appleton-Century-Crofts, 1956.

Hinton, B. L. Environmental frustration and creative problem solving. *J. applied Psychol.,* 1968, 52, 211–217.

Himmelfarb, S., and Senn, D. J. Forming impressions of social class: Two tests of an averaging mode. *J. pers. soc. Psychol.,* 1969, 12, 38–51.

Hoepfner, R., Nihira, K., and Guilford, J. P. Intellectual abilities of symbolic and semantic judgment. *Psychol. Monogr.,* 1966, 80, No. 624.

Hoffman, P. J. The paramorphic representation of clinical judgment. *Psychol. Bull.,* 1960, 57, 116–131.

Hoffman, P. J. Assessment of the independent contributions of predictors. *Psychol. Bull.,* 1962, 59, 77–80.

Hoffman, P. J., Slovic, P., and Rorer, L. G. An analysis-of-variance model for the assessment of configural cue utilization in clinical judgment. *Psychol. Bull.,* 1968, 69, 338–349.

Holland, J. L., and Baird, L. L. The preconscious activity scale: The development and validation of an originality measure. *J. creative Behav.,* 1968, 2, 217–225.

Hollingworth, H. L. The inaccuracy of movement. *Arch. Psychol.,* 1909, No. 13.

Hollingworth, H. L. The central tendency of judgment. *J. Philos. Psychol. & Scientific Method,* 1910, 7, 461–469.

Horn, M. D. The thousand and three words most frequently used by kindergarten children. *Childhood Educ.,* 1926, 3, 118–122.

Hovland, C. I., Harvey, O. J., and Sherif, M. Assimilation and contrast effects in reactions to communication and attitude change. *J. abnorm. soc. Psychol.,* 1957, 55, 244–252.

Hovland, C. I., and Weiss, W. Transmission of information concerning concepts through positive and negative instances. *J. exp. Psychol.,* 1953, 45, 175–182.

Howat, M. G. Transfer in production and judgment with input information varied. Unpublished Ph.D. thesis, Michigan State University, 1962.

Hull, C. L. Quantitative aspects of the evolution of concepts. *Psychol. Monogr.,* 1920, 28, No. 123.

Hull, C. L. The mechanism of the assembly of behavior segments in novel combinations suitable for problem solution. *Psychol. Rev.,* 1935, 42, 219–245.

Humphrey, G. *Thinking: An introduction to its experimental psychology.* New York: Wiley, 1951.

Hunt, E. B., and Hovland, C. I. Order of consideration of different types of concepts. *J. exp. Psychol.,* 1960, 59, 220–225.

Hunt, E. B. *Concept learning.* New York: Wiley, 1962.

Hunt, E. B., Marin, J. K., and Stone, P. *Experiments in induction.* New York: Academic Press, 1965.

Hunt, J. McV., and Cofer, C. N. Psychological deficit. In J. McV. Hunt (Ed.), *Personality and the behavior disorders.* New York: Ronald Press, 1944.

Hunt, W. A., and Volkmann, J. The anchoring of an affective scale. *Amer. J. Psychol.,* 1937, 49, 88–92.

Hunter, I. M. L. The solving of three-term series problems. *British J. Psychol.,* 1957, 48, 286–298.

Hunter, I. M. L. Further studies on anagram solving. *British J. Psychol.,* 1961, 52, 161–165.

Huttenlocher, J. Constructing spatial images: A strategy in reasoning. *Psychol. Rev.,* 1968, 75, 550–560.

Hyman, R. On prior information and creativity. *Psychol. Rep.,* 1961, 9, 151–161.

Imai, S., and Garner, W. R. Discriminability and preference for attributes in free and constrained classification. *J. exp. Psychol.,* 1965, 69, 596–608.

Indow, T., and Togano, K. On retrieving sequence from long-term memory. *Psychol. Rev.,* 1970, 77, 317–331.

Inhelder, B., and Piaget, J. *The growth of logical thinking from childhood to adolescence.* New York: Basic Books, 1958.

Inhelder, B., and Piaget, J. *The early growth of logic in the child.* New York: Harper & Row, 1964.

Ipsen, G. Über Gestaltaufassung. Erörterung des Sanderschen Parallelogramms. *Neue psychologische Studien,* 1926, *1,* 167–278.

Irwin, F. W., and Smith, W. A. S. Further tests of theories of decision in an "expanded judgment" situation. *J. exp. Psychol.,* 1956, *52,* 345–348.

Irwin, F. W., Smith, W. A. S., and Mayfield, J. F. Tests of two theories of decision in an "expanded judgment" situation. *J. exp. Psychol.,* 1956, *51,* 261–268.

Isaacs, I. D., and Duncan, C. P. Reversal and nonreversal shifts within and between dimensions in concept formation. *J. exp. Psychol.,* 1962, *64,* 580–585.

Isaacs, S. *Intellectual growth in young children.* London: Routledge & Kegan Paul, 1930.

Jacobsen, T. L., and Asher, J. J. Validity of the concept constancy measure of creative problem solving. *J. gen. Psychol.,* 1963, *68,* 9–19.

Jacobson, L. I., Elenewski, J. J., Lordahl, D. S., and Liroff, J. H. Role of creativity and intelligence in conceptualization, *J. pers. soc. Psychol.,* 1968, *10,* 431–436.

Jahoda, G. Children's concepts of nationality: A critical study of Piaget's stages. *Child Develop.,* 1964, *35,* 1081–1092.

Janis, I. L., and Frick, F. The relationship between attitudes toward conclusions and errors in judging logical validity of syllogisms. *J. exp. Psychol.,* 1943, *33,* 73–77.

Jeffrey, W. E. Variables affecting reversal-shifts in young children. *Amer. J. Psychol.,* 1965, *78,* 589–595.

Jenkins, J. J. Language and thought. In J. F. Voss (Ed.), *Approaches to thought.* Columbus, Ohio: Merrill, 1969.

Jenkins, J. J., Russell, W. A., and Suci, G. J. An atlas of semantic profiles for 360 words. *Amer. J. Psychol.,* 1958, *71,* 688–699.

Jennings, J. W., and Johnson, D. M. Context effects in production and judgment. *J. Psychol.,* 1963, *56,* 53–59.

John, E. R. Contributions to the study of the problem-solving process. *Psychol. Monogr.,* 1957, *71,* No. 447.

Johnson, D. M. Confidence and speed in the two-category judgment. *Arch. Psychol.,* 1939, No. 241.

Johnson, D. M. Confidence and the expression of opinion. *J. soc. Psychol.,* 1940, *12,* 213–220.

Johnson, D. M. Confidence and achievement in eight branches of knowledge. *J. educ. Psychol.,* 1941, *32,* 23–36.

Johnson, D. M. Generalization of a scale of values by the averaging of practice effects. *J. exp. Psychol.,* 1944, *34,* 425–436.

Johnson, D. M. A systematic treatment of judgment. *Psychol. Bull.,* 1945, *42,* 193–224.

Johnson, D. M. How a person establishes a scale for evaluating his performance. *J. exp. Psychol.,* 1946, *36,* 25–34.

Johnson, D. M. Generalization of a reference scale for judging pitch. *J. exp. Psychol.,* 1949a, *39,* 316–321.

Johnson, D. M. Learning function for a change in the scale of judgment. *J. exp. Psychol.,* 1949b, *39,* 851–860.

Johnson, D. M. The central tendency of judgment as a regression phenomenon. *Amer. Psychol.,* 1952, *7,* 281.

Johnson, D. M. *The psychology of thought and judgment.* New York: Harper & Row, 1955.

Johnson, D. M. Serial analysis of thinking. In E. Harms (Ed.), Fundamentals of psychology: The psychology of thinking. *Ann. N.Y. Acad. Sci.,* 1960, *91,* 66–75.

Johnson, D. M. Unpublished report (the data were collected by Charles Rhynard). Michigan State University, 1960.

Johnson, D. M. Formulation and reformulation of figure-concepts. *Amer. J. Psychol.,* 1961, *74,* 418–424.

Johnson, D. M. Reanalysis of experimental halo effects. *J. applied Psychol.*, 1963, 47, 46–47.

Johnson, D. M. Solution of anagrams. *Psychol. Bull.*, 1966, 66, 371–384.

Johnson, D. M. Improvement of problem solving processes. Final Report, Project No. 5-0705, Office of Education, U.S. Department of Health, Education, and Welfare. Michigan State University, 1968.

Johnson, D. M., and Hall, E. R. Organization of relevant and irrelevant words in the solution of verbal problems. *J. Psychol.*, 1961, 52, 99–104.

Johnson, D. M., and Jennings, J. W. Serial analysis of three problem-solving processes. *J. Psychol.*, 1963, 56, 43–52.

Johnson, D. M., and Kelly, K. Reexamination of training against atmosphere and conversion errors in syllogistic reasoning. Unpublished paper, Michigan State University, 1971.

Johnson, D. M., and King, C. R. Systematic study of end anchoring and central tendency of judgment. *J. exp. Psychol.*, 1964, 67, 501–506.

Johnson, D. M., Lincoln, R. E., and Hall, E. R. Amount of material and time of preparation for solving problems. *J. Psychol.*, 1961, 51, 457–471.

Johnson, D. M., Lynch, D. O., and Ramsay, J. G. Word frequency and verbal comparisons. *J. verb. Learn. & verb. Behav.*, 1967, 6, 403–407.

Johnson, D. M., and Mullally, C. W. The correlation-and-regression model for category judgments. *Psychol. Rev.*, 1969, 76, 205–215.

Johnson, D. M., and O'Reilly, C. A. Concept attainment in children: Classifying and defining. *J. educ. Psychol.*, 1964, 55, 71–74.

Johnson, D. M., Parrott, G. L., and Stratton, R. P. Production and judgment of solutions to five problems. *J. educ. Psychol.*, 1968, 59, Monogr. Suppl. No. 6.

Johnson, D. M., and Rhoades, C. Measurement of a subjective aspect of learning. *J. exp. Psychol.*, 1941, 28, 90–92.

Johnson, D. M., and Stratton, R. P. Evaluation of five methods of teaching concepts. *J. educ. Psychol.*, 1966, 57, 48–53.

Johnson, D. M., and Vidulich, R. N. Experimental manipulation of the halo effect. *J. applied Psychol.*, 1956, 40, 130–134.

Johnson, D. M., and Zerbolio, D. J. Relations between production and judgment of plot-titles. *Amer. J. Psychol.*, 1964, 77, 99–105.

Johnson, E. S. An information-processing model of one kind of problem solving. *Psychol. Monogr.*, 1964, 78, No. 581.

Johnson, P. J. Nature of mediational responses in concept-identification problems. *J. exp. Psychol.*, 1967, 73, 391–393.

Johnson, P. J., and White, R. M., Jr. Concept of dimensionality and reversal shift performance in children. *J. exp. child Psychol.*, 1967, 5, 223–227.

Johnson, T. J., and Van Mondfrans, A. P. Order of solutions in ambiguous anagrams as a function of word frequency of the solution words. *Psychon. Sci.*, 1965, 3, 565–566.

Johnson-Laird, P. N., and Tagart, J. How implication is understood. *Amer. J. Psychol.*, 1969, 82, 367–373.

Johnson-Laird, P. N., and Wason, P.C. A theoretical analysis of insight into a deductive problem. *Cognitive Psychol.*, 1970, 1, 134–148.

Jones, S. The effect of a negative qualifier in an instruction. *J. verb. Learn. & verb. Behav.*, 1966a, 5, 497–501.

Jones, S. Decoding a deceptive instruction. *British J. Psychol.*, 1966b, 57, 405–411.

Juda, A. *Höchstbegabung*. Munich, Germany: Urban & Schwarzenberg, 1953. (Reviewed by F. J. Kallmann and G. S. Baroff. *Ann. Rev. Psychol.*, 1955, 6, 304–305.)

Judson, A. J., and Cofer, C. N. Reasoning as an associative process: I. "Direction" in a simple verbal problem. *Psychol. Rep.*, 1956, 2, 469–476.

Kagan, J., Moss, H. A., and Sigel, I. E. Psychological significance of styles of conceptualization. In J. C. Wright and J. Kagan (Eds.), Basic cognitive processes in children. *Monogr. Soc. Res. Child Develop.*, 1963, 28, 73–118.

Kagan, J., Rosman, B. L., Day, D., Albert, J., and Phillips, W. Information processing in the child: Significance of analytic and reflective attitudes. *Psychol. Monogr.*, 1964, *78*, No. 578.

Kaplan, I. T., and Carvellas, T. Effect of word length on anagram solution time. *J. verb. Learn. & verb. Behav.*, 1968, *7*, 201–206.

Kaplan, I. T., and Schoenfeld, W. N. Oculomotor patterns during the solution of visually displayed anagrams. *J. exp. Psychol.*, 1966, *72*, 447–451.

Karlins, M., and Lamm, H. Information search as a function of conceptual structure in a complex problem-solving task. *J. pers. soc. Psychol.*, 1967, *5*, 446–459.

Katona, G. *Organizing and memorizing*. New York: Columbia Univ. Press, 1940.

Kaufman, E. L., Reese, T. W., Volkmann, J., and Rogers, S. *Accuracy, variability and speed of adjusting an indicator to a required bearing*. So. Hadley, Mass.: Mt. Holyoke College, 1947.

Keislar, E. R. ,and Stern, C. Differentiated instruction in problem solving for children of different mental ability levels. *J. educ. Psychol.*, 1970, *61*, 445–450.

Kelly, E. L., and Fiske, D. W. *The prediction of performance in clinical psychology*. Ann Arbor, Mich.: Univ. Michigan Press, 1951.

Kendler, H. H., and D'Amato, M. F. A comparison of reversal shifts and non-reversal shifts in human concept formation behavior. *J. exp. Psychol.*, 1955, *49*, 165–174.

Kendler, H. H., and Karasik, A. D. Concept formation as a function of competition between response produced cues. *J. exp. Psychol.*, 1958, *55*, 278–283.

Kendler, H. H., and Kendler, T. S. Inferential behavior in preschool children. *J. exp. Psychol.*, 1956, *51*, 311–314.

Kendler, H. H., and Kendler, T. S. Vertical and horizontal processes in problem solving. *Psychol. Rev.*, 1962, *69*, 1–16.

Kendler, H. H., and Watson, G. W. Conceptual behavior as a function of associative strength between representational responses. *J. verb. Learn. & verb. Behav.*, 1968, *7*, 321–325.

Kendler, T. S. Concept formation. *Ann. Rev. Psychol.*, 1961, *12*, 447–472.

Kendler, T. S. Inferential behavior in children: II. The influence of order of presentation. *J. exp. Psychol.*, 1961, *61*, 442–448.

Kendler, T. S. Learning and problem solving: Comments on Professor Gagné's paper. In A. W. Melton (Ed.), *Categories of human learning*. New York: Academic Press, 1964a.

Kendler, T. S. Verbalization and optional reversal shifts among kindergarten children. *J. verb. Learn. & verb. Behav.*, 1964b, *3*, 428–436.

Kendler, T. S., and Kendler, H. H. Inferential behavior in children as a function of age and subgoal constancy. *J. exp. Psychol.*, 1962, *64*, 460–466.

Kendler, T. S., and Kendler, H. H. An ontogeny of optional shift behavior. *Child Develop.*, 1970, *41*, 1–27.

Kendler, T. S., Kendler, H. H., and Learnard, B. Mediated responses to size and brightness as a function of age. *Amer. J. Psychol.*, 1962, *75*, 571–586.

Kennedy, J. E. The paired-comparison method and central tendency in esthetic judgments. *J. applied Psychol.*, 1961, *45*, 128–129.

Kessen, W., and Kuhlman, C. Thought in the young child. *Monogr. Soc. Res. Child Develop.*, 1962, *27*, 41–63.

Kettner, N. W., Guilford, J. P., and Christensen, P. R. A factor-analytic study across the domains of reasoning, creativity, and evaluation. *Psychol. Monogr.*, 1959, *73*, No. 479.

King, G. F., Ehrmann, J. C., and Johnson, D. M. Experimental analysis of the reliability of observations of social behavior. *J. soc. Psychol.*, 1952, *35*, 151–160.

King, F. J., Roberts, D., and Kropp, R. P. Relationship between ability measures and achievement under four methods of teaching elementary set concepts. *J. educ. Psychol.*, 1969, *60*, 244–247.

Kintsch, W. *Learning, memory, and conceptual processes*. New York: Wiley, 1970.

Klausmeier, H. J., and Meinke, D. L. Concept attainment as a function of instructions concerning the stimulus material, a strategy, and a principle for securing information. *J. educ. Psychol.,* 1968, 59, 215–222.

Klein, S. P., Frederiksen, N., and Evans, F. R. Anxiety and learning to formulate hypotheses. *J. educ. Psychol.,* 1969, 60, 465–475.

Kleinmuntz, B. The processing of clinical information by man and machine. In B. Kleinmuntz (Ed.), *Formal representation of human judgment.* New York: Wiley, 1968.

Knight, K. E. Effect of effort on behavioral rigidity on a Luchins water jar task. *J. abnorm. soc. Psychol.,* 1963, 66, 190–192.

Koestler, A. *The act of creation.* New York: Macmillan, 1964.

Kogan, N., and Wallach, M. A. *Risk taking: A study in cognition and personality.* New York: Holt, Rinehart and Winston, 1964.

Koltuv, B. B. Some characteristics of intrajudge trait intercorrelations. *Psychol. Monogr.,* 1962, 76, No. 552.

Komorita, S. S. A model for decision-making under risk. *Amer. J . Psychol.,* 1964, 77, 429–436.

Krantz, D. L., and Campbell, D. T. Separating perceptual and linguistic effects of context shifts upon absolute judgments. *J. exp. Psychol.,* 1961, 62, 35–42.

Krumboltz, J. D., and Christal, R. E. Relative pilot aptitude and success in primary pilot training. *J. applied Psychol.,* 1957, 41, 409–413.

Lampel, A. K., and Anderson, N. H. Combining visual and verbal information in an impression-formation task. *J. pers. soc. Psychol.,* 1968, 9, 1–6.

Larimer, G. S. Ambiguity and nearness of anchors as factors in assimilation. *Amer. J. Psychol.,* 1965, 78, 414–422.

Larimer, G. S., and White, B. J. Some effects of monetary reward and knowledge of results on judgment. *J. exp. Psychol.,* 1964, 67, 27–32.

Laughlin, P. R. Incidental concept formation as a function of creativity and intelligence. *J. pers. soc. Psychol.,* 1967, 5, 115–119.

Laughlin, P. R. Information specification in the attainment of conditional concepts. *J. exp. Psychol.,* 1969, 79, 370–372.

Lee, L. C., Kagan, J., and Rabson, A. The influence of a preference for analytic categorization upon concept acquisition. *Child Develop.,* 1963, 34, 433–442.

Lee, S. S. Transfer from lower-level to higher-level concept. *J. verb. Learn. & verb. Behav.,* 1968, 7, 930–937.

Lee, S. S., and Gagné, R. M. Effects of chaining cues on the acquisition of a complex conceptual rule. *J. exp. Psychol.,* 1969, 80, 468–474.

Lefford, A. The influence of emotional subject matter on logical reasoning. *J. gen. Psychol.,* 1946, 34, 127–151.

Le Furgy, W. G. The induction of anchoring effects in absolute judgements through differential reinforcement. *J. Psychol.,* 1966, 63, 73–81.

Lehman, H. C. The creative years: Oil paintings, etchings, and architectural works. *Psychol. Rev.,* 1942, 49, 19–42.

Lehman, H. C. *Age and achievement.* Princeton, N.J.: Princeton Univ. Press, 1953.

Lehman, H. C., and Gamertsfelder, W. S. Man's creative years in philosophy. *Psychol. Rev.,* 1942, 49, 319–343.

Lemke, E. A., Klausmeier, H. J., and Harris, C. W. Relationship of selected cognitive abilities to concept attainment and information processing. *J. educ. Psychol.,* 1967, 58, 27–35.

Lennenberg, E. H. Understanding language without ability to speak. *J. abnorm. soc. Psychol.,* 1962, 65, 419–425.

Levine, M. Human discrimination learning: The subset-sampling assumption. *Psychol. Bull.,* 1970, 74, 397–404.

Levitt, E. E., and Zuckerman, M. The water-jar test revisited: The replication of a review. *Psychol. Rep.,* 1959, 5, 365–380.

Levy, L. H. Context effects in social perception. *J. abnorm. soc. Psychol.*, 1960, *61*, 295–297.

Levy, L. H. Originality as role-defined behavior. *J. pers. soc. Psychol.*, 1968, *9*, 72–78.

Lincoln, J. W. Developing a creativeness in people. In S. J. Parnes and H. F. Harding (Eds.), *A source book for creative thinking*. New York: Scribners, 1962.

Lindgren, H. C. Brainstorming and the facilitation of creativity expressed in drawing. *Percept. mot. Skills*, 1967, *24*, 350.

Lindgren, H. C., and Lindgren, F. Brainstorming and orneriness as facilitators of creativity. *Psychol. Rep.*, 1965a, *16*, 577–583.

Lindgren, H. C., and Lindgren, F. Creativity, brainstorming, and orneriness: A cross-cultural study. *J. soc. Psychol.*, 1965b, *67*, 23–30.

Little, K. B., and Lintz, L. M. Information and certainty. *J. exp. Psychol.*, 1965, *70*, 428–432.

Lockhead, G. R. Identification and the form of multidimensional discrimination space. *J. exp. Psychol.*, 1970, *85*, 1–10.

Long, B. H., and Ziller, R. C. Dogmatism and predecisional information search. *J. applied Psychol.*, 1965, *49*, 376–378.

Long, L. L., and Welch, L. The development of the ability to discriminate and match numbers. *J. genetic Psychol.*, 1941, *59*, 377–387.

Lovell, K. Concepts in mathematics. In H. J. Klausmeier and C. H. Harris (Eds.), *Analyses of concept learning*. New York: Academic Press, 1966.

Luchins, A. S. Mechanization in problem solving. *Psychol. Monogr.*, 1942, *54*, No. 248.

Luchins, A. S., and Luchins, E. H. Reactions to inconsistencies: Phenomenal versus logical contradictions. *J. gen. Psychol.*, 1965, *73*, 47–65.

Luria, A. R. *The role of speech in the regulation of normal and abnormal behavior*. New York: Liveright, 1961.

MacKinnon, D. W. The nature and nurture of creative talent. *Amer. Psychol.*, 1962, *17*, 484–495.

MacRae, A. W. Channel capacity in absolute judgment tasks: An artifact of information bias? *Psychol. Bull.*, 1970, *73*, 112–121.

Magaro, P. A. The effect of imagined anchors on adaptation-level. *Amer. J. Psychol.*, 1966, *79*, 195–204.

Maier, N. R. F. Reasoning in humans: I. On direction. *J. comp. Psychol.*, 1930, *10*, 115–143.

Maier, N. R. F. Reasoning in humans: II. The solution of a problem and its appearance in consciousness. *J. comp. Psychol.*, 1931, *12*, 181–194.

Maier, N. R. F. Reasoning in humans: III. The mechanisms of equivalent stimuli and of reasoning. *J. exp. Psychol.*, 1945, *35*, 349–360.

Maier, N. R. F., and Burke, R. J. Response availability as a factor in the problem-solving performance of males and females. *J. pers soc. Psychol.*, 1967, *5*, 304–310.

Maier, N. R. F., Julius, M., and Thurber, J. A. Studies in creativity: Individual differences in the storing and utilization of information. *Amer. J. Psychol.*, 1967, *80*, 492–519.

Maltzman, I., Belloni, M., and Fishbein, M. Experimental studies of associative variables in originality. *Psychol. Monogr.*, 1964, *78*, No. 580.

Maltzman, I., Bogartz, W., and Breger, L. A procedure for increasing word association originality and its transfer effects. *J. exp. Psychol.*, 1958, *56*, 392–398.

Maltzman, I., Brooks, L. O., Bogartz, W., and Summers, S. S. The facilitation of problem solving by prior exposure to uncommon responses. *J. exp. Psychol.*, 1958, *56*, 399–406.

Maltzman, I., Eisman, E., Brooks, L. O., and Smith, W. M. Task instructions for anagrams following different task instructions and training. *J. exp. Psychol.*, 1956, *51*, 418–420.

Maltzman, I., and Morrisett, L. Different strengths of set in the solution of anagrams. *J. exp. Psychol.*, 1952, *44*, 242–246.

Maltzman, I., and Morrisett, L. Effects of task instructions on solution of different classes of anagrams. *J. exp. Psychol.*, 1953, 45, 351–354.

Maltzman, I., Simon, S., Raskin, D., and Licht, L. Experimental studies in the training of originality. *Psychol. Monogr.*, 1960, 74, No. 493.

Mandler, G. From association to structure. *Psychol. Rev.*, 1962, 69, 415–427.

Mandler, G., and Stephens, D. The development of free and constrained conceptualization and subsequent verbal memory. *J. exp. child Psychol.*, 1967, 5, 86–93.

Mandler, J. M., and Mandler, G. *Thinking: From association to Gestalt.* New York: Wiley, 1964.

Manis, M. The interpretation of opinion statements as a function of recipient attitude. *J. abnorm. soc. Psychol.*, 1960, 60, 340–344.

Manis, M. Comment on Upshaw's "Own attitude as an anchor in equal-appearing intervals." *J. abnorm. soc. Psychol.*, 1964, 68, 689–691.

Manis, M. Context effects in communication. *J. pers. soc. Psychol.*, 1967, 5, 326–334.

Manis, M., Gleason, T. C., and Dawes, R. M. The evaluation of complex social stimuli. *J. pers. soc. Psychol.*, 1966, 3, 404–419.

Manske, M. E., and Davis, G. A. Effects of simple instructional biases upon performance in the unusual uses test. *J. gen. Psychol.*, 1968, 79, 25–33.

Mayzner, M. S. Verbal concept attainment: A function of the number of positive and negative instances presented. *J. exp. Psychol.*, 1962, 63, 314–319.

Mayzner, M. S., and Tresselt, M. E. Anagram solution times: A function of letter order and word frequency. *J. exp. Psychol.*, 1958, 56, 376–379.

Mayzner, M. S., and Tresselt, M. E. Anagram solution times: A function of transition probabilities. *J. Psychol.*, 1959, 47, 117–125.

Mayzner, M. S., and Tresselt, M. E. Anagram solution times: A function of word transition probabilities. *J. exp. Psychol.*, 1962, 63, 510–513.

McGarvey, H. R. Anchoring effects in the absolute judgment of verbal materials. *Arch. Psychol.*, 1943, No. 281.

McGuire, W. J. A syllogistic analysis of cognitive relationships. In M. J. Rosenberg, et al. (Eds.), *Attitude organization and change.* New Haven, Conn.: Yale Univ. Press, 1960.

McNemar, O. W. An attempt to differentiate between individuals with high and low reasoning ability. *Amer. J. Psychol.*, 1955, 68, 20–36.

McNemar, Q. Lost: Our intelligence? Why? *Amer. Psychol.*, 1964, 19, 871–882.

Meadow, A., and Parnes, S. J. Evaluation of training in creative problem solving. *J. applied Psychol.*, 1959, 43, 189–194.

Meadow, A., Parnes, S. J., and Reese, H. Influence of brainstorming instructions and problem sequence on a creative problem solving test. *J. applied Psychol.*, 1959, 43, 413–416.

Mednick, M. T., and Andrews, F. M. Creative thinking and level of intelligence. *J. creative Behav.*, 1967, 1, 428–431.

Mednick, M. T., Mednick, S. A., and Jung, C. C. Continual association as a function of level of creativity and type of verbal stimulus. *J. abnorm. soc. Psychol.*, 1964, 69, 511–515.

Mednick, S. A. The associative basis of the creative process. *Psychol. Rev.*, 1962, 69, 220–232.

Mednick, S. A., and Halpern, S. Ease of concept attainment as a function of associative rank. *J. exp. Psychol.*, 1962, 64, 628–630.

Meltzer, L. Scientific productivity in organizational settings. *J. soc. Issues*, 1956, 12, 32–40.

Mendelsohn, G. A., and Griswold, B. B. Differential use of incidental stimuli in problem solving as a function of creativity. *J. abnorm. soc. Psychol.*, 1964, 68, 431–436.

Merrifield, P. R., Guilford, J. P., Christensen, P. R., and Frick, J. W. The role of intellectual factors in problem solving. *Psychol. Monogr.*, 1962, 76, No. 529.

Merrifield, P. R., Guilford, J. P., and Gershon, A. The differentiation of divergent-production abilities at the sixth-grade level. Reports from the Psychological Laboratory, University of Southern California,1963, No. 27.

Merrill, D. The C score as an indication of general vocabulary. Unpublished paper, Michigan State University, 1950.

Merrill, M. D. Correction and review on successive parts in learning a hierarchial task. *J. educ. Psychol.*, 1965, 56, 225–234.

Meyer, D. E. Differential effects of knowledge of results and monetary reward upon optimal choice behavior under risk. *J. exp. Psychol.*, 1967, 75, 520–524.

Meyers, C. R. Journal citations and scientific eminence in contemporary psychology. *Amer. Psychol.*, 1970, 25, 1041–1048.

Miller, G. A. The magical number seven, plus or minus two: Some limits on our capacity for processing information. *Psychol. Rev.*, 1956, 63, 81–97.

Miller, G. A. Some psychological studies of grammar. *Amer. Psychol.*, 1962, 17, 748–762.

Miller, G. A., Galanter, E., and Pribram, K. H. *Plans and the structure of behavior.* New York: Holt, Rinehart and Winston, 1960.

Miller, H., and Bieri, J. End anchor effects in the discriminability of physical and social stimuli. *Psychon. Sci.*, 1965, 3, 399–340.

Miller, L., Meyer, D. E., and Lanzetta, J. T. Choice among equal expected value alternatives: Sequential effects of winning probability level on risk preferences. *J. exp. Psychol.*, 1969, 79, 419–423.

Milton, G. A. The effects of sex-role identification upon problem-solving skill. *J. abnorm. soc. Psychol.*, 1957, 55, 208–212.

Milton, G. A. Sex differences in problem solving as a function of role appropriateness of the problem content. *Psychol. Rep.*, 1959, 5, 705–708.

Mitler, M. M., and Harris, L. Dimension preference and performance on a series of concept identification tasks in kindergarten, first-grade, and third-grade children. *J. exp. child Psychol.*, 1969, 7, 374–384.

Moore, O. K., and Anderson, S. B. Modern logic and tasks for experiments on problem solving behavior. *J. Psychol.*, 1954, 38, 151–160.

Morgan, J. J. B. Credence given to one hypothesis because of the overthrow of its rivals. *Amer. J. Psychol.*, 1945, 58, 54–64.

Morgan, J. J. B., and Carrington, D. H. Graphic instruction in relational reasoning. *J. educ. Psychol.*, 1944, 35, 536–544.

Morgan, J. J. B., and Morton, J. T. The distortion of syllogistic reasoning produced by personal convictions. *J. soc. Psychol.*, 1944, 20, 39–59.

Morgan, W. J., and Morgan, A. B. Logical reasoning: With and without training. *J. applied Psychol.*, 1953, 37, 399–401.

Mosher, F. A., and Hornsby, J. R. On asking questions. In J. S. Bruner, R. R. Olver and P. M. Greenfield (Eds.), *Studies in cognitive growth.* New York: Wiley, 1966.

Mostofsky, D., and Green, E. Two-category judgment task with available anchors. *Proc. 74th Ann. Convention Amer. Psychol. Assoc.*, 1966, 73–74.

Murphy, G. *An historical introduction to modern psychology.* New York: Harcourt, Brace, Jovanovich, 1949.

Murphy, G., and Murphy, L. B. *Experimental social psychology.* New York: Harper & Row, 1931.

Murphy, G., Murphy, L. B., and Newcomb, T. M. *Experimental social psychology.* New York: Harper & Row, 1937.

Murray, F. S., and Gregg, R. E. Reception versus selection procedures in concept learning. *J. exp. Psychol.*, 1969, 82, 571–572.

Myers, C. R. Journal citations and scientific eminence in contemporary psychology. *Amer. Psychol.*, 1970, 25, 1041–1048.

Nash, H. The judgment of linear proportions. *Amer. J. Psychol.*, 1964, 77, 480–484.

Natadze, R. Beitrag zur Methode der Begriffsbildungsforschung. Z. f. Psychologie, 1962, 167, 66–79.

Neimark, E. D. Effect of differential reinforcement upon information-gathering strategies in diagnostic problem solving. J. exp. Psychol., 1967, 74, 406–413.

Neimark, E. D. Development of comprehension of logical connectives: Understanding of "or." Psychon. Science., 1970, 21, 217–219.

Neimark, E. D., and Lewis, N. The development of logical problem-solving strategies. Child Develop., 1967, 38, 107–117.

Neisser, U. Cognitive psychology. New York: Appleton-Century-Crofts, 1967.

Neisser, U., and Weene, P. Hierarchies in concept attainment. J. exp. Psychol., 1962, 64, 640–645.

Newell, A., Simon, H. A., and Shaw, J. C. Elements of a theory of human problem solving. Psychol. Rev., 1958, 65, 151–166.

Newton, J. Judgment and feedback in a quasi-clinical situation. J. pers. soc. Psychol., 1965, 1, 336–342.

Noizet, G. Influence de la nature verbale des résponse sur l'ancrage perceptif. In Hommage à Andre Rey. Brussels: Dessart, 1967.

Öbrink, J. An experimental investigation of confidence. Ph.D. thesis, Uppsala University, Uppsala, Sweden, 1948.

Olczak, P. V., and Kaplan, M. F. Originality and rate of response in association as a function of associative gradient. Amer. J. Psychol., 1969, 82, 157–167.

Oléron, P. Recherches sur le développement mental des sourds-muets: Contribution à l'étude du problème "language et pensée." Paris: Centre National de la Recherche Scientifique, 1957.

Oléron, P. Étude sur l'apprehension des mots. Revue Psychologie Française, 1961, 6, 21–31.

Oléron, P. Les activities intellectuelles. Paris: Presses Universitaires de France, 1964.

Oléron, P., Gumusyan, S., and Moulinou, M. Extension des concepts et usage du langage. Revue Psychologie Française, 1966, 11, 149–161.

Olson, D. R. Language and thought: Aspects of a cognitive theory of semantics. Psychol. Rev., 1970, 77, 257–273.

Olton, R. M., and Crutchfield, R. S. Developing the skills of productive thinking. In P. Mussen, J. Langer, and M. V. Covington (Eds.), New directions in developmental psychology. New York: Holt, Rinehart and Winston, 1969.

Orne, M. T. On the social psychology of the psychological experiment: With particular reference to demand characteristics and their implication. Amer. J. Psychol., 1962, 17, 776–783.

Osborn, A. F. Applied imagination. New York: Scribners, 1953.

Osgood, C. E. A behavioristic analysis of perception and language as cognitive phenomena. In Contemporary approaches to cognition. Cambridge, Mass.: Harvard Univ. Press, 1957.

Osgood, C. E. Meaning cannot be r_m? J. verb. Learn. & verb. Behav., 1966, 5, 402–407.

Osgood, C. E., Suci, G. J., and Tannenbaum, P. H. The measurement of meaning. Urbana, Ill.: Univ. Illinois Press, 1957.

Osler, S. F., and Fivel, M. W. Concept attainment: I. The role of age and intelligence in concept attainment by induction. J. exp. Psychol., 1961, 62, 1–8.

Osler, S. F., and Weiss, S. R. Studies in concept attainment: III. Effect of instructions at two levels of intelligence. J. exp. Psychol., 1962, 63, 528–533.

Ostrum, T. M. Perspective as an intervening construct in the judgment of attitude statements. J. pers. soc. Psychol., 1966, 3, 135–144.

Overstreet, J. D., and Dunham, J. L. Effect of number of values and irrelevant dimensions on dimension selection and associative learning in a multiple-concept problem. J. exp. Psychol., 1969, 79, 265–268.

Page, M. M. Social psychology of a classical conditioning of attitudes experiment. *J. pers. soc. Psychol.*, 1969, 11, 177–186.

Paige, J. M., and Simon, H. A. Cognitive processes in solving algebra word problems. In B. Kleinmuntz (Ed.), *Problem solving: Research, method, and theory*. New York: Wiley, 1966.

Paivio, A. Mental imagery in associative learning and memory. *Psychol. Rev.*, 1969, 76, 241–263.

Parducci, A. Learning variables in the judgment of single stimuli. *J. exp. Psychol.*, 1954, 48, 24–30.

Parducci, A. Direction of shift in judgment of single stimuli. *J. exp. Psychol.*, 1956a, 51, 169–178.

Parducci, A. Incidental learning of stimulus frequencies in the establishment of judgment scales. *J. exp. Psychol.*, 1956b, 52, 112–118.

Parducci, A. Range-frequency compromise in judgment. *Psychol. Monogr.*, 1963, 77, No. 565.

Parducci, A. Category judgment: A range-frequency model. *Psychol. Rev.*, 1965, 72, 407–418.

Parducci, A., Calfee, R. C., Marshall, L. M., and Davidson, L. P. Context effects in judgment: Adaptation level as a function of the mean, midpoint, and median of the stimuli. *J. exp. Psychol.*, 1960, 60, 65–77.

Parducci, A., and Marshall, L. M. Supplementary report: The effects of the mean, midpoint, and median upon adaptation level in judgment. *J. exp. Psychol.*, 1961, 61, 261–262.

Parducci, A., and Marshall, L. M. Assimilation vs. contrast in the anchoring of perceptual judgments of weight. *J. exp. Psychol.*, 1962, 63, 426–437.

Parducci, A., Perrett, D. S., and Marsh, H. W. Assimilation and contrast as range-frequency effects of anchors. *J. exp. Psychol.*, 1969, 81, 281–288.

Parducci, A., Thaler, H., and Anderson, N. H. Stimulus averaging and the context of judgment. *Perception & Psychophysics*, 1968, 3, 145–150.

Parnes, S. J. Effects of extended effort in creative problem solving. *J. educ. Psychol.*, 1961, 52, 117–122.

Parnes, S. J., and Meadow, A. Effects of "brainstorming" instructions on creative problem solving by trained and untrained subjects. *J. educ. Psychol.*, 1959, 50, 171–176.

Parnes, S. J., and Meadow, A. Evaluation of persistence of effects produced by a creative problem-solving course. *Psychol. Rep.*, 1960, 7, 357–361.

Parrott, G. L. The effects of premise content on accuracy and solution time in syllogistic reasoning. Unpublished Master's thesis, Michigan State University, 1967.

Parrott, G. L. The effects of instructions, transfer, and content on reasoning time. Unpublished Ph.D. thesis, Michigan State University, 1969.

Payne, D. A., Krathwohl, D. R., and Gordon, J. The effect of sequence on programmed instruction. *Amer. educ. Res. J.*, 1967, 4, 125–132.

Pelz, D. C., and Andrews, F. M. *Scientists in organization: Productive climates for research and development*. New York: Wiley, 1966.

Peters, R. S. (Ed.). *Brett's history of psychology*. New York: Macmillan, 1953.

Peterson, C. R., and Beach, L. R. Man as an intuitive statistician. *Psychol. Bull.*, 1967, 68, 29–46.

Pettigrew, T. F. The measurement and correlates of category width as a cognitive variable. *J. Pers.*, 1958, 26, 532–544.

Pezzoli, J. A., and Frase, L. T. Mediated facilitation of syllogistic reasoning. *J. exp. Psychol.*, 1968, 78, 228–232.

Philip, B. R. Generalization and central tendency in the discrimination of a series of stimuli. *Canad. J. Psychol.*, 1947, 1, 196–204.

Piaget, J. *The language and thought of the child*. New York: Harcourt, Brace, Jovanovich, 1926.

Piaget, J. *Judgment and reasoning in the child.* New York: Harcourt, Brace, Jovanovich, 1928.

Piaget, J. *The moral judgment of the child.* London: Routledge and Kegan Paul, 1932.

Piaget, J. Le langage et la pensée du point de vu génétique. In G. Révész (Ed.), Thinking and speaking. *Acta Psychologica,* 1954, *10,* 51–60.

Piaget, J. Review of studies in cognitive growth, by Bruner, Olver, and Greenfield. *Contemp. Psychol.,* 1967, 7, 12.

Pieper, W. J. The effect of two situational variables on creative problem solving abilities. Unpublished Master's thesis, Michigan State University, 1965.

Podell, H. A. Two processes of concept formation. *Psychol. Monogr.,* 1958, 72, No. 468.

Podell, J. E., and Amster, H. Evaluative concept of a person as a function of the number of stimulus traits. *J. pers. soc. Psychol.,* 1966, 4, 333–336.

Pollack, I. The information of elementary auditory displays. *J. acoust. soc. Amer.,* 1952, 24, 745–749.

Pollay, R. W. A model of decision times in difficult decision situations. *Psychol. Rev.,* 1970, 77, 274–281.

Postman, L. J., and Miller, G. A. Anchoring of temporal judgments. *Amer. J. Psychol.,* 1945, 58, 43–53.

Postman, L. J., and Page, R. Retroactive inhibition and psychophysical judgment. *Amer. J. Psychol.,* 1947, 60, 367–377.

Poulton, E. C. The new psychophysics: Six models for magnitude estimation. *Psychol. Bull.,* 1968, 69, 1–19.

Prentice, J. L. Semantics and syntax in word meaning. *J. verb. Learn. & verb. Behav.,* 1966, 5, 279–284.

Rabin, A. I. Statistical problems involved in Rorschach patterning. *J. clin. Psychol.,* 1950, 6, 19–21.

Rambo, W. W. Absolute judgment of a restricted distribution of context stimuli. *J. gen. Psychol.,* 1962, 66, 169–178.

Rambo, W. W. The contribution of series and standard stimuli to absolute judgments of numerousness. *J. gen. Psychol.,* 1964, 71, 247–255.

Rambo, W. W., and Johnson, E. L. Practice-effects and the estimation of adaptation-level. *Amer. J. Psychol.,* 1964, 77, 106–110.

Rambo, W. W., and Watson, R. W. An empirical comparison of two theories of judgment. *J. gen. Psychol.,* 1962, 66, 235–240.

Raskin, E. Comparison of scientific and literary ability; a biographical study of eminent scientists and men of letters of the nineteenth century. *J. abnorm. soc. Psychol.,* 1936, 31, 20–35.

Ray, W. S. Verbal compared with manipulative solution of an apparatus problem. *Amer. J. Psychol.,* 1957, 70, 289–290.

Ray, W. S. Originality in problem solving as affected by single- versus multiple-solution problems. *J. Psychol.,* 1966, 64, 107–112.

Reed, H. B. Factors influencing the learning and retention of concepts: I. The influence of set. *J. exp. Psychol.,* 1946, 36, 71–87.

Reed, H. B. The learning and retention of concepts: V. The influence of form of presentation. *J. exp. Psychol.,* 1950, 40, 504–511.

Reed, H. B., and Dick, R. D. The learning and generalization of abstract and concrete concepts. *J. verb. Learn. & verb. Behav.,* 1968, 7, 486–490.

Reed, J. B. *The speed and accuracy of discriminating differences in hue, brilliance, area, and shape.* So. Hadley, Mass.: Mt. Holyoke College, 1951.

Rees, H. J., and Israel, H. E. An investigation of the establishment and operation of mental sets. *Psychol. Monogr.,* 1935, 46, No. 210.

Reese, H. W., and Parnes, S. J. Programming creative behavior. *Child Develop.,* 1970, 41, 413–423.

Reitman, W. R. *Cognition and thought.* New York: Wiley, 1965.

Restle, F. The selection of strategies in cue learning. *Psychol. Rev.*, 1962, *69*, 329–343.

Révész, G. Thinking and speaking. *Acta Psychologica*, 1954, *10*, 1–206.

Rhine, R. J. The relation of achievement in problem solving to rate and kind of hypotheses produced. *J. exp. Psychol.*, 1959, *57*, 253–256.

Richards, J. M., Holland, J. L., and Lutz, S. W. Prediction of student accomplishment in college. *J. educ. Psychol.*, 1967, *58*, 343–355.

Ridley, D. R., and Birney, R. C. Effects of training procedures on creativity test scores. *J. educ. Psychol.*, 1967, *58*, 158–164.

Riegel, K. F., Riegel, R. M., and Levine, R. S. An analysis of associative behavior and creativity. *J. pers. soc. Psychol.*, 1966, *4*, 50–56.

Rimoldi, H. J. A. A technique for the study of problem solving. *Educ. psychol. Measurement*, 1955, *15*, 450–461.

Rimoldi, H. J. A., Devane, J., and Haley, J. Characterization of processes. *Educ. psychol. Measurement*, 1961, *21*, 383–392.

Rimoldi, H. J. A., Fogliatto, H. M., Erdmann, J. B., and Donnelly, M. B. Problem solving in high school and college students. Psychometric Laboratory, Loyola University, Chicago, 1964.

Rinsland, H. D. *A basic vocabulary of elementary school children.* New York: Macmillan, 1945.

Rodwan, A. S., and Hake, H. W. The discriminant-function as a model for perception. *Amer. J. Psychol.*, 1964, *77*, 380-392.

Rogers, S. The anchoring of absolute judgments. *Arch. Psychol.*, 1941, No. 261.

Rokeach, M. *The open and closed mind.* New York: Basic Books, 1960.

Rokeach, M., and Rothman, G. The principle of belief congruence and the congruity principle as models of cognitive interaction. *Psychol. Rev.*, 1965, *72*, 128–142.

Rommetveit, R. Stages in concept formation and levels of cognitive functioning. *Scand. J. Psychol.*, 1960, *1*, 115–124.

Rommetveit, R., and Kvale, S. Stages in concept formation: III. Further inquiries into the effects of an extra intention to verbalize. *Scand. J. Psychol.*, 1965, *6*, 65–74.

Ronning, R. R. Anagram solution times: A function of the "ruleout" factor. *J. exp. Psychol.*, 1965, *69*, 35–39.

Rosenbaum, M. E., Arenson, S. J., and Panman, R. A. Training and instructions in the facilitation of originality. *J verb. Learn. & verb. Behav.*, 1964, *3*, 50–56.

Rosenbaum, M. E., and Levin, I. P. Impression formation as a function of source credibility and the polarity of information. *J. pers. soc. Psychol.*, 1969, *12*, 34–37.

Rosenthal, T. L., Zimmerman, B. J., and Durning, K. Observationally induced changes in children's interrogative classes. *J. pers. and soc. Psychol.*, 1970, *16*, 681–688.

Ross, J., and Di Lollo, V. A vector model for psychophysical judgment. *J. exp. Psychol., Monogr. Suppl.*, 1968a, *77*, No. 3, Part 2.

Ross, J., and Di Lollo, V. Category scales and contrast effects with lifted weights. *J. exp. Psychol.*, 1968b, *78*, 547–550.

Roughead, W. G., and Scandura, J. M. "What is learned" in mathematical discovery. *J. educ. Psychol.*, 1968, *59*, 283–289.

Russell, D. H. *Children's thinking.* Boston, Mass.: Ginn & Co., 1956.

Safren, M. A. Associations, set, and the solution of word problems. *J. exp. Psychol.*, 1962, *64*, 40–45.

Saidullah, A. Experimentelle Untersuchungen über den Geschmacksinn. *Arch. f. d. ges. Psychol.*, 1927, *60*, 457–484.

Saltz, E., and Sigel, I. E. Concept overdiscrimination in children. *J. exp. Psychol.*, 1967, *73*, 1–8.

Sarbin, T. R., Taft, R., and Bailey, D. E. *Clinical inference and cognitive theory.* New York: Holt, Rinehart and Winston, 1960.

Sargent, S. S. Thinking processes at various levels of difficulty. *Arch. Psychol.*, 1940, No. 249.

Sarris, V. Adaptation-level theory: Two critical experiments on Helson's weighted-average model. *Amer. J. Psychol.*, 1967, 80, 331–344.

Sarris, V. Ankerreiz-Effekte bei Tonhöhenbeurteilungen: Uberprüfung des Adaptations-niveau-Modells. Bericht über den 26 Kongress. In *Auftrage der Deutschen Gesellschaft für Psychologie*. Göttingen Verlag für Psychologie, 1969, 399–405.

Saugstad, P. An analysis of Maier's pendulum problem. *J. exp. Psychol.*, 1957, 54, 168–179.

Scandura. J. M. Learning verbal and symbolic statements of mathematical rules. *J. educ. Psychol.*, 1967, 58, 356–364.

Schaefer, C. E., and Anastasi, A. A biographical inventory for identifying creativity in adolescent boys. *J. applied Psychol.*, 1968, 52, 42–48.

Scheerer, M. Cognitive theory. In G. Lindzey (Ed.), *Handbook of social psychology*. Cambridge, Mass.: Addison-Wesley, 1954.

Schmidt, C. F. Personality impression formation as a function of relatedness of information and length of set. *J. pers. soc. Psychol.*, 1969, 12, 6–11.

Schneider, C. Unpublished report. Michigan State University, 1963.

Schroder, H. M., and Rotter, J. B. Rigidity as learned behavior. *J. exp. Psychol.*, 1952, 44, 141–150.

Schvaneveldt, R. W., and Kroll, N. E. A. Effects of cue associations in concept shifts. *J. verb. Learn. & verb. Behav.*, 1968, 7, 474–478.

Schwartz, S. H. Trial-by-trial analysis of processes in simple and disjunctive concept-attainment tasks. *J. exp. Psychol.*, 1966, 72, 456–465.

Segall, M. H. The effect of attitude and experience on judgments of controversial statements. *J. abnorm. soc. Psychol.*, 1959, 58, 61–68.

Segel, R. J., and Johnson, P. J. Consistency in type of solution to concept identification problems. Unpublished paper, University of New Mexico, 1969.

Sellin, T., and Wolfgang, M. E. *The measurement of delinquency*. New York: Wiley, 1964.

Sells, S. B. The atmosphere effect: An experimental study of reasoning. *Arch. Psychol.*, 1936, No. 200.

Shapiro, R. J. Creative research scientists. *Psychologie Africana*, 1968, Monogr. Suppl. No. 4.

Shelly, M. W., and Bryan, G. L. *Human judgments and optimality*. New York: Wiley, 1964.

Shepard, R. N. On subjectively optimum selection among multiattribute alternatives. In M. W. Shelly and G. L. Bryan (Eds.), *Human judgments and optimality*. New York: Wiley, 1964.

Shepard, R. N., Hovland, C. I., and Jenkins, H. M. Learning and memorization of classifications. *Psychol. Monogr.*, 1961, 75, No. 517.

Sherif, C. W. Social categorization as a function of latitude of acceptance and series range. *J. abnorm. soc. Psychol.*, 1963, 67, 148–156.

Sherif, C. W., Sherif, M., and Nebergall, R. E. *Attitude and attitude change*. Philadelphia, Pa.: Saunders, 1965.

Sherif, M., and Hovland, C. I. *Social judgment: Assimilation and contrast effects in communication and attitude change*. New Haven, Conn.: Yale Univ. Press, 1961.

Sherif, M., Taub, D., and Hovland, C. I. Assimilation and contrast effects of anchoring stimuli on judgments. *J. exp. Psychol.*, 1958, 55, 150–155.

Shulman, L. S. Review of Wallach and Kogan's Modes of thinking in young children. *Amer. educ. Res. J.*, 1966, 3, 305–309.

Shulman, L. S., and Keislar, E. R. *Learning by discovery: A critical appraisal*. Chicago: Rand McNally, 1966.

Shulman, L. S., Loupe, M. J., and Piper, R. M. Studies of the inquiry process. East Lansing, Michigan: Educational Publication Services, College of Education, Michigan State Univ., 1968.

Sidowski, J. B., and Anderson, N. H. Judgments of city-occupation combinations. *Psychon. Sci.,* 1967, 7, 279–280.

Sieber, J. E., and Lanzetta, J. T. Some determinants of individual differences in predecision information-processing behavior. *J. pers. soc. Psychol.,* 1966, 4, 561–571.

Sigel, I. E. Developmental trends in the abstraction ability of children. *Child Development,* 1953, 24, 131–144.

Sigel, I. E. The distancing hypothesis: A causal hypothesis for the acquisition of representational thought. Unpublished paper, Merrill-Palmer Institute, Detroit, Michigan, 1968.

Sigel, I. E., Saltz, E., and Roskind, W. Variables determining concept conservation in children. *J. exp. Psychol.,* 1967, 74, 471–475.

Simon, H. A., and Barenfeld, M. Information-processing analysis of perceptual processes in problem solving. *Psychol. Rev.,* 1969, 76, 473–483.

Simon, H. A., and Kotovsky, K. Human acquisition of concepts for sequential patterns. *Psychol. Rev.,* 1963, 70, 534–546.

Simpson, M. E., and Johnson, D. M. Atmosphere and conversion errors in syllogistic reasoning. *J. exp. Psychol.,* 1966, 72, 197–200.

Sinclair-de-Zwart, H. Developmental psycholinguistics. In D. Elkind and J. H. Flavell (Eds.), *Studies in cognitive development.* New York: Oxford Univ. Press, 1969.

Slack, C. W. Some characteristics of the "range effect." *J. exp. Psychol.,* 1953, 46, 76–80.

Slovic, P. Cue-consistency and cue-utilization in judgment. *Amer. J. Psychol.,* 1966, 79, 427–434.

Slovic, P. Analyzing the expert judge: A descriptive study of a stockbroker's decision processes. *J. applied Psychol.,* 1969a, 53, 255–263.

Slovic, P. Differential effects of real versus hypothetical payoffs on choices among gamblers. *J. exp. Psychol.,* 1969b, 80, 434–437.

Slovic, P., and Lichtenstein, S. Relative importance of probabilities and payoffs in risk taking. *J. exp. Psychol. Monogr.,* 1968, 78, No. 3, Part 2.

Slovic, P., Lichtenstein, S., and Edwards, W. Boredom-induced changes in preferences among bets. *Amer. J. Psychol.,* 1965, 78, 208–217.

Smedslund, J. *Multiple-probability learning.* Olso: Akademisk Forlag, 1955.

Smedslund, J. The acquisition of conservation of substance and weight: II. External reinforcement of conservation of weight and of the operations of addition and subtraction. *Scand. J. Psychol.,* 1961a, 2, 71–84.

Smedslund, J. The acquisition of conservation of substance and weight in children: III. Extinction of conservation of weight acquired "normally" and by means of empirical controls on a balance. *Scand. J. Psychol.,* 1961b, 2, 85–87.

Smedslund, J. Psychological diagnostics. *Psychol. Bull.,* 1969, 71, 237–248.

Smith, H. C. *Sensitivity to people.* New York: McGraw-Hill, 1966.

Smith, K., and Hardy, A. H. Effects of context on the subjective equation of auditory and visual intensities. *Science,* 1961, 134, 1623–1624.

Smith, W. J., Albright, L. E., Glennon, J. R., and Owens, W. A. The prediction of research competence and creativity from personal history. *J. applied Psychol.,* 1961, 45, 59–62.

Smoke, K. L. Negative instances in concept learning. *J. exp. Psychol.,* 1933, 16, 583–588.

Sommer, R., Anchor-effects and the semantic differential. *Amer. J. Psychol.,* 1965, 78, 317–318.

Staats, A. W. Verbal and instrumental response-hierarchies and their relationship to problem-solving. *Amer. J. Psychol.,* 1957, 70, 442–446.

Staats, A. W. Experimental demand characteristics and the classical conditioning of attitudes. *J. pers. soc. Psychol.,* 1969, 11, 187–192.

Staats, A. W., Staats, C. K., and Heard, W. G. Denotative meaning established by classical conditioning. *J. exp. Psychol.,* 1961, 61, 300–303.

Staats, C. K., and Staats, A. W. Meaning established by classical conditioning. *J. exp. Psychol.*, 1957, 54, 74–80.

Stanley, J. C. Analysis of unreplicated three-way classifications, with applications to rater bias and trait independence. *Psychometrika*, 1961, 26, 205–219.

Stellwagen, M. S. Discontinuity in the development of a set for anagrams. Unpublished paper, Michigan State University, 1968.

Stern, C. Labeling and variety in concept identification with young children. *J. educ. Psychol.*, 1965, 56, 235–240.

Stern, C. Acquisition of problem-solving strategies in young children and its relation to verbalization. *J. educ. Psychol.*, 1967, 58, 245–252.

Stevens, S. S. The direct estimation of sensory magnitudes—loudness. *Amer. J. Psychol.*, 1956, 69, 1–25.

Stevens, S. S. Adaptation-level vs. the relativity of judgment. *Amer. J. Psychol.*, 1958, 71, 633–646.

Stevens, S. S. On the operation known as judgment. *Amer. Sci.*, 1966a, 54, 385–401.

Stevens, S. S. A metric for the social consensus. *Science*, 1966b, 151, 530–541.

Stevens, S. S., and Greenbaum, H. B. Regression effect in psychophysical judgment. *Perception & Psychophysics*, 1966, 1, 439–446.

Stilson, D. W., and Maroney, R. J. Adverbs as multipliers: Simplification and extension. *Amer. J. Psychol.*, 1966, 79, 82–88.

Stratton, R. P. Atmosphere and conversion errors in syllogistic reasoning with contextual material and the effect of differential training. Unpublished Master's thesis, Michigan State University, 1967.

Stratton, R. P. Response hierarchies in productive thinking. Ph.D. thesis, Michigan State University, 1970.

Stratton, R. P., and Brown, R. Improving creative thinking by training in the production and-or judgment of solutions. *J. educ. Psychol.*, 1972 (In press).

Stratton, R. P., Parrott, G. L., and Johnson, D. M. Transfer of judgment training to production and judgment of solutions on a verbal problem. *J. educ. Psychol.*, 1970, 61, 16–23.

Suchman, J. R. The child and the inquiry process. In A. H. Passow and R. R. Leeper (Eds.), *Intellectual development: Another look*. Washington, D.C.: Assoc. Supervision & Curriculum Develop., 1201 Sixteenth Street, N. W., 1964.

Suchman, R. T., and Trabasso, T. Stimulus preference and cue function in young children's concept attainment. *J. exp. child. Psychol.*, 1966, 3, 188–198.

Summers, D. A., and Hammond, K. R. Inference behavior in multiple-cue tasks involving both linear and nonlinear relations. *J. exp. Psychol.*, 1966, 71, 751–757.

Summers, S. A. The learning of responses to multiple weighted cues. *J. exp. Psychol.*, 1962, 64, 29–34.

Summers, S. A., Summers, R. C., and Karkau, V. T. Judgments based on different functional relationships between interacting cues and a criterion. *Amer. J. Psychol.*, 1969, 82, 203–211.

Suppes, P. On the behavioral foundations of mathematical concepts. In L. N. Morrisett and J. Vinsonhaler (Eds.), Mathematical learning. *Monogr. Soc. Res. Child Develop.*, 1965, 30, 60–96.

Suppes, P. Mathematical concept formation in children. *Amer. Psychol.*, 1966, 21, 139–150.

Sweeny, E. J. Sex differences in problem solving. Technical Report, Stanford University, Stanford, Calif., 1953, No. 1.

Tabory, L., and Thurlow, W. Judgments of the loudness of a series of tones with two different range expectancies. *J. gen. Psychol.*, 1959, 60, 167–172.

Tagatz, G. E. Effects of strategy, sex, and age on conceptual behavior of elementary school children. *J. educ. Psychol.*, 1967, 58, 103–109.

Tajfel, H. The anchoring effects of value in a scale of judgment. *British J. Psychol.*, 1959, 50, 294–304.

Tajfel, H., and Bruner, J. S. The relation between breadth of category and decision time. *British J. Psychol.*, 1966, 57, 71–75.

Tate, M. W., Stanier, B., and Harootunian, B. Differences between good and poor problem-solvers. School of Education, University of Pennsylvania, Philadelphia, 1959.

Taylor, C. L., and Haygood, R. C. Effects of degree of category separation on semantic concept identification. *J. exp. Psychol.*, 1968, 76, 356–359.

Taylor, C. W., and Barron, F. (Eds.), *Scientific creativity: Its recognition and development.* New York: Wiley, 1963.

Taylor, C. W., and Holland, J. Predictors of creative performance. In C. W. Taylor (Ed.), *Creativity: Progress and potential.* New York: McGraw-Hill, 1964.

Taylor, C. W., Smith, W. R., and Ghiselin, B. The creative and other contributions of one sample of research scientists. In C. W. Taylor and F. Barron (Eds.), *Scientific creativity: Its recognition and development.* New York: Wiley, 1963.

Taylor, D. W., Berry, P. C., and Block, C. H. Does group participation when using brainstorming facilitate or inhibit creative thinking? *Admin. Sci. Quart.*, 1958, 3, 23–47.

Terborg, R. H. Order effects in learning a scale of judgment. Unpublished Master's thesis, Michigan State University, 1966.

Terborg, R. H. Dissipation of functional fixedness by means of conceptual grouping tasks. Ph.D. thesis, Michigan State University, 1968.

Terman, L. M. Scientists and nonscientists in a group of 800 gifted men. *Psychol. Monogr.*, 1954, 68, No. 7.

Terman, L. M., and Oden, M. H. *Genetic studies of genius, Vol. 5.* Stanford, Calif.: Stanford Univ. Press, 1958.

Thorndike, E. L., and Lorge, I. *The teacher's word book of 30,000 words.* New York: Teachers College Press, Teachers College, Columbia Univ., 1944.

Tighe, L. S., and Tighe, T. J. Discrimination learning: Two views in historical perspective. *Psychol. Bull.*, 1966, 66, 353–370.

Tighe, T. J., and Tighe, L. S. Differentiation theory and concept-shift behavior. *Psychol. Bull.*, 1968a, 70, 756–761.

Tighe, T. J., and Tighe, L. S. Perceptual learning in the discrimination processes of children: An analysis of five variables in perceptual pretraining. *J. exp. Psychol.*, 1968b, 77, 125–134.

Titchener, E. B. *Lectures on the experimental psychology of the thought-processes.* New York: Macmillan, 1909.

Torgerson, W. S. *Theory and methods of scaling.* New York: Wiley, 1958.

Torrance, E. P. *Guiding creative talent.* Englewood Cliffs, N.J.: Prentice-Hall, 1962.

Torrance, E. P. Role of evaluation in creative thinking. Bureau of Educational Res., University of Minnesota, 1964.

Torrance, E. P. *Rewarding creative behavior.* Englewood Cliffs, N.J.: Prentice-Hall, 1965.

Torrance, E. P. The Minnesota studies of creative behavior: National and international extensions. *J. creative Behav.*, 1967, 1, 137–154.

Torrance, E. P., and Harmon, J. A. Effects of memory, evaluative and creative reading sets on test performance. *J. educ. Psychol.*, 1961, 52, 207–214.

Trabasso, T. Verification of conceptual rules. *Proc. 75th Ann. Convention Amer. Psychol. Assoc.*, 1967, 41–42.

Trabasso, T., and Bower, G. Presolution reversal and dimensional shifts in concept identification. *J. exp. Psychol.*, 1964, 67, 398–399.

Trabasso, T., and Staudenmayer, H. Random reinforcement in concept identification. *J. exp. Psychol.*, 1968, 77, 447–452.

Traub, R. E. Importance of problem heterogeneity to programed instruction. *J. educ. Psychol.*, 1966, 57, 54–60.

Treffinger, D., and Ripple, R. E. Developing creative problem solving abilities and related attitudes through programed instruction. *J. creative Behav.*, 1969, 3, 105–110.

Tresselt, M. E. The influence of amount of practice upon the formation of a scale of judgment. *J. exp. Psychol.*, 1947, 37, 251–260.

Tresselt, M. E. Similarity in stimulus material and stimulus task on the formation of a new scale of judgment. *J. exp. Psychol.*, 1965, 69, 241–245.

Tresselt, M. E. Uni-polar or bi-polar scales of judgment. *Psychon. Sci.*, 1965, 3, 365.

Triandis, H. C., and Fishbein, M. Cognitive interaction in person perception. *J. abnorm. soc. Psychol.*, 1963, 67, 446–453.

Tucker, M. F., Cline, V. B., and Schmitt, J. R. Prediction of creativity and other performance measures from biographical information among pharmaceutical scientists. *J. applied Psychol.*, 1967, 51, 131–138.

Turchoie, R. M. The relation of adjacent inhibitory stimuli to the central tendency effect. *J. gen. Psychol.*, 1948, 39, 3–14.

Turner, W. M., and Rains, J. D. Differential effects of "brainstorming" instructions upon high and low creative subjects. *Psychol. Rep.*, 1965, 17, 753–754.

Turnure, C., and Wallach, L. The influence of contextual variation on the differentiation of parts from wholes. *Amer. J. Psychol.*, 1965, 78, 481–485.

Tversky, A. Intransitivity of preferences. *Psychol. Rev.*, 1969, 76, 31–48.

Underwood, B. J., and Richardson, J. Verbal concept learning as a function of instructions and dominance level. *J. exp. Psychol.*, 1956, 51, 229–238.

Upshaw, H. S. Own attitude as an anchor in equal-appearing intervals. *J. abnorm. soc. Psychol.*, 1962, 64, 85–96.

Upshaw, H. S. A linear alternative to assimilation-contrast: A reply to Manis. *J. abnorm. soc. Psychol.*, 1964, 68, 691–693.

Upshaw, H. S. The effect of variable perspective on judgments of opinion statements for Thurstone scales: Equal-appearing intervals. *J. pers. soc. Psychol.*, 1965, 2, 60–69.

Van de Geer, J. P. *A psychological study of problem solving.* Haarlem, Netherlands: Uitgeverij de Toorts, 1957.

Van de Geer, J. P., and Jaspers, J. M. F. Cognitive functions. *Ann. Rev. Psychol.*, 1966, 17, 145–176.

Vannoy, J. S. Generality of cognitive complexity-simplicity as a personality construct. *J. pers. soc. Psychol.*, 1965, 2, 385–396.

Volkmann, J. Scales of judgment and their implications for social psychology. In J. H. Rohrer and M. Sherif (Eds.), *Social psychology at the crossroads.* New York: Harper & Row, 1951.

von Wright, J. M., and Mikkonen, V. Changes in repeated reproduction of weight as a function of adaptation level. *Scand. J. Psychol.*, 1964, 5, 239–248.

Vygotsky, L. S. *Thought and language* (Edited and translated by E. Hanfmann and G. Vakar). Cambridge, Mass.: M.I.T. Press, 1962.

Walker, C. M., and Bourne, L. E. The identification of concepts as a function of amounts of relevant and irrelevant information. *Amer. J. Psychol.*, 1961, 74, 410–417.

Wallace, J. Concept dominance, type of feedback, and intensity of feedback as related to concept attainment. *J. educ. Psychol.*, 1964, 55, 159–166.

Wallach, L. The complexity of concept-attainment. *Amer. J. Psychol.*, 1962, 75, 277–283.

Wallach, M. A., and Kogan, N. *Modes of thinking in young children.* New York: Holt, Rinehart and Winston, 1965.

Wallach, M. A., and Wing, C. W., Jr. *The talented student: A validation of the creativity-intelligence distinction.* New York: Holt, Rinehart and Winston, 1969.

Wallas, G. *The art of thought.* New York: Harcourt, Brace, Jovanovich, 1926.

Ward, J. H. Comments on "The paramorphic representation of clinical judgment." *Psychol. Bull.*, 1962, 59, 74–76.

Ware, R., and Harvey, O. J. A cognitive determinant of impression formation. *J. pers. soc. Psychol.*, 1967, 5, 38–44.

Warr, P. B., and Coffman, T. L. Personality, involvement and extremity of judgment. *British J. soc. clin. Psychol.*, 1970, 9, 108–121.

Warren, T. F., and Davis, G. A. Techniques for creative thinking: An empirical comparison of three methods. *Psychol. Rep.*, 1969, *25*, 207–214.

Washburn, M. F., Haight, D., and Regensburg, J. The relation of the pleasantness of color combinations to that of colors seen singly. *Amer. J. Psychol.*, 1921, *32*, 145–146.

Wason, P. C. The processing of positive and negative information. *Quart. J. exp. Psychol.*, 1959, *11*, 92–107.

Wason, P. C. On the failure to eliminate hypotheses in a conceptual task. *Quart. J. exp. Psychol.*, 1960, *12*, 129–140.

Wason, P. C. Response to affirmative and negative binary statements. *British J. Psychol.*, 1961, *52*, 133–142.

Wason, P. C. The effect of self-contradiction on fallacious reasoning. *Quart. J. exp. Psychol.*, 1964, *16*, 30–34.

Wason, P. C. Reasoning about a rule. *Quart. J. exp. Psychol.*, 1968, *20*, 273–281.

Wason, P. C. Regression in reasoning. *British J. Psychol.*, 1969, *60*, 471–480.

Wason, P. C., and Johnson-Laird, P. N. Proving a disjunctive rule. *Quart. J. exp. Psychol.*, 1969, *21*, 14–20.

Wason, P. C., and Jones, S. Negatives: Denotation and connotation. *British J. Psychol.*, 1963, *54*, 299–307.

Weaver, H. E., and Madden, E. H. "Direction" in problem solving. *J. Psychol.*, 1949, *27*, 331–345. ·

Wegryn, J. Using anchor points to increase the color channel capacity. Unpublished Master's thesis, Michigan State University, 1964.

Weiss, B. Movement error, pressure variation, and the range effect. *J. exp. Psychol.*, 1955, *50*, 191–196.

Weiss, W. Effect of response system on development of standards for end categories. *Psychol. Rep.*, 1963a, *13*, 543–546.

Weiss, W. Scale judgments of triplets of opinion statements. *J. abnorm. soc. Psychol.*, 1963b, *66*, 471–479.

Weiss, W., and Ten Eyck, P. H. Effects on judgment of changes in the response scale. *Psychol. Rep.*, 1960, *7*, 487–495.

Weisskopf-Joelson, E., and Eliseo, T. S. An experimental study of the effectiveness of brainstorming. *J. applied Psychol.*, 1961, *45*, 45–49.

Welch, L. A behavioristic explanation of concept formation. *J. genetic Psychol.*, 1947, *71*, 201–222.

Wells, H. Effects of transfer and problem structure in disjunctive concept formation. *J. exp. Psychol.*, 1963, *65*, 63–69.

Werner, H. *Comparative psychology of mental development.* New York: Harper & Row, 1940.

Werner, H., and Kaplan, E. The acquisition of word meanings: A developmental study. *Monogr. Soc. Res. Child Develop.*, 1950, *15*, No. 51.

Wertheimer, M. Productive thinking. New York: Harper & Row, 1945.

Westcott, M. R. On the measurement of intuitive leaps. *Psychol. Rep.*, 1961, *9*, 267–274.

Westcott, M. R. *Psychology of intuition.* New York: Holt, Rinehart and Winston, 1968.

Westcott, M. R., and Ranzoni, J. Correlates of intuitive thinking. *Psychol. Rep.*, 1963, *12*, 595–613.

Wever, E. G., and Zener, K. E. The method of absolute judgment in psychophysics. *Psychol. Rev.*, 1928, *35*, 466–493.

Wheeler, D. Studies in the development of reasoning in school children. *British J. stat. Psychol.*, 1958, *11*, 137–159.

Whimbey, A. E., and Ryan, S. F. Role of short-term memory and training in solving reasoning problems mentally. *J. educ. Psychol.*, 1969, *60*, 361–364.

White, B. J. Availability of categories and contrast-effects in judgment. *Amer. J. Psychol.*, 1964, *77*, 231–239.

White, B. J., and Alter, R. D. Dogmatism, authoritarianism, and contrast effects in judgment. *Percept. mot. Skills,* 1965, *20,* 99–102.

White, B. J., Alter, R. D., Snow, M. E., and Thorne, D. E. Use of instructions and hypnosis to minimize anchor effects. *J. exp. Psychol.,* 1968, *77,* 415–421.

White, R. K. Note on the psychopathology of genius. *J. soc. Psychol.,* 1930, *1,* 311–315.

White, R. M., Jr. Effects of some pretraining variables on concept identification. Cognitive Processes Report, University of Colorado, Boulder, 1967, No. 105.

Whorf, B. L. *Language, thought, and reality* (Ed. J. B. Carroll). New York: Wiley, 1956.

Wiggins, J. G. Some relationships between stimulus structure and ambiguity in the solution of anagrams. *J. clin. Psychol.,* 1956, *12,* 332–337.

Wiggins, N., and Hoffman, P. J. Three models of clinical judgment. *J. abnorm. Psychol.,* 1968, *73,* 70–77.

Wiggins, N., Hoffman, P. J., and Taber, T. Types of judges and cue utilization in judgments of intelligence. *J. pers. soc. Psychol.,* 1969, *12,* 52–59.

Wilkins, M. C. The effect of changed material on ability to do formal syllogistic reasoning. *Arch. Psychol.,* 1928, No. 102.

Willingham, W. W., and Jones, M. B. On the identification of halo through analysis of variance. *Educ. psychol. Measurement,* 1958, *18,* 403–407.

Willis, R. H. Stimulus pooling and social perception. *J. abnorm. soc. Psychol.,* 1960, *60,* 365–373.

Wilson, R. C., Guilford, J. P., and Christensen, P. R. The measurement of individual differences in originality. *Psychol. Bull.,* 1953, *50,* 362–370.

Winters, R. W., and Johnson, D. M. Attention and the establishment of a scale of judgment. *J. exp. Psychol.,* 1969, *81,* 603–605.

Wishner, J. Reanalysis of "Impressions of personality." *Psychol. Rev.,* 1960, *60,* 365–373.

Witkin, H. A., Dyk, R. B., Faterson, H. F., Goodenough, D. R., and Karp, S. A. *Psychological differentiation: Studies of development.* New York: Wiley, 1962.

Wittrock, M. C. Replacement and nonreplacement strategies in children's problem solving. *J. educ. Psychol.,* 1967, *58,* 69–74.

Wittrock, M. C., and Keislar, E. R. Verbal cues in the transfer of concepts. *J. educ. Psychol.,* 1965, *56,* 16–21.

Wittrock, M. C., Keislar, E. R., and Stern, C. Verbal cues in concept identification. *J. educ. Psychol.,* 1964, *55,* 195–200.

Wohlwill, J. F. The abstraction and conceptualization of form, color, and number. *J. exp. Psychol.,* 1957, *53,* 305–309.

Wohlwill, J. F. A study of the development of the number concept by Scalogram analysis. *J. genetic Psychol.,* 1960, *97,* 345–377.

Wohlwill, J. F., and Lowe, R. C. Experimental analysis of the development of the concept of number. *Child Develop.,* 1962, *33,* 153–167.

Wolff, J. L. Concept-shift and discrimination-reversal learning in humans. *Psychol. Bull.,* 1967, *68,* 369–408.

Woodrow, H. Weight discrimination with a varying standard. *Amer. J. Psychol.,* 1933, *45,* 391–416.

Woodworth, R. S. Situation-and-goal set. *Amer. J. Psychol.,* 1937, *50,* 130–140.

Woodworth, R. S. *Experimental psychology.* New York: Holt, Rinehart and Winston, 1938.

Woodworth, R. S. Reinforcement of perception. *Amer. J. Psychol.,* 1947, *60,* 119–124.

Woodworth, R. S., and Sells, S. B. An atmosphere effect in formal syllogistic reasoning. *J. exp. Psychol.,* 1935, *18,* 451–460.

Woolum, S. J. The verbal context paradigm. Ph.D. thesis, Michigan State University, 1970.

Woolum, S. J., and Johnson, D. M. Concept acquisition as a function of frequency of occurrence in verbal context. *Psychon. Sci.,* 1969, *14,* 199–200.

psychophysical judgment in which confidence increases with the physical difference between two stimuli. But the amount of information was also a factor. After 20 pairs of cards had been seen, confidence reached averages of 50, 59, and 69, respectively.

Anyone who has studied statistics would ask next about the variability of the numbers. The experimenters raised this question also and found that, in general, confidence in deciding between the two packs decreased as the standard deviation of the difference increased. Similar results were obtained when they gave the subjects just one pack of cards, with positive and negative numbers, asking whether the mean was greater or less than zero. With other factors held constant, the confidence of college students, like that of statisticians, increases as a function of the familiar statistic t (Little and Lintz, 1965).

CONFIDENCE AND ACCURACY

The old question about the relation between confidence and accuracy takes two forms. If we ask whether those who express their judgments with the most confidence are the most accurate, the answer comes from interindividual correlations, and these exhibit much variation depending on the materials judged. College students taking multiple-choice tests of vocabulary in eight fields of knowledge and reporting their confidence in each choice showed correlations between confidence and accuracy of .13 to .45 for the seven academic fields and .76 for sports vocabulary (Johnson, 1941). Words can be judged for spelling as well as meaning, and the same correlations can be computed. In judging which of four versions of a word was correctly spelled, the correlations between confidence and accuracy were above .60 (Adams and Adams, 1961).

The question about confidence and accuracy can also be posed for a single judge. Will he be more accurate in those judgments that he makes with more confidence? In general, a change in the materials or conditions of judgment that increases accuracy increases confidence. In the comparative judgment, confidence and accuracy are related (as noted above) because both are related to the stimulus difference. A learning experiment can be arranged so that confidence and accuracy rise in parallel (Johnson and Rhoades, 1941). Thus it frequently happens that those judgments given with the most confidence are the most accurate (Öbrink, 1948).

These statements apply to homogeneous objects, but the same question arises for heterogeneous objects of judgment. Will the judge be most confident in the field he knows best? This question was investigated by intraindividual correlations between confidence and accuracy on eight vocabulary tests (Johnson, 1941), and a mean correlation of .46 was obtained. In general, the students were most confident on the tests on which they got their best scores, but there was considerable variability. Kelly and Fiske (1951), after studying the prediction of performance in clinical psychology from heterogeneous data, demonstrated that confidence of judgment cannot be taken as a guide to correctness of judgment. The motivation for accuracy is quite straightforward but the motivation for an expression of confidence, like

Worthen, B. R. Discovery and expository task presentation in elementary mathematics. *J. educ. Psychol., Monogr. Suppl.*, 1968, *59*, No. 1, Part 2.

Wyer, R. S., and Dermer, M. Effect of context and instructional set on evaluations of personality-trait adjectives. *J. pers. soc. Psychol.*, 1968, *9*, 7–14.

Yonge, G. D. Structure of experience and functional fixedness. *J. educ. Psychol.*, 1966, *57*, 115–120.

Youniss, J., and Furth, H. G. Learning of logical connectives by adolescents with single and multiple instances. *J. educ. Psychol.*, 1967, *58*, 222–230.

Zavalloni, M., and Cook, S. W. Influence of judges' attitudes on ratings of favorableness of statements about a social group. *J. pers. soc. Pyschol.*, 1965, *1*, 43–54.

Zimbardo, P. G. Verbal ambiguity and judgmental distortion. *Psychol. Rep.*, 1960, *6*, 57–58.

INDEXES

INDEX
OF TOPICS

INDEX
OF NAMES

72 73 74   7 6 5 4 3 2 1